# Biographical Dictionary
of American Educators

# Biographical Dictionary of American Educators

edited by JOHN F. OHLES

Volume 3

GREENWOOD PRESS

WESTPORT, CONNECTICUT
LONDON, ENGLAND

**Library of Congress Cataloging in Publication Data**

Main entry under title:

Biographical dictionary of American educators.

Includes index.
1. Educators—United States—Biography.  I.     Ohles, John F.
LA2311.B54         370'.973 [B]     77-84750
ISBN 0-8371-9893-3

Library of Congress Catalog Card Number: 77-84750
ISBN: 0-8371-9893-3 (set)
        0-8371-9896-8 (vol. 3)

First published in 1978

Greenwood Press, Inc.
51 Riverside Avenue, Westport, Connecticut 06880

Printed in the United States of America

10  9  8  7  6  5  4  3  2

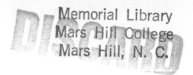
# CONTENTS

# Biographical Dictionary
# of American Educators

# R

**RAMBAUT, Mary Lucinda Bonney.** B. June 8, 1816, Hamilton, New York, to Benjamin and Lucinda (Wilder) Bonney. M. 1888 to Thomas Rambaut. Ch. none. D. July 24, 1900, Hamilton, New York.

Mary Lucinda Bonney was educated at the Hamilton (New York) Academy and later at Emma Willard's Troy (New York) Female Seminary. She then spent fifteen years teaching at numerous positions in various locations: Jersey City, New Jersey; New York City and DeRuyter, New York; Troy Female Seminary, Beaufort and Roberville, South Carolina; Providence, Rhode Island; and Miss Phelp's School in Philadelphia, Pennsylvania.

Because of the experiences she gained as both a student and a teacher in private schools, Bonney appreciated the value of educating young women. In 1850 she opened the Chestnut Street Female Seminary in Philadelphia with the aid of a friend and former Troy Seminary teacher, Harriette A. Dillaye. In 1883 the school moved to Ogontz, Pennsylvania, and was renamed the Ogontz School for Young Ladies, with Bonney its senior principal until her retirement in 1888.

As a social reformer Bonney played an active part in creating public awareness of unjust government policies against the American Indians and served as first president of the Woman's National Indian Association. Under her leadership, the association developed educational programs for Indians and sponsored missions, libraries, schools, and loan funds.

Bonney also helped found the Woman's United Missionary Society. While the society delegate to a world missionary convention in London, England, in 1888, she met and married the Reverend Thomas Rambaut, a fellow delegate and former president of William Jewell College.

REFERENCES: *AC; DAB; NAW; NCAB* (6:100); *TC; WC; WWW* (I); *NYT*, July 26, 1900, p. 7.                                    *Karen L. Hadley*

**RANDALL, Samuel Sidwell.** B. May 27, 1809, Norwich, New York, to Perez and Betsey Parker (Edmunds) Murray Randall. M. October 29, 1829, to Lucy Ann Briede. M. to Sarah Bassett Hubbell. Ch. five. D. June 3, 1881, Morrisania, New York.

Samuel Sidwell Randall was educated at Oxford (New York) Academy and at Hamilton College in Clinton, New York, where he studied for two years. He studied law in a Norwich, New York, law office and was admitted to the bar in 1830.

Randall practiced law in Norwich (1830–36) and was deputy clerk of the state legislature (1836–37). He served as clerk (1837) and general deputy superintendent of common schools (1838–54) in the state department of common schools. He proposed a separation of the offices of superintendent of public instruction and secretary of state, the reinstitution of the office of county superintendent of schools, and a permanent tax to support the common schools; the measures were implemented by 1867. He was superintendent of the Brooklyn (New York) public schools for a short time, returned to the state department, and ran for election as state superintendent of public instruction. Defeated by Victor M. Rice (q.v.), he became superintendent of the New York City public schools in 1854 and served to his retirement in 1870.

Randall was the author of *A Digest of the Common-School System of the State of New York* (1844), *Incentives to the Cultivation of Geology* (1846), *Mental and Moral Culture and Popular Education* (1850), *The Common School System of the State of New York* (1851), *Principles of Popular Education* (1868), *History of the State of New York* (1870), and *History of the Common School System of the State of New York* (1871). He was editor of the *District School Journal* (1845–52) and associate editor of the *American Journal of Education and College Review* and *Northern Light*.

REFERENCES: *AC; DAB; NCAB* (18:184); *NYT,* June 4, 1881, p. 5; *WWW* (H).                                             *Carey W. Brush*

**RAUB, Albert Newton.** B. March 28, 1840, Leesburg, Pennsylvania, to John and Maria (Miller) Raub. M. September 15, 1861, to Martha Jennie Lovett. M. September 2, 1876, to Lydia Maria (Chamberlin) Bridgman. Ch. nine. D. February 4, 1904, Newark, Delaware.

Albert Newton Raub, college president and educational author, was educated in district schools in Lancaster County, Pennsylvania. He received the B.S. degree (1860) from the Pennsylvania State Normal School at Millersville (later, Millersville State College).

He was principal of the Union School of Bedford, Pennsylvania, in 1860 and took charge of the Cresson, Pennsylvania, school system, which he completely reorganized (1861–64). He served as superintendent of the Ashland (Pennsylvania) public schools (1864–66). Raub was professor of English literature and rhetoric at Keystone State Normal College (later, Kutztown State College) in Kutztown, Pennsylvania (1866–68). From 1868 to 1877 he was principal of the Lock Haven, Pennsylvania, High School. He worked to reorganize the school and became superintendent of the city's schools.

Following a year as county superintendent of schools in Clinton County, Pennsylvania, he returned to Lock Haven as superintendent of schools. The State Normal School of Lock Haven (later, Lock Haven State College) was organized under his direction, and he was elected its first principal in

1877. In 1884 he resigned from his position at the normal school and spent a year revising the textbooks he had been writing through the years. From 1885 to 1888 he was principal of Delaware College (later, the University of Delaware). During his tenure as president, Delaware College grew rapidly in the number of students and facilities and the educational program. He was instrumental in establishing a policy that admitted students from Delaware without tuition charges.

Raub wrote many books and published them in his firm of Raub and Company. Among his books were *The Normal Speller* (1865), *Plain Educational Talks with Parents and Teachers* (1869), *The Elementary Arithmetic* (1877), *The Complete Arithmetic* (1877), *The Normal Reader* (five volumes, 1878), *Lessons in English* (1880), *Studies in English and American Literature* (1882), *School Management* (1882), *Methods of Teaching* (1883), *Grammatical Analysis by Diagrams* (1885), *Practical Rhetoric and Composition* (1887), *Punctuation and Letter Writing* (1887), *Hints and Helps on English Grammar* (1889), *Practical Arithmetic* (1895), *Practical Language Works for Beginners* (1895), and *Helps in the Use of Good English* (1897). He was editor and owner of a weekly educational journal, *The Educational News*, and was educational editor of the *Pottsville* (Pennsylvania) *Standard*.

Raub was president of the Pennsylvania State Teachers' Association (1871). He was awarded honorary degrees by the College of New Jersey (later, Princeton University), Lafayette College, and Ursinus College.

REFERENCES: *NCAB* (38:425); *TC*                          *Gorman L. Miller*

**RAUCH, Frederick Augustus.** B. July 27, 1806, Kirchbracht, Prussia (Germany), to Heinrich and Friederike (Haderman) Rauch. M. 1833 to Phebe Bathiah Moore. Ch. none. D. March 2, 1841, Mercersburg, Pennsylvania.

After receiving the Ph.D. (1827) degree from the University of Marburg, Germany, Frederick Rauch studied at the universities of Giessen and Heidelberg and was professor extraordinarius at Giessen. An expression of political sympathies against the government resulted in his resignation from Heidelberg, where he was about to be appointed professor ordinarius.

Rauch emigrated to the United States as a political refugee in 1831. He taught music for a time and then taught German at Lafayette College in Easton, Pennsylvania. He was principal of a high school in York, Pennsylvania (1832–35), connected with the seminary of the German Reformed church. He was ordained a minister in 1832 and was also appointed professor of biblical literature at the seminary (1832–35). The seminary and academy were moved to Mercersburg in 1834, where Rauch organized the academy into Marshall College in 1835 and became its first president (1836–41). The college later merged with Franklin College into Franklin and Marshall College at Lancaster, Pennsylvania.

At the college, he and others formed the doctrinal system of Mercersburg theology, which influenced religious beliefs and worship in the United States. Rauch wrote *Psychology or a View of the Human Soul, including Anthropology* (1840), which was the first attempt to unite American and German mental philosophy. He also wrote *Vorlesungen über Goethe's Faust* (1830). E. B. Gerhart edited a selection of Rauch's sermons, *The Inner Life of the Christian,* published posthumously in 1856. He received an honorary degree from Heidelberg University.

REFERENCES: *AC; DAB; NCAB* (11:62); *TC; WWW* (H).

*John M. Ivanoff*

**RAY, Joseph.** B. November 25, 1807, near Wheeling, Virginia (later, West Virginia), to n.a. M. n.a. Ch. n.a. D. April 17, 1865, Cincinnati, Ohio.

Joseph Ray began teaching in Cincinnati when he was sixteen years old. He attended Washington (Pennsylvania) College, Athens (Ohio) College (later, Ohio University), and the Ohio Medical College in Cincinnati, where he earned the M.D. degree (1830). He was a surgeon at the Cincinnati Hospital and professor of mathematics at Woodward College from 1834 to 1851. The college was converted into a high school with Ray as its principal (1851–56).

Ray was noted for his mathematics textbooks, which continued to be published in many editions after his death. They include *The Little Arithmetic* (1834), *Ray's Eclectic Arithmetic* (1837), *Ray's Arithmetic* (three volumes, 1843–44), *Ray's Algebra* (two volumes, 1848–52), *The Child's Arithmetic* (1853), *Mental Arithmetic* (1853), *Practical Arithmetic* (1853), *Ray's Higher Arithmetic* (1856), and *Intellectual Arithmetic* (1857). He also wrote *Calumny Refuted* (1855). Ray designed his text series to be gradual and progressive, mastery of one book being necessary before the student could advance to the next.

Ray was active in professional groups, serving as president of the Ohio State Teachers' Association (1852). He was elected president of the board of directors of the Cincinnati House of Refuge in 1849.

REFERENCES: *NCAB* (1:349); *WWW* (H); James J. Burns, *Educational History of Ohio* (Columbus, Ohio: Historical Publishing Co., 1905); John A. Nietz, *Old Textbooks* (Pittsburgh: University of Pittsburgh Press, 1961). *Sally H. Wertheim*

**RAYMOND, George Lansing.** B. September 13, 1839, Chicago, Illinois, to Benjamin Wright and Amelia (Porter) Raymond. M. July 31, 1872, to Mary Elizabeth Blake. Ch. one. D. July 11, 1929, Washington, D.C.

George Lansing Raymond, pioneer in aesthetics education, was graduated from Phillips Academy in Andover, Massachusetts, in 1858. He received the A.B. (1862) and A.M. (1865) degrees from Williams College in Williamstown, Massachusetts, and was graduated from the Princeton

(New Jersey) Theological Seminary in 1865. He studied art in Europe (1865–68).

Ordained a Presbyterian minister in 1870, he served a church in Darby, Pennsylvania (1870–74). Raymond was professor of oratory at Williams College (1874–80) and professor of oratory and aesthetic criticism (1880–93) and aesthetics (1893–1905) at Princeton (New Jersey) University. From 1905 to 1912, he was a professor of aesthetics at George Washington University in Washington, D.C. He retired to Los Angeles, California, in 1912 and returned to Washington in 1917.

A prolific author, Raymond wrote *Colony Ballads* (1876), *Ideals Made Real* (1877), *Orators Manual* (1877), *Modern Fishers of Men* (1879), *A Life in Song* (1886), *Poetry as a Representative Art* (1886), *Ballads of the Revolution* (1887), *Sketches in Song* (1887), *The Genesis of Art Form* (1893), *The Writer* (1893), *Art in Theory* (1894), *Pictures in Verse* (1894), *Rhythm and Harmony in Poetry and Music* (1895), *Painting, Sculpture and Architecture* (1899), *The Representative Significance of Form* (1900), *The Aztec God and Other Dramas* (1900), *Ballads and Other Poems* (1901), *The Essentials of Aesthetics* (1907), *Psychology of Inspiration* (1908), *Dante and Collected Verse* (1909), *Fundamentals in Education, Art and Civics* (1911), *Suggestions for the Spiritual Life* (1912), *The Mountains About Williamstown* (1913), and *Ethics and Natural Law* (1920). Marion Mills Miller compiled some of Raymond's writings in *A Poet's Cabinet* (1914) and *An Art Philosopher's Cabinet* (1915).

Raymond was a member of many American and foreign scholarly organizations and received honorary degrees from Rutgers and Williams colleges and Princeton University.

REFERENCES: *DAB; NCAB* (8:457); *NYT,* July 12, 1929, p. 23; *TC; WWAE* (I); *WWW* (I).                                                                 *John F. Ohles*

**RAYMOND, John Howard.** B. March 7, 1814, New York, New York, to Eliakim and Mary (Carrington) Raymond. M. May 12, 1840, to Cornelia E. Morse. Ch. nine. D. August 14, 1878, Poughkeepsie, New York.

John Howard Raymond attended Columbia College (1828) and was graduated from Union College in Schenectady, New York, with the A.B. (1832) and A.M. (1835) degrees. He studied law and was admitted to the bar in 1835 but did not practice law. He studied theology at Madison College (later, Colgate University) in Hamilton, New York, and was graduated in 1838.

Raymond was appointed a tutor in Hebrew at Madison College (1837–39) and professor of rhetoric and English literature (1839–49). He accepted a position at the new University of Rochester, New York, as professor of history and belles lettres (1850–55). He organized and was president of the Brooklyn Collegiate and Polytechnic Institute (1856–64). His success at

Brooklyn led to an invitation to assume the presidency of Vassar College at Poughkeepsie, New York, succeeding Milo Parker Jewett *(q.v.)*, founder with Matthew Vassar of the institution. Raymond served as president and professor of mental and moral philosophy to 1878. He succeeded in reorganizing the administration, faculty, and curriculum and acted as chaplain of the college.

Raymond was the author of several pamphlets and sermons. He was awarded an honorary degree by the University of Rochester in 1855.

REFERENCES: *AC; DAB; NCAB* (5:234); *NYT,* August 16, 1878, p. 8; *TC; WWW* (H).                                          *George R. Berrian*

**READ, Daniel.** B. June 24, 1805, near Marietta, Ohio, to Ezra Read and his wife n.a. M. 1826 to Alice Brice. Ch. five, including Theodore Read, a Union general in the Civil War. D. October 3, 1878, Keokuk, Iowa.

Daniel Read was educated at a Marietta, Ohio, academy and later attended Ohio University in Athens, where he was graduated with the A.B. (1824) and A.M. (1827) degrees.

Read was principal of the preparatory department at Ohio University (1824–35). He was a professor of ancient languages (1836–38) and taught Latin and political economy (1839–42) at Ohio University and was professor of languages (1843–56) and acting president (1853–54) at Indiana State Normal School (later, State University) in Terre Haute.

He moved to the University of Wisconsin and became professor of mental and moral philosophy (1856–67). While at Wisconsin, Read became closely associated with John Hiram Lathrop *(q.v.)*, who was president of the University of Missouri. Read became Lathrop's successor in 1867 and rebuilt and reorganized the university. He expanded into new fields of instruction, correlated the curriculum to the public schools, removed the university operation from partisan politics and sectarian influences, and allowed women to enroll as students. Read provided programs for classical education and for industrial, technical, professional, and graduate education. He established a strong course of study for teacher training, founding the College of Normal Instruction in 1867.

After a long struggle Read opened the school of law (1872), completing the program of expansion he had announced in 1866. Later the school of medicine was established (1873). Read became president emeritus in 1876. He received an honorary degree from Indiana Asbury (later, DePauw) University (1853).

REFERENCES: *AC; DAB; NCAB* (8:185); *TC; WWW* (H); Frank F. Stephens, *A History of the University of Missouri* (Columbia: University of Missouri Press, 1962), pp. 194–99; Jonas Viles, *The University of Missouri: A Centennial History* (Columbia, Mo.: E. W. Stephens Co., 1939), pp. 111–27, 160–75.                          *James R. Layton*

**READ, Gerald Howard.** B.June 28, 1913, Akron, Ohio, to Charles Luther and Clara (Beck) Read. M. June 5, 1941, to Victoria C. Twarog. Ch. one.

Gerald H. Read attended the public schools of Akron, Ohio, and was graduated with both the A.B. and B.S. magna cum laude degrees from Kent State University (1936). He received the A.M. (1938) and Ph.D. (1950) degrees from Ohio State University; both his master's thesis and doctoral dissertation concerned education in Cuba. In the summer of 1941 he conducted research on Cuban schools at the University of Havana.

After serving as a junior high school principal in Tallmadge, Ohio (1938–41), and teacher of Spanish at Perrysburg, Ohio (1941–42), Read was appointed assistant professor at Kent State University in 1943 where he retired in 1976 as Endowed Professor of Comparative and International Education. He was one of the founders of the Comparative (and International) Education Society serving as secretary-treasurer (1955–66) and treasurer (1966–73). With William W. Brickman *(q.v.)* of New York University, Read organized and directed the first international seminars under the Comparative Education Society from 1956. In 1957 Read and Brickman negotiated the first exchange of professional materials and displays and tours to the U.S.S.R. Read was instrumental in negotiating an agreement in 1973 with the Peoples Republic of China for seminars to China; he headed the resultant first tour in 1974.

Active in professional associations, Read served as vice-president (1954–64) and president (1964–66) of Kappa Delta Pi and on the commission on International Education of Phi Delta Kappa (1958–68). He wrote *The Changing Soviet School* (with George Z. F. Bereday and William W. Brickman, 1960), and contributed articles to professional journals. He served as director of the Research Center for the Study of Socialist Education from 1969 and was a consultant to the United States State Department and Office of Education.

REFERENCES: *LE* (V); *Who's Who in the Midwest*, 12th ed. (Chicago: Marquis, 1970). *John F. Ohles*

**REAVIS, William Claude.** B. August 18, 1881, Francisco, Indiana, to Franklin and Sarah (Wood) Reavis. M. June 14, 1907, to Anna Lanpher. Ch. none. D. June 1, 1955, Chicago, Illinois.

William Claude Reavis began teaching in rural schools (1899–1905) before completing baccalaureate studies. He received the A.B. degree (1905) from Oakland (Indiana) City College and completed the Ph.B. (1908) and M.A. (1911) degrees at the University of Chicago. He received the Ph.D. degree there in 1925.

Reavis was principal of Indiana high schools at Francisco (1905–07) and Hazelton (1907–08) and was superintendent at Oakland City (1908–12). He moved to St. Louis, Missouri, where he became principal of the Pierre

Laclede School (1912–17) and was professor of educational sociology at Harris Teachers College (1917–18). He became superintendent of schools in Alton, Illinois, in 1918. After three years Reavis returned to the University of Chicago as principal of its high school (1921–27). In 1927 he became a professor in the department of education, holding that post until his retirement in 1947.

Reavis was noted as a consultant to public school systems throughout the United States. He was the author of *Pupil Adjustment in Junior and Senior High Schools* (1926), *Office Practices in Secondary Schools* (with Robert C. Woellner, 1930), *The Elementary School, Its Organization and Administration* (with others, 1931), *Guidance Programs* (1932), *Relations of School Principals to Central Administrative Office in Large Cities* (1937), *Administering the Secondary School* (1940), *Duties of School Principals* (1941), *The Teacher and Educational Administration* (with Charles H. Judd, *q.v.*, 1942), *Administering the Elementary School* (with others, 1953), and *The Effective School Principal* (1954).

He was editor of *Masters' Theses in Secondary School Administration* (1929), *Critical Issues in School Administration* (1938), *Democratic Practices in School Administration* (1939), *Evaluating the Work of the School* (1940), *Administrative Adjustments Required by Socio-Economic Change* (1941), *The School and the Urban Community* (1942), *War and Post-War Responsibilities of American Schools* (1943), *Significant Aspects of American Life and Postwar Education* (1944), *Forthcoming Developments in American Education* (1945), and *Educational Administration* (1946).

Reavis was active in the National Education Association on the commission of problems of school administration of the Department of Superintendents that produced the twelfth yearbook (1934) and the committee that produced the seventh yearbook of the Department of Supervisors and Directors of Instruction (1934). He was a member of the Illinois State Teachers College Board and of many other professional organizations.

REFERENCES: *LE* (III); *WWAE* (VIII); *WWW* (III); *NYT,* June 3, 1955, p. 23.                                                                    *Robert V. Shuff*


**REDWAY, Jacques Wardlaw.** B. May 5, 1849, near Murfreesboro, Tennessee, to John Wesley and Lady Alexandrina (Wardlaw) Redway. M. September 21, 1893, to Lilian Burnham Von Ebert. M. September 11, 1924, to Katherine Virginia Clark. Ch. none. D. November 6, 1942, Mount Vernon, New York.

Jacques Redway was a prominent geographer of the late nineteenth and early twentieth centuries and the author of many geography, history, and meteorological textbooks. He was orphaned after the Civil War; his father and two brothers were killed while serving in the Confederate army, and his mother died soon after. In 1865 he began to study medicine in Chicago but soon dropped these studies to go West, traveling by horseback over the Oregon Trail. For the next few years he worked as scout, pony express rider, reporter for the *Portland Oregonian,* and prospector in Oregon and California.

Redway took a special course in mining engineering at the University of California and studied at the University of Munich (Germany). He was connected with various mines in California and Arizona as an engineer or superintendent (1870–80). He became an instructor of chemistry at the University of California. He was appointed professor of physical geography and geology at the California State Normal School (later, University of California, Los Angeles) in Los Angeles (1883–85), where he met James Monteith and wrote a geography text for a series Monteith was producing.

Redway went to New York in 1885. He was a lecturer on geography and political economy on the staff of the Institute of the University of the State of New York in 1898. His major activity to 1913 was writing geography books and traveling in the Western Hemisphere and Europe to lecture and gather material for his books. He was one of the first to suggest that the physical environment is a major factor in determining racial distribution and political history.

A major producer of geography books, Redway wrote *New Physical Geography for Grammar and High Schools and Colleges* (1884), *Butter's Elementary Geography* (1888), *Manual of Geography and Travel* (1888), *The Teacher's Manual of Geography* (1889), *Natural Advanced Geography* (1891), *Natural Elementary Geography* (1897), *Elementary Physical Geography* (1900), *The New Basis of Geography* (1901), *Commercial Geography* (1903), *Inquiries Concerning the First Landfall of Columbus* (1907), *The Treeless Plains of America* (1907), *Natural Introductory Geography* (with Russell Hinman, 1907), *Natural School Geography* (with Russell Hinman, 1907), and *Geography, Commercial and Industrial* (1923). He edited Sir John Mandeville's *Travels and Voyages* (1898) and Alexander W. Kinglake's *Eothen* (1898) and wrote three school histories: *The Making of the Empire State* (1904), *The Making of the American Nation* (1905), and *Redway School History* (1910). He also wrote a travel book for juveniles, *All Around Asia* (1910).

Redway became interested in meteorology and established a meteorological laboratory in Mount Vernon, New York (later a part of the United States Weather Bureau). He wrote *Handbook of Meteorology* (1921) and *The Story of Weather* (1932). Redway was a contributor to several encyclopedias and scientific journals. He was a fellow of the Royal Geographic Society of England and an honorary fellow of the National University of La Plata, Argentina.

REFERENCES: *AC; NCAB* (31:85); *TC; WWW* (II); *NYT,* November 7, 1942, p. 15. *Carol O'Meara*

**REED, David Allen.** B. October 3, 1850, Troy, New York, to Orville and Elizabeth (Allen) Reed. M. to Gratia R. Chapin. Ch. five. D. April 28, 1932, Springfield, Massachusetts.

David Allen Reed was graduated from Hamilton College in Clinton, New York, in 1877 and studied in Germany for two years at Bonn and Leipzig universities (1878–80) before returning to enter Auburn (New York) Seminary. He was graduated in 1881 and became minister of the Hope Congregational Church in Springfield, Massachusetts.

Recognizing the need for specially trained workers for the Young Men's Christian Association (YMCA) movement and for lay persons to assist with church activities, Reed founded and became first president of the School for Christian Workers in Springfield in 1885. The two departments separated in 1890 into the YMCA Training School and the Bible Normal School, with Reed president of both; he retired as president of the training school in 1891. He was also president of a third institution he founded to teach young men skilled industrial trades, the Christian Industrial and Training School. The International YMCA College became Springfield College, the Hartford School of Religious Education became the Hartford Theological Seminary, and the Christian Industrial and Training School became Springfield Technical High School.

A fourth school Reed inaugurated in Springfield was the French-Protestant College, established to provide Christian education for the foreign born; in 1894 it became American International College. Reed sought to merge these four schools into a Christian university. Although he was not successful, his efforts did lead to the permanent establishment of all four institutions. He retired in 1896.

Reed was the author of *Outline of the Fundamental Doctrines of the Bible* (1893). He was a trustee of Massachusetts Home Missionary Society and of the institutions he founded.

REFERENCES: Laurence L. Doggett, *Man and a School* (New York: Association Press, 1943); Lawrence K. Hall, *Doggett of Springfield* (Lebanon, Pa.: Somers Printing Co., 1964); Harry Andrew Wright, *The Story of Western Massachusetts* (New York: Lewis Historical Publishing Co., 1949), vol. 3.                                    *Thomas L. Bernard*

**REEVE, Tapping.** B. October, 1744, Brookhaven, New York, to Abner Reeve and his wife (n.a.). M. 1771 to Sarah (Sally) Burr. M. 1799 to n.a. Ch. one. D. December 13, 1823, Litchfield, Connecticut.

Tapping Reeve was graduated from the College of New Jersey (later, Princeton University) in 1763 and was a teacher and headmaster at a school in Elizabethtown, New Jersey (1763–67). From 1767 to 1770 he was a tutor at the College of New Jersey. In 1771 he moved to Connecticut and studied law in the office of Judge Jesse Root at Hartford.

Admitted to the bar in 1772, Reeve moved to Litchfield, Connecticut, and opened a law practice. Law students read the law with Reeve, and he began to give regular instruction in law in his office. In 1784 he established the Litchfield Law School and was its sole instructor until 1798, when he was joined by James Gould *(q.v.)*.

Reeve was a state's attorney in 1788, became a member of the legislature, and served on the state council. He was appointed judge of the Connecticut superior court in 1798, serving until 1814, when he became chief justice of the state; he retired in 1816. He wrote *The Law of Baron and Femme* (1816) and *A Treatise on the Law of Descents in the Several United States of America* (1825).

During the Revolution, Reeve was appointed by the Connecticut Assembly to a committee to travel about the state to arouse interest in the war; he was active in raising recruits. He was a frequent contributor of political articles, one of which led to an indictment for libeling President Thomas Jefferson. As a judge he worked for change in the law regarding the property of married women. He was an agent for the Connecticut Bible Club and was active in a local temperance movement. He received honorary degrees from Middlebury College and the College of New Jersey.

REFERENCES: *AC; DAB; NCAB* (6:175); *TC; WWW* (H).

> *Joseph P. Cangemi*
> *Thomas E. Kesler*

**REEVE, William David.** B. September 11, 1883, Edwardsport, Indiana, to Charles and Martha (McLin) Reeve. M. June 16, 1911, to Isabel Jaensch. Ch. one. D. February 16, 1961, New York, New York.

William Reeve spent his early life in rural Indiana. He received the B.S. degree (1909) from the University of Chicago and the Ph.D. degree (1924) from the University of Minnesota.

Reeve served in Indiana as a teacher in rural schools (1902–03) and at the high school at Bicknell (1904–05) and as a principal at Edwardsport (1905–07) and at Sanborn (1907–08). He taught mathematics at University High School in Chicago (1910–14); he was head of the mathematics department (1915–21) and principal of the University (of Minnesota) High School (1921–23). He was a professor of mathematics at Teachers College, Columbia University, from 1924 until his retirement in 1949. Reeve believed in higher standards of preparation for teachers and crusaded for improved mathematics teaching.

He wrote sixteen textbooks, including *General Mathematics* (1919), *Essentials of Algebra* (1926), *Essentials of Trigonometry* (1927), *The Teaching of Junior High School Mathematics* (1927), *Texts and Tests in Plane Geometry* (1933), *Workbooks in General Mathematics grades 7, 8, and 9* (1941), *Texts and Tests in Algebra* (1941), *Essential Mathematics*

(1943), and *Teaching Problems in High School Mathematics* (1946). He
was editor of the second through twentieth yearbooks of the National
Council of Teachers of Mathematics and was editor of *Mathematics
Teacher* (1928–50).

Reeve was president of Tau Kappa Epsilon (1918–21) and was awarded
the Honor Key from Phi Delta Kappa. He was a member of the Joint
Committee on the Place of Mathematics in Secondary Schools (1934–36)
and the New York Society for Experimental Study of Education (vice-
president).

REFERENCES: *LE* (III); *WWAE* (XVI); *WWW* (IV); *NYT,* February 17,
1961, p. 28.                                                    *Robert McGinty*

**REID, Ira de Augustine.** B. July 2, 1901, Clifton Forge, Virginia, to Daniel
A. and Willie R. (James) Reid. M. October 15, 1925, to Gladys Russell
Scott. M. August 12, 1958, to Anne M. Cooke. Ch. one. D. August 15, 1968,
Haverford, Pennsylvania.

Ira de A. Reid, the first black full-time professor at New York University, grew up in Pennsylvania, where he attended public schools in
Harrisburg and Philadelphia. Moving to Georgia with his family, Reid
attended Morehouse Academy and Morehouse College in Atlanta in 1917;
he moved to West Virginia on the death of his father. He served in the army
in World War I and returned to Morehouse College where he received the
A.B. degree (1922). He was awarded the M.A. degree (1925) from the
University of Pittsburgh, Pennsylvania, and the Ph.D. degree (1939) from
Columbia University.

Reid taught social sciences at Texas College in Tyler, Texas (1922–23),
and taught at the Douglas High School in Huntington, West Virginia
(1923–24). He was industrial and research secretary for the New York
Urban League for Social Work among Negroes (1925–28) and director of
research for the National Urban League, where he made surveys of racial
problems in several American cities (1928–34). He was a professor of
sociology at Atlanta (Georgia) University (1934–46) and professor of educational sociology in the School of Education at New York University
(1946–47). In 1947 he became professor of sociology and chairman of the
department of sociology and anthropology at Haverford (Pennsylvania)
College, where he remained to his retirement in 1966. He was a visiting
director of the department of extramural studies at the University College
in Ibadan, Nigeria (1962), and Danforth Distinguished Professor of Sociology at the International Christian University in Tokyo, Japan.

The author of several books and reports, Reid wrote *The Negro Immigrant* (1939), *In a Minor Key* (1940), and *Sharecroppers All* (with Arthur F.
Raper, 1941), edited *Racial Desegregation and Integration* (1956), and
was editor of *Phylon* (1943–47). He was a member of the advisory council

for teacher grants of the Danforth Foundation, an advisory committee of the United States Department of Labor (1940–42), the Governor's Commission on Higher Education for Pennsylvania (1956–68), the Philadelphia Commission on Higher Education (1958–68), and the Governor's Commission on Police Brutality (1964). He was a fellow of the American Association for the Advancement of Science and the American Sociological Association (vice-president, 1954) and a member of several associations, including the Eastern Sociological Society (president, 1955) and the Urban League of Philadelphia (president). He received honorary degrees from Morehouse (1953) and Haverford (1967) colleges.

REFERENCES: *CB* (July 1946 and October 1968); *NYT*, August 17, 1968, p. 27; *WWW* (V); *Publishers Weekly* 194 (September 2, 1968): 38; *Who's Who in Colored America*, 7th ed. (Brooklyn, N.Y.: Burckel & Associates, 1950). *John F. Ohles*

**REINHARDT, Aurelia Isabel Henry.** B. April 1, 1877, San Francisco, California, to William Warner and Mary Rogers (Merritt) Henry. M. December 4, 1909, to George Frederick Reinhardt. Ch. two. D. January 28, 1948, Palo Alto, California.

Aurelia Henry Reinhardt was one of forty girls admitted to San Francisco (California) Boys' High School in 1888. Reinhardt entered the University of California at Berkeley in 1894 where she received the B.Litt. degree (1898). In 1901 she enrolled in graduate school at Yale University under Albert Stanburrough Cook (*q.v.*) and received the Ph.D. degree in 1905. She spent 1905 and 1906 at Oxford (England) University on a fellowship from the Association of Collegiate Alumnae.

An instructor of English at the University of Idaho (1898–1901), Reinhardt was professor of English at the State Normal School (later, Lewis-Clark State College) at Lewiston, Idaho (1901–08). Her marriage to George F. Reinhardt from 1909 to his death in 1914 was followed by an appointment as lecturer in English at the University of California (1914–16) and service as president of Mills College in Oakland, California (1916–43). Reinhardt tripled the enrollment at Mills in the first decade of her presidency.

Reinhardt wrote several essays published by the National Education Association and edited *The Monarchia* of Dante Alighieri (1904), *Epicoene, or The Silent Woman* by Ben Jonson in Yale Studies in English XXXI (1906). She was moderator of the Unitarian Churches of America (1940–42), a member of the National Committee on Mobilization for Human Needs (1935–37), a trustee of the American Councils of the Institute of Pacific Relations and the Pacific Geography Association, and chairman of the department of education of the General Federation of Women's Clubs. She served as president of the American Association of University Women (1923–27) and was the recipient of several honorary degrees from American colleges and universities.

REFERENCES: *CB* (May 1941); *DAB* (supp. 4); *LE* (I); *NAW; NYT,* January 29, 1948, p. 23; *WWAE* (I); *WWW* (II); George Percy Hedley, *Aurelia Henry Reinhardt: Portrait of a Whole Woman* (Oakland, Calif.: Mills College, 1961).                                              *Karen Wertz*

**REMSEN, Ira.** B. February 10, 1846, New York, New York, to James Vanderbilt and Rosanna (Secor) Remsen. M. April 5, 1875, to Elizabeth Mallory. Ch. two. D. March 4, 1927, Carmel, California.

Ira Remsen entered the New York Free Academy (later, the College of the City of New York) at the age of fourteen but left before receiving a degree. Later he was awarded the A.B. degree with the academy's class of 1865. He earned the M.D. degree (1867) from the College of Physicians and Surgeons of Columbia University. He had little interest in medicine, however, and never practiced. He went to Germany and studied chemistry under Justus Liebig and Jacob Volhard at the University of Munich and under Friedrich Wöhler and Rudolph Fittig at the University of Göttingen where he earned the Ph.D. degree (1870). He assisted Fittig at the University of Tübingen from 1870 to 1872.

Remsen taught at Williams College in Williamstown, Massachusetts (1872–76). He was the first professor of chemistry at Johns Hopkins University in Baltimore, Maryland (1876–1913), director of the chemistry laboratory (1876–1908), secretary of the academy council (1887–1908), and president of Johns Hopkins (1901–13). At Johns Hopkins he promoted research as the primary function of a university.

Remsen had a great influence on the development of science education in the United States. He attracted to Johns Hopkins a group of brilliant students who later held important academic positions at other universities. Among the contributions of his laboratory were the discoveries of saccharin and Remsen's law concerning the prevention of oxidation in methyl.

Remsen published 156 research papers and was the author of important textbooks, including *The Principles of Theoretical Chemistry* (1876), *An Introduction to the Study of Compounds of Carbon, or Inorganic Chemistry* (1885), *Introduction to the Study of Chemistry* (1887), *The Elements of Chemistry* (1888), *Inorganic Chemistry* (1889), *A Laboratory Manual* (1889), and *Chemical Experiments* (1895). He translated *Organic Chemistry* by Rudolph Fittig (1873) and founded the *American Chemical Journal* (1879) and edited it until 1914 when it merged with the *Journal of the American Chemical Society.*

He was president of the American Association for the Advancement of Science, the National Academy of Sciences (1907–13), and the Society for the Chemical Industry (1910–11). He received the medal of the Society for the Chemical Industry in 1904, the Priestley Medal from the American

Chemical Society in 1923, and honorary degrees from eight universities.

REFERENCES: *DAB; DSB; EB; NCAB* (37:52); *WWW* (I); B. Harrow, *Eminent Chemists of Our Time* (New York: D. Van Nostrand Co., 1929), p. 197; *NYT,* March 6, 1927, sec. 2, p. 11; *School and Society* 25 (March 12, 1927): 321.                                        *B. Richard Siebring*

**RENNER, George Thomas, Jr.** B. July 11, 1900, Winfield, Kansas, to George Thomas and Mildred May (Dodd) Renner. M. June 12, 1924, to Mayme Margaret Pratt. Ch. one. D. October 14, 1955, Leonia, New Jersey.

George Thomas Renner, Jr., attended public schools in Kansas and Oklahoma and entered Cornell College in Mount Vernon, Iowa, where he received the B.A. degree (1922). He received the M.A. (1924) and Ph.D. (1927) degrees from Columbia University.

Renner was a science teacher and director of athletics at the Anita, Iowa, high school (1920–21) and a lecturer in economic geography (1922–26) and instructor in geography (1926–27) at the Columbia University School of Business. Associate professor and chairman of the department of geography at the State University of Washington (1927–33), Renner was a geographer with the Iowa Forest and Waste Land Survey (1933–34) and an agricultural economist and consultant geographer in Washington with governmental resources planning agencies (1934–43). He was also associated with Teachers College, Columbia University, where he served as visiting associate professor of education (1936–37), associate professor of geography and chairman of the department (1937–39), and professor of geography (1939–55). He was an associate member of the faculty of philosophy of Columbia University (1950–53).

Renner's special interests in the discipline of geography were in the fields of climatology, geonomics, social and cultural geography, and geopolitics. He was active in city and regional planning and conservation. Renner was a member of the President's Technical Committee on National Regional Planning (1935) and educational consultant and member of the aviation educational research project of the Civil Aeronautics Administration (1942–47). During World War I Renner served in France with the Army Artillery Corps, and during World War II he served as consultant and lecturer to the United States Army General Staff. He was geographical consultant to the Continental Air Command, United States Air Force (1950–51), educational consultant on Air Force Academy matters to the Headquarters Command of the air force (1951–53), and lecturer on economics and industrial geography at the United States Military Academy during the later years of his career.

Renner was a prolific writer; among his books were *Primitive Religion in the Tropical Forests—A Study in Social Geography* (1927), *World Climate Regions* (1930), *Regional Factors in National Planning and Development* (with J. Crane, M. Dimock, and J. Gaus, 1935), *Geography—An Intro-duction to Human Ecology* (with C. L. White, 1936), *North America—A Geography Reader* (1936), *Land Planning Procedure—Suggestions to State Planning Boards* (with others, 1936), *Conservation and Citizenship* (with W. H. Hartley, 1940), *World Map for the Air Age* (1942), *Geographi-cal Education for the Air Age* (1942), *Conservation of Natural Resources—An Educational Approach to the Problem* (1942), *Home Geography* (with E. H. Reeder, 1944), and *World Economic Geography* (with others, 1951). He contributed the geographical section of the *King's English Dictionary* (1929) and articles to many popular and professional journals, and he made ten educational sound films. He was educational map editor for the Denoyer-Geppart Company, geographical editor for Thomas Y. Crowell Company, and special map editor for Rand, McNally & Company. He served as associate editor of the *Journal of Geography* (1938–55), editor of the international forum department of *The Social Studies* (1939–43), and member of the editorial staff of *Building America* (1942–44). Renner was a founder of the Pacific Geographical Society and active in the National Council of Geography Teachers (elected fellow, 1949 and posthumously awarded the Distinguished Service Award, 1956). Ren-ner was a member of many other professional and service organizations. He received an honorary degree from Cornell College (1943).

REFERENCES: *NCAB* (45:290); *WWAE* (XIV); *WWW* (III); *NYT,* Octo-ber 15, 1955, p. 15.                                              *J. Franklin Hunt*

**REVEL, Bernard.** B. September 17, 1885, Kaunas, Lithuania, to Nahum Shraga and Leah (Gitilevitz) Revel. M. to Sarah Travis. Ch. two. D. December 2, 1940, New York, New York.

Bernard Revel studied at the Yeshiva School at Telsche, Lithuania. He emigrated to the United States in 1906 and studied at the University of Pennsylvania and New York University, where he received the M.A. degree (1909). He received the Ph.D. degree (1911) from Dropsie College in Philadelphia, Pennsylvania.

Revel moved to Tulsa, Oklahoma, where he was a pioneer in the refining of natural gas. In 1915 he was persuaded to become president of Isaac Elchanan Theological Seminary in New York City. He opened the semi-nary to laymen and teachers and founded the Talmud'cal Academy (1916), the first combined high school and yeshiva (school of talmudic studies) in the United States. In 1928 he founded Yeshiva College (later, University) as an extension of the seminary. Yeshiva was the first Jewish liberal arts college and was the first effort to combine traditional talmudic and modern secular studies in higher education. Revel was president of the institution (1928–40) and established the graduate school of Jewish studies, which was named for him.

A leader of modern Jewish Orthodoxy, Revel contributed to the study of Jewish religious law and the teachings of the Karaite sect. He was the author of *Karaite Halakah and Its Relation to Sadducean, Samaritan and Philonian Halakah* (1913) and *Pseudo-Jonathan on the Pentateuch* (n.d.). He was an associate of the Hebrew encyclopedia *Ozar Yisrael* (1913). He was a fellow of the Jewish Academy of Arts and Sciences (vice-president, 1927–40) and honorary president of the Union of Orthodox Rabbis of the United States and Canada.

REFERENCES: *DAB* (supp. 2); *NYT,* December 2, 1940, p. 23; *WWAE* (VIII); *WWW* (I); *Encyclopedia Judaica* (New York: Macmillan, 1972).

*John F. Ohles*

**REVELS, Hiram Rhoades.** B. September 1, 1822, Fayetteville, North Carolina, to n.a. M. 1850 to Phoebe A. Bass. Ch. two. D. January 16, 1901, Aberdeen, Mississippi.

Hiram Rhoades Revels attended a private school in Fayetteville, North Carolina, and moved to Liberty, Indiana, in 1844 where he enrolled in a Quaker school. While in Indiana he attended an African Methodist Episcopal (AME) church and became interested in the church's struggle for political and educational freedom for blacks. He enrolled in an AME seminary in Ohio and was ordained (1854) and attended Knox College in Nashville, Tennessee.

Revels was an itinerant preacher to free blacks and slaves (1854–60). He taught at a high school for blacks and served a church in Baltimore, Ohio, in 1860. He helped organize two black regiments for service in the Union army during the Civil War in Maryland and Missouri and taught school in St. Louis, Missouri (1863–64). He served congregations in several border and southern states before arriving with the Union army in Vicksburg, Mississippi, at the end of the war to serve as chaplain for black troops and to work in the Freedmen's Bureau.

Revels organized churches in Kansas and Missouri (1865–67) and settled in Natchez, Mississippi, in 1868 where he was appointed alderman and state senator. He was elected by the state senate to fill the unexpired term in the United States Senate of Jefferson Davis, the ex-president of the Confederacy, and was the first black United States senator (1870–71).

Upon the return of Revels to Mississippi, Governor James Lusk Alcorn named him president of Alcorn Agricultural University (later, Alcorn Agricultural and Mechanical College) at Oakland (later Lorman), Mississippi, an institution that became the first black land-grant college in the nation. Revels publicly favored the enfranchisement of white southerners and associated himself more and more with the southern Democrats. Amid controversy and unrest with Mississippi blacks, he resigned the presidency of Alcorn. He left the Republican party to work actively on

behalf of southern Democrats. He lost black support while gaining acceptance from the white power structure. He was named secretary of state for
Mississippi and was again appointed president of Alcorn College in 1877, a
position he held until he retired in 1883.

Revels edited the *Southwestern Christian Advocate,* a religious journal.
He spent the remaining years of his life assisting with church activities and
occasionally teaching classes at Rust College in Holly Springs, Mississippi.

REFERENCES: *AC; DAB; NCAB* (11:405); *NYT,* January 17, 1901, p. 9;
*TC; WWW* (H); John P. Davis, ed., *The American Negro Reference Book*
(Englewood Cliffs, N.J.: Prentice-Hall, 1966); Wilhelmena S. Robinson,
*International Library of Negro Life and History: Historical Negro Biog-
raphies* (New York: Publishers Co., 1968); G. A. Sewall, "Hiram Rhoades
Revels: Another Evaluation," *Negro History Bulletin* 38 (December
1974): 336–39; Julius Eric Thompson, "Hiram R. Revels, 1827–1901: A
Biography" (Ph.D. diss., Princeton University, 1973).     *Exyie C. Ryder*

**RICE, Fenelon Bird.** B. January 2, 1841, Greensburg, Ohio, to David
Lyman and Emily (Johnson) Rice. M. September 26, 1863, to Helen Maria
Libby. Ch. one. D. October 26, 1901, Oberlin, Ohio.

Fenelon B. Rice attended Hillsdale (Michigan) College (1858–61) where
his father was on the board of trustees. He was graduated from the Boston
Music School in 1863 where he had studied with J. W. Tufts, B. F. Baker,
and Edwin Bruce. He studied at the Leipzig (Germany) Conservatory with
B. R. Papperitz, E. F. E. Richter, Ignaz Moscheles and Louis Plaidy
(1867–69).

Rice was an instructor at Hillsdale College (1863–67) and at Oberlin
(Ohio) College (1869–1901) and was director of the Oberlin Conservatory
of Music and professor of music from 1871. The conservatory developed
into a leading school of music under Rice, who organized the institution
after European schools, particularly the Leipzig Conservatory. He established a program that provided broad musical experiences and emphasized
the study of classical music literature. He was successful in obtaining funds
for a new physical plant for the conservatory.

Rice was director of Oberlin's Musical Union (1871–1901) and president
of the Music Teachers National Association (1880–81).

REFERENCES: *DAB; WWW* (H); Nicholas Slonimsky, *The International
Cyclopedia of Music and Musicians,* 6th ed. (New York: Dodd, Mead &
Co., 1952).                                                  *J. K. Ward*

**RICE, James Edward.** B. March 12, 1865, Aurora, Illinois, to James Roder-
ick and Emmeline (Wing) Rice. M. September 14, 1898, to Elsie Van
Buren. M. October 31, 1936, to Louise E. (Scott) Dawley. Ch. six. D.
October 25, 1953, Miami, Florida.

James E. Rice received his preparatory education at Granville Military Academy in North Granville, New York, and later studied at Cornell University in Ithaca, New York, where he received the B.S. degree in agriculture (1890). At Cornell Rice conducted the first experiments in poultry feeding in an American college. In 1889 he perfected a trap nest for egg laying; the trap nesting system laid the foundation for pedigree poultry breeding as a scientific industry.

Following graduation in 1890, Rice continued at the college of agriculture for a year establishing the first formal course in poultry husbandry in an American college. In 1892 he farmed in Bucks County, Pennsylvania, and returned a year later to New York State to continue farming as a partner in the firm of White and Rice, which operated the Fernwood Fruit and Poultry Farm at Yorktown (1893–1903). He lectured to farmers' institutes in New York, New Jersey, Maryland, and Minnesota during the winters. He developed a gasoline heated brooder that enabled two hundred or more chicks to be brooded at one time.

Rice returned to Cornell University in 1903 as assistant professor to establish the first department of poultry husbandry in the United States. He was head of the department from 1907 until his retirement in 1934.

He wrote over a hundred bulletins and coauthored *Practical Poultry Management* (with Harold E. Botsford, 1925) and *Judging Poultry* (with Golden O. Hall and Dean R. Marble, 1930). He was editor of the Poultry Science Series of textbooks.

Rice was chairman of the United States delegation to the First World Poultry Congress at the Hague, the Netherlands (1921), general chairman of the Seventh Congress in Cleveland, Ohio (1939), and president of the Eighth Congress in Copenhagen, Denmark (1948). He founded and served twice as president of the World Poultry Science Association and was founder, fellow, and president of the American Poultry Science Association and founder and president of the Northeastern Poultry Producers Council. The poultry industry presented the James E. Rice Memorial Library to Cornell University.

REFERENCES: *NCAB* (45:319); *NYT*, October 27, 1953, p. 27; *WWW* (V).                                                             *Prodeep K. Paul*

**RICE, John Andrew.** B. February 1, 1888, Lynchburg, South Carolina, to John Andrew and Anna Bell (Smith) Rice. M. December 28, 1914, to Nell Aydelotte. M. 1942 to Dikka Moen. Ch. four. D. November 17, 1968, Silver Springs, Maryland.

John Andrew Rice attended the Webb School in Bellbuckle, Tennessee, and was graduated with the B.A. degree (1911) from Tulane University in New Orleans, Louisiana. He was selected as a Rhodes Scholar from Louisiana and studied at the University of Oxford, England (1911–14), where he received the B.A. degree. He continued his studies at the University of Chicago (1916–18).

Rice taught at the Webb School (1914–16) and served with the Military Intelligence Division of the United States Army in Washington, D.C. (1918–19). He was an associate professor of classics at the University of Nebraska (1916–26) and was chairman of the classics department (1926–28). He was professor of classics at Rutgers University in New Brunswick, New Jersey, and also was head of the department of classics at the New Jersey College for Women (later, Douglass College) from 1928 to 1930. Rice was professor of classics at Rollins College in Winter Park, Florida (1930–33). A caustic critic of teaching and teachers, Rice conflicted with colleagues and administrators at Nebraska and Rollins.

In 1933 Rice and three fellow professors left Rollins College to establish Black Mountain College in North Carolina. An experiment in pure democracy, Black Mountain had a limited enrollment of 125 students. There was no set curriculum, regulations, or discipline, and routine tasks were assigned voluntarily. Artistic and musical accomplishments were stressed, and artists, composers, and poets were on the instructional staff. The college was directed by a rector, who was elected yearly by a vote of the faculty; Rice served four terms as rector (1934–39).

Rice left Black Mountain in 1940 to write, and the college was discontinued in the 1950s. Rice wrote articles, the autobiographical *I Came Out of the 18th Century* (1942), for which he was co-winner of the Harper 125th Anniversary Award, and *Local Color* (1947).

REFERENCES: *NYT*, November 28, 1968, p. 37; John Andrew Rice, "Black Mountain College," *Progressive Education* 11 (April 1934): 271–74; "Brilliant Critic," *Time* 40 (November 23, 1942): 88–90.

*John F. Ohles*

RICE, Joseph Mayer. B. May 20, 1857, Philadelphia, Pennsylvania, to Mayer and Fanny (Sohn) Rice. M. October 10, 1900, to Deborah Levinson. Ch. two. D. June 24, 1934, Philadelphia, Pennsylvania.

Joseph Rice was educated in the public schools of Philadelphia and New York City. He studied at the College of the City of New York and earned the M.D. degree (1881) from the College of Physicians and Surgeons of Columbia. Rice practiced in New York hospitals (1881–84) and had a successful private practice in New York City (1884–88). He studied psychology and pedagogy in Germany at the universities of Jena and Leipzig (1888–90) and also studied European school systems.

His interest in the prevention of disease among children led to his study of child development. Rice believed that children's efforts in school were not adequately rewarded by the results of the school experience. He abandoned his medical practice to engage in an extensive eight-year study of one hundred or more school systems in the United States and Europe. He proposed that it would be necessary to determine how long it took most teachers to teach a subject to determine the amount of time a student should spend in learning a specific task.

Rice returned to the United States in 1890 and studied American schools under the sponsorship of *Forum* magazine. The study was published in 1893 as *The Public School System of the United States*. Rice was editor of *Forum* from 1897 to 1907.

Rice disagreed with the popular theory that the more time allotted to a subject each day, the more rapidly a child would learn. He conducted a study on children's learning to spell; his study and findings led to his preparation of *The Rational Spelling Book* (1898). He also wrote *Scientific Management in Education* (1913) and *The People's Government* (1915). Rice founded the Society of Educational Research in 1903.

REFERENCES: *NCAB* (12:203); *NYT,* June 25, 1934, p. 15; *WWW* (I).

*Ted Beach*

**RICE, Thurman Brooks.** B. August 17, 1888, Landers, Indiana, to Robert Tilton and Ruth (Porter) Rice. M. September 1, 1910, to Ada Charles. M. March 29, 1923, to Ruby Orene Caster. Ch. six. D. December 27, 1952, Indianapolis, Indiana.

Thurman Brooks Rice spent his career in Indiana, where he attended public schools in Grant County and received the B.S. degree (1909) from Marion Normal College (later, Marion College) in Indianapolis, the B.Pd. degree (1912) from Valparaiso University, the B.A. degree (1913) from Muncie Normal Institute (later, Ball State University), and the B.A. (1914), M.A. (1917), and M.D. (1921) degrees from Indiana University.

Rice taught in Huntington County public schools (1906–08) and in the Wheeler high school (1910–12). He was an instructor in biology at Winona College (1914–16) and joined the faculty of Indiana University in 1916 where he became professor of public health and department chairman (1945–52). Rice directed the Indiana State Board of Health laboratory (1924–26) and was secretary (1942–45) and chairman of the division of health and physical education (1936–42) and consultant on public health (1945–52). He was assistant director of the Indiana Division of Public Health (1933–36) and state health commissioner (1942–45).

The author of many articles in scientific journals, Rice wrote *Conquest of Disease* (1927), *Racial Hygiene* (1929), *Textbook of Applied Bacteriology* (1932), *The Human Body* (1937), *Public Safety* (1937), *Living* (1940), *Microbiology and Pathology* (with Fern Coy, 1942), *March Against Cancer* (1946), *Sex, Marriage and Family* (1946), *Effects of Alcoholic Drinks, Tobacco, Sedatives, Narcotics* (with Rolla N. Harger, 1949), and *Low-Sodium Diet* (1951). He also wrote the Sex Education series (1933).

He was a fellow of the American Medical Association and a member of many professional and scientific groups. He received the Ravdin Medal of the School of Medicine of Indiana University.

REFERENCES: *NCAB* (41:27); *NYT,* December 28, 1952, p. 48; *WWW* (III).                                                                       *John F. Ohles*

**RICE, Victor Moreau.** B. April 5, 1818, Mayville, New York, to William and Rachel (Waldo) Rice. M. November 26, 1846, to Maria L. Winter. Ch. none. D. October 17, 1869, Oneida, New York.

Victor Moreau Rice grew up in Chautauqua County, New York, and was educated at Allegheny College in Meadville, Pennsylvania. After graduation in 1841 he taught for eight months and studied law in Mayville, New York, and at Buffalo, New York, with Millard Fillmore. He was admitted to the bar in 1845, but taught penmanship, Latin, and bookkeeping in a private school, which became Buffalo High School. He began teaching in the Buffalo public schools in 1846 and in 1852 was elected superintendent of schools. In 1854, Rice became the first elected superintendent of public instruction in New York State. Reelected in 1857, Rice resigned in 1860 to run successfully as a New York State assemblyman for one term. In 1862 and 1865 he was reelected superintendent of public instruction.

By the time Rice left office in 1868, there were seven normal schools in New York, largely a result of his efforts. A milestone in his career was the act of 1856 under which a state tax of three quarters of a mill was imposed on the assessed value of personal and real property for the support of public schools. This increased state taxes for schools by over two hundred thousand dollars. In 1867 the rate bill (payment for each school-age child by the parent) was abolished by the legislature, making public schools free in New York State. Rice was responsible for the codification of New York's school laws. Rice edited *The Cataract* in 1846. He was president of the New York State Teachers Association in 1853.

REFERENCES: *AC; DAB; NCAB* (14:178); *WWW* (H); William D. Murphy, *Biographical Sketches of the State Officers and Members of the Legislature of the State of New York in 1861* (Albany, N.Y.: The author, 1861), pp. 252–54; *NYT,* October 20, 1869, p. 5; Zoraida E. Weeks, "The Fight for Free Schools," *New York State Education* 54 (April 1967): 10–11.                                                                 *Wayne Mahood*

**RICE, William North.** B. November 21, 1845, Marblehead, Massachusetts, to William and Caroline Laura (North) Rice. M. April 12, 1870, to Elizabeth Wing Crowell. Ch. two. D. November 13, 1928, Delaware, Ohio.

W. North Rice attended Wesleyan University in Middletown, Connecticut, where he received the A.B. degree (1865). He was awarded the Ph.D. degree (1867) from the Sheffield Scientific School of Yale University. He was the first to receive the doctorate in geology from Yale. He studied at the University of Berlin, Germany (1867–68), and traveled and studied in Europe (1892–93 and 1911–12).

Rice spent his academic career at Wesleyan University as professor of geology and natural history (1867–1918), librarian (1868–69), and acting president (1907, 1908–09, and 1918). He also served with the United States Fish Commission (1873–74) and the United States Geological Survey (1891–92) and was superintendent of the Connecticut State Geological and Natural History Survey (1903–16).

He was the author of *Geology of Bermuda* (1884), *Science Teaching in the Schools* (1889), *Twenty-five Years of Scientific Progress* (1894), *Christian Faith in an Age of Science* (1903), *Manual of the Geology of Connecticut* (with H. E. Gregory, 1906), *Return to Faith* (1916), *Through Darkness to Dawn* (1917), *Poet of Science* (1919), and *Science and Religion* (1925). He edited *Dana's Text-Book of Geology* (1897).

A fellow of the American Association for the Advancement of Science (vice-president and chairman of section E, 1905–06) and the Geological Society of America (vice-president, 1911), Rice was a charter member and president of the American Society of Naturalists (1891) and the Connecticut Council of Education (1902–05). He was active in the Methodist Episcopal church as chairman of the board of examiners of the New York East Conference (1896–1925) and a member of the Council of Connecticut Federation of Churches (president, 1910–11 and 1919–20 and secretary, 1913–19). He received honorary degrees from Syracuse and Wesleyan universities.

REFERENCES: *AC; DAB; NCAB* (12:264); *TC; WWW* (I). *John F. Ohles*

**RICHARDS, Charles Russell.** B. June 30, 1865, Boston, Massachusetts, to Charles C. and Josephine (Gleason) Richards. M. 1917 to Hilda Muhlhauser. M. 1926 to Mildred Batchelder. Ch. none. D. February 21, 1936, New York, New York.

Shortly after completing the S.B. degree at the Massachusetts Institute of Technology (1885), Charles Russell Richards moved to New York City. He became director of the department of science and technology at Pratt Institute (1888–98), director of the department of manual training at Teachers College, Columbia University (1898–1908), and director of Cooper Union (1908–23). Richards became director (1923) and vice-president (1927) of the American Association of Museums and executive vice-president of the New York Museum of Science and Industry (1930).

While he was in these administrative positions, he directed and published surveys and other studies on industrial and vocational education. The Federal Education Bureau published his report, *Progress in Industrial Education During the Year 1910–1911* (1912). *How Shall We Study the*

*Industries for the Purposes of Vocational Education?* (1914) gave practical advice on the construction of questionnaires. *The Gary Public Schools: Industrial Work* (1918) was commissioned by the Gary, Indiana, school board.

Under the auspices of the National Society for Vocational Education and the New York State education department, Richards undertook a survey of institutions giving instruction in the industrial arts. The final report, *Art in Industry* (1922), called for educating the public taste, viewing artistry as a commercial asset, and providing adequate training for designers. *The Industrial Museum* (1925) focused on history, organization, and administration, and *Industrial Art and the Museum* (1927) described specific European museums of applied art. Richards argued that American museums should incorporate both fine and applied arts under the same roof. As an officer of the American Federation of Arts, he edited three catalogs: *International Exhibition of Ceramic Art* (1928–29), *International Exhibition of Contemporary Glass and Rugs* (1929–30), and *Decorative Metalwork and Cotton Textiles* (1930–31). He was associate editor of *Manual Training Magazine* (1903–11).

Among other activities, Richards was a trustee of the Children's Aid Society of New York (1904–16), a founder and first secretary of the National Society for the Promotion of Industrial Education, and a member of the Corporation of the Massachusetts Institute of Technology (1909–14). He received the Michael Friedsam Medal (1936) and the French Legion of Honor.

REFERENCES: *WWW* (I); *NYT*, February 22, 1936, p. 15; "Honor to Professor Richards: Michael Friedsam Medal Award," *Industrial Education Magazine* 38 (January 1936): 7a; C. A. Bennett *(q.v.)*, "Charles R. Richards, Industrial Arts Educator," *Industrial Education Magazine* 38 (May 1936): 140–41.                                  *David Delahanty*

**RICHARDS, Ellen Henrietta Swallow.** B. December 3, 1842, Dunstable, Massachusetts, to Peter and Fanny Gould (Taylor) Swallow. M. June 4, 1875, to Robert Hallowell Richards. Ch. none. D. March 30, 1911, Jamaica Plain, Massachusetts.

Ellen H. Richards, the founder of home economics, was educated by her parents for the first twenty-five years of her life. In 1868 she was accepted at Vassar College in Poughkeepsie, New York, as a special student, was admitted to the senior class the next fall, and received the A.B. degree in 1870. She was interested in science, especially astronomy, which she studied with Maria Mitchell *(q.v.)*. She was the first woman to be admitted to Massachusetts Institute of Technology (MIT) in Boston, where she received the B.S. degree (1873). She was awarded the M.A. degree (1873) from Vassar. Although she continued graduate study at MIT for two years, she did not receive a doctorate because the heads of the departments did not wish a woman to be the first to receive the D.S. in chemistry.

In 1875 she married Professor Robert Hallowell Richards of MIT, who developed the institute's noted metallurgical and mining engineering laboratories. Richards devoted most of her life to the education of women. During her undergraduate study at MIT she taught a chemistry course at Girls' High School in Boston. She solicited the aid of the Women's Education Association of Boston to establish a Woman's Laboratory at MIT and taught there during the seven years of its existence (1876–84). In 1884 MIT established a chemical laboratory for the study of sanitation with Ellen Richards as an instructor in sanitary chemistry. During her twenty-seven years at the laboratory, she developed a program in sanitary engineering, the first in any university.

Richards was the author of *Chemistry of Cooking and Cleaning* (1882), *Food Materials and their Adulteration* (1886), *Home Sanitation: A Manual for Housekeepers* (with Marion Talbot, *q.v.*, 1887), *The Cost of Living* (1889), *Domestic Economy as a Factor in Public Education* (1889), *Air, Water, and Food* (1900), *First Lesson in Minerals* (1900), *The Cost of Food* (1900), *First Lessons in Food and Diet* (1905), *The Art of Right Living* (1905), *Sanitation in Daily Life* (1907), *Laboratory Notes on Industrial Water Analysis: A Survey Course for Engineers* (1908), *Conservation by Sanitation* (1911), and *Euthenics: The Science of Controllable Environment* (1912).

Richards was founder of the American Association of University Women and the Rumford Kitchen, a New England kitchen that provided nutritious school lunches. She issued bulletins on nutrition, established a school of housekeeping, organized the Lake Placid Conferences that resulted in the new field of home economics, and became the first president of the American Home Economics Association. She was the first woman elected to membership in the American Institute of Mining and Metallurgical Engineers (1882). She was in demand as a lecturer and received an honorary degree from Smith College in 1910.

REFERENCES: *AC; DAB; NAW; NCAB* (7:343); *NYT*, March 31, 1911, p. 11; *TC; WC; WWW* (I).                   *Agnes Fenster Ridley*

**RICHARDS, Linda (Melinda Ann) Judson.** B. July 27, 1841, near Potsdam, New York, to Sanford and Betsy (Sinclair) Richards. M. no. D. April 16, 1930, Boston, Massachusetts.

Linda Richards was known as America's first trained nurse and as a pioneer in nursing education. Richards spent much of her early childhood in Vermont, where she attended common schools in Lyndon and an academy at Barton. Orphaned while a teenager, she lived with the family of a physician and assisted in caring for his patients.

Richards went to Boston City Hospital in 1870 to work as an assistant nurse and to receive training in nursing, but, disillusioned with the poor quality of nursing, she left after three months. In 1872 she enrolled in the first American nursing school organized under Susan Dimock at the New England Hospital for Women and Children. Working in the hospital for a year and attending twelve lectures, she completed the course and was awarded the school's first diploma.

Richards served as superintendent of several nursing schools based on the Nightingale system, including the Bellevue Training School in New York City (1874) and the Boston Training School, which later became the Massachusetts General Hospital School of Nursing (1875–77). She resigned from her post to travel to England to study the Nightingale system and to meet and talk to Florence Nightingale. Upon her return to Boston in 1878, she helped to develop a training school at Boston City Hospital, which was a basic part of the hospital's organization. Richards developed programs of regular classroom instruction for student nurses. She demanded cleanliness and order in the hospital. Her work gave prestige to the professional training of nurses.

Under the auspices of the Congregational church, Richards traveled to Japan in 1886 where she opened the first training school for nurses in Japan. Upon her return to the United States in 1891, her health deteriorated, and she served in a number of posts for short periods of time as she was able. Among these assignments were directing the Philadelphia Visiting Nurses Society (1891) and reorganizing the New England Hospital for Women and Children (1893–94), the Brooklyn Homeopathic Hospital (1894–95), and the Hartford (Connecticut) Hospital (1895–97). She was director of training schools at Massachusetts hospitals for the insane at Taunton and Worcester and at Kalamazoo, Michigan.

Richards served as the first president of the American Society of Superintendents of Training Schools (1894) and contributed to the founding of the *American Journal of Nursing* (1900). The National League for Nursing established the Linda Richards Award in 1962.

REFERENCES: *NAW; NYT,* April 18, 1930, p. 23; Lena Dixon Dietz, *History and Modern Nursing* (Philadelphia: F. A. Davis Co., 1963); Josephine A. Dolan, *Goodnow's History of Nursing* (Philadelphia: W. B. Saunders Company, 1964); Isabel M. Stewart *(q.v.)* and Anne L. Austin, *A History of Nursing* (New York: G. P. Putnam's Sons, 1962).

*Marjorie E. Souers*

**RICHARDS, William.** B. August 22, 1793, Plainfield, Massachusetts, to James and Lydia (Shaw) Richards. M. October 30, 1822, to Clarissa Lyman. Ch. at least six. D. November 7, 1847, Honolulu, Hawaii.

William Richards was graduated from Williams College in Williamstown, Massachusetts, in 1819 and from Andover (Massachusetts) Theological Seminary in 1822.

Richards was ordained as a missionary and went to the Hawaiian Islands. He settled on the island of Maui where he preached, taught, was physician and artisan, and translated some of the Bible into Hawaiian. In 1837 he returned to the United States as agent of the Sandwich Islands mission to encourage world evangelism. He returned to Hawaii in 1838 as chaplain, teacher, and interpreter for the king and chiefs and through them influenced the writing of the Hawaiian Bill of Rights of 1839, the Constitution of 1840, and laws enacted from 1838 to 1842. Richards was sent in 1842 to negotiate recognition of the Hawaiian government by the United States, Great Britain, and France. He returned to the islands in 1845, was president of the board of commissioners to settle land titles (1846–47) and served as the first minister of public instruction (1846–47).

Richards was the author of *Memoir of Keopuolani, Late Queen of the Sandwich Islands* (published anonymously, 1825), and he edited the *Translation of the Constitution and Laws of the Hawaiian Islands* (1842). He translated thirteen books of the Bible into Hawaiian and assisted with seven others. He also prepared several Hawaiian schoolbooks.

REFERENCES: *AC; DAB; NCAB* (4:533); *WWW* (H).

*Lawrence S. Master*

**RICHARDS, Zalmon.** B. August 11, 1811, Cummington, Massachusetts, to Nehemiah and Betsy (Packard) Richards. M. 1836 to Minerva Todd. M. August 19, 1874, to Mary F. Mather. Ch. one. D. November 1, 1899, Washington, D.C.

Zalmon Richards attended country and private schools in Cummington, Massachusetts, and became a teacher in a country school at the age of seventeen. He was a graduate of Williams College in 1836, where he studied under Mark Hopkins *(q.v.)*.

Richards held teaching and school administrative positions in Massachusetts and New York for twelve years and became active in organizing training institutes for teachers. He moved to Washington, D.C., in 1849 to become principal of the preparatory department of Columbian College (later, George Washington University). He organized the Union Academy in 1851, but the successful private high school was forced to close at the outbreak of the Civil War when the predominantly southern student body withdrew.

Richards helped organize the Washington, D.C., Young Men's Christian Association in 1852 and served as its first president. He played a central role in founding the National Teachers' Association, (later, National Education Association) and was elected its first president in 1857. He was elected president of the Common Council of the District of Columbia in

1867 and became the first superintendent of schools in the capital, an office he was instrumental in creating. One of the most active lobbyists on behalf of the bill creating the United States Department of Education, he was Commissioner Henry Barnard's *(q.v.)* first appointment to that agency staff.

He wrote *Teachers' Manual* (1880), *Natural Arithmetic* (1885), and a historical sketch of the National Educational Association (1891). He maintained a private school in his home during his final years.

REFERENCES: *DAB; NCAB* (13:578); *WWW* (H); *Washington Post,* November 2, 1899; Donald R. Warren, *To Enforce Education: A History of the Founding Years of the U.S. Office of Education* (Detroit: Wayne State University Press, 1974); Allen Culling Clark, "Zalmon Richards, Educator," *Records of the Columbian Historical Society* (Washington: The Society, 1942), pp. 42–43.

**RICHARDSON, Charles Francis.** B. May 29, 1851, Hallowell, Maine, to Moses Charles and Mary Savary (Wingate) Richardson. M. April 12, 1878, to Elizabeth Miner. Ch. none. D. October 8, 1913, Sugar Hill, New Hampshire.

The son of a physician and the town librarian of Hallowell, Maine, Charles Francis Richardson attended Hallowell Academy and Augusta (Maine) High School. He was graduated from Dartmouth College in Hanover, New Hampshire, with the A.B. (1871) and A.M. (1874) degrees.

Richardson showed an early interest in writing and literature; he published two amateur papers before he was eleven years old and at fourteen had become a writer for local periodicals. He taught at the South Berkshire Institute in New Marlborough, Massachusetts (1871–72), and joined the staff of the *New York Independent* as literary editor (1872–78). He served as editor of the *Sunday School Times* of Philadelphia (1878–80) and *Good Literature* in New York City (1880–82). He returned to Dartmouth in 1882, where he began a twenty-nine-year service as Winkley Professor of Literature, remaining until 1911.

Richardson's major work, *American Literature, 1607–1885* (two volumes, 1886–88), was influential in the last decade of the nineteenth century. He also wrote *The College Book* (with Henry A. Clark, 1878), *Primer of American Literature* (1878), *The Cross*, a book of religious verse (1879), *The Choice of Books* (1881), *The End of the Beginning*, a romance (1896), and *A Study of English Rhyme* (1909). He edited James Fenimore Cooper's *Last of the Mohicans* (1897), *Poe's Complete Work* (1902), and *Daniel Webster for Young Americans* (1903).

He received two honorary degrees.

REFERENCES: *AC; DAB; NCAB* (9:95); *TC; WWW* (I); *NYT,* October 9, 1913, p. 13.                                      *William W. West*

**RICHARDSON, Leon Burr.** B. April 14, 1878, Lebanon, New Hampshire, to Orlando Joseph and Mary M. (Burr) Richardson. M. June 20, 1906, to Alice Millicent Warnock. Ch. three. D. October 25, 1951, Hanover, New Hampshire.

Leon Burr Richardson entered Dartmouth College in Hanover, New Hampshire, in 1896 and retained his close association with the college for more than half a century. Richardson received the B.A. (1900) and M.A. (1902) degrees from Dartmouth and in 1902 was appointed instructor in chemistry. In 1946 the board of trustees of the college named him New Hampshire Professor of Chemistry in recognition of his long and devoted service. He retired from the active faculty in 1948.

Respected as a well-known chemist who authored two widely adopted texts, Richardson was also recognized for his pioneering efforts to rationalize the curricula of liberal arts colleges. In 1924–25 he was granted a leave to study universities in the United States, Canada, England, and Scotland. As a result of this study, he wrote "A Study of the Liberal College," which provided the basis for a major revision of the Dartmouth curriculum. In the same year, he presented a paper, "The Liberal College and Vocationalism," before the Association of American Universities, which attracted national attention and resulted in curricula revision at many colleges and universities throughout the country.

Among his books are *General Chemistry* (1927), *A Laboratory Manual of General Chemistry* (with Andrew J. Scarlett, 1928), *History of Dartmouth College* (two volumes, 1932), *William E. Chandler, Republican* (1940), and *Brief College Chemistry* (with Andrew J. Scarlett, 1942). He edited *An Indian Preacher in England* (1933). He was president of the New Hampshire Academy of Sciences (1922) and an examiner in chemistry for the College Entrance Examination Board. He served on many local boards, including the Hanover school board (1919–25). Dartmouth awarded him an honorary Litt.D. in 1933.

REFERENCES: *LE* (II); *NCAB* (39: 92); *NYT*, October 26, 1951, p. 24.
*Edward J. Durnall*

**RICHMAN, Julia.** B. October 12, 1855, New York, New York, to Moses and Theresa (Melis) Richman. M. no. D. June 24, 1912, Neuilly, France.

Julia Richman, social progressive and educational pioneer, attended the Huntington (Long Island, New York) and New York City public schools. Graduating from P.S. 50, she enrolled in a two-year teacher training program at the Normal College of the City of New York. She was graduated at the age of sixteen and taught school against the advice of her parents.

Richman taught in New York City public schools, including P.S. 59 and P.S. 73 (1881–84), when she became New York City's first Jewish and first woman school principal. She served as principal of the girls' department at

P.S. 77 for nineteen years (1884–1903). She instituted special classes for bright, average, and slow pupils. She was chosen the first woman district superintendent in Manhattan and the third in the city in 1903.

In her district Richman formed classes for the mentally retarded and accelerated classes for those old enough to seek employment. She established probationary schools for truant and disruptive students and established a foundation for the Bureau of Child Guidance. She introduced eye examinations, a limited school lunch program, and services of guidance counselors for school dropouts. She was director of the girls' branch of the Public Schools Athletic League (1905–12). She resigned in 1912 and died in France where she had gone to improve her facility in French.

Coauthor of *Pupil's Arithmetic* (n.d.), Richman was the author of *Good Citizenship* (1908) and numerous articles in professional journals. She was a founder of the Educational Alliance (member of the board of directors and chairman of the committee on education). A girls' high school in Manhattan and the Julia Richman Athletic League were named in her honor.

REFERENCES: *NAW; NYT,* June 26, 1912, p. 13; Selma C. Berrol, "Superintendent Julia Richman: A Social Progressive in the Public Schools," *Elementary School Journal* 72 (May 1972): 402–11.

*Kathryn D. Lizzul*

**RICKER, Nathan Clifford.** B. July 24, 1843, Acton, Maine, to Ebenezer and Mary (Stacy) Ricker. M. August 25, 1875, to Mary Carter Steele. Ch. one. D. March 19, 1924, Urbana, Illinois.

Nathan Clifford Ricker attended local Acton, Maine, public schools; his family moved to Springvale, Maine, where he was largely self-educated while working at his father's mill. He taught in a country school (1861–62) and spent the winter of 1862–63 in Washington, D.C., while his father was engaged in military duties. A temporary visit in 1867 to an uncle in La Harpe, Illinois, led to his enrollment in Illinois Industrial University (later, University of Illinois) as a student of architecture, where he received the B.S. (1873) and M.Arch. (1878) degrees. At the suggestion of the university president, John Milton Gregory *(q.v.),* Ricker traveled in Europe and studied at the Bauakademie in Berlin, Germany (1873).

Ricker taught architecture at Illinois from 1873 to his retirement in 1917 and was dean of the college of engineering (1878–1905). Under Ricker's leadership, about a fourth of the students of architecture in the United States were enrolled in the University of Illinois in 1900. He established a graduate program and organized an engineering experiment station. He played a major role in passage of the Illinois Architectural Act in June 1897 and was a member of the board of examiners for architects (1897–1917), serving as chairman from 1899 to 1917. He was chairman of the Commission to Codify the Building Laws of Illinois (1911–12). He served on a number of architectural competition juries. He designed several buildings at the University of Illinois.

Ricker was the author of *Elementary Graphical Statics and Construction of Trussed Roofs* (1885), *Treatise on Design and Construction of Roofs* (1912), *Simplified Formulas and Tables for Floors, Joists and Beams; Roofs, Rafters, and Purlins* (1913), and three bulletins published by the Engineering Experiment Station. He translated over forty volumes of architectural works from French and German, including Otto Wagner's *Moderne Architektur* [The brickbuilder] (1901), and a dictionary of French medieval architecture.

Ricker received an honorary degree from the University of Illinois in 1900, and the university named the Ricker Library of Architecture in his honor (1917).

REFERENCES: *WWW* (I); *Alumni Record,* University of Illinois, 1918, p. 2; Alan K. Laing, *Nathan Clifford Ricker: Pioneer in Architectural Education* (Champaign: University of Illinois, 1973).     *John F. Ohles*

**RICKOFF, Andrew Jackson.** B. August 23, 1824, near New Hope, New Jersey, to n.a. M. to Rebecca Davis. Ch. three. D. March 30, 1899, Berkeley, California.

Andrew Jackson Rickoff moved from New Jersey to Cincinnati, Ohio, with his parents when he was six years old. He attended public schools, was tutored by a brother, and attended Woodward College in Cincinnati.

Rickoff began to teach at a country school near Cincinnati (1840). About 1844 he was superintendent of the Portsmouth (Ohio) schools and was an assistant (1849–50) and principal (1850–53) in a Cincinnati public school. He was appointed the first nonelective superintendent of the Cincinnati public schools (1853–58), where he organized the grammar school as an intermediate school between district and high schools and relieved principals of teaching responsibilities so that they could supervise the teaching staff.

From 1858 to 1867 he conducted a successful private school in Cincinnati and accepted an offer to serve as superintendent of the Cleveland, Ohio, schools (1867–82). Rickoff gained a national reputation in Cleveland, where he reorganized the school system, conducted a teachers' institute for a week before the opening of school, established a one-year normal school, started a school for incorrigibles, staffed grammar schools with women principals, and designed and supervised the construction of six school buildings noted for their effectiveness of ventilation and heating. Opposition to Rickoff arose in 1881, and he moved to Yonkers, New York, as superintendent (1882–83). He served as a textbook author and editor for D. Appleton, publishers, and took charge of Felix Adler's *(q.v.)* school for workingmen in 1888. Ill health and the deaths of his son and, later, his wife led to his retirement to California.

Rickoff was the author of *Mental and Written Arithmetic* (1885), *Numbers Applied* (1886), and *First Lessons in Arithmetic* (1891), and he prepared with William T. Harris *(q.v.)* and Mark Bailey the popular Appleton Readers series. Active in professional affairs, Rickoff was president of the Ohio State Teachers' Association (1855), the National Teachers' Association (later, National Education Association) in 1859, and the Ohio State Board of Examiners for teachers. He was awarded honorary degrees by several colleges and universities.

REFERENCES: *A C; NCAB* (4:556); Samuel P. Orth, *A History of Cleveland, Ohio* (Chicago: S. J. Clarke, 1910).                      *Elaine F. McNally*

**RIDPATH, John Clark.** B. April 26, 1840, Putnam County, Indiana, to Abraham and Sally (Matthews) Ridpath. M. December 22, 1862, to Hannah R. Smythe. Ch. five. D. August 1, 1900, New York, New York.

John Clark Ridpath was graduated from Indiana Asbury University (later, DePauw University) in 1863. He was a teacher, then principal, of the academy at Thorntown, Indiana (1864–66), and was superintendent of schools at Lawrenceburg, Indiana (1866–69).

Ridpath returned to Indiana Asbury in 1869 as professor of English literature and normal instruction. He was professor of belles lettres and history (1871–82) and, as his interests turned more to history, became professor of history and political science from 1882 until his retirement in 1885. He also served as librarian (1869–79) and was vice-president (1879–85). As vice-president Ridpath was influential in securing a large contribution from Washington C. DePauw, a wealthy Indiana citizen. As part of the negotiations Ridpath advocated and took the lead in renaming the university after DePauw.

While at DePauw Ridpath wrote *History of the United States, Prepared Especially for Schools* (1875), *A Popular History of the United States of America* (1876), *The Life and Work of James A. Garfield* (1881), and the *Cyclopedia of Universal History* (1885). Most of his writing was done after he retired from DePauw in 1885 and became literary editor of Jones Brothers Publishing Company in Cincinnati, Ohio. The company published several of his works in German, including the first United States history to be translated into German. Other important works by Ridpath include *The Great Races of Mankind* (four volumes, 1893), *History of the World* (1897), *William E. Gladstone* (1898), *James G. Blaine* (1893), and the monumental Ridpath Library of Universal Literature, twenty-five volumes, which he edited in 1898. He also edited *The Arena* (1897–98). Ridpath was awarded an honorary degree by Syracuse University in 1879. DePauw University established a chair in history in his honor in 1919.

REFERENCES: *AC; DAB; NCAB* (6:485); *TC; WWW* (I); George B. Manhart, *DePauw Through the Ages* (Greencastle, Ind.: DePauw University, 1962); *Review of Reviews* 22 (September 1900): 281; *Independent* 52 (November 22, 1900): 2795.                    *Harris L. Dante*

**RIESMAN, David.** B. September 22, 1909, Philadelphia, Pennsylvania, to David and Eleanor (Fleisher) Riesman. M. July 15, 1936, to Evelyn Hastings Thompson. Ch. four.

David Riesman distinguished himself as a lawyer, sociologist, and educator. He received his early education in Philadelphia and attended Harvard University where he received the A.B. (1931) and LL.B. (1934) degrees.

After a year as a research fellow, he served as a law clerk under Supreme Court Justice Louis Brandeis (1935–36) and practiced law in Boston (1936–37) before becoming a professor of law at the University of Buffalo (New York) from 1937 to 1941. Riesman was a visiting research fellow at Columbia University (1941–42) and deputy assistant district attorney for New York County (1942–43). He worked for the Sperry Gyroscope Company in Lake Success, New York, for three years and in 1946 began an association with the University of Chicago as professor of social science that lasted to 1958, when he became Henry Ford Professor of Social Sciences at Harvard.

Riesman authored or coauthored a dozen books. Early in his career he wrote three works on law, including *The American Constitution and International Labour Legislation* (1941). He gained a reputation as a social scientist with the publication of *The Lonely Crowd: A Study of the Changing American Character* (1950). His other works include *Faces in the Crowd* (with Nathan Glazer, 1952), *Thorstein Veblen* (1953), *Individualism Reconsidered and Other Essays* (1954), *Abundance for What? and Other Essays* (1963), *The Academic Revolution* (with Christopher Jencks, 1969), and *Academic Transformation* (with Verne A. Stadtman, 1973). He wrote numerous articles in professional journals and served on the editorial boards of a number of publications, including *American Quarterly, American Scholar, Sociology of Education,* and *University Quarterly.*

Riesman speculated that industrialized society was heading toward a situation of saturation in population growth with the role of the peer group becoming a chief determinant of individual behavior. His areas of study included the sociology of higher education, intra- and inter-institutional competition and cooperation, and problems of financing and organizing higher education. He was a member of professional and scholarly associations and was a member of the Carnegie Commission for the Study of Higher Education (from 1967) and the advisory council for the Peace Corps, a fellow of the Center for Advanced Studies in Behavioral Sciences

(1968–69), and a trustee of the Institute for Policy Studies in Washington, D.C. He received many honorary degrees.

REFERENCES: *CA* (5–8); *CB* (January 1955); *NCAB* (I:257); *WW* (XXXIX); *WWAE* (XVI).                                    *James M. Vosper*

**RIGGS, Kate Douglas Wiggin.** See **WIGGIN, Kate Douglas.**

**RITTER, Frederic Louis.** B. June 22, 1834, Strasbourg, Germany, to n.a. M. to n.a. M. 1867 to Frances Malone Raymond. Ch. two. D. July 6, 1891, Antwerp, Belgium.

Frederic Louis Ritter showed a talent for music at an early age. He studied under Hans Schletterer in Strasbourg, Franz Hauser in Fennestrange, and Georges Kastner, a relative of his mother, in Paris, France. He also studied under several master teachers in Germany (1850–52). He returned to Fennestrange in Lorraine province of France to teach at the Protestant Seminary in 1852. In 1856 he accompanied his parents to America.

Ritter settled in Cincinnati, Ohio, where he taught music for several years and established the Cecilia Vocal Society and a philharmonic orchestra. He presented many concerts where a large number of important works were heard for the first time in the United States. In 1861 he moved to New York City where he conducted the Sacred Harmonic Society (1862–69) and Arion Male Chorus Society and directed the first musical festival held in New York City (1867). He was appointed professor of music at Vassar College in Poughkeepsie, New York, in 1867 and held the position until his death in 1891.

Ritter gained an international reputation as a writer on musical subjects. His most important work was *A History of Music in the Form of Lectures* (1870–74). He also wrote *Woman as a Musician* (1876), *Some Famous Songs* (1878), *Music in America* (1883), *Music in England* (1883), *Manual of Musical History* (1886), *Musical Dictation* (1887–88), and *Practical Harmony* (1888). He collaborated with J. Ryland Kendrick in compiling *Laudamus: A Hymnal* (1877) and edited *The Realm of Tones*. He wrote many compositions including three symphonies, a symphonic poem "Stella," a concert overture "Othello," several concertos, and some chamber music.

Ritter received an honorary degree from the University of the City of New York in 1878.

REFERENCES: *AC; DAB; NCAB* (7:426); *NYT*, July 7, 1891, p. 5; *TC; WWW* (H); Nicholas Slonimsky, ed., *Baker's Biographical Dictionary of Musicians,* 5th ed. (New York: G. Schirmer, 1958).

*Edward B. Goellner*

**RIVLIN, Harry N.** B. December 30, 1904, New York, New York, to Samuel and Jennie (Feldman) Rivlin. M. August 23, 1928, to Eugénie Graciany. Ch. two.

Harry Rivlin was born, educated, and earned a reputation as an expert in urban education in New York City. He received the B.S.S. degree (1924) from the City College of New York (CCNY), the A.M. degree (1926) from Teachers College, Columbia University, and the Ph.D. degree in psychology (1930) from Columbia University.

After six years as a high school English teacher in Brooklyn, Rivlin joined the city's higher educational system where he remained for thirty-six years. He was assistant professor of education at CCNY (1930–39), associate professor and department chairman at Queens College (1939–57), and dean of teacher education at City University of New York (CUNY) from 1957 to 1966.

At Queens College and CUNY he introduced new programs in undergraduate and graduate studies. From June 1961 to February 1962 he was the acting president of CCNY. Rivlin was dean of the school of education at Fordham University (1966–73); he was the first person of the Jewish faith to hold such a high academic position at the Jesuit-run institution. After his resignation as dean, Fordham named him John Mosler Professor of Urban Education (from 1973).

He contributed to professional journals, served on the editorial board of *Educational Forum* (1963–67), and wrote, coauthored, or edited a dozen books, including *Functional Grammar* (1930), *Educating for Adjustment* (1936), *Know Your Language* (1941), *Encyclopedia of Modern Education* (1943), *Teaching Adolescents in Secondary Schools* (1948), *Improving Children's Learning Ability* (1953), *Improving Your Learning Ability* (1953), *Growth, Teaching, and Learning* (1957), *The First Years in College* (editor, 1965), *The Preparation of Urban Teachers* (1968), *Conflicts in Urban Education* (editor with Sheldon Marcus, 1970), and *Cultural Pluralism in Education* (editor with Madelon Stent and William Hazard, 1973).

Among many professional activities, he was a member of the Interstate Teachers Conference (president, 1953–54) and the Advisory Board on Teacher Education of the New York State Education Department (chairman, 1963–67) and served with the Leadership Training Institute (director, 1969–73). He was a trustee of the Center for Urban Education (1965–71) and the Bank Street College (from 1971). He was a fellow of the American Psychological Association and the American Educational Research Association and a member of the National Society of College Teachers of Education (president, educational psychology division, 1952–54) and the John Dewey Society (director).

He was the recipient of medals and awards by several colleges and universities and by Phi Beta Kappa. CUNY established the Harry N. Rivlin Fellowship.

REFERENCES: *LE* (V); *WW* (XXXIX); *NYT,* March 6, 1966, p. 30, September 17, 1972, p. 57; Russell W. Calkins, ed., *Who's Who in American College and University Administration 1970–71* (New York: Crowell-Collier Educational Corporation, 1970).          *David Delahanty*

**ROARK, Ruric Nevel.** B. May 19, 1859, Greenville, Kentucky, to Martin Jefferson and Nancy (David) Roark. M. 1881 to Mary Creegan. Ch. three D. April 14, 1909, Cincinnati, Ohio.

Ruric Nevel Roark received his early education in the Greenville (Kentucky) public schools, Greenville Academy, and from private collegiate tutors. He earned the B.S. degree in 1881 and later the M.Pd. degree from the National Normal University in Lebanon, Ohio.

Roark taught at the normal school (1881–85). He was principal of the Glasgow (Kentucky) Normal School (1885–89) and dean of the department of pedagogy of the State College of Kentucky (later, University of Kentucky) in Lexington (1889–1905). With other educators he sponsored a movement to establish separate teacher-training institutions in Kentucky, which led to establishment of two state normal schools in 1906. Roark was elected president of one, Eastern Kentucky State Normal School (later, Eastern Kentucky University) at Richmond. He held that position until his death. After his death, his wife was president (1909–10) and continued there for several years as dean of women.

Roark was a leader in progressive education in Kentucky. He was the author of *Psychology in Education* (1895), *Method in Education* (1899), *General Outline of Pedagogy* (1900), and *Economy in Education* (1905). He was a member of professional associations, an honorary fellow of Clark University (1905–06), and received an honorary degree from the National Normal University.

REFERENCES: *DAB; WWW* (I).                    *Joseph P. Cangemi*
                                             *Thomas E. Kesler*

**ROBB, Isabel Adams Hampton.** B. 1860, Welland, Ontario, Canada, to Samuel James and Sarah Mary (Lay) Hampton. M. July 11, 1894, to Hunter Robb. Ch. two. D. April 15, 1910, Cleveland, Ohio.

Isabel Adams Hampton Robb was educated in a Welland, Ontario, Canada, preparatory school and was graduated from St. Catherines (Ontario) Collegiate Institute, receiving a teaching certificate. She moved to New York City to attend the newly established Bellevue Hospital School for Nurses and completed the two-year course in 1883.

Robb spent two years at St. Paul's House in Rome, Italy, where nursing care was available to American and British citizens. Returning to the United States, she was superintendent of nurses in the Cook County Hospital Illinois Training School for Nurses in Chicago (1886–89). She moved to the nursing school at the new Johns Hopkins (University) Hospital in Baltimore, Maryland, as superintendent of nurses and director of the training school. She continued at Johns Hopkins to 1894, when she was married and moved to Cleveland, Ohio.

Robb was the author of *Nursing: Its Principles and Practice* (1893), *Nursing Ethics* (1903), and *Educational Standards for Nurses* (1907). She was active in the movement to professionalize nursing and improve standards for nursing education. In Chicago she introduced the first graded course of study for nurses in the country, and at Johns Hopkins she laid the basis for a professional three-year nursing program and a standard workday of eight hours.

She was the leader in the founding in 1894 and president (1908) of the American Society of Superintendents of Training Schools for Nurses of the United States and Canada (later, National League of Nursing Education) and founder (1897) and first president (1897–1901) of the Nurses' Associated Alumnae of the United States and Canada (later, American Nurses' Association).

REFERENCES: *NAW; Cleveland Plain Dealer,* April 16, 1910, p. 1.

*Patricia L. Earls*

**ROBERTS, Oran Milo.** B. July 9, 1815, Laurens County, South Carolina, to Obe and Margaret (Ewing) Roberts. M. December 1837 to Frances W. Edwards. M. December 1887 to Catherine E. Border. Ch. seven. D. May 19, 1898, Austin, Texas.

At ten years of age, Oran Milo Roberts shared responsibility with an older brother in the operation of the family farm in Alabama to which they had moved when their father died. Educated in an academy and in county schools, he entered the University of Alabama in 1833, graduating in 1836. He studied law and was admitted to the bar in 1837.

Roberts practiced law in Talladega and Ashville, Alabama (1837–41), and served one term in the Alabama legislature. He moved west in 1841 to practice law in San Augustine, Texas, where he rose rapidly in his profession. Appointed district attorney by the president of Texas, Sam Houston, on February 6, 1844, he served a two-year term, which was followed by an appointment as district judge by the first governor of Texas, J. Pinkney Henderson, an appointment he held until 1851. He was elected associate justice of the supreme court of Texas on February 1, 1857.

Active in the slavery controversy, Roberts was elected president of the convention in Austin in 1861 that submitted the secession ordinance to the people for vote. He resigned from the court in 1861 and in 1862 raised the

Eleventh Texas Infantry Regiment for the Confederate army, which he served with distinction as commanding officer (1862–64). While still in command of his unit in Louisiana, Roberts was elected to replace Chief Justice Royall T. Wheeler in 1864, a position he filled until the collapse of the Confederacy in 1865. Elected to the United States Senate in August 1865, he was not allowed to take his seat.

Roberts practiced law for eight years at Tyler and Gilmer, Texas, and also conducted a law school at Gilmer. He served as chief justice of the supreme court of Texas from January 1874. He was elected governor of Texas in 1878 and was reelected in 1880. The outstanding achievement of his administration was the founding and organization of the University of Texas. Ill health caused his retirement from politics, but he served as professor of law at the university from 1883 until his retirement in 1893.

Roberts wrote *A Description of Texas, Its Advantages and Resources* (1881), *The Elements of Texas Pleading* (1890), *Our Federal Relations from a Southern View of Them* (1892), and two chapters in D. G. Wooten's *Comprehensive History of Texas* (1899).

He was president of the Texas Historical Society (1874) and received an honorary degree from the University of Alabama (1881).

REFERENCES: *AC; DAB; NCAB* (9:73); *TC; WWW* (H).

*Bruce D. Mattson*

**ROBERTS, Robert Jeffries.** B. January 29, 1849, England, to Jefferson and Elizabeth (Dant) Roberts. M. April 28, 1873, to Sarah Anne Sherman. Ch. three. D. December 28, 1920, Boston, Massachusetts.

R. J. Roberts sailed from Liverpool, England, to the United States at the age of four. Completing a course of study at the Phillips Street School in Boston, Massachusetts, he worked as a messenger and delivery clerk for Western Union Company. He later trained as a woodturner and mechanic.

In 1869 Roberts joined the Tremont Gymnasium in Boston and worked with Dio Lewis *(q.v.)*, the pioneer of light gymnastics, at the Essex Street Gymnasium and with B. Windship, a celebrated strongman and graduate of Harvard Medical School. In 1868 he taught swimming at Bruce's Bath and gymnastics at the Union Gymnasium in Boston.

In 1875 the Young Men's Christian Association (YMCA), seeking an instructor who had knowledge of both the gymnasium and the association, selected Roberts as its superintendent. He was a stimulating teacher whose body-building methods held wide appeal. The first to develop a leaders' corp of assistant instructors, Roberts trained thirty men in the mid-1880s. Roberts was employed to work with Luther Gulick *(q.v.)* in the YMCA School for Christian Workers in Springfield, Massachusetts, to conduct a course for training superintendents for YMCA gymnasiums (1887–89). He was director of a gymnasium in Utica, New York (1889–91), and was recalled in 1891 to head the Boston YMCA, where he remained until his death.

Robert's influence as a pioneer of the new gymnastics was based on his concept of light, systematic, and scientific exercise to promote health and strength. He did not approve of competition as an incentive for exercise, viewing it as indefensible for ethical reasons. His chief concern was for the health needs of the average person. He believed that a gymnasium should be a "hall of health."

Roberts invented a variety of gymnasium apparatus, including the barbell, dumbbells, horizontal bars, overhead ladder, mats, medicine ball, low and overhead parallel bars, pulley weights, ring shower, indoor running track, vaulting bar, indoor shot, and jumping weight and rubber-soled shoes. He edited a column for the *Watchman* and wrote *100 Health Hints* (1891), *Home Dumb-Bell Drill* (1894), and articles for *Young Men's Era*.

REFERENCES: *Boston's Young Men* 9 (January 1, 1921); C. Howard Hopkins, *History of YMCA in North America* (New York: Association Press, 1951); Fred E. Leonard, *Pioneers of Modern Physical Training*, 2d ed. (New York: Association Press, 1922).                  *Kathryn D. Lizzul*

**ROBERTSON, William Schenck.** B. January 11, 1820, Huntington, New York, to Samuel and Dorcas (Platt) Robertson. M. April 15, 1850, to Ann Eliza Worcester. Ch. at least two, including Alice Mary Robertson, member of Congress from Oklahoma. D. June 16, 1881, Muskogee, Oklahoma.

William Schenck Robertson, pioneer educator of Indians, was graduated from Union College in Schenectady, New York, in 1842. He studied medicine but decided to become a teacher.

After teaching in several New York state academies Robertson joined the Presbyterian church and volunteered for service as a teacher in Indian schools. In 1849 he was assigned the principalship of a mission school for Creek Indians at Tullahassee, Indian Territory (later, Oklahoma). He completed the school building and opened the school in January 1850, working under Robert McGill Loughridge *(q.v.),* superintendent of the school.

Robertson, Loughridge, and other missionaries were expelled by the Indians during the Civil War. Robertson taught school in Mattoon (1862–63) and Centralia (1863–64), Illinois, and was assigned to an orphanage in Highland, Kansas (1864–66). Ordained a Presbyterian minister in 1866, he returned to Tullahassee at the request of the Creeks. He participated in the annual Indian fair held at Muskogee and was in charge of the Indian educational exhibit at the Centennial Exhibition at Philadelphia, Pennsylvania, in 1876. He continued with his work to his death.

Robertson published *Our Monthly* newspaper printed in Creek on a small printing press. He and his wife prepared first and second readers written in Creek and, following the work of Loughridge, he began translating the New Testament into Creek, a task completed after his death by his wife and published in 1887.

REFERENCES: *DAB; WWW* (H); *Chronicles of Oklahoma* 37 (Spring 1959).                                                                    *John F. Ohles*


**ROBINSON, Ezekiel Gilman.** B. March 23, 1815, Attleboro, Massachusetts, to Ezekiel and Cynthia (Slack) Robinson. M. February 21, 1844, to Harriet Richards Parker. Ch. six. D. June 13, 1894, Boston, Massachusetts.

Ezekiel Gilman Robinson spent his boyhood on the family farm and attended schools, which in his opinion "did him more harm than good," and academies at New Hampton, New Hampshire, and Pawtucket, Rhode Island. He "drifted aimlessly into and through college . . . only during the last year to see what I might and ought to have done." He was licensed to preach by his Baptist church in Pawtucket before he was graduated from Brown University (1838).

He worked for a short time for the American Tract Society, studied on the graduate level at Brown, and entered Newton (Massachusetts) Theological Institution. He was graduated in 1842 and served his first pastorate at the Cumberland Street Baptist Church in Norfolk, Virginia (1843–44); in 1845 he served as chaplain at the University of Virginia.

He was pastor of the Old Cambridge (Massachusetts) Baptist Church (1845–46) and then became professor of biblical interpretation in the recently established Baptist Theological Institute at Covington, Kentucky. When the school was torn with dissension over the question of slavery, Robinson became pastor of the Cincinnati (Ohio) Ninth Street Baptist Church (1848). In 1853 he assumed the professorship of biblical theology at Rochester (New York) Theological Seminary and became president in 1860. He left Rochester in 1872 to accept the presidency of Brown University, where he also taught moral philosophy and metaphysics.

Before he resigned from Brown in 1889, he had led the university to doubled financial support and endowments, new buildings, and a strengthened academic program. Robinson lectured at Crozier Theological Seminary in Chester, Pennsylvania, and was professor of ethics and apologetics at the University of Chicago from 1892 to his death.

Robinson translated Augustus Neander's *Planting and Training of the Christian Church* (1865). He was the author of *Relation of the Church to the Bible* (1866), *Principles and Practice of Morality* (1881), *Christian Evidences* (1895), and *Christian Character, Baccalaureate Sermons* (1896). His lectures at Rochester were published in *Christian Theology* (1844), and those at Yale University in 1882 were published in *Lectures on*

*Preaching* (1883). Many of his articles appeared in the *Christian Review,* which he edited (1859–64).

REFERENCES: *AC; DAB; NCAB* (8:26); *NYT,* June 14, 1894, p. 1; *TC; WWW* (H). *M. Jane Dowd*

**ROBINSON, Frederick Bertrand.** B. October 16, 1883, Brooklyn, New York, to Henry Duval and Emma Louise (Ravn) Robinson. M. June 30, 1909, to Julia Marie Randolph. Ch. two. D. October 19, 1941, New York, New York.

Frederick Bertrand Robinson received the A.B. degree (1904) from the College of the City of New York and the M.A. (1906) and Ph.D. (1907) degrees from New York University.

A teacher in the New York City schools (1904–06), Robinson was a member of the faculty of the City College of New York as a teacher of economics and head of the department of economics (1918), assistant director (1910), and director (1915–27) of the evening session. He developed the largest evening program of instruction in the world. He organized and directed the first course for training New York City civil service employees and the first summer session that was equivalent to half a regular term. He was the organizer and director of the division of vocational subjects and civil administration, dean of the school of business administration and civic administration (1920), acting president (1926), and president (1927–39).

Robinson was the author of *Effective Public Speaking* (1914) and *Business Costs* (with others, 1921) and was business manager and associate editor of *City College Quarterly* (1908–18), associate editor of *English Journal* (1915–22), editor of the *Public Speaking Review* (1913–14), and editor in chief of the College of the City of New York Commerce, Civics and Technology Series (1917). He drew up the legislation for the board of higher education for the City of New York and was the first provost (1926). He was a lecturer on economic theory at the New York University graduate school (1908–09) and a lecturer for the New York City board of education (1907–27).

A member of many organizations, Robinson was active in the American League for Human Rights (chairman, 1933), the Association of Urban Universities (secretary-treasurer, 1914–27 and president, 1917), the Danish-American History Society (vice-president), the Goethe Society (honorary vice-president), and the Association of Colleges and Universities of the State of New York (president, 1930). He received honorary degrees from Manhattan College, Temple University, and the University of Pittsburgh.

REFERENCES: *LE* (I); *NCAB* (C:115); *NYT,* October 20, 1941, p. 17, October 21, 1941, pp. 20, 22, October 22, 1941, p. 23; *WWAE* (VIII); *WWW* (I); *School and Society* 54 (October 25, 1941): 353. *John F. Ohles*

**ROBINSON, James Harvey.** B. June 29, 1863, Bloomington, Illinois, to James Harvey and Latricia Maria (Drake) Robinson. M. September 1, 1887, to Grace Woodville Read. Ch. none. D. February 16, 1936, New York, New York.

After graduating from the public schools of Bloomington, Illinois, James Harvey Robinson spent a brief time at a state normal school but soon left for a year of travel in Europe. Upon his return to Bloomington he worked in a general store and a bank. He followed his brother to Harvard University where he obtained the A.B. (1887) and A.M. (1888) degrees. He returned to Europe and received the Ph.D. degree (1890) from the University of Freiburg, Germany.

In 1891 Robinson returned to the United States to teach at the University of Pennsylvania. In 1895 he resigned to accept an appointment as professor of European history at Columbia University. He left Columbia in 1919 to help establish the New School for Social Research in New York City. Two years later he withdrew entirely from teaching and devoted the remainder of his life to research and writing.

Robinson is best known for his advocacy of the new history. Robinson and others, including Charles Beard *(q.v.)* and John Dewey *(q.v.)*, were committed to a fundamental reform of the study and teaching of history. They sought to transform history from a narrow and sometimes sterile examination of past politics into a comprehensive and vital study of the daily lives and achievements of the common man. Robinson campaigned for the new history by writing popular histories and textbooks for schools and colleges and serving on several national committees appointed to examine the secondary school curriculum. The recommendations of two of these committees, the Committee of Five of the American Historical Association (1911) and the National Education Association's Committee on Social Studies of the Commission on the Reorganization of Secondary Education (1916), reflected Robinson's views and set a pattern that persisted for more than fifty years.

Robinson was the author or editor of twenty-four books and many articles on American and European history, the teaching of history, and history for the general reader. Among his books were *The German Bundesrath* (1891), *Petrarch* (with H. W. Rolfe, 1899), *An Introduction to the History of Western Europe* (1903), *Readings in Modern European History* (two volumes, 1904–05), *The Development of Modern Europe* (two volumes, with C. A. Beard, 1907), *The New History* (1911), *Medieval and Modern Times* (1915), *The Mind in the Making* (1921), *The Humanizing of Knowledge* (1923), and *The Ordeal of Civilization* (1926). He was editor of *Annals* of the American Academy of Political and Social Science (1891–95) and associate editor of the *American Historical Review* (1911–20).

Robinson was a fellow of the American Association for the Advancement of Science and the Royal Historical Society and a member of other associations, including the American Historical Association (president, 1929). He received honorary degrees from the University of Utah (1922) and Tufts College (1924).

REFERENCES: DAB (supp. 2); *LE* (I); *NCAB* (C:28); *NYT*, February 17, 1936, p. 17; *TC; WWW* (I); Luther V. Hendricks, *James Harvey Robinson: Teacher of History* (New York: King's Crown Press, 1946).

N. *Ray Hiner*

**ROBINSON, Stillman Williams.** B. March 6, 1838, Reading, Vermont, to Ebenezer and Adeline (Williams) Robinson. M. December 29, 1863, to Mary Elizabeth Holden. M. April 12, 1888, to Mary Haines. Ch. three. D. October 3, 1910, Columbus, Ohio.

Stillman Williams Robinson received his early education in the district school in Reading, Vermont. Upon graduation he tried farming but disliked it and was apprenticed as a machinist in 1855. After saving enough money he entered the University of Michigan in January 1861 as an engineering student and received the C.E. degree (1863).

After graduation Robinson was an assistant engineer in the federal survey of the Great Lakes. He returned to the University of Michigan as an assistant in engineering, geodesy, and mining (1866–70). Illinois Industrial University (later, University of Illinois) hired Robinson to establish a department of mechanical engineering in 1870, and he became dean of the college of engineering in 1878. However, he left in 1878 to accept the professorship of physics at Ohio State University where he continued until his retirement in 1895. He was inspector of railways in Ohio (1880–84) and was consulting engineer for the Santa Fe Railroad (1888–90) and Lick Observatory (1887).

Robinson established a successful business with his son, Erdis, in 1903. It later became the Robinson-Houchin Optical Company of Columbus, Ohio.

Robinson acquired over forty patents, of which ten were concerned with shoe manufacturing. His first invention was developed while a student, and it won an award and prize at the Philadelphia Centennial Exposition of 1876. Among his inventions were a clock escapement, a steam rock drill, value gearing for steam engines, improvement of the telephone, and an automatic airbrake mechanism.

Among his publications were *Teeth of Gear Wheels* (1876), *Railroad Economics* (1882), *Strength of Wrought Iron Bridge Members* (1882), *Compound Steam Pumping Engines* (1884), and *Principles of Mechanism* (1896). He was a fellow of the American Association for the Advancement of Science and the Society for the Promotion of Engineering Education and a member of many professional associations. Robinson received several awards and medals at expositions in 1876 and 1903 and an honorary degree from Ohio State University (1896).

REFERENCES:*AC; DAB; NCAB* (35:150); *TC; WWW* (I). *Alfred J. Ciani*

**ROEMER, Joseph.** B. September 25, 1884, Sugar Grove, Kentucky, to Adolph and Sallie Trice (Tuck) Roemer. M. June 15, 1911, to Louise Beasley. Ch. one. D. July 1, 1955, Leesburg, Florida.

Joseph Roemer attended local Sugar Grove, Kentucky, schools, Western Kentucky State Normal School (later, Western Kentucky University) in Bowling Green, and the University of Kentucky where he received the B.S. degree (1914). He studied at the George Peabody College for Teachers in Nashville, Tennessee, and was awarded the A.M. (1915) and Ph.D. (1919) degrees. He was the first to be awarded a doctorate from Peabody. He also engaged in postgraduate studies at Columbia University (1924–25).

Roemer began to teach in Kentucky rural schools (1903–06). After completing a business course at Bowling Green Business University (1907), he worked in a Bowling Green bank. He was principal of the demonstration school at Peabody (1914–16) and headed the education department of Sam Houston State Teachers College (later, State University) at Huntsville, Texas (1916–20). He was a professor of secondary education and visitor of high schools at the University of Florida in Gainesville (1920–31).

Returning to Peabody as professor of secondary education in 1931, Roemer was director of instruction of Peabody Junior College and Demonstration School (1931–36), dean of the Junior College (1936–41) and became dean of the college in 1941, serving until 1952. He was particularly interested in extracurricular activities in secondary schools.

Roemer served the military government in Germany after World War II as director of teacher education (1949–52). He helped McMurry College in Abilene, Texas, establish a graduate teacher education program (1952–55).

Roemer was a coauthor of many articles and books, including *Extra Curricular Activities* (1926), *Readings in Extra Curricular Activities* (1929), *The Administration of the Modern Secondary School* (1931), *Secondary School Administration* (1932), *Basic Student Activities* (1935), *Gentleman Commander* (1936), *My Activity Book* (1937), and *Dean of Boys in High School* (1939).

Roemer was active in professional organizations as president of the Southern Association of Colleges and Secondary Schools (1931–32), the Florida Young Men's Christian Association (1921–31), and the Florida Education Association (1926). He was awarded an honorary degree from Tampa (Florida) University (1938).

REFERENCES: *LE* (III); *WWAE* (XIV); *WWW* (III); James Gee, "Joseph Roemer—He Gladly Taught," *The Peabody Reflector* (May–June 1956); "In Memoriam," *The Peabody Reflector* (June–July 1955): 181; *NYT*, July 3, 1955, p. 33; Macon Sawrie, "Dr. Joseph Roemer," *The Peabody Reflector* (June 1941): 219–20.                    *John F. Ohles*

**ROGERS, Carl Ransom.** B. January 8, 1902, Oak Park, Illinois, to Walter A. and Julia (Cushing) Rogers. M. August 28, 1924, to Helen Martha Elliott. Ch. two.

Carl Ransom Rogers, the leader of nondirective, client-centered theory of psychotherapy, enrolled at the University of Wisconsin with the intention of majoring in agriculture. He decided to enter the Protestant ministry and took part in the World Student Christian Federation Conference in China in 1922. He was graduated from the University of Wisconsin with the B.A. degree (1924) and entered Union Theological Seminary in New York City. Deciding not to continue in religious studies, he enrolled in courses in psychology and psychiatry at Teachers College, Columbia University. Awarded a fellowship to the new Institute for Child Guidance, Rogers received the M.A. (1928) and Ph.D. (1931) degrees from Teachers College.

In 1928 Rogers became a psychologist for the child study department of the Society for the Prevention of Cruelty to Children in Rochester, New York, and directed the agency from 1930 to 1938. In 1939 he helped establish the Rochester Guidance Center and became its first director.

Rogers became a professor in clinical psychology at Ohio State University in 1940, teaching treatment and counseling methods to graduate students. In 1944 Rogers served as psychological consultant to the United States Army Air Force. He was director of counseling services of the United Service Organizations (1944–45). Rogers was professor of psychology at the University of Chicago (1945–57) and executive secretary of the university-connected Counseling Center, which he had helped to establish. Invited to lecture at the University of Wisconsin as Knapp Visiting Professor, Rogers remained for seven years as professor of psychology and psychiatry (1957–63). Rogers was named a fellow of the Center for Advanced Study in the Behavioral Sciences at Palo Alto, California (1962–63) and spent ten years at La Jolla at the Western Behavioral Sciences Institute (1964–68) and as resident fellow at the Center for Studies of the Person (1968–74).

Rogers was the author of *Measuring Personality Adjustment in Children* (1931), *Clinical Treatment of the Problem Child* (1939), *Counseling and Psychotherapy* (1942), *Counseling with Returned Servicemen* (with J. Wallen, 1946), *Client-Centered Therapy* (1951), *Psychotherapy and Personality Change* (with others, 1954), *On Becoming a Person* (1961), *The*

*Therapeutic Relationship and Its Impact* (with others, 1967), *Freedom to Learn* (1969), *Carl Rogers on Encounter Groups* (1970), and *Becoming Partners: Marriage and Its Alternatives* (1972). He was editor of Studies of the Person Series (with W. R. Coulson) and *Psychotherapy and Personality Change* (with Rosalind Dymond, 1954).

Named to the American Academy of Arts and Sciences (1961), Rogers received the Distinguished Scientific Contribution Award (1956) and the first Distinguished Professional Contribution Award (1972) from the American Psychological Association. He was cited for outstanding research by the American Personnel and Guidance Association (1955 and 1961) and was awarded the Nicholas Murray Butler Medal by Columbia University (1955), was named Humanist of the Year by the American Humanist Association (1964), and received an award from the American Board of Professional Psychology (1968). Rogers was a founder of the American Association for Applied Psychology (chairman, clinical section, 1942–44, president, 1944–45) and was vice-president of the American Orthopsychiatric Association (1944–45). He was president of the American Psychological Association (1946–47) and headed the division of clinical and abnormal psychology (1949–50). He was a charter member of the American Academy of Psychotherapists (president, 1956–58). He received honorary degrees from Lawrence College and Gonzaga University.

REFERENCES: *CA* (1–4); *CB* (December 1962); *LE* (III); *WW* (XXXVIII); *WWAE* (XIII); "Carl R. Rogers," *Education* 95 (Winter 1974): 101–02; Frank Milhollan and Bill E. Forisha, *From Skinner to Rogers; Contrasting Approaches to Education* (Lincoln, Neb.: Professional Educators Publications, 1972); "Person to Person," *Time* 70 (July 1, 1957): 34–35.                              *Harold G. MacDermot*

**ROGERS, Elizabeth Ann.** B. November 2, 1829, St. Erth, Hayle, Cornwall, England, to James and Ann (Ellis) Rogers. M. no. D. February 20, 1921, Honolulu, Hawaii.

Elizabeth Ann Rogers grew up in Cornwall, England, and became interested in an Anglican religious order, the Congregation of Religious of the Society of the Most Holy Trinity. In 1864 the order established a house and school on the Hawaiian island of Maui. In 1865 Queen Emma of Hawaii visited the order in England seeking assistance for the education of Hawaiian girls. Rogers met the queen and entered the order in 1866 as Sister Beatrice.

In 1866 Rogers, two other religious, and Lydia Sellon, founder and mother of the order, traveled to Honolulu, Hawaii, where they established St. Andrews' Priory School for girls. The school was staffed by the original sisters and transfers from Lahaina, Maui, when the first school was closed in 1877. On the death of the other teachers, the school continued with

Rogers and Ellen Albertina Polyblank (Sister Albertina). When the order closed its mission in Hawaii, Rogers and Polyblank were granted permission to remain at the school.

In 1902 Hawaii came under the jurisdiction of the American Protestant Episcopal church, and in 1918 control of the school was assumed by the Community of the Transfiguration of Cleveland, Ohio. The sisters retired in 1902 and continued to live on the school grounds to their deaths.

REFERENCES: *NAW; Hawaiian Monthly Chronicle,* August 1930, pp. 9–10; *Honolulu Advertiser,* February 21, 1921.          *Betty S. Harper*

**ROGERS, Harriet Burbank.** B. April 12, 1834, North Billerica, Massachusetts, to F. Calvin and Ann (Faulkner) Rogers. M. no. D. December 12, 1919, North Billerica, Massachusetts.

Harriet Burbank Rogers was graduated from Massachusetts State Normal School in West Newton, Massachusetts (later, Framingham State College), in 1851 and taught in several country schools and in Westford (Massachusetts) Academy. In 1863 she accepted as a private student a deaf girl, Fanny Cushing, whose parents wanted her to learn to speak. Although the manual alphabet and sign language were the current mode of educating the deaf in the United States, Rogers employed an oral method she read was used in schools for the deaf in Germany. Fanny Cushing successfully learned to speak by feeling the teacher's breath and voice vibrations and creating the same breath and voice production herself.

Rogers was associated with Gardiner Greene Hubbard, whose deaf daughter later became the wife of Alexander Graham Bell *(q.v.),* in opening a school in 1866 at Chelmsford, Massachusetts, with five deaf students, using an oral approach to instruction. John Clarke of Northampton, Massachusetts, contributed an endowment to establish the Clarke Institute for Deaf Mutes (later Clarke School for the Deaf) at Northampton; the institute was granted a state charter in 1867. Rogers served as director of the school until 1886 when ill health forced her resignation.

Rogers visited Europe in 1871 and 1872 where she studied the German schools for the deaf that used oral instruction exclusively. In the United States controversy was beginning over which method of instruction should be accepted. The oralists, mostly women, advocated teaching with the oral method with great zeal, while the manualists, mostly men, looked down on the innovators.

Rogers's efforts were successful when the 1886 convention of the American Educators of the Deaf went on record favoring efforts to include the teaching of speech and lipreading to deaf students. In 1870 the American Association to Promote the Teaching of Speech to the Deaf was formed.

REFERENCES: *DAB; NAW; WWW* (IV).          *Judy Egelston-Dodd*

**ROGERS, Henry Wade.** B. October 10, 1853, Holland Patent, New York, to n.a. M. June 22, 1876, to Emma Ferdon Winner. Ch. none. D. August 16, 1926, Pennington, New Jersey.

Henry Wade Rogers, educator and jurist, grew up as the adopted son of an uncle for whom he was named, Henry W. Rogers. After residing in Buffalo, New York, the family moved to Ann Arbor, Michigan. Rogers attended the University of Michigan where he received the B.A. (1874) and M.A. (1877) degrees and was admitted to the bar. Following brief periods practicing law in Minnesota and New Jersey, Rogers was appointed Tappan Professor of Law at the University of Michigan (1882) and served as dean of the law school (1885–90).

He was appointed president of Northwestern University in Evanston, Illinois, where he spent ten successful years (1890–1900). His administration was marked by significant growth and development and reorganization of the university over strong opposition. A scientific department was established, new buildings were constructed, and student enrollment nearly doubled.

Rogers was a member of the faculty at the Yale University School of Law (1900–21), serving as dean from 1903 to 1916. From 1913 to his death in 1926, he was judge of the federal circuit court of appeals in New York City.

Rogers's most significant work was as dean at Yale. The school adopted the case method of instruction, required the college degree for admission, and restricted faculty to full-time teachers.

Rogers authored several legal treatises, including *Illinois Citations* (1881), *The Law of Expert Testimony* (1883), *Introduction to Constitutional History as Seen in American Law* (1889), and *Two Centuries of American Law* (1901). He was associate editor of *Johnson's Universal Encyclopedia* (eight volumes, 1893–97), a contributor to a number of major reference encyclopedias, and the author of many articles.

He was active in professional associations, including the Association of American Law Schools (president, 1906) and the American Bar Association as chairman of the Section on Legal Education (1893–94) and the Committee on Legal Education and Admission to the Bar (1906–17, 1919). He served the Methodist Episcopal church as president of the General Layman's Association. He received several honorary degrees.

REFERENCES: *DAB; NCAB* (26:50); *TC; WWW* (I); *NYT*, August 17, 1926, p. 21.                                    *Joe L. Green*

**ROGERS, William Barton.** B. December 7, 1804, Philadelphia, Pennsylvania, to Patrick Kerr and Hannah (Blythe) Rogers. M. June 20, 1849, to Emma Savage. Ch. none. D. May 30, 1882, Boston, Massachusetts.

William Barton Rogers received his elementary and secondary education from his father and the Baltimore (Maryland) public schools. He was graduated in 1822 from the College of William and Mary in Williamsburg, Virginia, where his father was professor of natural philosophy and chemistry.

Rogers taught mathematics and studied the classics at William and Mary (1822–25). With his brother James he conducted a school in Windsor, Maryland (1825–28), and in 1827 delivered two series of lectures before the Maryland Institute in Baltimore. On the death of his father in 1828, Rogers was appointed to succeed him as professor of natural philosophy and chemistry at William and Mary. In 1835 he became professor of natural philosophy at the University of Virginia and served as chairman of the faculty (1844–45), a position equivalent to president of the university. His administration was marked by student riots that were quelled by civil authorities. He served as state geologist for Virginia (1835–42) and with his brother Henry conducted a geological survey of the state.

In 1853 Rogers moved to Boston where he engaged in scientific activities under the Boston Society of Natural History and the American Academy of Arts and Sciences. He was inspector of gas and gas meters for the state of Massachusetts (1861–64). With his brother Henry he made provisional plans for a polytechnic institution in Boston, plans that resulted in approval by the Massachusetts legislature in 1861 of an act to charter the Massachusetts Institute of Technology (MIT). Rogers served as first president of MIT from 1862 to 1870, when ill health forced his retirement. When his successor, John D. Runkle *(q.v.)*, resigned in 1878 Rogers served again as president and also as professor of geology and physics to his final retirement in 1882.

Rogers was the author of *Strength of Materials* (1838), *Elements of Mechanical Philosophy* (1852), and annual geological survey reports that were published in 1884 as *A Reprint of Annual Reports and Other Papers on the Geology of the Virginias*. He was a founding member of the National Academy of Sciences (president, 1878–82), chairman of the Association of American Geologists and Naturalists (1847), and president (1848 and 1876) of the successor American Association for the Advancement of Science. He was corresponding secretary of the American Academy of Arts and Sciences (1863–69), founder and first president of the American Association of Social Science (1865), and a member of other American and foreign societies. He received honorary degrees from Hampden-Sydney and William and Mary colleges and Harvard University.

REFERENCES: *AC; DAB; NCAB* (7:410); *NYT,* May 31, 1882, p. 5; *TC; WWW* (H); "In Memory of William Barton Rogers," *Society of Arts* (Boston: Massachusetts Institute of Technology, 1882); *Philadelphia Press,* May 31, 1882; Emma Savage Rogers, *The Life and Letters of William Barton Rogers* (Boston: Massachusetts Institute of Technology, 1896); W. S. W. Ruschenberger, "A Sketch of the Life of Robert E.

Rogers, with Biographical Notices of His Father and Brothers," *Proceedings of the American Philosophical Society* 23 (1896); F. A. Walker, "William Barton Rogers," *National Academy of Science, Biographical Memoirs* (New York: 1895), vol. 3.                              *Walter F. C. Ade*

**ROOT, George Frederick.** B. August 30, 1820, Sheffield, Massachusetts, to Frederick Ferdinand and Sarah (Flint) Root. M. August 1845 to Mary Olive Woodman. Ch. six, including Clara Louisa Burnham, author. D. August 6, 1895, Bailey's Island, Maine.

As a youngster, George Root taught himself to play several instruments. In 1838 he studied under A. N. Johnson and George J. Webb in Boston and assisted Lowell Mason *(q.v.)* at the Boston Academy of Music. In 1841 Root moved to New York City to become a singing teacher at Abbott's School for Young Ladies and also taught at the Rutgers Female Institute, Miss Haines' School for Young Ladies, Union Theological Seminary, and the New York State Institution for the Blind.

In 1853, following further vocal study in Paris, he established the New York Normal Institute with Lowell Mason; they conducted the institute in New York from 1853 to 1856. The first faculty included Root, Mason, William Bradbury *(q.v.)*, and Thomas Hastings. The institute was moved to North Reading, Massachusetts (1856–58). Root was successful in preparing teachers. Following the example of Lowell Mason, he organized musical conventions in various parts of the country to acquaint teachers in the newest methods in singing instruction. Root continued this practice for many years, which was an important factor in the extension and development of music education. With Mason, he is credited with introducing singing as a regular branch of study in American education.

In 1859, Root joined his brother, E. T. Root, in managing a music store in Chicago. When it was destroyed in the 1871 fire, the firm's assets were acquired by the John Church Co. of Cincinnati, Ohio; Root continued as the Chicago representative of the business firm, which still carried his name. He conducted teacher-training classes in music education during the school summer vacations. Some classes were housed at the University of Chicago, which awarded him the honorary doctor of music degree (1881).

Root's compositions were originally written to provide materials for his classes, but encouraged by commercial success, Root adopted the pen name "Wurzel" (German for "root") to publish his compositions, including some for the Christy Minstrels. Later his compositions were published under his own name. He composed several popular Civil War songs, including "The Battle Cry of Freedom," "Tramp, Tramp, Tramp, the Boys Are Marching," "Just Before the Battle, Mother," and "The Vacant Chair." He composed over two hundred songs and compiled over seventy other publications in the field of music.

He was the author of several books, including the autobiographical *The Story of a Musical Life* (1891), *Root's Harmony and Composition* (1892), *Don't, A Friendly Attempt to Correct Some Prevalent Errors in Music Terminology* (1895), and *The New Choir and Congregation* (1907).

REFERENCES: *AC; DAB; NCAB* (9:384); *TC; WWW* (H); James Duff Brown, *Biographical Dictionary of Musicians* (New York: Verlag, 1970), pp. 520–21; Frank J. Metcalf, *American Writers and Compilers of Sacred Music* (New York: Russell and Russell, 1967), pp. 189–93; *NYT*, August 8, 1895, p. 2; Nicolas Slonimsky, ed., *Baker's Biographical Dictionary of Musicians*, 5th ed. (New York: G. Schirmer, 1958), p. 1366.

*Jo Ann Kaufman*

**RORER, Sarah Tyson Heston.** B. October 18, 1849, Richboro, Pennsylvania, to Charles Tyson and Elizabeth (Sager) Heston. M. February 23, 1871, to W. Albert Rorer. Ch. three. D. December 27, 1937, Colebrook, Pennsylvania.

Sarah Tyson Heston Rorer's father opened a chemistry laboratory and apothecary shop in Buffalo, New York. She was graduated from East Aurora (New York) Academy in 1869. She married in 1871 and moved to Philadelphia, Pennsylvania, where she enrolled in a domestic science course at the New Century Club in 1879.

In 1880 Rorer taught the domestic science course at the New Century Club and in 1883 established the Philadelphia School of Domestic Science where she continued as principal to 1903. Preferring light meats, fruits, and vegetables to rich, heavy foods, Rorer conducted classes for girls, women, and professional cooks, taught cooking and hygiene to destitute girls, and provided a yearly scholarship for a black girl. She provided courses of weekly lectures for nurses at Women's Hospital, students at Women's Medical College, and fourth-year students at the University of Pennsylvania. She established a two-year normal course for teachers of the domestic arts.

Rorer gained a national reputation on the publication of the *Philadelphia Cookbook* (1886). She was also the author of *New Cook Book* (1902), *My Best 250 Recipes* (1907), *Home Candy Making* (1911), *Canning and Preserving* (1912), *New Salads* (1912), *Bread-Making* (n.d.), *Made Over Dishes* (1912), *Sandwiches* (1912), *Hot Weather Dishes* (n.d.), *How to Use a Chafing Dish* (1912), *Diet for the Sick* (1914), and *A Key to Simple Cookery* (1917). She was editor and part owner of *Table Talk* (1886–92) and *Household* (1893–97). The *Ladies' Home Journal* purchased *Household* in 1897, and Rorer served on the *Journal* staff from 1897 to 1911. In 1914 she became head of the cooking department of *Good Housekeeping*.

A director of the Chautauqua movement, Rorer organized cooking classes in rural Pennsylvania. She was director of home economics kitchens for the Chicago (1893) and St. Louis (1904) expositions and was invited to conduct demonstrations at the Paris (France) Exposition (1900). She continued active and delivered a paper, "Early Dietetics," to the Pennsylvania Dietetic Association at the age of eighty-five.

REFERENCES: *NAW; NCAB* (16:232); *TC; WWW* (I); Gertrude Bosler Biddle and Sarah Dickenson Lowrie, eds., *Notable Women of Pennsylvania* (Philadelphia: University of Pennsylvania Press, 1942).

M. *Jane Dowd*

**ROSE, Mary Davies Schwartz.** B. October 31, 1874, Newark, Ohio, to Hiram B. and Martha (Davies) Schwartz. M. September 15, 1910, to Anton Richard Rose. Ch. one. D. February 1, 1941, Edgewater, New Jersey.

Mary Davies Schwartz Rose was graduated from the Wooster (Ohio) high school (1892) and Denison University in Granville, Ohio, where she received the B.Litt. degree (1901). She studied at the Mechanics Institute in Rochester, New York (1901–02), and received the B.S. degree in home economics (1906) from Teachers College of Columbia University. She was given a special fellowship to engage in graduate study in physiological chemistry at Yale University with Lafayette Mendel and received the Ph.D. degree in 1909.

Rose was a high school home economics teacher in Wooster, Ohio (1899–1901), and Fond du Lac, Wisconsin (1902–05). She was an assistant at Teachers College, Columbia University (1906–07), and taught nutrition there from 1909, becoming professor of nutrition in 1921.

A contributor of articles to journals in the fields of nutrition and home economics, Rose was the author of *Laboratory Handbook for Dietetics* (1912), *Feeding the Family* (1916), *Everyday Foods in War Time* (1918), *Foundations of Nutrition* (1927), and *Teaching Nutrition to Boys and Girls* (1932).

Rose served as deputy director of the Bureau of Conservation of the Federal Food Board (1918–19) and a member of the nutrition committee of the Health Organization of the League of Nations (from 1935), the council of foods of the American Medical Association (from 1933), and the American Institute of Nutrition (president, 1937–38). She was a fellow of the American Association for the Advancement of Science and the American Public Health Association and a member of other professional organizations.

REFERENCES: *DAB* (supp. 3); *NAW; NYT*, February 2, 1941, p. 46; *WWW* (I); Grace McLeod, "Mary Schwartz Rose," *Journal of Home Economics* 33 (April 1941): 221–24; Benjamin R. Andrews, "Mary Schwartz Rose, 1874–1941," *School and Society* 53 (April 26, 1941): 538; Henry C. Sherman, "Mary Schwartz Rose," *Teachers College Record* 42 (March 1941): 544–45.                                    *Roberta Sorensen*

**ROSSKOPF, Myron Frederick.** B. October 2, 1907, Fairmont, Minnesota, to Joseph and Alvina (Meyer) Rosskopf. M. to Frances Clark. Ch. two. D. January 31, 1973, Ridgefield, Connecticut.

Myron Frederick Rosskopf received his early education in public schools in Minneapolis, Minnesota, and was graduated from the University of Minnesota with the B.A. (1928) and M.A. (1930) degrees and from Brown University in Providence, Rhode Island, with the Ph.D. degree in mathematics in 1934.

Rosskopf was assistant director and director of the mathematics groups in an eight-year study for the Progressive Education Association (1936–40). He served in the United States Army Air Force (1941–45). He was associate professor in mathematics and education at Syracuse University from 1948 to 1952. From 1952 to 1956 he was associate professor of mathematics and education at Columbia University. He joined the faculty of Teachers College, Columbia University, as a professor of mathematics and education in 1956, and in 1971 he was named the first Clifford Brewster Upton Professor of Mathematical Education at the college. Rosskopf served as chairman of the department of mathematical education at the college from 1966 until his death in 1973.

One of the country's leading mathematics educators, Rosskopf was an authority on the teaching of mathematics and preparation of mathematics teachers. He was one of the first mathematicians in the United States to engage in research in the Piagetian cognitive development theory of mathematical learning.

Rosskopf was the author or coauthor of over thirty books, including *Logic in Elementary Mathematics* (with Robert M. Exner, 1959), *Modern Mathematics* (two volumes with others, 1964–66), and *Geometry; a Perspective View* (with Joan C. Levine and Bruce R. Vogeli, 1969). He was editor of *Teaching Secondary School Mathematics* (1970) (the thirty-third yearbook of the National Council of Teachers of Mathematics) and *Piagetian Cognitive Development Theory and Mathematical Education* (1971). Rosskopf was editor of the *New York State Mathematics Teachers Journal* (1954–56) and *Mathematics Student Journal* (1961–64) and associate editor of *Mathematics Teacher* (1953–59) and member of the editorial panel (1969–73).

Rosskopf was a Fulbright lecturer at the University of Oslo, Norway. He was director of the Conference on the Piaget Type of Research in Mathematical Education held by the National Council of Teachers in Mathematics at Columbia University. He was elected to a three-year term on the board of directors of the National Council of Teachers of Mathematics (1972).

REFERENCES: *CA* (5–8); *NYT,* February 1, 1973, p. 38; *American Men of Science,* 11th ed. (New York: Bowker, 1967).     *Virginia Taylor*

**RUFFNER, Henry.** B. January 16, 1790, Shenandoah County, Virginia, to David and Ann (Brumbach) Ruffner. M. March 31, 1819, to Sarah Lyle. M. to Laura J. Kirby. Ch. four, including William Henry Ruffner (q.v.). D. December 17, 1861, Kanawha County, Virginia (later, West Virginia).

Henry Ruffner, one of Virginia's pioneer educators, entered the classical school of Dr. Joseph McElhenney in Lewisburg, Virginia, at the age of nineteen, studying for three years. He enrolled in Washington College (later, Washington and Lee University) in Lexington, Virginia, in 1812, completed the four-year course in a year and a half, and received the B.A. degree (1813). He taught language courses at the college, studied theology with George Baxter, president of Washington College, in 1814, and was licensed to preach by the Presbyterian church in 1815.

Ruffner organized the first Presbyterian church in the Kanawha Valley and a private classical school in Charleston, Virginia (later, West Virginia). In 1819 he became professor of languages at Washington College and was acting president three times before becoming president (1836–48).

Ruffner was a delegate to the convention held in Clarksburg, Virginia, in 1841 to study the educational needs of the state and to make recommendations to the legislature. He proposed a comprehensive plan for a system of district schools supported by taxes levied by the districts, similar to the one adopted by the state in 1870. Ruffner's plan proposed the organization of a system of district schools under proper supervision, with support for these schools primarily from the Virginia Literary Fund, supplemented by a tax on property. The plan was rejected by the legislature.

He wrote *The Fathers of the Desert* (two volumes, 1850), *A Discourse on the Duration of Future Punishment* (1823), *Against Universalism* (n.d.), and a novel *Judith Bensaddi* (n.d.). He received honorary degrees from the College of New Jersey (1838) and Washington College (1849).

REFERENCES: *AC; DAB; NCAB* (3:164); *TC; WWW* (H); C. C. Pearson, "William Henry Ruffner: Reconstruction Statesman of Virginia," *The South Atlantic Quarterly* 20 (January 1921): 25–31 and (April 1921): 137–51.                                                              *S. S. Britt, Jr.*

**RUFFNER, William Henry.** B. February 11, 1824, Lexington, Virginia, to Henry (q.v.) and Sarah (Lyle) Ruffner. M. September 3, 1850, to Harriet Ann Gray. Ch. four. D. November 24, 1908, Asheville, North Carolina.

William Henry Ruffner was graduated with the A.B. (1842) and M.A. (1845) degrees from Washington College (later, Washington and Lee University) in Lexington, Virginia. He studied at the Union Theological Seminary in Hampden-Sydney, Virginia (later in New York City), and Princeton (New Jersey) Theological Seminary. After a two-year chaplaincy (1849–51) at the University of Virginia he was ordained on January 14, 1852, by the presbytery of Philadelphia.

Chronic throat trouble compelled his resignation from the ministry in

1853. Ruffner was a farmer for sixteen years until his election in 1870 as the first state superintendent of schools in Virginia with the support of General Robert E. Lee. He wrote the school law of Virginia. He served to 1882 when a shift in political alliances resulted in inadequate support for his reelection. Ruffner became the first president of the State Female Normal School (later, Longwood College) at Farmville, Virginia, in 1884. He served until 1887 when he became a land surveyor.

Ruffner also served as trustee at Washington College (1865–76) and at the state's new Agricultural and Mechanical College (later, Virginia Polytechnic Institute and State University) in Blacksburg. He was the author of a number of reports as superintendent, *History of Washington and Lee University* (1893), and *Charity and the Clergy* (n.d.). He served for a number of years as editor of the department of public instruction's *Educational Journal of Virginia*. He received an honorary degree from Washington and Lee University.

REFERENCES: *AC; DAB; NCAB* (12:526); *TC; WWW* (I); *Asheville* (North Carolina) *Gazette,* November 25, 1908.          *Glen I. Earthman*


**RUGG, Harold Ordway.** B. January 17, 1886, Fitchburg, Massachusetts, to Edward Francis and Merion Abbie (Davidson) Rugg. M. September 4, 1912, to Bertha Miller. M. August 25, 1930, to Louise Krueger. M. 1947 to Elizabeth Howe Page. Ch. three. D. May 17, 1960, Woodstock, New York.

Harold O. Rugg was graduated from high school in Fitchburg, Massachusetts (1902), and received the B.S. degree (1908) from Dartmouth College in Hanover, New Hampshire, and the C. E. degree (1909) from the Thayer School of Civil Engineering at Dartmouth. He was awarded the Ph.D. degree (1915) from the University of Illinois.

Rugg taught engineering at James Milliken University in Decatur, Illinois (1909–11), and at the University of Illinois (1911–15). He taught courses in educational administration, statistics, and psychology at the University of Chicago (1915–20), was professor of education at Teachers College of Columbia University (1920–51), and was school psychologist at Columbia's Lincoln School. He was a Fulbright Scholar in Egypt (1952–53) and visiting professor at the University of Puerto Rico (1953–54). A leading progressive educator, he came under attack by opponents of progressive education who fought the use of his instructional materials and advocated the banning of his books from libraries.

Rugg assembled teams of graduate students and teachers to assist him in writing and compiling the Rugg Social Science Pamphlets (twelve volumes, 1921–28), which were among the most popular social studies materials published at the time. He also wrote *Statistical Methods Applied to Education* (1917), *A Primer of Graphics and Statistics* (1925), *The Child-Centered School* (1930), *Culture and Education in America* (1931), *The*

*Great Technology* (1933), *American Life and the School Curriculum* (1936), *That Men May Understand* (1941), *Now Is the Moment* (1943), *Foundations of American Education* (1947), *The Teacher in the School and Society* (1950), *The Teacher of Teachers* (1952), and *Imagination* (1963), published posthumously. He was the author of thirteen of the fourteen volumes of the Man and His Changing Society Series (1929–45) and was founder and editor of the New World Education Series. He edited *Readings in the Foundation of Education* (two volumes, 1940), was editor of the *Journal of Educational Psychology* (1920–31) and *Frontiers of Democracy* (1939–43), was on the editorial board of *Social Frontier* (1934–39), and was social studies editor of *Scholastic Magazine* (1930–40).

Rugg was active in many professional organizations and was a fellow of the American Statistical Association and the American Association for the Advancement of Science. He was a founder of the National Council for the Social Studies, president of the Educational Research Association (1921–22), and American representative on the New Education Fellowship from 1932. He was the recipient of honorary degrees from Dartmouth College and the University of Tasmania, Australia.

REFERENCES: *CB;* (May 1941 and June 1960); *LE* (III); *NCAB* (G: 543); *NYT,* May 18, 1960, p. 41; *WWW* (IV); Harold O. Rugg, *That Men May Understand* (New York: Doubleday, Doran, 1941).    *Murry R. Nelson*

**RUNKLE, John Daniel.** B. October 11, 1822, Root, New York, to Daniel and Sara (Gordon) Runkle. M. 1862 to Catharine Robbins Bird. Ch. four. D. July 8, 1902, Southwest Harbor, Maine.

John Daniel Runkle was educated in public schools and academies in Canajoharie, Ames, and Cortland, New York. He taught for three years (1844–47) in the academy at Onondaga, New York, continuing his study of mathematics through the requirements for college entrance. In 1847 he entered the Lawrence Scientific School of Harvard University. He was graduated with the B.S. degree in 1851 and received the honorary M.A. degree for high scholarship.

In 1858 Runkle founded *Mathematical Monthly* and served as editor. Runkle became associated with a group of men who were working on a proposal for an advanced educational institution, the Massachusetts Institute of Technology, which opened in the spring of 1865. Runkle was a member of the original faculty of ten and was appointed the institute's first secretary. In 1868 Runkle was appointed acting president, and he was president from 1870 to 1878.

Seeing a need for shopwork experience for students, Runkle developed the School of Mechanic Arts. Admission to the school was limited to boys at least fifteen years of age who were qualified to enter high school. The school gave those who wished to enter an industrial career some experience in industry.

Runkle wrote a textbook, *Elements of Plane Analytic Geometry* (1886), *The Manual Element in Education* (n.d.), and numerous reports on mathematical material, and he worked on the *American Ephemeris and Nautical Almanac* from 1849 to 1884. He received honorary degrees from Hamilton College (1869) and from Wesleyan University (1871).

REFERENCES: *AC; DAB; NCAB* (6:350); *TC; WWW* (I).

*Lee H. Smalley*

**RUSBY, Henry Hurd.** B. April 26, 1855, Franklin, New Jersey, to John and Abigail (Holmes) Rusby. M. October 5, 1887, to Margaretta Hanna. Ch. three. D. November 18, 1940, Sarasota, Florida.

Henry Hurd Rusby began his long career as a botanist, pharmacologist, and explorer at the age of fifteen, when he initiated a study of flowering plants in his neighborhood. He began his education at the local school in Franklin, New Jersey, where his teacher encouraged his interest in plants. He prepared himself for a career in teaching by attending the Massachusetts State Normal School (later, Westfield State College) at Westfield, Massachusetts (1872–74). After several years as a teacher, he received an M.D. degree from the University Medical College of New York University (1884).

He made botanical explorations for the Smithsonian Institution in the American Southwest (1880–81, 1883) and Latin America (1885–87, 1896, 1917, 1921–22). He was professor of botany, physiology, and materia medica at Columbia University (1889–1930) and professor of materia medica of the university and Bellevue Hospital Medical College (1897–1902); he became dean of the college in 1901. Rusby served as drug expert and pharmacognosist in the Bureau of Chemistry, United States Department of Agriculture. He fought successfully to stop the common use of decomposed ergot in medical preparations for use in childbirth. Although his formal education in botany was minimal, Rusby learned firsthand from plants rather than from books. He received recognition as one of the country's outstanding experts on medicinal botany.

A partial list of books Rusby wrote includes *Morphology and Histology of Plants* (1899), *Wild Vegetable Foods of the United States* (1906), *Fifty Years of Materia Medica* (1907), *Manual of Botany* (1911), and *Properties and Uses of Drugs* (1930). In addition to his scholarly activities, Rusby engaged in political activities to bring about reforms in pharmacy. His efforts helped bring about the standardization of drugs and medicines by chemical analysis, passage of the Pure Food and Drug Act of 1906, and elevation of professional standards for pharmacists.

Rusby was active in professional organizations, serving as president of the American Pharmaceutical Association (1909–10). An honorary member of medical and pharmaceutical societies in Great Britain and Mexico, he was honorary curator of the Economic Museum of the New

York Botanical Garden. He was awarded honorary degrees by the Philadelphia College of Pharmacy and Science and Columbia University.

REFERENCES: *DAB* (supp. 2); *NCAB* (A:172); *TC; WWW* (I); *NYT,* November 19, 1940, p. 23; *Science* 93 (January 17, 1941): 53; *School and Society* 52 (November 23, 1940): 523.                     B. Richard Siebring

**RUSH, Benjamin.** B. December 24, 1745, Philadelphia, Pennsylvania, to John and Susanna (Hall) Rush. M. January 11, 1776, to Julia Stockton. Ch. thirteen, including Richard Rush, American statesman. D. April 19, 1813, Philadelphia, Pennsylvania.

In 1752 Benjamin Rush became the ward of his uncle, Samuel Finley, under whom he prepared for college in a Nottingham (Maryland) classical school. He was graduated with the A.B. (1760) and A.M. (1763) degrees from the College of New Jersey (later, Princeton University) and studied medicine under John Redman in Philadelphia, Pennsylvania (1761–66). He studied medicine at the University of Edinburgh, Scotland, where he received the M.D. degree (1768). He spent a year in further study in London, England, and Paris, France.

On his return to Philadelphia, Rush began the practice of medicine and was the first professor of chemistry in the colonies at the Philadelphia Medical College (1769–91). He was professor of the institutes of medicine in the merger of the medical college with the University of Pennsylvania (1792–1813) and also was professor of theory and practice (1796–1813). He was a member of the Continental Congress and a signer of the Declaration of Independence. He served in the American Revolution as surgeon to the Pennsylvania navy (1775–76) and was surgeon-general and physician-general in the Continental army (1777–78). He was surgeon to the Pennsylvania Hospital (1784–1813), established the first free dispensary in the country (1786), and was port physician of Philadelphia (1790–93). From 1799 to 1813 he served as treasurer of the United States Mint.

Rush was the author of the first American chemistry text, *A Syllabus of a Course of Lectures on Chemistry* (1790), and one of the first American books on personal hygiene, *Sermons to Gentlemen upon Temperance and Exercise* (1792). He also wrote *Essays on the Mode of Education Proper to a Republic* (1786), *Medical Inquiries and Observations* (five volumes, 1789–98), *Account of the Philadelphia Society for the Establishment of Charity Schools* (1796), *Essays, Literary, Moral and Philosophical* (1798), *Sixteen Introductory Lectures* (1811), and *Diseases of the Mind* (1812).

An organizer (1774) and president (1803) of the Pennsylvania Society for the Abolition of Slavery, Rush was president of the Philadelphia Medical Society, founder and vice-president of the Philadelphia Bible Society, and founder of the Philadelphia College of Physicians (1787). He participated in founding the American Philosophical Society (vice-president, 1800) and Dickinson College in Carlisle, Pennsylvania (1783). Rush received an honorary degree from Yale College (1812).

REFERENCES: *AC; DAB; DSB; EB; NCAB* (3:333); *TC; WWW* (H); George W. Corner, ed., *The Autobiography of Benjamin Rush* (Princeton, N.J.: Princeton University Press, 1948); David F. Hawke, *Benjamin Rush: Revolutionary Gadfly* (New York: The Bobbs-Merrill Co., 1971).

*Samuel A. Farmerie*

**RUSSELL, Albert Jonathan.** B. January 15, 1831, Petersburg, Virginia, to William Hathaway and Sarah Ann (Iseman) Russell. M. to n.a. Roberts. M. October 1865 to Abby M. Baker. Ch. none. D. January 17, 1896, Jacksonville, Florida.

Albert Jonathan Russell was graduated from Anderson Seminary in Petersburg, Virginia. He went to Lake City, Florida, in 1859 and to Jacksonville, Florida, where he practiced architecture. At the outbreak of the Civil War in 1861, he enlisted in the Confederate army where he served as a second lieutenant in the Second Florida Infantry Volunteers.

At the close of the war, Russell resumed his business. In 1865 and in 1874, he was elected to the Jacksonville city council and was chosen chairman of the board of public instruction of Duval County, Florida, in 1876. In 1877 Russell was elected county superintendent of Duval County, Florida, and served from 1877 to 1884, when Governor William D. Bloxham appointed him state superintendent of public instruction, a position he filled until 1893.

Russell was the last appointed state superintendent of public instruction in Florida under the constitution of 1868 and the first elected under the constitution of 1885. He was the father of the school law of 1889, which provided for a system of county high schools in the state of Florida, the first organized public school system for Florida.

REFERENCES: *Life and Labors of Albert Jonathan Russell* (Jacksonville, Fla.: DeCosta Printing Co., 1897); *History of the Florida Education Association 1886–87 to 1956–57* (Tallahassee: Florida Education Association, 1958).

*Freeman R. Irvine, Jr.*

**RUSSELL, Harry Luman.** B. March 12, 1886, Poynette, Wisconsin, to Ephriam Fred and Lucinda Estella (Waldron) Russell. M. December 20, 1893, to Hannah May Delany. M. July 27, 1932, to Susanna Cocroft Headington. Ch. two. D. April 11, 1954, Madison, Wisconsin.

Harry Luman Russell received the B.S. (1888) and M.S. (1890) degrees from the University of Wisconsin. In 1890 he went abroad to study at the University of Berlin, Germany, the Pasteur Institute in Paris, France, and the Naples (Italy) Zoological Laboratory. He studied under the direction of Robert Koch and Louis Pasteur. He was awarded the Ph.D. degree (1892) by Johns Hopkins University.

Russell's long professional association with the University of Wisconsin began in 1893, when he became assistant professor of bacteriology. He was the prime mover in establishing the department of bacteriology, the first department of its kind at a major American university. He served as dean of the college of agriculture and director of the Wisconsin Experiment Station (1907–31). During his tenure as dean, the college became one of the most highly respected agricultural colleges in the country. The departments of agricultural education, home economics, agricultural journalism, agricultural economics, and rural sociology were established, and agricultural extension was organized.

Russell engaged in pioneer work in the study of the relation of bacteria to bovine tuberculosis, improvement of the milk pasteurization process, and development with Stephen M. Babcock of a cold-curing process for cheese. After his retirement in 1931, Russell continued to serve the University of Wisconsin as director of the Wisconsin Alumni Research Foundation to 1939.

He was the author of *Agricultural Bacteriology* (1898) and *Public Water Supplies* (with F. E. Turneaure, 1910) and coauthored with E. G. Hastings *Experimental Dairy Bacteriology* (1909), *Dairy Bacteriology* (1919), and *Agricultural Bacteriology* (1921).

Russell was instrumental in the establishment of the Wisconsin State Hygiene Laboratory and served as its first director (1903–08). He also led the campaign to establish a state tuberculous sanitarium (1905) and served as president of the advisory board. He represented the International Education Board in surveying educational institutions in the Far East (1925–26). He was a fellow of the American Association for the Advancement of Science and was a member of the Wisconsin Academy of Science and the Washington Academy of Sciences. He received an honorary degree from the University of Wisconsin (1934).

REFERENCES: *LE* (II); *NCAB* (43:32); *WWW* (V); E. H. Beardsley, *Harry L. Russell and Agricultural Science in Wisconsin* (Madison: University of Wisconsin Press, 1969); *Dictionary of Wisconsin Biography* (Madison: State Historical Society of Wisconsin, 1960), p. 310.

*B. Richard Siebring*

**RUSSELL, James Earl.** B. July 1, 1864, Hamden, New York, to Charles and Sarah (McFarlane) Russell. M. June 19, 1889, to Agnes Fletcher. M. January 24, 1929, to Alice F. Wyckoff. Ch. four, including William Fletcher Russell *(q.v.)*. D. November 4, 1945, Trenton, New Jersey.

James Earl Russell attended local New York rural schools and the Delaware Academy in Delhi, New York. He was awarded a New York State Regents' scholarship to Cornell University in Ithaca and earned the A.B. degree (1887) with honors in philosophy. He studied in Germany at the universities of Jena, Leipzig, and Berlin (1893–95) and received the Ph.D. degree (1894) from the University of Leipzig, where he studied under Wilhelm Wundt.

He taught in secondary schools (1887–90) and was principal of the Cascadilla School in Ithaca, New York (1890–93). On his return to the United States from Germany in 1895 he became professor of philosophy and pedagogy at the University of Colorado (1895–97), where he re-organized the teacher-training program. In 1897 he became head of the department of psychology at Teachers College, whose affiliation with Columbia University was in jeopardy. Russell was instrumental in saving the affiliation and within three months was named dean of Teachers College. He was Barnard Professor of Education at Columbia (1904–27). He built a strong faculty, which included Edward L. Thorndike *(q.v.)*, David Snedden *(q.v.)*, Paul Monroe *(q.v.)*, George D. Strayer *(q.v.)*, and William H. Kilpatrick *(q.v.)*. He arranged for John Dewey *(q.v.)* to lecture at Teachers College. Under his leadership Teachers College was transformed from a struggling institution of 169 students in 1897 to a position of pre-eminence among professional schools of education with an enrollment of nearly five thousand when he retired in 1927. He was instrumental in the establishment of the Speyer School, the Lincoln School, the International Institute, the Institute of Educational Research, and the Institute of Child Welfare as integral parts of Teachers College.

Russell's books include *The Extension of University Teaching in England and America* (1895), *The Function of the University in the Training of Teachers* (1900), *German Higher Schools* (1907), *Industrial Education* (1912), *The Trend in American Education* (1922), *Founding Teachers College* (1937), and *Heredity in Dairy Cattle* (1945). The last book was published shortly before his death and reflects his avocational interest in the scientific breeding of dairy cattle. He was a contributor to professional and scholarly journals in education and was editor of the American Teaching Series.

An organizer and first president (1926–30) of the American Association of Adult Education, Russell held membership in other professional associations. He served as the European agent for the Bureau of Education (1893–95). He was a member of the New Jersey State Board of Health (1932–40). He received honorary degrees from six colleges and universities in the United States and Canada.

REFERENCES: *CB* (December 1945); *DAB* (supp. 3); *NYT,* November 5, 1945, p. 19; *LE* (I); *TC; WWW* (II); "James Earl Russell, 1864–1945," *Teachers College Record* 47 (February 1946): 285–309; W. C. Bagley *(q.v.)*, "James Earl Russell: 1864–1945," *School and Society* 63 (November 17, 1945): 317.                          *Erwin H. Goldenstein*

**RUSSELL, William.** B. April 28, 1798, Glasgow, Scotland, to Alexander and Janet (Jamieson) Russell. M. August 22, 1821, to Ursula Wood. Ch. one. D. August 16, 1873, Lancaster, Massachusetts.

William Russell studied at the University of Glasgow, Scotland (1811–15). Because he could not make the required journey to Oxford or Cambridge universities, he was not awarded a degree. He contracted a pulmonary ailment that made it necessary to seek a warmer climate and sailed for Georgia in 1817.

In 1818 Russell conducted a private school in Savannah, Georgia, in connection with Chatham Academy, where he became principal (1821–22). He moved to New Haven, Connecticut, where he and his wife operated a school. In 1825 he became headmaster of the Hopkin's Grammar School in New Haven and tutored Yale College students in elocution and oratory. Again suffering ill health, he moved to Boston, where he taught elocution in several schools and to Harvard University students.

In 1830 Russell moved to Philadelphia, Pennsylvania, and established a school for girls affiliated with the Germantown Academy. He established a girls' school in Philadelphia (1833–38). In 1838 he and James E. Murdock opened a school of speech in Boston. He resided in Andover, Massachusetts, where he taught and lectured from 1842 to 1844 at Phillips Academy, Andover Theological Seminary, and Abbot Academy. He also lectured at the Theological Institute in East Windsor, Connecticut.

Russell moved to Medford, Massachusetts, in 1846 but continued to lecture to various schools and also periodically at Brown University in Providence, Rhode Island, Union Theological Seminary and the College of New Jersey (later, Princeton University). In 1849 he founded the Merrimack (New Hampshire) Normal Institute, which was discontinued in 1852. In response to an invitation from Lancaster, Massachusetts, he opened the New England Normal Institute in 1853, closing it in 1855 because of ill health. Russell resided in Lancaster until his death in 1873, devoting his time to lecturing and writing for various teachers' journals.

Russell wrote *Manual of Mutual Instruction* (1826), *Lessons in Enunciation* (1830), *Rudiments of Gesture* (1838), *American Elocutionists* (1844), *Orthophony; or the Cultivation of the Voice* (1845), *Exercises in Elocution* (1841), *Russell's Elementary Series* (1845–47), *Pulpit Elocution* (1846), *Exercises on Words* (1856), and *Normal Training* (1863). He edited the *American Journal of Education* (1825–29) and founded the *Journal of Education* in Philadelphia in 1832.

REFERENCES: *AC; DAB; WWW* (H).                              *John W. Schifani*

**RUSSELL, William Fletcher.** B. May 18, 1890, Delhi, New York, to James Earl *(q.v.)* and Agnes (Fletcher) Russell. M. June 17, 1913, to Clotilda Desjardins. Ch. three. D. March 26, 1956, Washington, D.C.

William Fletcher Russell, successor to his father as dean of Teachers

College of Columbia University, was graduated from Cornell University in Ithaca, New York, receiving the A.B. degree (1910); he was a scholar and honorary fellow (1912–14) at Teachers College, where he received the Ph.D. degree (1914).

Russell was a teacher of history and economics at the high school (1910–11) and assistant professor of history and sociology (1911–12) at Colorado State Teachers College (later, University of Northern Colorado) at Greeley. He taught secondary education at George Peabody College for Teachers in Nashville, Tennessee (1914–17), and was dean of the college of education at the State University of Iowa (1917–23). He joined the faculty of Teachers College, Columbia University, where he was professor of education (1923–36), Barnard Professor of Education (1936–54), associate director of the International Institute (1923–27), dean (1927–49), and president (1949–54). He was deputy director of the Foreign Operations Administration (later, International Cooperation Administration) in Washington, D.C. (1954–56). Russell was a leader in the field of international and comparative education. He established the Advanced School of Education, the Congress on Education for Democracy (1939), and the Citizenship Education Project (1949) at Teachers College.

Russell was the author of *Economy in Secondary Education* (1916), *Schools in Siberia* (1919), *The Short Constitution* (with M. J. Wade, 1921), *School Finance in Iowa Cities* (1921), *The Financing of Education in Iowa* (with others, 1925), *Liberty vs. Equality* (1936), *The New "Common Sense"* (1941), and *The Meaning of Democracy* (with T. H. Briggs, *q.v.*, 1941). He edited volume 1 of *The Rise of a University* (1937).

During World War I, Russell was director of the educational section, Russian division of the Committee on Public Information (1918–19), and he was an expert for the United States War Department in World War II. He was a member of the China Educational Commission (1921–22), the National Advisory Committee on Education (1928–31), and the American Youth Commission of the American Council on Education (1935–42), and was chairman of the American delegation to the World Federation of Educational Associations (1925–27) and president of the World Organization of the Teaching Profession (1947–52). He was chairman of the American Council on Education (1933–35), director of the National Citizenship Education Program of the United States Department of Justice (1941–45), and chairman of the Advisory Committee on Human Relations of the New York City Board of Education (1945–47). He was decorated by the governments of Yugoslavia, France, and Bulgaria and received honorary degrees from American and foreign colleges and universities.

REFERENCES: *CB* (June 1956); *LE* (III); *NYT,* March 27, 1956, p. 35; *WWAE* (VIII); *WWW* (III); *Educational Record* 37 (October 1956): 348–49.                                                                                   *John F. Ohles*

**RYAN, Will Carson, Jr.** B. March 4, 1885, New York, New York, to Will C. and Sarah (Hobby) Ryan. M. June 20, 1908, to Isabel E. Van Dewater. Ch. five. D. May 28, 1968, Alexandria, Virginia.

Awarded the A.B. degree summa cum laude (1907) by Harvard University, Will Carson Ryan, Jr., pursued graduate studies at Columbia University (1907–11). He enrolled in a doctoral program in guidance at George Washington University in Washington, D.C., where he received the Ph.D. degree (1918).

Ryan taught French and German in a Nutley, New Jersey, high school (1908–09) and German at the University of Wisconsin (1911–12) before working as an editor (1912–17) and director (1917–20) of the information bureau in the United States Office of Education. He was educational editor of the *New York Evening Post* for one year (1920–21).

Ryan was head of the department of education (1921–30) at Swarthmore (Pennsylvania) College, where he achieved a national reputation in teacher training and student counseling. He was director of education (1930–35) for the United States Indian Service in the Department of the Interior, was on the staff of the Commonwealth Fund (1935–36), and was staff associate for the Carnegie Foundation for the Advancement of Teaching (1936–40). He was Kenan Professor of Education at the University of North Carolina, where he headed the department of education (1940–48), retiring in 1956.

He was the author of several books, including *The Literature of American School and College Athletics* (1929), *Vocational Guidance in Public Schools* (1938), *Mental Health through Education* (1938), *Studies in Early Graduate Education* (1939), and *Essentials of Educational Psychology* (with others, 1947). He was associate editor of *School and Society* (1921–27) and editor of *Vocational Guidance Bulletin* (1915–18), *High School Journal* (1940–49), and *Understanding the Child* (1941).

A founder of the National Vocational Guidance Association, he served as secretary (1915–18) and president (1926–27). Ryan traveled abroad seventeen times on educational missions and conducted educational surveys on schools in Saskatchewan, Canada, and Santo Domingo, Puerto Rico, and on Friends' schools, Indian schools, schools of the Virgin Islands, and mental health and education for the Commonwealth Fund of New York City. From 1946 to 1948, he spent many months in China as a consultant in child welfare for the United China Relief organization. He received an honorary degree from George Washington University in 1932.

REFERENCES: *LE* (III); *WWAE* (XVI); *WWW* (V); *NYT,* June 2, 1968, p. 76.                                              *Vernon Lee Sheeley*

# S

**SABIN, Ellen Clara.** B. November 29, 1850, Sun Prairie, Wisconsin, to Samuel Henry and Adelia M. (Bordine) Sabin. M. no. D. February 2, 1949, Madison, Wisconsin.

Ellen (also called Ella) Clara Sabin spent her early years on farms in Wisconsin and attended the University of Wisconsin from 1865 to 1868. Her father moved his family of eleven to Eugene, Oregon, in 1872.

Sabin began her teaching career as a teacher and principal in Sun Prairie (1866) and Madison, Wisconsin (1869–72). In Oregon she established a one-room school (1872–73) and taught in Portland (1873–85). She spent a year studying in Europe, augmenting her earlier education (1885–86). On her return to Oregon, she became superintendent of the Portland schools (1887–90), an unusual position for a woman in a city the size of Portland.

In 1891 Sabin returned to Fox Lake, Wisconsin, to become president of Downer College, a college for women. She continued to serve as president until 1921 of the then combined Milwaukee-Downer College (later, merged with Lawrence College to Lawrence University). During her tenure as college president, she received her first college degrees: honorary doctorates from Beloit (Wisconsin) and Grinnell (Iowa) colleges.

Sabin's rural beginnings, life in the West, and years of teaching experience in a waterfront area of Portland led her to view education from a practical point of view. She helped her students in Portland get jobs and ensured that Milwaukee-Downer College offered degree programs in home economics, nursing, and occupational therapy along with courses leading to the traditional liberal arts degree.

Sabin was active in civic and professional organizations and served as a juror of educational exhibits at the Chicago Exposition of 1893 and as a member of the National Council of Education (1886–92) and the Wisconsin State Board of Education (1912–23).

REFERENCES: *NAW; NYT,* February 3, 1949, p. 23; *WC; WWW* (II); *Wisconsin Journal of Education* 81 (March 1949): 28.          *Rita S. Saslaw*

**SABIN, Florence Rena.** B. November 9, 1871, Central City, Colorado, to George Kimball and Rena (Miner) Sabin. M. no. D. October 3, 1953, Denver, Colorado.

Although she was born in the mining camp country of Colorado, Florence Rena Sabin received her education in the East, first attending Vermont Academy in Saxtons River, Vermont, and then Smith College in Northampton, Massachusetts, from which she received the B.S. degree in 1893. To earn money to attend medical school, she taught mathematics for two years at Wolfe Hall, a girls' school in Denver, Colorado, and zoology for one year at Smith College. She was the first woman to matriculate at Johns Hopkins University in Baltimore, Maryland, and was its first woman graduate, receiving the M.D. degree in 1900. While at Johns Hopkins, Sabin constructed a model of the brain stem of a newborn child; it served as the original for numerous copies.

After receiving the M.D. degree, Sabin served as an intern at Johns Hopkins Hospital (1900–01). She was awarded a fellowship in anatomy by the Baltimore Association for Promoting University Education of Women and resumed her studies at Johns Hopkins Medical School. In 1902 she was appointed to the anatomy teaching staff as the first woman faculty member at Johns Hopkins and became professor of histology in 1917, the first woman to reach the rank in an American college of medicine. She conducted significant research in development of the lymphatic system and on studies of human blood.

In 1924 Sabin was the first woman to join the staff of the Rockefeller Institute for Medical Research in New York City where she took charge of a department devoted to the study of blood and blood diseases in 1925. In 1938 she resigned and retired to Denver, Colorado. Her retirement ended in 1944 when the governor of Colorado asked her to revamp the state's public health system. Her work resulted in eight bills known as the Sabin health bills, of which seven were passed in 1947. Sabin was manager of health and charity for the city of Denver from 1948 to 1951 and chairman of the new Department of Health and Hospitals from 1951 until shortly before her death.

Sabin wrote *An Atlas of the Medulla and Mid-Brain* (1901), *Biography of Franklin Paine Mall* (1934), and numerous articles. She was the first woman member of the National Academy of Sciences and was a member of many other medical and scholarly associations, including the American Association of Anatomists (vice-president, 1908–09, and president, 1924–26) and the Society of Experimental Biology and Medicine (councillor, 1932). She represented American anatomists at the opening of the Peking Union Medical College in China (1921) and in 1924 was named by the League of Women Voters as one of the twelve greatest American women. She received the *Pictorial Review's* achievement award for women (1929), the M. Carey Thomas Award from Bryn Mawr College (1935), the Trudeau Medal from the National Tuberculosis Association (1945), the first Jane Addams Medal, the Lasker Foundation Award (1951), the American Women's Association Medal, the Elizabeth Blackwell Citation from the New York Infirmary, and a medal for distinguished public service from General Rose Memorial Hospital in Denver in 1951. She was awarded honorary degrees by fourteen colleges and universities. The new cancer wing at the University of Colorado Medical Center was dedicated as the Florence Rena Sabin Building for Research in Cellular Biology (1951). A statue of Sabin was placed in Statuary Hall in the Capitol in Washington, D.C.

REFERENCES: *CB* (April 1945); *LE* (I); *NCAB* (40:12, C:288); *WWW* (III); *NYT,* October 4, 1953, p. 89; *Wilson Library Bulletin* 28 (December 1953): 328.                                                        *Carol O'Meara*

**SACHAR, Abram Leon.** B. February 15, 1899, St. Louis, Missouri, to Samuel and Sarah (Abramowitz) Sachar. M. June 6, 1926, to Thelma Horwitz. Ch. three.

Abram Leon Sachar received the B.A. and M.A. degrees from Washington University in St. Louis, Missouri, in 1920. He studied at Harvard University (1918–19) and Emmanuel College, Cambridge (England) University, from which he received the Ph.D. degree in 1923.

From 1923 to 1929 he was an instructor in history at the University of Illinois, where he also directed the first Hillel Foundation in the United States (1929–33). He was national director of B'nai B'rith Hillel Foundations in Champaign, Illinois, from 1933 until 1948, when he was named first president of the newly founded Brandeis University in Waltham, Massachusetts. Brandeis was the first nonsectarian Jewish-sponsored university in the United States. During Sachar's presidency, Brandeis grew quickly, achieved a national reputation for excellence, and established a graduate school of arts and sciences and the Florence Heller School for Advanced Studies in Social Welfare. On his retirement in 1968, Sachar was named chancellor of the university.

Sachar was the author of *Factors in Jewish History* (1927), *A History of the Jews* (1929), which won the Anisfield-Wolf Award in 1965, *The Jew in the Contemporary World, Sufferance Is the Badge* (1939), and *A Host at Last* (1976), memoirs of his years at Brandeis. He also edited *Religion of a Modern Liberal* (1932).

Sachar was the host of a popular public television series, "The Course of Our Times," first aired in 1970 and 1971, and lectured in many cities and towns in the United States and Canada. He was a trustee and adviser to many foundations and academic institutions in the United States, Canada, and Israel. He belonged to numerous professional organizations and was a member of the American Council on Education (1953), the Massachusetts Commission on Fulbright Awards (1962), and the United States Advisory Commission on International Education and Cultural Affairs (1967). He was the recipient of honorary degrees from many colleges and universities.

REFERENCES: *CB* (November 1949); *LE* (IV); *NCAB* (I:416); *WW*

(XXXVIII); Abram L. Sachar, *A Host at Last* (Boston: Little, Brown, 1976).                                                          *Frederik F. Ohles*

**SACHS, Julius.** B. July 6, 1849, Baltimore, Maryland, to Joseph and Sophia (Baer) Sachs. M. June 23, 1874, to Rosa Goldman. Ch. two. D. February 2, 1934, New York, New York.

Julius Sachs received the A.B. (1867) and A.M. (1871) degrees from Columbia University. He engaged in postgraduate study in Germany at the universities of Würzburg, Berlin, and Göttingen, and at Rostock University from which he received the Ph.D. degree (1871). He was particularly influenced by Hermann Souppe of Göttingen University, a professor of teaching methods.

Upon his return to America, Sachs opened the Sachs Collegiate Institute School for Boys in New York City in 1872, hoping to provide a model for the improvement of American secondary schools and teaching methods at a time when American colleges and universities had raised their standards and were dissatisfied with the established secondary schools. He also trained teachers at the school. He continued the boys' school to 1904 and also served as principal of Sachs School for Girls (1891-1907). He joined the faculty of Teachers College, Columbia University, as professor of secondary education (1902-17).

Sachs wrote *The American Secondary School and Some of Its Problems* (1912). He contributed to the *Educational Review* (1905-18) and published a number of articles. Sachs was president of the Schoolmasters Association of New York (1889), the American Philosophical Association (1890-91), the Headmasters Association of the United States (1899) and the New York Society of Archaeological Institute of America (1900-03). He was a member of the Latin conference committee of the Committee of Ten (1892) and the Latin auxiliary of the Philological Society Committee of Twelve (1896) and secondary school representative on the College Entrance Examination Board (1900-07). He received an honorary degree from Columbia University.

REFERENCES: *DAB; LE* (I); *NCAB* (13:560); *NYT,* February 3, 1934, p. 13; *WWW* (I).                                                          *Barbara Ruth Peltzman*

**SAFFORD, Anson Peacely-Killen.** B. February 14, 1830, Hyde Park, Vermont, to David and Lydia (Peacely-Killen) Safford. M. July 24, 1869, to Jennie L. Tracey. M. December 19, 1877, to Margarita Grijalva. M. 1881 to Soledad Bonillas. Ch. three. D. December 15, 1891, Tarpon Springs, Florida.

Considered to be the father of Arizona education, Anson Peacely-Killen Safford was orphaned in 1849 and was left with the responsibility of managing the family farm and raising the siblings.

In 1850 he left Illinois and migrated to California, traveling throughout California and the Southwest in search of gold (1850–56). He entered politics, successfully running for the California legislature (1856). He was chairman of the education committee, which drafted California's original school legislation. He left the legislature to manage a business in San Francisco (1859–62), moving to Nevada to become Humbolt County recorder. He was appointed surveyor-general by President Andrew Johnson in 1867, also serving as one of three members of the Nevada School Board, which wrote and lobbied for the passage of the first comprehensive education legislation for Nevada.

On April 7, 1869, he was appointed governor of the Arizona Territory by President Ulysses S. Grant. In his first address to the Arizona territorial legislature, he proposed free public educational opportunities for all young people of the territory and submitted a comprehensive school law during his first year in office. Similar to the law he had assisted in developing for Nevada, it provided that the education system would be financed by tax monies with one superintendent for each county and a superintendent for the territory; the governor was to serve as ex-officio superintendent. Safford established the territorial school system, assisting in identifying and hiring the first teachers and paid for some books and supplies from personal funds.

Safford was forced by ill health to resign as governor on April 5, 1877. He left Arizona in 1877, traveled east, and founded the city of Tarpon Springs, Florida, where he died.

REFERENCES: *NYT,* December 17, 1891, p. 2; John C. Bury, *The Historical Role of Arizona's Superintendent of Public Instruction* (Phoenix: Arizona State Department of Education, 1974), 1: 34–71; Howard R. Lamar, "Carpetbaggers Full of Dreams: A Functional View of the Arizona Pioneer Politician," *Arizona and the West* 7 (1965): 187–206; Jay J. Wagoner, *Arizona Territory 1863–1912: A Political History* (Tucson: University of Arizona Press, 1970), pp. 101–24; Stephen B. Weeks, *History of Public School Education in Arizona* (Washington, D.C.: Government Printing Office, 1918), pp. 18–36; Eugene E. Williams, "The Territorial Governors of Arizona: Anson Peacely-Killen Safford," *Arizona Historical Review,* 7 (January 1936): 71–84.                    *Joseph Engle*

**SALISBURY, Albert.** B. January 24, 1843, Lima, Wisconsin, to Oliver and Emily (Gravath) Salisbury. M. November 20, 1866, to Abba A. Maxson. M. August 28, 1883, to Agnes Hosford. Ch. five. D. June 2, 1911, Whitewater, Wisconsin.

Albert Salisbury was instructed by his mother and at the district school in Rock County, Wisconsin. He entered Milton (Wisconsin) Academy (later, Milton College) at the age of eighteen but left in 1863 to enlist in the

Thirteenth Wisconsin Infantry. He returned to Wisconsin after the Civil War and worked as a farmer, nurseryman, and rural schoolteacher. He attended Milton (Wisconsin) College where he received the A.B. (1870), A.M. (1872), and Ph.D. (1888), degrees.

He was principal of Brodhead (Wisconsin) High School (1870–73) and instructor of history and first conductor of teachers' institutes at the State Normal School (later, University of Wisconsin—Whitewater) in Whitewater, Wisconsin (1873–82). He was superintendent of the American Missionary Association schools for southern freedmen and western Indians at Atlanta, Georgia (1882–85). He returned to Whitewater as president of the normal school (1885–1911). Salisbury supported the establishment of a state school for the feebleminded; in 1895 a state institution for the feebleminded was established in Chippewa Falls. He worked for improvement of instruction in rural schools.

He wrote many books, including *Historical Sketch of Normal Instruction in Wisconsin, 1846–1876* (1876), *Phonology and Orthoëpy* (1879), *The Duty of the State to the Feeble-Minded* (1890), *Historical Sketches of the First Quarter-Century of the State Normal School at Whitewater* (1893), *The Rural School Problem* (1897), *Theory of Teaching and Elementary Psychology* (1905), and *School Management: A Textbook for County Training Schools and Normal Schools* (1911).

Salisbury was a trustee of the Wisconsin State School for the Deaf at Delavan and president of the Wisconsin Teachers' Association.

REFERENCES: *DAB; NCAB* (11:384); *WWW* (I); *Milwaukee Sentinel,* June 3, 1911; *Whitewater Register,* June 9, 1911.    *Lawrence S. Master*

**SAMAROFF, Olga.** B. August 8, 1882, San Antonio, Texas, to Carlos and Jane (Loening) Hickenlooper. M. 1900 to Boris Loutzky. M. April 24, 1911, to Leopold Stokowski. Ch. one. D. May 17, 1948, New York, New York.

Christened Lucie Mary Olga Agnes Hickenlooper, Olga Samaroff was educated at the Ursuline Convent in Galveston, Texas, and took piano lessons at an early age from her maternal grandmother. Her talent was recognized early, and on the advice of Edward MacDowell, Vladimir de Pachmann, and William Steinway, she traveled to Paris, France, with her grandmother where she studied under Antoine François Marmontel and Ludovic Breitner (1894–97). At the age of fourteen, she was the first American girl to win a piano scholarship at the Conservatoire de musique. She engaged in academic studies at the Convent of the Holy Sacraments and studied piano with Ernst Jedliczka and Ernest Hutcheson in Berlin (1901–03).

After a brief marriage and retirement from music, she returned to music to support her family. She took the name Samaroff from an ancestor and debuted at Carnegie Hall in 1905. A series of European and American concerts followed. In 1909 she was considered one of the world's foremost pianists.

After another leave from concert work, Samaroff returned to an active career in 1923, following a divorce from Leopold Stokowski. She joined the faculty of the new Juilliard Graduate School of Music in New York City where she taught for the rest of her life (1925–48). In 1929 Samaroff was appointed head of the piano department of the Philadelphia Conservatory of Music where she taught once a week for ten years. She was a guest lecturer at American universities.

Samaroff was music critic for the *New York Evening Post* (1926–27) and wrote *The Laymen's Music Book* (1935), *The Listener's Music Book* (1937), *The Magic World of Music* (1936), *A Music Manual* (1937), and an autobiography, *An American Musician's Story* (1939).

Samaroff founded the Schubert Memorial to provide a debut with a symphony orchestra for gifted students (1928). She developed a music course for laymen used at the David Mannes Music School and Town Hall in New York and in Philadelphia and Washington, D.C. She was a founder of the Musician's Emergency Fund of New York (1931) to aid needy musicians during the Depression. Samaroff was a delegate to the International Music Education Contest in Prague (1936) and a judge at the piano contest organized by Queen Mother Elisabeth of Belgium (1938).

She received honorary degrees from the University of Pennsylvania (1931) and from the Cincinnati (Ohio) Conservatory of Music (1943). Her students established the Olga Samaroff Memorial Fund for a home for music students in New York City.

REFERENCES: *CB* (March 1946); *DAB* (supp. 4); *NAW; NCAB* (36:96); *WWW* (II); *NYT*, May 18, 1948, p. 23; Olga Samaroff, *An American Musician's Story* (New York: W. W. Norton, 1939).

*Barbara Ruth Peltzman*

**SAMMARTINO, Peter.** B. August 15, 1904, New York, New York, to Guy and Eva (Amendola) Sammartino. M. December 5, 1933, to Sylvia Scaramelli. Ch. none.

Peter Sammartino, founder and president of Fairleigh Dickinson University, attended Stuyvesant High School in New York City and the City College of New York, graduating with the B.S. degree (1924). He received the M.A. (1928) and Ph.D. (1931) degrees from New York University and also studied at the Sorbonne in Paris, France.

From 1924 to 1928, Sammartino taught in New York City elementary and junior high schools and at Townsend Harris High School. He was a member of the faculty of the City College of New York (1928–33) and was chairman of the language department at New College, an experimental unit of Teachers College, Columbia University (1933–41).

While at New College, Sammartino participated in a survey of problems of higher education in the Rutherford, New Jersey, area, which demonstrated a lack of opportunities for high school graduates to attend college. Sammartino developed a plan for a college in the area, recruited sixteen high school principals to support the plan, and persuaded Fairleigh S. Dickinson, an industrial executive, to purchase and donate a ten-acre estate in Rutherford for a college. With financial support from people in the area, a two-year Fairleigh Dickinson Junior College was opened with 153 students in 1942, increased to 650 by 1945, and expanded to a second campus in Teaneck, New Jersey, in 1953. Four-year courses were offered in 1948 and permission was granted in 1956 to change the name to Fairleigh Dickinson University. The university expanded to a third campus in Madison, New Jersey, and enrolled nearly twenty thousand students in 1972.

Sammartino was the author of articles published in professional journals and *French in Action* (1933), *Il Primo Libro* (1936), *Survey of French Literature* (1937), *Grammaire simple et lectures facile* (1938), *Community College in Action* (with Ellsworth Tompkins, 1950), *President of a Small College* (1954), *Multiple Campuses* (1964), and *Of Castles and Colleges* (1972). He was associate editor of *Clearing House* and *Literary Review*.

Sammartino was a member of many organizations, serving as president of the New Jersey chapter of the American Association for the United Nations, the International Association of University Presidents (1965), and the Ereved Foundation (1957). He was a member of the President's Commission on Higher Education, received awards from foreign governments, including Italy and France, and was awarded honorary degrees by several American and foreign universities.

REFERENCES: *CA* (57–60); *CB* (December 1958); *NCAB* (I: 230); *WW* (XXXVI); *WWAE* (XXII).                    *John F. Ohles*

**SANCHEZ, George Isidore.** B. October 4, 1906, Barela, New Mexico, to Telesfor and Juliana Sanchez. M. June 15, 1925, to Virginia Romero. M. August 30, 1947, to Luisa G. Guerroro. Ch. two. D. April 5, 1972, Austin, Texas.

George I. Sanchez (Jorge Isidore Sanchez y Sanchez) was reared in New Mexico and Arizona. He taught and administered a one-room country school (1923–30) while attending the University of New Mexico where he earned the B.A. degree (1930). He received the M.S. degree (1931) from the University of Texas and the Ed.D. degree (1934) from the University of California.

He was director of the division of information and statistics for the New Mexico State Department of Education (1930–35). As a research assistant for the Julius Rosenwald Fund, he surveyed rural schools in Mexico and the southwestern United States. During 1937 and 1938 he directed the National Pedagogical Institute for Venezuela's Ministry of Education. He was at the University of New Mexico (1938–40) and surveyed the Taos, New Mexico, schools. In 1940 Sanchez was appointed professor of Latin American education at the University of Texas in Austin, a position he held to his death.

He was a relentless advocate of social justice and advanced the thesis that Mexican-Americans were a colonized people, subjugated and then forgotten. Into the late 1960s and early 1970s, he continued his battle for social justice, challenging Texas school policy and teacher education, and advocating bilingual-bicultural education for Mexican-American students.

Sanchez wrote the landmark text on Mexican-Americans, *The Forgotten People: A Study of New Mexicans* (1940). He also wrote *Mexico, A Revolution by Education* (1938), *The Development of Higher Education in Mexico* (1944), *The People: A Study of the Navajos* (1948), *Arithmetic in Maya* (1961), *The Development of Education in Venezuela* (1963), and *Mexico* (1965).

Sanchez was national president of the League of United Latin American Citizens (1941–42), worked for the Office of Coordinator of Inter-American Affairs in Washington, D.C. (1943–44), was president of the Southwest Council on Education of Spanish-Speaking People (1945–72), and served on President John F. Kennedy's Citizens Committee on a New Frontier Policy in the Americas (1960). He was a consultant to many government agencies and was a member of professional associations, including the New Mexico Education Association (president).

REFERENCES: *LE* (III); *WW* (XXXVI); *Who's Who in the South and Southwest* (Chicago: Marquis, 1952).                    *Ricardo L. Garcia*

**SANDERS, Charles Walton.** B. March 24, 1805, Newport, New York, to Jacob and Lydia (Martin) Sanders. M. August 2, 1842, to Elizabeth Barker. Ch. three. D. July 5, 1889, New York, New York.

Charles Walton Sanders was sent by his father to a local school at four years of age. The family moved to Homer, New York, where he completed his education and became a licensed teacher (1821).

He taught in the public schools of Homer and Cortland County (1821–38) and moved to New York City. In 1829 he was elected county inspector of schools and served in that position for several years.

From 1838 to 1863 Sanders engaged in writing schoolbooks. He was said to have written over sixty books, of which a few were *Metrical Stories in Chimistry* [sic] *and Natural Philosophy* (1842), *Sanders' Pictorial Primer* (1846), *Sanders New Speller* (1862), *Sanders' Young Ladies Reader* (1864), *The Union Speller* (1865), *Sanders' Analysis of English Words* (1859), and a schoolbook series that included *The School Reader* (1840–

52), *Sanders Union* (1862–68), and *The School Singer* (with William Batchelder Bradbury, *q.v.*, 1842–50). Sanders added songs at the end of readers to encourage singing in school.

Sanders participated in professional activities and was present at the organization of the New York State Teachers' Association in 1845. He was also active in the temperance movement.

REFERENCES: *DAB; NCAB* (2:257); *WWW* (H); *NYT,* July 6, 1889, p. 5.                                                            *Barbara Ruth Peltzman*

**SANDERS, Daniel Jackson.** B. February 15, 1847, Winnsboro, South Carolina, to B. William and Laura Sanders. M. September 16, 1880, to Fannie T. Price. Ch. nine. D. March 6, 1907, Charlotte, North Carolina.

Daniel Jackson Sanders was permitted by his slave master to learn to read and write. He was apprenticed to a shoemaker, left his master's home in 1866, and settled in Chester, South Carolina. While working as a shoemaker he was instructed by W. B. Knox and attended Brainerd Institute at Chester (1869–70). He was principal of the Chester public schools. Ordained to the Presbyterian ministry in 1870 he attended Western Theological Seminary at Allegheny (later, Pittsburgh), Pennsylvania, and was graduated in 1874.

Sanders was pastor of the Chestnut Street Presbyterian Church in Wilmington, North Carolina (1874–86). He was principal of city schools in Wilmington (1875–91). He visited England and Scotland in 1875 for the Board of Missions for Freedmen, where he raised funds for an endowment fund for Biddle University (later, Johnson C. Smith University) to provide scholarships for students preparing for missionary work in Africa. Sanders was elected the first black president of Biddle University and served from 1891 to his death in 1907.

Active in the Presbyterian church, Sanders was the first black moderator of both the Yadkin and Cape Fear presbyteries and served as stated clerk in the Atlantic and Yadkin presbyteries and the Catawba synod. He attended the general councils of Presbyterian churches at Toronto, Canada (1892), and Washington, D.C. (1898), and was a member of many Presbyterian general assemblies. He was a delegate to meetings of the Alliance of Reformed Churches Holding the Presbyterian System at Toronto, Canada; Liverpool, England; and Washington, D.C. He received two honorary degrees from Lincoln University and an honorary degree from Biddle University.

REFERENCES: *DAB; TC; WWW* (I).                                  *Anne R. Gayles*

**SANFORD, Maria Louise.** B. December 19, 1836, Saybrook, Connecticut, to Henry E. and Mary (Clark) Sanford. M. no. D. April 21, 1920, Washington, D.C.

Maria Sanford entered a country school at the age of four. She attended an academy in Meriden, Connecticut, and was graduated from the New Britain (Connecticut) Normal School (later, Central Connecticut State College) in 1855.

Starting in 1852 at Gilead, she taught in rural and town schools in Connecticut and by 1859 was a teacher in New Haven. In 1867 she accepted a position teaching in Parkersville, Pennsylvania, where she ran unsuccessfully for the office of county superintendent of schools (1869). She spoke often to teachers' institutes and other groups about education and gained a reputation that led to her appointment in 1869 as teacher of English and history at Swarthmore (Pennsylvania) College, a Quaker college founded in 1864. She was professor of history at Swarthmore, one of the first women in the United States to hold that position. Personal problems contributed to her decision to resign from Swarthmore in 1879, and she spent the next year lecturing.

William Watts Folwell (q.v.), president of the University of Minnesota, met Sanford in 1880 at the Chautauqua (New York) Institute and engaged her as an assistant professor of rhetoric and elocution. During her stay at Minnesota (1880–1909), she chaired the department, which became the largest in the university.

Sanford continued to give public lectures after retirement. She was active in many organizations. On the occasion of her eightieth birthday, in 1916, the University of Minnesota held a statewide convocation in her honor. In 1958 her statue was placed in the national Capitol in Washington as one of Minnesota's two representatives in Statuary Hall.

REFERENCES: *NAW; NCAB* (20:67); *WWW* (I); *Acceptance of the Statue of Maria L. Sanford* (Washington, D.C.: Government Printing Office, 1960); *NYT,* April 22, 1920, p. 11; Barbara Stuhler and Gretchen Kreuter (eds.), *Women of Minnesota: A Beginning History* (St. Paul: Minnesota Historical Society, 1977).                    *Susan Margot Smith*

**SANFORD, Robert Nevitt.** B. May 31, 1909, Chatham, Virginia, to Thomas Ryland and Margaret (Taylor) Sanford. M. June 15, 1931, to Christine Dickson. Ch. seven.

R. Nevitt Sanford attended the University of Richmond, Virginia, where he received the A.B. degree (1925). He received the M.A. degree from Columbia University (1930) and the Ph.D. degree (1934) from Harvard University. He also studied at Boston Psychoanalytic Institute.

Sanford was a psychologist at the Norfolk (Massachusetts) Prison Colony (1932–35) and was a research psychologist with the Harvard Growth Studies of School Children (1935–40). In 1940 Sanford joined the department of psychology of the University of California at Berkeley and remained there to 1961. Fired from California for refusing to sign the faculty loyalty oath, he was later reinstated and cleared by the courts. He was also a research associate at the Institute of Child Welfare (1940–45), associate director of the Institute of Personality Assessment and Research (1949–53), and coordinator of the Mary Conover Mellon Fund at Vassar College (1952–58). He was professor of psychology at Stanford (California) University and director of the Cooperative Commission for the Study of Alcoholism (1961–67). He was a visiting professor at the Graduate Theological Union and Starr King School for the Ministry (1967–68). In 1968 he established and was president of the Wright Institute in Berkeley, California. Sanford was a pioneer in the application of psychoanalysis, ego psychology, human development, and systems theory in education.

Among Sanford's publications were *Physique, Personality and Scholarship* (with others, 1943), *The Authoritarian Personality* (with others, 1950), *The American College* (1962), *Self and Society* (1966), *Where Colleges Fail* (1967), *Search for Relevance* (1969), and *Issues in Personality Theory* (1970). He was coeditor of "The Activist Corner" column in the *Journal of Social Issues* (from 1968). He was active in professional associations and was a member of the board of directors of the American Civil Liberties Union of Northern California, the American Psychological Association (1959), and the Social Science Research Council (1959–61). He was president of the Social and Psychological Studies Society (1957). He received honorary degrees from the universities of Notre Dame (1967) and Nevada (1968).

REFERENCES: *LE* (V); *WW* (XXXVI); "Gold Medal Educators," *Education* 92 (November–December 1971): unpaged.     *Harry L. Summerfield*

**SARGENT, Dudley Allen.** B. September 28, 1849, Belfast, Maine, to Benjamin and Caroline (Rogers) Sargent. M. April 7, 1881, to Ella Fraser Ledyard. Ch. one. D. July 21, 1924, Peterboro, New Hampshire.

Dudley Allen Sargent was one of several physicians who played a major role in the development of physical education. About the age of thirteen he began practicing with dumbbells and Indian clubs. As his gymnastic skills improved he gave exhibitions and worked for two seasons as a circus and vaudeville performer. He attended Bowdoin College in Brunswick, Maine, and received the A.B. (1875) and A.M. (1887) degrees. He received the M.D. degree (1878) from Yale College.

He became director of gymnastics at Bowdoin College in 1869 and became director of the gymnasium at Yale College in 1875. Sargent went to New York City where he attended clinics and opened the Institute for Physical Training and Therapy (1878–79). He lectured at the Chautauqua (New York) Assembly in the summer of 1879. He was director of the gymnasium and assistant professor of physical training at Harvard University (1879–89). The Hemenway Gymnasium opened in 1879 at Harvard with Sargent as director to 1919. An annex at Radcliffe College was opened in 1881 as a private venture of Sargent's; it evolved into the Normal School of Physical Training, a one-year normal school for teachers of physical education and continued to 1916, when it became the Sargent School for Physical Education with Sargent as president. He began the Harvard Summer School of Physical Education in 1887. Sargent retired in 1919 at the age of seventy, but continued to teach to his death.

Sargent's collection and classification of statistics on the anthropometry of college students and the charts of male and female students set a standard for comparison for all later observations. He invented many mechanical devices for adapting exercises to the changed conditions of the modern city. His normal school assumed a leading position in the training of teachers of physical education.

Sargent was the author of *Universal Test for Strength, Speed and Endurance* (1902), *Health, Strength and Power* (1904), and *Physical Education* (1906).

He played a major role in the organization of the American Association for the Promotion of Physical Training (later, the American Physical Education Association) and was president (1890–95). He was active in the formation of the Society of Directors of Physical Education in Colleges (president, 1899).

REFERENCES: *DAB; NCAB* (7:97); *WWW* (I); *NYT,* July 22, 1924, p. 15; Ledyard W. Sargent, ed., *Dudley Allen Sargent: An Autobiography* (Philadelphia: Lea & Febiger, 1927).                                       *Curtis C. Stone*

**SARGENT, Epes.** B. September 27, 1813, Gloucester, Massachusetts, to Epes and Hannah Dane (Coffin) Sargent. M. May 10, 1848, to Elizabeth W. Weld. Ch. none. D. December 30, 1880, Boston, Massachusetts.

After his father's move to Boston, Epes Sargent entered the Boston Latin School in 1823 and was graduated in 1829. He attended Harvard University but did not complete his studies.

In the early 1830s he worked for the *Boston Daily Advertiser* and later the *Boston Daily Atlas,* for which he was Washington correspondent (1837–39). He also worked for Samuel G. Goodrich *(q.v.)* preparing the Peter Parley books and writing poetry for the *Token.* He went to New York City where he worked for the *New York Mirror* and the *New World* (1839–47) and established *Sargent's New Monthly Magazine* (1843). He returned to Boston to edit the *Boston Transcript* (1847–53).

While a newspaperman, he found time to produce a number of literary works, including two plays, *The Bride of Genoa* (1837) and *Velasco* (1838), a fifteen-volume drama collection, *Modern Drama* (1846–58), and a volume of poetry, *Songs of the Sea* (1847). His later works include plays, novels, and collections of poetry.

Sargent is known as the author or editor of several textbooks, including *The Standard Speaker* (1852), *The Etymological Reader* (1872), and the series of Standard Readers and New American Readers (with Amasa May, 1871). Despite the popularity of the McGuffey Readers, Sargent and other textbook writers were able to enjoy considerable financial success with their schoolbooks.

REFERENCES: *AC; DAB; NCAB* (7:243); *TC; WWW* (H); *NYT*, January 1, 1881, p. 5.                                    *Charles V. Partridge*

**SARGENT, Walter.** B. May 7, 1868, Worcester, Massachusetts, to Lucius Manlius and Clara Fatima (Allen) Sargent. M. July 17, 1901, to Emma Florence Bailey. Ch. none. D. September 19, 1927, Chicago, Illinois.

Walter Sargent, artist and educator, was graduated from the Worcester (Massachusetts) Academy in 1885 and studied art at the Massachusetts Normal Art School (later, Massachusetts College of Art) in Boston. His art technique and his ideas on the teaching of art were further developed when he attended the Academy of Colarossi and the Academy of Delucluse, both in Paris, France. Upon returning to the United States he was a special student at Harvard University.

Sargent was Massachusetts state supervisor of drawing (1903–06) and director of drawing and manual training for the city of Boston (1906–09). He was hired as a professor of art education at the University of Chicago (1909–24) and was professor and chairman of the department of art from 1924 to his death. During his professional career, he lectured widely on art topics.

Sargent exhibited his art at the Boston Art Club, the Society of American Artists (New York), the American Artists Exhibition (Chicago), the Pennsylvania Academy (Philadelphia), the Corcoran Gallery (Washington), and the Albright Gallery (Buffalo, New York). He wrote *Modelling in Public Schools* (1909), *Fine and Industrial Arts in Elementary Schools* (1912), *How Children Learn to Draw* (1916), *Art Education in the United States* (1918), and *The Enjoyment and Use of Color* (1923).

REFERENCES: *NYT*, September 20, 1927, p. 29; *WWW* (I); *Indiana Education Magazine* 29 (December 1927): 193–94; *School Arts Magazine* 25 (January 1926): 259; H. T. Bailey, "Walter Sargent: Teacher of Art," *School Arts Magazine* 27 (December 1927): 194–98.

*LeRoy Barney*

**SARTAIN, Emily.** B. March 17, 1841, Philadelphia, Pennsylvania, to John and Susannah Longmate (Swaine) Sartain. M. no. D. June 17, 1927, Philadelphia, Pennsylvania.

Emily Sartain was born into a family of eminent engravers and artists. Showing artistic ability, she was encouraged and taught by her father. At an early age, she was the only woman mezzotint engraver in America and Europe. She studied painting under Christian Schussele at the Pennsylvania Academy of Fine Arts (1864–70) and studied oils in Paris under Evariste Luminais (1871–75). The Paris salon accepted two of her paintings and one, a genre entitled *The Reproof,* won a medal at the Philadelphia Centennial Exposition (1876).

In 1886 she became principal of the Philadelphia School of Design for Women, the first school in America teaching industrial arts to women. She held this position until her retirement in 1920, when she became principal emeritus. Sartain revised the school's curriculum, rejecting the English pattern of instruction in which students copied great masters in favor of the French method, which stressed the use of perspective and live models. Believing that commercial art and fine arts required the same skills, she organized a rigorous curriculum for commercial artists, which encouraged them to produce work of aesthetic value.

Sartain was art editor of the magazine *Our Continent* (1881–83) and of Ellen C. H. Rollins' *New England Bygones,* published in 1883. She represented the United States at the International Congress of Instruction in Drawing in Paris, France (1900), and Berne, Switzerland (1904). She sponsored art and literary clubs in Philadelphia. For service to art and education, she received many medals, certificates, and diplomas, including one from the London Society of Literature, Science and Art.

REFERENCES:*AC; DAB; NAW; NCAB* (13:326); *NYT,* June 19, 1927, p. 23; *TC; WC; WWW* (I).                                              *M. Jane Dowd*

**SAYLOR, John Galen.** B. December 12, 1902, Carleton, Nebraska, to John Oliver and Ella (Rothrock) Saylor. M. June 1, 1927, to Helen Smith. Ch. three.

J. Galen Saylor attended the Carleton, Nebraska, public schools and received the B.A. degree (1922) with a major in history from McPherson (Kansas) College. He received the M.A. (1934) and Ph.D. (1941) degrees from Columbia University.

Saylor was a teacher of mathematics in Kansas high schools in Holton (1922–23) and Ramona (1924–25) and was a high school principal in Waverly, Nebraska (1925–29). He was superintendent of the Waterloo, Iowa, public schools (1929–35). He became research director for the Nebraska State Education Association in Lincoln (1936–38) and research associate at Columbia University (1938–40).

His appointment as associate professor of secondary education at the University of Nebraska in 1940 was interrupted by service with the United States Navy (1942–46). At the close of World War II he rejoined the Nebraska faculty, served as department chairman (1949–68), and retired in 1971. He was a Fulbright Professor at the University of Jyvaskyla, Finland

(1962–63). He also was a lecturer and consultant to universities in the United States and Europe, as well as a consultant to the United States High Commission for Germany after World War II.

Saylor is well known for his books on curriculum coauthored with William M. Alexander, including *Secondary Education: Basic Principles and Practices* (1950) and *Curriculum Planning: Basic Principles and Practices* (1954). He also wrote *Factors Associated with Cooperative Programs of Curriculum Development* (1941), *Junior College Studies* (with others, 1949), *Modern Secondary Education* (1959), *Curriculum Planning for Modern Schools* (1966), *The High School: Today and Tomorrow* (1971), and *Planning Curriculum for Schools* (1974). He wrote extensively for educational journals and contributed to several encyclopedias.

Saylor was a member of the Association for Supervision and Curriculum Development (president, 1965–66), the Nebraska Congress of Parents and Teachers (president, 1953–56), and the National Congress of Parents and Teachers (treasurer, 1958), in addition to being active in many other state and national professional groups. He was a delegate to the White House Conference in 1960, to a conference on programmed instruction in Berlin, Germany, in 1963, and to the World Confederation of Organizations of the Teaching Profession in Seoul, Korea, in 1966. He was a trustee of the Joint Council on Economic Education (1964–67). Saylor was awarded an honorary degree by McPherson College.

REFERENCES: *CA* (19–20); *LE* (V); *WW* (XXXI); *Who's Who in the Midwest*, 10th ed. (Chicago: Marquis, 1966).     *Erwin H. Goldenstein*

**SCARBOROUGH, William Sanders.** B. February 16, 1852, Macon, Georgia, to Jeremiah and Frances Scarborough. M. August 2, 1881, to Sarah C. Bierce. Ch. none. D. September 9, 1926, Wilberforce, Ohio.

William Sanders (or Saunders) Scarborough, a former slave, was president of Wilberforce University and a leading expert on foreign languages. He was initially educated by the American Missionary Association in Lewis, Georgia, and received the A.B. (1875) and M.A. (1878) degrees from Oberlin (Ohio) College and the Ph.D. degree (1892) from Kentucky State Normal School for Colored Persons (later, Kentucky State College) in Frankfort.

He was born of slave parents and was a slave until 1865; his parents could read and write and encouraged him in his studies. His interest in language was the result of Bible study, which was encouraged by the missionary association that sponsored his education. To help pay his living costs during his undergraduate days, he taught at black teachers' colleges in Albany and Bloomingburg, Ohio.

He was principal of Paine Institute for Blacks in Cokesbury, South Carolina (1875–77). In 1877 Scarborough was appointed instructor of classical Greek at Wilberforce (Ohio) University and was professor of Hellenistic Greek at the Payne Theological Seminary at Wilberforce University and professor of classical Greek, head of the classical college, and vice-president (1895–1908). He assumed the presidency of Wilberforce in 1908 and remained in that position until his retirement in 1920. From 1920 until his death, he was employed by the United States Department of Agriculture where he conducted an investigation that was published in a bulletin, *Tenancy and Ownership Among Negro Farmers in Southampton County, Virginia* (1926).

He was considered by many to be the preeminent scholar of his race. His writings include *First Lessons in Greek* (1881), *Theory and Functions of the Thematic Vowel to the Greek* (1884), *Birds of Aristophanes: A Theory of Interpretation* (1886), and numerous articles on the Negro question. An organizer for black civil rights in Ohio in 1883, he was a publication editor for the African Methodist Episcopal church and a delegate to that church's ecumenical conference in London in 1901 and to its Congress of Races in 1911. He was a member of many professional and literary associations and vice-president of the American Negro Academy.

He was the first postmaster of the village of Wilberforce in 1879. He was the recipient of honorary degrees from Liberia (West Africa) College (1882), Morris Brown College (1908), and St. Columbia's College in England (1909).

REFERENCES: *AC; DAB; NCAB* (12:55); *NYT,* September 12, 1926, p. 29; *WWW* (I); William J. Simmons, *Men of Mark* (New York: Arno Press and The New York Times, 1968), pp. 410–18.          *Leo D. Leonard*


**SCATES, Douglas Edgar.** B. December 11, 1898, San Diego, California, to Walter Bennett and Louise (Roberts) Scates. M. December 26, 1922, to Marjorie Lee Baldwin. M. July 4, 1952, to Alice Virginia Yeomans. Ch. two. D. November 16, 1967, Gainesville, Florida.

Douglas Edgar Scates was graduated from Whitworth College in Spokane, Washington, with the B.A. degree (1922) and received the Ph.D. degree (1926) from the University of Chicago.

After serving as assistant to the examiner and instructor in education at the University of Chicago (1923–26), he became an assistant professor of education at Indiana University (1926–29). Scates served as the director of the bureau of research of the Cincinnati Public Schools (1929–39) and professor at Duke University (1939–48) in Durham, North Carolina.

Scates served with the Office of the Secretary of War, with the personnel research section (1946–47), and as director of research in scientific personnel for the American Council on Education (1948–50). He was a visiting professor at Queens College in New York City and administrative assistant to the dean of teacher education (1950–52). He was a consultant for the Office of Naval Research and the Human Resources Research Institute of the United States Air Force (1950–52). In 1953 Scates became professor of education and was a consultant for the statistics laboratory at the University of Florida (1955–62). Scates also was a research specialist for the American Social Health Association in New York City (1954–55).

Scates coauthored *The Methodology of Educational Research* (with C. V. Good, *q.v.*, and A. S. Barr, *q.v.*, 1936) and *Methods of Research* (with C. V. Good, 1954). He was chairman of the editorial board and editor of the *Review of Educational Research* and served on the editorial staffs of the *Journal of Educational Research, Journal of the American Statistical Association,* and *Journal of Teacher Education.*

He was a fellow of the American Association for the Advancement of Science and a member of the American Educational Research Association (president, 1947–48), the American Statistical Association (vice-president, 1941), the Ohio Conference of Statisticians (president, 1933), and other professional organizations.

REFERENCES: *LE* (III); *WWAE* (XVI); *WWW* (V).        *Paul L. Ward*

**SCHAEFFER, Nathan Christ.** B. February 3, 1849, near Kutztown, Pennsylvania, to David and Esther Anna (Christ) Schaeffer. M. July 8, 1800, to Anna Ahlum. Ch. seven, including John A. Schaeffer, college president. D. March 15, 1919, Lancaster, Pennsylvania.

Nathan Christ Schaeffer received the A.B. (1869) and Ph.D. (1879) degrees from Franklin and Marshall College in Lancaster, Pennsylvania. He studied at the Theological Seminary of the Reformed Church in Lancaster, Pennsylvania, and completed his studies in Germany at Tübingen, Berlin, and Leipzig (1873–75).

Upon his return, he taught Latin for two years at Franklin and Marshall. He became principal of the Keystone State Normal School (later, Kutztown State College) in Kutztown, Pennsylvania, in 1877 and held that position for sixteen years. From 1893 until his death in 1919, Schaeffer served as superintendent of the State Department of Public Instruction in Pennsylvania. As superintendent, he directed the expansion of public education in the state, persuaded the legislature to increase appropriations for schools, set common standards for secondary education, increased teachers' salaries, and lowered tuition in state normal schools.

Among Schaeffer's books were *Bible Readings for Schools* (1897), *Thinking and Learning to Think* (1900), and *History of Education in Pennsylvania* (1907). He was interested in religious education and the relations between church and state. He edited the *Pennsylvania School Journal* while he was superintendent of public instruction.

Schaeffer was chancellor of the Pennsylvania Chautauqua at Mount

Gretna (1902–05) and president of the National Educational Association (1905–07). He served on the Pennsylvania Commission on Industrial Education, a commission to codify and revise the state school laws, the Dental Council, the Bureau of Medical Education and Licensure, and the National Council of Education. He received two honorary degrees from Dickinson College.

REFERENCES: *DAB; NCAB* (22:454); *TC; WWW* (I); *NYT,* March 16, 1919, p. 20.                                    *Jacob L. Susskind*

**SCHELLING, Felix Emanuel.** B. September 3, 1858, New Albany, Indiana, to Felix and Rose (White) Schelling. M. March 7, 1886, to Caroline Derbyshire. M. 1939 to Gertrude Bueb. Ch. two. D. December 15, 1945, Mount Vernon, New York.

Because of poor health and the mobility of his family, Felix Emanuel Schelling was taught by private tutors and his mother. He entered the University of Pennsylvania with sophomore standing, studied English and the classics, and was graduated with the A.B. (1881), LL.B. (1883), and A.M. (1884) degrees.

Schelling practiced law in Philadelphia and in 1886 became a teacher of English at the University of Pennsylvania; he became John Welsh Centennial Professor of History and English Literature (1893) and department head (1895). In 1929 he was appointed Felix E. Schelling Professor and continued in that position until he retired in 1934. He was the creator of the modern English language and literature department at the University of Pennsylvania and was one of the foremost scholars of the Elizabethan drama in America.

Schelling was a prolific writer; his books include *Literary and Verse Criticism of the Reign of Elizabeth* (1891), *Life and Works of George Gascoigne* (1893), *A Book of Elizabethan Lyrics* (1896), *A Book of Seventeenth Century Lyrics* (1899), *The English Chronicle Play* (1902), *History of Elizabethan Drama* (1908), *English Literature During the Lifetime of Shakespeare* (1910), *The English Lyric* (1913), *A History of English Drama* (1914), *Elizabethan Playwrights* (1925), and *Pedagogically Speaking* (1929). He edited many literary works.

A member of honorary and professional organizations, Schelling received honorary degrees from several American colleges and universities.

REFERENCES: *DAB* (supp. 3); *LE* (I); *NCAB* (A:426); *TC; WWW* (II); *NYT,* December 16, 1945, p. 40.                           *S. S. Britt, Jr.*

**SCHEVILL, Rudolph.** B. June 18, 1874, Cincinnati, Ohio, to Ferdinand August and Johanna (Hartmann) Schevill. M. May 22, 1912, to Margaret Erwin. M. June 4, 1939, to Isabel Magana. Ch. three. D. February 17, 1946, Berkeley, California.

Rudolph Schevill was graduated from Yale University with the B.A. degree (1896). After continuing his studies in Europe at the Sorbonne, the Collège de France, and the Universidad Central in Madrid, Spain, he received the Ph.D. degree (1898) from the University of Munich, Germany. He spent fifteen months in study and travel in Mexico and Latin America (1903–04).

Schevill's teaching career began at Bucknell University in Lewisburg, Pennsylvania, where he taught French and German (1899–1900). Moving to Yale in 1900, he taught German, French, and Spanish to 1910. He became professor of Spanish at the University of California at Berkeley in 1910, serving to his retirement in 1944.

Schevill was internationally known for his studies in Spanish literature. Of his books, *Ovid and the Renascence in Spain* (1913), *The Dramatic Art of Lope de Vega* (1918), and the biography *Life of Cervantes* (1919) were important in the field of Hispanism. His greatest achievement was as coeditor of the eighteen-volume *Complete Works of Cervantes* (1914–41). He also edited *The Dramatic Works of Luis Velez de Guevara* (1937).

In 1942 the Hispanic Society of America awarded Schevill the Medal of Arts and Literature. He was a fellow of the American Academy of Arts and Sciences and president of the Modern Language Association of America (1943). He was a corresponding member of many foreign societies.

REFERENCES: *DAB;* (supp. 4); *LE* (I); *NCAB* (35:35); *WWW* (II); *NYT,* February 19, 1946, p. 25.                                    *John L. Flynn*

**SCHLESINGER, Hermann Irving.** B. October 11, 1882, Minneapolis, Minnesota, to Louis and Emily (Stern) Schlesinger. M. April 2, 1910, to Edna M. Simpson. Ch. two. D. October 3, 1960, Chicago, Illinois.

Hermann Schlesinger's student and professional career was spent at the University of Chicago. He earned the B.A. (1903) and Ph.D. (1905) degrees there. He spent two years in Germany studying under W. Nernst and J. Theile. Soon afterward he returned to Chicago to begin his forty-one-year teaching career.

Schlesinger developed and taught general chemistry and science survey courses. Among his major contributions to science education was his pioneer work in visual media. He produced and directed seven films covering the fundamental principles of general chemistry. Among the first educational films produced, they were used for several decades in high schools and colleges throughout the United States. His technique for the preparation of the boron hydrides opened a new field of research and contributed to the development of jet and rocket fuels.

Schlesinger's contributions to chemical research were published in more than sixty scientific papers. He was the author of *General Chemistry* (1925). He was a fellow of the American Association for the Advancement of Science and a member of professional associations, including the American Chemical Society (chairman of the Chicago section, 1930–31). Schlesinger received the Priestly Medal, the Willard Gibbs Medal, and the United States Navy Distinguished Public Service Award.

REFERENCES: *WWW* (IV); *Chemical and Engineering News* 38 (1960): 131; *NYT,* October 4, 1960, p. 43.                      *B. Richard Siebring*

**SCHNEIDER, Herman.** B. September 12, 1872, Summit Hill, Pennsylvania, to Anton and Sarah (Wintersteen) Schneider. M. December 1899 to Jesse Schober. M. July 27, 1904, to Louise Bosworth. Ch. none. D. March 28, 1939, Cincinnati, Ohio.

Herman Schneider was graduated from Lehigh University in Bethlehem, Pennsylvania, with the B.S. degree (1894). He pursued a career as a civil engineer (1894–99) and was an instructor of civil engineering at Lehigh University (1899–1903).

Schneider taught at the University of Cincinnati (1903–06) where he developed the idea of a cooperative plan of education in which students alternated periods of study with periods of employment related to their major fields. The plan was first tried at Cincinnati when Schneider was dean of the college of engineering (1906–29). He served as president of the University of Cincinnati from 1929 to 1932. Schneider was known as the Father of Cooperative Education. In his lifetime cooperative education was adopted at thirty other institutions of higher learning and at many high schools.

Schneider wrote articles and books, including *Education for Industrial Workers* (1915), *Thirty Years of Educational Pioneering: The Philosophy of the Cooperative System and Its Practical Test* (1935), and *The Problem of Vocational Guidance* (1938). He was a member of the Committee on School Inquiry of New York, New York (1911–13), and consultant to the New York Board of Education (1914–15). He received the Lamme Medal (1936) and was awarded honorary degrees by the universities of Pittsburgh (1911) and Cincinnati (1933).

REFERENCES: *DAB* (supp. 2); *LE* (I); *NCAB* (37:277); *WWW* (I); J. E. Barbeau, *Cooperative Education in America: Its Historical Development, 1906–1971* (Boston: Northeastern University, 1973); J. E. Barbeau, "The Spirit of Man: The Educational Philosophy of Dean Schneider," *Journal of Cooperative Education* 7 (May 1971): 1-7; *NYT,* March 29, 1939, p. 23; C. W. Park, *Ambassador to Industry: The Idea and Life of Herman Schneider* (New York: Bobbs-Merrill, 1943); C. W. Park, "Genesis of the Cooperative Idea," *Journal of Engineering Education* 33 (January 1943): 410–16; R. Walters, "Herman Schneider's Contributions to Engineering Education," *The Bent of Tau Beta Pi* (February 1943): 11–14.

*Joseph E. Barbeau*

**SCHORLING, Raleigh.** B. August 15, 1887, Batesville, Indiana, to Henry and Catherine Schorling. M. July 26, 1916, to Marie Louise Oury. Ch. three. D. April 22, 1950, Ann Arbor, Michigan.

From the age of two, Raleigh Schorling was raised by John and Dorothea Kammeyer. He was graduated from Indiana State Normal College (later, Indiana State University) (1909) and received the B.A. degree (1911) from the University of Michigan. The University of Chicago awarded him the M.A. degree (1915), and he received the Ph.D. degree (1925) from Columbia University.

Schorling was a public school teacher (1904–07) and the first principal of Columbia University's experimental Lincoln School (1917–22). He was an organizer and first principal of the University High School (1922–26) and the first director of student teaching programs at the University of Michigan. He was professor of education at Michigan from 1926 to his death. He developed the first laboratory course for college credit in making audio-visual aids and the first comprehensive program of internships in teaching for prospective teachers in Michigan.

Schorling authored or coauthored over two hundred books, including *A Tentative List of Objectives* (1920), *Modern School Mathematics* (books 1 and 2, 1935), *Education and Social Trends* (1936), *Modern School Algebra* (1936), *Mathematics in Life* (1937), *Modern School Geometry* (1938), *Fundamental Mathematics* (books 1 and 2, 1944), *Mathematics in Life* (1946), and *Mathematics for the Consumer* (1947). His best-known books outside of mathematics were in student teaching. In 1940 he published *Student Teaching*. The first textbook on the subject, it was widely used in teacher-training programs. He also wrote *Swords into Ploughshares* (1946) and *A Bill of Rights for Teachers* (1947). He was a member of professional organizations and a fellow of the American Association for the Advancement of Science.

REFERENCES: *LE* (III); *NCAB* (38:477); *WWAE* (VIII); *WWW* (III); R. S. Rickard, "Story of My Father," *Mathematics Teacher* 44 (February 1951): 69–75; *NYT,* April 23, 1950, p. 95.                           *Daniel L. Paul*

**SCHURZ, Margarethe Meyer.** B. August 27, 1833, Hamburg, Germany, to Heinrich Christian Meyer and his wife n.a. M. July 6, 1852, to Carl Schurz, United States senator. Ch. four. D. March 15, 1876, Hamburg, Germany.

Margarethe Meyer Schurz was a pioneer kindergarten teacher in Wisconsin. While assisting her sister in managing a Froebelite kindergarten in London, England, in 1852, she met and married Carl Schurz and accompanied him to the United States. They settled in Watertown, Wisconsin, in 1856, where Margarethe Schurz was credited with opening what is sometimes considered to have been the first American kindergarten.

Schurz was said to have converted Elizabeth Peabody *(q.v.)* to the Froebel philosophy at an 1859 meeting in Boston, Massachusetts. A semi-invalid for many of her forty-two years, Schurz returned to her hometown of Hamburg, Germany, after the death of a daughter, remaining there for the last nine years of her life.

REFERENCES: *NAW; NYT,* March 17, 1876, p. 19; *Dictionary of Wisconsin Biography* (Madison: State Historical Society of Wisconsin, 1960), pp. 320–21; Carl Schurz, *Reminiscences of Carl Schurz* (New York: McClure, 1907–08); Agnes Snyder, *Dauntless Women in Childhood Education, 1856–1931* (Washington, D.C.: Association for Childhood Education International, 1972). *Lawrence S. Master*

**SCHWEICKHARD, Dean Merrill.** B. August 5, 1892, Mankato, Minnesota, to Daniel Louis and Mary Isabelle (Ashworth) Schweickhard. M. June 14, 1917, to Mildred Parmelee. Ch. one.

Dean Merrill Schweickhard received the A.B. degree (1916) from the University of Wisconsin and the M.A. degree (1927) from the University of Minnesota.

He was a teacher at Lyle, Minnesota (1912–13), an elementary school principal at Kinney, Minnesota (1913–14), and a high school teacher at Sioux City, Iowa (1916–17). He became a professor of trade and industrial education at Purdue University in Lafayette, Indiana (1919–20), and the director of vocational education at Clinton, Iowa (1920–22). He was a captain in the United States Army School of Military Aeronautics (1918).

In 1922 Schweickhard became field supervisor of the Minnesota State Department of Education. He held that position until 1930 when he became assistant superintendent of Minneapolis (Minnesota) public schools, a position he held until 1943. He taught summers at various colleges and universities throughout the United States. Schweickhard became Minnesota commissioner of education in 1943 and held the position through December 1961.

He published numerous articles in the *Minnesota Journal of Education* and other scholarly and professional journals. He wrote *Industrial Arts in Education* (1928). He was particularly interested in vocational education and school consolidation.

Schweickhard was a member of professional associations, including the Minnesota Vocational Education Association (president, 1934–36), the Minnesota State Teachers Retirement Fund (president), the War-Navy Committee (education member, 1947–50), the Federal Commission on Life Adjustment of Youth (1947–50), the Minnesota State Commission on School District Reorganization (executive secretary), the Minnesota State Commission for Study of Higher Education (chairman), the State Teachers College Board (secretary), and the Council of Chief State School Officers

(president, 1957). He received an honorary degree.
    REFERENCES: *LE* (III); *WW* (XXXI); *WWAE* (XVI).
                                              *Winifred Wandersee Bolin*

**SCOTT, John Work.** B. November 27, 1807, York County, Pennsylvania, to Andrew Scott and his wife (n.a.). M. to Phebe Anna Jenkins. Ch. six. D. July 25, 1879, Charlotte, North Carolina.

John Work Scott was graduated from Jefferson College, Canonsburg, Pennsylvania, in 1827. After three years of teaching, he studied theology with Samuel Martin in Chanceford, Pennsylvania, and entered Princeton (New Jersey) Seminary, receiving the D.D. degree (1832). He served churches in Ohio, including Poland (1832–36), Three Springs, and Steubenville (1836–47).

Scott was founder and principal of the Grove Academy at Steubenville (1836–47), principal of the Lindsley Institute in Wheeling, Virginia (later, West Virginia) from 1847 to 1853, and president of Washington (Pennsylvania) College (1853–65). In 1865 Scott took charge of the Woodburn Female Seminary and Monongalia Academy in Morgantown, West Virginia, remaining in charge of both until they were donated to the state in 1867 to help found a state land-grant college (West Virginia University). He was one of West Virginia University's first teachers and served as professor of languages and, at times, as vice-president (1867–79). In 1873 he assumed the chair of mental and moral sciences, which was usually assigned to the president. As acting president of West Virginia University (1875–77), he sought to enroll women, in part to increase enrollment. West Virginia accepted some women students in 1889 and was open to them on an equal basis with men in 1897.

In 1879 Scott taught in Charlotte, North Carolina, at Biddle (later Johnson C. Smith) University, a Presbyterian-maintained classical and theological school for Negroes. In his last years he suffered failing sight and lived on a farm near Ridgeway, North Carolina. He received two honorary degrees.

    REFERENCES: *NCAB* (20:460); *TC;* Charles H. Ambler, *A History of Education in West Virginia from Early Colonial Times to 1949* (Huntington, W. Va.: Standard Printing and Publishing Co., 1951); James Morton Callahan, *History of West Virginia* (Chicago: American Historical Society, 1923), vol. 1; Alfred Nevin, ed., *Encyclopaedia of the Presbyterian Church of the United States of America* (Philadelphia: Presbyterian Encyclopaedia Publishing Co., 1884).                    *John P. Burgess*

**SCOTT, Miriam Finn.** B. August 9, 1882, Vilna, Russia, to Moses and Gittel (Seletchnick) Finn. M. June 24, 1904, to Leroy Scott. Ch. three. D. January 6, 1944, New York, New York.

Miriam Finn Scott's family emigrated from Russia to New York City in 1893. At the age of sixteen (1898), she directed New York's first building rooftop recreational program with about a thousand children as her daily responsibility. She received the A.B. degree (1903) from Hunter College and continued graduate study at Barnard College and Columbia University.

Scott was director of children's work at the University Settlement in New York City (1899–1903) and was director of a program in Speyer School under the direction of Columbia University, which involved women who were studying academic programs while participating in social work.

Children's problems became her special concern, and she opened a school, the Children's Garden, in her own home to study child development. She developed systematic procedures for studying play patterns. She conducted intelligence testing as games, observing the children as they took play objects from shelves to see what they did with them, how long they played with them, and generally how they responded to other people.

In addition to close observation of children to determine the nature of children's problems, she investigated the home environment and the school. She believed the child is part of a total and unique system and has specific ways of responding to the total environment. She discussed with parents the reasons for a child's behavior and was able to provide insight and direction on ways that parents could relate to the child. Asked by the New York City Board of Education in 1935 to work with adults, she lectured to audiences interested in family development, effective parenthood, and the understanding of young children; she also conducted a private practice. She wrote *How to Know Your Child* (1915), which was translated into Russian and German. It was one of the first books on education of children to be published in Soviet Russia. She was also the author of *Meeting Your Child's Problem* (1922). Scott conducted radio programs on parent education over several stations (1934–37).

REFERENCES: *NCAB* (36:419); *NYT,* January 7, 1944, p. 17; *WWW* (II); John William Leonard, ed., *Woman's Who's Who in America* (New York: American Commonwealth Co., 1914).                              *Edythe Margolin*

**SCOTT, Walter Dill.** B. May 1, 1869, Cooksville, Illinois, to James Sterling and Henrietta (Sutton) Scott. M. July 21, 1898, to Anna Marcy Miller. Ch. two. D. September 23, 1955, Evanston, Illinois.

Walter Dill Scott was graduated from the Illinois State Normal School (later, Illinois State University) in Normal (1891) and received the B.A. degree (1895) from Northwestern University in Evanston, Illinois. He attended McCormick Theological Seminary in Chicago, Illinois (1895–98), studied in Europe, and received the Ph.D. degree from the University of Leipzig, Germany (1900).

After returning to the United States, he taught education and psychology (1901–20) at Northwestern University and was director of the psychological laboratory (1901–08). He was also a professor of advertising and applied psychology from 1902 and head of the department of psychology.

On leaves of absence, he organized and directed the Bureau of Salesmanship Research at Carnegie Institute of Technology (later, Carnegie-Mellon University) in Pittsburgh, Pennsylvania (1916–17), and served as the director of a committee on rating officers and on classifying personnel for the United States Army (1917–18). He initiated a system by which enlisted men were classified for assignment in the service during World War I and devised aptitude tests for officer candidates. His system was modified for use during World War II.

In 1920 Scott was elected president of Northwestern University, serving until he retired in 1939. During his presidency financial contributions increased, the Chicago campus was established, fifty-seven new buildings were erected in Chicago and Evanston, the endowment was increased, the faculty doubled in size, and the course offerings were expanded. He instituted an extensive program of adult education and established the Medill School of Journalism (1921).

Scott was cooperating editor of *Psychology Bulletin* and was chairman of the editorial board of the *American Readers' Encyclopedia* (1948–55). He was the author of *Theory in Advertising* (1903), *Psychology of Public Speaking* (1907), *Psychology of Advertising* (1909), *Influencing Men in Business* (1911), *Increasing Human Efficiency* (1911), *Psychology of Advertising in Theory and Practice* (1921), *Science and Common Sense in Working with Men* (1921), *The Life of Charles Deering* (1929), and *Biography of John Evans* (1939), and he coauthored many other books.

A pioneer in applying psychology to industrial management, personnel, advertising, and sales techniques, he was a consultant for industry. In 1918 Scott and his associates organized the Scott Company in New York City, a consultant and engineering firm in the field of industrial personnel. He served as director of the Division of Psychology and Anthropology of the National Research Council (1919–20). He was a trustee of a Century of Progress, Chicago (1933–34) and Presbyterian Theological Seminary, Chicago. During World War II, he served as chairman of the United States Solid Fuels Advisory War Council (1941–46).

He was the recipient of the Distinguished Service Medal of the United States (1919) and was decorated with a cross (1933) and was made a chevalier of the French Legion of Honor (1938). He was a member of many civic and professional organizations, including the American Council on Education (chairman, 1927) and the American Psychological Association (president, 1918–19). He received two honorary degrees.

REFERENCES: *LE* (III); *NCAB* (42:328); *WWAE* (VIII); *WWW* (III);

*Newsweek* 46 (October 3, 1955): 80; *Wilson Library Bulletin* 30 (November 1955): 220.                                                      *Lawrence S. Master*

**SEARS, Barnas.** B. November 19, 1802, Sandisfield, Massachusetts, to Paul and Rachel (Granger) Sears. M. July 6, 1830, to Elizabeth Griggs Corey. Ch. five. D. July 6, 1880, Saratoga Springs, New York.

Barnas Sears studied for the ministry with Parson Cooley of East Granville, Massachusetts. Sears entered the grammar school of Brown University in Providence, Rhode Island, and continued at Brown University, graduating with high honors in 1825. He studied at Newton (Massachusetts) Theological Institution, graduating in 1828. In 1827 he was ordained pastor of the First Baptist Church of Hartford, Connecticut, but resigned his pastorate in the spring of 1829 because of ill health.

Sears was professor of ancient languages at Hamilton (New York) Literary and Theological Institution (later, Colgate University) from 1829 to 1836. He served as a resident licentiate at Andover (Massachusetts) Theological Seminary in 1830 and spent two years studying theology in Germany and France (1833–35). Sears was professor of Christian theology at Newton (Massachusetts) Theological Institution (1836–48) and served as president (1839–48). In 1848 Sears succeeded Horace Mann *(q.v.)* as secretary and general agent of the Massachusetts Board of Education and was credited with making permanent the educational reforms that Mann had initiated.

In 1855 Sears became president and professor of moral philosophy at Brown University, where he effected major changes in the administrative structure of the university. He established a system of scholarships, revised the grading system, improved research methods, abolished minor penalties in college discipline, and expanded the physical plant.

In 1867 the Peabody Fund for the promotion of education in the South was established, and chairman Robert C. Winthrop asked Sears to formulate a proposal for administering the fund. His plan was accepted, and he was invited to become the fund's general agent. In 1867 Sears left Brown University and moved to Staunton, Virginia, to work for the Peabody Fund. He devoted himself to that work almost to the time of his death (1867–80).

Barnas Sears was the author of *A Grammar of the German Language* (1842), *Classical Studies: Essays on Ancient Literature and Art* (with others, 1843), *The Ciceronian: Or the Prussian Method of Teaching the Elements of the Latin Language* (1844), *Life of Martin Luther* (1850), *Discourse at Centennial Celebration of Brown University* (1864), and *Objections to Public Schools Considered* (1875). He was editor of *Roget's Thesaurus of English Words and Phrases* (1853). He edited the *Christian Review* (1836–39).

Sears was a fellow of the American Academy of Arts and Sciences and of Brown University (1841–51). He was awarded honorary degrees by Harvard University and Yale College.

REFERENCES: *AC; DAB; NCAB* (8:24); *TC; WWW* (H); Walter C. Bronson, *The History of Brown University, 1764–1914* (Providence: The university, 1914); J. L. M. Curry *(q.v.), A Brief Sketch of George Peabody and a History of the Peabody Education Fund Through Thirty Years* (New York: Negro Universities Press, 1969); *NYT*, July 7, 1880, p. 5; Earle H. West, "The Life and Educational Contributions of Barnas Sears" (Ph.D. diss., George Peabody College for Teachers, 1961).    *Fredrick Chambers*

**SEASHORE, Carl Emil.** B. January 28, 1866, Mörlunda, Sweden, to Carl Gustaf and Emily Charlotta (Borg) Seashore. M. June 7, 1900, to Mary Roberta Holmes. Ch. four. D. October 16, 1949, Lewiston, Idaho.

Carl Emil Seashore left Sweden with his parents when he was two years old and settled in Iowa in 1869. He attended Gustavus Adolphus College in St. Peter, Minnesota, where he was graduated with the A.B. degree (1891). He received the Ph.D. degree (1895) from Yale University.

Seashore was an assistant at the psychological laboratory at Yale (1895–97). He joined the staff of the State University of Iowa, where he was assistant professor of philosophy (1897–1902) and professor of psychology (1902–36) and served as head of the psychology department (1905–36) and dean of the graduate school (1908–36). He was a leading psychologist in the United States and a pioneer in psychological testing in the field of music.

His first major publication was *Elementary Experiments in Psychology* (1908). He also wrote *Psychology in Daily Life* (1913), *The Psychology of Musical Talent* (1919), *Introduction to Psychology* (1922), *Learning and Living in College* (1927), *Trends in Graduate Study* (1931), *Psychology of Music* (1941), *Pioneering in Psychology* (1942), and *Psychology and Life in Autobiography* (1949). He was editor of University of Iowa Studies in Psychology (volumes 2–12) and Studies in the Psychology of Music.

He authored numerous articles for professional journals. He developed the Seashore Measures of Musical Talent (1919), a series of tests intended to identify the musical aptitudes of students. These tests purported to measure differences in auditory discrimination of pitch, loudness, rhythm, time, timbre, and tonal sequence. The tests were used extensively in secondary schools and colleges in the United States and in Europe.

Seashore was a member of several learned societies and organizations, including the National Academy of Sciences, the American Psychological Association (president, 1911), the Western Philosophical Association (president, 1909), and the National Research Council (chairman, division of anthropology and psychology, 1933–39), and he was a fellow of the

American Association for the Advancement of Science and the Society of Experimental Psychologists. He received six honorary degrees.

REFERENCES: *DAB* (supp. 4); *NCAB* (A: 227); *TC; WWAE* (I); *WWW* (II); *NYT,* October 18, 1949, p. 27; M. Metfessel, "Carl Emil Seashore: 1866–1949," *Science* 111 (June 30, 1950): 713–17; *National Education Association Journal* 38 (December 1949): 714; *Oxford Companion to Music,* 10th ed. (New York: Oxford University Press, 1970); G. D. Stoddard *(q.v.),* "Carl Emil Seashore: 1866–1949," *American Journal of Psychology* 63 (July 1950): 456–62. *Robert H. Niederkorn*

**SEELEY, Levi.** B. November 21, 1847, Harpersfield, New Jersey, to Levi and Hanna (Thorpe) Seeley. M. July 24, 1886, to Marie Hesse. Ch. none. D. December 23, 1928, Trenton, New Jersey.

In 1871, at the age of twenty-four, Levi Seeley was graduated from the Albany Normal School (later, State University of New York at Albany). He was a student in Germany from 1883 to 1886 when he was awarded the Ph.D. degree by the University of Leipzig.

Educator, author, perennial student, and traveler, Seeley served in various educational posts. He was principal of New York public schools at Orient (1871–74), New Hamburgh (1874–75), and Patchogue (1875–81). He was superintendent of the Lansingburg (New York) schools (1881–83) and principal of the Cobleskill public schools (1886–87). In 1887 Seeley moved from New York to Lake Forest, Illinois, where he was principal of Ferry Hall Seminary until 1894, when he returned to Europe for a year of study and travel. From 1895 to 1918 he served as professor of pedagogy at Trenton (New Jersey) Normal School (later, Trenton State College).

Seeley wrote several books on education theory and practice, including *The American Common School System* (1886, his thesis at Leipzig), *The Grube System of Numbers* (1887), *The Grube Idea* (1890), *The German Common School System and Its Lessons to America* (1896), *History of Education* (1899), *The Foundations of Education* (1901), *A New School Management* (1903), *Seeley's Question Book* (1905), *Elementary Pedagogy* (1906), and *Teaching, Its Aims and Methods* (1915). He received an honorary M.A. degree (1871) from Williams College.

REFERENCES: *NYT,* December 24, 1928, p. 13; *WWW* (I). *Albert Nissman*

**SEELYE, Julius Hawley.** B. September 14, 1824, Bethel, Connecticut, to Seth and Abigail (Taylor) Seelye. M. October 23, 1854, to Elizabeth Tillman James. Ch. four. D. May 12, 1895, Amherst, Massachusetts.

Julius Hawley Seelye was graduated from Amherst (Massachusetts) College with high honors (1849) and from Auburn (New York) Theological Seminary (1852). He studied philosophy and theology for one year at the

University of Halle, Germany (1852), and was ordained as pastor of the First Dutch Reformed Church in Schenectady, New York (1853).

In 1858 Seelye accepted the chair of philosophy at Amherst College and continued there until his death. He became president of Amherst upon the death of William Augustus Stearns in 1876. He established a student self-government system that came to be known as the Amherst plan, which proved successful at Amherst and influenced other colleges and universities. Under the Amherst plan students settled disciplinary matters in the college senate. He was interested in building character and educating the whole person. Under Seelye's leadership the financial resources of the college were increased, the physical plant was enlarged, and standards for admission and graduation were raised.

Seelye published many articles on political and religious subjects. He translated the *History of Philosophy* by Albert Schwegler (1856), and he edited and revised L. P. Hickok's *Empirical Psychology* (1882) and *System of Moral Science* (1880). He wrote *Christian Missions* (1875), *Duty* (1891), and *Citizenship* (1894). A series of lectures he delivered in India in 1872 was published as *Lectures to Educated Hindus* (1873).

Seelye was appointed a member of the Massachusetts commission for the revision of the tax laws in 1874. He served in the United States House of Representatives (1875–77) and was a trustee of Clarke Institute for Deaf Mutes and Smith College where his brother Laurenus Clark Seelye *(q.v.)* was president. He received honorary degrees from Union and Columbia colleges.

REFERENCES: *A C; DAB; NCAB* (6:157); *TC; WWW* (H); *N YT,* May 13, 1895, p. 2.                                                          *Michael R. Cioffi*

**SEELYE, Laurenus Clark.** B. September 20, 1837, Bethel, Connecticut, to Seth and Abigail (Taylor) Seelye. M. November 17, 1863, to Henrietta Chapin. Ch. seven. D. October 12, 1924, Northampton, Massachusetts.

Clark Seelye was the youngest son of a large family, which included Julius Hawley Seelye *(q.v.)*. He was prepared for college by an older brother, a minister. He was graduated from Union College, Schenectady, New York, in 1857 and attended Andover (Massachusetts) Theological Seminary (1858–59), but frail health caused his family to send him to Europe where he traveled throughout Western Europe, Palestine, and Egypt. He completed theological studies in Germany at the universities of Berlin and Heidelberg (1861–62).

Seelye served as minister of the North Congregational Church at Springfield, Massachusetts (1863–65), but he left because of poor health and from 1865 to 1873 was professor of rhetoric, oratory, and English literature at Amherst (Massachusetts) College.

He left Amherst in 1873 to help establish Smith College in Northampton,

Massachusetts, and served as president (1873–1910). Admissions standards and degree requirements at Smith College were to compare with those of New England colleges for men. Women were to be housed in groups of twenty to fifty in units dubbed the "cottage" plan. On Seelye's retirement in 1910, Smith was the largest institution of its kind in the world.

Seelye was the author of *The Early History of Smith College* (1923). He was a member of the board of supervisors of Smith's Agricultural School and the Rockefeller Foundation. He was awarded honorary degrees by Union, Amherst, and Smith colleges.

REFERENCES: *AC; DAB; NCAB* (38;376); *TC; WWW* (I); *NYT,* October 13, 1924, p. 17.                                        *Thomas L. Wilton*

**SEERLEY, Homer Horatio.** B. August 13, 1848, near Indianapolis, Indiana, to Thomas and Louisa Ann (Smith) Seerley. M. July 9, 1878, to Clara E. Twaddle. Ch. three. D. December 23, 1932, Cedar Falls, Iowa.

Homer Horatio Seerley received the Ph.B. degree (1873), the bachelor's diploma (1875), and the A.M. degree (1876) from the State University of Iowa.

He was a teacher (1873–75) and superintendent of schools (1875–86) at Oskaloosa, Iowa. He was president of Iowa State Teachers' College at Cedar Rapids (1886–1928), which was later called University of Northern Iowa. Under Seerley, the college gained national prominence as a teacher-training institution.

Seerley was the author of *History and Civil Government of Iowa* (with L. W. Parish, 1897), *The Country School* (1912), and *Geography of Iowa* (1916). He delivered many addresses to professional groups, including the annual meetings of the National Education Association.

He was president of the Iowa State Teachers' Association (1884), the National Educational Association (department of normal schools, 1898), the National Council of Education (1919–21), the American State Teachers College Council (1919), and the American Council on Education (1918). He was the recipient of two honorary degrees.

REFERENCES: *LE* (I); *WWAE* (I); *WWW* (IV).                    *John F. Ohles*

**SELVIDGE, Robert Washington.** B. August 11, 1872, Moundview, Missouri, to James S. and Susannah J. (Kirby) Selvidge. M. October 11, 1908, to Ivy F. Harner. Ch. two. D. November 16, 1941, Columbia, Missouri.

Robert Selvidge was graduated from Bradley Polytechnical Institute (later, Bradley University) of Peoria, Illinois, with the B.S. degree (1907) and received the M.A. degree (1908) from Columbia University.

Selvidge taught in rural and village schools until 1895, was superintendent of schools in Johnson County, Missouri (1895–97), and taught in the high school at Joplin, Missouri (1900–03). He was a professor of manual arts at Louisiana Industrial Institute (later, Louisiana Tech University) at Ruston (1903–07), and he taught at the University of Missouri (1908–13) and the George Peabody College for Teachers in Nashville, Tennessee (1913–19). From 1918 to 1921 Selvidge worked as a district vocational director and supervisor of instruction in special schools for the War Department.

He returned to the University of Missouri in 1919 as professor of industrial education and was chairman of the department of mechanical engineering (1925–41). His use of the individual instruction sheet was an early development in individualized instruction techniques.

Selvidge was the author of a number of publications, including *How to Teach a Trade* (1923) and *Individual Instruction Sheets—How to Write and How to Use Them* (1926) and was joint author of *Teaching the Manual Arts* (1910) and *Principles of Trade and Industrial Teaching* (with Verne C. Frykland, 1930). He was editor of the Selvidge Series of Instruction Manuals.

Selvidge was a member of the American Society of Military Engineers, the American Society of Mechanical Engineers, and the Western Drawing and Manual Training Association (president, 1914). He was a fellow of the American Association for the Advancement of Science.

REFERENCES: *LE* (I); *WWW* (II); W. T. Bawden, "Tribute to Professor Selvidge," *Industrial Arts and Vocational Education* 31 (January 1942): 40; *School and Society* 54 (December 27, 1941): 615.          *Lee H. Smalley*

**SETON, Elizabeth Ann Bayley.** B. August 28, 1774, New York, New York, to Richard and Catherine (Charlton) Bayley. M. January 25, 1794, to William Magee Seton. Ch. five. D. January 4, 1821, Emmitsburg, Maryland.

Rejected by their stepmother, Elizabeth Ann Bayley Seton and her older sister were cared for by relatives for months at a time. She was educated in the private Mama Pompelion's School in New York City.

Seton was the mother of five children and was active in New York City society and charitable work. She helped organize the Widow's Society. She came to be called a Protestant sister of charity. Her husband suffered ill health and died in 1803 in Pisa, Italy, where they had gone seeking a better climate for him. In Italy she was influenced by Catholic friends, and she joined the Catholic church in 1805 after she returned to the United States.

Unsuccessful in operating a school in New York, she accepted an invitation to move to Baltimore, Maryland, where she opened a school (1808). In 1809 she took her first religious vows before Archbishop John Carroll and founded a religious community, the Sisters of Charity of St. Joseph, in Emmitsburg, Maryland. It became a religious order in 1812 and engaged in teaching and nursing. The St. Joseph's School (later, College) was established in 1809, and Mother Seton offered a free education to poor local girls. Seton came to be called the foundress of the parochial school in the United States.

The Sisters of Charity became established in Philadelphia and New York City, and a branch was being organized in Baltimore by Seton's death in 1821. The order came to staff schools and hospitals in the United States and in many other countries. The Catholic church recognized Elizabeth Seton by acknowledging her as a saint through a formal process of canonization completed on September 14, 1975, the first such recognition accorded a native-born American.

REFERENCES: *AC; DAB; EB; NAW; NCAB* (2:436); *TC; WWW* (H); Joseph I. Dirvin, *Mrs. Seton, Foundress of the American Sisters of Charity* (New York: Farrar, Straus and Cudahy, 1962); *New Catholic Encyclopedia* (New York: McGraw-Hill, 1967).                    *Karen Kennelly*

**SEWALL, May Eliza Wright Thompson.** B. May 27, 1844, Milwaukee, Wisconsin, to Philander Montague and Mary Weeks (Brackett) Wright. M. 1872 to Edwin W. Thompson. M. October 30, 1880, to Theodore Lovett Sewall. Ch. none. D. July 22, 1920, Indianapolis, Indiana.

May Eliza Wright Sewall showed great academic promise as a child. Following a brief teaching career in Waukesha, Wisconsin, she decided to seek a college education. Disappointed because she could not attend Yale College as her father had, she entered Northwestern Female College (later, Northwestern University) in Evanston, Illinois, where she was awarded the B.L. (1866) and M.A. (1871) degrees.

After serving as a teacher and principal in Corinth and Plainwell, Michigan, and in Franklin, Indiana, she moved to Indianapolis, Indiana, following her marriage to Edwin W. Thompson in 1872. They both taught at what later became Shortridge High School; after Thompson's death in 1875, she continued her teaching career there.

In 1880, she married Theodore Lovett Sewall, who conducted a boys' school in Indianapolis. In 1882 the Sewalls founded the Girls' Classical School of Indianapolis, which became noted for its rigorous curriculum. Theodore L. Sewall died in 1895, and May Sewall remained as the head of the school until 1907.

May Sewall assisted in the formation of many women's clubs, including the General Federation of Women's Clubs, the Western Association of Collegiate Alumnae (forerunner of the American Association of University Women), and the International Council of Women. She served as chairman of the executive committee of the National Woman Suffrage Association (1882–90) and as United States representative to the Paris Exposition of 1900. At the Panama-Pacific Exposition in San Francisco in 1915, Sewall presided over the International Conference of Women Workers to Promote

Permanent Peace. Later that same year, she sailed with other pacifists on the peace ship *Oscar II* in an unsuccessful attempt to stop the war in Europe.

Sewall edited a women's column in the *Indianapolis Times* and wrote many monographs on education and reform. She wrote or edited a number of books, including *Higher Education of Women in the Western States of the U.S.A.* (n.d.), *History of the Woman Suffrage Movement in Indiana* (n.d.), *The World's Congress of Representative Women* (two volumes, 1894), *Women, World War, and Permanent Peace* (1915), and *Neither Dead Nor Sleeping* (1920).

REFERENCES: *DAB; NAW; NCAB* (19:108); *NYT,* July 24, 1920, p. 9; *TC; WC; WWW* (I).                                                    *Marjorie E. Souers*

**SEYBOLT, Robert Francis.** B. February 25, 1888, Kearny, New Jersey, to George Strickland and Mary Bethel (Best) Seybolt. M. December 29, 1913, to Ottilie Turnbull. M. December 26, 1926, to Frances B. Plummer. M. June 7, 1933, to Leora E. Hopkins. M. June 1, 1950, to Lynn Ruth Livingston. Ch. none. D. February 5, 1951, Hollywood, Florida.

Robert F. Seybolt received the Ph.B. (1910) and A.M. (1911) degrees from Brown University and the Ph.D. degree (1916) in history from Columbia University.

He served as a professor of history at the University of Wisconsin (1913–20). He was professor of the history of education at the University of Illinois (1920–46) and was named professor of humanities in 1946, a post he held until his death.

Seybolt wrote extensively of life in the American colonies and was a major author of works on the history of education in America. His works include *Apprenticeship and Apprenticeship Education in Colonial New England and New York* (1917), *The Colonial Citizen of New York City* (1918), *The Evening School in Colonial America* (1925), *Source Studies in Colonial Education* (1925), *The Public Schools of Colonial Boston* (1935), *The Private Schools of Colonial Boston* (1935), *The Public Schoolmasters of Colonial Boston* (1939), and *The Town Officials of Colonial Boston* (1939). He translated several educational documents from Latin and German, including *The Manuale Scholarium* (1921), *Renaissance Student Life* (1927), and *The Autobiography of Johannes Rutzbach* (1933).

He was a fellow of the American Association for the Advancement of Science, the Royal Historical Society, and the Royal Society of the Arts and a member of numerous historical and literary organizations in the United States and England.

REFERENCES: *LE* (III); *NCAB* (39:449); *WWAE* (VIII); *WWW* (III).                                                                    *James Ogan*

**SHAFER, Helen Almira.** B. September 23, 1839, Newark, New Jersey, to Archibald and Almira (Miller) Shafer. M. no. D. January 20, 1894, Wellesley, Massachusetts.

The daughter of a Congregational minister, Helen Almira Shafer received her education in the Albion (New York) Seminary. She was graduated from Oberlin (Ohio) College (1863). After teaching for two years in New Jersey, she taught for over ten years at Central High School in St. Louis, Missouri. Superintendent of the St. Louis schools William T. Harris *(q.v.)* (later United States commissioner of education) enthusiastically praised her teaching methods and the results they produced.

Shafer was appointed professor of mathematics and head of the department at Wellesley College in 1877. Under her direction the department became one of the strongest mathematics departments for undergraduates in the country. She gave courses in the history of geometry and in determinants despite the lack of adequate textbooks in English.

In 1888 Shafer became president of Wellesley and served in the position to her death in 1894. Under Shafer, the college curriculum was changed; over sixty new courses were added, providing opportunities for students to select elective courses of study. New admission standards were instituted, and local Greek letter societies were encouraged.

Shafer was awarded an honorary M.A. degree (1877) by Oberlin College and was the second woman in the United States to be awarded the LL.D. degree (Oberlin, 1893).

REFERENCES: *AC; DAB; NCAB* (7:328); *TC; WC; WWW* (H); *NYT,* January 20, 1894, p. 8; *Wellesley College 1875–1975—A Century of American Women* (Wellesley, Mass.: Wellesley College, 1975).

*Janet Durand Thomas*

**SHAHAN, Thomas Joseph.** B. September 11, 1857, Manchester, New Hampshire, to Peter and Mary Anne (Carmody) Shahan. M. no. D. March 9, 1932, Washington, D.C.

The son of Irish immigrants of modest means, Thomas Joseph Shahan attained prominence as an educator, churchman, historian, and theologian. He attended public school in Millbury, Massachusetts, and received his seminary training at the Sulpician College, Montreal, Ontario, Canada, and at the North American College in Rome, Italy. After his ordination on June 3, 1882, he became secretary to the Catholic bishop of Hartford, Connecticut, where he demonstrated organizational and planning skills.

Shahan studied in Berlin and Paris for two years (1889–91) to prepare to teach at the Catholic University of America in Washington, D.C. He was professor of church history and patrology at Catholic University from 1891 until 1909, when he became rector of the university. As rector he enlarged the faculty fourfold and tripled the endowment. He retired in 1928.

His works include numerous articles on history and theology. He contributed articles and was associate editor of *Catholic Encyclopedia* (1905–29). Among his published works were *The Blessed Virgin in the Catacombs* (1892), *Giovanni Baptista de Rossi* (1900), *The Beginnings of Christianity* (1903), *The Middle Ages, Sketches and Fragments* (1904), *St. Patrick in History* (1904), and *The House of God* (1905). He also translated Otto Bardenhewer's *Patrologie* (1908). He was the editor of *Catholic University Bulletin* (1895–1909).

He founded the Catholic Educational Association and was its president (1909–28). He helped found the National Conference of Charities, the Catholic Sisters College, and the American Catholic Historical Association. He is credited with inspiring the building of the National Shrine of the Immaculate Conception. In 1914 he was named titular bishop of Germanicopolis. Shahan was a fellow of the Medieval Academy of America (1926). He received honorary degrees from Georgetown University and the University of Louvain.

REFERENCES:*DAB; LE* (I); *NCAB* (5: 531); *NYT,* March 10, 1932, p. 21; *WWW* (I); *New Catholic Encyclopedia* (New York: McGraw-Hill, 1967).

*James M. Vosper*

**SHALER, Nathaniel Southgate.** B. February 22, 1841, near Newport, Kentucky, to Nathaniel Burger and Ann Hinde (Southgate) Shaler. M. 1862 to Sophia Penn Page. Ch. two. D. April 10, 1906, Cambridge, Massachusetts.

Nathaniel Southgate Shaler was the son of a physician who settled in Kentucky after graduating from the Harvard University Medical School. At the age of ten Shaler studied Latin and mathematics at the Newport, Kentucky, military post school and took drawing lessons across the river in Cincinnati, Ohio. In his middle teens, he studied Greek and Latin classics and the philosophies of Hegel and Kant. At the age of seventeen he was sent to the Harvard preparatory school and enrolled in the Lawrence School of Science at Harvard University in 1859. A favorite student of Louis Agassiz (*q.v.*), he received the B.S. degree (1862).

He returned to Kentucky and served in the Union army during the Civil War (1862–64). In 1864 he was at Harvard assisting Agassiz as a lecturer in paleontology and in the museum of comparative zoology. He received the Sc.D. degree (1865) from Harvard and left the following year to travel and study abroad. He returned to Harvard in 1868 as professor of paleontology (1868–87), professor of zoology (1888–91), and dean of the Lawrence Scientific School (1891–1906).

In 1874 he was appointed state geologist of Kentucky and spent his summers there. During the summers of 1875 and 1876 he conducted Camp Harvard in the Cumberland Gap, a summer school of geology, which lead to the establishment of the Harvard summer school at Cambridge. As state geologist for Kentucky and while in charge of the Atlantic Coast Division of the United States Geological Survey (1884–1900), Shaler collected data on foot for most of the distance from Florida to Maine. He established one of the first laboratories for testing road materials and served on many local, state, and national committees. He served as president of the Geological Society of America (1895).

Shaler wrote many of the annual reports of the United States Geological Survey and was the author of *Illustrations of the Earth's Surface* (with William Morris Davis, *q.v.*, 1881), *A First Book in Geology* (1884), *Kentucky, A Pioneer Commonwealth* (1885), *Aspects of the Earth* (1889), *Sea and Land* (1891), *Nature and Man in America* (1891), *The Story of Our Continent*, a school text (1892), *Beaches and Tidal Marshes of the Atlantic Coast* (1895), *Domesticated Animals* (1895), *American Highways* (1896), *Armada Days*, a dramatic sketch (1898), *Outlines of the Earth's History* (1898), *The Individual, a Study of Life and Death* (1900), *Elizabeth of England, a Dramatic Romance* (five volumes, 1903), *A Comparison of the Features of the Earth and the Moon* (1903), *The Neighbor, the Natural History of Human Contacts* (1904), *The Citizen: A Study of the Individual and the Government* (1904), and *Man and the Earth* (1905), and he edited *The United States of America* (1894).

REFERENCES: *AC; DAB; DSB; NCAB* (9:315); *NYT,* April 11, 1906, p. 11; *TC; WWW* (1); John E. Wolff, "Memoir of Nathaniel Southgate Shaler," *Geological Society of America: Bulletin* 18 (1907): 592–608.

*Isadore L. Sonnier*

**SHARP, Katharine Lucinda.** B. May 21, 1865, Elgin, Illinois, to John William and Phebe (Thompson) Sharp. M. no. D. June 1, 1914, Saranac Lake, New York.

Katharine Lucinda Sharp was seven years old when her mother died in 1872, and she was sent to live with relatives in Dundee and Elgin, Illinois. She attended Elgin Academy and at the age of sixteen enrolled in Northwestern University in Evanston, Illinois, where she earned the Ph.B. (1885) and Ph.M. (1889) degrees.

Sharp taught at Elgin Academy (1886–88) and was assistant librarian of the new Scoville Institute in Oak Park, Illinois (later the Oak Park Public Library), in 1888. Deciding to become a librarian, in 1890 she entered the New York State Library School at Albany directed by Melvil Dewey (*q.v.*). She was graduated with the B.L.S. (1892) and M.L.S. (1906) degrees. She organized the Adams Memorial Library in Wheaton, Illinois (1891), and the public library in Xenia, Ohio (1892). She was in charge of organizing the "Comparative Library Exhibit" for the New York State Library School shown at the Chicago World's Fair (1893).

Sharp was librarian and head of the department of library economy at the newly established Armour Institute of Technology in Chicago, the first library school in the Midwest (1893–97). The school was moved to the University of Illinois in 1897 with Sharp as professor of library economy, head librarian, and director of the Illinois Library School. The library school granted the B.L.S. degree based on a two-year curriculum, which required two years of college courses for admission. Sharp believed that a college degree should be a requirement to enroll in the library school. While she was director, the entrance requirement was established as three years of college in 1903 and the college degree in 1911. She retired in 1907 and was second vice-president at the Lake Placid (New York) Club organized by Melvil Dewey.

Sharp was active in professional organizations, including the American Library Association (council member, 1895–1905, and vice-president, 1898 and 1907) and the Illinois Library Association (president, 1903–04). She wrote frequently for library periodicals and was the author of *Illinois Libraries* (five volumes, 1906–08), a historical survey of the libraries in the state. She received an honorary degree from the University of Illinois (1907).

REFERENCES: *DAB; NAW; TC; WWW* (I).                    *Darlene E. Fisher*

**SHATTUCK, Joseph Cummings.** B. February 28, 1835, Marlborough, New Hampshire, to Abraham and Jerusha H. (French) Shattuck. M. August 17, 1858, to Hattie Mason Knight. Ch. three. D. May 15, 1921, Denver, Colorado.

Joseph Cummings Shattuck was educated at Westminster (Vermont) Academy and enrolled at Wesleyan University in Middletown, Connecticut. He dropped out of Wesleyan because of financial problems in 1857 and traveled to Camden County, Missouri, where he taught school to 1860.

With the outbreak of the Civil War, he returned east, teaching in Phillipsburg, New Jersey, and New Hampshire. In December 1862 he returned to Missouri and served as appointments clerk in the quartermaster's office in Lebanon. He worked for a railroad (1864–65) and returned to teaching in Camden County (1866–67). After a period as a salesman, Shattuck joined the Union Colony and traveled to Greeley, Colorado, in 1870.

The first graded school in Greeley was organized by Shattuck in 1871, and he served as principal in 1873. He was a trustee (1871–76) and vice-president of the colony (1872–76). He was elected to the Colorado territorial legislature in 1874 and was the first to be elected to the office of state superintendent of public instruction in 1876. He was reelected in 1878 and 1882, serving to 1885.

Shattuck joined the University of Denver in 1885 and served as treasurer, dean, and business manager. He guided the university through serious financial difficulties and served as a member of the executive committee past the age of eighty and as a trustee to his death.

Shattuck was active in church affairs and was editor of the *Rocky Mountain Christian Advocate*. He served a term as mayor of South Denver.

REFERENCES: *Education in Colorado* (Denver: News Print Co., 1885), p. 84; *The Encyclopedia of the New West* (Marshall, Tex.: United States Biographical Publishing Co., 1881), pp. 32-33; *History of the City of Denver, Arapahoe County, and Colorado* (Chicago: O. L. Baskin & Co., 1880), p. 578; *Rocky Mountain News* (Denver), May 16, 1921, p. 1; James Norland, "Our Long Lane of Distress," *University of Denver Magazine* 1 (March 1964): 5-7. *John F. Ohles*

SHEATS, William Nicholas. B. March 5, 1851, Auburn, Georgia, to John Lemuel and Ann Elizabeth (Jackson) Sheats. M. November 14, 1877, to Mary Susan Williams. Ch. none. D. July 19, 1922, Tallahassee, Florida.

William Nicholas Sheats was graduated from Emory College in Oxford, Georgia (later Emory University in Atlanta, Georgia), with the A.B. (1873) and A.M. (1876) degrees after working on Florida farms from 1866 to earn money to finance a college education. He began teaching with O. D. Scott at Fletcher Institute in Thomasville, Georgia (1873–74), and was principal of a school in Camilla, Georgia (1874–77). He returned to Florida in 1877 and taught as first assistant to E. P. Carter at the East Florida Seminary at Gainesville.

While teaching in Gainesville, Sheats was elected superintendent of public instruction in Alachua County (1880) and was reelected four times, serving in that position to 1892. During his term as county superintendent, he was elected a delegate to the state constitutional convention of 1885, and prepared the educational provisions in article XII of the new constitution.

At the Tampa State Democratic convention in 1892, Sheats was nominated superintendent of public instruction of the state. He was elected and served three successive terms (1893–1905). While state superintendent, he prepared and secured the enactment of most of the school laws of Florida that constituted the state school system for generations. Defeated for reelection in 1904, he served eight years as principal of high schools in the state. While he was principal of the Lakeland High School, he ran again for state superintendent and was elected and reelected, serving to his death in 1922.

Sheats was active in the Methodist church as a delegate to general conferences of the church and was awarded an honorary degree by Stetson University in 1913.

REFERENCES: *WWW* (I); *Who Was Who in Florida* (Huntsville, Ala.: Strode Publishers, 1973). *Freeman R. Irvine, Jr.*

**SHEDD, William Greenough Thayer.** B. June 21, 1820, Acton, Massachusetts, to Marshall and Eliza (Thayer) Shedd. M. October 7, 1845, to Lucy Ann Myers. Ch. four. D. November 17, 1894, New York, New York.

William Greenough Thayer Shedd received his early education at Westport, New York. He entered the University of Vermont at the age of fifteen and was graduated in 1839. He spent three years at Andover (Massachusetts) Theological Seminary, and was graduated in 1843.

Shedd was pastor of the Congregational church at Brandon, Vermont (1843–45), and was ordained in 1844. He was copastor at the Brick Presbyterian Church in New York City. From 1845, he was engaged in teaching and writing. He was professor of English literature at the University of Vermont (1845–52), professor of rhetoric, theology, and church history at Auburn (New York) Theological Seminary (1852–54), and professor of ecclesiastical history and lecturer on pastoral theology at Andover Theological Seminary (1854–62). He was professor at Union Theological Seminary in New York City (1863–90).

Shedd was a defender of Calvinism and a disciple of Coleridge, in spite of his increasing conservatism in the face of progressive theological thinking. In his last years he opposed the higher criticism put forth by a famous colleague, Charles A. Briggs, a way of thinking that later prevailed.

Among Shedd's books were *Lectures upon the Philosophy of History* (1856), *Discourses and Essays* (1856), *The Confessions of Augustine* (1860), *Literary Essays* (1878), and *Dogmatic Theology* (1888–94), his best-known work. He was awarded honorary degrees by the Auburn Theological Seminary (1857) and the University of the City of New York (later, New York University) in 1876.

REFERENCES: *AC; DAB; NCAB* (7:318); *NYT,* November 11, 1894, p. 2; *TC; WWW* (H). *Joseph P. Cangemi*
*Thomas E. Kesler*

**SHELDON, Edward Austin.** B. October 4, 1823, near Perry Center, New York, to Eleazor and Laura (Austin) Sheldon. M. May 16, 1849, to Frances Ann Bradford Stiles. Ch. five, including Mary Downing Sheldon Barnes (*q.v.*). D. August 26, 1897, Oswego, New York.

Edward Austin Sheldon was educated in local district schools and the newly opened Perry Center (New York) Academy. He attended Hamilton College in Clinton, New York (1844–47), but was forced to leave for health reasons. He moved to Oswego, New York, in 1847, where he engaged in an unsuccessful nursery business.

Concerned with the needs for schooling the immigrant and poor children in Oswego, Sheldon was the major organizer of the Orphan and Free School Association of Oswego in 1848. A "ragged school" for impoverished children was opened under the sponsorship of the association.

SHELDON, William Evarts [1175]

In 1849 Sheldon and J. D. Higgins opened a private school, Oswego Seminary. Appointed superintendent of the Syracuse (New York) public schools in 1851, Sheldon had established a graded organization of the schools and established night schools and school libraries before he resigned in 1853 to return to Oswego. While secretary of the Oswego board of education, a position equivalent to school superintendent, he organized the Oswego free public school system. In 1859 he founded an unclassified school for workers unable to attend regular schools.

In 1859 Sheldon first established classes for teachers that became the Oswego Primary Training School in 1861. He served as principal of the normal school and continued in that position when it became a state-supported institution and the state's first normal school in 1865. In 1869 he relinquished the post of superintendent of Oswego schools. He was introduced to Pestalozzian teaching methods and materials at the National Museum in Toronto, Canada, and became an enthusiastic promoter of Johann Heinrich Pestalozzi. He recruited Margaret E. M. Jones from London, England (1861–62) and another Pestalozzian expert, Hermann Krüsi *(q.v.)* in 1862. During Sheldon's tenure (1862–97), the Oswego State Normal and Training School became a major teacher-training institution in the country and the center of Pestalozzian influence and the object method of instruction.

Sheldon was the author of *A Manual of Elementary Instruction* (1862), *Lessons on Objects* (1863), *First Reading Book and Phonic Cards* (1863), *Teachers' Manual of Instruction in Reading* (1875), and *Autobiography of Edward Austin Sheldon,* edited by his daughter, Mary Downing Sheldon Barnes, and published in 1911. He was also the author of the Sheldon Readers series (1872–75) and Primary and Graded Spellers (1875–76). Sheldon was awarded honorary degrees by Hamilton College (1869) and the board of regents of the University of the State of New York (1875).

REFERENCES: *A C; DAB; EB; NCAB* (7:67); *NYT*, August 27, 1897, p. 7; *WWW* (H); Mary D. S. Barnes *(q.v.), Autobiography of Edward Austin Sheldon* (New York: Ives-Butler Co., 1911); Dorothy Rogers, *Oswego; Fountainhead of Teacher Education* (New York: Appleton-Century-Crofts, 1961); A. E. Winship, *Great American Educators* (New York: Weiner, 1900), pp. 145-61.                          *John F. Ohles*

SHELDON, William Evarts. B. 1832, Dorset, Vermont, to Julius King and Harriet (Newell) Sheldon. M. July 30, 1854, to Mary Ames Soule. Ch. three. D. April 16, 1900, Boston, Massachusetts.

William Sheldon attended Burr Seminary in Manchester, Vermont (1847–48 and 1850–53). Graduating in 1853, he became principal of a high school in East Abington (later, Rockland), Massachusetts, to 1858. He established a system of graded schools and instituted reforms in instruction and administration that resulted in requests to address many teachers' institutes and societies.

He was supervising principal of Boston primary schools and principal of Boston's Hancock School (1864–67). He initiated reforms based on Pestalozzian principles. Sheldon resigned from the Boston public schools to join a wool merchant firm in Boston (1867–69) and was principal of the Waltham (Massachusetts) grammar school from 1869. He was business manager of the *Boston Daily News* (c. 1873).

Sheldon was nationally known as a leader of progressive education movements and reforms. He published many articles and was well known for his addresses at teachers' organizations. He was editor of the *Massachusetts Teacher* (1860–65) and coeditor of *American Teacher* (1883–87). He was a founder of the *Journal of Education* in 1877 and served as advertising manager (1877–1900). He was an organizer of the National Teachers' Association (later, National Education Association), served as secretary (1882–83 and 1885–86) and as president (1887), and was instrumental in organizing the kindergarten department. He was president of the Plymouth County Teachers Association (1857), the Middlesex County Teachers' Association (1861–62), the Massachusetts Teachers' Association (1862–64), and the American Institute of Instruction (1867). He helped organize the Society of Arts (1862), which later was part of a merger that resulted in the formation of the Massachusetts Institute of Technology.

REFERENCES: *DAB; NCAB* (5:542); *WWW* (H); *Boston Transcript,* April 17, 1900.

*E. A. Scholar*
*Karen Wertz*

**SHEPARD, James Edward.** B. November 3, 1875, Raleigh, North Carolina, to Augustus and Hattie E. (Whitted) Shepard. M. November 7, 1895, to Annie Day Robinson. Ch. two. D. October 6, 1947, Durham, North Carolina.

James Edward Shepard received the Ph.G. degree (1894) in pharmacy from Shaw University in Raleigh, North Carolina, and the A.M. degree (1913) from Selma (Alabama) University.

He was a pharmacist (1894–98), a clerk in the office of the recorder of deeds in Washington, D.C. (1898–99), deputy collector of internal revenue in Raleigh, North Carolina (1900–05), and superintendent of fieldwork among blacks in the International Sunday School Association (1905–10).

In 1910 Shepard was instrumental in establishing the National Religious Training School and Chautauqua of Durham to give six weeks of instruction to black educators and clergymen to correct some of the educational deficiencies he had identified with the Sunday School Association. Bankrupt and auctioned in 1915, the school was bought and refinanced by Mrs. Russell Sage and reorganized as the National Training School to prepare teachers. In 1923 Shepard was able to obtain state support for the institution, and eventually it was named North Carolina Central University. The school prospered under Shepard's leadership and state support, and a school of law was added in 1940 and the school of library science in 1941. He served as president of the institution from 1910 until his death in 1947 and earned a national reputation as an educator.

Shepard was a charter member (1898) of the North Carolina Mutual Life Insurance Company, a founder and trustee of the Mechanics and Farmers Bank of Durham, and a trustee of Lincoln Hospital and the Lincoln School for Nurses in Durham. He was a member of the executive committee of the North Carolina Industrial Association.

Shepard was a field worker for the International Sunday School Association. He was a delegate and the only black speaker at the World's Sunday School Convention in Rome, Italy (1907). He traveled extensively in Europe, Africa, and Asia where he was a major spokesman for improved life for blacks in America. He received three honorary degrees.

REFERENCES: *DAB* (supp. 4); *LE* (I); *NCAB* (33:33); *WWW* (II); J. H. Franklin, *From Slavery to Freedom,* (New York: Alfred A. Knopf, 1963); *NYT,* October 7, 1947, p. 27; *Journal of Negro History* 33 (January 1948): 118–19.                                        *Don C. Locke*

**SHERA, Jesse Hauk.** B. December 8, 1903, Oxford, Ohio, to Charles Hypes and Jessie (Hauk) Shera. M. November 3, 1928, to Helen May Bickham. Ch. two.

Jesse Hauk Shera was awarded the B.A. degree (1925) in English literature from Miami (Oxford, Ohio) University, and he obtained the M.A. degree (1927) from Yale University and the Ph.D. degree (1944) in library science from the University of Chicago.

His library career began when he took a temporary job as an assistant cataloger at Miami University (1927–28). The advent of the Depression and the scarcity of teaching positions prompted him to choose librarianship as a career. From 1928 to 1940, Shera was associated with a special program sponsored at Miami by the Scripps Foundation for Research in Population Problems.

Shera was associate director of libraries at the University of Chicago (1944–47) and taught in the graduate library school (1947–52). In 1952 he was chosen dean of the school of library science at Western Reserve University (later, Case Western Reserve University) in Cleveland, Ohio, a post he held until his retirement in 1970. Under his leadership, the school gained international prominence for developing advanced ideas and techniques in librarianship and information science. Its center for documentation and communications research was the first of its kind to be associated with any library school.

Shera was a prolific writer, with articles and book reviews numbering in the hundreds. Among his books were *The Foundations of the Public*

*Library* (1949), *Bibliographic Organization* (with Margaret E. Egan, 1951), *Historians, Books, and Libraries* (1953), *Libraries and the Organization of Knowledge* (1965), *Documentation and the Organization of Knowledge* (1966), *Sociological Foundations of Librarianship* (1971), and *Foundations of Education for Librarianship* (1972). He was editor of *American Documentation* (1953–60) and Western Reserve University Press (1954–59) and was editor-in-chief of Wiley-Interscience Texts in Documentation and Library Science.

Shera was a member of presidential commissions, including those for the employment of the handicapped and library research and education. He was a delegate to the United Nations Educational, Scientific, and Cultural Organization's International Conference in Paris, France (1950), and the International Conference on Bibliographic Classification at Dorking, England (1957). He was a trustee of the Council of National Library Associations. He received the Beta Phi Mu, Melvil Dewey, and Joseph W. Lippincott awards. He was a member of many organizations, including the Association of American Library Schools (president, 1964–65) and the Ohio Library Association (president, 1963–64).

REFERENCES: *CA* (5–8); *CB* (June 1964); *LE* (V); *WW* (XXXVIII); Kathleen Molz, "A Profile of Jesse Shera," *Bulletin of Bibliography* 26 (April 1969): 33–36.                                              Gary D. Barber

**SHERWIN, Thomas.** B. March 26, 1799, Westmoreland, New Hampshire, to David and Hannah (Pritchard) Sherwin. M. June 10, 1836, to Mary King Gibbons. Ch. three. D. July 23, 1899, Dedham, Massachusetts.

Thomas Sherwin was sent at the age of seven to live with an uncle in Temple, New Hampshire, on the death of his mother. He attended his sister's district school for a while and studied with a Dartmouth student, Solomon P. Miles. At the age of fourteen, Sherwin was apprenticed to a clothier in Groton, Massachusetts, where he learned the trade and studied some Latin. In 1819 he left Groton to teach in the district school in Harvard, Massachusetts, and then prepared for college at the academies at Groton and Ipswich, Massachusetts. Despite a serious illness and part-time teaching duties at Groton and Leominster to pay tuition, he was graduated from Harvard University tenth in his class in 1825.

Sherwin was headmaster at Lexington (Massachusetts) Academy (1826) and a mathematics tutor at Harvard (1827). In 1828 Sherwin opened a private school for boys in Boston and joined his boyhood tutor, Solomon P. Miles, in 1829 to become a submaster at Boston's English High School, the first American high school. When Miles resigned, Sherwin was the unanimous choice to succeed him as the school's third headmaster (1837–69). The school became a model for public secondary schools across the country.

He wrote two mathematics textbooks, *Elementary Treatise on Algebra* (1841) and *Common School Algebra* (1845). He was a member of the editorial board of the *Massachusetts Teacher* from its founding in 1853 and was a frequent contributor.

Sherwin was a founding member of the American Institute of Instruction in 1830 (president, 1853–54) and the Massachusetts Teachers' Association in 1845 (first vice-president and president, 1849–50). He participated in founding the Massachusetts Institute of Technology (1861) of which he was a director and counselor until his death. Sherwin was elected to membership in the American Academy of Arts and Sciences.

REFERENCES: *AC; DAB; NCAB* (11:350); *WWW* (H).     *Stephen J. Clarke*

**SHIELDS, Thomas Edward.** B. May 9, 1862, Mendota, Minnesota, to John and Bridget (Burke) Shields. M. no. D. February 15, 1921, Washington, D.C.

The son of immigrant Irish parents, Thomas Edward Shields left home and entered St. Francis Seminary in Milwaukee, Wisconsin, in 1882, where he was soon recognized as outstanding in philosophy and science. He went to St. Thomas Seminary in St. Paul, Minnesota (1885–91). He was ordained by Archbishop John Ireland *(q.v.)* in 1891. While at St. Thomas he published the *Index Omnium* in 1888. He earned the A.M. degree (1892) from St. Mary's Seminary in Baltimore, Maryland, and the Ph.D. degree in biology (1895) from Johns Hopkins University in Baltimore.

After seven years as a seminary teacher and parish priest in Minnesota, Shields joined the staff of Catholic University in Washington, D.C., in 1902, becoming professor of psychology and education. He was a founder and the first dean of Catholic Sisters College of Catholic University (1911–21). He encouraged summer schools to upgrade the education of Catholic nuns. He founded the Catholic Correspondence School (1904–09). Frequently misunderstood and at times the object of strong opposition, Shields nevertheless fought to raise educational standards and make religious training less rigid.

He wrote several works, including *Psychology of Education* (1904), *The Education of Our Girls* (1907), *The Teaching of Religion* (1907), *Religion, First Book* (1908), *Second Book* (1909), *Third Book* (1910), *Third Reader* (1910), *Fourth Reader* (1915), *Fifth Reader* (1915), *The Making and Unmaking of a Dullard* (1909), *Teacher's Manual of Primary Methods* (1912), *The Philosophy of Education* (1917), and *Religion, Fourth Book* (1918). He established the Catholic Educational Press in 1908 and *The Catholic Educational Review* in 1911 and served as editor (1911–21).

REFERENCES: *DAB; WWW* (I); *New Catholic Encyclopedia* (New York: McGraw-Hill, 1967).     *James M. Vosper*

**SHINN, Josiah Hazen.** B. March 29, 1849, Russellville, Arkansas, to Josiah Carlock and Elizabeth Frances (Gilpin) Shinn. M. to Mildred Carlton Williams. Ch. one. D. September 3, 1917, Washington, D.C.

Josiah Hazen Shinn, a native of Arkansas, grew up and attended school in Kentucky and Ohio. He was graduated from Ohio Normal School and attended Northwestern Ohio University (later, Ohio Northern University) in Ada.

He was an instructor at schools in Kentucky and Ohio and then returned to Arkansas in 1882 where he taught high school in the Russellville school district. In 1884 he was made principal of the Russellville Male and Female High School, which also included the lower grades. He taught at Magnolia, Arkansas (1884–85). He became institute director for the state superintendent of public instruction (1885–90). He was president of the Arkansas State Teachers Association in 1886; he took a leading role in the establishment of a state normal school at Mount Nebo.

Shinn was state superintendent of public instruction from 1890 to 1894. He persuaded the legislature to make an appropriation for teacher education and thus established the first Chautauqua in Arkansas. He also established six district normal schools, opened for three-month terms, and state normal schools at Stuttgart, Morrilton, and Jonesboro with nine-month terms.

Shinn was a student of history, in particular, Arkansas history. He was the author of several books, including *History of the American People* (1893), *The History of Arkansas* (1898), *The History of Education in Arkansas* (1900), *Pioneers and Makers of Arkansas* (1908), and *History of Russia* (n.d.). He was the founder of the *Southern School Journal* (1889) and founded and edited *The Arkansas Teacher* (1884–85).

Some years before his death, he went to Washington, D.C., where he worked as an accountant for the Bureau of Indian Affairs. He devoted much of his time to statistical work for the Senate and House in the Congressional Library.

REFERENCES: *Centennial History of Arkansas* (Chicago: S. J. Clarke Publishing Co., 1922); vol. 1; *Courier Democrat* (Russellville, Arkansas), September 20, 1917; T. M. Stinnett and Clara B. Kennan, *All This and Tomorrow Too* (Little Rock: Arkansas Education Association, 1969), pp. 73-90.                                           *Allen Lee Thornell*

**SHIPPEN, William, Jr.** B. October 16, 1736, Philadelphia, Pennsylvania, to William and Susannah (Harrison) Shippen. M. 1760 to Alice Lee. Ch. nine. D. July 11, 1808, Germantown, Pennsylvania.

William Shippen, pioneer medical educator, received his early education at an academy headed by Samuel Finley in Nottingham, Maryland. He studied at the College of New Jersey (later, Princeton University), from which he was graduated in 1754. He then studied medicine under his father until 1757, when he went to London, England, to study. Later he went to the University of Edinburgh (Scotland) where he received the M. D. degree (1761).

He returned to Philadelphia in 1762 with a number of anatomical drawings and casts to start teaching anatomy; the first classes were conducted in the State House. In his teaching he performed dissections of human bodies, which aroused public animosity. His dissecting rooms were mobbed, and he once narrowly escaped from a mob. His courses were successful, and he offered courses on midwifery to medical students and to women who intended to practice midwifery.

In 1765 Shippen became professor of anatomy and surgery at the newly established medical school at the College of Philadelphia. He was appointed chief physician and director-general of the hospital in the Continental army in New Jersey in 1776. On April 11, 1777, Congress made him chief physician and director general of the Continental Army Hospital. Shippen submitted a plan for the reorganization of the Army Medical Department that was adopted by Congress.

Shippen was a member of the staff at the Pennsylvania Hospital in 1778, but resigned to serve with the United States Army. The army subjected Shippen to a court-martial on charges of financial irregularities in his department. He was acquitted and remained chief of the medical department of the Continental army until his resignation in 1781. In 1791 he rejoined the hospital staff and served until 1802.

The legislature repealed the charter of the College of Philadelphia in 1779 and created the University of the State of Pennsylvania (later, University of Pennsylvania). Shippen accepted a chair in the new school, and he became professor of anatomy, surgery, and midwifery at the University of Pennsylvania (1791). He was one of the founders of the College of Physicians of Philadelphia and was president from 1805 to 1808.

REFERENCES: *AC; DAB; NCAB* (10:384); *TC; WWW* (H); Ralph H. Major, *A History of Medicine* (Springfield, Ill.: Charles C Thomas Publisher, 1954), vol. 2.                                              *Richard M. Coger*

**SHORES, Louis.** B. September 14, 1904, Buffalo, New York, to Paul and Ernestine (Lutenberg) Shores. M. November 19, 1931, to Geraldine Urist. Ch. none.

Louis Shores, a leader in library education, received the A.B. degree (1926) from the University of Toledo (Ohio), the M.S. degree (1927) from the City College of New York, the B.S. degree (1928) from Columbia University, and the Ph.D. degree (1934) from George Peabody College for Teachers in Nashville, Tennessee.

Shores was reference librarian and professor at the New York Public

Library (1926–28) and at Fisk University in Nashville, Tennessee (1928–33). He served as librarian (1933–37) and director of the library school at George Peabody College (1933–46). He was dean of the library school and professor at Florida State University in Tallahassee from 1946 to his retirement in 1967. He served with the United States Air Force during World War II.

Shores was the author of *Origins of the American College Library, 1636-1800* (1935), *Bibliographies and Summaries in Education* (1936), *Highways in the Sky* (1947), *Mark Hopkins' Log and Other Essays* (1965), *The Library-College* (1966), and *Around the Library World in 76 Days* (1967) and coauthor of *Basic Reference Books* (1939) and *Challenges to Librarianship* (1953). He was editor of *Basic Reference Sources* (1954) and *Journal of Library History* (1965–68). He contributed many articles to library and educational journals. He was associate editor (1946–60) and editor from 1960 of *Collier's Encyclopedia*.

Active in professional associations, he was a director of the Association of College and Reference Librarians and president of the Southeastern Library Association (1950–52) and the Florida Library Association (1953). He was awarded the Beta Phi Mu Award (1967) and Mudge Citation (1967). He was awarded an honorary degree by Dallas Baptist College.

REFERENCES: *CA* (15–16); *LE* (III); *WW* (XXXVIII); *WWAE* (XVI).

*Dan L. Isaacs*

**SHOWALTER, Noah David.** B. February 22, 1869, Cass County, Nebraska, to Noah and Nancy (Shoopman) Showalter. M. March 12, 1895, to Arra Belle Thomas. Ch. five. D. August 4, 1937, Olympia, Washington.

Noah David Showalter introduced principles that shaped education in the state of Washington. He left Nebraska in 1891 for the Northwest. He attended the State Normal School (later, Central Washington State College) at Ellensburg, Washington, the University of Idaho (1893–96), and Idaho State Normal School (later, Lewis-Clark State College) at Lewiston, where he earned a teacher's certificate (1899). He earned the B.A. (1907) and M.A. (1908) degrees from the State College of Washington (later, Washington State University) at Pullman. He also studied at Stanford University and Teachers College, Columbia University.

Showalter served in Washington as a teacher in Whitman County rural schools (1894–95) and superintendent at Farmington (1899–1903) and Oakesdale (1903–05), and he was Whitman County superintendent of schools (1905–09). His rural school experiences led him to develop the first rural demonstration schools in the Northwest and to write a handbook for rural school administrators.

In 1909 he was head of the rural department of the State Normal School in Cheney (later, Eastern Washington State College) and became president in 1910. Shortly after his arrival, the main building burned to the ground in 1912, and he was faced with a state legislature that wanted to abandon the school in a time of teacher surplus. He was able to have the main building rebuilt and started a construction program that shaped the campus. Promoting the improved preparation of teachers, he helped draft legislation to upgrade teacher certification standards and implemented a four-year teacher preparation curriculum. Enrollment for the normal school went from 650 to 1,875 during his sixteen-year tenure.

Showalter resigned as president of the normal school in 1926 to manage his extensive real estate investments; he then entered politics and campaigned successfully for state superintendent of schools in 1928. He served two terms ending in 1936. At his prodding, the legislature passed a state school support bill and an improved certification standard for teachers. As state superintendent, Showalter encouraged schools to adopt child-centered curricula and build libraries. The office of state superintendent grew under his leadership to include departments of research and statistics, vocational education, and Indian education.

Showalter was the author of *A Handbook for Rural School Affairs* (1920) and served on the Washington educational code commission, the state board of education, and the joint board of higher curricula. He attended the World Conference on Education (1923) at San Francisco, California, where he was one of the founders and a trustee of the World Federation of Educational Associations. He was a member of many other professional organizations. He received an honorary degree from the College of Puget Sound in 1920.

REFERENCES: *LE* (I); *WWW* (I); Zita Lichtenberg, ed., *Washington Schools in the Good Old Days,* (Olympia, Wash.: Superintendent of Public Instruction, 1969), pp. 17–19; J. Orin Oliphant, *The Educational Services of President N. D. Showalter* (Spokane, Wash.: Inland American Printing Co., 1926); J. Orin Oliphant, *History of the State Normal School at Cheney, Washington* (Spokane, Wash.: Inland-American Printing Co., 1924), p. 81.                                        *Michael A. Balasa*

**SHUSTER, George Nauman.** B. August 27, 1894, Lancaster, Wisconsin, to Anthony and Elizabeth (Nauman) Shuster. M. June 25, 1924, to Doris Cunningham. Ch. one. D. January 25, 1977, South Bend, Indiana.

George Nauman Shuster interrupted his studies at the University of Notre Dame to serve in World War I and received the certificate of aptitude from the University of Poitiers, France. On his return to Notre Dame, he received the A.B. (1915) and A.M. (1920) degrees. He was a student of literature at Columbia University (1924–26) and received the Ph.D. degree (1940) from Columbia.

In 1924 he became managing editor of *Commonweal,* the weekly magazine edited by Catholic laymen; he resigned in 1937 rather than compromise his anti-Franco views. Shuster was head of the department of English at Notre Dame (1920–24) and taught English at Brooklyn (New York) Polytechnic Institute (1924–25) and St. Joseph's College for Women in Brooklyn, New York (1924–35). He was a fellow of the Social Service Research Council of Columbia University in Germany (1937–39).

On his return from Germany, Shuster was dean and acting president (1939–40) and president (1940–60) of Hunter College of the City University of New York. He was selected by the New York City Board of Higher Education because he was a leading Catholic liberal who could function effectively with Catholics and non-Catholics and with conservatives and liberals. As president he successfully withstood attempts by communists to gain influence at Hunter and efforts by the archbishop of New York to influence his stand on controversial issues. Hunter College gained in stature during Shuster's presidency. The college opened its doors to a number of distinguished refugees from nazism. With the end of World War II, Shuster served as deputy high commissioner for Germany, responsible for Bavaria (1950–51).

Turning down an offer to become chancellor of the municipal college system of New York City, Shuster returned to Notre Dame in 1960 to serve as special assistant to president Theodore M. Hesburgh. He developed the Center for the Study of Man in Contemporary Society, which attracted considerable foundation support and sponsored notable research.

Shuster was a prolific writer. Among his books are *Catholic Spirit in Modern English Literature* (1922), *Newman—Prose and Poetry* (1925), *English Literature* (1926), *The Hill of Happiness* (1926), *The Catholic Spirit in America* (1927), *The Eternal Magnet* (1929), *The Catholic Church and Current Literature* (1929), *The Germans* (1932), *Strong Man Rules* (1934), *Like a Mighty Army* (1935), *Brother Flo* (1938), *Look Away* (1939), *The English Ode* (1940), *Cultural Cooperation and the Peace* (1952), *Religion Behind the Iron Curtain* (1954), and *In Silence I Speak* (1956). He translated several books into English and was editor of Century College Texts in English (from 1932).

He was active in professional and civic affairs as an adviser to the American delegation to the London Conference on International Education (1945) and was a delegate to the United Nations Educational, Scientific, and Cultural Organization Conference in Paris, France (1946, 1958), chairman of the board of trustees of the Institute for International Education (1945), president of the Pestalozzi Foundation (1955), and the recipient of awards from several foreign countries and honorary degrees from many American and foreign colleges and universities.

REFERENCES: *CB* (October 1960); *LE* (III); *NCAB* (H:89); *NYT,* January 27, 1977, p. 38; *WW* (XXXVIII); Vincent P. Lannie, ed., *On the*

*Side of Truth* (Notre Dame, Ind.: University of Notre Dame Press, 1974). *Robert Hassenger*

**SIBLEY, Frederick Hubbard.** B. June 24, 1872, Oxford, Massachusetts, to Sumner and Maria Florence (Miller) Sibley. M. June 10, 1909, to Annabelle Pearson. Ch. two. D. April 2, 1941, Reno, Nevada.

Frederick Hubbard Sibley was graduated from Brown University in Providence, Rhode Island, with the Ph.B. degree (1898). During the next five years he served an apprenticeship in a machine shop and worked as a draftsman, and he attended night school at the Massachusetts Institute of Technology and at the Case School of Applied Science, (later, Case Western Reserve University) in Cleveland, Ohio, where he received the M.S. (1903) and M.E. (1905) degrees.

He was appointed an instructor in drawing and mechanical design at Case (1903) and assistant professor of mechanical engineering (1905–08). He became professor and head of the department of mechanical engineering at the University of Alabama (1908–12) and accepted the same positions at the University of Kansas in 1912. He was also director of the Fowler Shops and a consultant engineer to Kansas oil companies.

In 1920 he was appointed dean of the College of Engineering at the University of Nevada and held this position until his death. During Sibley's deanship both he and the college gained a national reputation. The college doubled its enrollment, expanded its curriculum, developed the Mackay School of Mines, and gained a reputation for scholarship and research. Sibley's initial research was on the flow of steam through nozzles; he later studied a wide variety of engineering problems, including concrete structural design, the efficiency of gear teeth, petroleum cracking, thermodynamics, and the strength of steel at high temperatures.

He authored many professional articles, was coauthor of *Elementary Mechanical Drawing* (1905), and wrote *A Textbook of Pure Mechanism* (1914) and *Engineering Thermo-Dynamics* (1930), a widely used standard text on the subject. He also wrote a historical novel, *Manchaung* (1937).

Sibley was a fellow of the American Association for the Advancement of Science and he held memberships in the American Society of Mechanical Engineers (president, Nevada chapter), the Society for Promotion of Engineering Education (president, West Coast chapter), and many other engineering organizations.

REFERENCES: *LE* (I); *NCAB* (36:61); *WWW* (I); *NYT,* April 4, 1941, p. 21. *Robert H. Truman*

**SILL, Anna Peck.** B. August 9, 1816, Burlington, New York, to Abel and Hepsibah (Peck) Sill. M. no. D. June 18, 1899, Rockford, Illinois.

Anna Sill, a pioneer in the education of women, attended the local rural school and Phipps' Union Seminary in Albion, New York (1837).

She taught in the Barre, New York, district school (1836–37) and at Phipps' Seminary (1838–43). She conducted a seminary for young ladies in Warsaw, New York (1843–46), and was head of the female department of Cary Collegiate Institute in Oakfield, New York (1846–49).

Congregationalist and Presbyterian leaders asked Sill to open a private girls' school in Rockford, Illinois, as an affiliate to Beloit (Wisconsin) Seminary. She began classes in 1849 with about sixty students in a furnished rent-free building and with little other support. In addition to donations from Rockford citizens for a school building, Sill secured funds from New York and New England to finance a second building to accommodate rising enrollments. She was appointed principal in 1852. With an emphasis on biblical and classical studies, Sill inaugurated a three-year course in 1854, a four-year course was instituted in 1865, and college degrees were conferred in 1882. Sill retired in 1884, living on the campus to her death. In 1892 the name of the institution was changed to Rockford College.

REFERENCES: *DAB; EB; NAW; WWW* (H).                     *M. Ann Dirkes*

**SILL, Edward Rowland.** B. April 29, 1841, Windsor, Connecticut, to Theodore and Elizabeth (Newberry) Roland Sill. M. February 1867 to Elizabeth Newberry Sill. Ch. none. D. February 27, 1887, Cleveland, Ohio.

Edward Rowland Sill was considered one of the great teachers of his time. His family moved to Cleveland, Ohio, where he was orphaned in 1853, and he lived with an uncle, Elisha Noyes Sill, in Cuyahoga Falls, Ohio. After a year of preparation at Phillips Academy in Exeter, New Hampshire, and another brief period at the preparatory school of Western Reserve College at Hudson, Ohio (later, Case Western Reserve University in Cleveland, Ohio), Sill attended Yale College where he was graduated in 1861. He was on the editorial board of the *Yale Literary Magazine* (1860–61) and, as class poet, delivered the class poem. He attended Harvard Divinity School in 1867.

Upon graduation from Yale, Sill began several years of drifting. He sailed around the Horn to California, where he worked as a post office clerk in Sacramento and a bank teller in Folsom. In 1866 he returned east to Cuyahoga Falls. In 1867 he moved to Brooklyn, New York, where he taught in a boys' school, translated Heribert Rau's *Mozart, A Biographical Romance,* and served as literary critic for the New York *Evening Mail.*

He returned to Ohio, where he taught school in Wadsworth (1868–69) and was superintendent of schools at Cuyahoga Falls (1869–70). In 1871 he taught classics and English in the Oakland (California) high school. Sill joined the faculty of the University of California as professor of English language and literature. He remained at the university until 1882, when he returned to Cuyahoga Falls, Ohio.

Sill was best known as a poet; his books include *Field Notes* (1868), *The Hermitage and Later Poems* (1868), *The Venus of Milo and Other Poems* (1883), *Poems* (1887), and *Hermione and other Poems* (1889).

His collected prose was published posthumously as *The Prose of Edward Rowland Sill* (1900) and his verse as *The Poems of Edward Rowland Sill* (1902).

REFERENCES: *AC; DAB; EB; NCAB* (7:249); *TC; WWW* (H).

*William W. West*

SILLIMAN, Benjamin. B. August 8, 1779, Trumbull, Connecticut, to Gold Selleck and Mary (Fish) Silliman. M. September 17, 1809, to Harriet Trumbull. M. September 17, 1851, to Sarah Isabella (McClellan) Webb. Ch. nine, including Benjamin Silliman, Jr. *(q.v.)*, scientist and professor at Yale University. D. November 24, 1864, New Haven, Connecticut.

Benjamin Silliman helped establish the independence of science from the classical curriculum. He matriculated at Yale College at the age of thirteen and pursued the classical curriculum. He was graduated in 1796, studied law in New Haven with Simeon Baldwin, and was admitted to the bar in 1802.

Silliman was a tutor at Yale (1799–1802) and was appointed Yale's first professor of chemistry and natural history in 1802. Given two years to qualify himself for teaching those subjects, he read widely and studied with James Woodhouse *(q.v.)* of the University of Pennsylvania. He delivered his first lectures at Yale in 1804 and was sent to Europe in 1805 to engage in further study and to search for books. In 1813 he helped establish the Yale Medical School and in 1818 founded *The American Journal of Science and Arts,* the oldest scientific journal in the United States, which he and his descendants edited for the next century.

Silliman made practical geological surveys, was a consultant for coal and gold mining, and isolated various chemical elements. But it was as a teacher, lecturer, and editor of various scientific textbooks that he gained recognition for science and himself. He prepared the way for the acceptance of science in the college curriculum but did not anticipate a future conflict between science and religion.

Silliman was the author of *Journals of Travel in England, Holland, and Scotland* (1810), *A Short Tour Between Hartford and Quebec* (1820), *Elements of Chemistry in the Order of Lectures Given in Yale College* (two volumes, 1830, 1831), *Consistency of Discoveries of Modern Geology with the Second History of the Creation and Deluge* (1837), and *Narrative of a Visit to Europe in 1851* (two volumes, 1853), and he edited William Henry's *Elements of Chemistry* (1808) and Robert Blakewell's *Introduction to Geology* (1829).

Retiring in 1853 as professor emeritus, Silliman continued his research. Shortly before his death he was appointed by Congress to the corporation that established the National Academy of Sciences. He was admitted to the American Philosophical Society in 1805. He was the first president (1840) of the American Association of Geologists and Naturalists (later, the American Association for the Advancement of Science). He was a member of American and foreign scientific societies. He was awarded honorary degrees by Bowdoin and Middlebury colleges. The rock-forming mineral Sillimanite was named for him.

REFERENCES: *AC; DAB; DSB; NCAB* (2:285); *TC; WWW* (H); John S. Brubacher *(q.v.)* and Willis Rudy, *Higher Education in Transition* (New York: Harper & Row, 1968); *NYT,* November 25, 1864, p. 4; John F. Fulton and Elizabeth H. Thomson, *Benjamin Silliman, 1779–1864, Pathfinder in American Science* (New York: H. Schuman, 1947).

*Jack K. Campbell*

**SILLIMAN, Benjamin, Jr.** B. December 4, 1816, New Haven, Connecticut, to Benjamin *(q.v.)* and Harriet (Trumbull) Silliman. M. May 14, 1840, to Susan Huldah Forbes. Ch. seven. D. January 14, 1885, New Haven, Connecticut.

Benjamin Silliman was greatly influenced by his father, a professor of chemistry and natural history in Yale College from 1802 to 1853, the most prominent and influential scientific man in America during the first half of the nineteenth century. As soon as he was graduated from Yale (1837) and received the A.M. degree (1840), Silliman became a teaching assistant to his father.

In 1846 he was appointed professor of practical chemistry and assisted in establishing the school of applied chemistry at Yale, which became the Sheffield Scientific School. He succeeded his father as professor of chemistry in the Yale Medical School and Yale College in 1853 and continued with the Scientific School to 1869, Yale College to 1870, and the Yale Medical School to his death in 1885.

He gave the first lectures in America on agricultural chemistry in New Orleans (1845–46). From 1849 to 1854, he spent some time as professor of chemistry in the medical department of the University of Louisville, Kentucky. He was a consultant in chemical and mining problems and made an important contribution when he investigated characteristics of petroleum for a company that owned the land on which Edwin L. Drake later drilled the first oil well in Pennsylvania.

His best-known books were two college texts, *First Principles of Chemistry* (1847) and *First Principles of Physics* (1859). He was also the author of *American Contributions to Chemistry* (1874) and was editor with Charles R. Goodrich of *The World of Science, Art, and Industry* (1854) and *The Progress of Science and Mechanism* (1854). He was associate editor (1838–64) and editor (1864–85) of the *American Journal of Science,* founded by his father.

He was a member of the Association of American Geologists and Naturalists, which became the American Association for the Advancement of Science in 1847. He was one of the fifty original members of the National Academy of Sciences, incorporated in 1863. Silliman served as a member of the New Haven common council (1845–49). He received honorary degrees from the University of South Carolina and Jefferson Medical College.

REFERENCES: *AC; DAB; DSB; NCAB* (2:386); *TC; WWW* (H); *American Journal of Science* 129 (February 1885): 85; *Nature* 31 (1885): 343; *NYT*, January 15, 1885, p. 5. *Saul Barron*

**SILVIUS, George Harold.** B. April 4, 1908, Virdi, Minnesota, to George A. and Mell (Goodwin) Silvius. M. August 29, 1931, to Josephine O. Edinger. Ch. one.

G. Harold Silvius earned the B.S. degree (1930) from Stout Institute (later, University of Wisconsin-Stout) in Menomonie, Wisconsin, the M.A. degree (1937) from Wayne State University in Detroit, Michigan, and the Ed.D. degree (1946) from Pennsylvania State University.

Silvius was a teacher of industrial arts in the Detroit public schools at the Parker School (1929–31) and Post Intermediate School (1931–35); he served as a critic teacher for Wayne State University (1935–40), and he taught at the Durfee Intermediate School (1940–41). He was assistant supervisor (1941–45) and supervisor (1945–46) of vocational education for the Detroit public schools. In 1946 he joined the faculty of Wayne State University where he was professor of industrial education and chairman of the department (1946–70).

Silvius wrote books in the field of industrial, vocational, and technical education, including *Safe Work Practices in Sheet Metal Work* (with Gerald Baysinger, 1948), *The Student Planning Book* (with Gerald Baysinger, 1941), *Teaching Successfully the Industrial Arts and Vocational Subjects* (with Estell H. Curry, 1953), *Safe Practices in Woodworking and Plastics* (with others, 1954), *Teaching Multiple Activities in Industrial Education* (with Estell H. Curry, 1956), and *Organizing Course Materials for Industrial Education* (with Ralph C. Bohn, 1961). He also contributed many articles to professional journals, including biographical sketches of distinguished educators to the *Journal of Industrial Teacher Education*. He was the editor for industrial arts of the *American Vocational Journal* (1957–63).

A member of many professional associations, Silvius was president of the National Association of Industrial and Technical Teacher Educators (1947–48), vice-president of the industrial arts division (1953–56), and vice-president (1963–66) of the American Vocational Association.

REFERENCES:*CA* (5–8); *LE* (III); *WW*(XXXVIII); *WWAE* (XXII); Leslie H. Cochran, "Dedication to G. Harold Silvius," *Journal of Industrial Teacher Education* 7 (Spring 1970): 5-8.                    *William D. Wolansky*

**SIMPSON, Roy E.** B. March 15, 1893, Santa Rosa, California, to George L. and Luella M. (Heath) Simpson. M. May 16, 1919, to Olive Shields. Ch. three.

Roy E. Simpson was graduated from the Santa Rosa (California) high school and studied at Heald's Business College in San Francisco, Armstrong College in Berkeley, and the University of California at Berkeley. He received the A.B. degree from Pomona College and the M.A. degree (1931) from Claremont College.

Simpson's entire career was spent in California. He taught at Anderson Union High School (1915–17) and left to enlist in the United States Army, which he served as ordnance sergeant (1917–19). Simpson returned to Anderson and became principal of the high school there (1919–27). He was principal of Emerson Junior High School in Pomona (1927–29), became principal of the Pomona Evening High School in 1930, and served as principal of both schools until 1933. He was district superintendent of Gilroy Union High School District and Gilroy Elementary School District (1933–37), city superintendent of schools at Santa Cruz (1937–39), and district superintendent of the South Pasadena-San Marino Union High School District and South Pasadena Elementary School District (1939–45).

He was appointed head of the public school system of California in 1945, serving until 1963. Simpson was a dynamic and innovative leader during the post–World War II era. He was a member of the Shasta County (California) Board of Education (1919–27) and president of the Association of California Public School Superintendents (1944) and national Council of Chief State School Officers (1953–54) and a member and officer of many other councils, boards, and commissions. He received three honorary degrees.

REFERENCES: *LE* (III); *WW* (XXXII); *WWAE* (XIX); "Appointment of Superintendent of Public Instruction," *California Schools* 16 (December 1945): 241; "Highlights of a Seventeen-Year Administration as Superintendent of Public Instruction," *California Schools* 32 (December 1962): 421-28; *Who's Who in the West* 8th ed. (Chicago: Marquis, 1962).
*Stratton F. Caldwell*

**SINNOTT, Edmund Ware.** B. February 5, 1888, Cambridge, Massachusetts, to Charles Peter and Jessie Elvira (Smith) Sinnott. M. June 24, 1916, to Mabel H. Shaw. Ch. three. D. January 6, 1968, New Haven, Connecticut.

Edmund Ware Sinnott, noted American botanist and educator, was the son of teachers. His father, a Harvard University graduate, taught geography and geology in the normal school at Bridgewater, Massachusetts, where Edmund Sinnott was graduated from high school.

Sinnott received the A.B. (1908), A.M. (1910), and Ph.D (1913) degrees from Harvard University. He began his career at Harvard as an Austin teaching fellow (1908–10), a Sheldon traveling fellow for botanical research in Australasia (1910–11), an assistant in botany (1911–12), and an instructor at the Forestry School and Bussey Institute (1913–15). He was professor of botany and genetics at Connecticut Agricultural College (later, University of Connecticut) at Storrs (1915–28), professor at Barnard College of Columbia University (1928–39), and professor at Columbia University (1939–40).

Sinnott joined the Yale University faculty in 1940 as Sterling Professor of Botany (1940–56) and chairman of the department of botany (1940–50), and was director of the Sheffield Scientific School and chairman of the division of science (1945–56) and dean of the graduate school (1950–56). Under Sinnott's leadership there was great growth in botanical studies, and the Sheffield School continued as one of the nation's best scientific research centers. He also served as director of the Osborn Botanical Laboratory and the Marsh Botanical Gardens while at Yale. Sinnott was noted for his research in plant genetics and promoted the concept of developing the brotherhood of man through the brotherhood of science.

He was the author of *Botany Principles and Problems* (1923), *Principles of Genetics* (with L. C. Dunn, 1925), *Cell and Psyche* (1950), *Two Roads to Truth* (1953), *The Biology of the Spirit* (1955), *Matter, Mind and Man* (1957), *Plant Morphogenesis* (1960), *The Bridge of Life* (1963), *Meetinghouse and Church in Early New England* (1963), and *The Problem of Organic Form* (1963). For a number of years Sinnott was editor-in-chief of the *American Journal of Botany*. He also wrote many papers on the subjects of anatomy, morphogenesis, and inheritance in the higher plants.

Active in many professional organizations, Sinnott was a fellow of the American Association for the Advancement of Science (vice-president, 1935, president, 1948), the American Society of Naturalists (president, 1945), and the Botanical Society of America (president, 1937). He was on the board of managers of the New York Botanical Gardens. He received honorary degrees from Northeastern and Lehigh universities.

REFERENCES: *CB* (October 1948); *LE* (III); *NCAB* (H:191); *WWW* (IV); *NYT,* January 7, 1968, p. 84. *Rebecca L. Sparks*

**SISSON, Edward Octavius.** B. May 24, 1869, Gateshead, England, to George and Mary (Arnott) Sisson. M. November 29, 1899, to Nellie May Stowell. M. July 3, 1947, to Astrid Honoria Seron. Ch. two. D. January 24, 1949, Monterey, California.

Edward O. Sisson was brought to the United States from England in 1882. He received the B.Sc. degree (1886) from Kansas State Agricultural College (later, Kansas State University) in Manhattan. He attended the University of Chicago, where he was awarded the A.B. degree (1893). He studied at the University of Berlin, Germany (1903–04) and received the Ph.D. degree (1905) from Harvard University.

A public school teacher and principal (1886–91), Sisson was principal of South Side Academy in Chicago, Illinois (1892–97). He was the director of Bradley Polytechnic Institute (later, Bradley University) in Peoria, Illinois (1897–1904). He was an assistant professor of education at the University of Illinois (1905–06), professor of education and director of the department of education at the University of Washington (1906–12), and head of the department of education at Reed College in Portland, Oregon (1912–13). Sisson was Idaho's first commissioner of education (1913–17) under the "Idaho plan" of reorganization of the state's public schools. Under his direction, the school laws were consolidated and simplified, teacher certification was made simpler and more flexible, and the school term was increased from five to seven months. He was president of the University of Montana (1917–21). From 1921 to his retirement in 1939 he was professor of philosophy at Reed College.

Sisson was the author of *The Essentials of Character* (1910), *The Social Emergency* (with others, 1913), *Principles of Secondary Education* (1914), and *Educating for Freedom* (1925). He was a fellow of the Philosophy of Education Society and president of its Pacific division in 1939. A member of many other professional organizations, he was awarded honorary degrees by the University of Montana (1935) and Reed College (1947).

REFERENCES: *LE* (II); *NYT,* January 25, 1949, p. 23; *WWAE* (XIII); *WWW* (I); *School and Society* 69 (February 5, 1949): 98. *John F. Ohles*

**SKINNER, Burrhus Frederic.** B. March 20, 1904, Susquehanna, Pennsylvania, to William Arthur and Grace Madge (Burrhus) Skinner. M. November 1, 1936, to Yvonne Blue. Ch. two.

B. F. Skinner received the A.B. degree (1926) from Hamilton College in Clinton, New York, and the M.A. (1930) and Ph.D. (1931) degrees from Harvard University.

Skinner sought to make a living as a writer but was not successful and turned to the study of psychology. He was a research fellow for the National Research Council at Harvard (1931–33) and a junior fellow of the Harvard Society of Fellows (1933–36). He taught psychology at the University of Minnesota (1936–45) and was professor of psychology and chairman of the department of psychology at Indiana University (1945–48). He joined the Harvard University faculty as professor of psychology in 1948 and became Edgar Pierce Professor in 1958.

Skinner became the chief exponent of operationism or operant behaviorism. He developed an air crib for baby care toward the end of World War II and the Skinner box, which was used in psychological research of the behavior of pigeons and rats. He developed programmed instruction and the teaching machine.

Skinner was the author of *Behavior of Organisms* (1938), *Walden Two* (1948), *Science and Human Behavior* (1953), *Verbal Behavior* (1957), *Schedules of Reinforcement* (with C. B. Ferster, 1957), *Cumulative Record* (1959), *The Analysis of Behavior* (with J. G. Holland, 1961), *The Technology of Teaching* (1968), *Contingencies of Reinforcement* (1969), and *Beyond Freedom and Dignity* (1971).

A Guggenheim Fellow (1944–45), Skinner was a member of many scientific and psychological associations and was the recipient of the Howard Crosby Warren Medal (1942) and the Hoyt Vandenberg trophy. He received several honorary degrees.

REFERENCES:*CA* (9–12); *CB* (January 1964); *LE* (III); *WW* (XXXVI); *WWAE* (XVI); Edwin H. Boring and Lindzey Gardner, eds., *A History of Psychology in Autobiography* (New York: Appleton-Century-Crofts, 1967); Burrhus Frederic Skinner, *Particulars of My Life* (New York: Alfred A. Knopf, 1976). *C. Roy Rylander*

**SKINNER, Charles Rufus.** B. August 4, 1844, Union Square, New York, to Avery and Charlotte Prior (Stebbins) Skinner. M. October 16, 1873, to Elizabeth Baldwin. Ch. six. D. June 30, 1928, Pelhamwood, New York.

Charles Rufus Skinner was educated in the district school and at Mexico (New York) Academy and Clinton Liberal Institute in Oswego County, New York.

He served on the Watertown board of education from 1875 to 1884. A member of the state legislature from 1877 to 1881, he was chairman of the committee on railroads and advocated a five-cent fare on the New York elevated railway. In 1881 he was elected as representative to Congress to finish the unexpired term of Thomas Collier Platt and was reelected and served until 1885; his chief interest was in postal matters.

After a year of editorial work, he became deputy state superintendent of public instruction in 1886, supervisor of teachers' institutes and teacher-training classes in 1892, and state superintendent of public instruction in 1895. He believed that the state should concentrate its educational efforts on the elementary schools, leaving the high schools and colleges to private enterprise and endowment. In 1904, when the department of public instruction merged with the state board of regents through legislation that Skinner himself sponsored, his position ceased to exist.

From 1906 to 1911 he was assistant appraiser of merchandise for the port of New York. He was librarian of the state assembly (1913–14) and in 1915 was given the newly created post of legislative librarian. Under him the legislative library became a quick reference library in which everything was arranged alphabetically. He retired in 1925.

Skinner was the author of *Watertown, New York, A History of Its Settlement and Progress* (1876), *New York Question Book* (1890), *Arbor Day Manual* (1891), *Manual of Patriotism for the Schools of New York* (1900), *The Bright Side* (1909), and *History and Government of New York* (1918).

He was president of the National Educational Association (1896–97). He received honorary degrees from Hamilton College, Colgate University, and Tufts University.

REFERENCES: *AC; DAB; NCAB* (10:388); *TC; WWW* (I); *NYT* July 1, 1928, p. 25.                                        *Paul J. Schafer*

**SLAGLE, Robert Lincoln.** B. March 7, 1865, Hanover, Pennsylvania, to William Augustus and Margaret Elizabeth (Stine) Slagel. M. May 28, 1896, to Gertrude Anna Riemann. Ch. none. D. January 29, 1929, near Indianapolis, Indiana.

Robert Lincoln Slagel, pioneer educator of South Dakota, received the A.B. (1887) and A.M (1890) degrees from Lafayette College in Easton, Pennsylvania, and the Ph.D. degree (1894) from Johns Hopkins University in Baltimore, Maryland. He studied nutrition at Wesleyan University in Middletown, Connecticut, with Wilbur Olin Atwater *(q.v.),* (1894–95).

Slagle was professor of natural sciences for a year at the Collegiate Institute in Groton, South Dakota, and professor of chemistry at South Dakota Agricultural College (later, South Dakota State University) from 1895 to 1897. He was professor of chemistry (1897–1906), secretary to the board of regents (1898–99), and president (1899–1906) of the South Dakota School of Mines (later, School of Mines and Technology). He returned to South Dakota Agricultural College as president (1906–14) and was president of the University of South Dakota (1914–29). During his tenure at the University of South Dakota, the enrollment tripled and the physical plant was enlarged. The university became a major regional institution under Slagle.

A fellow of the American Association for the Advancement of Science, Slagle was awarded honorary degrees from Lafayette College (1922) and the University of South Dakota (1927).

REFERENCES: *NCAB* (25:411); *NYT,* January 30, 1929, p. 21; *WWW* (I).                                        *John F. Ohles*

**SLOANE, William Milligan.** B. November 12, 1850, Richmond, Ohio, to James Renwick Willson and Margaret Anna Wylie (Milligan) Sloane. M. December 27, 1877, to Mary Espy Johnston. Ch. four. D. September 11, 1928, Princeton, New Jersey.

William Milligan Sloane was educated at Martha Washington Collegiate Institute in New York City and Columbia College (later, University) from which he received the A.B. (1868) and A.M. (1871) degrees. He studied at Berlin and Leipzig, Germany, and received the Ph.D. degree (1876) from the University of Leipzig.

He taught in the private Newell School (1868–72) and traveled to Europe as private secretary and research assistant to George Bancroft, United States minister to Germany, assisted Bancroft in writing the *History of the United States,* and was third secretary to the legation. Sloane returned to the United States and was assistant professor of Latin (1876–83) and professor of history and political science (1883–96) at the College of New Jersey (later, Princeton University). From 1896 to his retirement in 1916, Sloane was Seth Low Professor of History at Columbia University. He was Roosevelt Exchange Professor at the University of Berlin, Germany (1912–13).

Sloane was the author of *Life and Works of James Renwick Sloane* (1888), *The French War and the Revolution* (1893), *Life of James McCosh* (1896), *Napoleon Bonaparte, A History* (four volumes, 1896), *The French Revolution and Religious Reform* (1901), *The Balkans* (1914), *Party Government in the United States* (1914), *The Powers and Aims of Western Democracy* (1919), and *Greater France in Africa* (1924). He was editor of the *Princeton Review* (1886–89).

Active in professional associations, Sloane was president of the American Historical Association (1911), the American Academy of Arts and Letters (1920), and the National Institute of Arts and Letters (1910). He was decorated by France and Sweden and received honorary degrees from Columbia, Princeton, and Rutgers universities.

REFERENCES: *AC; DAB; NCAB* (21:95); *NYT,* September 12, 1928, p. 27; *TC; WWW* (I). *Gail Pasciuta Reigel*

**SMALL, Albion Woodbury.** B. May 11, 1854, Buckfield, Maine, to Albion Keith Parris and Thankful Lincoln (Woodbury) Small. M. June 20, 1881, to Valeria von Massow. Ch. one. D. March 24, 1926, Chicago, Illinois.

Albion Small was graduated with the A.B. degree (1896) from Colgate University in Hamilton, New York, and from Newton (Massachusetts) Theological Institution in 1879. Deciding not to enter the ministry, he studied in Berlin and Leipzig, Germany, from 1879 to 1881. He earned the Ph.D. degree (1889) from Johns Hopkins University in Baltimore, Maryland.

Upon his return to the United States, Small was appointed professor of history and political economy at Colby College in Waterville, Maine (1881–88), and was a reader in history at Johns Hopkins (1888–89). In 1889 he became Colby's fourth president and occupied the Babcock Chair of

Intellectual and Moral Philosophy. He was appointed head of the department of sociology at the University of Chicago in 1892 and was dean of the
graduate school of arts, literature, and science (1904–24).

Small was distinguished in sociology as one of the four founding fathers
of the discipline of sociology. Among his more than three hundred writings,
the most noted are *General Sociology* (1905), *Adam Smith and Modern
Sociology* (1907), *The Cameralists* (1909), *The Meaning of Social Science*
(1910), and what is regarded by many as his major work, *Between Eras:
From Capitalism to Democracy* (1913). His last book, *Analysis of Sociology,* appeared in 1924. He was founder and editor of the *American Journal
of Sociology* (1895–1926).

Small was vice-president and a member of the organizing committee of
the World's Congress of Arts and Sciences at the Louisiana Purchase
Exposition in St. Louis (1904). He received an honorary degree from Colby
College (1900).

REFERENCES: *DAB; NCAB* (25:242); *NYT,* March 25, 1926, p. 23; *TC;
WWW* (I).                                              *Arthur J. Newman*

**SMART, James Henry.** B. June 30, 1841, Center Harbor, New Hampshire,
to William Hutchings and Nancy (Farrington) Smart. M. July 21, 1870, to
Mary H. Swan. Ch. two. D. February 21, 1900, Lafayette, Indiana.

James H. Smart received his early education in his father's school and in
the Concord (New Hampshire) high school.

He began his teaching career in the public schools of Claremont, New
Hampshire (1859), and was a teacher and principal in New Hampshire
schools (1860–63). He was principal of intermediate schools at Toledo,
Ohio (1863–65) and served as superintendent of the Fort Wayne, Indiana,
city schools (1865–75). During his administration the Fort Wayne school
system attained excellent status for discipline, scholarship, and general
progress, and he satisfactorily resolved problems between the public and
parochial schools. To have access to a better teaching staff, he established
at Fort Wayne one of the first teacher-training schools west of the Allegheny Mountains. He was the first school administrator in the Midwest to
employ special teachers in the public schools in art, music, reading, and
writing.

In 1874, he was elected Indiana state superintendent of public instruction
and served to 1881. He was instrumental in raising teaching standards,
promoting secondary education, and establishing uniform courses of study
in the state. He was a publisher's agent in Indiana from 1881 to 1883.

In 1883 Smart was appointed president of Purdue University (1883–
1900). Under his leadership, the university developed into one of the
largest, best equipped, and most prosperous technical schools in the
United States. He was particularly instrumental in the development of the

schools of engineering. A school of pharmacy was also organized under Smart.

Smart was author of *A Manual of School Gymnastics* (1864), *Commentary on the School Law of Indiana* (1881), and *Teachers Institutes* (1885), and edited *The Indiana Schools and the Men Who Have Worked in Them* (1876).

Smart was assistant commissioner for Indiana to the Vienna (Austria) Exposition (1872), United States commissioner at the Paris (France) Exposition (1878), and United States commissioner at the Agricultural Congress at the Hague in the Netherlands (1891). He was president of the Indiana State Teachers Association (1871), the National Educational Association (1881), and the American Association of Agricultural Colleges and Experiment Stations (1890). He was a member of the Indiana State Board of Education for twenty-seven years. He received honorary degrees from Dartmouth College and Indiana University.

REFERENCES:*DAB; NCAB* (6:106); *WWW* (I). *Donna H. Wernz*

**SMITH, Bunnie Othanel.** B. May 29, 1903, Clarksville, Florida, to Isma Isaac and Lula (Cox) Smith. M. August 29, 1929, to Tommie Naomi Harkey. Ch. two.

B. O. Smith received the B.S. degree (1925) from the University of Florida at Gainesville and the M.A. (1932) and Ph.D. (1938) degrees from Columbia University.

Smith was an assistant principal at the Bay County (Florida) High School (1925–26), science teacher at Brooksville, Florida (1926–27), and high school principal and supervising principal at Tallahassee, Florida (1927–30). He was an assistant professor at the University of Florida (1930–37). He taught at the University of Illinois at Urbana-Champaign until his retirement (1937–70) and was chairman of the department of history and philosophy of education from 1966. He returned to Florida and was affiliated in 1970 with the University of South Florida at Tampa. Smith made contributions of basic importance to several areas of educational analysis. He conducted studies of the concepts, methodology, and limits of education as a discipline and contributed to curriculum theory. He was a pioneer in the analytic study of educational concepts and was a leader in the improvement of teacher education.

Smith was the author of *Logical Aspects of Educational Measurement* (with others, 1938), *The Improvement of Practical Intelligence* (with others, 1943), *Fundamentals of Curriculum Development* (with others, 1950), *Social Foundations of Education* (with others, 1951), *A Study of the Logic of Teaching* (with Milton Meux, 1952), *Democracy and Excellence in Secondary Education* (with others, 1963), *A Study of the Strategies of Teaching* (with others, 1967), and *Teachers for the Real World* (1969). He edited *Language and Concepts in Education* (with R. H. Ennis, 1961) and *Research in Teacher Education* (1971). He was editor of *Progressive Education* (1947–52), assistant editor of *Curriculum Journal* (1934–40), and a member of the editorial board of the *Encyclopedia of Educational Research* (1960) and *Journal of Teacher Education* (1959–62).

Active in professional associations, Smith was president of the National Society of College Teachers of Education (1949) and the Philosophy of Education Society (1956–57). He was vice-president of the American Educational Research Association (1967–69). He was chairman of the advisory council of the Association of Organizations of Teacher Education. Smith received the Centennial Award of the University of Florida (1953) and the John Dewey Society Award (1975).

REFERENCES: *LE* (IV); *WW* (XXXVIII).                           *Ronald D. Szoke*

**SMITH, Charles Alfonso.** B. May 28, 1864, Greensboro, North Carolina, to Jacob Henry and Mary Kelly (Watson) Smith. M. November 8, 1905, to Susie McGee Heck. Ch. three. D. June 13, 1924, Annapolis, Maryland.

C. Alfonso Smith attended the Greensboro, North Carolina, public schools and was graduated from Davidson (North Carolina) College with the A.B. (1884) and A.M. (1887) degrees. He received the Ph.D. degree (1893) from Johns Hopkins University in Baltimore, Maryland.

Smith taught for four years in three North Carolina communities and served as an instructor of English at Johns Hopkins (1890–93) and as professor of English language and literature at Louisiana State University (1893–1902). He was a professor of English at the University of North Carolina (1902–07) and also was head of the English department (1907–09) and dean of the graduate department (1903–09). In 1909 Smith became Edgar Allan Poe Professor of English at the University of Virginia, serving to 1917, when he became head of the department of English at the United States Naval Academy in Annapolis, Maryland. He continued at Annapolis to his death.

Smith was distinguished by his writing, including among his books *Repetition and Parallelism in English Verse* (1894), *An Old English Grammar* (1896), *Elementary English Grammar* (1903), *Studies in English Syntax* (1906), *The American Short Story* (1912), *What Can Literature Do for Me?* (1913), *O. Henry Biography* (1916), *Keynote Studies in Keynote Books of the Bible* (1919), and *New Words Self-Defined* (1919). He was the author of several collections of literary works and was coauthor of the Smith-McMurry Language Series (with Lida B. McMurry, 1919) and editor-in-chief of *Library of Southern Literature* (seventeen volumes, 1907–23). While at the University of North Carolina, he founded and edited *Studies in Philology*.

Smith was Roosevelt Professor of American History and Institutions at the University of Berlin, Germany (1910–11). Active in professional and literary organizations, he was president of the central division of the Modern Language Association of America (1897–99) and founder of the Virginia Folk-Lore Society. He was the recipient of three honorary degrees. He was a brother of Henry Louis Smith *(q.v.)*.

REFERENCES: *DAB; NYT*, June 14, 1924, p. 11; *WWW* (I). *John F. Ohles*

**SMITH, Daniel B.** B. July 14, 1792, Philadelphia, Pennsylvania, to Benjamin and Deborah (Morris) Smith. M. 1824 to Esther Morton. Ch. one. D. March 29, 1883, Germantown, Pennsylvania.

Daniel B. Smith was educated at a Friend's school in Burlington, New Jersey, under John Griscom *(q.v.)*, a noted Quaker educator. Smith developed an interest in the physical sciences and became an apprentice in pharmacy at John Biddle's drugstore in Philadelphia, Pennsylvania. Upon completion of his training, Smith became a partner to Biddle. Smith established his own pharmacy in 1819 and continued in that business to 1849.

Smith was active in the founding of the Philadelphia College of Pharmacy (1821) and served as its third president from 1829 to 1854. From 1834 to 1846 Smith also taught English literature and chemistry at Haverford (Pennsylvania) School (later, College). In 1846 Smith returned to the active practice of pharmacy but sold his drugstore in 1849 to devote his time to experimental work at his laboratory outside Philadelphia.

Smith was the author of *The Principles of Chemistry for the Use of Schools, Academies and Colleges* (1837) and *The Dispensatory of the United States of America* (with George B. Wood, *q.v.*, and Franklin Bache, 1833). He gained his reputation in large part by contributing articles to professional journals, including the *Journal of the Philadelphia College of Pharmacy* (later, *American Journal of Pharmacy*).

Smith was a founder of the Apprentices' Library (1820), the Franklin Institute (1824), the Historical Society of Pennsylvania (first secretary, 1825), and the House of Refuge (1828). He was the first president of the American Pharmaceutical Association (1852).

REFERENCES: *AC; DAB; NCAB* (5:343); *WWW* (H).

*Barbara Ruth Peltzman*

**SMITH, David Eugene.** B. January 21, 1860, Cortland, New York, to Abram P. and Mary E. (Bronson) Smith. M. January 19, 1887, to Fanny Taylor. M. November 5, 1940, to Eva May Luse. Ch. none. D. July 29, 1944, New York, New York.

David Eugene Smith attended school in Cortland, New York, and received the Ph.B. (1881), Ph.M. (1884), and Ph.D. (1887) degrees from Syracuse (New York) University and the M.Pd. degree (1898) from Michigan State Normal College (later, Eastern Michigan University) at Ypsilanti. He also studied in Europe at various times, including in 1907–08.

He practiced law with his father in Cortland (1881–84) and taught mathematics at the State Normal School (later, State University of New York College) at Cortland (1884–91), and at Michigan State Normal College (1891–98). He was principal of the State Normal School at Brockport, New York (1898–1901), and became professor of mathematics at Teachers College, Columbia University, in 1901, remaining there to his retirement in 1926. Smith exerted a major influence on mathematics education in the United States and on the history of mathematics. He established the first secondary education methods course in the United States.

A prolific writer, Smith was the author or collaborator of many textbooks. Among his writings were *Plane and Solid Geometry* (with Wooster W. Beman, 1895), *History of Modern Mathematics* (1896), *Higher Arithmetic* (1898), *Teaching of Elementary Mathematics* (1900), *Elements of Algebra* (1900), *Geometric Paper Folding* (1901), *Academic Algebra* (1902), *Rara Arithmetica* (1908), *Teaching of Arithmetic* (1909), *Hindu-Arabic Numerals* (with L. C. Karpinski, 1911), *Teaching of Geometry* (1911), *A History of Japanese Mathematics* (with Y. Mikami, 1914), *Number Stories of Long Ago* (1919), *Our Indebtedness to Greece and Rome in Mathematics* (1922), *Progress of Mathematics in the Last Twenty-five Years* (1923), *History of Mathematics* (two volumes, 1923, 1925), *Source Book of Mathematics* (1929), *History of Mathematics in America before 1900* (with Jekuthiel Ginsburg, 1934), *Poetry of Mathematics and other Essays* (1934), and *The Wonderful Wonders of 1, 2, 3* (1937). He was editor of *A Portfolio of Portraits of Eminent Mathematicians* (part 1, 1905, part 2, 1906, and part 1, 1936, part 2, 1937).

He served as mathematics editor for many encyclopedias, including *New International Encyclopedia* (1902–06), *Monroe's Cyclopedia of Education* (1911–13), and *Encyclopaedia Britannica* (1927). He was editor of the *Bulletin of the American Mathematical Society* (1902–20) and associate editor of *The American Mathematical Monthly* (1916). He helped found and was associate editor of *Scripta Mathematica* in 1932.

Smith was active in many professional associations as president of the International Commission on the Teaching of Mathematics (1928–32 and honorary president, 1932–44) and the Mathematical Association of America (1920–21) and founder and president of the History of Science Society (1927). He was a fellow of the American Association for the Advancement of Science and the Medieval Academy of America. He received the Gold Star of the Order of Elmi from the government of Persia (1933) and was the recipient of three honorary degrees.

REFERENCES: *DAB* (supp. 3); *LE* (II); *NCAB* (E:218); *TC; WWW* (II); *NYT,* July 30, 1944, p. 35.                                    *Charles E. Davis*

**SMITH, Dora Valentine.** B. February 14, 1893, Minneapolis, Minnesota, to Alexander Warden and Jane (Deas) Smith. M. no.

Born on Valentine's Day, Dora Smith was given the middle name Valentine. She was graduated from West High School in Minneapolis, Minnesota, and received the A.B. (1916), A.M. (1919), and Ph.D. (1929) degrees from the University of Minnesota. She also studied at the University of London, England (1920–21), and Teachers College of Columbia University (1928–29).

Smith was a high school teacher at Long Prairie, Minnesota (1916–17), and an English teacher and supervisor of student teachers at the University High School at the University of Minnesota (1917–27); she continued as a professor of education and director of graduate students and research in English teaching at Minnesota to her retirement in 1958. She taught at St. George's College in London, England (1920–21), and the Lincoln School of Teachers College, Columbia University (1927–28). A leader in English education, she was responsible for training two generations of leaders in English language arts.

Smith's publications include *Reading and Literature* (three volumes, with E. M. Haggerty, 1928), *Teaching English in the Junior High School* (with E. H. Webster, 1925), *Instruction in English,* monograph No. 20 of the National Survey of Secondary Schools (1932), *Evaluating Instruction in Elementary School English* (1937), and *Evaluating Instruction in Secondary School English* (1937). She was editor and director of the National Council of Teachers of English Commission on the English curriculum reports, *The English Language Arts* (1952), *Language Arts for Today's Children* (1954), and *The English Language Arts in Secondary Schools* (1956). She was a frequent contributor to professional journals.

Smith was president of the National Conference for Research in English (1937–38) and the National Council of Teachers of English (1936–37). She was chairman of the elementary section of the National Council of Teachers of English (1942–45) and director of the curriculum commission of the National Council of Teachers of English from 1946. She was a consultant in English on the National Survey of Secondary Schools conducted by the United States Office of Education (1931–32) and consultant in English to the New York Regents' Inquiry (1936–37). She was a member of the Advisory Committee on Secondary Education to the United States Office of Education from 1949. She received an honorary degree from Rhode Island College of Education.

REFERENCES: *LE* (III); *WW* (XXVIII); *WWAE* (VIII); R. H. Beck, "Educational Leadership, 1906–1956," *Phi Delta Kappan* 37 (January 1956): 164. *William W. West*

**SMITH, Eleanor.** B. June 15, 1858, Atlanta, Illinois, to Willard Newton and Matilda (Jaspersen) Smith. M. no. D. June 30, 1942, Midland, Michigan.

Eleanor Smith, pioneer in public school music, attended school in Chicago, Illinois. She was graduated from the Cook County (Illinois) Normal School and attended the Hershey School of Music in Chicago, where she studied voice under Fannie Root and musical composition under Frederic Grant Gleason. She traveled to Berlin, Germany, where she studied vocal music with Julius Hay and musical composition with Meritz Meszkewski.

After studying in Europe (1887–91) she taught music at the Chicago (Illinois) Kindergarten College. She taught at the Chicago Normal School for Teachers with Francis Parker *(q.v.)* and with John Dewey *(q.v.)* at the school of education of the University of Chicago (1901–10). She was active in promoting the teaching of music in the public schools. In association with Jane Addams' Hull House, she founded the Hull House School of Music in 1893 and was its director until she retired in 1935.

Smith was well known as a writer of textbooks, including *Songs of Life and Nature* (1898), *Eleanor Smith Music Course* (four volumes, 1908), *Eleanor Smith Music Course Manual* (1909), *Eleanor Smith Music Primer* (1911), and Modern Music Series (1898–1910). She also compiled *The Children's Hymnal* (with others, 1918) and *Song Devices and Jingles* (1920) and composed "The Quest," "Hull House Songs," and three operettas, *Trolls Holiday, A Fable in Flowers,* and *The Merman's Bride.*

REFERENCES: *NCAB* (35:499); *NYT,* July 1, 1942, p. 25; John William Leonard, ed., *Woman's Who's Who of America* (New York: American Commonwealth Co., 1914). *LeRoy Barney*

**SMITH, Francis Henney.** B. October 18, 1812, Norfolk, Virginia, to Francis Henney and Anna (Marsden) Smith. M. June 9, 1835, to Sara Henderson. Ch. seven. D. March 21, 1890, Lexington, Virginia.

Francis Henney Smith was graduated from the United States Military Academy at West Point, New York, in 1833 and was commissioned a second lieutenant. He taught geography, history, and ethics at West Point (1834–36). Resigning his commission in 1836, he accepted the position of professor of mathematics at Hampden-Sydney (Virginia) College.

In 1839 he was appointed the first superintendent with the rank of major and professor of mathematics at the newly founded Virginia Military Institute (VMI) in Lexington, Virginia. For fifty years (1839–89) Smith administered VMI and changed its emphasis from the preparation of teachers to practical application of the sciences. Early in his career he arranged an instructional exchange with Washington College (later, Washington and Lee University), also in Lexington. In 1846 he introduced the first course in industrial chemistry in the South emphasizing the practical use of scientific knowledge. Burned in 1864, VMI continued in operation in Richmond, Virginia, and by October 1865 was back in Lexington. When Smith resigned as superintendent, VMI was one of the foremost military schools in the country.

Smith translated Jean Baptiste Biot's *Analytical Geometry* (1840) and wrote *American Statistical Arithmetics* (with Robert M. T. Duke, 1845), *The Best Methods of Conducting Common Schools* (1849), *College Reform* (1850), *An Elementary Treatise on Algebra* (1855), and *The Virginia Military Institute,* published posthumously in 1912.

REFERENCES: *AC; DAB; NCAB* (26:297); *TC; WWW* (H).

*Charles A. Reavis*

**SMITH, Harold Babbitt.** B. May 23, 1869, Barre, Massachusetts, to Samuel Francis and Julia Asenath (Babbitt) Smith. M. June 15, 1894, to Laura Dertha Smith. M. September 28, 1911, to Persis Helen Smith. Ch. three. D. February 9, 1932, Worcester, Massachusetts.

After graduation from Barre (Massachusetts) High School, Harold Babbitt Smith attended Cornell University where he received a degree in mechanical engineering in 1891. He began graduate studies at Cornell but went to the University of Arkansas in 1892 as professor of electrical engineering. In 1893 he left Arkansas to accept a position as head designer and electrical engineer for the Elektron Manufacturing Company of Springfield, Massachusetts.

Smith resumed his academic career later in 1893 as professor of electrical engineering at Purdue University in Lafayette, Indiana, where he founded the electrical engineering department and served as director of the school of engineering until 1896. He taught at Worcester (Massachusetts) Polytechnic Institute from 1896 to 1931, where he established and headed the electrical engineering department. Worcester received national recognition for its excellent electrical engineering department.

Smith was recognized as a pioneer in electrical engineering education and was known in both academic circles and in industry. He was active as a consulting engineer and was an engineer and designer for the Westinghouse Electric and Manufacturing Company of Pittsburgh, Pennsylvania (1905–13). He was an innovator in the development of high-voltage power transmission equipment and carried on extensive research in dielectric equipment, anenomena, and electric stress distribution.

During World War I Smith was an associate member of the Naval Consulting Board and consultant to a special board concerning antisubmarine devices. He was a fellow of the American Association for the Advancement of Science and the American Institute of Electrical Engineering (director, 1920–24, vice-president, 1924–26, president, 1929–30) and was a member of the American Engineering Council (1930–32) and

other professional associations.
REFERENCES: DAB; WWW (I); NYT, February 10, 1932, p. 23.
                                                    Jordan Greer

**SMITH, Henry Lester.** B. April 2, 1876, Bloomington, Indiana, to Samuel Thomas Wishard and Sarah Ellen (Cathcart) Smith. M. February 3, 1915, to Johnnie Wilson Rutland. Ch. three. D. October 25, 1963, Bloomington, Indiana.

Henry Smith studied at Indiana University, receiving the A.B. (1898) and A.M. (1899) degrees, and at Columbia University, where he received the M.A. (1910) and Ph.D. (1916) degrees.

He was a principal at the Hayden (Indiana) high school (1897). He also served Indiana schools as principal (1899–1901) and superintendent (1901–05) at Brookville and supervising principal at Indianapolis (1905–08). He was appointed superintendent of the United States government schools in the Panama Canal Zone (1908–09).

Smith was superintendent of schools at Bloomington, Indiana (1909–15), and an instructor in school administration at Indiana University (1911–15). He spent a year as assistant superintendent of schools in Minneapolis, Minnesota (1915–16). Returning to Indiana from Minneapolis, he began a long career as dean of the school of education at the University of Indiana (1916–46). Under Smith's leadership, the university established programs for training school nurses and librarians, a department for training teachers in physical education, a course in special education for the handicapped, and a division of visual aids.

On a leave of absence from the university in 1918–19, he was director of the rehabilitation division of the Federal Board for Vocational Education. He was a state consultant in school construction planning and was director of the state division of schoolhouse construction (1949–56). He was research director of the Palmer Foundation (1947–57).

Smith authored many books, including *Practice of Medicine as a Vocation* (1919), *Teaching as a Vocation* (1919), *Suggestions on School Planning* (1924), *Education in Latin America* (with Harold Littel, 1934), *An Introduction to Education* (with Velous Martin, 1941), *Comparative Education* (1941), *Education in Mexico* (1942), *Educational Research, Principles, and Practices* (1944), *One Hundred Fifty Years of Grammar Textbooks* (with others, 1946), and *Character Education in the Public Schools of the U.S.* (1948). He coauthored several school textbooks and compiled bibliographies on educational subjects. He was editor of Educational Publications and on the editorial board of *Education Digest* and *Educational Abstracts*. He also made local and national radio broadcasts of his views on education.

Smith was president of the National Education Association (1934), the department of superintendence of the National Education Association, the National Council of Education (1925–31), the Indiana State Teachers' Association (1921–22), the Indiana Council on Education (1938–40), and the National Association of Colleges and Departments of Education (1942). He was secretary-general of the World Federation of Education Associations (1941–47). He received an honorary degree from Butler University.

REFERENCES: *LE* (III); *NCAB* (I:212); *WWAE* (XII); *WWW* (IV); *NYT,* October 27, 1963, p. 88.      *Karen H. Westerman*

SMITH, Henry Louis. B. July 30, 1859, Greensboro, North Carolina, to Jacob Henry and Mary Kelly (Watson) Smith. M. August 4, 1896, to Julia Lorraine Dupuy. Ch. seven. D. February 27, 1951, Greensboro, North Carolina.

Henry Louis Smith received the A.B. (1881) and A.M. (1886) degrees from Davidson (North Carolina) College and attended the University of Virginia (1886–87), where he received the Ph.D. degree (1890).

Smith organized and was first principal of Selma (North Carolina) Academy (1881–86). Smith was first interested in physics and served as professor of physics and astronomy in Davidson College (1887–1901). Early in his career at Davidson, he organized regular laboratory work for students in physics and geology. Practical surgery benefited from Smith's experiments with x-rays in which he made a photograph of a hand to find the position of a bullet. This was believed to have been the first x-ray picture made in the United States. Smith continued to experiment with the x-ray, promoted its use by surgeons, and originated the use of x-ray with surgical cases in the United States.

Smith's greatest contribution was as a college and university president. He became president of Davidson College in 1901 and remained as president for eleven years. During his term the number of students tripled, the physical plant, the college endowment and the faculty doubled, and the college's entrance requirements were standardized.

Smith accepted the presidency of Washington and Lee University in Lexington, Virginia, in 1912, continuing to his retirement in 1930. Under Smith, the faculty and student enrollment of Washington and Lee doubled and the endowment fund increased.

Smith lectured on the sciences, education, and topics of civic concern. His books include *YourBiggest Job* (1920), *America Interwoven with Great Britain* (1921), *The Culture Afforded by Scientific Study* (1922), *Enriching One's Vocabulary* (1936), *Climbing Upward* (1937), and *This Troubled Century* (1947).

Smith was president of the North Carolina Teachers' Assembly (1889) and the Association of Virginia Colleges (1914–15). He was a member of the American Academy of Political and Social Science, the American

Association for the Advancement of Science, and the American Society for Broader Education (director). He received an honorary degree from the University of North Carolina in 1899. He was a brother of Charles Alfonso Smith *(q.v.)*.

REFERENCES: *LE* (I); *NCAB* (40:46); *NYT* February 28, 1951, p. 27; *WWAE* (XI); *WWW* (III); Ollinger Crenshaw, *General Lee's College* (New York: Random House, 1969); *Wilson Library Bulletin* 25 (April 1951): 639.                                                          *Earl W. Thomas*

**SMITH, John.** B. December 21, 1752, Rowley, Massachusetts, to Joseph and Elisabeth (Palmer) Smith. M. to Mary Cleaveland. M. to Susan Mason. Ch. two. D. April 30, 1809, Hanover, New Hampshire.

John Smith prepared for college at Dummer Academy. He entered Dartmouth College in Hanover, New Hampshire, in 1771 and was graduated with the B.S. degree in 1773.

Smith was preceptor at Moor's Charity School and studied theology under Eleazar Wheelock *(q.v.)*, a Dartmouth president. He was a tutor at the college from 1774 to 1778. In 1778 he declined a pastorate in Connecticut to accept the chair of languages at Dartmouth, where he was professor until his death. Smith was college librarian for thirty years (1779–1809) and associate pastor (1773–87) and pastor (1787–1809) of the college church.

He was an expert in the Samaritan, Chaldaic, and Arabic languages. His publications include *Hebrew Grammar* (1772), *The New Hampshire Latin Grammar* (1802), and edition of Cicero's *De Oratore* (1804), and *Greek Grammar* (1809). His wife Susan Mason Smith edited his memoirs, which were published in 1843.

He was a trustee of Dartmouth (1788–1809). He received an honorary degree from Brown University (1803).

REFERENCES: *AC; NCAB* (9:95); *WWW* (H).          *Michael R. Cioffi*

**SMITH, John Rubens.** B. January 23, 1775, Convent Garden, London, England, to John Raphael and Hanna (Croome) Smith. M. April 14, 1809, to Elizabeth Pepperal Sanger. Ch. one, John Rowson Smith, artist. D. August 21, 1849, New York, New York.

John Rubens Smith, painter, drawing master, engraver, and art teacher, learned draftsmanship from his father, John Raphael Smith, a mezzotint engraver. By the age of twenty-one Smith had exhibited in the Royal Academy of Art. He had shown some fifty of his paintings, including many portraits, in the annual exhibitions of the Royal Academy (1796–1811).

He moved to the United States by 1809 and established himself as an artist in Boston, Massachusetts, where he executed a series of topographical water colors that depicted many local landmarks, including Beacon Hill and Old South Church. He and his family moved to Brooklyn, New York, where he established a drawing academy (1814). He moved to Philadelphia, Pennsylvania, in the 1830s where he established another drawing school. Among Smith's students were several eminent artists.

Smith was the author of a number of books, including *The Juvenile Drawing-Books* (1847), *A Compendium of Picturesque Anatomy* (1827), and *A Key to the Art of Drawing the Human Figure* (1831). Under the pseudonym Neutral Tint, he engaged in many literary controversies, which led to his exclusion from the National Academy of Design.

REFERENCES: *DAB; WWW* (H); George C. Croce and David H. Lawrence, *The New-York Historical Society's Dictionary of Artists in America* (New Haven, Conn.: Yale University Press, 1957).      *Roger H. Jones*

**SMITH, Nathan.** B. September 30, 1762, Rehoboth, Massachusetts, to John and Elizabeth (Ide) Hills Smith. M. January 16, 1791, to Elizabeth Chase. M. September 1794 to Sarah Hall Chase. Ch. ten. D. January 26, 1829, New Haven, Connecticut.

Nathan Smith is also reported to have died in July 1829 and in 1828. He was a physician, surgeon, and educator; he founded the medical departments at Dartmouth, Yale, and Bowdoin colleges. In his youth he helped his father farm in Massachusetts and Chester, Vermont, where he served in the militia and spent approximately two years during the later part of the Revolutionary War on the northern frontier of Vermont. At the age of twenty-two while engaged in teaching school, he assisted Josiah Goodhue of Putney, Vermont, in an operation at Chester, Vermont. He decided to become a physician, spent a year in preparation, and for three years was a pupil, assistant, and apprentice to Dr. Goodhue. He began the practice of medicine at Cornish, New Hampshire, in 1787. He attended the Institute of Medicine at Harvard University (1789–90) and received the M.B. degree (1790).

Smith returned to his medical practice in Cornish and gave some private instruction in medicine. The three medical schools in the United States were located at Harvard and Columbia colleges and the University of Pennsylvania. Smith believed there should be a medical school more centrally located in New England and proposed establishing a professorship of theory and practice of medicine to the trustees of Dartmouth College in Hanover, New Hampshire. He spent a year of study abroad in Glasgow and Edinburgh, Scotland; and London, England. In August 1798 the trustees formally approved his plan and elected him professor, a position he held until 1814. The medical department expanded under his leadership.

Smith became professor in surgery and medicine at Yale College and persuaded the Connecticut legislature to appropriate money for a medical building, medical library, and botanical garden. He continued as head of the Yale medical department to his death in 1828. In 1824 he organized the medical department of Bowdoin College in Brunswick, Maine, and delivered a series of lectures on medicine and surgery. He gave similar lectures at the University of Vermont (1822–25) where his son, Nathan Ryno Smith, had established a department of medicine.

Smith was the author of *Practical Essays on Typhus Fever* (1821) and *Medical and Surgical Memoirs* with addenda by his son, Nathan R. Smith. He edited the *American Medical Review* (1824–26). He was elected president of the Vermont State Medical Society in 1811 and received honorary M.D. degrees from Dartmouth College and Harvard University.

REFERENCES: *AC; DAB; NCAB* (3:153); *TC; WWW* (H).

*C. Roy Rylander*

**SMITH, Nila Banton.** B. October 10, 1890, in Altoona, Michigan, to George Addison and Ella (Banton) Smith. M. no. D. December 13, 1976, Los Angeles, California.

Nila Banton Smith was graduated with the Ph.B. degree summa cum laude from the University of Chicago (1928) and received the M.A. (1929) and Ph.D. (1932) degrees from Columbia University.

She returned to Michigan in 1928 and was supervisor of reading in the Detroit public schools to 1933. She was head of the department of education at Greensboro (North Carolina) College (1933–34) and dean of the school of education at Whittier (California) College (1934–37). She served as associate professor of education at Indiana University (1937–39), professor of education at the University of Southern California (1939–49), and director of reading instruction at New York University (1949–63). She was Distinguished Service Professor of Education at Glassboro (New Jersey) State College (1963–68) and taught at the University of Southern California from 1968.

She wrote *One Hundred Ways of Teaching Silent Reading* (1925), *Picture Story Reading Lessons* (with S.A. Courtis, *q.v.,* 1925), *American Reading Instruction* (1934), *Adventures in Teacher Education* (1937), *Learning to Read* (1945), *Frontiers Old and New* (with Stephen F. Bayne, 1947), *Distant Doorways* (edited with Stephen F. Bayne, 1956), *On the Long Road* (with Stephen F. Bayne, 1956), *The Best in Children's Literature* (1962), *Reading Instruction for Today's Children* (1963), *Read Faster and Get More from Your Reading* (1968), and *Be a Better Reader* (1970–71).

Smith was president of the International Reading Association (1963–64), a member of the Association for Childhood Education, and other professional organizations. She received a citation merit award from the International Reading Association.

REFERENCES: *CA* (21–22); *LE* (IV); *WW* (XXVI); *Who's Who of American Women,* 9th ed. (Chicago: Marquis, 1975).              *Joan Duff Kise*

**SMITH, Payson.** B. February 11, 1873, Portland, Maine, to John Parker and Margaret (Bolton) Smith. M. April 18, 1898, to Carrie Emily Swasey. Ch. one. D. March 11, 1963, Portland, Maine.

Payson Smith was educated at Westbrook Seminary in Portland, Maine, and Tufts College (later, University) in Medford, Massachusetts, from which he received the A.M. degree (1903).

Smith was an instructor at Westbrook Academy (1897–99) and was principal of the Canton (Maine) high school (1899–1901). He was superintendent of schools at Rumford (1901–03) and Auburn (1904–07), Maine. Smith served as state superintendent of public schools of Maine (1907–17) and commissioner of education for Massachusetts (1917–35). He was an advocate of vocational and industrial education and a pioneer in the vocational school movement. He introduced home economics and manual training in Maine normal schools and initiated summer schools in Maine. He lectured on educational administration and was a member of the faculty of the graduate school of education at Harvard University (1935–40) and was professor of education at the University of Maine (1940–50).

Active in professional associations, Smith was chairman of the committee on teacher education for the American Council on Education (1938) and active in the National Education Association as a member of the Educational Policies Commission and the committee for a national academy of education of the National Council of Education. He was president of the Institute for Instruction and chairman of the national committee for the Horace Mann Centenary (1937). He was a member of the National Conference on Financing Education (1933) and a consultant to the President's Advisory Committee on Education (1938). He received several honorary degrees from American colleges and universities.

REFERENCES: *LE* (III); *WWAE* (VIII); *WWW* (IV). *Charles W. Ryan*

**SMITH, Samuel Stanhope.** B. March 16, 1750, Pequea, Pennsylvania, to Robert and Elizabeth (Blair) Smith. M. June 28, 1775, to Ann Witherspoon. Ch. nine. D. August 21, 1819, Baltimore, Maryland.

Samuel Stanhope Smith was said to have studied Latin and Greek at the age of six in his father's academy. He was graduated from the College of New Jersey (later, Princeton University) with the A.B. (1769) and A.M. (1772) degrees. He was licensed to preach in 1773 and was ordained to the Presbyterian ministry in 1774.

Smith was an assistant in his father's academy (1769–70) and a tutor at the College of New Jersey (1770–73). He served as a missionary in western Virginia (1774–75) and was a pastor in churches at Cumberland and Briery, Virginia. Smith founded and was first president of Hampden-Sydney (Virginia) Academy (later, College) from 1775 to 1779. He was professor of moral philosophy (1779–95) and vice-president (1786–95) of the College of

New Jersey and succeeded John Witherspoon *(q.v.)*, his father-in-law, as president (1795–1811).

Smith was an effective administrator, repairing damage to the college suffered during the Revolution, providing a unique course incorporating the humanities and sciences, and restoring discipline among the students. He was the author of *An Essay on the Causes of the Variety of Complexion and Figure of the Human Species* (1787), *Lectures on the Evidence of the Christian Religion* (1790), *Sermons* (1801), *Lectures on the Subjects of Moral and Political Philosophy* (two volumes, 1812), *A Continuation of Ramsey's History of the United States* (n.d.), and *Principles of Natural and Revealed Religion* (1815).

Secretary of the board of trustees of the College of New Jersey (1781–95), he was a member of the committee that drew up the plan for the organization of the Presbyterian church (1786) and was an honorary member of the American Philosophical Society. He received honorary degrees from Yale College (1783) and Harvard University (1810).

REFERENCES: *AC; DAB; NCAB* (2:21); *TC; WWW* (H); Samuel Holt Monk, "Samuel Stanhope Smith: Friend of Rational Liberty," in Willard Thorp, ed., *The Lives of Eighteen from Princeton* (Princeton: Princeton University Press, 1946).                                   *Joseph P. Cangemi*
*Thomas E. Kesler*


**SMITH, Thomas.** B. July 17, 1808, Lancaster, Pennsylvania, to n.a. M. 1828 to Martha McKay. M. to Hannah Rydall. Ch. four. D. August 1885, Little Rock, Arkansas.

Thomas Smith was eight years old when his father died, leaving a widow with eight children. The boy worked on a nearby farm, attended district school during the winter, and married and began to teach school at the age of twenty. He moved to West Newton, Pennsylvania, where he taught and studied medicine with Dr. John Hassen. In 1834 he attended a medical school in Cincinnati, Ohio, for a year and practiced medicine. In 1848 he was graduated with honors from the medical school.

After six years of medical practice in Cincinnati, Smith moved to Keokuk, Iowa, engaged in a prosperous practice, and taught in a local medical school. He moved to St. Louis and volunteered for service in the Union army in 1861. In 1864 he joined a group of wealthy migrants to Arkansas seeking to engage in planting cotton and settled in Helena to practice medicine.

In 1868 he was a delegate to the Arkansas constitutional convention in Little Rock, served on the education committee, and helped write the articles on education. He became the first state superintendent of public instruction, serving from 1868 to 1872. During his term, he directed the first statewide census of school-age children, organized the state's school system, established the state teachers' association, and established the state's first educational journal.

Smith left the state but returned in 1881 and practiced medicine to his death. He served as the first president of the Arkansas State Teachers' Association (1869–71) and editor of the *Arkansas Journal of Education* for three years.

REFERENCES: T. M. Stinnett and Clara B. Kenman, *All This and Tomorrow Too* (Little Rock: Arkansas Education Association, 1969).

*John F. Ohles*

**SMITH, William.** B. September 7, 1727, Aberdeen, Scotland, to Thomas and Elizabeth (Duncan) Smith. M. June 3, 1758, to Rebecca Moore. Ch. eight. D. May 14, 1803, Philadelphia, Pennsylvania.

After attending King's College at the University of Aberdeen, Scotland, and studying for the Anglican ministry (1743–47), William Smith left without a degree or ordination and served as a parochial schoolmaster.

Smith emigrated to America in 1751 and served as a tutor on Long Island, New York. He drew up a plan for a mechanic's school in 1753 and sent a copy to Benjamin Franklin *(q.v.),* who suggested that he should teach at the College of Philadelphia (later, University of Pennsylvania). In 1753 he returned to England where he was ordained in the Anglican church and claimed the right to the M.A. degree. He returned to Pennsylvania in 1754 where he taught at the College of Philadelphia and became first provost of the college (1755–79). He proposed a plan for the college that embraced the widest course of study and variety of subjects of any other college in America at the time.

During the French and Indian War, Smith was jailed for libelous statements he made about the Pennsylvania legislature. He was in England (1762–64) where he sought funds for the college. In 1779 the Pennsylvania legislature revoked the charter of the college and Smith moved to Chestertown, Maryland, where he served as rector of the Chester parish (1779–89). He established a classical seminary that was chartered as Washington College; he served as president of the college from 1782 to 1789. Smith returned to the College of Philadelphia as provost when the charter was restored in 1789 and continued to his retirement in 1791.

Smith was the author of *Brief Account of the Province of Pennsylvania* (1775), *Bouquet's Expedition Against the Western Indians* (1765), and *Poems of Nathaniel Evans with Memoirs* (1772).

Active in church affairs, Smith presided over the first convention of the American branch of the church in Philadelphia (1760) and the third convention in Perth Amboy, New Jersey (1764). He was president of the convention that organized the Protestant Episcopal church in Maryland and was elected first bishop, but his election was not ratified. He was secretary of the board of trustees of the College of Philadelphia (1764–90) and president of St. Andrews Society of Philadelphia and of a society to care for widows and children of Protestant Episcopal clergymen.

REFERENCES: *AC; DAB; NCAB* (1:340); *TC; WWW* (H); Albert Frank Gegenheimer, *William Smith: Educator and Churchman* (Philadelphia: University of Pennsylvania Press, 1943); Thomas Firth Jones, *A Pair of Lawn Sleeves: A Biography of William Smith (1727–1803)* (Philadelphia: Chilton, 1972).                                     *Walter F. C. Ade*

**SMITH, Zachariah Frederick.** B. January 7, 1827, Henry County, Kentucky, to Zachariah and Mildred (Dupuy) Smith. M. 1852 to Sue Helm. M. 1890 to Anna Pitman. Ch. three. D. July 5, 1911, Louisville, Kentucky.

Zachariah (in some accounts called Zachary) Frederick Smith began his formal education at Bacon College in Harrodsburg, Kentucky (a forerunner of Kentucky University), which eventually merged with Transylvania University in Lexington, Kentucky. He served as a curator (trustee) of Kentucky University and in the same capacity under the merged university. He was the last living curator among the original Transylvania University curators.

Smith was a farmer to 1860, when he became president of Henry College, New Castle, Kentucky. He served as president of the college during and after the Civil War. In 1867 he ran successfully for the office of superintendent of public instruction, serving until 1871. During his tenure, he improved the public schools by supporting schools through increased taxes, extending educational opportunities for the state's youth, and raising standards for teachers and school commissioners and trustees.

Smith became president of the Cumberland and Ohio Railroad but resigned in 1873 to become associated with the Austin and Pacific Railroad and other railroads under construction in the Southwest.

Smith wrote several histories, including *History of Kentucky* (1886), *School History of Kentucky* (1889), *Memoirs of the Mother of Henry Clay* (1900), *The Battle of New Orleans* (1904), and *History of Reformation of the Nineteenth Century, 1800–1832* (n.d.). He served as an official with D. Appleton and Company, publishers. He founded and served twelve years as president of the Kentucky Christian Education Society.

REFERENCES: *AC; NCAB* (9:546); *WWW* (I); *Biographical Encyclopedia of Kentucky of the Dead and Living Men of the Nineteenth Century* (Cincinnati: J. M. Armstrong and Co., 1878), pp. 239-40; Barksdale Hamlett, "History of Education in Kentucky," *Bulletin of Kentucky Department of Education* 7 (July 1914): 105-10; Alvin Fayette Lewis, *History of Higher Education in Kentucky,* U.S. Bureau of Education Circular of Information No. 3 (Washington, D.C.: Government Printing Office, 1899); *Louisville Courier Journal,* July 5, 1911; Robert Peter,

*Transylvania University: Its Origins, Rise, Decline, and Fall* (Louisville: John P. Morton and Co., 1896), pp. 176-77; Mary Young Southard and Ernest C. Miller, eds., *Who's Who in Kentucky* (Louisville: Standard Printing Co., 1936), p. 250. *Robert D. Neill*

**SMYTH, William.** B. February 2, 1797, Pittston, Maine, to Caleb and Abiah (Colburn) Smyth. M. 1827 to Harriet Porter. Ch. nine. D. April 4, 1868, Brunswick, Maine.

William Smyth received his early education in local schools. At the age of seventeen his parents died, and he assumed the responsibility for his younger brother and sister. To provide for them he enlisted in the army during the War of 1812, taught at a private school, and assisted the principal of an academy in Gorham, Maine. Smyth also prepared himself for college and entered Bowdoin College in 1820 as a junior, graduating as valedictorian in 1822, even though he was almost blind. He then completed a year at Andover (Massachusetts) Theological Seminary.

He joined the faculty of Bowdoin College in 1823 as a professor of Greek and was professor of mathematics (1828-68). He was a college professor of the old school, a competent scholar who was an able teacher with a wide variety of interests. He introduced the use of a blackboard in teaching algebra to his students.

Smyth authored a series of textbooks that were widely used; his algebra book was highly acclaimed. Among his works were *Plane Trigonometry* (1828), *Algebra* (1830), *Elementary Algebra For Schools* (1833), *Lectures on Modern History* (1849), *Treatise on Algebra* (1852), *Plane Trigonometry, Surveying and Navigation* (1855), *Analytical Geometry* (1855), and *Elements of the Differential and Integral Calculus* (1856).

Smyth was interested in public schools and served seventeen years as a member of the Brunswick (Maine) board of agents. He was influential in establishing graded schools in the state of Maine. He participated in antislavery activities, and his home was a station in the underground railroad. A licensed Congregational preacher, he received the D.D. degree from Bowdoin College in 1863.

REFERENCES: *AC; DAB; NCAB* (10:474); *TC; WWW* (H).
*Robert McGinty*

**SNAVELY, Guy Everett.** B. October 26, 1881, Antietam, Maryland, to Charles Granville and Emma (Rohrer) Snavely. M. September 27, 1905, to Ada Rittenhouse. M. April 6, 1950, to Louise Hutcheson. M. July 17, 1964, to Madelyn Hale. Ch. three. D. March 12, 1974, Birmingham, Alabama.

At the age of fifteen Guy Everett Snavely enrolled as a Romance language student at Johns Hopkins University in Baltimore, Maryland, from which he received the A.B. (1901) and Ph.D. (1908) degrees. He was an instructor in the Maryland Nautical Academy in Easton, Maryland (1901–02), and was part owner and vice-principal of Milton Academy in Baltimore, Maryland (1902–05).

Snavely joined the faculty of Allegheny College in Meadville, Pennsylvania, teaching Latin and French (1906–19) and served as registrar from 1908. During World War I he was granted leave from Allegheny to assume the southern directorship of the American Red Cross. He served as dean of Converse College in Spartanburg, South Carolina (1919–21). He was president of Birmingham-Southern College in Birmingham, Alabama (1921–38). Under his leadership Birmingham-Southern assumed a significant pioneering role in in-service education and experienced an unprecedented growth in enrollment, a major expansion of physical facilities, and a fourfold increase in endowments.

In 1937 the Association of American Colleges named Snavely its executive director, a post he held until 1954. Under Snavely the association made marked strides in providing an effective voice for college administrators, in stimulating an interest in the fine arts on member campuses, and in assisting colleges to develop more adequate funding programs. He was an adviser to the United States Information Service (1954–55) and returned to the presidency of Birmingham-Southern (1955–57), where he was named chancellor (1957), a position he held until his death.

Snavely was a frequent contributor to philosophical, religious, and educational journals and was the author of *Choose and Use Your College* (1941), *A Short History of the Southern Association of Colleges and Secondary Schools* (1945), *The Church and the Four Year College* (1955), and *A Search for Excellence: Memoirs of a College Administrator* (1964).

Active in many organizations, Snavely was a director of the National Conference of Christians and Jews (1950–53) and a member of the executive committee of the American Council on Education (1927–30 and 1933–36, vice-president, 1937) and National Advisory Committee on Education (1929). He was president of the Association of American Colleges (1929), the Association of Alabama Colleges (1926), and the Alliance Francaise (from 1945) and national president of Kappa Phi Kappa (1927–31) and Omicron Delta Kappa (1935–37). He was the recipient of twenty-six honorary degrees from American colleges and universities.

REFERENCES: *CA* (5–8); *CB* (April 1951); *LE* (IV); *NCAB* (E:339); *WWAE* (XII); *WWW* (VI); *Liberal Education* 60 (May 1974): 153-55; Joseph H. Parks and Oliver C. Weaver, Jr., *Birmingham-Southern College, 1856–1956* (Nashville: The Parthenon Press, 1957); Wilbur Dow Perry, *A History of Birmingham-Southern College, 1856–1931* (Nashville: Methodist Publishing House, 1931); Guy E. Snavely, *A Search for Excellence* (New York: Vantage, 1964); *Time* 63 (January 11, 1954): 47.

*David E. Luellen*

**SNEDDEN, David Samuel.** B. November 19, 1868, Kavilah, California, to Samuel and Anna (O'Keefe) Snedden. M. June 30, 1898, to Genevra Sisson. Ch. six. D. December 1, 1951, Palo Alto, California.

Taught to read, write, and spell by his mother, David Samuel Snedden first attended school at the age of fourteen and enrolled in a new district one-room school that was opened in 1884. He received the A.B. (1890) and M.A. (1892) degrees from St. Vincent's College in Los Angeles and a second A.B. degree (1897) from Stanford (California) University. He was awarded the A.M. (1901) and Ph.D. (1907) degrees from Teachers College, Columbia University.

Snedden taught school in California at Fairview (1890–91) and Fillmore (1891–92) and was a teacher and grammar and high school principal at Santa Paula (1892–95). He was superintendent of schools at Paso Robles, California (1897–1900). Snedden was an assistant professor of education at Stanford University (1901–05) and adjunct professor of education at Columbia University (1905–09).

Snedden was the first Massachusetts state commissioner of education (1909–16). A pioneer in educational sociology, he was an exponent of education for social efficiency and a leader in the extension of vocational education. In 1916 Snedden returned to Columbia University as professor of education and continued until his retirement in 1935.

Snedden was the author of *Administration of Education for Juvenile Delinquents* (1906), *School Reports and School Efficiency* (with William H. Allen, 1907), *Educational Administration in the United States* (with Samuel Dutton, q.v., 1908), *Problems of Vocational Education* (1911), *Problems of Educational Readjustment* (1914), *Problems of Secondary Education* (1917), *Vocational Education* (1920), *Sociological Determiniation of Objectives in Education* (1921), *Educational Sociology* (1922), *What's Wrong with American Education?* (1927), *Educational Sociology for Beginners* (1928), *Toward Better Schools* (1931), *American High Schools and Vocational Schools in 1960* (1931), *Toward Better Education* (1931), *Education for Political Citizenship* (1934), and *Introductory Sociology for Teachers* (1935). He was editor of *Vocational Education* (from 1922).

Active in professional associations, Snedden was the first president of the National Society for Vocational Education (1918–20).

REFERENCES: *LE* (II); *WWAE* (VIII); *WWW* (V); W. T. Bawden, *q.v.,* "David Samuel Snedden," *Industrial Arts and Vocational Education* 41 (April 1952): 8A; Walter H. Drost, *David Snedden and Education for Social Efficiency* (Madison: University of Wisconsin Press, 1967); *School and Society* 74 (December 15, 1951): 382.                    *David C. Gardner*

**SNYDER, Franklyn Bliss.** B. July 25, 1884, Middletown, Connecticut, to Peter Miles and Grace (Bliss) Snyder. M. June 15, 1909, to Winifred Perry Dewhurst. Ch. two. D. May 11, 1958, Evanston, Illinois.

The son of a Congregational minister, Franklyn Bliss Snyder was graduated from Beloit (Wisconsin) College in 1905 and received the A.M. (1907) and Ph.D. (1909) degrees from Harvard University. He was a fellow in English at Beloit (1905–06) and a Thayer Fellow at Harvard (1908–09).

Northwestern University was the focal point of Snyder's life. His presence was felt for four decades as he rose from instructor of English in 1909 to professor (1918–49). He was appointed dean of the graduate school in 1934. Three years later he became vice-president and dean of faculties of the university. In 1939 he was elected president of Northwestern University, a post he held for a decade. In 1936 he was Alexander Lecturer at the University of Toronto.

Snyder made numerous contributions to English journals and magazines. He also published *The English of Business* (with Ronald S. Crane, 1921), *A Book of American Literature* (with E. D. Snyder, 1927), *The Life of Robert Burns* (1932), and *The Life of Robert Burns—His Personality, His Reputation and His Art* (1936). He edited *A Book of English Literature* (with R. G. Martin, 1916).

He served many professional and civic groups. He was a trustee of Beloit College and the Carnegie Foundation for the Advancement of Teaching, an honorary member of the board of governors of the National College of Education, a member of the board of directors of the Evanston Hospital Association, and a member (1940) and president (1941) of the board of visitors of the United States Naval Academy. He received the Navy Civilian Distinguished Service Award in 1949. He was elected a fellow of the Society of Antiquaries of Scotland (1932). Snyder also held memberships in a number of other organizations. He received many honorary degrees.

REFERENCES: *LE* (III); *NCAB* (F:236); *WWAE* (XIII); *WWW* (III); *NYT* May 12, 1958, p. 29.                                                      *Jerry L. Johns*

**SOARES, Theodore Gerald.** B. October 1, 1869, Abridge, England, to Augusto and Kathleen Mary (Carbery) Soares. M. July 10, 1894, to Lillian May Martin. Ch. one. D. November 20, 1952, Pasadena, California.

Theodore Gerald Soares began his education in London, England, schools and worked as a clerk. When he was seventeen years old, his family emigrated to the United States, settling in Minneapolis, Minnesota. He attended the University of Minnesota where he received the B.A. (1891) and A.M. (1892) degrees. He was granted the Ph.D. (1894) and B.D. (1897) degrees from the University of Chicago.

Ordained in the Baptist ministry (1894), Soares served in Illinois as pastor of churches in Rockford (1894–99), Galesburg (1899–1902), and Oak Park (1902–05). In addition to his pastoral duties, he was an extension lecturer on biblical literature at the University of Chicago. In 1906 he was appointed professor of homiletics and religious education at Chicago and remained there to 1930. From 1919 to 1925 he was in charge of the Hyde Park Congregational Church in Chicago.

Soares joined the faculty of the California Institute of Technology as professor of philosophy and ethics in 1930 and continued in that position until he retired as professor emeritus in 1945. In 1930 he resigned from the Baptist denomination and became a member of the Congregational and Unitarian fellowships, serving as minister of the Neighborhood Church in Pasadena, California, until 1945.

Soares was nationally known as a speaker. He was special speaker for the Young Men's Christian Association at United States Army camps in 1918. In 1927 he gave the Earl Lectures at the Pacific School of Religion. He was a member of the board of preachers at Harvard University (1922–30 and 1931–39).

Soares's books include *The Supreme Miracle and Other Sermons* (1904), *His Life Series* (1905), *Heroes of Israel* (1909), *Lessons from the Great Teachers* (with Lillian Soares, 1911), *A Baptist Manual* (1911), *The Social Institution and Ideals of the Bible* (1915), *Studies in Comradeship* (1919), *A Study of Adult Life* (1923), *How to Enjoy the Bible* (1924), *Religious Education* (1928), *The Story of Paul* (1930), *Three Typical Beliefs* (1937), *The Origins of the Bible* (1941), and *The Growing Concept of God in the Bible* (1943). He served as a member of the board of editors of *The Biblical World* and *The American Journal of Theology*.

Soares was active on the Council on Religious Education (president, 1914–16) and was a founder of the Religious Education Association (president, 1921–24). He received honorary degrees from Knox College and Meadville Theological School.

REFERENCES: *LE* (II); *NCAB* (42:508); *WWW* (V); *Religious Education* 48 (March–April 1953): 80.                                             *Darlene E. Fisher*

**SOLDAN, Frank Louis.** B. October 20, 1842, Frankfurt am Main, Germany, to Johann Justin and Caroline (Elssman) Soldan. M. 1862 to Ottilie Bernhard. Ch. one. D. March 27, 1908, St. Louis, Missouri.

F. Louis Soldan was educated in Germany prior to emigrating to the United States in 1863 and became a United States citizen in 1882. He attended St. Louis (Missouri) Law School (1869–70) but did not complete the studies.

Soldan opened an academy for young ladies in 1863 and continued there until he was appointed an instructor of modern languages in Central High School in St. Louis (1868). He was assistant superintendent in charge of instruction in the German language (1870–71) and principal of St. Louis Normal School (1871–95). The high school and normal school merged (1887) with Soldan as principal. He was superintendent of instruction for St. Louis schools from 1895 to his death.

Soldan became an associate of William Torrey Harris *(q.v.)*. Under their leadership St. Louis became an educational center. Soldan was a pioneer in city school educational administration. His system of administering schools and supervision of instruction gained wide recognition. He aided South Carolina in establishing normal institutes for teachers.

Soldan translated Hegel's *Philosophy of Religion* and many of Horace's selections. He wrote *Grube's Method: Two Essays on Elementary Instruction in Arithmetic* (1881) and *The Century and the School, and Other Educational Essays* (1912). He was active in professional associations, including the National Educational Association (president, 1885). He received an honorary degree from the University of South Carolina.

REFERENCES: *DAB; NCAB* (12:516); *NYT,* March 28, 1908, p. 9; *St. Louis Post-Dispatch,* March 28, 1908; Selwyn K. Troen, *The Public and the Schools: Shaping the St. Louis System, 1838–1920* (Columbia: University of Missouri Press, 1975).                    *James R. Layton*
                                                            *Mary Paula Phillips*

**SOPHOCLES, Evangelinus Apostolides.** B. c. 1805, Tsangarada, Thessaly, Greece, to Apostolides Sophocles and his wife (n.a.). M. no. D. December 17, 1883, Cambridge, Massachusetts.

Evangelinus Apostolides Sophocles, classicist and neo-Hellenist, was born between 1800 and 1808 (he concealed the exact date). He was educated in a school in Cairo, Egypt, that belonged to the monastery of St. Catherine on Mt. Sinai and throughout his life maintained friendly relations with the Sinaitic monks. Sent to the United States in 1829 under the auspices of the American Board of Commissioners for Foreign Missions, he studied at Monson (Massachusetts) Academy. He entered Amherst (Massachusetts) College but withdrew for health reasons.

Sophocles taught at Mount Pleasant Classical Institute (later, Amherst Academy) at Amherst (c. 1830–34) and was an instructor in mathematics at Hartford and New Haven, Connecticut (1834–42). In 1842 he was appointed tutor in Greek at Harvard University and served there to his death in 1883, with the exception of a period of inactivity because of ill health (1845–47).

Sophocles was the author of *A Greek Grammar for the Use of Learners* (1835), *First Lessons in Greek* (1839), *Greek Exercises* (1841), *A Romaic Grammar* (1842), *Greek Lessons* (1843), *A Catalogue of Greek Verbs* (1844), *History of the Greek Alphabet* (1848), and *Greek Lexicon of the Roman and Byzantine Periods* (1870).

Sophocles made two trips to Greece, collecting valuable books he brought back to the United States. He was awarded an honorary master's degree by Yale College (1837) and Harvard University (1847) and an honorary doctorate from Western Reserve University (1862) and Harvard (1868).

REFERENCES: *AC; DAB; NCAB* (5:239); *NYT,* December 18, 1883, p. 5; *WWW* (H).                                                      *Albert S. Weston*

**SORIN, Edward Frederick.** B. February 6, 1814, Ahuille, France, to n.a. M. no. D. October 31, 1893, South Bend, Indiana.

After studying at the University of Paris, France, Edward Frederick Sorin entered the Catholic diocesan seminary at Le Mans, France, and was ordained in 1840. He joined the newly formed Congregation of the Holy Cross.

He responded to a plea of Bishop Celestine de la Hailandière of Vincennes, Indiana, for missionary volunteers and emigrated with six other brothers to the United States in 1841. In 1842 Celestine Hailandière offered Sorin land near South Bend, Indiana, if he would establish a college in two years. Sorin accepted the challenge and appealed for more men from France.

The Indiana legislature granted a charter, and the University of Notre Dame Du Lac held its first commencement in June 1844. Sorin served as president to 1865 and remained on the board of trustees to his death in 1893. He became provincial superior of the order of the Holy Cross in the United States in 1857 and directed missionary work in parts of Illinois, Indiana, and Michigan. In 1843 he invited a group of Sisters of Holy Cross to his province and founded and was superior general of the order in the United States, which was located in Bertrand, Michigan, in 1844. Sorin selected Eliza Maria Gillespie *(q.v.)* (Mother Angela) to head the community. During the Civil War he organized priests and nuns to care for wounded soldiers.

In 1868 Sorin was elected superior general of the Congregation of the Holy Cross and directed the order's educational and missionary programs in the United States, Canada, France, and India. He was credited with the establishment of the Laetare Medal (1883) and founded the periodical *Ave Maria* (1865). He assisted at the Plenary Council in Baltimore, Maryland, in 1883. He was decorated by the French government as an Officer of Public Instruction.

REFERENCES: *AC; DAB; TC; New Catholic Encyclopedia* (New York: McGraw-Hill, 1967); Francis Wallace, *Notre Dame* (New York: David McKay & Co., 1969).                                                     *James M. Vosper*

**SOULÉ, George.** B. May 14, 1834, Barrington, New York, to Ebenezer and Cornelia Elizabeth (Hogeboom) Soulé. M. September 6, 1860, to Mary Jane Reynolds. Ch. nine. D. January 26, 1926, New Orleans, Louisiana.

George Soulé was graduated from the Sycamore (Illinois) Academy in 1853 and Jones's Commercial College in St. Louis, Missouri, in 1856.

Soulé moved to New Orleans, Louisiana, in 1856 where he opened a business school, the Soulé Commercial College and Literary Institute. The school was a success and was granted a charter in 1861. Soulé served in the Confederate army (1862–65). Returning to New Orleans in 1865, he reopened the school, which had been closed and its assets confiscated by the Union army. He continued as head of the increasingly successful school until his death in 1926.

Soulé was the author of textbooks, including *Practical Mathematics* (1872), *Analytic and Philosophic Commercial and Exchange Calculator* (1872), *Contractions in Numbers* (1873), *Intermediate Philosophic Arithmetic* (1874), *New Science and Practice of Accounts* (1881), *Gems of Business Problems* (1885), *Manual of Auditing* (1892), *Partnership Settlements* (1893), and *Practical Mathematics* (1895).

A lecturer on education and public issues and active in fraternal affairs, Soulé was vice-president of the American Unitarian Association and president of the Business Educators' Association of America. He received an honorary degree from Tulane University in 1918.

REFERENCES: *AC; DAB; NCAB* (1:510); *NYT,* January 27, 1926, p. 23; *WWW* (I); P. J. Rinderle, "South's Oldest Business School," *Roosevelt Review* (New Orleans: Roosevelt Hotel, 1954).                    *Joe L. Green*

**SPALDING, Catherine.** B. December 23, 1793, Charles County, Maryland, to Ralph Spalding and his wife (n.a.). M. no. D. March 20, 1858, Nazareth, Kentucky.

On the death of her father, Catherine Spalding moved with her mother and sister from Maryland to Kentucky in 1799. Her mother died two years later, and Spalding grew up with relatives. With six other young women, Spalding became a charter member of the Sisters of Charity in Nazareth, organized in Bardstown, Kentucky, in 1813.

Elected the first mother superior, Spalding directed the community in gaining self-sufficiency and building a chapel (1816) and establishing a boarding school (1818), a pioneer academy in Kentucky. Among the schools she established in Kentucky were St. Vincent's Academy in Union County and the Academy of St. Catherine's in Scott County (1823), which was moved to Louisville in 1834. She also founded the Pioneer Academy in Louisville (1831), the first Catholic school in the city, and St. Frances School in Owensboro (1850). In 1836 she founded St. Vincent's (later, St. Joseph's) Infirmary in Louisville.

During a cholera epidemic in 1833 she established a home for children orphaned in the epidemic. St. Vincent's Orphanage in Louisville became her major interest to her death.

The Catherine Spalding College (formerly Nazareth College) was located in Louisville and conducted by the Sisters of Charity of Nazareth.

REFERENCES: *AC; DAB; WWW* (H); *New Catholic Encyclopedia* (New York: McGraw-Hill, 1967). *James M. Vosper*

**SPALDING, John Lancaster.** B. June 2, 1840, Lebanon, Kentucky, to Richard Martin and Mary Jane (Lancaster) Spalding. M. no. D. August 25, 1916, Peoria, Illinois.

John Lancaster Spalding, outstanding intellectual of the American Catholic hierarchy, attended St. Mary's College near Lebanon, Kentucky, and Mount St. Mary's College in Emmitsburg, Maryland; he received the A.B. degree (1859) from Mount St. Mary's of the West College in Cincinnati, Ohio. He studied at the American College in Louvain, France, receiving the S.T.B. (1862) and S.T.L. (1864) degrees. He was ordained to the priesthood in 1863 and studied in Germany and Italy before returning to the United States in 1865.

Spalding assisted at the cathedral in Louisville, Kentucky, and was a secretary to the bishop of Louisville. He also was a pastor to black Catholics in the city. He served as theologian at the Second Plenary Council of Baltimore in 1866 and was chancellor of the diocese of Louisville. In 1872 after the death of his uncle, Archbishop Martin John Spalding of Baltimore, he went to New York City where he wrote *The Life of the Most Rev. M. J. Spalding* (1873) and served as director of schools for St. Michael's parish. He was appointed first bishop of Peoria, Illinois (1877–1908), where he emphasized the development of parochial schools, which increased under his administration from twelve to seventy. He supported girls' academies and founded a boys' high school, Spalding Institute (1899).

A proponent of a national Catholic seminary, he delivered a noted sermon, "The Higher Education of the Priesthood," at the council in Baltimore (1884) and was a member of the committee that planned the Catholic University of America, established in Washington, D.C., in 1888. He supported the education of women and the establishment of Trinity College (1900) and Sisters College of Catholic University (1911).

Spalding was the author of a number of books, including *Education and the Higher Life* (1890), *Things of the Mind* (1894), *Means and Ends of Education* (1895), *Thoughts and Theories of Life and Education* (1897), *Opportunity and Other Essays* (1898), *Aphorisms and Reflections* (1901), *Socialism and Labor* (1902), *Agnosticism and Education* (1902), and *Glimpses of Truth* (1903).

Spalding was active in the Irish Catholic Colonization Association (president, 1879). He was a trustee of Catholic University (1884–1907) and was in charge of the Catholic educational exhibit at the Columbian Exposition at Chicago, Illinois (1893). He was awarded honorary degrees by

Western Reserve and Columbia universities.

REFERENCES: *AC; DAB; NCAB* (10:44); *NYT,* August 26, 1916, p. 7; *TC; WWW* (I); *New Catholic Encyclopedia* (New York: McGraw-Hill, 1967).                                                    *James M. Vosper*

**SPARKS, Jared.** B. May 10, 1789, Willington, Connecticut, to Joseph and Eleanor (Orcutt) Sparks. M. October 16, 1832, to Frances Anne Allen. M. May 21, 1839, to Mary Crowninshield Silsbee. Ch. six. D. March 15, 1866, Cambridge, Massachusetts.

Jared Sparks was twenty years old when he entered Phillips Academy in Exeter, New Hampshire. He entered Harvard University in 1811 and was graduated in 1815. After teaching in Lancaster, Massachusetts, he returned to Harvard as a tutor in mathematics and natural philosophy. He studied divinity, receiving the A.M. degree in 1819.

Sparks became a Unitarian minister in Baltimore, Maryland, and edited the monthly *Unitarian Miscellany* (1821–23). He was chaplain of the United States Congress in 1821. In 1823 he resigned his post, traveled in the west, then moved to Boston where he bought the *North American Review,* which he edited and directed (1824–31).

In 1825 Sparks began many years of work collecting papers and writing biographies from the early American Republic. He traveled to Europe to gather material for his work. He was named McLean Professor of Ancient and Modern History at Harvard University in 1839. The first professor of nonecclesiastical history in the United States, he organized Harvard's history department and sought recognition of American history as an academic subject but was not successful. He was president of Harvard for four years (1849–53).

Sparks was the author of many books, including *Letters on the Protestant Episcopal Church* (1820), *Comparative Moral Tendency of Trinitarian and Unitarian Doctrines* (1823), *Life of John Ledyard* (1828), *Life of Gouverneur Morris* (three volumes, 1832), and *Remarks on American History* (1837), and he was editor of *Essays and Tracts on Theology* (six volumes, 1825–26), *The Diplomatic Correspondence of the American Revolution* (twelve volumes, 1829–30), *The Writings of George Washington* (twelve volumes, 1829–30), and *The Life of George Washington* (1839). He was editor of *The Works of Benjamin Franklin* (ten volumes, 1836–40), the Library of American Biography (twenty-five volumes in two series, 1834–38 and 1844–48), and *Correspondence of the American Revolution* (four volumes, 1854). He was the originator and first editor of the *American Almanac and Repository of Useful Knowledge* (1830–61).

Sparks was a member of scholarly associations and was a fellow of the American Academy, corresponding secretary of the American Antiquarian Society, and vice-president of the Massachusetts Historical Society. He was a member of the Massachusetts board of education (1837–40). He was awarded honorary degrees by Dartmouth College (1841) and Harvard University (1844).

REFERENCES: *AC; DAB; EB; NCAB* (5:433); *NYT*, March 15, 1866, p. 5; *TC; WWW* (H); H. B. Adams *(q.v.), The Life and Writings of Jared Sparks* (Freeport, N.Y.: Books for Libraries Press, 1893), 2 vols.

*Lawrence S. Master*

SPAULDING, Frank Ellsworth. B. November 30, 1866, Dublin, New Hampshire, to William and Abby Roxanna (Stearns) Spaulding. M. October 17, 1895, to Mary Elizabeth Trow. Ch. four. D. June 6, 1960, La Jolla, California.

Frank Ellsworth Spaulding received the A.B. degree (1889) from Amherst (Massachusetts) College. He studied at the University of Leipzig, Germany (1891–92), the Sorbonne in Paris, France (1892–93), and the University of Berlin, Germany (1893). He received the A.M. and Ph.D. degrees (1894) from the University of Leipzig.

Spaulding was an instructor at the Amherst (Massachusetts) Summer School of Languages (1889, 1890) and Louisville (Kentucky) Military Academy (1889–91). He was superintendent of schools at Ware, Massachusetts (1895–97), Passaic, New Jersey (1897–1904), Newton, Massachusetts (1904–14), Minneapolis, Minnesota (1914–17), and Cleveland, Ohio (1917–20). He was professor of education at the Yale University graduate school (1920–39) and organized the Yale department of education and was chairman of the department (1920–29).

Spaulding wrote *Richard Cumberland als Begrunder der englischen Ethik* (1894), *The Individual Child and His Education* (1904), *The Passaic Primer* (with Catherine T. Bryce, 1904), *The Page Story Reader* (with C. T. Bryce, 1906), *The Aldine Reader* (eight volumes, with C. T. Bryce, 1907), *Learning to Read: A Manual for Teachers* (with C. T. Bryce, 1907), *Graded School Speller* (seven volumes, with William D. Miller, 1908), *The Aldine Language Books* (three volumes, with C. T. Bryce and Huber G. Buehler, 1913–17), *One School Administrator's Philosophy: Its Development* (1952), and *School Superintendent in Action in Five Cities* (1955). He founded *The Individual Child and His Education,* a quarterly journal (1903–04).

Spaulding was a member of the army educational commission of the American Expeditionary Force during World War I. He participated in many school surveys of major American cities. A member of professional associations, he was a member of the General Education Board (1917–20), chairman of the educational advisory committee of the New York State Economic Council (1934–35), and a member of the Massachusetts Commission on Immigration (1913–14). He was a trustee of Adelbert College of Western Reserve University. He received honorary degrees from Clark and Yale universities and Amherst College.

REFERENCES: *LE* (III); *NCAB* (D:264); *NYT,* June 8, 1960, p. 39; *WWAE* (XIII); *WWW* (IV).                              *Lawrence S. Master*

**SPENCER, Platt Rogers.** B. November 7, 1800, East Fishkill, New York, to Caleb and Jerusha (Covell) Ide Spencer. M. April 1828 to Persis Duty. Ch. eleven. D. May 16, 1864, Geneva, Ohio.

Platt Rogers Spencer's family moved in 1810 from New York to live in Ashtabula County, Ohio. As a child Spencer showed an interest in penmanship and criticized the handwriting found on public bulletin boards. Because paper was scarce and expensive, Spencer developed his calligraphic ability on any available materials—sand, snow, ice, and leather. He taught his first writing class in 1815. From 1816 to 1821 Spencer worked as a merchant's clerk and bookkeeper.

In his early twenties, Spencer developed a unique style of penmanship characterized as sloping, semiangular, and easy to embellish. He pointed out the similarities of his writing style with natural forms. Spencer had little formal education and was primarily self-taught. From 1821 to 1824 he studied literature, Latin, and law, taught penmanship in a common school, and worked as an accountant.

Spencer's system of penmanship gained widespread recognition. He placed emphasis on the monetary and aesthetic benefits that could be derived from using his system. He held classes in a schoolhouse built of logs on his farm in Geneva, Ohio, and traveled to academies and business colleges to promote his system of calligraphy. Through his classes and public lectures, Spencer gained many advocates who taught others the Spencerian or Semi-Angular system of penmanship.

He wrote *System of Business and Ladies' Penmanship* (1848), *Key to Spencerian Penmanship* (1864), and other publications. Spencer gave addresses on temperance, slavery, and universal education. He believed he was the first person in the United States to advocate total abstinence from alcohol as the solution to alcohol abuse. Spencer was one of the founders of the Ashtabula County Anti-Slavery Society.

REFERENCES: *AC; DAB; NCAB* (8:11); *TC; WWW* (H).      *Joe Adams*
*Edward Nussel*

**SPRAGUE, Homer Baxter.** B. October 19, 1829, Sutton, Massachusetts, to Jonathan and Mary Ann (Whipple) Sprague. M. December 28, 1854, to Antoinette Elizabeth Pardee. Ch. four. D. March 23, 1918, Newton, Massachusetts.

Homer Baxter Sprague studied at Leicester (Massachusetts) Academy and entered Yale College, from which he received the A.B. (1852) and M.A. (1855) degrees. He studied law and was admitted to the bar in 1854. He earned the Ph.D. degree (1873) from the University of New York (later, New York University).

Sprague practiced law in Worcester, Massachusetts (1855–56) and New Haven, Connecticut (1859–61). He was principal of the Worcester High School (1856–59) and sat on the New Haven board of education (1860–61). He wrote numerous articles for anti-slavery literature, raised a volunteer company, and served as an officer during the Civil War. Sprague was wounded and taken prisoner of war.

Following the war he returned to education as a principal of the Connecticut Normal School (later, Central Connecticut State College) at New Britain (1866–67). When he became a member of the house of representatives of Connecticut (1868) he furthered education, especially in public schools, through his influence as chairman of the education committee. He taught English literature and rhetoric at Cornell University in Ithaca, New York (1868–70), was principal of Adelphi Academy in Brooklyn, New York (1870–75), and was headmaster of Girls' High School in Boston, Massachusetts (1876–85).

Sprague founded the Martha's Vineyard (Massachusetts) Summer Institute in 1879 and served as president of Mills College in Oakland, California (1885–86). He is most noted as president of the University of North Dakota (1887–91). During his presidency, the university made marked progress in student enrollment and scholastic standards. He was an extension lecturer (1892–96) and professor (1896–1900) at Drew Theological Seminary in Madison, New Jersey, and edited the department of rhetoric in the *Students' Journal* (1898–1903).

Among the many publications Sprague authored are *Fellowship of Slaveholders* (1857), *Free Text Books for Public Schools* (1879), *American Liberty* (1900), *The Two Parties* (1900), *The Assassination* (1901), *The Nation's Honor Roll* (1902), *Right and Wrong in Our Civil War* (1903), *The People's Party* (1904), *Recollections of Henry Ward Beecher* (1905), *The True Macbeth* (1909), *Appreciation of Daniel C. Gilman* (1910), *War Pensions and Promises* (1910), *Caesar and Brutus* (1911), *The Elevation of His Satanic Majesty* (1912), *The European War—Its Cause and Cure* (1914), and *Lights and Shadows in Confederate Prisons* (1915).

He was first president of the North Dakota Teachers' Association (1888), president of the American Institute of Instruction (1883–85), and a councillor of the National Educational Association (1887–88). He received an honorary degree from Temple University.

REFERENCES: *DAB; NCAB* (24:65); *NYT,* March 24, 1918, p. 13; *WWW* (I).                                                            *Marjorie E. Souers*

**SPROUL, Robert Gordon.** B. May 22, 1891, San Francisco, California, to Robert and Sarah Elizabeth (Moore) Sproul. M. September 6, 1916, to Ida Amelia Wittschen. Ch. three. D. September 10, 1975, Berkeley, California.

Robert G. Sproul attended the University of California, from which he received the B.S. degree (1913). He worked for the efficiency department of the city of Oakland, California (1913–14), and became cashier for the University of California at Berkeley (1914–18).

Sproul served the University of California to his retirement in 1958 as assistant comptroller and assistant secretary of the board of regents (1918–20), comptroller and secretary of the board of regents (1920–30), vice-president (1925–30), and president (1930–58). Sproul's long tenure survived several controversies, including confrontation with student groups opposing military conscription in 1940 and a faculty loyalty oath ordered by the board of regents in 1949. Under his leadership the University of California gained an international reputation, particularly in scientific research.

The author of articles in professional journals, Sproul was active in many organizations and was a member of the California State Committee on Agricultural Education (1921–23), the Commission on the Revision of the California Constitution (1929–30 and 1964–65, cochairman, 1964), the California State Board of Social Welfare (1928–31), and the California Citizens Advisory Committee on the Public Educational System (1958–61). He was a member of many advisory boards, including the national Red Cross (chairman) and the United States Civil Rights Commission (1958–60), and was senior adviser to the American Group on the Allied Commission on Reparations (1945). He was on the governing boards of many groups and institutions, including the Carnegie Foundation for the Advancement of Teaching (1939–58) and the Rockefeller Foundation (1939–56).

Sproul was a special ambassador to Korea (1956). He received more than twenty honorary degrees from American colleges and universities. He received the Benjamin Ide Wheeler Distinguished Service Award from the University of California (1934) and became an honorary fellow of Stanford University in 1941. He was decorated by the governments of France, Rumania, and Italy.

REFERENCES: *CB* (July 1945); *LE* (III); *NCAB* (C:387); *NYT,* September 12, 1975, p. 36; *WW* (XXXVIII); *WWAE* (XIII); *WWW* (VI).

*Barbara Ruth Peltzman*

**SQUIRES, James Duane.** B. November 9, 1904, Grand Forks, North Dakota, to Vernon Purinton and Ethel Claire (Wood) Squires. M. September 5, 1928, to Catherine Tuttle. Ch. two.

James Duane Squires received the A.B. degree (1925) from the University of North Dakota, the A.M. degree (1927) from the University of

Minnesota, and the Ph.D. degree (1933) from Harvard University.

Squires was a high school teacher at Dickinson, North Dakota (1925–26), and was a graduate assistant at the University of Minnesota (1926–27). He was a professor of history at Mayville (North Dakota) State Teachers College (later, Mayville State College) from 1927 to 1931. He became professor of history at Colby Junior College in New London, New Hampshire, in 1933 and was chairman of the social studies department in 1935 and chairman of the summer forum in 1942.

Squires was the author of *Aeronautics in the Civil War* (1937), *The First and Second World Wars* (1945), *A History of the New Hampshire Young Men's Christian Association* (1944), *Mirror to America* (1952), *Experiment in Cooperation* (1953), *Community Witness* (1954), *The Granite State: A History of New Hampshire, 1923–1955* (1956), and *New Hampshire: A Student's Guide to Localized History* (1966), and he was coauthor of *Western Civilization* (1942).

Active in church affairs, Squires was president of the New Hampshire Council of Churches (1945–47), the New Hampshire Baptist Convention (1946–49), and the New Hampshire Council of Churches and Religious Education (1945–48). He was a member of the Board of Education and Publications of the American Baptist Convention. He was a member of the National Commission on Governmental Reorganization (1949). He was president of the New England Association of Social Studies Teachers.

REFERENCES: *CA* (5–8); *WW* (XXXVI); *WWAE* (XIV).

*John F. Ohles*

**STANLEY, Albert Augustus.** B. May 25, 1851, Manville, Rhode Island, to George Washington and Augusta Adaline (Jefferds) Stanley. M. December 27, 1875, to Emma F. Bullock. M. December 1, 1921, to Dorothea Oestreicher. Ch. one. D. May 19, 1932, Ann Arbor, Michigan.

Albert Augustus Stanley moved with his parents in 1865 to Slatersville, Rhode Island, where he attended local schools. He showed an early ability and interest in music; by the age of fourteen he was a church organist. He studied at the Leipzig (Germany) Conservatory (1871–75), graduating in 1875.

Stanley taught at Ohio Wesleyan College in Delaware, Ohio (1875–76), and was organist at Grace Church in Providence, Rhode Island (1876–88). He was appointed professor of music at the University of Michigan (1888–1921) and was director of the University School of Music (1903–21). Stanley organized the Ann Arbor School of Music into the University School of Music. He established the annual Ann Arbor May Festival in 1894, a music event he conducted to 1921.

Composer of a variety of musical forms, Stanley was the author of a compilation of four compositions, *Greek Themes in Modern Musical Settings* (1924), compiler of the *Catalogue of the Stearns Collection of Musi-*

*cal Instruments* (1918), and author of *Musical Instruments in Their Socio-logical Relations* (n.d.). He was active in professional organizations as a founder of the American College of Musicians (1884) and the American Guild of Organists (1896). He was secretary, treasurer, and president of the Music Teachers' National Association (1883–95), twice president of the Michigan Music Teachers' Association, examiner for the American College of Music (1893), vice-president of the American Museum of Music, and representative to the Internationale Musik Gesellschaft (president of the American section, 1899–1912). He received honorary degrees from the University of Michigan and Northwestern University.

REFERENCES: *DAB; NYT,* May 20, 1932, p. 19; *WWW* (I); Nicholas Slonimsky, ed., *The International Cyclopedia of Music and Musicians,* 6th ed. (New York: Dodd, Mead, 1952).                              *John F. Ohles*

**STEARNS, Eben Sperry.** B. December 23, 1819, Bedford, Massachusetts, to Samuel and Abigail (French) Stearns. M. August 27, 1854, to Ellen Augusta Kuhn. M. 1880 to Betty Irwin. Ch. four. D. April 11, 1887, Nashville, Tennessee.

Eben (changed from Ebenezer) Sperry Stearns was graduated from Phillips Academy in Andover, Massachusetts, and then received the B.A. degree from Harvard University (1841). He taught at schools for young women in Ipswich, Massachusetts, and at Portland, Maine, before receiving the M.A. degree (1846) from Harvard.

Stearns organized the Female High School in Newburyport, Massachusetts, and was principal until he succeeded Cyrus Peirce *(q.v.)* as principal of the State Normal School at West Newton, Massachusetts (1849). While he was principal, the school was moved to Framingham, Massachusetts. In 1855 he became the principal of the Female Academy at Albany, New York, where he stayed for fourteen years. He organized and administered the Robinson Female Academy in Exeter, New Hampshire (1869).

In September 1875 he was selected by the board of the Peabody Fund as the first president of the State Normal School in Nashville, Tennessee, and was appointed chancellor of the University of Nashville, a post he held to his death. Under Stearns, the State Normal School was kept in Nashville despite attempts to move it to Georgia. Under his leadership, a system of scholarships was instituted to help students from distant parts of the South. Later (1889) the institution took the name of Peabody Normal College and, in 1909, received $2 million from the Peabody Education Fund and took the name George Peabody College for Teachers. Through its graduates, the college exerted a great influence on the development of education in the South.

A speech by Stearns on the ninth anniversary of his appointment to the college was published as *Historical Sketch of the Normal College at*

*Nashville, Tennessee* (1885). He was the recipient of honorary degrees.
REFERENCES: *DAB; NCAB* (8:133); *NYT,* April 12, 1887, p. 2; *TC; WWW* (H). *Alfred J. Ciani*

**STEELE, Joel Dorman.** B. May 14, 1836, Lima, New York, to Allen and Sabra (Dorman) Steele. M. July 7, 1859, to Esther Baker. Ch. none. D. May 25, 1886, Elmira, New York.

J. Dorman Steele studied at the Boys' Classical Institute in Albany, New York, under Charles Anthon *(q.v.)* and at the Boys' Academy in Troy, New York. He taught in district schools to finance his education at Genesee College (later, Syracuse University) from which he was graduated in 1858.

Steele was an instructor (1858–59) and principal (1859–61) of Mexico (New York) Academy. He served in the Union army, organized and was captain of the Eighty-first New York Volunteers, and was wounded at the Battle of Seven Pines near Fair Oaks, Virginia (1862). Steele was principal of Newark (New Jersey) High School (1863–66) and the Elmira (New York) Free Academy (1866–72). He retired to write textbooks in 1872.

While at Elmira, Steele taught science and prepared outlines of instruction that later became the basis for his Fourteen Weeks Series of science texts. Among the books in the series were *Chemistry* (1867), *Astronomy* (1868), *Natural Philosophy* (1869), *Geology* (1870), *Human Physiology* (1873), *Zoology* (1875), and *Answers to the Practical Questions in Steele's Sciences* (1869). Steele also wrote *Barnes Popular History of the United States* (1875) and, with his wife, other volumes in the Barnes Brief History Series, including *France* (1874), *Ancient Peoples* (1883), *Mediaeval and Modern Peoples* (1883), *General History* (1883), *History of Greece* (1883), and *History of Rome* (1884). Steele has been credited with popularizing the study of science through his texts.

Steele was active in professional associations, including the New York State Teachers' Association (president, 1870), and was a fellow of the Geological Society of London, England. A trustee of Syracuse University, he left the university a fifty thousand dollar endowment to establish a chair in theistic science. His widow donated the Steele Memorial Library in Elmira, New York, in his honor. He was awarded an honorary degree by the regents of the University of the State of New York in 1870.

REFERENCES: *AC; DAB; NCAB* (3:265); *WWW* (H); John A. Nietz, *Old Textbooks* (Pittsburgh: University of Pittsburgh Press, 1961).
*Richard W. Gates*

**STEINHAUS, Arthur H.** B. October 4, 1897, Chicago, Illinois, to Henry D. and Rose (Daehler) Steinhaus. M. June 23, 1921, to Eva Kunzmann. Ch. one. D. February 8, 1970, Lansing, Michigan.

Arthur Steinhaus attended George Williams College in Downers Grove, Illinois, where he received the B.P.E. (1921) and M.P.E. (1926) degrees. At the University of Chicago, he was awarded the S.B. (1920), M.S. (1925), and Ph.D. (1928) degrees.

Steinhaus joined the faculty of George Williams College, originally a college founded to train personnel for the Young Men's Christian Association (YMCA), as an instructor in biological science (1920). He became a professor of physiology (1928), director of the Division of Health and Physical Education (1953), and dean of the faculty (1954) until his retirement in 1962. His leadership was central in the training of YMCA physical directors and the growth and development of twentieth-century YMCA physical education.

A commitment to physiological research was central to numerous publications Steinhaus produced focusing upon the physiology of muscle, blood and exercise, the harmful effects of smoking, the relationship of boxing to brain damage, the importance of good posture and relaxation, and the contributions of health education and physical education to health, fitness, and the development of the whole person. Among his better-known publications were a series of twenty-four articles, "Physiology in the Service of Physical Education," in the *Journal of Health and Physical Education*. He also wrote *Tobacco and Health* (1939), *More Firepower for Health Education* (1945), *How to Keep Fit and Like It* (1957), and *Toward an Understanding of Health and Physical Education* (1963).

During World War II Steinhaus served as a consultant to the secretary of the navy on physical fitness and rehabilitation, was a member of the Civilian Advisory Committee for the United States Navy Physical Fitness Program, and was chief of the Division of Physical Education and Health Activities of the United States Office of Education.

Steinhaus served as president of the Illinois American Association of Health, Physical Education and Recreation (AAHPER) (1948–49), the Midwest district of AAHPER (1955–56), and the American Academy of Physical Education (1943–45). He received the Roberts-Gulick Award (1940), the William G. Anderson Award (1951), the Clark Hetherington Award (1963), and the Luther Halsey Gulick Award (1969), all special honors accorded distinguished members of the physical education profession.

REFERENCES: *CA* (19–20); *LE* (III); *WWAE* (XIV); WWW (V); Marie W. Mitchell, "Arthur H. Steinhaus, 1897–1970," *Journal of Health, Physical Education and Recreation* 41 (May 1970): 90; *NYT*, February 10, 1970, p. 43; Arthur Weston, *The Making of American Physical Education* (New York: Appleton-Century-Crofts, 1962).                    *Stratton F. Caldwell*

**STERLING, John Ewart Wallace.** B. August 6, 1906, Linwood, Ontario, Canada, to William and Annie (Wallace) Sterling. M. August 7, 1930, to Anna Marie Shaver. Ch. three.

J. E. Wallace Sterling received the B.A. degree (1927) from the University of Toronto, Ontario, Canada, and the M.A. degree (1930) from the University of Alberta in Edmonton, Alberta, Canada. He was awarded the Ph.D. degree (1938) from Stanford (California) University.

Sterling was a lecturer in history at Regina (Saskatchewan) College (1927–28) and was an assistant in history, athletic director, and football coach at the University of Alberta. He was a research staff member of the Hoover Library of War, Revolution and Peace (1932–37) and an instructor in history (1935–37) at Stanford University. He was an assistant and associate professor of history (1937–45) at California Institute of Technology at Pasadena and became Edward S. Harkness Professor of History and Government in 1945. He also was secretary of the faculty (1941), chairman of the faculty (1944), and a member of the executive committee (1945).

In 1948 Sterling was appointed director of the Henry E. Huntington Library and Art Gallery in San Marino, California, an internationally famous center for scholars in English and American literature and history. He became president of Stanford University in 1949 and retired as chancellor in 1968.

Sterling was a news analyst for the Columbia Broadcasting System with radio station KNX in Hollywood, California (1942–48). He edited *Features and Figures of the Past* (with others, 1939).

A member of many organizations, Sterling was a fellow of the Social Science Research Council and the American Geographical Society and was president of the Association of American Universities (1961–63). He was a civilian faculty member (1947) and member of the board of consultants (1948–52) of the National War College and of the board of visitors to the United States Naval Academy (1956–58). He received more than twenty honorary degrees from American and foreign colleges and universities and was decorated by the governments of Great Britain, Germany, France, Japan, and Austria.

REFERENCES: *CB* (January 1951); *LE* (V); *NCAB* (H:208); *NYT*, May 10, June 4, July 6, August 20, 1968, *WW* (XXXIX); *WWAF* (XVI); "Hello and Goodbye," *Time* 52 (November 29, 1948):52.

*Stratton F. Caldwell*

**STETSON, William Wallace.** B. June 17, 1849, Greene, Maine, to Reuben and Christiana (Thompson) Stetson. M. July 4, 1871, to Rebecca Jane Killough. Ch. none. D. July 1, 1910, Auburn, Maine.

William Wallace Stetson attended local schools in Greene, Maine, and taught in local district schools at age fifteen. He taught during the winter months and worked on his father's farm the rest of the year.

He left Maine in 1868 and settled in Illinois. Although he had little formal education, he held the position of superintendent of schools in Rockford, Illinois, from 1880 to 1885. He also served as superintendent of schools in Auburn, Maine, from 1885 to 1895 and was Maine state superintendent of public schools from 1895 to 1907.

Stetson was the author of *History and Civil Government of Maine* (1898), and a number of his other writings were published by his wife as *Ideals and Essentials in Education* (1911). Active in professional organizations, Stetson was president of the Northern Illinois Teachers' Association (1883), the Maine Pedagogical Society (1890–91), the American Institute of Instruction (1894–95), and the department of superintendence of the National Educational Association (1905). He received honorary degrees from Colby (1902) and Monmouth (1907) colleges.

REFERENCES: *DAB; NCAB* (17: 206); *WWW* (I); Kermit S. Nickerson, *150 Years of Education in Maine* (Augusta: State of Maine, Department of Education, 1970), pp. 21–22.                                    *William G. Ellis*

**STEVENS, Georgia Lydia.** B. May 8, 1870. Boston, Massachusetts, to Henry James and Helen (Granger) Stevens. M. no. D. March 28, 1946, New York, New York.

Georgia Lydia Stevens attended Elmhurst, the convent school of the Society of the Sacred Heart in Providence, Rhode Island (1882–84), and Mrs. Gillian's School in Boston, Massachusetts. She studied music in Boston and at the Hoch Conservatorium in Frankfurt am Main (Germany) in 1888. Returning to the United States she continued her studies under Charles Martin Loeffler in Boston.

Stevens became a music performer and teacher, giving violin concerts and private lessons and teaching the violin at Elmhurst. She became a convert to Catholicism in 1895 and entered the Society of the Sacred Heart at Kenwood, New York, in 1906. She completed her religious training under Janet Erskine Stuart in Roehampton, England, and Ixelles, Belgium, and taught at the Sacred Heart Academy in Roehampton (1908–13). She returned to the United States from Belgium in 1914 and taught at Manhattanville Academy (later, College), then located in New York City. With the assistance of Justine Bayard (Cutting) Ward, Stevens founded a professorship of liturgical music (1916), which became the Pius X Institute and the Pius X School of Liturgical Music at Manhattanville College of the Sacred Heart in 1931. The program sought to stimulate a return to the use of the Gregorian chant and sacred polyphony and to emphasize the participation of worshipers in music and liturgy.

Stevens wrote the Tone and Rhythm series of textbooks (1935–45) in which she emphasized her methods of teaching music.

REFERENCES: *NAW; NYT,* March 29, 1946, p. 23; Joseph I. Malloy,

"Death of Mother Georgia Stevens," *Catholic World* 163 (May 1946): 180; *Commonweal* 43 (April 12, 1946): 638; *New Catholic Encyclopedia* (New York: McGraw-Hill, 1967).                                    *James M. Vosper*

**STEWART, Cora Wilson.** B. January 17, 1875, Farmers, Rowan County, Kentucky, to Jeremiah and Annie Eliza (Halley) Wilson. M. to Ulysses Grant Carey. M. 1904 to Alexander T. Stewart. Ch. none. D. December 9, 1958, Tryon, North Carolina.

Cora Wilson Stewart moved with her family to Morehead, Kentucky, in 1890, where she attended Morehead Normal School (later, Morehead State University). She began to teach as an assistant instructor in the Morehead public schools at the age of fifteen. She received a teaching certificate in 1892 and continued her education during school recesses at the National Normal University in Lebanon, Ohio (1892 and 1893). In 1898 she enrolled in Wilbur R. Smith's Commercial College in Kentucky and in 1899 became the first woman instructor at the school.

Stewart served as both principal and superintendent of the Rowan County (Kentucky) schools. In 1911 she initiated schools to assist illiterate adults of Rowan County to learn to read and write. Operated at night, the schools came to be known as Moonlight Schools. By 1914 the program was expanded into a statewide program as Governor James B. McCreary of Kentucky, responding to a letter from Stewart, proposed the Kentucky Illiteracy Commission. Established by the legislature, a commission was appointed with Stewart as chairman. The program was recognized by the United States Bureau of Education and gained national attention.

Stewart was the author of books, including textbooks used in her schools. Among her writings were *Soldier's First Book* (1917), *Moonlight Schools* (1922), *Mother's First Book* (1930), and the Country Life Readers Series (1915). She was editor of *The Rowan County Messenger,* a simple newspaper for her students.

In 1926 President Calvin Coolidge appointed Stewart director of the National Illiteracy Crusade, and President Herbert Hoover named her director of the National Illiteracy Commission in 1929. She was chairman of the illiteracy committee of the World Federation of Education Associations and Kentucky chairman of the Illiteracy Commission of the National Education Association. She was president of the Kentucky Education Association (1912). She received the Clara Barton and Ella Flagg Young (1930) medals and awards from *Pictorial Review* magazine (1924), the Kentucky Education Association, and the General Federation of Women's Clubs (1941).

REFERENCES: *LE* (II); *WW* (XV); Willie E. Nelms, Jr., "Cora Wilson Stewart and the Crusade Against Illiteracy in Kentucky," *The Register* 74 (January 1976); Mary M. Stroh, *Eyes to See* (Austin, Tex.: Delta Kappa Gamma Society, 1947).                                    *Roger H. Jones*

**STEWART, Isabel Maitland.** B. January 14, 1878, Chatham, Ontario, Canada, to Frank B. and Elizabeth (Farquharson) Stewart. M. no. D. October 7, 1963, New York, New York.

Isabel Maitland Stewart was educated to become a schoolteacher in Canada at the Manitoba Normal School, Chatham Collegiate Institute, and Winnipeg Collegiate Institute. She was employed as an elementary schoolteacher in Manitoba, Canada (1896–1900).

Growing restless with teaching and developing an interest in nursing, she entered nurses' training at the age of twenty-two. She studied at the School of Nursing, Winnipeg General Hospital, and at Teachers College, Columbia University, where she received the B.S. (1911) and A.M. (1913) degrees.

Stewart was nursing supervisor at Winnipeg General Hospital School of Nursing (1906–08). She moved to New York City and taught at Teachers College, Columbia University. She began as an instructor in the department of nursing education (1909) and became chairman of the division of nursing education (1925–47). Prior to assuming responsibility for directing the nursing program at Teachers College, she worked under the leadership of M. Adelaide Nutting (q.v.), whom she replaced in 1925. Stewart's major interest was in the development of nursing curricula. She developed the first program to prepare nursing faculties.

She wrote *A Short History of Nursing* (with Lavinia L. Dock, 1920) and *Education of Nurses* (1943). She was editor of Macmillan Nursing Education Monographs. She published the first nursing research journal as one of the series of *Nursing Education Bulletins*.

Stewart was active in the National League of Nursing Education (served on many committees and secretary, 1915–16), and vice-president, 1920–21), the Association of Collegiate Schools of Nursing (secretary, 1933–36), and president, 1936–44), the International Council of Nurses (chairman, committee on education, 1925–47), the Florence Nightingale International Foundation of London, England (committee on management, 1937–46), and the American Council on Education (second vice-president, 1944–45). She was a consultant on nursing education for the United States Public Health Service (1940–47) and a consultant and chairman of the committee on nursing education and personnel for the War Manpower Commission (1943–46).

In 1961 she was honored by the establishment of a development fund at Teachers College to endow the Isabel Stewart Research Professorship in Nursing.

REFERENCES: *LE* (III); *WWAE* (XIII); *WWW* (IV); Teresa Christy, *Cornerstone for Nursing Education* (New York: Teachers College Press, 1969); *NYT,* October 7, 1963, p. 31; *The Reminiscences of Isabel M. Stewart,* tape recorded interviews from the Oral History Research Office,

Columbia University, 1961; Edna Yost, *American Women of Nursing* (Philadelphia: J. B. Lippincott, 1947). *Elaine L. La Monica*

**STEWART, Joseph Spencer.** B. September 23, 1863, Oxford, Georgia, to Joseph Spencer and Rebecca Hannah (Starr) Stewart. M. August 19, 1890, to Selma M. Hahr. Ch. six. D. March 25, 1934, Athens, Georgia.

J. S. Stewart was graduated from Emory College in Oxford (later, Atlanta), Georgia, with the A.B. degree (1883) and received the A.M. degree (1897) from the University of Georgia.

Principal of the Cherokee Institute in Cave Spring, Georgia (1883–89), Stewart was president of the Harwood Seminary in Marietta, Georgia (1889–91). He was superintendent of schools in Marietta (1891–95) where he organized the public school system and developed the schools into a system comparable to the best in the country.

Stewart was president of North Georgia Agricultural College (later, North Georgia College) in Dahlonega (1897–1903). He was professor of secondary education and state high school inspector (1903–34) at the University of Georgia. He led the development of high schools in Georgia and provided a model for the rest of the South. Constitutional amendments were passed in 1910 incorporating high schools into the state educational system. From eleven secondary schools in 1905, Georgia had 393 approved high schools in 1930. In 1897 Stewart was appointed by the governor to plan the curriculum for a system of district agricultural schools, and in 1905 he began to organize cotton and corn clubs for boys in the state. He was the director of the university's summer school from 1922.

The author of *Georgia Oratory* (1933), Steward was editor of the *High School Quarterly* from 1912. He served on the Commission on the Reorganization of Secondary Education of the National Education Association (1914–24), was vice-president of the Southern Association of Colleges (1921), founder and president of the Georgia High School Association (1908), and president of the Georgia Education Association (1905–06). He received an honorary degree from the University of Georgia (1913).

REFERENCES: *LE* (1); *WWW* (1); Dorothy Orr, *A History of Education in Georgia* (Chapel Hill: University of North Carolina Press, 1950); Wylly Folk St. John, "How Secondary Education Was Rescued in Georgia," *The* (Atlanta) *Constitution,* May 18, 1930. *Ernest D. Riggsby*

**STEWART, William Mitton.** B. September 5, 1859, Draper, Utah, to Isaac M. and Elizabeth (White) Stewart. M. December 16, 1883, to Sarah E. Vincent. Ch. five. D. August 26, 1913, Salt Lake City, Utah.

William Mitton Stewart was graduated from the University of Deseret (later, University of Utah) in 1881 and became the principal of the Draper (Utah) schools (1881–85).

Stewart was elected superintendent of schools for Salt Lake County (Utah) in 1885 and served to 1888. He was instrumental in improving instructional methods and standards in the schools of the county and in achieving a better organization of the schools. He also was principal of the Nineteenth Ward School in Salt Lake City, which he developed into a model school (1885–88). He became director of the state normal school at the University of Deseret (1888–1913). Stewart served three terms as a regent of the University of Utah. In 1907 he received an honorary degree from the University of Utah. Stewart has been called Utah's greatest educator and Father of Education in the West.

*REFERENCES: NCAB* (20:363).                                               *Thomas A. Barlow*

**STILES, Ezra.** B. November 29, 1727, North Haven, Connecticut, to Isaac and Keria (Taylor) Stiles, M. February 10, 1757, to Elizabeth Hubbard. M. October 17, 1782, to Mary (Cranston) Checkley. Ch. eight. D. May 12, 1795, New Haven, Connecticut.

Ezra Stiles was graduated from Yale College in 1746, studied theology, and was licensed to preach by the New Haven ministerial association in 1749. He gave up the pulpit in 1752 to study law. He was admitted to the bar in 1753 and practiced to 1755 when he returned to preaching.

A tutor at Yale (1749–55), Stiles delivered an oration in Latin on the occasion of a visit of Benjamin Franklin *(q.v.)* to Yale in 1755 and formed a friendship that lasted to Franklin's death. Stiles took charge of a church in Newport, Rhode Island (1756), but moved to a church in Portsmouth, New Hampshire, in 1777 when Newport was occupied by British troops. In Newport he had assisted in the founding of Rhode Island College (later, Brown University) in Providence (1764).

Stiles was appointed president of Yale College in 1778 and served in that post to his death. He also was professor of ecclesiastical history (1778–95) and of divinity after the death of Naphtali Daggett in 1780. He was recognized as the leading theologian of his time. Under his leadership, Yale was strengthened and secularized.

Stiles was the author of *Prospect of the City of Jerusalem* (1742), *Looking-Glass for Changelings* (1743), *The Declaration of the County of New Haven Concerning the Rev. George Whitefield* (1745), *The Character and Duty of Soldiers* (1755), *The United States Elevated to Glory and Honor* (1783), *Account of the Settlement of Bristol, R.I.* (1785), and *History of Three of the Judges of Charles I* (1794). Stiles left unfinished an *Ecclesiastical History of New England,* along with his diary and forty-five volumes of manuscripts.

He was the first president of the Connecticut Society for the Abolition of Slavery (1790) and a member of the American Philosophical Society. He received honorary degrees from Yale and Dartmouth colleges, the College of New Jersey, and the University of Edinburgh, Scotland.

REFERENCES: *AC; DAB; EB; NCAB* (1:167); *TC; WWW* (H); Franklin B. Dexter, ed., *The Literary Diary of Ezra Stiles* (New York: Charles Scribner's, 1901). Francis Parsons, *Six Men of Yale* (New Haven: Yale University Press, 1939).                                      *Robert C. Morris*

STILLÉ, Charles Janeway. B. September 23, 1819, Philadelphia, Pennsylvania, to John and Maria (Wagner) Stillé. M. April 12, 1846, to Anna Dulles. Ch. none. D. August 11, 1899, Philadelphia, Pennsylvania.

Charles Janeway Stillé prepared for college at schools in Pennsylvania and New Jersey and enrolled in Yale College in 1835. He was graduated in 1839 as class valedictorian. He read law with Joseph R. Ingersoll and was admitted to the bar. He often traveled to Europe to study literature and history.

Stillé joined the faculty of the University of Pennsylvania in 1866 as professor of English literature and belles lettres. At his prompting, elective courses were introduced in the curriculum in 1867. He became provost in 1868. Under his leadership courses in science, music, and dentistry were first offered, and community relations and university finances improved. Disagreements with the trustees over the conduct of the institution led to Stillé's resignation in 1880. He continued to teach in the university for one year, after which he traveled and engaged in writing.

Stillé was the author of *Studies in Medieval History* (1882), *Life and Times of John Dickinson* (1891), and *Major-General Anthony Wayne and the Pennsylvania Line in the Continental Army* (1893). He wrote *History of the United States Sanitary Commission* (1866) after serving on that body during the Civil War. He was president of the Historical Society of Pennsylvania for eight years and received an honorary degree from Yale University.

REFERENCES: *AC; DAB; NCAB* (1:344); *NYT,* August 12, 1899, p. 7; *WWW* (I); Saul Sack, *History of Higher Education in Pennsylvania* (Harrisburg: Pennsylvania Historical and Museum Commission, 1963).                                      *Samuel A. Farmerie*

STIMSON, John Ward. B. December 16, 1850, Paterson, New Jersey, to Henry C. and Julia M. (Atterbury) Stimson. M. to Mary R. (n.a.). Ch. six. D. June 13, 1930, Corona, California.

Landscape painter, author, and educator, John Ward Stimson was graduated from Yale College in 1872. He traveled to France where he was a pupil of Alexandre Cabanel and Jacquesson de la Chevreuse at the Ecole des beaux arts, Paris. After graduation from the Beaux arts he remained in Europe to continue art studies for six years in Italy, Belgium, Holland, and England.

Upon returning to the United States, Stimson first settled in New York City, where he combined painting with preparing illustrations for magazines. Active in the field of education, Stimson served as a lecturer and art teacher on the faculty of Princeton University. For five years he was director of the Metropolitan Museum School and in 1888 was the founder and, for twelve years, the director of the Artist-Artisan Institute in New York. He was director of the School of Fine and Industrial Arts in Trenton, New Jersey, and concurrently served as lecturer and instructor at the Art Students' League in New York.

Stimson was editor of *The Arena* and author of *The Law of Three Primaries* (n.d.), *Principles and Methods in Art Education* (1892), *To Teach Boys How to Live: The New Education* (1910), *The Gate Beautiful; Being Principles and Methods in Vital Arts Education* (1903), and *Wandering Chords* (1903), a collection of poems.

REFERENCES: *WWW* (I); *The Art Digest* (June 1930): 16; James Carr, ed., *Mantle Fielding's Dictionary of American Painters, Sculptors and Engravers* (New York: James F. Carr Publisher, 1965); *NYT*, June 15, 1930, sec. 2, p. 6.                                    *Roger H. Jones*

**STIMSON, Rufus Whittaker.** B. February 20, 1868, Palmer, Massachusetts, to Horace W. and Harriet A. (Hunt) Stimson. M. October 4, 1899, to Helen Morris. Ch. none. D. May 1, 1947, Hyannis, Massachusetts.

Rufus W. Stimson, leader in agricultural education, was graduated from Harvard University, from which he received the A.B. (1895) and A.M. (1896) degrees. He received the B.D. degree (1897) from the Yale Divinity School.

Stimson was professor of English, ethics, and public speaking at the Connecticut Agricultural College (later, University of Connecticut) from 1897 to 1901 and was acting president (1901–02) and president (1902–08) of the college. He became the first director of Smith's Agricultural School and Northampton School Industries in Northampton, Massachusetts (1908–11). The school was established as a result of the Douglas Commission of Massachusetts, which issued a report in 1906 calling for the establishment of industrial schools in local communities. The Smith school was the first permanent school of vocational agriculture in Massachusetts. Founded with state aid and a private endowment from the Smith Charities, it became a prototype for other schools.

In an effort to establish a practical program based on school-home cooperation, Stimson developed the home-project plan. Projects consisted of units of farm production, which were studied at school and carried out by the students on their home farms under the supervision of teachers. Stimson's plan received national attention and was credited with influencing vocational programs established by the Smith-Hughes Act of 1917.

In 1911 Stimson was appointed Massachusetts state supervisor of vocational agricultural education. He supervised state-aided agricultural programs in the schools and promoted improvement in classroom instruction. He organized "conferences on wheels," in which groups of agricultural instructors visited the classrooms of a colleague to judge student achievement. He assisted Paul Hanus *(q.v.)* of Harvard University in conducting a study of the Hampton (Virginia) Normal and Agricultural Institute (1916–17).

Hc was chairman of the college section of the American Association of Agricultural Colleges and Experimental Stations (1905) and president of the Association for the Advancement of Agricultural Teaching. He was awarded a gold medal at the Panama Pacific Exposition in San Francisco, California (1915).

REFERENCES: *LE* (I); *WWW* (IV); *Agricultural Education Magazine* 20 (August 1947): 29; *Daily Hampshire Gazette* (Northampton, Mass.), February 8, 1908, May 2, 1947; *Our Friend and Guest, Rufus W. Stimson,* pamphlet issued at testimonial dinner at Hotel Sheraton, Boston, February 21, 1938.                                    *William Kornegay*

**STODDARD, Francis Hovey.** B. April 25, 1847, Middlebury, Vermont, to Solomon and Frances Elizabeth (Greenwood) Stoddard. M. May 14, 1873, to Lucy M. Smith. Ch. one. D. February 6, 1936, New York, New York.

Francis Hovey Stoddard's father was professor of languages at Middlebury (Vermont) College. Stoddard received the A.B. (1869) and A.M. (1886) degrees from Amherst (Massachusetts) College. He studied at Oxford University in England from 1884 to 1886 and received the Ph.D. degree from the Western University of Pennsylvania (later, University of Pittsburgh) in 1896.

Stoddard was employed in cotton manufacturing in Northampton, Massachusetts, in 1873. He was an instructor in English at the University of California (1886–88) and became a professor of English and literature at New York University in 1888. He was dean of the college of arts and pure sciences there from 1911 to 1914, when he retired. He advocated and used the inductive teaching method in his classes.

Stoddard was the author of *The Modern Novel* (1883), *The Ideal in Literature* (1884), *Psycho-Biography* (1885), *Women in the English Universities* (1886), *The Caedmon Poems* (1887), *The Conditions of Labor in England* (1887), *Miracle Plays and Mysteries* (1887), *Tolstoi and Matthew Arnold* (1890), *The Uses of Rhetoric* (1890), *Inductive Work in College Classes* (1890), *Literary Spirit in the Colleges* (1893), *The Study of the English Language* (1899), *Lord Byron, Introduction to His Works* (1899), *The Evolution of the English Novel* (1900), and *Life of Charles Butler* (1903), and he edited *Poems of National Spirit* (1904). He edited the

Macmillan Pocket Classics. He was awarded honorary degrees by Amherst College, the Western University of Pennsylvania, and New York University.

REFERENCES: *AC; LE* (I); *NCAB* (27:105); *NYT,* February 7, 1936, p. 20; *TC; WWW* (I).                                                    *Earl W. Thomas*


**STODDARD, George Dinsmore.** B. October 8, 1897, Carbondale, Pennsylvania, to Eugene and Charlotte (Dinsmore) Stoddard. M. December 26, 1925, to Margaret Trautwein. Ch. five.

George Dinsmore Stoddard received the B.A. degree (1921) from Pennsylvania State College (later, University), a diploma from the University of Paris in 1923, and the Ph.D. degree (1925) from the University of Iowa.

Stoddard taught at the University of Iowa from 1925 to 1942. He directed the Iowa Child Welfare Research Station (1928–42), was dean of the graduate college (1936–42), and headed the psychology department (1938–39). In 1942 he became president of the University of the State of New York and state commissioner of education. He left in 1946 to become president of the University of Illinois (1946–53). He was later dean of the school of education (1956–60) and chancellor and executive vice-president at New York University (1960–64), where he was Distinguished Professor of Education from 1964 to 1967. He was vice-chancellor and chancellor for academic affairs at Long Island University from 1967 to 1969.

Stoddard's major research was centered on tests and measurement and educational and child psychology. He made a significant impact on psychological circles with studies showing that environmental factors influence intelligence and that the intelligence level of an individual, previously thought to be stationary throughout life, can be raised by improving his environment.

Stoddard was the author of *Iowa Placement Examinations* (1925), *Tests and Measurement in High School Instruction* (with G. M. Ruch, 1927), *The General Shop* (with L. V. Newkirk, 1928), *Getting Ideas from the Movies* (with P. W. Holaday, 1933), *Child Psychology* (with B. L. Wellman, 1934), *Manual of Child Psychology* (with B. L. Wellman, 1936), *The Meaning of Intelligence* (1943), *Tertiary Education* (1944), *Frontiers in Education* (1945), and *On the Education of Women* (1950).

Stoddard was a member of many educational conferences and missions around the world. He was a delegate to the United Nations Educational, Scientific, and Cultural Organization (UNESCO) general conferences seven times, and was chairman of the United States General Commission to UNESCO from 1949 to 1952. He belonged to many professional organizations, was a fellow of the American Association for the Advancement of Science, chairman of the American Council on Education (1946–47), and vice-chairman of the national committee of the mid-century White House

Conference on Children and Youth. He was the recipient of many honorary degrees from American colleges and universities.

REFERENCES: *CB* (July 1946); *LE* (III); *NCAB* (G:112); *WW* (XXXI); *WWAE* (VIII); Robert J. Havighurst *(q.v.)*, ed., *Leaders in American Education* (Chicago: University of Chicago Press, 1971).

John C. Meyer

**STODDARD, John Fair.** B. July 20, 1825, Greenfield, New York, to Phineas and Marilda (Fair) Stoddard. M. October 18, 1865, to Elizabeth Ann Platt. Ch. one. D. August 6, 1873, Kearney, New Jersey.

John Fair Stoddard attended school in New York at the Montgomery Academy in Orange County, the Nine Partners' School in Dutchess County, and the State Normal College (later, State University of New York at Albany), from which he was graduated in 1847. He received the A.M. degree (1853) from the University of the City of New York (later, New York University).

Stoddard taught in a district school in 1843 and served as president of Liberty (Pennsylvania) Normal Institute (1847–51), University of Northern Pennsylvania (1851–54), and the Lancaster County (Pennsylvania) Normal School (1855–57). In 1857 he opened a teachers' college on the site of the discontinued University of Northern Pennsylvania, but a fire destroyed the buildings a few weeks later. He established the Susquehanna County Normal School at Montrose (1857–59). He moved to New York City in 1859 and was principal of Grammar School No. 10.

Stoddard was the author of *The American Intellectual Arithmetic* (1849), *Practical Arithmetic* (1852), *Philosophical Arithmetic* (1853), *University Algebra* (1857), *Stoddard's Rudiments of Arithmetic* (1863), *Stoddard's Complete Arithmetic* (1868), and *School Arithmetic* (1869). His works attained great popularity. Annual sales of his books reached two hundred thousand copies and by 1888 over two and one-half million had been published. His first manuscript, *The American Intellectual Arithmetic*, followed the Pestalozzian trend. The book was rated as one of the best mental arithmetics in the *Report of the Commissioner of Education for the Year 1897–98*.

A frequent speaker at teachers' institutes, Stoddard was president of the Pennsylvania State Teachers Association (1867) and received the honorary A.M. degree from the University of the City of New York.

REFERENCES: *AC; DAB; WWW* (H); John A. Nietz, *Old Textbooks* (Pittsburgh: University of Pittsburgh Press, 1961).          *Albert Nissman*

**STOKOWSKI, Olga. See SAMAROFF, Olga.**

**STONE, John Charles.** B. January 11, 1867, Albion, Illinois, to James Scott and Elizabeth Sarah (Hocking) Stone. M. August 5, 1891, to Gertrude

Lucia Walser. Ch. two. D. May 21, 1940, St. Petersburg, Florida.

John Charles Stone was graduated from Southern Collegiate Institute in 1885 and taught for nine years in the public schools of Edwards County, Illinois. In 1894 he entered Indiana University and was graduated with the A.B. and A.M. degrees in 1897.

Stone was head of the department of mathematics and physics at Elgin (Illinois) high school (1897–98) and Lake Forest (Illinois) Academy (1898–1900) and from 1900 to 1909 was associate professor of mathematics at Michigan State Normal College (later, Eastern Michigan University) at Ypsilanti. He became professor of mathematics at the State Teachers College (later, Montclair State College) in Montclair, New Jersey, where he remained until 1935 when he retired as professor emeritus. Stone was a special lecturer at extramural courses of New York University (1920).

Stone was the author of *Method in Geometry* (1904), *The Teaching of Arithmetic* (1905), *Essentials of Algebra* (with James F. Millis, 1907), *The Modernization of Arithmetic* (1914), *Method in Arithmetic* (1916), *A Higher Arithmetic* (with James F. Millis, 1917), *How to Teach Primary Numbers* (1921), *Elementary Algebra* (with Howard F. Hart, 1924), *How to Teach Elementary Arithmetic* (1928), *First Year Algebra* (1928), *Modern Plane Geometry* (with Virgil S. Mallory, 1929), *Mathematics for Everyday Use* (with V. S. Mallory, 1925), and *A First Course in Algebra* (with V. S. Mallory, 1936). He was the author of textbook series, including the Southworth-Stone Arithmetics (three volumes, with Gordon A. Southworth, 1904), Stone-Millis Arithmetics (three volumes, with James F. Millis, 1912), Junior High School Mathematics (three volumes, 1919), the Stone Arithmetics (1925), the New Mathematics (four volumes, 1926), and the Unit Mastery Arithmetics (six volumes, with C. N. Mills, 1932). He was a member of several professional associations.

REFERENCES: *CB* (1940); *NCAB* (31:473); *NYT,* May 23, 1940, p. 23; *WWW* (I); *Publishers Weekly* 137 (June 8, 1940): 2224.

*Nicholas A. Branca*

**STONE, Lucinda Hinsdale.** B. September 30, 1814, Hinesburg, Vermont, to Aaron and Lucinda (Mitchell) Hinsdale. M. June 10, 1840, to James Andrus Blinn Stone. Ch. three. D. March 14, 1900, Kalamazoo, Michigan.

Lucinda Hinsdale Stone was raised by her widowed mother, an advocate of education for women. Stone studied with a class of boys at the Hinesburg (Vermont) Academy and was mocked for her desire to go to college. After graduation from the academy she taught in Vermont at the Burlington and Middlebury female seminaries. She served three years in Natchez, Mississippi, as a tutor to a planter's children, fostering her antislavery beliefs.

In 1840 she married James A. B. Stone, a Baptist minister who was director of a preparatory branch of the Kalamazoo (Michigan) University (later, College). He was president of Kalamazoo College for twenty years, and Lucinda Stone served as principal of the female department of the college. She encouraged her students to develop independent thinking as well as useful character. James Stone resigned from the college in 1863, and Lucinda Stone resigned the next year.

She continued to work for women's education by organizing schools and women's clubs and advising them of study materials. From 1867 to 1888 she led girls on educational tours of Europe and the Near East. A proponent of coeducation, she succeeded in her fight for admission of women to the University of Michigan in 1870. She advocated appointment of women to the university faculty; one woman was appointed in 1896. She received an honorary degree from the University of Michigan (1891), and a scholarship was established in her memory in 1903.

REFERENCES: *NAW; NCAB* (13:198); *WC. Nancy Baldrige Julian*

**STORY, Joseph.** B. September 18, 1779, Marblehead, Massachusetts, to Elisha and Mehitable (Pedrick) Story. M. December 9, 1804, to Mary Lynde Oliver. M. August 27, 1808, to Sarah Waldo Wetmore. Ch. seven, including William W. Story, artist and author. D. September 10, 1845, Cambridge, Massachusetts.

Joseph Story attended Marblehead (Massachusetts) Academy and was graduated from Harvard University, from which he received the A.B. (1798) and A.M. (1801) degrees. He studied law with Samuel Sewall in Marblehead and Samuel Putnam in Salem, Massachusetts, and was admitted to the bar in 1801.

Story practiced law in Salem and became active in politics as a state representative (1805–07 and 1810–11) and a member of the United States Congress (1808–09). He was appointed associate justice of the United States Supreme Court in 1811 and held the office to his death. On the court Story supported the nationalist positions of John Marshall and was influential in major decisions concerning the extension of federal powers and development of a uniform commercial law, the sanctity of contracts, and exclusive federal jurisdiction over fugitive slaves.

In 1829 Story became Dane Professor of Law at Harvard University and served to 1845. With Simon Greenleaf *(q.v.)* Story was credited with the establishment of the Harvard Law School as a major institution of legal education in the United States.

Story was the author of many important books on the law, including *Commentaries on the Law of Bailments* (1832), *Commentaries on the Constitution of the United States* (three volumes, 1833), *Commentaries on the Conflict of Laws* (1834), *Commentaries on Equity Jurisprudence* (two volumes, 1835–36), *Equity Pleadings* (1838), *Law of Agency* (1839), *Law of*

*Partnership* (1841), *Law of Bills of Exchange* (1843), and *Law of Promissory Notes* (1845). He also wrote *The Power of Solitude* (1804) and *Selection of Pleadings in Civil Actions* (1805).

An overseer of Harvard University (1818–25), Story was a fellow of the American Academy of Arts and Sciences and the Massachusetts Historical Society. He received honorary degrees from Brown and Harvard universities and Dartmouth College.

REFERENCES: *AC; DAB; EB; NCAB* (2:468); *TC; WWW* (H); Gerald T. Dunne, *Justice Joseph Story and the Rise of the Supreme Court* (New York: Simon and Schuster, 1970); James McClellan, *Joseph Story and the American Constitution* (Norman: University of Oklahoma Press, 1971); William W. Story, *Life and Letters of Joseph Story,* 2 vols. (Boston: C. C. Little and J. Brown, 1851).                                                   *Morgan D. Dowd*

**STOWE, Calvin Ellis.** B. April 26, 1802, Natick, Massachusetts, to Samuel and Hepzibah (Biglow) Stow. M. 1832 to Eliza Tyler. M. January 6, 1836, to Harriet Elizabeth Beecher. Ch. seven. D. August 22, 1886, Hartford, Connecticut.

Although the death of his father when he was six left his mother in poverty, Calvin E. Stowe was able to attend the local district school. He was apprenticed at the age of twelve to a papermaker and earned money to continue his education at Bradford Academy and Gorham (Maine) Academy. As a young man he changed the spelling of his name to Stowe. He attended Bowdoin College in Brunswick, Maine, from which he received the A.B. (1824) and A.M. (1827) degrees. He was graduated from Andover (Massachusetts) Theological Seminary in 1829 and in his senior year translated *John's History of the Hebrew Commonwealth* from the German.

Stowe was librarian and instructor at Bowdoin College (1824–25). After graduation from Andover, he was editor of the *Boston Recorder,* a religious journal (1829–30), and became professor of Greek at Dartmouth College in Hanover, New Hampshire (1830–32). In 1832 Stowe accepted the chair of biblical literature at Lane Theological Seminary in Cincinnati, Ohio, and served there to 1850. In 1850 he became Collins Professor of Natural and Revealed Religion at Bowdoin College and in 1852 professor of sacred literature at Andover Theological Seminary. He accompanied his wife on three visits to Europe in the 1850s and resigned from Andover in 1864 because of failing health. The family moved to Hartford, Connecticut, and purchased a winter home at Mandarin, Florida.

Stowe regarded the common school movement as necessary to the development of the West. He was one of the founders of the Western Literary Institute and College of Teachers, an organization to promote public education, in Cincinnati in 1833 and advocated public schools as a means to Americanize immigrants. He wrote the influential *Report on*

*Elementary Instruction in Europe* in 1837 after spending a year in Europe to purchase books for Lane Theological Seminary and gather information and report on the state of public education in various European countries for the Ohio legislature. Stowe was especially impressed by the educational system of Prussia and recommended that Ohio follow the Prussian pattern of state support, teacher training, and course of study. Ten thousand copies of the *Report* were distributed to every school district in Ohio, and it was reprinted by the legislatures of Massachusetts, Michigan, North Carolina, Pennsylvania, and Virginia.

Stowe also wrote *Introduction to the Criticism and Interpretation of the Bible* (1835), *The Religious Element in Education* (1844), *The Right Interpretation of the Sacred Scriptures* (1853), and *Origin and History of the Books of the Bible* (1867). He was awarded honorary degrees by Miami and Indiana universities and Dartmouth College.

REFERENCES: *AC; DAB; NCAB* (10:140); *NYT*, August 23, 1886, p. 5; *TC; WWW* (H); Edgar W. Knight *(q.v.)*, ed., *Reports on European Education by John Grissom, Victor Cousin, Calvin E. Stowe* (New York: McGraw-Hill, 1930); Charles Edward Stowe, *Life of Harriet Beecher Stowe, Compiled from Her Letters and Journals* (Boston: Houghton, Mifflin and Co., 1891). *Harris L. Dante*

**STOWELL, Thomas Blanchard.** B. March 29, 1846, Perry, New York, to David Page and Mary Ann (Blanchard) Stowell. M. August 3, 1869, to Mary Caroline Blakeslee. Ch. two. D. July 29, 1927, Los Angeles, California.

Thomas Blanchard Stowell attended Genesee College (later part of Syracuse University) in Lima, New York, where he obtained the A.B. (1865) and A.M. (1868) degrees and Syracuse University where he received the Ph.D. degree (1881).

He was principal of Addison (New York) Academy (1865–66) and Union School in Morrisville, New York (1866–67). He taught mathematics at Genesee Wesleyan Seminary (1867–68) and in 1868 moved to Leavenworth, Kansas, where he was principal of Morris High School. He returned to New York to head the department of natural sciences in the State Normal School (later, State University of New York College) at Cortland (1868–69) and was principal of the State Normal and Training School (later, State University of New York College) at Potsdam, New York (1869–89). At Potsdam he reorganized the high school. In 1884 Stowell employed Julia Ettie Crane *(q.v.)* as a music teacher. She established the Crane Normal Institute at Potsdam in 1886 and developed a personal and institutional reputation in the education of music teachers.

In 1889 Stowell went to the University of Southern California in Los Angeles to organize the department of education. From 1889 to 1909 he developed the teacher education program and organized a graduate program. Stowell was dean of the new school of education from 1918 until 1919, when he retired.

Stowell was a frequent contributor of articles and monographs on the nervous system of the domestic cat, alcoholism, and subjects in education. He was a fellow of the American Association for the Advancement of Science and belonged to other professional organizations. He was awarded an honorary degree by St. Lawrence University in 1909. The Stowell Research Library in education at the University of Southern California was named in his honor.

REFERENCES: *NCAB* (21:429); *NYT,* July 30, 1927, p. 15; *WWW* (I).

*Walter J. Sanders*

**STRANG, Ruth May.** B. April 3, 1895, Chatham, New Jersey, to Charles Garrett and Ann (Bergen) Strang. M. no. D. January 3 1971, Amityville, Long Island, New York.

Ruth May Strang was educated at Adelphi Academy in Brooklyn, New York, and studied home economics at Pratt Institute in Brooklyn (1914–16). She studied at Teachers College, Columbia University, where she received the B.S. degree (1922) in home economics and the M.A. (1924) and Ph.D. (1926) degrees.

Strang first taught home economics in the New York City schools (1917–20) and was a research assistant and research fellow at Teachers College (1923–27). She joined the faculty at Teachers College in 1929 and continued there to her retirement in 1960. She taught at the University of Arizona (1960–68) and accepted the Peter Sandiford Professorship at the Ontario Institute for Education at the University of Toronto, Ontario, Canada, in 1968.

Strang's early interest at Columbia was in the area of guidance and student personnel; she became a national leader in the field. Prior to her work, the field of guidance and counseling was viewed as the responsibility of a specialist, but she furthered the concept that teachers should accept the role of counseling students. Her later interests focused on reading and the education of gifted children.

Strang wrote many important books in the field of education, including *Subject Matter in Health Education* (1926), *A Personnel Study of Deans of Women* (with S. M. Sturtevant, *q.v.,* 1928), *An Introduction to Child Study* (1930), *The Role of the Teacher in Personnel Work* (1932), *Personal Development and Guidance in College and Secondary Schools* (1934), *Behavior and Background of Students in College and Secondary Schools* (1937), *Counseling Techniques in Colleges and Secondary Schools* (1937), *Problems in the Improvement of Reading in Colleges and Secondary Schools* (1938), *Group Activities in Colleges and Secondary Schools*

(1941), *Educational Guidance: Its Principles and Practice* (1947), *An Introduction to Child Study* (1951), *The Role of the Teacher in Personnel Work* (1953), *The Adolescent Views Himself* (1957), *Helping Your Gifted Child* (1960), *Helping Your Child Improve His Reading* (1962), and *Diagnostic Teaching of Reading* (1964), and she was editor of *Understanding and Helping the Retarded Reader* (1965). She was editor of the *Journal of the National Association of Women Deans and Counselors* (1935–60). She collaborated with others in preparing the series Teen Age Tales and Gateways to Readable Books.

Strang was active in professional associations as a member of the National Association of Women Deans and Counselors (chairman of the research committee, 1930–39), the American Association for Gifted Children (treasurer and director), the International Council for the Improvement of Reading Instruction (board of directors), the National Society for the Study of Education (chairman, 1960), and the National Association for Remedial Teaching (president, 1955–56). She was a fellow of the American Association for the Advancement of Science, the American Public Health Association, the American Association of Applied Psychology, and Her Majesty's Royal Society of Health in England.

REFERENCES: *CA* (1–4); *CB* (December 1960); *LE* (III); *WWAE* (XXII); Robert J. Havighurst *(q.v.)*, ed., *Leaders in American Education* (Chicago. University of Chicago Press, 1971); *NYT*, January 5, 1971, p. 39; *Who's Who of American Women*, 6th ed. (Chicago, Marquis, 1969).

*Diana Scott*

**STRAYER, George Drayton.** B. November 29, 1876, Wayne, Pennsylvania, to Daniel Jacob Reese and Mary Anna Walton (Ott) Strayer. M. September 17, 1903, to Cora Bell. Ch. four. D. September 29, 1962, Princeton, New Jersey.

George D. Strayer was graduated with the A.B. degree (1903) from Johns Hopkins University in Baltimore, Maryland, after transferring there from Bucknell University in Lewisburg, Pennsylvania. He received the Ph.D. degree (1905) from Columbia University.

Strayer was a teacher and principal in public schools in Pennsylvania and Maryland from 1893 to 1903. He taught at Teachers College, Columbia University, from 1905 until he retired in 1943. He was director of the division of field studies in the Institute of Educational Research (1921–42) and director of the division of organization and administration of education (1937–42).

Strayer became a national leader in school administration. He directed or participated in more than eighty school surveys that assessed the efficiency of schools, especially in terms of cost management. He published more than a hundred articles, most of which treated topics in the administration and management of schools and school systems. He was the author of *City School Expenditures* (1905), *The Teaching Process* (1911), *Retardation and Elimination in Schools and Colleges* (1911), *Educational Administration* (with E. L. Thorndike, *q.v.*, 1913), *How to Teach* (with Naomi Norsworthy, *q.v.*, 1917), *The Classroom Teacher* (with N. L. Engelhardt, *q.v.*, 1920), *Problems in Educational Administration* (with others, 1925), *School Building Problems* (with N. L. Engelhardt, 1927), and *Principles of Teaching* (with others, 1936). He wrote arithmetic series with C. B. Upton, including Strayer-Upton Arithmetics (1928), Strayer-Upton Junior Mathematics (1928), and Strayer-Upton Practical Arithmetics (three volumes, 1934). He was editor of the American Educational Series.

Active in professional associations, Strayer was president of the National Education Association (1918–19) and the National Society for the Study of Education (1918–19). He was a fellow of the American Association for the Advancement of Science and a member of the National Advisory Committee on Education (1929–33). He was director of the Educational Finance Inquiry (1921–25) and the school campaign for the National War Savings Committee of the United States Treasury (1918). He was a member of the Educational Policies Commission (1935–45) and chairman of the Commission on the Emergency in Education (1919–22). He received the Butler Silver Medal for educational administration (1923) and was the recipient of several honorary degrees.

REFERENCES: *LE* (III); *NCAB* (A:377); *NYT,* October 1, 1962, p. 31; *WWAE* (XVI); *WWW* (IV).                    *W. Richard Stephens*

**STRONG, Edward Kellogg, Jr.** B. August 18, 1884, Syracuse, New York, to Edward Kellogg and Mary Elizabeth (Graves) Strong. M. September 12, 1911, to Margaret Tower Hart. Ch. three. D. December 4, 1963, Menlo Park, California.

Edward K. Strong, Jr., developer of the Strong Vocational Interest Inventory, was educated in the Bloomington, Illinois, and Bay City, Michigan, public schools. He received the B.S. (1906) and M.S. (1909) degrees from the University of California in Berkeley and the Ph.D. degree (1911) from Columbia University.

Strong was an assistant at Barnard College (1909–10) and was a research fellow and a lecturer in the extension department at Columbia (1911–14). He was a professor of psychology and the psychology of education at George Peabody College for Teachers at Nashville, Tennessee (1914–19). He was professor and head of the department of vocational education at Carnegie Institute of Technology (later, Carnegie-Mellon University) in Pittsburgh, Pennsylvania (1919–23), and head of the Bureau of Educational Research at Carnegie (1921–23). In 1923 Strong was professor of psychology in the graduate school of business at Stanford University and served to his retirement in 1949. He also was director of vocational interest research at Stanford from 1932 to his death.

A contributor of many articles to psychological journals, Strong was the author of *Relative Merits of Advertising* (1911), *Introductory Psychology for Teachers* (1919), *Psychology for Selling Life Insurance* (1927), *Job Analysis and the Curriculum* (with R. S. Uhrbrock, 1923), *Psychology of Selling and Advertising* (1925), *Change of Interests with Age* (1931), *Japanese in California* (1933), *The Second Generation Japanese Problem* (1934), *Psychological Aspects of Business* (1938), *Vocational Interests of Men and Women* (1943), *The Use of Vocational Interest Scales in Planning a Medical Career* (with H. C. Tucker, 1952), and *Vocational Interests Eighteen Years After College* (1955).

A member of professional organizations, Strong was a fellow of the American Association for the Advancement of Science and the American Psychological Association, and president of the Southern Society of Philosophy and Psychology (1919) and the Western Psychological Association (1933). He was awarded the Butler Silver Medal from Columbia University (1944) and the American Personnel and Guidance Association Research Award (1953).

REFERENCES: *LE* (III); *NCAB* (51:254); *NYT*, December 6, 1963, p. 35; *WWW* (IV); John G. Darley, "Edward Kellogg Strong, Jr.," *Journal of Applied Psychology* 48 (April 1964): 72–74. *John F. Ohles*

**STRONG, Frank.** B. August 5, 1859, Venice, New York, to John Butler and Mary (Foote) Strong. M. June 24, 1890, to Mary Evelyn Ransom. Ch. four. D. August 6, 1934, Lawrence, Kansas.

Frank Strong was graduated from the Auburn (New York) high school and from Yale University with the A.B. (1884), A.M. (1893), and Ph.D. (1897) degrees. He studied law and was admitted to the bar in 1886.

Strong was a high school Greek and mathematics teacher at Auburn, New York (1885–86), and practiced law in Kansas City, Kansas (1886–88). He was principal of a high school in St. Joseph, Missouri (1888–92), superintendent of schools in Lincoln, Nebraska (1892–95), and lecturer in history at Yale (1897–99).

Strong was president of Oregon State University in Corvallis (1899–1902) and chancellor of the University of Kansas at Lawrence (1902–20). On his retirement as president in 1920, he was professor of constitutional law to 1934. He was an effective university administrator. At Kansas the student body and faculty were increased in size, and schools of medicine, education, and nursing were established, summer sessions were instituted, and many academic departments were added to the university.

A contributor to professional journals, Strong was the author of *Life of*

*Benjamin Franklin* (1898), *A Forgotten Danger to the New England Colonies* (1898), *Cromwell's West Indian Expedition, 1654–55* (1899), and *Government of the American People* (1901).

He was active in professional associations, including the Kansas State Teachers' Association (president, 1910) and the National Association of State Universities (president, 1915), and was a member of the Kansas State Board of Education (1902–20). He was a delegate to the Association of American Universities (1912–20), president of the Kansas Tuberculosis Association (from 1920), and a member of the board of education of the Northern convention of the Baptist Church (1913–15). He was the recipient of several honorary degrees.

REFERENCES: *NCAB* (13:440, B:217); *NYT,* August 7, 1934, p. 17; *TC; WWW* (I).                                                                       *Lew E. Wise*

**STRONG, James Woodward.** B. September 29, 1833, Brownington, Vermont, to Elijah Gridley and Sarah Ashley (Partridge) Strong. M. September 3, 1861, to Mary Davenport. Ch. three. D. February 24, 1913, Northfield, Minnesota.

James Woodward Strong attended college preparatory school and Beloit (Wisconsin) College where he received the A.B. (1858) and A.M. (1861) degrees. He was graduated from the Union Theological Seminary in New York City in 1862 and was ordained as a Congregational minister.

Strong worked in a printing shop, in a book store, and as a schoolteacher in Vermont (1846–51). His family moved to Beloit, Wisconsin, in 1851 where Strong was a city clerk (1854–55) and superintendent of schools (1855–56) while attending Beloit College. He served churches at Brodhead, Wisconsin (1862–64), and Faribault, Minnesota (1865–70).

In 1867 Strong joined other Congregationalists in establishing a college in Northfield, Minnesota. He was a trustee during the organization of the college (1867–70) and was the first president of the college, which was named after William Carleton, a major benefactor of the new institution. He built Carleton into one of the leading colleges in the Northwest. He retired in 1903.

Strong was active in church affairs as an elected member of the American Board of Commissioners for Foreign Missions (1872), was president of the Minnesota State Home Missionary Society (1872–1905), and was a member of the International Council (1899). He attended most of the National Congregational Councils from 1865 to 1901 and was twice moderator of the Minnesota State Association of Congregational Churches. He was awarded honorary degrees by Beloit College (1872) and Illinois College (1896).

REFERENCES: *AC; DAB; NCAB* (24:50); *TC; WWW* (I).    *John F. Ohles*

**STRUCK, Ferdinand Theodore.** B. March 18, 1886, Hamburg, Germany, to Ludwig Christian Nicholous and Bertha (Runge) Struck. M. November 25, 1915, to Alice Edith Clark. Ch. three. D. November 22, 1943, State College, Pennsylvania.

F. Theodore Struck was brought to the United States from Germany by his parents in 1893. They settled in Oregon, where Struck was graduated from high school at Hood River in 1907 and received the B.S. degree and certificate in engineering from the University of Oregon in 1911. He studied at Teachers College, Columbia University, from which he received the M.A. (1914) and Ph.D. (1920) degrees.

Struck was a journeyman carpenter and drafter. He was a student assistant in the University of Oregon wood shops in 1909, taught shopwork and drawing at Stadium High School in Tacoma, Washington (1911–13), was director of the New Jersey Industrial School in West Orange (1914–15), and served as head teacher at Essex County Vocational School in West Orange (1915–18).

Struck moved to Pennsylvania where he spent the rest of his career in education. He was associate professor and professor of agricultural education at Pennsylvania State College (later, Pennsylvania State University) from 1918 to 1920. He was state supervisor of industrial education and assistant director and director of the vocational bureau in the state department of public instruction in Harrisburg (1920–26). He returned to Pennsylvania State College in 1926 as professor and head of the industrial education department, a position he held until his death.

Struck was the author of *Construction and Repair Work for the Farm* (1923), *Methods in Industrial Education* (1930), and *Creative Teaching* (1938). He contributed extensively to various educational journals and wrote many technical reports at Pennsylvania State College and the Pennsylvania State Department of Public Instruction.

Struck was instrumental in the establishment of the professional fraternity for industrial education, Iota Lambda Sigma. While adviser for the Alpha chapter of the fraternity at Pennsylvania State College, he established the Grand Chapter and was first president (1931); he remained on the national advisory council. He was trustee (1938–39) and president (1940–41) of the National Association of Industrial Teacher Trainers and was active in many other associations.

REFERENCES: *LE* (II); *WWAE* (XI); *WWW* (II); *Industrial Arts and Vocational Education* 33 (February 1944), supp. 20. *Prodeep K. Paul*
*Henry J. Sredl*


**STRYKER, Melancthon Woolsey.** B. January 7, 1851, Vernon, New York, to Isaac Pierson and Alida Livingston (Woolsey) Stryker. M. September

27, 1876, to Clara Elizabeth Goss. Ch. six. D. December 6, 1929, Rome, New York.

Melancthon Woolsey Stryker, clergyman and college president, received his early education in Rome, New York, schools. He studied at Hamilton College in Clinton, New York, for three years, worked for a year at the New York City Young Men's Christian Association, and returned to Hamilton and was graduated with the B.A. degree (1872), receiving high distinction in oratory, the classics, and English literature. He studied at Auburn (New York) Theological Seminary, preached a year in Bergen, New York, and returned to Auburn where he was graduated in 1876.

Stryker was ordained and installed as pastor of Calvary Presbyterian Church, Auburn (1876), and served the First Presbyterian Church of Ithaca, New York (1877–83), and the Second Congregational Church of Holyoke, Massachusetts (1883–85). He was pastor of the Fourth Presbyterian Church in Chicago, Illinois, where he attracted national attention by his preaching; his church became one of the most influential in Chicago.

In 1892 he accepted the presidency of Hamilton College, a post he held for twenty-five years. In addition to administrative responsibilities, Stryker was pastor of the college church, taught classes in biblical subjects and ethics, continued to be concerned with the department of public speaking, and served as choir director. During his tenure, the college erected eight new buildings, beautified the campus, acquired more land, built an athletic field, and enlarged and strengthened the faculty. While other colleges were changing their curricula, he upheld the classic tradition of Hamilton, but he also advocated athletics as a desirable part of college life.

His publications, about forty in number, include a translation of the entire New Testament from the Greek, *Hymns and Verses* (1883), *Songs of Miriam* (1888), *Letters of James the Just* (1895), *Hamilton, Lincoln and Other Addresses* (1895), *Well by the Gate* (sermons, 1903), *Attempts at Verse* (1911), *English Bible Versions and Origins* (1915), *Lincoln's Land and Other Verse* (1921), *Ethics in Outline* (1923), *Embers* (collected verse, 1926), and *Corbula* (1929). He compiled and edited collections of religious music and wrote the Hamilton College song, "Carissima."

Stryker received several honorary degrees. After his retirement he served as a trustee of Hamilton College to his death.

REFERENCES: *AC; DAB; NCAB* (26:142); *NYT*, December 27, 1929, p. 21; *TC; WWW* (I); W. Pilkington, *Hamilton College: A History, 1812–1962* (Clinton, N.Y.: Hamilton College, 1962), pp. 213–28.

*J. Franklin Hunt*

**STUBBS, Joseph Edward.** B. March 19, 1850, Ashland, Ohio, to Joseph Deyarmon and Mary Jane (Gray) Stubbs. M. July 10, 1873, to Ella A. Sprengle. Ch. five. D. May 27, 1914, Reno, Nevada.

Joseph E. Stubbs was born and reared in Ashland, Ohio. After graduating from Ashland High School (1868), he entered Ohio Wesleyan University in Delaware, Ohio, from which he received the B.A. (1873) and M.A. (1876) degrees. He was graduated from Drew Theological Seminary (later, Drew University) in Madison, New Jersey, in 1875. He was ordained to the Methodist Episcopal church ministry in 1874.

While attending Ohio Wesleyan University Stubbs served as high school principal and tutor in Latin and Greek at Delaware, Ohio, and was superintendent of schools in Ashland (1880–86). Stubbs was chosen president of Baldwin University (later, Baldwin-Wallace College) in Berea, Ohio, in 1886 and served in that capacity to 1894. He took a leave of absence in 1890 to study and visit abroad at the universities of Berlin, Halle, Heidelberg, and Leipzig, Germany, and Oxford, England.

Stubbs was president of the University of Nevada (1894–1914). He was credited with elevating the university curriculum and raising its academic standards. He introduced expanded high school–level offerings at the university and encouraged the establishment of high schools in the state. He established university extension programs in Nevada, which expanded the influence of the institution throughout the state. During his presidency, Clarence Mackay, the most notable early patron of the University of Nevada, began making a series of gifts to the institution, totaling more than $1.5 million, including the establishment of the Mackay School of Mines.

Stubbs was active in professional associations, serving as a director of the National Education Association (1895–1908) and president of the Association of American Agricultural Colleges and Experimental Stations (1899–1900) and the College Association of Ohio (1891–92). He was a delegate to the Ecumenical Conference in London, England (1901), and a member of the Permanent American Commission for Study of Agricultural Finance, Production, Distribution and Rural Life (1913–14). He received an honorary degree from German Wallace College in 1890.

REFERENCES: *NCAB* (16:42); *NYT,* May 28, 1914, p. 13; *TC; WWW* (I); Samuel Bradford Doten, *An Illustrated History of the University of Nevada* (Reno: University of Nevada, 1924); James W. Hulse, *The University of Nevada, A Centennial History* (Reno: University of Nevada Press, 1974); *Nevada State Journal,* May 28, 1914.

*Joan W. Thompson*

**STUDEBAKER, John Ward.** B. June 10, 1887, McGregor, Iowa, to Thomas Henderson and Mary (Dorcas) Studebaker. M. December 25, 1909, to Elinor Regina Winberg. Ch. one.

John Ward Studebaker worked his way through Leander Clark College in Toledo, Iowa, as a union bricklayer, graduating with the A.B. degree in 1910. He earned the A.M. degree (1917) from Columbia University.

His first professional position was as high school principal and coach at

Guthrie Center, Iowa (1910–11). He moved to Mason City, Iowa, where he was an elementary and junior high school principal (1911–14). In 1914 Studebaker became assistant superintendent of schools in Des Moines, Iowa, moving into the superintendency in 1920. He installed an itemized budget, an equal pay scale, and reorganized the building program. He instituted an adult education program, possibly the first in the nation. He was the national director of the Junior Red Cross during World War I.

Studebaker was United States commissioner of education from 1934 to 1948. He resigned as superintendent in Des Moines in 1937 after a three-year leave of absence. As commissioner he organized an adult education program, extending nationwide the successful public forums he had begun in Des Moines. He proposed educational activities for the Civilian Conservation Corps and the National Youth Administration. He supported educational opportunity for blacks, strengthened the department's library division, and instituted the Teacher of the Year selection and the Life Adjustment Program. He proposed the year-round school schedule.

During World War II he proposed and carried out the National Defense Training Program. He administered the High School Victory Corps, defense savings stamp and bond sales, and conservation activities. Later he helped organize support for school lunches, the GI Bill of Rights, high school credit for military experience, and the Zest for Democracy program to fight communist ideas in high schools and colleges. Studebaker prepared the way for an equalization fund to provide equal educational opportunities in the states for teacher training and aid to school construction.

Studebaker was the author of *Our Country's Call to Service* (1918), *The American Way* (1935), *Plain Talk* (1936), and *Mathematics and Life* (with G. M. Ruch, 1937). He coauthored series of arithmetic textbooks, including Number Stories (three volumes, 1941–43), Understanding Numbers (1942), Standard Service Arithmetics (1929), and Study Mathematics Series (books 3–8, 1943–46). He received honorary degrees from several American universities.

REFERENCES: *CB* (May 1942); *LE* (III); *WW* (XXIX); *WWAE* (XV).

*Paul C. Pickett*


**STURTEVANT, Julian Monson.** B. July 26, 1805, Warren, Connecticut, to Warren and Lucy (Tanner) Sturtevant. M. August 31, 1829, to Elizabeth Maria Fayerweather. M. March 3, 1941, to Hannah Fayerweather. Ch. ten. D. February 11, 1886, Jacksonville, Illinois.

At the age of eleven, Julian Monson Sturtevant moved with his family from Warren, Connecticut, to Tallmadge, Ohio, where he attended an academy and returned to Connecticut in 1822 to attend Yale College. Graduating in 1826, he studied theology at Yale Divinity School and was ordained to the Congregational ministry in 1829.

Sturtevant and his first bride went west with Theron Baldwin *(q.v.)* and settled in Jacksonville, Illinois, where he was the first teacher at Illinois College (1830). He served as professor of mathematics, natural philosophy, and astronomy (1831–44) and president and professor of mental science and the science of government (1844–76). After stepping down as president, he continued on the faculty to 1885.

Sturtevant was a religious and educational leader in the Midwest. He delivered the opening sermon at the first National Council of Congregational Churches in Boston in 1865. He became a radical abolitionist and, as a friend of Abraham Lincoln, went to England during the Civil War to enlist support for the Union. He successfully worked to keep Illinois College free from narrow sectarian control and ensured relative freedom in discussion of theological issues.

Sturtevant wrote articles for periodicals, *Economics, or the Science of Wealth* (1877), *The Keys of Sect* (1880), and an autobiography published posthumously.

REFERENCES:*AC; DAB; NCAB* (13:601); *NYT,* February 12, 1886, p. 5; *WWW* (H); J. M. Sturtevant, Jr. (ed.), *Julian M. Sturtevant. An Autobiography* (New York: F. N. Revell, 1896).                    *John F. Ohles*

**STURTEVANT, Sarah Martha.** B. February 22, 1881, Sonora, California, to Andrew and Martha (Doe) Sturtevant. M. no. D. December 18, 1942, Modesto, California.

Educated in California at Sacramento and Oakland high schools, Sarah M. Sturtevant studied at the University of California at Berkeley from which she received the A.B. degree (1904). Fifteen years later (1919) she enrolled at Teachers College, Columbia University, where she completed work for the A.M. degree (1920) and was awarded the Teachers College diploma for "Adviser of Women."

Sturtevant was vice-principal and teacher of history and English at the Fort Bragg (California) Union High School (1904–12). She taught English at the Anna Head School in Berkeley (1912–15) and Fremont High School in Oakland (1915–18), and was dean of girls at Fremont High School (1918–19). Upon her return from Teachers College to California in 1920 Sturtevant was appointed supervisor of school activities, dean of girls, and instructor in education at University High School at the University of California (1920–22). She taught at Teachers College, Columbia University, as associate professor (1923–34) and professor (1934–42).

The author of several articles published in educational journals, Sturtevant coauthored with Ruth Strang *(q.v.) A Personnel Study of Deans of Women in Teachers Colleges and Normal Schools* (1928) and *A Personnel Study of Deans of Girls in High School* (1929), and coedited *Deans at Work* (with Harriet Hayes, 1930) and *Trends in Personnel Work* (with others, 1940).

A member of the National Association of Deans of Women, Sturtevant served as president of the New York State Association of Deans (1927–33). She was a member of the executive committee of the American Council of Guidance and Personnel Associations (1934–35) and served as first woman chairperson (1935–36). She was a member of the committee of fifteen on secondary education of the California High School Teachers Association (1922–23), the National Committee to Survey Secondary Education (1930), and the Associated Boards for Christian Colleges in China. She received an honorary degree from Russell Sage College (1939).

REFERENCES: *LE* (II); *NYT,* December 19, 1942, p. 19; *WWAE* (VIII); *WWW* (II).                                            *Vernon Lee Sheeley*

**SUHRIE, Ambrose Leo.** B. February 28, 1874, New Baltimore, Pennsylvania, to Francis and Mary Theresa (Topper) Suhrie. M. August 15, 1906, to Rosa R. Ritchie. M. August 5, 1950, to Alice Noggle Judson. Ch. two. D. February 19, 1956, Pasadena, California.

Ambrose L. Suhrie received a teacher's certificate in 1891 from Southwestern State Normal School (later, California State College) at California, Pennsylvania, and the Ph.B. degree (1906) from John B. Stetson University in De Land, Florida. He studied at Wooster (Ohio) College (1903–05) and the University of Chicago (1906) and became a Harrison Fellow at the University of Pennsylvania from which he received the A.M. (1911) and Ph.D. (1912) degrees.

Suhrie first taught at the Suhrie School in New Baltimore, Pennsylvania, and was a public school teacher, principal, and superintendent in Pennsylvania (1891–1902). He was professor of education at Stetson University (1906–10) and director of the normal department (1912–14) at Georgia Normal and Industrial College at Milledgeville (later, Georgia College). He was head of the department of education and director of the extension division at the State Normal School at West Chester, Pennsylvania (1914–15) and director of practice teaching at the University of Pennsylvania (1915–18). From 1918 to 1924 he was dean of the Cleveland (Ohio) School of Education.

Suhrie moved to New York University in 1924 to organize the department of normal school and teachers' college as one of the first graduate programs in education. He was a leader in the development of teacher education programs, helping coordinate state programs of preservice and in-service education of teachers, upgrading certification standards and requirements, and improving faculty-student relationships. He retired in 1942 and served as a consultant for a study of black colleges for the General Education Board in New York City (1943–44) and was an educational consultant to the Southern Missionary College of the Seventh-Day Adventist church in Collegedale, Tennessee, from 1945 to his death.

A founder and editor (1939–42) of the *Journal of Teacher Education,*

Suhrie was the author of *The Inductive Determination of Educational Method* (1915), *New Possibilities in Education* (1916), *Problems in Teacher Training* (1926), and *Teacher of Teachers* (1955). He also wrote the Spell-to-Write Spelling Series (with Robert P. Kochler, 1928) and the Story World Series (with Myrtle Garrison Gee, 1954). He was associate editor of *New Jersey Journal of Education* (1926–28).

Suhrie founded and was first president (1926–32) of the Eastern States Association of Professional Schools for Teachers, secretary of the joint conference committee of the Cleveland School of Education and Western Reserve University (1920–24), chairman of the teacher-training section of the New York Society for the Experimental Study of Education (1926–30), and a member of many other professional associations. He received an honorary degree from Stetson University in 1919.

REFERENCES: *LE* (I); *NYT*, February 21, 1956, p. 33; *WWAE* (I); *WWW* (III); Ambrose L. Suhrie, *Teacher of Teachers* (West Rindge, N.H.: Topside, 1955). *T. S. Geraty*

**SUMNER, William Graham.** B. October 30, 1840, Paterson, New Jersey, to Thomas and Sarah (Graham) Sumner. M. April 17, 1871, to Jeannie Whittemore Elliott. Ch. three. D. April 12, 1910, Englewood, New Jersey.

William Graham Sumner attended the public schools in Hartford, Connecticut, before entering Yale College in 1859 from which he received the A.B. degree (1863). He studied at Göttingen, Germany, and Oxford, England (1863–66).

Sumner was made a deacon of the Protestant Episcopal church in 1867 and was ordained a priest in 1869. He was rector of the Church of the Redeemer in Morristown, New Jersey (1870–72), and accepted the newly created chair of political and social science at Yale in 1872 where he remained until his retirement in 1908.

Sumner was the author of *A History of American Currency* (1874), *Lectures on the History of Protection in the United States* (1875), *Life of Andrew Jackson* (1882), *What Social Classes Owe Each Other* (1882), *Collected Essays in Political and Social Sciences* (1883), *Protectionism* (1885), *The Financier* (1892), *Finances of the Revolution* (1892), *A History of Banking in the United States* (1896), and *Folkways* (1907).

Sumner was a member of the New Haven, Connecticut, board of aldermen (1873–76) and an active member of the State Board of Education (1882–1910). He participated in the development of teacher education in the state and the certification of teachers. He was a member of the board of visitors of the United States Naval Academy and was president of the American Sociological Society at the time of his death. He received honorary degrees from the University of East Tennessee (1884) and Yale University (1909).

REFERENCES: *AC; DAB; EB; NCAB* (25:8); *NYT,* April 13, 1910, p. 11; *WWW* (I); A. G. Keller, "William Graham Sumner," *American Journal of Sociology* 15 (May 1910): 832–35; *New Haven Evening Register,* April 13, 1910; Harris E. Starr, *William Graham Sumner* (New York: Henry Holt and Co., 1925).                                   *Arthur E. Soderlind*

**SUNDERLAND, Eliza Jane Read.** B. April 19, 1839, Huntsville, Illinois, to Amasa and Jane (Henderson) Read. M. December 7, 1871, to Jabez Thomas Sunderland. Ch. three. D. March 3, 1910, Hartford, Connecticut.

Eliza Jane Read Sunderland started teaching at the age of fifteen with the intention of attending Mount Holyoke Seminary (Massachusetts). She enrolled in Mount Holyoke, graduating in 1865. She received the Ph.B. (1889) and Ph.D. (1892) degrees from the University of Michigan.

Although she was offered a position at Mount Holyoke, she was unable to accept it because of problems at home. She took a position in the high school at Aurora, Illinois, in 1866 and was principal of the school (1867–71), one of the first women in the United States to head a public secondary school. The school became a model school for the state of Illinois.

She taught school in Chicago, Illinois, and Ann Arbor, Michigan (1877–98). Sunderland's chief interest was religion, and she sought a broader religious faith. Although not ordained, she preached in many churches. She was involved in many matters concerned with promoting a better quality of life, including temperance, the advancement of women, the improvement of education, and religion.

Sunderland wrote many religious articles and pamphlets. She contributed "Importance of the Study of Comparative Religions" to *The World's Congress of Religions* (1894), and collaborated with Jabez Sunderland on *James Martineau and His Greatest Book* (1905). She also wrote *Stories from Genesis* (1890) and *Heroes and Heroines* (1895). She was an associate editor of the *Illinois Social Science Journal* (1878).

Sunderland was the chief organizer of the Women's Western Unitarian Conference (first president, 1882–87) and a member of the Association for the Advancement of Women (vice-president and director, 1885–95). She was a featured speaker at the World's Parliament of Religions and at the Congress of Women in Chicago (1893).

REFERENCES: *DAB; NCAB* (10:219); *WC; WWW* (I). *Maxine Huffman*

**SUTTON, William Seneca.** B. August 12, 1860, Fayetteville, Arkansas, to James Tilton and Francena Lavenia (Martin) Sutton. M. June 12, 1884, to Anna Blackman Erwin. Ch. two. D. November 26, 1928, Austin, Texas.

William Seneca Sutton received the B.A. degree from the University of Arkansas at the age of eighteen (1878) and the M.A. degree in 1880.

After teaching a year in an Arkansas country school, he became a principal (1879–80) and superintendent (1880–83) in Fayetteville, Arkansas. He went to Ennis, Texas, as a high school principal for three years and to Houston as high school principal (1886–87) and superintendent (1887–97). During his public school career he served as president of the Texas State Teachers Association (1896) and principal of the State School of Methods (1894–96), working in both for the better preparation of teachers and public support of schools.

Fron 1897 until his death Sutton was a member of the faculty of the University of Texas in Austin; he was head of the department of pedagogy, founder and dean (1898–1918) of the university summer school, dean of the school of education (1909–28), which he was instrumental in separating from the college of arts, and acting president (1923–24).

Sutton coauthored Pupils' Series of Arithmetics (with W. H. Kimbrough, 1892), *Sutton and Bruce's Arithmetic* (with W. H. Bruce, *q.v.*, 1906), and *Schoolroom Essentials* (with Paul W. Horn, 1911), and wrote *Problems in Modern Education* (1913).

Among the associations he helped organize were the Texas Conference on Education (1907), the Texas Academy of Sciences (president, 1910–11), and the National Society for the Scientific Study of Education (president, 1908–09). He also was active in the National Society of College Teachers of Education (president, 1908–09) and the University Commission on Race Questions in the South (chairman, 1915). He was awarded an honorary degree from the University of Arkansas (1905). Sutton Hall at the University of Texas was named in his honor.

REFERENCES: *DAB; NCAB* (21:436); *NYT,* November 27, 1928, p. 31; *WWW* (IV). *D. Richard Bowles*

**SUZZALLO, Henry.** B. August 22, 1875, San Jose, California, to Peter and Anne (Suzzallo) Suzzallo. M. February 8, 1912, to Edith Moore. Ch. none. D. September 25, 1933, Seattle, Washington.

The son of poor Portuguese immigrants, Henry Suzzallo worked his way through school and became a leading figure in American education. He received the A.B. degree (1899) from Stanford (California) University and the A.M. (1902) and Ph.D. (1905) degrees from Columbia University.

Suzzallo was a principal of California schools (1896–97 and 1899–1901), instructed at Stanford from 1902, and was lecturer (1903–05) at Columbia University and deputy superintendent of San Francisco public schools for five months in 1903, 1904, and 1907. He was an instructor and lecturer at California normal schools in San Francisco (1902–03) and San Jose (1905–07). He was an assistant professor of education at Stanford (1905–07), adjunct professor of elementary education (1907–09), and professor of the philosophy of education (1909–15).

In 1915 Suzzallo was selected president of the University of Washington in Seattle. He successfully led the University of Washington to a position as a major educational institution. He planned the development of the physical plant, began an extensive building program, and sought public funds to support the university. His aggressive efforts to improve financial support led to his dismissal by the governor of Washington in 1926.

Suzzallo lectured in Europe on American education for the Carnegie Foundation for the Advancement of Teaching (1926–28). He was a specialist in higher education for the foundation (1927–29), director of the National Advisory Committee on Education (1929–30), and president of the Carnegie Foundation for the Advancement of Teaching from 1930 to his death.

A contributor to professional journals, Suzzallo was editor of the Riverside Educational Monographs from 1909. He was active in professional associations as a fellow of the American Association for the Advancement of Science, president of the National Association of State Universities (1921–22), director of the American Federation of the Arts, a member of the *Annals* editorial committee of the American Academy of Political and Social Science and the committee on higher education of the North Central Association of Colleges and Secondary Schools (1929–33), and a member at large of the division of states' relations of the National Research Council (1919–23). He was a trustee of the Carnegie Foundation for the Advancement of Teaching (1919, and chairman of the board 1926–33), the Carnegie Corporation of New York, the National Council of Education (1926–33), and Stevens Institute of Technology (1927–33). He was a member of advisory boards to the universities of Denver and Wyoming and Colorado College and was a member of the Washington state boards of education and vocational education. He received honorary degrees from several American universities and was decorated by the government of Italy. The library at the University of Washington was dedicated to his memory shortly after his death.

REFERENCES: *DAB; LE* (I); *NCAB* (C:21, 24:39); *NYT,* September 26, 1933, p. 21; *WWAE* (IV); *WWW* (I); *School and Society* 38 (September 30, 1933): 440; "Dr. Henry Suzzallo," *Seattle Post-Intelligencer,* August 1, 1975, p. A4.                                        *Michael A. Balasa*

**SWAIN, David Lowry.** B. January 4, 1801, Asheville, North Carolina, to George and Caroline (Lowry) Swain. M. January 12, 1824, to Eleanor H. White. Ch. two. D. August 27, 1868, Chapel Hill, North Carolina.

David Lowry Swain studied at Newton Academy in Asheville, North Carolina, and attended the University of North Carolina for four months in 1821. He read law in the office of John Louis Taylor and was admitted to the bar in 1823; he engaged in a successful law practice.

Swain was a legislator from Buncombe County (1824–26 and 1828–29). He was elected solicitor of the Edenton (North Carolina) District in 1827, rode the circuit once, and resigned. In 1830 he became a member of the board of internal improvements and was elected judge of the Superior Court of Law and Equity (1831–32). In 1832 Swain was the youngest man to be elected governor of North Carolina, serving to 1835.

From 1835 to his death Swain served as president of the University of North Carolina. From nearly ninety students in 1835, the student body grew to almost five hundred in 1860. Swain was a delegate to the convention in Montgomery, Alabama, that organized the Confederate government. He served as an adviser to the governor of North Carolina during the Civil War and was a special emissary to General William Tecumseh Sherman in April 1865 to arrange terms of surrender to the Union army. He served as an adviser on matters of reconstruction to President Andrew Johnson (1865–68).

Swain was a founder of the North Carolina Historical Society and a trustee (1831–68) and president of the board (1832–35) of the University of North Carolina. He was the founder of *University of North Carolina Magazine*. Swain received honorary degrees from the College of New Jersey (1841) and Yale College (1842). Swain County, North Carolina, was named in his honor in 1871.

REFERENCES: *AC; DAB; NCAB* (4:424); *TC; WWW* (H).

*Linda C. Gardner*

**SWAIN, Joseph.** B. June 16, 1857, Pendleton, Indiana, to Woolston and Mary Ann (Thomas) Swain. M. September 22, 1885, to Frances Morgan. Ch. none. D. May 19, 1927, Philadelphia, Pennsylvania.

Joseph Swain was graduated from Indiana University with the A.B. (1883) and M.S. (1885) degrees. He studied mathematics and astronomy at the University of Edinburgh, Scotland (1885–86).

Swain was an assistant instructor in mathematics (1883–85) and biology (1884–85) and associate professor of mathematics and biology and professor of mathematics and astronomy (1886–91) at Indiana University. He was professor of mathematics at Leland Stanford Junior University (later, Stanford University) in California (1891–93) and president of Indiana University (1893–1902). He was president of Swarthmore (Pennsylvania) College (1902–21). He was noted for his support for improved living conditions for teachers and his progressive ideas about higher education. The enrollment at Swarthmore tripled while he was president, and many new departments were added to the college, including those of political science, psychology, and education.

Swain was active in professional associations, serving as president of the National Education Association (1913–14), the Indiana State Teachers' Association (1894), and the higher education section of the National Educational Association (1898). He was a member of the board of the World Peace Foundation and vice-president and a member of the board of trustees of the Public Education Association of Philadelphia, Pennsylvania. He was awarded five honorary degrees by American colleges and universities.

REFERENCES: *NCAB* (6:355); *NYT,* May 20, 1927, p. 19; *TC; WWW* (I); *School and Society* 25 (June 4, 1927): 661–62.                        *John F. Ohles*

**SWETT, John.** B. July 31, 1830, Pittsfield, New Hampshire, to Eben and Lucretia (French) Swett. M. May 8, 1862, to Mary Louise Tracy. Ch. six. D. August 22, 1913, Alhambra, California.

John Swett, Father of the Public School System in California, attended school in New Hampshire at Pittsfield (1843–47) and Pembroke (1848–50) academies and the Merrimack Normal Institute at Reed's Ferry, New Hampshire, under William Russell *(q.v.)* in 1851.

Swett taught in the winter term in district schools (1847–51) and joined the gold rush to California, sailing around Cape Horn in 1852. He was principal of the Rincon School in San Francisco (1853–62). He was California state superintendent of public instruction (1862–67). He was successful in obtaining legislative support for taxes for the schools, established a teacher certification system, and provided for uniform textbooks in the state. He organized the state teachers' association and wrote the first workable school law. He held teachers' institutes and participated in the founding of the *California Teacher* in 1863.

Swett was principal of the Denman School in San Francisco (1868–70 and 1873–76) and was deputy superintendent of the San Francisco public schools (1870–73). He was principal of the Girls' High and Normal School (1876–89) and superintendent of schools in San Francisco (1890–94). He retired to his ranch near Martinez, California, in 1894.

Swett wrote *Common School Readings* (1865), *History of the Public School System of California* (1876), *Methods of Teaching* (1880), *School Elocution* (1886), *American Public Schools: History and Pedagogics* (1900), and *Public Education in California* (1911). He collaborated with William Swinton *(q.v.)* in writing several language arts and geography textbooks (1872–76). He was editor-in-chief of the *California State Educational Journal* (1864–68). He was awarded honorary degrees in 1866 by the College of California and Dartmouth College and by the University of California in 1913.

REFERENCES: *DAB; NCAB* (10:523); *NYT,* August 24, 1913, p. 11; *WWW* (I); Will S. Cluff, Jr., "The Contributions of John Swett to Free Public Education in California" (Ed.D. diss., University of the Pacific, 1954).                                                            *J. Marc Jantzen*

**SWINTON, William.** B. April 23, 1833, Salton, Scotland, to William and Jane (Currie) Swinton. M. May 4, 1853, to Catherine Linton. Ch. five. D. October 24, 1892, Brooklyn, New York.

William Swinton's family emigrated from Scotland to Canada in 1843. He attended Knox College in Toronto, Ontario, a Presbyterian preparatory school that later became one of the colleges of the University of Toronto. He entered Amherst (Massachusetts) College but completed only part of the freshman year.

In 1852 Swinton became professor of languages at Edgeworth Female Seminary in Greensboro, North Carolina. He taught at the Mount Washington Collegiate Institute in New York City (1855–58) while studying for the Presbyterian ministry. From 1858 to 1869 Swinton was on the staff of the *New York Times* and during the Civil War became a special field correspondent. His criticism of leading generals, including Ambrose Burnside and Ulysses S. Grant, resulted in his exclusion from army camps. In 1867 he traveled in the South visiting and collecting materials for a history of the war. He returned to the *Times* as literary critic.

In 1869 Swinton became professor of belles lettres at the newly established University of California at Berkeley, but he opposed the policies of the president, Daniel Coit Gilman *(q.v.)*, and resigned in 1874. He returned to Brooklyn and engaged in a financially successful career writing school textbooks.

Among his books were *Rambles Among Words* (1858), *The Times Review of McClellan: His Military Career Reviewed and Exposed* (1864), *The Twelve Decisive Battles of the War* (1867), *Campaigns of the Army of the Potomac* (1866), *A Condensed History of the United States* (1870), *History of the New York 7th Regiment During the War of Rebellion* (1870), and *Outlines of the World's History* (1875). He also wrote the World Book Series (1871), Language Series (1873–74), and juvenile informational books. He edited *Masterpieces of English Literature* (1880) and *Treasury of Tales* (1885).

Swinton received an honorary A.M. degree from Amherst College in 1866 and was awarded a gold medal for a textbook series at the Paris (France) Exposition in 1878.

REFERENCES: *AC; DAB; NCAB* (11:488); *NYT,* October 26, 1892, p. 5; *TC; WWW* (H); John A. Neitz, *Old Textbooks* (Pittsburgh: University of Pittsburgh Press, 1961). *Barbara Ruth Peltzman*

**SYMONDS, Percival Mallon.** B. April 18, 1893, Newtonville, Massachusetts, to Joseph Ainsworth and Abbie Kendall (Mallon) Symonds. M. December 25, 1922, to Johnnie Pirkle. Ch. none. D. August 6, 1960, Salem, Massachusetts.

Percival M. Symonds was graduated from Harvard University with the A.B. degree (1915) and received the A.M. (1920) and Ph.D. (1923) degrees from Columbia University.

Symonds was a teacher at Punchard High School in Andover, Massachusetts (1915–17), and Worcester (Massachusetts) Academy (1917–18). He was an assistant and instructor at Teachers College of Columbia University (1921–22) and professor of education and psychology at the University of Hawaii (1922–24). He returned to Teachers College in 1924 and continued there to his retirement in 1958. He was chairman of the division of theory and techniques of measurement (1933–37) and head of the department of research methods (1937–42). He was a leader in educational measurement and research.

Symonds was the author of many books, including *Measurement in Education* (1927), *Ability Standards for Standardized Achievement Tests in High School* (1927), *The Nature of Conduct* (1928), *Tests and Interest Questionnaires in the Guidance of High School Boys* (1930), *Diagnosing Personality and Conduct* (1931), *Mental Hygiene of the School Child* (1934), *Psychological Diagnosis in Social Adjustment* (1934), *Measurement of Personality Adjustment of High School Pupils* (with C. E. Jackson, 1935), *Education and Psychology of Thinking* (1936), *Psychology of Parent and Child Relations* (1939), *Dynamics of Human Adjustment* (1946), *Dynamic Psychology* (1949), *Adolescent Fantasy* (1949), *Dynamics of Parent-Child Relations* (1949); *Ego and the Self* (1951); *Dynamics of a Psychotherapy* (volume 1, 1956, volume 2, 1957, and volume 3, 1958), *What Education Has to Learn from Psychology* (1958), and *From Adolescent to Adult,* published posthumously in 1961. He was on the editorial board of *Journal of Educational Psychology, Journal of Educational Research, Psychological Monographs, Sociatry, Personality,* and *Nervous Child.*

Symonds was a diplomate and fellow of the American Psychological Association (president of educational psychology division, 1947–48) and a fellow of the American Orthopsychiatric Association, the American Association for the Advancement of Science (secretary of section Q, 1937–39), the Society for Projective Techniques, and the Rorschach Institute. He was president of the American Educational Research Association (1956–57).

REFERENCES: *LE* (III); *NCAB* (46:7); *NYT,* August 8, 1960, p. 21; *WWW* (IV).                                                    *John M. Ivanoff*

# T

**TABA, Hilda.** B. December 7, 1902, Estonia, to Robert and Lusa (Leht) Taba. M. no. D. July 6, 1967, Burlingame, California.

After earning the B.A. degree (1926) from the University of Tartu in her native Estonia, Hilda Taba came to the United States. She completed the

M.A. degree (1927) at Bryn Mawr (Pennsylvania) College and was awarded the Ph.D. degree (1932) from Columbia University, where she studied under John Dewey *(q.v.)*.

Taba served as director of curriculum in Dalton, Ohio (1934–35), and was appointed assistant professor of education at Ohio State University (1936–38) where she was on the field evaluation staff. She was assistant professor of education at the University of Chicago (1939–40) and was director of the curriculum laboratory (1939–45). She was director of an experimental intergroup project in New York City sponsored by the American Council on Education (1945–48). As a result of the experimental project, the Center of Intergroup Education was established at the University of Chicago under a grant from the National Council of Christians and Jews. Taba returned to Chicago and directed the center (1948–51). She served as professor of education at San Francisco (California) State College (later, San Francisco State University) from 1959 to 1967 and was appointed professor of educational administration shortly before her death.

Taba served as a consultant to many local institutions and school districts. She took part in the United Nations Educational, Scientific, and Cultural Organization seminars in Paris and Brazil. She engaged in research on the relations between ethnic groups, curriculum processes, and the development of cognitive processes in children.

A prolific writer, she contributed many articles to professional journals. She edited Studies of Intergroup Education, a series describing research conducted under the auspices of the American Council of Education. She also wrote *The Dynamics of Education* (1932), *School Culture: Studies of Participation and Leadership* (1955), *Curriculum Development: Theory and Practice* (1962), and *A Teacher's Handbook for Elementary Social Studies* (1967), and coauthored *Adolescent Personality and Character* (with Robert J. Havighurst, *q.v.*, 1949), *Thinking in Elementary School Children* (with others, 1964), and *Teaching Strategies for the Culturally Disadvantaged* (with Deborah Elkins, 1966).

REFERENCES: *LE* (III); *NCAB* (54:113); *NYT*, July 8, 1967, p. 25; *Who's Who of American Women*, 3rd ed. (Chicago: Marquis, 1963); R. L. Brown, "Taba Rediscovered," *School Teacher* 40 (November 1973): 30–33.

*Mary Harshbarger*


**TAFT, Horace Dutton.** B. December 28, 1861, Cincinnati, Ohio, to Alphonso and Louisa Maria (Torrey) Taft. M. June 29, 1892, to Winifred S. Thompson. Ch. none. D. January 28, 1943, Watertown, Connecticut.

The son of a United States attorney general, brother of a president of the United States, and uncle of a United States senator, Horace Dutton Taft was raised and educated in Cincinnati, Ohio, graduating from Woodward High School before going to Yale University. He was graduated from Yale with the A.B. (1883) and M.A. (1893) degrees. He returned home in 1883 to study law at Cincinnati Law School and was admitted to the bar in 1885. He practiced law briefly with his older brother, William Howard Taft, before deciding to become a teacher.

In 1877 Taft returned to Yale as a Latin tutor. Three years later he resigned and established a preparatory school for boys (which became coeducational in 1972). His school of ten boarders and seven day students grew sufficiently by 1893 to move from limited accommodations at Pelham Manor, New York, to larger facilities at Watertown, Connecticut.

Taft was an ideal private school headmaster. He was highly competent as an administrator, disciplinarian, classicist, and teacher. Taft School, which he and another teacher owned, was turned over to a board of trustees in 1927 permitting the solicitation of endowments. Taft raised some $2 million, which was mainly used for new buildings. At the time of his retirement in 1936, the school's enrollment was three hundred; it had become one of the outstanding preparatory schools for high-school boys in America. He was the author of the autobiographical *Memories and Opinions* (1942).

Taft was prominent in civic affairs. He spoke and wrote principally about city managership, the League of Nations, the merit system, and prohibition. He served on the board of trustees of two preparatory schools in addition to his own and was active in the Headmasters Association (president, 1908, and the New England Association of Colleges and Secondary Schools (president, 1918–19). He was awarded a number of honorary degrees.

REFERENCES: *CB* (March 1943); *LE* (I); *NCAB* (35:244); *WWW* (II); *NYT*, January 29, 1943, p. 19; Horace Dutton Taft, *Memories and Opinions* (New York: Macmillan Co., 1942).                                    *Robert H. Truman*

**TALBOT, Marion.** B. July 31, 1858, Thun, Switzerland, to Israel Tisdale and Emily (Fairbanks) Talbot. M. no. D. October 20, 1948, Chicago, Illinois.

Born in Thun, Switzerland, while her parents were in Europe, Marion Talbot was reared and educated in Boston, Massachusetts. Talbot attended Chauncy Hall School and the Girls' High School. She was admitted to Boston University, where she was graduated with the B.A. degree (1880). She enrolled in the Massachusetts Institute of Technology in 1881, left after one term, but returned later and received the B.S. degree (1888).

Talbot was a lecturer at the Lasell Seminary (later, Lasell Junior College) in Auburndale, Massachusetts (1888–90), and an instructor of domestic science at Wellesley (Massachusetts) College (1890–92). In 1892 she joined the faculty of the University of Chicago where she continued to 1925 as a teacher of sanitary science and household administration and also was dean of women (1892–1925) and dean of the Junior College of Science for women (1905–09). Talbot was the first to hold the position of dean of women in the United States.

Talbot was the author of *The Education of Women* (1910), *The Modern Household* (with Sophonisba P. Breckinridge, *q.v.*, 1912), *House Sanitation* (1912), *History of the American Association of University Women* (with Lois K. M. Rosenberry, 1930), and *More Than Love* (1936). She edited *Home Sanitation* (with Ellen H. Richards, *q.v.*, 1887).

After her retirement in 1925, Talbot served as acting president of Constantinople (Turkey) College for Women (1927–28 and 1931–32). In 1881 she joined her mother and others in establishing the Association of Collegiate Alumnae (later, American Association of University Women) and served as president and secretary for thirteen years. She was a fellow of the American Association for the Advancement of Science and the American Public Health Association, a member of the advisory committee of the Guggenheim Foundation, and the board of visitors of Wellesley College; and a trustee of Boston University. She was awarded honorary degrees by Cornell College and Boston and Tulane universities. The Marion Talbot Fellowship of the American Association of University Women was named in her honor.

REFERENCES: *NAW; NCAB* (36:425); *WWW* (II); *NYT,* October 21, 1948, p. 27; "Marion Talbot: In Memoriam," *American Association of University Women Journal* 42 (Winter 1949): 79–80.          *Olga Padron*

**TALL, Lida Lee.** B. November 17, 1873, Dorchester County, Maryland, to Washington and Sarah Elizabeth (Humphreys) Tall. M. no. D. February 21, 1942, Baltimore, Maryland.

Lida Lee Tall was graduated from Western High School in Baltimore, Maryland, and was a student in the normal extension courses of Johns Hopkins University in Baltimore. She studied summers at the University of Chicago (1904) and Columbia University (1905). She received the B.S. degree and bachelor's diploma in education (1914) from Teachers College of Columbia University.

Tall was a teacher and critic teacher in the Baltimore city schools and an instructor of education, literature, and history at the Teachers' Training School in Baltimore (1904–08). She was a supervisor of grammar grades (1908–17) and assistant superintendent of schools (1917–18) with the Baltimore County Schools. From 1918 to 1920 she was principal of the elementary department of the Lincoln School at Teachers College, Columbia University, and served as principal and president of the Maryland State Normal School (Teachers College in 1935 and, later, Towson State College) from 1920 to her retirement in 1938. In 1924 the Baltimore Teacher Training School was merged with the normal school and evolved into a four-year, degree-granting institution in 1935.

Tall was the author of *Bibliography of History for Schools and Libraries* (with others, 1910) and *How the Old World Found the New* (with Eunice F. Barnard, 1929) and compiler of *Baltimore County Course of Study* (with others, 1919). She was associate editor of *Atlantic Educational Journal* (1907–11).

Active in professional organizations, Tall was president of the Maryland State Teachers' Association (1935) and the Maryland Children's Aid Society (1938–42), first secretary of the Educational Society of Baltimore (1906), and secretary of the department of superintendence of the National Education Association (1916–17). She was an alumna trustee of Teachers College (1915–17) and was appointed by President Herbert Hoover to the National Advisory Committee on Education. She received a citation for her services to education from the governor of Maryland and received an honorary degree from the University of Maryland (1926).

REFERENCES: *LE* (II); *WWAE* (VIII); *WWW* (II); J. M. Gambrill, "Lida Lee Tall: An Appreciation," *School and Society* 56 (August 15, 1942): 129–30; *National Education Association Journal* (April 1942): 129; Baltimore, Maryland, *Evening Sun,* July 7, 1976.                    *John F. Ohles*

**TALMAGE, James Edward.** B. September 21, 1862, Hungerford, Berkshire, England, to James Joyce and Susannah (Preater) Talmage. M. June 14, 1888, to Mary May Booth. Ch. eight. D. July 27, 1933, Salt Lake City, Utah.

James Edward Talmage's family was converted to the Church of the Latter Day Saints and emigrated to the United States from England in 1876, settling in Utah. Talmage attended Brigham Young Academy (later, Brigham Young University) at Provo, Utah (1876–82), Lehigh University in Bethlehem, Pennsylvania (1882–83), and Johns Hopkins University in Baltimore, Maryland (1883–84). He received the B.S. degree (1891) from Lehigh and the Ph.D. degree (1896) from Illinois Wesleyan University at Bloomington, Illinois.

Talmage was professor of chemistry and geology at Brigham Young Academy (1884–88) and became president of Latter-Day Saints College in Salt Lake City, Utah (1888–93) and of the University of Utah (1894–97). He continued at the university as professor of geology after his resignation as president in 1897. He resigned his professorship in 1907 to become a consulting and mining geologist. Talmage was director of the Deseret Museum in Salt Lake City (1891–1919). He traveled in Europe six times for scientific purposes. He was a member of a geological party that crossed the Ural Mountains to Siberia in 1897.

He was the author of *First Book of Nature* (1888), *Domestic Science* (1891), *The Articles of Faith* (1899), *Tables for Blowpiper Determination of Minerals* (1899), *The Story of Mormonism* (1907), *The Great Apostasy* (1909), *The House of the Lord* (1912), *The Philosophy of Mormonism* (1914), *Jesus the Christ* (1915), *The Vitality of Mormonism* (1919), and *A Study of the Articles of Faith* (1924).

Talmage was a fellow of the Royal Microscopical Society (London, England), the Royal Scottish Geological Society, the Geological Society (London), the Geological Society of America, and the American Association for the Advancement of Science. He was a delegate from the Royal Society of Edinburgh to the International Geological Congress in St. Petersburg, Russia, in 1897. He was the recipient of several honorary degrees. He was ordained as an apostle of the Church of Jesus Christ of the Latter Day Saints and named to the Council of the Twelve in 1911.

REFERENCES: *DAB; NCAB* (16:19); *NYT,* July 28, 1933, p. 15; *WWW* (I). *John F. Ohles*

**TAPPAN, Eli Todd.** B. April 30, 1824, Steubenville, Ohio, to Benjamin and Betsy (Lord) Frazer Tappan. M. February 4, 1851, to Lydia L. McDowell. Ch. two. D. October 23, 1888, Columbus, Ohio.

Eli Todd Tappan was educated in the Steubenville (Ohio) public schools and by tutors in his father's home. He attended St. Mary's College in Baltimore, Maryland, but left in 1842 without receiving a degree to study law in the office of his father, who was in partnership with Edwin M. Stanton. He was admitted to the bar in 1846 and then founded a weekly newspaper, *Ohio Press,* in Columbus, Ohio, for which he was editor to 1848. He practiced law in Steubenville (1848–57), was elected mayor of Steubenville in 1852, and lectured to teachers on school organization and instructional methods. He was a teacher (1857–58) and school superintendent of the Steubenville public schools (1858–59).

Tappan was professor of mathematics at Ohio University in Athens (1859–60). He taught at the Mount Auburn Young Ladies' Institute near Cincinnati, Ohio (1860–65). He was appointed to the first Ohio State Board of School Examiners in 1864. In 1865 he returned to Ohio University where he served as professor of mathematics until 1868.

Tappan was appointed president of Kenyon College in Gambier, Ohio, in 1868. During his administration the college curriculum was revised and the campus chapel was completed. He resigned the presidency in 1875 but continued as professor of mathematics and political economy until 1887. He served as commissioner of the common schools of Ohio (1887–88).

Tappan wrote the *History of School Legislation of Ohio* in 1876, which formed part of the Ohio exhibit at the Centennial Exposition in Philadelphia that year. He contributed many articles to local and national educational journals and also was the author of *Treatise on Plane and Solid Geometry* (1867), *A Treatise on Geometry and Trigonometry* (1868), and *Elements of Geometry* (1885).

Tappan served as president of the Ohio Teachers' Association (1866), was active in the National Educational Association (treasurer, 1880–81, and president, 1883), and was a charter member of the National Council of Education (1880). He was the recipient of several honorary degrees.

REFERENCES: *AC; DAB; NCAB* (7:7); *TC; WWW* (H); Charles B. Galbreath, *History of Ohio* (Chicago: The American Historical Society, 1925), vol. 1.                                                   *Charles M. Dye*


**TAPPAN, Eva March.** B. December 25, 1854, Blackstone, Massachusetts, to Edmund March and Lucretia (Logée) Tappan. M. no. D. January 29, 1930, Worcester, Massachusetts.

Eva March Tappan was graduated from Vassar College in Poughkeepsie, New York (1875). She taught at Wheaton College in Norton, Massachusetts, for five years. She received the A.M. (1895) and Ph.D. (1896) degrees from the University of Pennsylvania. For the next seven years she was the department head of English at a high school in Worcester, Massachusetts.

Her first book was published in 1896 and other books followed. The success of her books encouraged her to leave the classroom in 1903 to spend full time writing. Her books include *Charles Lamb, The Man and the Author* (1896), *In the Days of Alfred the Great* (1900), *In the Days of William the Conqueror* (1901), *Old Ballads in Prose* (1901), *England's Story* (1901), *Our Country's Story* (1902), *In the Days of Queen Elizabeth* (1902), *The Christ Story* (1903), *In the Days of Queen Victoria* (1903), *Robin Hood, His Book* (1903), *A Short History of England's Literature* (1905), *The Golden Goose and Other Fairy Tales from the Swedish* (1905), *A Short History of America's Literature* (1906), *A Short History of England's and America's Literature* (1906), *American Literature with Selections from Colonial and Revolutionary Writers* (1907), *Letters from Colonial Children* (1908), *The Story of the Greek People* (1908), *The Chaucer Story Books* (1908), *European Hero Stories* (1910), *Dixie Kitten* (1910), *A Friend in the Library* (twelve volumes, 1910), *The Story of the Roman People* (1910), *An Old, Old Story Book* (1910), *Old World Hero Stories* (1911), *When Knights Were Bold* (1912), *The House with the Silver Door* (1913), *The Farmer and His Friends* (1916), *Diggers in the Earth* (1916), *Makers of Many Things* (1916), *Travelers and Traveling* (1916), *The Little Book of the Flag* (1917), *Our European Ancestors* (1918), *The Little Book of the War* (1918), *Food Saving and Sharing* (1918), *The Little Book of Our Country* (1919), *Hero Stories of France* (1920), *Heroes of Progress* (1921), *Ella, A Little School Girl of the Sixties* (1923), *American History Stories for Very Young Readers* (1924), *Stories of America for Very Young Readers* (1926), *The Story of Our Constitution* (1927), and *The Prince from No Where* (1928).

Tappan served during World War I as assistant editor for the United States Food Administration. She was a member of Phi Beta Kappa Society and the Boston Author's Club.

REFERENCES: *DAB; NCAB* (22:161); *NYT*, February 5, 1930, p. 14; *TC; WWW* (I).                                                    *Joan Duff Kise*

**TAPPAN, Henry Philip.** B. April 18, 1805, Rhinebeck on the Hudson, New York, to Peter and Ann (De Witte) Tappan. M. April 17, 1828, to Julia Livingston. Ch. five. D. November 15, 1881, Vevey, Switzerland.

Henry Philip Tappan taught for two years before entering Union College in Schenectady, New York. He studied there with Eliphalet Nott *(q.v.)*, a professor with progressive views on education, and was graduated with the B.A. degree (1825). He attended Auburn (New York) Theological Seminary, from which he was graduated in 1827.

Tappan became pastor of the Congregational church in Pittsfield, Massachusetts, in 1828 but retired from the ministry in 1832 because of ill health. He was professor of moral and intellectual philosophy at the University of the City of New York (later, New York University) from 1832 to 1838, when he retired from teaching to devote his time to writing. He was selected to be the first president of the University of Michigan in 1852. Tappan organized the university on the German pattern, providing for elective courses instead of a fixed curriculum. Under his leadership the University of Michigan became a model for later state universities. The science curriculum was put on an equal basis with the traditional classics curriculum. Students were given much freedom, and the university remained a secular institution. Tappan resigned in 1863 and lived in Europe until his death in 1881.

Tappan was the author of *Review of Edward's Inquiry into the Freedom of the Will* (1839), *Doctrine of the Will Determined by an Appeal to Consciousness* (1840), *Doctrine of Will Applied to Moral Agency and Responsibility* (1841), *Elements of Logic* (1844), *A Step from the New World to the Old and Back Again* (1852), and *Introduction to the Illustrious Personages of the Nineteenth Century* (1853).

He was president of the American Association for the Advancement of Science (1859) and was made a corresponding member of the French Imperial Institute (1856). He received honorary degrees from Union (1845) and Columbia (1854) colleges.

REFERENCES: *AC; DAB; NCAB* (1: 249); *NYT*, November 17, 1881, p. 5; *TC; WWW* (H); Henry S. Frieze, *q.v., A Memorial Discourse on the Life and Services of the Reverend Henry Philip Tappan* (Ann Arbor: University of Michigan Press, 1882).                        *Walter F. C. Ade*

**TAPPER, Thomas.** B. January 28, 1864, Canton, Massachusetts, to Thomas and Ellen (Whalley) Tapper. M. September 22, 1895, to Bertha Feiring Maas. M. November 20, 1920, to Maria Eugenia Keating. Ch. none. D. February 24, 1958, White Plains, New York.

Thomas Tapper studied music at the American College of Musicians, at New York University and in Europe. He returned to New York City where he was a lecturer and instructor at the Institute of Musical Art (1905–24) and also was director of the Music School Settlement (1907–09); he became head of the department of music at New York University (1908). He was director of the department of education for the J. C. Penney Company and was editor for the West Side Young Men's Christian Association. In his retirement he helped his wife operate a farm for Jersey cattle in Westchester County, New York.

Tapper was the author of many books, including *Chats with Music Students* (1890), *The Music Life* (1892), *Music Talks with Children* (1896), *Child's Music World* (1896), *Pictures from the Lives of Great Composers* (1900), *First Studies in Music Biography* (1900), *Music Life and How to Succeed in It* (1906), *First Year Harmony* (1908), *Youth and Opportunity* (1912), *Second Year Harmony* (1912), *First Year Melody Writing* (1912), *Essentials in Music History* (with P. Goetschius, *q.v.*, 1912), *First Year Music Theory* (1912), *First Year Analysis* (1914), *Education of the Music Teacher* (1914), *Child's Own Book of Great Musicians* (1915), *The Music Supervisor* (1916), *First Year Music History* (1926), *From Palestrina to Grieg* (1930), *First Year Counterpoint* (1935), and *Seven Keys to Success* (1939). He also wrote many series of music textbooks, including the Natural Course in Music (six volumes), Short Course in Music (two volumes), Harmonic Music Course (seven volumes), the Modern Graded Piano Course (nineteen volumes), and Students Repertoire of Piano Composition (two volumes). He was coeditor of the University Music Course.

Tapper was the editor of *The Musical Record and Review* (1903–04), *The Musician* (1904–07), and *The Dynamo* for the J. C. Penney Company (1916–32). He was a trustee of the New York College of Music and the Scudder School. He received an honorary degree from Bates College in 1911.

REFERENCES: *NYT,* February 25, 1958, p. 27; *TC; WWW* (III); Nicholas Slonimsky, ed., *Baker's Biographical Dictionary of Musicians,* 5th ed. (New York: G. Schirmer, 1958). *John F. Ohles*

**TARR, Ralph Stockman.** B. January 15, 1864, Gloucester, Massachusetts, to Silas Stockman and Abigail (Saunders) Tarr. M. March 28, 1892, to Kate Story. Ch. three. D. March 21, 1912, Ithaca, New York.

After being educated in the public elementary and high schools of Gloucester, Massachusetts, Ralph Stockman Tarr entered Harvard University as a special student at Lawrence Scientific School (1881). He was graduated from Harvard with the S.B. degree (1891).

During the summer of 1883, he worked under zoologists Alpheus Hyatt *(q.v.)* and Spencer F. Baird. He was employed by the Smithsonian Institution and the United States Fish Commission (1883–84), and he worked for the United States Geological Survey (1887–89) and the State Geological Survey of Texas (1889–90). He taught dynamic geology and physical geography at Cornell University in Ithaca, New York (1892), and was head of the department of physical geography (1906), a position he held until his death in 1912.

Tarr organized the Cornell Greenland Expedition (1896) and conducted the National Geographic Society's expeditions to Alaska (1909 and 1911). He studied the geological history of New York's Finger Lakes region and made surveys of the area for the United States Geological Survey. He was considered the foremost American authority on glaciers and earthquakes and contributed much new information in the field of glaciology.

Tarr was the author of many widely used textbooks, including *The Economic Geology of the United States* (1893), *Elementary Geology of the United States* (1893), *Elementary Physical Geography* (1897), the Cornell School Geographies (with F. M. McMurry, *q.v.*, 1900), *New Physical Geography* (1904), and *The Physical Geography of New York State* (1902). Published posthumously were *College Physiography* and *Alaskan Glacier Studies* (with L. Martin, 1914), which was awarded the gold medal of the Société de géographie de Paris. He contributed to *Johnson's Encyclopedia,* the *International Encyclopedia,* and the *Encyclopaedia Britannica* and was associate editor of the *Bulletin of the American Geographical Society* (1899–1911) and *The Journal of Geography* (1902–12).

Tarr served as a member of several professional societies, including the International Committee on Glaciers, the Royal Geographical Society of Vienna, the Geographical Society of London, and the Association of American Geographers (president, 1911–12).

REFERENCES: *DAB; NCAB* (10:311); *WWW* (I); *NYT,* March 22, 1912, p. 9. *Gary Howieson*

**TAUSSIG, Frank William.** B. December 28, 1859, St. Louis Missouri, to William and Adele (Wuerpel) Taussig. M. June 29, 1888, to Edith Thomas Guild. M. August 31, 1918, to Laura Fisher. Ch. four. D. November 11, 1940, Cambridge, Massachusetts.

Frank W. Taussig was educated in public and private schools in St. Louis, Missouri, and was graduated from Harvard University with the A.B. degree with highest honors in 1879. He also received the A.M. and Ph.D. degrees in 1883 and the LL.B. (1886) degree from Harvard. He served for a time as secretary to Harvard president Charles W. Eliot *(q.v.).*

He toured Europe and studied Roman law and political economy at the University of Berlin, Germany (1879–80).

Taussig taught political economy at Harvard (1882–1935) and was Henry Lee Professor (1901–35). He was a leading authority on tariff history and international trade and one of the most influential teachers of economics in America. He was a founder of the Harvard Graduate School of Business Administration. He served as chairman of the economics department and the division of history, government, and economics.

Taussig wrote *History of the Present Tariff, 1860–1883* (1885), *The Tariff History of the United States* (1888), *The Silver Situation in the United States* (1890), *Wages and Capital* (1896), *Principles of Economics* (1911), *Inventors and Money Makers* (1915), *Some Aspects of the Tariff Question* (1915), *Free Trade, the Tariff and Reciprocity* (1920), *International Trade* (1927), and *Origin of American Business Leaders* (1932). He was editor of the *Quarterly Journal of Economics* (1896–1937).

Taussig was chairman of the United States Tariff Commission (1917–19) and a member of the Advisory Committee on the Peace of Paris after World War I. He was president of the American Economic Association (1904–05). He was named commander of the Belgian Order of the Crown and chevalier of the Legion of Honor of France. He was a fellow in the American Academy of Arts and Sciences and a foreign member of the British and Italian academies. He received honorary degrees from Brown and Northwestern universities, University of Michigan, University of Bonn, Germany, and Cambridge (England) University.

REFERENCES: *CB* (1940); *DAB* (supp. 2); *LE* (I); *NCAB* (A:457 and 30:68); *WWW* (I); *NYT,* November 12, 1940, p. 23; Joseph A. Schumpeter, *Ten Great Economists from Marx to Keynes* (New York: Oxford University Press, 1951), pp. 191–221; Ben B. Seligman, *Main Currents in Modern Economics: Economic Thought since 1870* (New York: Free Press of Glencoe, 1962), pp. 623–28.                              *George G. Dawson*

**TAYLOR, Harold Alexander.** B. September 28, 1914, Toronto, Ontario, Canada, to Charles William and Elizabeth (Wilson) Taylor. M. November 8, 1941, to Grace Muriel Thorne. Ch. two.

Harold Taylor earned the B.A. (1935) and M.A. (1936) degrees in philosophy and literature from the University of Toronto. The Ph.D. degree was conferred on him in 1938 by the University of London, England.

Taylor was a member of the philosophy department at the University of Wisconsin in Madison from 1939 to 1945. During World War II he was a research associate in the Office of Scientific Research and Development (1943). He was president of Sarah Lawrence College in Bronxville, New York, from 1945 to 1959, serving on the faculty of the New School for Social Research from 1947 to 1949.

Taylor was the author of *On Education and Teaching* (1954) and *Art and the Intellect* (1960). He edited *Essays in Teaching* (1950), *Humanities in the Schools* (1968), *The World and the American Teacher* (1968), *The World as Teacher* (1969), *Students Without Teachers: The Crisis of the University* (1969), and *How to Change Colleges: Notes on Radical Reform* (1971), and he contributed articles to scholarly journals.

He was a member of the board of the Institute for International Order and Americans for Democratic Action, chairman of the National Research Council on Peace Strategy, and director of the League for Industrial Democracy. He received honorary degrees from several colleges and universities.

REFERENCES: *CA* (25–28); *CB* (1946); *LE* (V); "Taylor to Leave Sarah Lawrence," *NYT*, January 8, 1959, p. 31; *WW* (XXXVIII); *WWAE* (IV); David Boroff, "Sarah Lawrence," *Harpers Magazine* 217 (November 1958): 37–44.                    *Robert A. Waller*

**TAYLOR, John Orville.** B. 1807, Charlton, New Jersey, to n.a. M. n.a. D. January 18, 1890, New Brunswick, New Jersey.

John Orville Taylor was graduated from Union College in Schenectady, New York, in 1830. He attended Princeton (New Jersey) Theological Seminary but left before he finished the course.

Taylor taught school in Philadelphia, Pennsylvania, for two years. He engaged in a career promoting educational reforms, lecturing in the major cities of the country (1836–51). Taylor and James Wadsworth (*q.v.*) persuaded the New York State legislature to provide legislation establishing school libraries (1837). He was professor of popular education at the University of the City of New York (later, New York University) in 1837 and delivered a lecture on education to the United States Congress in 1838. He engaged in unsuccessful business ventures in New York City and retired to New Brunswick, New Jersey, in 1879.

Taylor was the author of *The District School* (1834), *The Farmer's School Book* (1837), *Satirical Hits on the People's Education* (1839), and *The First Lecture on Popular Education* (n.d.). He translated Victor Cousin's *Report on the Prussian School System* (1836) and was founder (1836) and editor of the monthly *Common School Assistant,* which was succeeded by a similar journal published by the state superintendent of public instruction.

REFERENCES: *AC; NYT,* January 19, 1890, p. 5.         *John F. Ohles*

**TAYLOR, Joseph Schimmel.** B. November 15, 1856, Passer, Pennsylvania, to Thomas and Mary (Schimmel) Taylor. M. 1884 to Katharine Moore Johnson. Ch. two, including Deems Taylor, composer of operas. D. July 3, 1932, Greensboro, Vermont.

Joseph S. Taylor was graduated from Millersville (Pennsylvania) Normal School (later, State College) in 1878. He also studied at Clark University in Worcester, Massachusetts.

Taylor moved to New York City where he was a public school teacher (1885–98), school principal (1898–1902), and district superintendent of schools (1902–27). He also lectured on teaching and school management at New York University for fourteen years, the College of the City of New York for three years, Hunter College for four years, and Brooklyn Institute for one year.

He wrote pedagogical books, including *Composition in the Elementary School* (1906), *Art of Class Management and Discipline* (1908), *Graded Movement Writing for Beginners* (with Margaret M. Hughes, 1910), *Word Study for the Elementary School* (1910), *Principles and Methods of Teaching Reading* (1912), *Handbook for Vocational Education* (1914), *Every Child's Language Book* (1925), and *Supervision and Teaching of Handwriting* (1926). He edited *A Teaching Plan of Grammar* (1916).

Taylor was a fellow of the American Association for the Advancement of Science and the New York Society for the Experimental Study of Education and a member of other professional associations. He was awarded the D.Ped. (1892) and Ph.D. (1924) degrees by New York University.

REFERENCES: *NYT,* July 4, 1932, p. 11; *WWW* (I); W. McAndrew, "Jo Taylor, Happy Schoolmaster," *School and Society* 36 (July 23, 1932): 115–16.                                                                     *John F. Ohles*

**TAYLOR, Samuel Harvey.** B. October 3, 1807, Londonderry, New Hampshire, to James and Persis (Hamphill) Taylor. M. December 8, 1837, to Caroline Persis Parker. Ch. four. D. January 29, 1871, Andover, Massachusetts.

Samuel Harvey Taylor attended Pinkerton Academy in Derry, New Hampshire, and was graduated from Dartmouth College in Hanover, New Hampshire, with the A.B. (1832) and A.M. (1835) degrees. He completed a course at Andover (Massachusetts) Theological Seminary (1837).

Taylor taught in district schools and worked on the family farm before he was a tutor at Dartmouth (1836–37). In 1837 he became principal of Phillips Academy in Andover, Massachusetts, and served there to his death in 1871. Under Taylor Phillips Academy achieved a reputation as one of the finest preparatory schools in the country.

A major classical scholar, Taylor was the author of *Method of Classical Study* (1861) and *Classical Study: Its Value Illustrated by Extracts from the Writings of Eminent Scholars* (1870). He edited *Bibliotheca Sacra* (1852–71). Taylor was awarded an honorary degree from Brown University in 1854.

REFERENCES: *AC; DAB; NCAB* (10:96); *TC; WWW* (H).

*Thomas L. Bernard*

**TAYLOR, William Septimus.** B. January 20, 1885, Beaver Dam, Kentucky, to Herschel Berry and Ellen Orah (Render) Taylor. M. February 3, 1923, to Helen Josephine Dodge. Ch. one. D. August 26, 1949, Lexington, Kentucky.

William Septimus Taylor received his early education in the Ohio County, Kentucky, schools and from Hartford (Kentucky) Academy. He received a diploma from the Western Normal School and Teachers College (later, Western Kentucky University) in Bowling Green in 1910, the B.S.A. degree (1912) from the University of Kentucky, the M.S. degree (1913) from the University of Wisconsin, and the Ph.D. degree (1924) from Columbia University.

Taylor began teaching in rural Kentucky schools at the age of eighteen. He taught two years at Hartford Academy (1905–07) while studying there and was an instructor at Western Normal School in 1910 and continued there after graduation. He was an associate professor of agricultural education at the University of Texas (1913–18). He was an agent for agricultural education of the Federal Board for Vocational Education (1918–19) and professor of rural education and head of the department of rural life at Pennsylvania State College (1919–20). Taylor was the assistant director of the Teacher's Bureau, Department of Public Instruction of Pennsylvania in Harrisburg (1920–22). He finished his career as dean of the college of education at the University of Kentucky (1923–49). He sought to raise the level of teacher training at the University of Kentucky and throughout Kentucky.

Taylor studied the English system of training teachers and the English school system in general at the University of London, England (1937–38). He reported his findings in a 135-page issue of the *Bulletin of School Service,* college of education, University of Kentucky (June 1939), entitled *Education in England.* He was also the author of *Development of Professional Education of Teachers in Pennsylvania* (1924), *Practical Arithmetic Workbooks* (with others, n.d.), and *An Introduction to Education* (with Jesse E. Adams, 1932). He was editor of the *Kentucky School Journal* (1927–34).

Taylor was a member of many organizations, including the National Education Association (chairman, committee on reorganization, 1936–37, and committee on academic freedom, 1939–43, state director, 1933–41, member of the executive committee, 1946–47), the Kentucky Education Association (president, 1928–29), the National Association of Colleges and Departments of Education (president, 1926–27, secretary-treasurer, 1941–47), and the Southern Association of Colleges and Secondary Schools (chairman, committee on curricular problems and research, 1946–47).

REFERENCES: *LE* (III); *NCAB* (39:285); *WWAE* (I); *WWW* (II).

*Earl W. Thomas*

**TEMPLE, Alice.** B. March 1, 1866, Chicago, Illinois, to John F. and Eliza Ann (Johnston) Temple. M. no. D. January 6, 1946, New Rochelle, New York.

Alice Temple grew up in Chicago and was graduated from a local high school. She was trained as a teacher at the Chicago Free Kindergarten Association (c. 1884) where she was a practice teacher (c. 1885–86) under the direction of Anna E. Bryan *(q.v.)* and continued as a teacher at the Free Kindergarten Association. Temple became principal after Bryan's illness and death (1901). In 1904 Temple resigned from the principalship to study at the University of Chicago and taught at the university department of kindergarten education. In 1909 she became director of the department and remained at Chicago to her retirement in 1932.

Temple organized the first university kindergarten-primary department at Chicago in 1913. The department established a three-year program and, later, a four-year bachelor's degree in education, setting a pattern for universities throughout the country. Temple was influenced by the philosophy of John Dewey *(q.v.)*, with whom she had studied at the University of Chicago.

Temple was a frequent contributor of articles to professional journals. She was the author of *Unified Kindergarten and First-Grade Teaching* (with Samuel C. Parker, 1928) and bulletins published by the University of Chicago and the United States Bureau (later, Office) of Education. She was active in editorial activities and was a contributor to *Childhood Education* and the yearbooks of the International Kindergarten Union (Association for Childhood Education, International).

Temple was active in the International Kindergarten Union and the successor Association for Childhood Education, International (committee member and chairman; president, 1925–27). She worked for the inclusion of a kindergarten division in the United States Bureau of Education.

REFERENCES: *LE* (I); *NYT,* January 7, 1946, p. 19; *Chicago Tribune,* January 7, 1946, p. 16; Agnes Snyder, *Dauntless Women in Childhood Education, 1856–1931* (Washington, D.C.: Association for Childhood Education International, 1972); *School and Society* 63 (January 12, 1946): 28; *Who's Who in Chicago,* 5th ed. (Chicago: Marquis, 1931).

*Barbara Ruth Peltzman*

**TENNENT, William.** B. 1673, Ireland, to n.a. M. May 15, 1702, to Catharine Kennedy. Ch. five. D. May 6, 1746, Neshaminy, Pennsylvania.

William Tennent was graduated from the University of Edinburgh, Scotland, in 1695, was ordained in the Irish Episcopal church in 1704, and became a priest in 1706.

Tennent emigrated with his family to America in 1716 or 1718 and settled in Philadelphia. He was admitted to the Presbyterian ministry in 1718 and served churches in East Chester and Bedford, New York, and Bensalem, Bucks County, Pennsylvania (1721–26). He settled at Neshaminy, Pennsylvania, in 1726. The Presbyterians required an educated clergy, but those who wished to enter church work had to go to New England or abroad to study. Tennent constructed a building in Neshaminy in 1736 and started a school for young men. Called the Log College the school became associated with the New Brunswick (New Jersey) Presbytery.

Tennent taught to 1742, or perhaps to his death. The school was closed, but its supporters and others organized the College of New Jersey (later, Princeton University).

REFERENCES: *AC; DAB; EB; NCAB* (5:469); *TC; WWW* (H); A. Alexander, *Biographical Sketches of the Founder and Principal Alumni of the Log College* (Princeton, N.J.: J. T. Robinson, 1845); Thomas Jefferson Wertenbaker, *Princeton 1746–1896* (Princeton, N.J.: Princeton University Press, 1946).                                            *Gorman L. Miller*

**TERMAN, Lewis Madison.** B. January 15, 1877, Johnson County, Indiana, to James William and Martha Parthenia (Cutsinger) Terman. M. September 18, 1899, to Anna Belle Minton. Ch. two. D. December 21, 1956, Palo Alto, California.

Lewis Terman earned the A.B. degree from Central Normal College in Danville, Indiana (1898), and Indiana University (1902). From 1903 to 1905 he was a fellow in psychology and education at Clark University in Worcester, Massachusetts, where he received the Ph.D. degree in 1905.

Terman taught in rural schools in Johnson County, Indiana (1894–95 and 1896–97), and was principal of the Johnson County high school (1898–1901). He was principal of the San Bernardino (California) high school (1905–06). He was professor of psychology and pedagogy at the State Normal School in Los Angeles (later, University of California at Los Angeles) from 1906 to 1910. From 1910 until his retirement in 1942, he was a member of the faculty of education at Stanford (California) University and was the head of the psychology department (1922–42).

During World War I Terman was on the army's Committee on the Classification of Personnel, where he devised the first group of intelligence tests, the army Alpha and Beta tests. Terman contributed the term "I.Q.," intelligence quotient, in 1916 when he published the first widely used test for measuring intelligence, the Stanford-Binet test, a revision of the Binet-Simon scale. He followed this work with a monumental thirty-year study of gifted children.

Terman's publications include *The Teacher's Health* (1913), *Health Work in the Schools* (with E. B. Hoag, 1914), *The Hygiene of the School Child* (1914), *The Measurement of Intelligence* (1916), *The Stanford Revision of the Binet-Simon Intelligence Scale* (1916), *The Terman Group*

*Test* (with others, 1920), *Genetic Studies in Genius* (with others, volume 1, 1925; volume 2, 1926; volume 3, 1930), *Mental and Physical Traits of a Thousand Gifted Children* (1925), *Sex and Personality: Studies in Masculinity and Femininity* (with Catherine Cox Miles, 1936), *Measuring Intelligence* (with Maud A. Merrill, 1937), *Marital Happiness* (1938), *The Terman-McNemar Test* (with Q. McNemar, 1942), *The Gifted Child Grows Up* (with Melita H. Oden, 1947), and published posthumously, *The Gifted Group at Mid-Life* (with Melita H. Oden, 1959).

Terman was president of the American Psychological Association (1923) and the American School Hygiene Association (1917) and was a fellow of the American Association for the Advancement of Science, the British Psychological Society, and the Educational Institute of Scotland. He received honorary degrees from four universities.

REFERENCES: *WWAE* (XVI); *WWW* (III); *NYT,* December 23, 1956, p. 31; H. J. Eysenck, W. Arnold and R. Meili, eds., *Encyclopedia of Psychology* (New York: Herder and Herder, 1972); E. R. Hilgard *(q.v.),* "Lewis Madison Terman, 1877–1956," *American Journal of Psychology* 70 (September 1957): 472–79; Carl A. Murchison *(q.v.),* ed., *A History of Psychology in Autobiography* (Worcester: Clark University Press, 1930), vol. 2, pp. 297–331; May V. Seagoe, *Terman and the Gifted* (Los Altos, Cal.: William Kaufmann, 1975); Robert R. Sears, "L. M. Terman, Pioneer in Mental Measurement," *Science* 125 (May 17, 1957): 978–79.

*Thomas E. Kesler*
*Joseph P. Cangemi*

**TEWKSBURY, Donald George.** B. April 9, 1894, Tunghsien, Hopei, China, to Elwood Gardner and Grace (Holbrook) Tewksbury. M. August 9, 1922, to Helen Taylor Plumb. Ch. one. D. December 8, 1958, New York, New York.

Donald George Tewksbury received his preliminary education at private schools in Tunghsien and Nanking, China, and in the United States. He attended the University of Nanking (1912–13), Peking (Christian) University (1914–15), and Oberlin (Ohio) College (1917–18), and he received the B.A. (1920), M.A. (1921), and Ph.D. (1932) degrees from Columbia University.

He taught and served as principal of the Kuling (China) American School (1915–16) and taught high school in East Orange, New Jersey (1921–22). He returned to China where he served as assistant professor of psychology and education at Yenching University, Peking (1922–27). He was visiting lecturer on Far Eastern civilization and culture at Sarah Lawrence College in Bronxville, New York (1928–33). He was research assistant and assistant and associate professor at Teachers College, Columbia University (1928–39).

Nicholas Murray Butler *(q.v.)*, president of Columbia, asked him in 1933 to serve as dean of Bard College and reorganize the educational program. Tewksbury introduced independent reading and study; small group seminars and personal tutorial conferences took the place of traditional classroom lectures. He introduced a midyear, off-campus period of independent reading and fieldwork.

Tewksbury was appointed director of New College, an experimental college for teachers associated with Teachers College (1938–39). He served in World War II and returned to Teachers College as professor of education in the department of social and philosophical foundations (1949–58), where he directed a program in international and intercultural education.

He was the author of *The Founding of American Colleges and Universities Before the Civil War* (1932) and *American Education and the International Scene* (1958). He compiled two volumes of source materials on Far Eastern political thought (1949, 1950).

He attended the Mexico City (Mexico) United Nations Educational, Scientific, and Cultural Organization General Conference (1947) and was a delegate to the Eleventh International Conference of the Institute of Pacific Relations in England (1947). He was one of four American educators invited by the Scandinavian countries to study their educational systems (1957). He was a member of many organizations and was first vice-president and president of the National Association of Foreign Student Advisors. He received an honorary degree from Bard College (1954).

REFERENCES: *LE* (III); *NCAB* (43:66); *WWAE* (VIII); *WWW* (III); *NYT,* December 10, 1958, p. 39; *Teachers College Record* 60 (April 1959): 408–10.                                                    *Michael R. Cioffi*

**THACH, Charles Coleman.** B. March 15, 1860, Athens, Georgia, to Robert Henry and Eliza Lockhart (Coleman) Thach. M. November 11, 1885, to Ellen Stanford Smith. Ch. five. D. October 3, 1921, Dalton, Georgia.

Charles Coleman Thach was graduated with the B.E. degree (1877) from Alabama Agricultural and Mechanical College (later, Auburn University). He studied at Johns Hopkins University in Baltimore, Maryland (1880–81).

Thach taught school at Hopkinsville, Kentucky. He was professor of modern languages at Austin College (Texas) (1881–82) and in 1885 joined the faculty of Alabama Polytechnic Institute as professor of English. He was elected its president in 1902 and held that office until he retired as president emeritus in 1920.

During his administration the school was greatly expanded and instructional departments were added, including mining and engineering, telephone engineering, drawing and machine design, animal husbandry, and architecture. In 1907 the institute participated in the supervision of the recently established county high schools in Alabama; farm demonstration work began in 1906 and became part of the extension service in 1914. Home demonstration work and summer conferences of teachers began in 1912. The department of education opened in 1915.

Thach was a member of many local and national organizations, including the Alabama History Commission (1898–1900), the Alabama Textbook Commission (1903), the Alabama Education Association (president, 1915), and the Alabama State Sunday School Association (president). He received two honorary degrees from the University of Alabama.

REFERENCES: *NCAB* (26:263); *WWW* (I); Henry S. Marks, comp., *Who Was Who in Alabama* (Huntsville, Ala.: Strode Publishers, 1972).

Donald C. Stephenson

**THAYER, Gideon French.** B. September 21, 1793, Watertown, Massachusetts, to Zephion and Susannah (Bond) Thayer. M. August 27, 1821, to Nancy Pierce. Ch. four. D. March 27, 1864, Keene, New Hampshire.

Gideon French Thayer was raised by a Boston tallow merchant after the early death of his parents. Thayer worked at a variety of jobs as a boy. He was apprenticed to a retail shoe merchant at the age of fourteen and remained with him for six years. He also studied to prepare for teaching and taught penmanship at the South Writing School of Boston in 1814. He resigned because of illness in 1818 and spent two years in New Orleans, Louisiana. He returned to Milton, Massachusetts, in 1820.

He opened a private school in Boston, which was noted for its gymnastic equipment and the use of Boston Common for exercise and games. He was able to purchase a building in Boston that became the Chauncy Hall School. The school was highly successful with a superior faculty. Thayer was an innovative educator, introducing a departmental organization of instruction and singing by note for all pupils. He resigned from Chauncy Hall School in 1855 and was president of an insurance company (1856–60).

Thayer became a popular lecturer on education; his lectures were published in professional journals. A series of articles was later published as *Letters to a Young Teacher* (1858). He was an editor of *Massachusetts Teacher* (1848) and editor of the *Quincy Patriot* (1851–52). He was a founder of the American Institute of Instruction (first secretary, 1830–31, and president, 1849–52), the American Association for the Advancement of Education, the Boston Public Library, the Massachusetts State Teachers' Association, and the Norfolk County Teachers' Association. He was a member of the Boston City Council (1839, 1844–48) and president of the Boston Dispensary (1840–46). He received honorary degrees from Brown (1854) and Harvard (1855) universities.

REFERENCES: *AC; DAB; NCAB* (7:532); *WWW* (H); Thomas Cushing,

"Memoir of Gideon F. Thayer," *New England Historical and Geneological Register* 19 (April 1865): 149–54.                    *Stuart B. Palonsky*

**THAYER, Sylvanus.** B. June 9, 1785, Braintree, Massachusetts, to Nathaniel and Dorcas (Faxon) Thayer. M. no. D. September 7, 1872, South Braintree, Massachusetts.

Sylvanus Thayer was a leader in establishing technological education in the United States. He was graduated from Dartmouth College in Hanover, New Hampshire, in 1807 and the Military Academy at West Point, New York, in 1808. He served with the corps of engineers engaged in building fortifications on New York and New England coasts and served in the War of 1812. In 1815 he was assigned to tour Europe, study military schools, and gather books and supplies for West Point. His views on education were influenced by that study of European institutions, particularly in France, where the Ecole polytechnique trained civil engineers as well as military officers.

Thayer was appointed superintendent of the United States Military Academy (1817–33). He chose the French model of rigidly prescribed courses and stringent competitive examinations. Although West Point was a military academy, Thayer successfully demanded scholarship, established high standards of achievement, formulated objective criteria of assessment, and attracted a qualified faculty. He assisted in establishing a curriculum suitable to what became the first technical and scientific college in the United States, the pioneer effort in teaching engineering.

The faculty was not limited to army officers, and in physics, mathematics, and engineering, it came to be regarded as the best in the United States. West Point became the source for engineers needed in the field and of teachers for the growing number of similar civilian engineering institutions being established, notably at Harvard, Yale, and the Thayer School of Architecture and Engineering, which Thayer endowed at Dartmouth in 1867. In addition to technical courses, the West Point curriculum included chemistry, general history, moral philosophy, law, geography, and ethics. Thayer introduced homogeneous class sections, daily recitations and weekly grades, competitive ranking, and public examinations. The honor system began under Thayer as a matter of mutual courtesy.

In the surge of Jacksonian democracy after 1828, Thayer and the academy came under growing criticism as an elitist and undemocratic institution; he resigned as superintendent in 1833 to live out his army career as a colonel of the corps of engineers until 1863.

REFERENCES: *AC; DAB; NCAB* (7:37); *TC; WWW* (H); Stephen E. Ambrose, *Duty, Honor, Country: A History of West Point* (Baltimore: Johns Hopkins Press, 1966); Thomas J. Fleming, *West Point: The Men and Times of the United States Military Academy* (New York: Morrow, 1969);

K. Bruce Galloway and Robert Bowie Johnson, Jr., *West Point: America's Power Fraternity* (New York: Simon & Schuster, 1973); *NYT,* September 8, 1872, p. 5.                                                    *Joseph C. Bronars, Jr.*

**THOMAS, Augustus Orloff.** B. February 21, 1863, Mercer County, Illinois, to William Lee and Mary Elizabeth (Cox) Thomas. M. June 14, 1894, to Ellamay Colvin. Ch. two. D. January 30, 1935, Washington, D.C.

Augustus Orloff Thomas earned the B.Sc. degree (1891) from Western Normal College in Bushnell, Illinois. He continued his formal education at Amity College in College Springs, Iowa, from which he received the Ph.B. (1894) and Ph.D. (1896) degrees. He earned the B. Ed. degree (1908) from the Nebraska State Teachers College (later, Peru State College) at Peru.

Thomas became principal of a public school at Cambridge, Nebraska, in 1891. Following two years in this position he served successively as superintendent of schools in the Nebraska communities of St. Paul (1893–96), Minden (1896–1901), and Kearney (1901–05). From 1905 to 1913 he organized and served as the first president of the Nebraska State Normal School (later, Kearney State College) at Kearney, the second normal school in the state. The matriculation of 863 students during the school's first year of operation was reported to be a record for new normal schools in the United States at that time; during the second year enrollment reached 1,181.

Thomas held the position of state superintendent for public instruction in Nebraska (1914–16). He left the Nebraska post to assume the state superintendency in Maine in 1917 and remained in that position until his retirement in 1929. He is credited with promoting many improvements in education in Maine, particularly in rural schools. Under his encouragement and direction new and modern schools were built, courses of instruction were improved, better textbooks were adopted, scientific methods of instruction were introduced, and evening schools were established.

He was associate editor of the *Western Journal of Education* and author of *Rural Arithmetic* (1916) and *A Boy's Choice of a Profession* (1921). He revised J. Sterling Mortin's two-volume *History of Nebraska* (1917).

While chairing the National Education Association's foreign relations committee, he sought to promote peace through the world's educational organizations. He called and presided over a world conference of educators in San Francisco in 1923; this meeting resulted in the organization of the World Federation of Education Associations. Thomas was elected its first president (1923–31); he became secretary-general in 1931. Under his leadership eighty organizations representing nearly two and one-half million teachers throughout the world became members of the federation.

Thomas also served as secretary of the Nebraska State Teachers

Association, acting secretary of the Mississippi Valley Historical Society, chairman of the Mississippi Valley History Teachers Association, and president of the normal school department of the National Education Association (1908). He was elected a fellow of the Educational Institute of Scotland and received an honorary degree from Bates College.

REFERENCES: *LE* (I); *NCAB* (C:499); *NYT,* January 31, 1935, p. 19; *WWAE* (I); *WWW* (I); *Nebraska Educational Journal* (March 1935).

*Erwin H. Goldenstein*

**THOMAS, Calvin.** B. October 28, 1854, near Lapeer, Michigan, to Stephen Van Rensselaer and Caroline Louisa (Lord) Thomas. M. March 25, 1880, to Jennie M. Sutton. M. June 16, 1884, to Mary Eleanor Allen. Ch. two. D. November 4, 1919, New York, New York.

Calvin Thomas was graduated from the University of Michigan with the A.B. (1874) and A.M. (1877) degrees and studied the classics in Leipzig, Germany (1877–78).

He was a high school teacher of Latin and Greek in Grand Rapids, Michigan (1874–77). On his return to America from Germany, he taught Greek and German at the University of Michigan (1878–96). In 1896 Thomas became professor of German languages and literature at Columbia College (later, University). He retired in 1914 but returned to head the department of German languages at Columbia during World War I.

Thomas edited a number of classic German texts for students, notably Goethe's *Torquato Tasso* (1888), *Hermann and Dorothea* (1891), and *Faust* (1892). Possibly his best-known work was *Goethe* (1917). He also wrote *A Practical German Grammar* (1895), *Life and Works of Schiller* (1901), and *German Literature* (1909). He was consulting editor of the *New Standard Dictionary* (1909). He reviewed books in the German and Scandinavian fields, mainly for the *Nation* magazine.

Thomas was a founder and president of the Modern Language Association of America (1896) and president of the American Dialect Society (1912). As chairman of a Modern Language Association committee of twelve in 1898, he made a report on the teaching of modern languages, which was printed by the United States Bureau of Education and aroused much discussion. He received an honorary degree from the University of Michigan (1904).

REFERENCES: *DAB; NCAB* (16:220); *TC; WWW* (I); *NYT,* November 5, 1919, p. 15.                                    *Ronald Iannarone*

**THOMAS, Frank Waters.** B. May 14, 1878, Danville, Indiana, to Erasmus Darwin and Mary (Roseborough) Thomas. M. September 2, 1908, to Ina Gregg. M. December 4, 1957, to Edith Archer Hover. Ch. three. D. October 11, 1970, Pasadena, California.

Frank Waters Thomas was educated in the Danville, Indiana, public schools and was graduated from Indiana State Normal School (later, Indiana State University) at Terre Haute in 1902. He received the A.B. degree (1905) from Indiana University, the A.M. degree (1910) from the University of Illinois, and the Ph.D. degree (1926) from Stanford (California) University.

Thomas taught (1906–10) and was principal (1910–11) in the academy of the University of Illinois and was principal of California high schools at Santa Monica (1911–13) and Sacramento (1913–17). He was head of the department of education and vice-president (1917–27) and president (1927–48) of Fresno Normal School. During his term as president, the Fresno school became Fresno State College (later, California State University, Fresno). Thomas established the school of agriculture and was a liberal administrator who permitted students to serve on university committees and voice their opinions on college policy that affected them.

Thomas was the author of *Training for Effective Study* (1921), *Principles and Technique of Teaching* (1927), *The Junior College* (1927), *Principles of Modern Education* (with A. R. Lang, 1937), and *An Experience in Health Education* (1950). He contributed to several anthologies and was editor of *California Journal of Secondary Education* (1948–51).

Thomas was active in professional associations as president of the American Association of Teachers Colleges (1938–39) and the California Society of Secondary Education and was a member of the National Commission on Teacher Education (1939–43). He received an honorary degree from Occidental College.

REFERENCES: *LE* (III); *WW* (XXXI); *WWAE* (XIV); *WWW* (VI); *Fresno (California) Bell,* October 11, 1970.                                    *John F. Ohles*

**THOMAS, Martha Carey.** B. January 2, 1857, Baltimore, Maryland, to James Carey and Mary (Whitall) Thomas. M. no. D. December 2, 1935, Philadelphia, Pennsylvania.

M. Carey Thomas was influenced by her mother's support of women's rights and her father's opposition to advanced education for women. She attended a Friends' school, the Howland Institute, and received the A.B. degree (1887) from Cornell University in Ithaca, New York. She attended Johns Hopkins University in Baltimore, Maryland, where she was prevented from sitting in classes. She was one of the first women to study at the University of Leipzig, Germany. Denied the right to receive the doctorate in a German university, she received the Ph.D. degree summa cum laude (1882) from the University of Zurich, Switzerland, as the first foreigner and the first woman to do so.

When Bryn Mawr (Pennsylvania) College was organized, Thomas's father and several other relatives were made trustees. She asked to be president of the new college but was dean and professor of English (1885–92). She was acting president (1892–94) and was appointed president, a position she held from 1894 to her retirement in 1922. More interested in administration than teaching, she believed that Bryn Mawr must maintain standards equal to or better than those of the leading men's colleges. She instituted entrance examinations equal to those at Harvard, adopted the Johns Hopkins' group system, and offered only courses in scholarly fields.

Thomas established the first graduate school connected with a women's college with resident fellowships and scholarships and founded eight European fellowships for study at Bryn Mawr, the first such fellowships awarded by any graduate school in the United States. She founded the first graduate school of economy and social research and established the first school for industrial workers on a college campus in a 1922 summer session. Thomas came into conflict with the faculty, and in 1915 a faculty revolt forced her to accept a chapter of the American Association of University Professors on the campus and faculty participation in governance of the college.

She was the author of *Education of Women* (1900). She was a founder of the Bryn Mawr School for Girls in Baltimore, founded the Association to Promote Scientific Research by Women (1900) and the International Federation of University Women, assisted in opening Johns Hopkins University Medical School to women (1893), and served as chairperson of the women's advisory committee of the medical school (1893–1915).

Thomas participated in the College Equal Suffrage League, was first president of the National College Women's Equal Suffrage League (1908), worked for the National American Woman Suffrage Association, and supported the National Woman's party in 1920. She believed in quality education for women and opposed protective legislation for women in industry.

She was awarded gold medals at expositions in Paris, France (1900), and St. Louis, Missouri (1904), and was the recipient of several honorary degrees.

REFERENCES: *DAB* (supp. 1); *NAW; NCAB* (13:84); *TC; WWW* (1); *NYT,* December 3, 1935, p. 25.                              *Barbara Ruth Peltzman*

**THOMPSON, Charles Oliver.** B. September 25, 1836, East Windsor Hill, Connecticut, to William and Eliza Welles (Butler) Thompson. M. May 14, 1862, to Maria Goodrich. Ch. three. D. March 17, 1885, Terre Haute, Indiana.

Charles Oliver Thompson was graduated from Dartmouth College in Hanover, New Hampshire, with the A.B. (1858) and A.M. (1861) degrees. He studied chemistry at Harvard University (1864–68) and technical education programs in Europe in 1868.

Thompson was principal of the Caledonia County Academy (later, Peacham Academy) in Peacham, Vermont (1858–64), and served as a civil engineer in Piermont, New York, for a short time in 1860. He was principal of the Cotting High School in Arlington, Massachusetts (1864–68), and was the first principal and professor of chemistry at the Worcester (Massachusetts) Free Institute of Industrial Science (later, Worcester Polytechnic Institute) from 1868 to 1882.

At Worcester Thompson set up a curriculum in which theoretical study of engineering was combined with practical work in machine shops that were in competition with commercial firms. His plan was adopted by similar schools. In 1883 Thompson became the first president of Rose Polytechnic Institute (later, Rose Hulman Institute of Technology) in Terre Haute, Indiana, where he served to his death.

Thompson was the author of *Manual Labor and School Work Combined* (with Andrew D. White, *q.v.*, 1870), *Robert Boyle, a Study in Biography* (1882), *Modern Polytechnic Schools* (1883), *Manual Training in the Public Schools* (1884), and *Hints Toward a Profession of Teaching* (1867). He was a member of scientific and scholarly organizations. He received honorary degrees from Dartmouth (1879) and Williams (1880) colleges.

REFERENCES: *AC; DAB; TC; WWW* (H).                          *K. J. Balthaser*

**THOMPSON, Hugh Smith.** B. January 24, 1836, Charleston, South Carolina, to Henry Tazewell and Agnes (Smith) Thompson. M. April 6, 1858, to Elizabeth Anderson Clarkson. Ch. seven. D. November 20, 1904, New York, New York.

Hugh Smith Thompson was educated in the Greenville, South Carolina, schools. He was graduated from the Citadel Academy (later, the Citadel) in Charleston, South Carolina (1856).

Thompson taught in the Arsenal Academy in Columbia, South Carolina, as an assistant professor of mathematics and French, holding the military rank of second lieutenant (1858–59), and was professor of French with the rank of first lieutenant (1859–61). He was promoted to captain and transferred to the Citadel Academy at Charleston as professor of belles lettres in 1861. He served with honor as the commander of an organized battalion in defense of Charleston Harbor during the Civil War. At the close of the war Thompson was elected principal and professor of the Columbia (South Carolina) Male Academy, which became one of the leading schools in the state. In 1876 he was elected superintendent of education in South Carolina and served to 1882. The modern development of the South Carolina public school system began under Thompson.

In 1882 Thompson was elected governor of the state of South Carolina and was reelected in 1884; he was credited with tax reform, economy, and efforts to improve education. He served as assistant secretary of the

United States Treasury (1886–89) and was appointed the Democratic member of the United States Civil Service Commission in 1889. He served to April 1892 when he became comptroller of the New York Life Insurance Company.

REFERENCES:*AC; DAB; NCAB* (24:78); *NYT,* November 21, 1904, p. 7; *TC; WWW* (I); *Cyclopedia of Eminent and Representative Men of the Carolinas* (Madison, Wis.: Brant & Fuller Publishers, 1892), 1: 531–36; Helen Kohn Hennig, *Great South Carolinians of a Later Date* (Chapel Hill: University of North Carolina Press, 1949), pp. 167–79.

*Dennis G. Wiseman*

**THOMPSON, Robert Ellis.** B. April 5, 1844, Lurgan, Ireland, to Samuel and Catherine (Ellis) Thompson. M. 1874 to Mary Ellis Neely. M. August 18, 1910, to Catherine Neely. Ch. three. D. October 19, 1924, Philadelphia, Pennsylvania.

Robert Ellis Thompson emigrated from Ireland with his family to Philadelphia, Pennsylvania, in 1857. He was educated in Philadelphia at Central High School. He was graduated from the University of Pennsylvania with the A.B. (1865) and A.M. (1868) degrees. He attended the Reformed Presbyterian Seminary in Philadelphia graduating in 1867. He received the Ph.D. degree (1870) from Hamilton College in Clinton, New York.

After serving a year as a supply pastor, Thompson returned to the University of Pennsylvania as an instructor in Latin and mathematics and served the university in many capacities for the next twenty-four years (1868–92). He was first dean of the Wharton School of Finance and Economy (1881–83) and continued to teach economics as Welsh Professor of History and English Literature (1883–92).

During his tenure at the University of Pennsylvania, Thompson became widely known as an author and lecturer. He supported protectionist economics, advocating high protective tariffs. He came into conflict with reformers who preached class conflict instead of a harmony of economic interests. His departure from the University of Pennsylvania was a result of conflict with younger members of the Wharton faculty and the university provost.

Thompson declined an offer to be president of Lake Forest (Illinois) College and a professorship at Princeton University to serve as principal of Central High School in Philadelphia (1894–1921). He was highly successful in the position and the school prospered.

Thompson was the author of *Social Science and National Economy* (1875), *Elements of Political Economy* (1881), *History of the Presbyterian Churches of America* (1895), *Political Economy for High Schools* (1895), *The National Hymn Book of the American Churches* (1893), *The Hand of God in American History* (1902), *Nature, the Mirror of Grace* (1907), *The*

*Historic Episcopate* (1910), *The Apostles as Every-Day Men* (1912), *The History of the Dwelling-House and Its Future* (1914), and lectures he delivered at Harvard, Yale, and Princeton universities. He was editor of *Penn Monthly* (1870–81) and *American Weekly* (1880–91) and served on the staff of the *Irish World* (1884–1924) and *Sunday School Times* (1892–1924).

Thompson received honorary degrees from the University of Pennsylvania and Muhlenberg College.

REFERENCES: *AC; DAB; NCAB* (10:18); *TC; WWW* (I); *NYT,* October 20, 1924, p. 17.                                                *Richard T. Rees*

**THOMPSON, Samuel Rankin.** B. April 17, 1833, South Shenango, Pennsylvania, to William and Mary (Latta) Thompson. M. 1859 to Lucy Gilmour. Ch. one. D. October 28, 1896, New Wilmington, Pennsylvania.

Samuel Rankin Thompson spent his early years on his father's farm. With only three months of preparation at an academy, he began teaching in Clarion County, Pennsylvania, at the age of fifteen. After eight years of teaching in winter and working on farms and in sawmills in summer, he entered Westminister College in Wilmington, Pennsylvania, where he received the A.B. (1863) and A.M. (1881) degrees.

Thompson was active in Pennsylvania as superintendent of schools for Crawford County (1860–65), professor of natural sciences and vice-president of the Edinboro State Normal School (later, Edinboro State College) from 1865 to 1867, and founder and principal of Pottsville High School (1867–68). He organized and administered a state normal school at Marshall College (later, University) in Huntington, West Virginia (1868–71).

Thompson had spent at least a year in Nebraska in his precollege years (1848–56) and returned there to the University of Nebraska as professor of agriculture and as the first dean of the college of agriculture (1872–75). He was principal of the Nebraska State Normal School at Peru (later, Peru State College) in 1876–77 and served as Nebraska superintendent of public instruction (1878–81). Before returning to the college of agriculture as professor of agriculture and didactics in 1882, he served for six months as interim superintendent of the Lincoln (Nebraska) public schools. He returned to Westminister College in 1884 as professor of physics, serving there to his death.

In Nebraska Thompson organized the state weather service and initiated a series of farmers' institutes. He introduced reforms into the public school system and secured important school legislation. He was the author of *A History of Higher Education in Pennsylvania* (edited by C. H. Haskins and W. I. Hull, 1902).

REFERENCES: *DAB; NCAB* (7:517); *WWW* (H); Robert Platt Crawford,

*These Fifty Years: A History of the College of Agriculture of the University of Nebraska* (Lincoln: University of Nebraska Press, 1925).

Erwin H. Goldenstein

**THOMPSON, William Oxley.** B. November 5, 1855, Cambridge, Ohio, to David Glenn and Agnes Miranda (Oxley) Thompson. M. September 21, 1882, to Rebecca Jane Allison. M. October 5, 1887, to Helen Starr Brown. M. June 28, 1894, to Estelle Godfrey Clark. Ch. three. D. December 9, 1933, Columbus, Ohio.

William Oxley Thompson entered Muskingum College in New Concord, Ohio, in 1870, attending only when he was not engaged as a farm worker or rural schoolteacher. He received the A.B. degree from Muskingum in 1878 and was employed as a teacher at an academy in Indiana, Pennsylvania. Deciding upon the ministry as his life's work, he received the M.A. degree from Muskingum College in 1881 and was graduated with honors from Western Theological Seminary, Allegheny (later, Pittsburgh), Pennsylvania, and was ordained in the Presbyterian ministry in 1882.

He served churches in Odebolt, Iowa, and Longmont, Colorado, where he also was president of a school known variously as Longmont Academy, Longmont College, and Synodical College. He was appointed president of Miami University of Ohio in Oxford in 1891. During his tenure he developed a reputation for dignified and eloquent leadership in the cause of higher education. He became president of Ohio State University in Columbus in 1899. Thompson led the university from a local college of 1,200 students in 1899 to a modern state university offering undergraduate and graduate programs, with a student body of over 12,000 by 1925, when he retired.

Thompson was president of the Association of American Agricultural Colleges and Experimental Stations (1903–04), the National Education Association (1905–06), and the National Association of State Universities (1910–11). He was a member of the board of education of the Columbus, Ohio, public school system during his tenure as president of the university. From 1905 to 1925 he was president of the Midland Mutual Life Insurance Company.

During World War I, Thompson played a role in the passage of the National Defense Act. In 1918 he was appointed chairman of the United States Agricultural Commission to England, France, and Italy overseeing food production and assistance to those countries during the war. He served as chairman of the controversial United States Anthracite Coal Commission in 1920. Thompson received many honorary degrees. After his retirement, he served as moderator of the General Assembly of the Presbyterian Church in the United States of America (1927).

REFERENCES: *DAB; LE* (I); *NCAB* (24:262); *NYT,* December 9, 1933, p.

15; *TC; WWW* (I); William A. Kinnison, *Building Sullivant's Pyramid: An Administrative History of the Ohio State University* (Columbus: Ohio State University Press, 1970); Thomas C. Mendenhall, ed., *History of the Ohio State University: Continuation of the Narrative from 1910 to 1925* (Columbus: Ohio State University Press, 1926), vol. 2; Wilbur H. Siebert, *History of the Ohio State University: The University in the Great War* (Columbus: The Ohio State University Press, 1934), vol. 4.

*Charles M. Dye*


**THOMSON, James Bates.** B. May 21, 1803, Springfield, Vermont, to n.a. M. to n.a. Coffin. Ch. n.a. D. June 21, 1883, Brooklyn, New York.

James Bates Thomson worked summers on the family farm and attended the local district school during the winter. He prepared for college at an academy in Plainfield, New Hampshire. He was graduated from Yale College (1834) and continued to study there, attending the lectures of Benjamin Silliman *(q.v.)*, Denison Olmsted *(q.v.)*, and others.

Thomson began to teach school in Springfield, Vermont, at the age of sixteen and moved to Massachusetts, where he was a teacher in the Juvenile Reform School in Boston and the Centre School in Brighton. After completing his studies at Yale, he was principal of an academy in Nantucket, Massachusetts (1835–42).

Ill health led to his resignation from the academy and a move in 1842 to Auburn, New York. In 1843 he participated as a mathematics instructor in the first teachers' institutes in New York State conducted in Ithaca, New York, by county superintendent J. S. Denman and presided over by Salem Town *(q.v.)*. He continued to participate in institutes in New York and other states for several years.

Thomson was asked by Jeremiah Day *(q.v.)*, president of Yale, to prepare an abridgement of Day's *Introduction to Algebra* (1814) for use in secondary schools. Thomson's revision was published in 1843. It was followed by *Mental Arithmetic* (1846), *Higher Arithmetic* (1847), *Rudiments of Arithmetic* (1853), *New Practical Algebra* (1877), *A Complete Intellectual Arithmetic* (1878), and *Complete Graded Arithmetic* (1882).

Thomson was a founder of the New York State Teachers Association in 1845 and served as its president. He was the recipient of honorary degrees from Hamilton College and the University of Tennessee.

REFERENCES: *AC;* Thomas E. Finegan *(q.v.)*, *Free Schools* (Albany: University of the State of New York, 1921); Hyland C. Kirk, *A History of the New York State Teachers Association* (New York: E. L. Kellogg, 1885); *NYT*, June 23, 1885, p. 4; John A. Nietz, *Old Textbooks* (Pittsburgh: University of Pittsburgh Press, 1961).                    *John F. Ohles*

**THORNDIKE, Edward Lee.** B. August 31, 1874, Williamsburg, Massachusetts, to Edward Roberts and Abigail Brewster (Ladd) Thorndike. M. August 29, 1900, to Elizabeth Moulton. Ch. five. D. August 9, 1949, Montrose, New York.

Edward Lee Thorndike, educator and experimental psychologist, received the B.A. degree (1895) from Wesleyan University in Middletown, Connecticut, the A.B. (1896) and A.M. (1897) degrees from Harvard University, and the Ph.D. degree (1898) from Columbia College (later, University).

He taught at the College for Women of Western Reserve University in Cleveland, Ohio (1898). He taught psychology at Columbia (1899–1940). He was director of the Columbia University division of psychology in the Institute of Educational Research (1922–40).

Thorndike regarded measurement as the key to scientific progress in education and psychology. He developed standard devices for testing animals that permitted investigation of animal psychology as scientific subject matter. His contributions to learning in humans involved the application of quantitative methods to the study of mental fatigue, memory, rate of learning, learning in adults, conditions of efficient learning, the correlation between various abilities and talents, and the influence of inheritance on intellectual functioning and character. He has been called the Father of Modern Educational Psychology.

Thorndike wrote more than 450 books, monographs, and articles. His works include *Educational Psychology* (1903), *Mental and Social Measurements* (1904), *Elements of Psychology* (1905), *Principles of Teaching* (1905), *Animal Intelligence* (1911), *The Original Nature of Man* (1913), *The Psychology of Learning* (three volumes, 1913–14), *The Teachers Word Book of 30,000 Words* (1921), *Psychology of Arithmetic* (1922), *The Measurement of Intelligence* (1926), *Fundamentals of Learning* (1932), *Thorndike Century Junior Dictionary* (1935), *Human Nature and The Social Order* (1940), *Thorndike Century Senior Dictionary* (1941), and *Man and His Works* (1949).

He was a member or fellow of numerous scientific and educational associations. He was president of the American Association for the Advancement of Science in 1934. Seven honorary degrees were conferred on him, two by European universities.

REFERENCES: *CB* (September 1941); *DAB* (supp. 4); *EB; LE* (III); *NCAB* (51:209); *WWAE* (VIII); *WWW* (II); *NYT*, August 10, 1949, p. 21; Geraldine Joncich, *The Sane Positivist: A Biography of Edward L. Thorndike* (Middletown, Conn.: Wesleyan University Press, 1968).

*Don C. Locke*

**THURSTON, Robert Henry.** B. October 25, 1839, Providence, Rhode Island, to Robert Lawton and Harriet (Taylor) Thurston. M. October 5, 1865, to Susan Taylor Gladding. M. August 4, 1880, to Lenora Boughton. Ch. three. D. October 25, 1903, Ithaca, New York.

Robert Henry Thurston was the son of one of the pioneer builders of the steam engine. Thurston attended Brown University in Providence, Rhode Island, from which he received the Ph.B. degree in 1859 and a certificate in civil engineering.

Thurston worked in his father's firm as a draftsman and as the firm's representative in Philadelphia. In March 1861 he entered the United States Navy as an engineering officer and served through the Civil War. At the close of the war he was assigned to the Naval Academy at Annapolis, Maryland, as an assistant professor of natural and experimental philosophy; he became head of the department (1866–71). He was professor of mechanical engineering at the newly founded Stevens Institute of Technology at Hoboken, New Jersey (1871–85). Thurston gained wide recognition as an engineer, scholar, and teacher. He formulated a plan of instruction in 1871 that became the foundation for the curriculum at Stevens.

In 1885 the trustees of Cornell University offered him the directorship of Sibley College, which he reorganized into a first-rate college of mechanical engineering. He was at Cornell to his death in 1903. He was the inventor of testing machines, engine governors, and other devices.

Thurston's major publications include *A History of the Growth of the Steam Engine* (1878), *Friction and Lubrication: Determinations of the Laws and Coefficients of Friction by New Methods and with New Apparatus* (1879), *The Materials of Engineering* (three volumes, 1883–84), *Stationary Steam Engines, Especially as Adapted to Electric Lighting Purposes* (1884), *A Treatise on Friction and Lost Work in Machinery and Millwork* (1885), *A Text-Book of the Materials of Construction, for Use in Technical and Engineering Schools* (1885), *Steam-Boilers Explosions in Theory and Practice* (1887), *A Manual of Steam Boilers* (1888), *Heat as a Form of Energy* (1890), *Reflections on the Motive Power of Heat* (1890), *A Handbook of Engine and Boiler Trials, and of the Indicator and Prony Brake* (1890), *Robert Fulton, His Life and Its Results* (1891), *A Manual of the Steam Engine: For Engineers and Technical Schools* (two volumes, 1891), *The Animal as a Machine* (1894), *Prime Motor* (1894), and *Laws of Energetics* (1894). He was editor of *Science* magazine and engineering editor of the *Universal,* and *Johnson's* and *Appleton's* encyclopedias.

Thurston was active in professional associations as a founder and first president of the American Society of Mechanical Engineers (1880–83) and was vice-president of the American Association for the Advancement of Science (1877, 1878, and 1884) and the American Institute of Mining Engineers (1878–79). He was a member of many federal and state commissions and was a delegate to international exhibitions at Vienna, Austria (1873), and Paris, France (1889). He was awarded three honorary degrees.

REFERENCES: *AC; DAB; NCAB* (4:479); *TC; WWW* (I); *NYT,* October 26, 1903, p. 1.                                                    *Joe L. Green*

**THURSTONE, Louis Leon.** B. May 29, 1887, Chicago, Illinois, to Conrad and Sophie (Stroth) Thurstone. M. July 17, 1924, to Thelma Gwinn. Ch. three. D. September 29, 1955, Chapel Hill, North Carolina.

Louis Leon Thurstone's father was a mathematics teacher and Lutheran minister and his mother was a musician and artist. Thurstone lived in Chicago, Illinois; Centerville, Mississippi; Stockholm, Sweden; and Jamestown, New York, during his formative years. He received the M.E. degree (1912) from Cornell University in Ithaca, New York, and the Ph.D. degree (1917) from the University of Chicago. Trained in electrical engineering at Cornell, he designed a motion-picture camera and projector before his graduation. He became interested in the application of psychology to engineering and in the importance of learning and teaching.

Thurstone taught engineering at the University of Minnesota (1912–14). He was professor of psychology at Carnegie Institute of Technology (later, Carnegie-Mellon University) in Pittsburgh, Pennsylvania (1915–23). He was professor of psychology (1923–38) and Charles F. Grey Distinguished Service Professor (1938–53) at the University of Chicago. He was interested in individual differences and conducted studies that led to contributions in test theory, psychophysics, attitude measurement, and multiple factor analysis. In 1953 he accepted a position as professor of education at the University of North Carolina where he founded the Psychometric Laboratory.

Thurstone was a prolific writer of books and monographs, professional journal articles, technical reports, and tests. His books include *The Learning Curve Equation* (1918), *The Nature of Intelligence* (1924), *Fundamentals of Statistics* (1924), *The Measurement of Attitude* (1929), *The Vectors of Mind* (1935), *Primary Mental Abilities* (1938), *Factorial Studies of Intelligence* (with Thelma G. Thurstone, 1941), *A Factorial Study of Perception* (1944), and *Multiple Factor Analysis* (1947). He founded *Psychometrika.*

Thurstone was a founder of the Psychometric Society (president, 1936) and president of the Midwestern Psychological Association (1930) and the American Psychological Association (1932). He was a fellow of the American Association for the Advancement of Science, the National Academy of Sciences, the American Philosophical Society, and the Swedish Psychological Society, and a member of many other scientific and professional associations. He was awarded an honorary degree by the University of Gothenberg, Sweden, in 1954.

REFERENCES: *EB; WWW* (III); Dael Wolfe, "Louis Leon Thurstone: 1887–1955," *American Journal of Psychology* 69 (March 1956): 131–34; H. J. Eysenck, W. Arnold, and R. Meili, eds., *Encyclopedia of Psychology* (New York: Herder and Herder, 1972); *NYT*, October 1, 1955, p. 19; Paul Horst, "L. L. Thurstone and the Science of Behavior," *Science* 122 (December 30, 1955): 1259–60.                          *Thomas E. Dinero*

**THWING, Charles Franklin.** B. November 9, 1853, New Sharon, Maine, to Joseph Perkins and Hannah Morse (Hopkins) Thwing. M. September 18, 1879, to Carrie Frances Butler. M. December 22, 1906, to Mary Gardiner Dunning. Ch. three. D. August 29, 1937, Cleveland, Ohio.

Charles Franklin Thwing was graduated from Phillips Academy in Andover, Massachusetts (1871). Admitted to Phi Beta Kappa when a sophomore, Thwing ranked second in his graduating class at Harvard University in 1876. He enrolled in Andover (Massachusetts) Theological Seminary in 1876, graduating in 1879. Ordained in the Congregational ministry, he accepted pastorates in Cambridge, Massachusetts (1879–86), and Minneapolis, Minnesota (1886–90).

Thwing was president of Western Reserve University and Adelbert College in Cleveland, Ohio (1890–1921), where he made his most significant and lasting contributions to American higher education. From a fledgling school with 246 students it developed into a university with increased faculty and buildings and over 2,000 students. The graduate school of liberal arts was established under Thwing's leadership, as well as schools in law, dentistry, pharmacy, and applied social sciences and programs in business education, religious education, and household administration. In cooperation with the city of Cleveland, he established the Cleveland School of Education (Cleveland Normal School). To enable the institution to serve its immediate area, he organized extension courses, adult education programs, and endowments for public lectures.

Thwing contributed to many publications and was editor of the *Chapel and Hymn Book,* associate editor and editor of the *Bibliotheca Sacra,* and editor-in-chief of the *Biographical History of Ohio.* He was the author of *The Reading of Books* (1883), *The Family* (with Carrie F. B. Thwing, 1886), *The Working Church* (1888), *Within College Walls* (1893), *The College Woman* (1894), *The American College in American Life* (1897), *The Best Life* (1898), *The Choice of a College* (1899), *College Administration* (1900), *The Youth's Dream of Life* (1900), *God in His World* (1900), *If I Were a College Student* (1902), *A Liberal Education and a Liberal Faith* (1903), *College Training and the Business Man* (1904), *A History of Higher Education in America* (1906), *Education in the Far East* (1909), *History of Education in the United States Since the Civil War* (1910), *Universities of the World* (1911), *Letters from a Father to His Son Entering College*

(1912), *The Coordinate System of Higher Education* (1913), *Letters from a Father to His Daughter Entering College* (1913), *Education According to Some Modern Masters* (1916), *The Ministry* (1916), *The Training of Men for the World's Future* (1916), *The College Gateway* (1918), *The American Colleges and Universities in the Great War* (1920), *Higher Education in Australia and New Zealand* (1922), *Human Australasia* (1923), *What Education Has the Most Worth!* (1924), *The College President* (1926), *Guides, Philosophers, and Friends* (1927), *The American and German University* (1928), *Education and Religion* (1929), *American Society— Interpretations of Educational and Other Forces* (1931), *Friends of Men* (1933), and *The American College and University—A Human Fellowship* (1935). He was editor of the *Chicago Advance* (1888–91).

Thwing served as secretary of the board of trustees of the Carnegie Foundation for the Advancement of Teaching (1905–21), president (1922–28) and life senator of the United Chapters of Phi Beta Kappa, and trustee of the Walter Hines Page School of International Relations at Johns Hopkins University and the Foreign Language Information Service. He was secretary of the American Board of Commissioners for Foreign Missions (1884) and a trustee of Anatolia (Greece) College. He belonged to many other local, national, and international organizations.

A staunch fighter against religious and racial prejudice and intolerance, Thwing supported efforts toward international peace; he received the first prize from the *Chicago Daily News* in its competition for a practical plan for world peace (1923) and was the recipient of a medal from the Cleveland Chamber of Commerce (1925). Thwing received honorary degrees from eight colleges and universities.

REFERENCES: *AC; DAB* (supp. 2); *LE* (I); *NCAB* (27:16); *TC; WWAE* (VIII); *WWW* (I); *NYT,* August 30, 1937, p. 21. *Charles M. Dye*

**TICKNOR, George.** B. August 1, 1791, Boston, Massachusetts, to Elisha and Elizabeth (Billings) Ticknor. M. September 18, 1821, to Anna Eliot. Ch. four. D. January 26, 1871, Boston, Massachusetts.

George Ticknor passed the entrance examination for Dartmouth College in Hanover, New Hampshire, at the age of nine, entered the junior class in 1805 at the age of fourteen, and was graduated with the A.B. (1807) and A.M. (1810) degrees. He studied Greek and Latin (1807–10) and read law (1810–13). He traveled in the United States (1814–15) and Europe, where he studied at the University of Göttingen in Germany (1815–17).

Admitted to the bar in 1813, Ticknor practiced law (1813–14) and was appointed professor of French and Spanish at Harvard University in 1817 and filled the position in 1819 on his return from Europe. Ticknor was an influential pioneer in organizing instruction. He advocated a division of the university into departments of related subjects and favored elective courses of study. He retired from Harvard in 1835 and spent three years in Europe.

Ticknor was the author of *Syllabus of a Course of Lectures on the History and Criticism of Spanish Literature* (1823), *Outlines of the Principal Events in the Life of Lafayette* (1825), *History of Spanish Literature* (three volumes, 1849), the first extensive survey of Spanish literature, and *A Life of William Hickling Prescott* (1864). He was a founder of the Boston Public Library (1852) and toured Europe (1856–57) collecting books for the library made possible by a gift of Joshua Bates. He donated his extensive collection of Spanish literature to the library. He was a fellow of the American Academy of Arts and Sciences, a member of other scholarly organizations, and a member of the board of visitors of the United States Military Academy at West Point, New York (1826). He received honorary degrees from Harvard University (A.M., 1814, and LL.D., 1850), Brown University (1850), Dartmouth College (1858), and the University of the State of New York (1864).

REFERENCES: *AC; DAB; NCAB* (6:477); *NYT,* January 27, 1871, p. 4; *TC; WWW* (H).                                               *Walter F. C. Ade*

**TIGERT, John James.** B. February 11, 1882, Nashville, Tennessee, to John James and Amelia (McTyeire) Tigert. M. August 25, 1909, to Edith Jackson Bristol. Ch. two. D. January 21, 1965, Gainesville, Florida.

John James Tigert, son of a clergyman, editor, and bishop of the Methodist Episcopal Church, South, and grandson of a president of Vanderbilt University, excelled at Vanderbilt as an athlete and a scholar, receiving the B.A. degree (1904). He completed postgraduate studies at Oxford (England) University as the first Rhodes scholar from Tennessee. He earned the M.A. degree at Oxford in 1915 after completing a seven-year apprenticeship and studied at the University of Minnesota (1916).

Upon his return to the United States from England, Tigert was a member of the faculty of Central Methodist College in Fayette, Missouri (1907–09). He became president of Kentucky Wesleyan College at Winchester (later, Owensboro), Kentucky, in 1909 at the age of twenty-seven. He served in that capacity until 1911 when he joined the faculty of the University of Kentucky where he was professor of philosophy and psychology (1911–17) and professor of psychology (1917–21). During World War I he served in Europe as an instructor in the Young Men's Christian Association and the Army Educational Corps (1918–19).

Returning to civilian life, Tigert was appointed United States commissioner of education by President Warren Harding (1921–28). He became president of the University of Florida in 1928. During his presidency, he established the general college to provide a general survey of knowledge during the first two years of study, developed a system of student self-government, organized the Institute of Inter-American Affairs, and organized the Southeastern Athletic Conference. He retired in 1947 and traveled to India, where he served as a member of the Indian Higher Education Commission. He was a visiting professor at the University of Miami in Coral Gables, Florida (1950–54).

Tigert wrote more than 275 books and articles, including *The Relation of Defective Vision to Retardation* (1916), *The Progress of Education in the Far West* (1923), *Democracy's Ideal of Education* (1925), *The New General College at the University of Florida* (1935), and *Bishop Holland Nimmons Mc Tyeire, Ecclestiastical and Educational Architect* (1955). He was the coauthor of *The Child—His Nature and His Needs* (1924), *The Book of Rural Life* (1925), and *High School Anthology* (1938).

A fellow of the Royal (London) Society of Arts and the International Institute of Arts and Letters, Tigert was president of Phi Delta Theta, was honored by the government of Denmark and the National Education Association, and received the Washington Bicentenary Medal. Tigert received many honorary degrees from American colleges and universities and was admitted to the National Football Hall of Fame. Tigert Hall at the University of Florida is named in his honor.

REFERENCES: *DAB; LE* (III); *NCAB* (F:246; 52:577); *NYT*, January 22, 1965, p 44; *WWAF* (XVI); *WWW* (IV); George C. Osborn, *John James Tigert American Educator* (Gainesville: University Presses of Florida, 1974)                                                          *John Steinert-Earls*

**TIPPETT, James Sterling.** B. September 2, 1885, Memphis, Missouri, to Edward Everett and Mary Olinda (Montgomery) Tippett. M. August 3, 1929, to Martha Louise Kelley. Ch. none. D. April 21, 1958, Chapel Hill, North Carolina.

James S. Tippett received the B.S. degree (1915) from the University of Missouri and studied on the graduate level at the University of Chicago (1915) and Columbia University (1921–28).

A rural schoolteacher in Scotland County, Missouri (1903–04), Tippett also taught in Missouri in the intermediate and high schools in Lancaster (1905–07), was principal and superintendent in Huntsville (1907–14) and Fayette (1914–17), and was an elementary school principal in Kansas City (1917–18). He was director of the demonstration school at George Peabody College for Teachers in Nashville, Tennessee (1918–22), teacher and special worker in the elementary division of the Lincoln School of Teachers College, Columbia University (1922–28), assistant professor of elementary education at the University of Pittsburgh, Pennsylvania (1928–30), and dean of the faculty at the Avon (Connecticut) Old Farms School (1930–32). He moved to North Carolina, where he was curriculum adviser to the Parker School District in Greenville, South Carolina (1934–39), and visiting lecturer in education at the University of North Carolina at Chapel Hill (1939–58). From 1939 he also was a professional writer of children's books.

Tippett was an important contributor to children's literature. Among his thirty books for youngsters were *Counting the Days* (1940), *I Live in a City* (1927), *I Spend the Summer* (1930), *Shadow and the Stocking* (1937), *Toys and Toy Makers* (1931), *A World to Know* (1933), and *I Know Some Little Animals* (1941). He also was the author of *School* (1927) and *School for a Growing Democracy* (with others, 1937). He collaborated in the Understanding Science Series of school texts. He was a member of professional associations.

REFERENCES: *LE* (III); *NCAB* (48:145); *NYT,* February 23, 1958, p. 92.                                                                          *J. W. Batten*

**TITCHENER, Edward Bradford.** B. January 11, 1867, Chichester, England, to John Bradford and Alice Field (Habin) Titchener. M. June 19, 1894, to Sophie Kellogg Bedlow. Ch. four. D. August 3, 1927, Ithaca, New York.

Edward Bradford Titchener was educated in England at Malvern College (1881–85) and Brasenose College of Oxford University. He received the B.A. (1890), M.A. (1894), and D.Sc. (1906) degrees from Oxford and studied experimental psychology under Wilhelm Wundt at the University of Leipzig, Germany, from which he received the Ph.D. degree (1892).

He returned to Oxford as an extension lecturer in biology (1892) and emigrated to the United States, where he joined the faculty of Cornell University in Ithaca, New York. He was appointed Sage Professor of Psychology and director of the psychological laboratory (1895), was professor in charge of music (1892–95), and became Sage Professor in the graduate school (1910–27). He was credited with developing psychology as a pure science and changing the study of psychology from traditional instruction to a laboratory subject.

Titchener translated a number of psychological books from German to English and was the author of *An Outline of Psychology* (1896), *A Primer of Psychology* (1898), *Experimental Psychology* (four volumes, 1901–05), *Elementary Psychology of Feeling and Attention* (1908), *Experimental Psychology of the Thought Processes* (1909), *A Textbook of Psychology* (1910), *A Beginner's Psychology* (1915), and *Systematic Psychology* (1924). He was the American editor of *Mind* (1894–1921) and associate editor (1895–1921) and editor (1921–25) of the *American Journal of Psychology*.

Titchener was a fellow of the American Association for the Advancement of Science, the Zoological Society of London, and the Royal (British) Society of Medicine. He was a foreign member of the Polish Academy of Arts and Science and a member of the international committees of the third through fifth congresses of psychology. He was vice-president of the sixth congress. He received four honorary degrees.

REFERENCES: *DAB; NCAB* (22:94); *WWW* (I); H. J. Eysenck, W. Arnold, and R. Meili, *Encyclopedia of Psychology* (New York: Herder and Herder, 1972); Robert M. Goldenson, *The Encyclopedia of Human Behavior* (New York: Doubleday & Co., 1970), vol. 2.

*Ronald Iannarone*

**TOLAND, Hugh Huger.** B. April 16, 1806, Guilder's Creek, South Carolina, to John and Mary (Boyd) Toland. M. 1833 to Mary Goodwin. M. 1844 to Mary Avery. M. 1860 to Mary B. (Morrison) Gridley. Ch. four. D. February 27, 1880, San Francisco, California.

Hugh Huger (sometimes Hughes) Toland was sent to school at the age of four, read about medicine as an adolescent, and worked in an apothecary shop. He studied medicine with George Ross and was graduated from a course in medicine at Transylvania University in Lexington, Kentucky, in 1828. He worked in a dissecting room in Lexington and spent over two years studying medicine in Paris, France.

Toland practiced medicine in Pageville, South Carolina (1828–30 and 1833–52). He developed a reputation as a surgeon while in South Carolina. In 1852 he moved to Stockton, California, and engaged in gold mining for a short time. He moved to San Francisco, California, in 1853 and practiced medicine, becoming the most notable surgeon on the Pacific Coast.

Toland established Toland Medical College in 1864, served as president, and was professor of surgery to his death in 1880. In 1873 Toland turned his college over to the University of California, where it continued as the Medical Center of the University of California in San Francisco. He wrote many important articles on medicine and a textbook, *Lectures on Practical Surgery* (1877).

REFERENCES: *DAB; WWW* (H); Henry Harris, *California's Medical Story* (San Francisco: J. W. Stacey, 1932).      *Stratton F. Caldwell*

**TOMLINS, William Lawrence.** D. February 4, 1844, London, England, to William and Sarah (Lawrence) Tomlins. M. 1868 to Elizabeth (Stripp) Squire. Ch. one. D. September 26, 1930, Delafield, Wisconsin.

William Lawrence Tomlins was a choirboy in London, England, and studied music with George A. Macfarren and Edward Silas. He was organist and choirmaster of a London church at the age of fifteen and a government inspector of music teachers at the age of eighteen. He was appointed examiner at the Tonic Sol-Fa College in London (1864).

Tomlins emigrated to the United States in 1870. He lived in Brooklyn, New York, and then moved to Chicago, Illinois, in 1875, where he demonstrated the orchestral organ for the Mason and Hamlin piano and organ manufacturer. In 1875 he became director of the Apollo Club male chorus, which became a mixed chorus in 1876. From 1883 he organized classes of schoolchildren for choral singing and began to instruct teachers of vocal music. In 1898 he resigned as conductor of the Apollo Club to devote full time to teaching. In 1903 he established the National Training School for Music Teachers in Chicago and became instructor of music teachers for the Chicago public schools in 1904. He spent two years in England teaching singing (1906–08).

Tomlins was the author of *Children's Songs and How to Sing Them* (1884) and was editor of *The Laurel Song Book* (1901).

REFERENCES: *DAB, NYT,* September 28, 1930, p. 26; *WWW* (IV); C. C. Birchard, "Tribute to William L. Tomlins," *Music Supervisor's Journal* 18 (May 1932): 14-15; *Music Supervisor's Journal* 17 (October 1930): 19; E. B. Birge *(q.v.),* "Recollections of W. L. Tomlins, Prophet," *Musician* 35 (December 1930): 23.                                                    *Thomas A. Barlow*

**TOMPKINS, Arnold.** B. September 10, 1849, near Paris, Illinois, to Henry and Delilah (Williams) Tompkins. M. December 23, 1875, to Jennie Snyder. Ch. none. D. August 12, 1905, Menlo, Georgia.

Arnold Tompkins grew up on his father's farm near Paris, Illinois, attending school during the winter and, when he was older, teaching in the local school when release from farm work was possible. He received his university education at Indiana University (1868), Butler University in Indianapolis, Indiana (1870), and Indiana State Normal School (later, Indiana State University) in Terre Haute, where he was graduated in 1880. He received the A.B. (1889) and M.A. (1891) degrees from Indiana University and studied on the graduate level at the University of Chicago and Ohio University in Athens, Ohio, where he received the Ph.D. degree (1897).

Tompkins began his teaching career near Paris, Illinois (1870), and became principal of a two-room school at Grand View, Illinois (1872). Upon graduation from Indiana State Normal School in 1880, he became school superintendent at Worthington, Indiana, and two years later was chosen superintendent in Franklin, Indiana. In 1885 he took charge of the English department at DePauw University (Indiana) and four years later became dean of the school. He was chosen chairman of the department of English in the Indiana State Normal School in 1890. He was professor of pedagogy at the University of Illinois from 1895 to 1899, when he became president of the Illinois State Normal University (later, Illinois State University). In 1900 he took over the presidency of the Chicago Normal School (later, Chicago State University), a position he held until his death in 1905.

As university president, Tompkins instituted reorganization in courses of study, insisting upon greater flexibility, different degrees of preparation, and freedom in the employment of methods. His theories and philosophy were embodied in his writings, which include *Science of Discourse* (1889), *Philosophy of Teaching* (1892), *Philosophy of School Management* (1895), and *Literary Interpretations or a Guide to the Teaching and Reading of Literature* (1896).

REFERENCES: *DAB; WWW* (I). *Lew E. Wise*

**TONNE, Herbert Arthur.** B. January 15, 1904, New York, New York, to F. Gustave and Anna Marie (Paulus) Tonne. M. December 22, 1928, to Henriette Kuhlmann. M. August 8, 1966, to Elizabeth Van De Veer. Ch. none.

Herbert A. Tonne attended New York City public schools and was graduated from Erasmus Hall High School. He spent two years working at the New York Stock Exchange before he followed the expectations of his parents and prepared to be a teacher. On the basis of study at City College of New York and New York University and home study courses from the University of Chicago, he enrolled at the University of Chicago and received the Ph.B. degree (1925) after a year of residence. He became interested in business education while studying with Paul S. Lomax *(q.v.)* and received the Ph.D. degree (1928) from New York University.

A teacher of social studies and commercial subjects at Elizabeth City, New Jersey, and New Rochelle, New York (1926–29), he joined the faculty of New York University in 1929, became department chairman in 1959, and remained there to his retirement in 1966. He then moved to the State University of New York at Albany to assist in developing a doctoral program in business education.

Tonne was the author of books on business education, including *Social-Business Education in the Secondary Schools* (with M. H. Tonne, 1932), *Business Education Basic Principles and Trends* (1939), *Consumer Education in the Schools* (1941), *Realistic Philosophy of Education* (1942), *Principles of Business Education* (1947), *Methods of Teaching Business Subjects* (with others, 1957) and *Principles of Business* (1969). He was the editor of *Research Bulletin of Commercial Education* (1930–32), *National Business Education Quarterly* (1932–36), *Journal of Business Education* (1938–51), and the *American Business Education Yearbook* (1955).

Active in professional associations, Tonne was president of the Gregg Teachers Association (1935), the Commercial Education Association (1937–38), the International Society of Business Education (American chapter, 1948–50), Delta Phi Epsilon (1954–55), and the National Business Education Association (1966–67). He was treasurer of the American Humanist Association. Tonne served as consultant to the Commercial Teacher Training College in Ankara, Turkey (1957). He was awarded the John Robert Gregg Award in Business Education in 1962.

REFERENCES: *LE* (III); *WW* (XXXVI); *WWAE* (XIV); "Herbert Tonne

Receives 1962 Gregg Award," *Balance Sheet* 44 (February 9, 1963): 268-69; "Dr. Tonne Honored," *Journal of Business Education* 41 (May 1966): 345.                                                                          *John F. Ohles*

**TOURJÉE, Eben.** B. June 1, 1834, Warwick, Rhode Island, to Ebenezer and Angelina (Ball) Tourjée. M. October 1855 to Abbie I. Tuell. M. October 1871 to Sarah Lee. Ch. four. D. April 12, 1891, Boston, Massachusetts.

Eben Tourjée (also spelled Tourgee) was employed in a calico mill at the age of eight and worked in a cotton mill in Harrisville, Rhode Island (1847–51). Governor Elisha Harris, owner of the mill, recognized Tourjée's musical talent and financed his attendance at the East Greenwich (Rhode Island) Academy where he received an academic education and private instruction in music. Tourjée studied music in Europe in 1863.

Tourjée clerked in a Providence, Rhode Island, music store in 1851 and was established as a music dealer and public school music teacher in Fall River, Massachusetts, in 1853. He opened a private music school in Fall River but moved to Newport, Rhode Island, where he engaged in private music instruction and playing the organ. He established a music school in 1859 connected with the East Greenwich Academy. He organized the Musical Institute of Providence (later, Providence Conservatory of Music) in 1864 and moved to Boston in 1867 where he and Robert Goldbeck *(q.v.)* established the New England Conservatory of Music in 1870.

Tourjée served as director of the New England Conservatory and also at Boston University as professor of sacred music (1868–72) and as organizer and dean of the college of music (1872–83). He moved the conservatory into an old hotel he purchased in 1882; for the rest of his life he struggled with serious financial problems.

Tourjée edited *Tribute of Praise* (1873) and *Chorus Choir* (1875) and was the author of *Plea for Music in the Public Schools* (n.d.) and *New England Conservatory Piano Method* (n.d.). He edited *Key-Note* (later, *Massachusetts Musical Journal*). He organized the chorus of the Peace Jubilee (1874) and conducted the choir of the Music Hall Society. He was the first president of the Music Teachers National Association (1876). He was awarded an honorary degree by Wesleyan University in 1866.

REFERENCES: *AC; DAB; NCAB* (7:324); *TC; WWW* (H).

*John F. Ohles*

**TOWN, Salem.** B. March 5, 1779, Belchertown, Massachusetts, to Israel, Jr., and Naomi (Stebbins) Town. M. March 26, 1807, to Abigail King. Ch. seven. D. February 24, 1864, Greencastle, Indiana.

Salem Town moved from Massachusetts to New York where he was principal of Granville (New York) Academy (1807–22). He moved to

Powelton, Georgia, in 1822, where he was principal of the Powelton Academy for a few years before he returned to Granville. He was reported to have enjoyed great success in Georgia where his students outnumbered the citizens of the town, and his academy attracted boarders who lived too far to commute to the school.

Town was principal of the Cayuga Academy in Aurora, New York, from 1829 to 1835, when he retired as principal because of ill health. He continued at the academy as a teacher of philology and lecturer on ancient and modern history and on the origin and progress of the arts and sciences. He retired from the academy in 1850.

Town wrote important schoolbooks, including *An Analysis of Derivative Words in the English Language* (1830), *Town's Spelling Book* (1839), *Town's Spelling and Defining Book* (1839), *The Grammar School Reader* (1850), and the *Town's Reader Series* (1844–55). The Progressive Reader Series was published in 1856 under the names of Salem Town and Nelson M. Holbrook; it seemed to be written primarily by Holbrook. *The Pronouncing Pictorial Primer* was published under Town's name in 1866, two years after his death. An active member of the Masonic order, he wrote *A System of Speculative Masonry* (1818).

Town was credited with serving as the chief instructor at the first teachers' institute in the United States held in Ithaca, New York, in April 1843. He served as a member of the New York State Senate.

REFERENCES: *AC:* Temple R. Hollcroft, *Brief History of Aurora, N.Y.,* rev. ed. (New York: Aurora Committee of the American Bicentennial, 1976); John A. Nietz, *Old Textbooks* (Pittsburgh: University of Pittsburgh Press, 1961); Dorothy Orr, *A History of Education in Georgia* (Chapel Hill: University of North Carolina Press, 1950). *John F. Ohles*

**TRABUE, Marion Rex.** B. April 30, 1890, Kokomo, Indiana, to Otto A. and Mary Emma (Long) Trabue. M. April 20, 1913, to Emma Wilkie Small. Ch. two. D. January 11, 1972, Annandale, Virginia.

Marion Rex Trabue was graduated from Northwestern University in Evanston, Illinois, with the A.B. degree (1911). He completed studies for the M.A. (1914) and Ph.D. (1915) degrees at Teachers College, Columbia University.

Trabue was principal of high schools at Fairbury (1911–12) and Hinsdale (1912–13), Illinois. He was a graduate assistant (1914–15), instructor (1915–17), and assistant professor of education (1917–22) and director of the bureau of educational services (1919–22) at Teachers College. In 1922 he became professor of education at the University of North Carolina in Chapel Hill where he remained to 1937. He served for nineteen years as dean of the college of education and director of summer sessions at Pennsylvania State University. In 1956 he retired to become Distinguished

Professor of Higher Education at the University of Kentucky (1956–72).

During World War I Trabue was a captain in the United States Army adjutant general's office. He pioneered with the war department as a psychological examiner and researcher directing the administration of Alpha and Beta tests to over one hundred thousand recruits. From 1934 to 1936 he was technical director of the Occupational Research program of the United States Employment Service, which produced the first *Dictionary of Occupational Titles* in 1949.

Trabue wrote *Completion-Test Language Scales* (1916), *Measure Your Mind* (with Francis P. Stockbridge, 1920), *Measuring Results in Education* (1924), *Trabue-Stevens Speller* (with B. A. Stevens, 1929), *Today's English* (with Bessie B. Goodrich, two volumes, 1935), *Spell to Write* (with B. A. Stevens, three volumes, 1941), and *Language Arts for Boys and Girls* (with Bessie B. Goodrich, 1941).

A member of professional organizations, Trabue was president of the American Educational Research Association (1925–26), the National Society of College Teachers of Education (1938–39), the National Conference on Research in English (1932–33), the National Association of Colleges and Departments of Education (1941–42 and 1946–47), the National Vocational Guidance Association (1944–46 and trustee, 1941–44), and the Council of Guidance and Personnel Associations (1945–46). He was a member of the federal council of the United States Employment Service (1934–39) and chairman of the emergency subcommittee on learning and training of the National Research Council (1941–43).

REFERENCES: *LE* (III); *NYT,* January 13, 1972, p. 44; *WWAE* (XIII); *WWW* (V).                                                      *Vernon Lee Sheeley*

**TRAVERS, Robert Morris William.** B. October 16, 1913, Bangalore, India, to Morris William and Dorothy (Gray) Travers. M. October 19, 1940, to Norma Colcaire. Ch. three.

Robert M. W. Travers's father was the first director of the Indian Institute of Science (1906–14). The Travers family left India in 1914 and returned to England where Travers attended the University of London (1932–35) and received the B.Sc. degree. He engaged in graduate study in England at Cambridge University (1935–36) and the University of London (1936–38) and in the United States at Teachers College, Columbia University (1938–41). He was a personal research assistant to Edward L. Thorndike *(q.v.)* at Teachers College and received the Ph.D. degree there in 1941. He became an American citizen in 1942.

Travers was an instructor at Ohio State University (1941–43) before joining the United States War Department in Washington, D.C., where he worked as a research psychologist (1943–45). Following World War II, Travers taught at the University of Michigan (1947–49) and for the Board of

Higher Education, New York City (1949–52). He served as the research administrator for the Air Force Personnel and Training Research Center in San Antonio, Texas (1952–58). He became chairman of the department of educational psychology at the University of Utah (1958–63) and was also the director of educational research (1963–65). He was appointed Distinguished University Professor at Western Michigan University at Kalamazoo in 1965.

During his tenure at Utah, Travers completed the works for which he became most well known: *An Introduction to Educational Research* (1958) and *Essentials of Learning* (1963). He also wrote *Man's Information System* (1970) and *Educational Psychology* (1973) and edited the *Second Handbook of Research on Teaching* (1973).

Travers was president of the educational psychology section of the American Psychological Association. He received the Department of the Army Civilian Meritorious Service citation (1945).

REFERENCES: *CA* (5–8); *LE* (V); *WW* (XXXIX); *American Men of Science*, 11th ed. (New York: R. R. Bowker, 1968).          *Kim Sebaly*

**TRAXLER, Arthur Edwin.** B. February 19, 1900, Irving, Kansas, to Edwin C. and Ora (Wells) Traxler. M. June 1, 1924, to Mabel Bobbi Yearout. Ch. one.

Arthur E. Traxler was graduated with the B.S. in Edn. degree (1920) from Kansas State Teachers College (later, Emporia Kansas State College) in Emporia and studied at the University of Chicago, from which he received the M.A. (1924) and Ph.D. (1932) degrees.

Traxler was superintendent of schools in Kansas at Holyrood (1918–19), Quincy (1920–22), Derby (1922–23), and Wakefield (1923–28). He was a psychologist at the University of Chicago high school (1931–36). He joined the Educational Records Bureau in New York City and served as executive director (1950–64) and president (1964–65). He was a part-time lecturer at the University of Miami in Coral Gables, Florida, from 1965.

A major contributor to literature in the fields of educational measurement, reading, and guidance, Traxler was the author of *The Measurement and Improvement of Silent Reading at the Junior High School Level* (1932), *The Use of Test Results in Diagnosis and Instruction in the Tool Subjects* (1936), *Read and Comprehend* (with P. E. Knight, 1937), *The Use of Test Results in Secondary Schools* (1938), *The Use of Tests and Rating Devices in the Appraisal of Personality* (1938), *The Nature and Use of Anecdotal Records* (1939), *The Nature and Use of Reading Tests* (1941), *Develop Your Reading* (with P. E. Knight, 1941), *Ten Years of Research in Reading* (1941), *Techniques of Guidance* (1945), *The Improvement of Reading* (with others, 1946), *How to Use Cumulative Records* (1947), *Introduction to Testing* (with others, 1952), *The Positive Value in Ameri-*

*can Education* (1959), and *Curriculum Planning to Meet Tomorrow's Needs* (1960). He was the editor of many reports for the Educational Records Bureau and the American Council on Education.

Traxler was active in professional associations as president of the American Educational Research Association (1950–51) and the National Council on Measurement in Education (1959–60) and vice-president of the American Association for the Advancement of Science (1956–57). He served on the Hartsdale, New York, board of education (1958–60) and was assistant director of college and professional testing programs of the American Institute of Accounting (1946–65).

REFERENCES: *CA* (21–22); *LE* (IV); *WW* (XXXVI); *WWAE* (XIII).

*John F. Ohles*

**TRENT, William Peterfield.** B. November 10, 1862, Richmond, Virginia, to Peterfield and Lucy Carter (Burwell) Trent. M. December 8, 1896, to Alice Lyman. Ch. two. D. December 6, 1939, Hopewell Junction, New York.

William Peterfield Trent was educated in private schools in Richmond, Virginia, and at Norwood's University School. He attended the University of Virginia, from which he received the B.Litt. (1883) and A.M. (1884) degrees. While at the university he edited the student magazine and wrote verse and literary criticism. From 1885 to 1887 Trent read law and taught in private schools in Richmond. He enrolled in Johns Hopkins University and engaged in graduate study in history with scholars, including Herbert Baxter Adams *(q.v.)* and Woodrow Wilson *(q.v.)*.

In 1888 Trent joined the faculty of the University of the South at Sewanee, Tennessee, where he founded and edited the *Sewanee Review* (1892–1900). He became influential in promoting the study of literary history as an integral part of history as a whole. Trent was a professor of English language and literature, acting professor of political economy and history, and, from 1894 to 1900, dean of the academic department. On the recommendation of Theodore Roosevelt, Brander Matthews, *q.v.,* and Nicholas Murray Butler, *q.v.,* Trent was appointed professor of English literature at Barnard College of Columbia University in 1900. He continued at Columbia to his retirement in 1929.

Trent was the author of *English Culture in Virginia* (1889), *Life of William Gilmore Simms* (1892), *Southern Statesmen of the Old Regime* (1897), *Robert E. Lee* (1899), *Verses* (1899), *John Milton, a Short Study of His Life and Works* (1899), *Authority of Criticism and Other Essays* (1899), *War and Civilization* (1901), *The Progress of the United States in the Century* (1901), *A History of American Literature, 1607-1865* (1903), *History of the United States for Schools* (with C. K. Adams, *q.v.,* 1903), *A Brief History of American Literature* (1904), *Greatness in Literature, and Other Papers* (1905), *Longfellow and Other Essays* (1910), *An Introduc-*

*tion to the English Classics* (with others, 1911), *Great American Writers* (with John Erskine, *q.v.,* 1912), *Defoe–How to Know Him* (1916), and *Verse Jottings* (1924). He edited *The Cambridge History of American Literature* (four volumes, with others, 1917–21). In 1910 he suggested that the Columbia University Press publish the first complete edition of Milton's works. He served as editor-in-chief until ill health forced him to resign in 1925. The eighteen-volume *Complete Writings of John Milton* was completed in 1938 by a group of Trent's former colleagues and students.

Trent received honorary degrees from Wake Forest University (1899) and the University of the South (1905).

REFERENCES *DAB* (supp. 2); *LE* (I); *NYT,* December 8, 1939, p. 25; *TC; WWW* (I); *American Historical Review* 45 (April 1940): 754-55; *School and Society* 50 (December 16, 1939): 795.                   *Carol O'Meara*

**TROWBRIDGE, John.** B. August 5, 1843, Boston, Massachusetts, to John Howe and Adeline (Richardson) Whitney Trowbridge. M. June 20, 1877, to Mary Louise (Thayer) Gray. Ch. none. D. February 18, 1923, Cambridge, Massachusetts.

John Trowbridge attended Boston Latin School and, on his eighteenth birthday, was admitted to the Lawrence Scientific School of Harvard University. Graduating summa cum laude with the B.S. degree (1865), his first teaching assignment was as a tutor in physics at Harvard (1866–69). In 1869 he became an assistant professor in physics at the Massachusetts Institute of Technology, but he returned to Harvard the next year.

Trowbridge has been credited with the design and implementation of laboratory techniques in science education. In 1870 he established a laboratory course of instruction and student research in physics at Harvard. Aware of the role of research in the advance of physics and dissatisfied with its status, Trowbridge proposed the establishment of a facility and staff dedicated to laboratory research. In 1884 the Jefferson Laboratory was built at Harvard for which Trowbridge solicited funds, provided the design, and supervised construction. In 1888 he assumed the directorship of the laboratory and was appointed Rumford Professor of Applied Science, a chair he held until his retirement in 1910.

Trowbridge conducted research with electrical phenomena and spectrum analysis. He investigated electrical conduction through gases, high-velocity propogation of electrical waves, and high-frequency electrical oscillations. In 1887 he instituted experiments that proved the presence of carbon and platinum in the sun. His major books include *The New Physics* (1884), *The Electrical Boy* (1891), *What Is Electricity?* (1896), and *Philip's Experiments in Electrical Science* (1898). The original scientific work conducted under his direction was compiled in *Contributions from the Physics Laboratory of Harvard College* (c. 1877). He wrote over fifty scientific papers. He was one of the editors of the *Annals of Scientific Discovery* (1869) and associate editor of the *American Journal of Science* (1880–1920).

Trowbridge was a member of professional associations and was a delegate to the International Congress of Electricians in Paris, France (1883), and the United States Congress of Electricians in Philadelphia (1884). He was a fellow of the American Academy of Arts and Sciences and served as secretary (1879–1884) and president (1884) of the physical sciences section of the American Association for the Advancement of Science. He received an honorary degree from Harvard University (1873).

REFERENCES:*AC; DAB; DSB; NCAB* (23:53);*NYT,* February 20, 1923, p. 17; *TC; WWW* (I); Allen G. Bebus, ed., *World Who's Who in Science* (Hannibal, Mo.: Western Publishing Co., 1968), p. 1689; Theodore Lyman, Theodore W. Richards, and George W. Pierce, "The Life and Services of Professor John Trowbridge," *Science* 57 (June 1, 1923): 631-32.

*Nicholas Celso III*

**TRUE, Alfred Charles.** B. June 5, 1853, Middletown, Connecticut, to Charles Kiddredge and Elizabeth Bassett (Hyde) True. M. November 23, 1875, to Emma Fortune. Ch. two. D. April 23, 1929, Washington, D.C.

Alfred Charles True was educated at Boston Latin School and was graduated from Wesleyan University in Middletown, Connecticut, where his father was a professor. He received the A.B. (1873) and A.M. (1876) degrees from Wesleyan, studied at Harvard University (1882–84), and received the Ph.D. degree (1886) from Erskine College in Due West, South Carolina.

True was principal of a high school in Essex, New York (1873–74), and was an instructor at the State Normal School (later, Westfield State College) at Westfield, Massachusetts (1875–82). He taught Latin and Greek at Wesleyan University (1884–88) where he became acquainted with Wilbur O. Atwater *(q.v.),* who founded the office of experiment stations in the United States Office of Agriculture. True followed Atwater to Washington, working as editor (1888–93) and director (1893–1915) of the office of experiment stations. First concerned with the dissemination of information about agricultural problems, he later assumed leadership in research on human nutrition and home economics education. He also promoted farmers' institutes as educational techniques.

In 1915 True became director of the States Relation Service, serving to 1923, when he became counselor to the secretary of agriculture for states' relations and engaged in writing monographs, including *A History of Agricultural Extension Work and Research in the United States, 1785–1923* (1928) and *A History of Agricultural Education in the United States, 1785–1923* (1929).

True was agricultural editor of the *New International Encyclopedia and Year-book,* a fellow of the American Association for the Advancement of Science, and a member of other organizations, including the Association of American Agricultural Colleges and Experiment Stations (president, 1914). He was a member of the advisory committee of the American Farm Bureau Federation. He was dean of seven national graduate school of agriculture meetings between 1902 and 1916. He received an honorary degree from Wesleyan University in 1906.

REFERENCES: *DAB; WWW* (I); C. H. Lane, "Our Leadership in Agricultural Education: Dr. A. C. True of the U.S.D.A.," *Agricultural Education* 1 (October 1929), 10; "Debt of Home Economics to Dr. True," *Journal of Home Economics* 21 (July 1929), 508-09; *Washington* (D.C.) *Daily News,* April 24, 1929.                                                         *John F. Ohles*

**TRUEBLOOD, Thomas Clarkson.** B. April 6, 1856, Salem, Indiana, to Jehu and Louise (Pritchard) Trueblood. M. September 1, 1881, to Carolyn Hobbs. Ch. two. D. June 4, 1951, Bradenton, Florida.

Thomas C. Trueblood was graduated with the A.M. degree (1886) from Earlham College in Richmond, Indiana, and studied elocution and oratory with James E. Murdock, S. S. Hamill, and Charles John Plumptre.

Trueblood and Robert I. Fulton founded a school of oratory in Kansas City, Missouri, in 1879. From 1884 to 1889 he lectured at the University of Missouri, Ohio Wesleyan University at Delaware, Ohio, the University of Kentucky, and the University of Michigan. He joined the faculty of the University of Michigan as professor of public speaking in 1889 and became chairman of the department; he retired as professor emeritus in 1926. He taught the first college credit course in public speaking and organized the department of speech at Michigan. Among his students were two future United States senators, Edgar E. Borah and Arthur H. Vandenberg. He was the first golf coach and continued for thirty-five years at the University of Michigan. He was credited with devising the locomotive cheer. He lectured at colleges and universities in California, Hawaii, and Japan (1910) and Australia and New Zealand (1917–18).

Trueblood was the author of *Choice Readings* (1884), *Practical Elocution* (with R. I. Fulton, 1893), *Patriotic Eloquence* (1900), *Standard Selections* (1907), *Essentials of Public Speaking* (1909), and *Standard British and American Eloquence* (1912). He edited *Honor Orations of the University of Michigan* (1898) and *Winning Speeches in the Northern Oratorical League* (1909).

Active in professional organizations, Trueblood was president of the National Speech Arts Association for two years. He organized the Northern Oratorical League (1890), the Central Debating League (1898), and the Midwest Debating League (1914) and presided at the organizing of Delta Sigma Rho Society for honors debaters and orators (1906). He was honorary president of both the National Association of Teachers of Speech and the Northern Oratorical League (1941–42). He received an honorary degree from Earlham College in 1921.

REFERENCES: *LE* (I); *NCAB* (42:138); *NYT,* June 5, 1951, p. 31; *WWW* (III); *School and Society* 73 (June 16, 1951): 383.                    *Dee Wyckoff*

**TUCKER, George.** B. August 20, 1775, St. George's Island, Bermuda, to Daniel and Elizabeth (Tucker) Tucker. M. October 1797 to Mary (Byrd) Farley. M. February 1802 to Maria Ball Carter. M. December 1828 to Louisa (Bowdoin) Thompson. Ch. five. D. April 10, 1861, Sherwood, Virginia.

George Tucker was descended from a prominent English family that had lived in Bermuda for over one hundred and fifty years. In 1795 at the age of twenty, Tucker decided to go to America to establish his career. Sponsored by St. George Tucker, a relative and wealthy landholder from Williamsburg, Virginia, he was welcomed by the Virginia Tidewater artistocracy. He enrolled in the College of William and Mary to prepare for reading the bar examination and received the A.B. degree (1797).

Tucker established a law practice in Richmond, Virginia, in 1800 and later practiced in Pittsylvania County and Lynchburg. He served in the Virginia legislature and for three terms in the United States House of Representatives (1819–25). Because of his friendship with Thomas Jefferson *(q.v.)* and James Madison, Tucker was invited to join the newly established University of Virginia as professor of ethics. As the oldest faculty member, he was made the first chairman of the faculty in 1825 and continued at the university until 1845.

George Tucker was a distinguished man of letters. He wrote about finance, economy, biography, and history and was the author of satire and novels. He advocated the economic ideas of Adam Smith and the population theory of Thomas Malthus. A strong nationalist, he believed that society progressed through increased industry and commerce. Originally opposed to slavery on principle, he later justified it on grounds of expediency.

Tucker's most important books on political economy were *The Laws of Wages, Profit and Rent Investigated* (1827), *The Theory of Money and Banks Investigated* (1839), and *Political Economy for the People* (1859). From his conversations with Jefferson, he wrote a two-volume biography, *Life of Thomas Jefferson* (1837). He also wrote *Essay on Cause and Effect* (1842), *Essay on the Association of Ideas* (1843), and *Essays, Moral and Philosophical* (1860). His major novels were *The Valley of the Shenandoah* (1824) and a satirical romance, *A Voyage to the Moon* (1827). He wrote the four-volume *History of the United States* (1856–58).

On his retirement from the university, Tucker moved to Philadelphia where he continued to write.

REFERENCES: *AC; DAB; NCAB* (7:521); *TC; WWW* (H); Robert Colin McLean, *George Tucker: Moral Philosopher and Man of Letters* (Chapel Hill: University of North Carolina Press, 1961).     *Harold D. Lehman*

**TUCKER, William Jewett.** B. July 13, 1839, Griswold, Connecticut, to Henry and Sarah White (Lester) Tucker. M. June 22, 1870, to Charlotte Henry Rogers. M. June 23, 1887, to Charlotte Barrell Cheever. Ch. three. D. September 29, 1926, Hanover, New Hampshire.

William Jewett Tucker received his education in the Plymouth, New Hampshire, schools and Kimball Academy at Meriden, New Hampshire. He received the A.B. degree (1861) from Dartmouth College in Hanover, New Hampshire, and entered Andover (Massachusetts) Theological Seminary in 1863. He served with the United States Christian Commission with the Union army during the Civil War and was graduated from Andover in 1866.

Tucker was a schoolteacher in Columbus, Ohio, from 1861 to 1863. Ordained to the ministry in 1867, he served churches in Fort Scott, Kansas (1866), Manchester, New Hampshire (1867–75), and New York City, where he preached in the Madison Square Church (1875–79). He was Bartlett Professor of Sacred Rhetoric at Andover Theological Seminary (1880–93). At Andover he pioneered in developing courses in sociology for divinity students, founded the Andover House settlement house, and was a founder of the *Andover Review*.

In 1893 Tucker became president of Dartmouth College. During his administration twenty new buildings were constructed, the college's financial condition was improved to the point where it was free of debt, the student body tripled in size, and the Tuck School of Business Administration was established. He retired from Dartmouth in 1909.

Tucker was the author of *The Making and Unmaking of the Preacher* (1898), *Personal Power* (1910), *Public Mindedness* (1910), *The Function of the Church in Modern Society* (1911), *The New Reservation of Time* (1916), and an autobiography, *My Generation* (1919). He was an editor of the *Andover Review* (1885–93).

Tucker was a trustee of Dartmouth College (1878–93), a fellow of the American Academy of Arts and Sciences, and a member of other organizations. He received six honorary degrees.

REFERENCES: *AC; DAB; NCAB* (24:242); *NYT*, September 30, 1926, p. 25; *TC; WWW* (I); William Jewett Tucker, *My Generation* (Boston: Houghton Mifflin Co., 1919).     *M. Jane Dowd*

**TURNER, Jonathan Baldwin.** B. December 7, 1805, Templeton, Massachusetts, to Asa and Abigail (Baldwin) Turner. M. October 22, 1835, to Rhodolphia S. Kibbe. Ch. seven. D. January 10, 1899, Jacksonville, Illinois.

Jonathan Baldwin Turner, an 1833 graduate of Yale College, joined the faculty of Illinois College at Jacksonville, Illinois, in 1833 as a teacher of rhetoric and belles lettres. He resigned in 1847 because of a disagreement with college officials over slavery and denominational questions. He became a leader in the movement for public schools in Illinois. The free school law of 1855 resulted largely from his efforts, and he was influential in the establishment in 1857 of Illinois State Normal University (later, Illinois State University), the first normal school in Illinois.

In 1850 Turner proposed the foundation of a state university for agricultural and general industrial classes. His suggestion attracted nationwide attention, and Congressman Justin Morrill of Vermont presented a bill to Congress in 1857 that reflected Turner's ideas. The bill was vetoed by President James Buchanan, but a similar bill, the Land Grant Act, was enacted in 1862. Turner was instrumental in the establishment in 1868 of the Illinois Industrial University (later, University of Illinois). He advocated an American system of education that would provide higher education for working-class children.

Turner engaged in agricultural experiments and promoted the Osage orange for farm hedges in an area where there was not enough timber to build fences. He invented and patented a cultivator, drill, and planter to plant Osage orange seeds and a corn planter and wheat drill.

Turner was the author of *Mormonism in All Ages* (1842), *The Three Great Races of Men* (1861), *Universal Law and Its Opposites* (1892), and *The Christ Word Versus the Church Word* (1895). He was editor of *Statesman*, an anti-slavery publication. He was an organizer of the Illinois State Teachers' Association in 1854 and was the first president of the Illinois State Historical Society in 1858.

REFERENCES: *DAB; WWW* (H); Mary Turner Carriel, *The Life of Jonathan Baldwin Turner* (Urbana: University of Illinois Press, 1961); Helen E. Marshall, *Grandest of Enterprises* (Normal: Illinois State Normal University, 1956).                                    *Claude A. Bell*

**TUTWILER, Henry.** B. November 16, 1807, Harrisonburg, Virginia, to Henry and Margaret (Lorchbaugh) Tutwiler. M. December 24, 1835, to Julia Ashe. Ch. eleven, including Julia Strudwick Tutwiler *(q.v.),* educator. D. September 22, 1884, Greene Springs, Alabama.

Henry Tutwiler was largely self-educated and entered the University of Virginia when it was opened in 1825. He was graduated in 1829 and studied law (1829–30). He joined the faculty of the University of Alabama as professor of ancient languages from its establishment in 1831 to 1837. In 1837 the faculty of the University of Alabama resigned en masse, and Tutwiler moved to the Industrial College at Marion, Alabama (1837–39). He taught in other Alabama colleges to 1847 when he opened and served as principal of the Greene Springs School for Boys near Havana, Alabama.

TUTWILER, Julia Strudwick [1315]

Called the Rugby of the South, the Greene Springs School enjoyed a wide reputation for a highly qualified faculty, an excellent academic program, which included an emphasis on science, and the treatment accorded to the individual student. Declining offers to the presidency of universities, Tutwiler continued to conduct the school to his death in 1884. He was a frequent contributor to periodicals.

REFERENCES: *AC; DAB; WWW* (H).                    *Dennis G. Wiseman*

**TUTWILER, Julia Strudwick.** B. August 15, 1841, Tuscaloosa, Alabama, to Henry *(q.v.)* and Julia (Ashe) Tutwiler. M. no. D. March 24, 1916, Birmingham, Alabama.

Julia Strudwick Tutwiler, daughter of an eminent Alabama educator, was sent to Philadelphia, Pennsylvania, to attend Madame Maroteau's boarding school for two years. When the Civil War started, Tutwiler returned to Alabama where she taught at her father's Greene Springs School. She attended Vassar College in Poughkeepsie, New York, for a semester in 1866. She traveled to Europe and studied at the Institute of Deaconesses in Kaiserswerth, Germany (1873–74). She became acquainted with vocational training for women prison inmates, teacher-training programs, and industrial and vocational education for women. She returned to Alabama and taught at Tuscaloosa Female College (1874–79).

Tutwiler was appointed coprincipal of Livingston (Alabama) Female Academy. She was instrumental in obtaining funds from the legislature to establish a normal school at the academy and served as president of the Alabama Normal College (later, Livingston State University). In 1879 Tutwiler became aware of conditions in the local jail and surveyed the prisons of Alabama. She successfully campaigned to abolish the convict-lease system and establish the South's first prison school in 1887. Women were admitted to the University of Alabama as a result of her efforts.

The author of song lyrics, Tutwiler wrote the state song "Alabama," "Dixie Now," "The Southern Yankee Doodle," and "Duty," a song used for the Robert E. Lee centennial. Active in professional associations, she was president of the department of elementary education of the National Educational Association (1891) and headed the prison and jail activities in Alabama for the Women's Christian Temperance Union. A building at the University of Alabama and the Julia Tutwiler Prison for Women were named in her honor. She was one of the first to be named to the Alabama Hall of Fame. The University of Alabama awarded her an honorary degree. She left her estate as a scholarship loan fund for the girls of Alabama.

REFERENCES: *DAB; NAW; NCAB* (15:101); *WC; WWW* (I); Helen Christine Bennett, *American Women in Civic Work* (New York: Dodd, Mead & Co., 1915); Anne Gary Pannell and Dorthea E. Wyatt, *Julia S. Tutwiler and Social Progress in Alabama* (Birmingham: University of Alabama Press, 1961).                    *Linda C. Gardner*

**TYLER, Moses Coit.** B. August 2, 1835, Griswold, Connecticut, to Elisha and Mary (Greene) Tyler. M. October 26, 1859, to Jeannette Hull Gilbert. Ch. two. D. December 28, 1900, Ithaca, New York.

Moses Coit Tyler attended public schools in Detroit, Michigan. He was a student at the University of Michigan but left to enter Yale College from which he received the A.B. (1857) and A.M. (1863) degrees. He studied theology at Yale (1857–58) and at Andover (Massachusetts) Theological Seminary (1858–59) and was ordained in 1859 as a Congregational minister. He was later ordained a deacon (1881) and priest (1883) in the Protestant Episcopal church.

Tyler served churches at Oswego (1859–60) and Poughkeepsie (1860–62), New York. He went to England in April 1863 where he lectured and wrote for American publications. He returned to the United States in December 1866 and was appointed professor of rhetoric and English literature at the University of Michigan in 1867. He did much to modernize instruction in literature and developed an interest in the interpretation of American colonial history. Tyler resigned from Michigan in 1873 and became literary editor of Henry Ward Beecher's *Christian Union* in New York, but returned to the University of Michigan in 1874. In 1881 he became the first professor of American history in the country at Cornell University in Ithaca, New York.

Tyler wrote numerous essays, reviews, and articles. He wrote a number of books, including *The Braunville Papers* (1869), *A History of American Literature During the Colonial Time, 1607-1765* (two volumes, 1878), *Manual of English Literature* (1879), *Life of Patrick Henry* (1887), *Three Men of Letters* (1895), *The Literary History of the American Revolution, 1763-1783* (two volumes, 1897), and *Glimpses of England* (1898).

A founder of the American Historical Association (1884), Tyler gained recognition as an authority on American colonial literature of the country and was recognized as a leader of critical rather than patriotic history. He received honorary degrees from Wooster (1875) and Columbia (1888) universities.

REFERENCES: *AC; DAB; EB; NCAB* (4:483); *NYT,* December 29, 1900, p. 7; *TC; WWW* (I); Howard Mumford Jones, *The Life of Moses Coit Tyler* (Ann Arbor: University of Michigan Press, 1933).     *Norman J. Bauer.*

**TYLER, Ralph Winfred.** B. April 22, 1902, Chicago, Illinois, to William Augustus and Ella Clara (Kimball) Tyler. M. August 31, 1921, to Flora Olivia Volz. M. August 1, 1947, to Louise M. Lingenfelder. M. August 28, 1955, to Mary Catherine McCord. Ch. three.

Ralph W. Tyler received the A.B. degree (1921) from Doane College in Crete, Nebraska, the A.M. degree (1923) from the University of Nebraska, and the Ph.D. degree (1927) from the University of Chicago.

In 1921 Tyler was a high school teacher in Pierre, South Dakota. He was an assistant supervisor of sciences at the University of Nebraska (1922–27), associate professor of education at the University of North Carolina (1927–29), associate professor of education (1929–31) and professor of education and research associate in the Bureau of Educational Research at the Ohio State University (1931–38). He went to the University of Chicago as chairman of the department of education (1938–48) and dean of social sciences (1948–53). He also served as university examiner at the University of Chicago (1938–53). In 1953 he became director of the Center for Advanced Study in Behavioral Sciences at Stanford, California, and retired in 1966.

Tyler edited *Service Studies in Higher Education* (1933), *Educational Evaluation* (1969), *Accountability in Education* (with Leon M. Lessinger, 1971), and *Crucial Issues in Testing* (with Richard M. Wolf, 1974) and wrote *Constructing Achievement Tests* (1934), *Appraising and Recording Student Progress* (1942), *Cooperation in General Education* (1945), *Basic Principles of Curriculum and Instruction* (1949), *What People Want to Read About* (with Douglas Waples, 1931), *Perspectives of Curriculum Evaluation* (with Robert M. Gagné and Michael Scriven, 1967), and *The Challenge of National Assessment* (1968).

From 1934 to 1942 Tyler served as director of evaluation for the Eight-Year Study of the Committee on the Relation of School and College of the Progressive Education Association. He served on many governmental, educational, and research agencies; he was director of the examinations staff of the United States Armed Forces Institute (1943–46), research adviser to the United States Office of Education, member of the board of directors of the National Society for Study of Education, and chairman of the Committee on Cooperative Education. He was a fellow of the American Association for the Advancement of Science (chairman of section Q, 1937). He received many honorary degrees.

REFERENCES: *LE* (III); *WW* (XXXII); *WWAE* (XVIII); D. W. Robinson, "Talk with Ralph Tyler," *Phi Delta Kappan* 49 (October 1967): 75-77.

*Paul L. Ward*

**TYLER, William Seymour.** B. September 2, 1810, Harford, Pennsylvania, to Joab and Nabby (Seymour) Tyler. M. September 4, 1839, to Amelia Ogden Whiting. Ch. four. D. November 19, 1897, Amherst, Massachusetts.

William Seymour Tyler was graduated from Amherst (Massachusetts) College in 1830 and studied theology at Andover (Massachusetts) Theological Seminary and with the Reverend Thomas H. Skinner of New York. He was licensed to preach in 1836 and was ordained a Congregational minister in 1859.

Tyler was appointed professor of Latin and Greek at Amherst College, remaining an active instructor of classics there until 1892. Throughout his teaching career he preached in several area churches. He played a major role in founding Williston Seminary in Easthampton, Massachusetts.

Tyler was the author of *Germania and Agricola of Tacitus* (1847), *Histories of Tacitus* (1848), *Prayer for Colleges* (1854), *Plato's Apology and Crito* (1859), *Memoir of Dr. Henry Lobdell* (1859), *Theology of the Greek Poets* (1867), *Plutarch on the Delay of the Diety* (with H. B. Hackett, 1867), *History of Amherst College* (1873), and *Demosthenes's Phillippics and Olynthiacs* (1875). Tyler's autobiography was published posthumously in 1912.

He served on the board of trustees of Williston Academy (president), Mount Holyoke Seminary, and Smith College. He received two honorary degrees from Harvard University and one from Amherst College.

REFERENCES: *AC; DAB; NCAB* (10:347), *NYT,* November 20, 1897, p. 7; *WWW* (H).                                    *Joseph M. McCarthy*

# U

**ULICH, Robert.** B. April 20, 1890, Lam bei Riedermühl, Bavaria, Germany, to Robert and Helene (Schaarschmidt) Ulich. M. November 16, 1929, to Elsa Braedstroem. M. December 30, 1948, to Mary Ewen. Ch. two. D. June 17, 1977, Stuttgart, Germany.

Robert Ulich attended the Humanistisches Gymnasium (1900–09) where he received a thorough preparation in Latin and Greek. After studying in Germany at the universities of Bremen, Munich, and Berlin, and at Neuchâtel, Switzerland, he received the Ph.D. degree (1915) from the University of Leipzig, Germany.

Ulich was a research and teaching assistant in the history of culture at the University of Leipzig and teacher of German literature at the Thomas Gymnasium in Leipzig. In 1918 he became a librarian at the University of Leipzig. He moved to the Ministry of Education of Saxony in 1921 where he served as assistant counselor in charge of the division of adult education (1921–23) and was counselor in charge of Saxon University (1923–33). He was also honorary professor of philosophy at the Dresden Institute of Technology (1928–33).

When Adolf Hitler and the National Socialist party came to power in 1933 Ulich, who opposed Nazi policy, left Germany. Arriving in the United States in 1934 he joined the faculty of Harvard University as a lecturer in comparative education. In 1936 he became professor of the history and philosophy of education and was appointed the first James Bryant Conant Professor of Education in 1954. He retired in 1960 but continued his research and writing. He moved to Germany in 1970.

Through his teaching and numerous publications, Ulich provided leadership in the fields of history of education, philosophy of education, and comparative education. He was the author of *Sequence of Educational Influences* (1935), *Fundamentals of Democratic Education* (1940), *History of Educational Thought* (1945), *Conditions of Civilized Living* (1946), *Three Thousand Years of Educational Wisdom* (1947), *Crisis and Hope in American Education* (1951), *The Human Career* (1955), *Professional Education as a Humane Study* (1956), *Philosophy of Education* (1961), and *The Education of Nations: A Comparison in Historical Perspective* (1961). He was a member of professional associations and received honorary degrees from Harvard, Clark and Korea universities.

REFERENCES: *LE* (III); *NYT*, June 18, 1977, p. 22; *WW* (XXVI); *WWAE* (XV); Robert J. Havighurst *(q.v.),* ed., *Leaders in American Education* (Chicago: University of Chicago Press, 1971); "Award to Professor Robert Ulich," *School and Society* 85 (November 9, 1957):341.

*William W. Brickman*

# V

**VAILE, Edwin Orlando.** B. November 21, 1843, Piqua, Ohio, to Jonathan and Elizabeth (Esterbrook) Vaile. M. July 14, 1870, to Emma Brainard. Ch. four. D. August 3, 1922, Oak Park, Illinois.

Edwin Orlando Vaile received his education in local public schools. At the age of seventeen, he became a teacher at Carlisle, Ohio. He served as a volunteer in the 131st Ohio Volunteer Infantry during the Civil War. Vaile returned to the classroom after the war and was appointed a school principal in Columbus, Ohio (1870). He later served as a principal in Cincinnati, Ohio, and Chicago, Illinois.

He was the author of two books that are considered landmarks in the history of education, *Pro and Con of Spelling Programs* (1877) and *Our Accursed Spelling* (1902). He founded (1880) and was editor of *Intelligence,* a weekly journal for teachers and a current-events periodical for primary grade children. He was credited with devising a phonetic alphabet and at the time of his death was engaged in compiling a series of reading books using this alphabet.

A pioneer in the spelling reform movement, Vaile was credited with theories and proposals that proved useful to modern linguists.

REFERENCES: *NCAB* (20:10); *Oak Park* [Ill.] *Reporter*, June 15, 1889, p. 4; *Oak Leaves* (Oak Park, Ill.), August 5, 1922, p. 12, and March 14, 1946, p. 116.

*LeRoy Barney*

**VALENTINE, Milton.** B. January 1, 1825, Uniontown, Maryland, to Jacob and Rebecca (Picking) Valentine. M. December 18, 1855, to Margaret G. Galt. Ch. four. D. February 7, 1906, Gettysburg, Pennsylvania.

Milton Valentine was raised on the family farm in Maryland and prepared for college by attending Taneytown (Maryland) Academy. He enrolled at Pennsylvania (later, Gettysburg) College in Gettysburg, Pennsylvania, at the age of twenty-one and was graduated with honors in 1850. Valentine then entered the Lutheran Theological Seminary in Gettysburg, and was ordained in 1852.

Although he was trained as a minister and his first professional experiences were in that capacity, he gained fame as an educator. Valentine served as principal of Emmaus (Middletown, Pennsylvania) Institute for four years and was professor of biblical and ecclesiastical history at the Lutheran Theological Seminary (1866–68), president of Gettysburg College (1868–84), and professor of theology and chairman of the faculty at the seminary (1884–1903). He gained a reputation as the leading Lutheran educator in America.

Valentine was a frequent contributor to church periodicals and served several terms as joint editor of the *Lutheran Quarterly*. His published works include *Natural Theology* (1885), *Theoretical Ethics* (1897), *Christian Truth and Life* (1898), and *Christian Theology* (1900).

Valentine was awarded honorary degrees by Gettysburg and Wittenberg colleges. Increasing age and impaired hearing led to Valentine's retirement in 1903.

REFERENCES: *AC; DAB; NCAB* (10:389); *TC; WWW* (I); Samuel G. Hefelbower, *The History of Gettysburg College*, (Gettysburg, Pa.: Gettysburg College, 1932); Abdel R. Wentz, *History of the Gettysburg Theological Seminary* (Philadelphia: United Lutheran Publication House, 1927).

*Samuel A. Farmerie*

**VALENTINE, Thomas Weston.** B. February 16, 1818, Northboro, Massachusetts, to Gill and Sabra (Wood) Valentine. M. to Harriet Dryden. Ch. five. D. April 4, 1879, Brooklyn, New York.

Thomas Weston Valentine was educated in the schools of Northboro, Massachusetts, and at Worcester (Massachusetts) Academy. Valentine began to teach at the age of eighteen in Lancaster, Massachusetts (1836), and in Northboro (1837–40), and he also spent one year teaching in Pennsylvania. He returned to teach for a year in Ashland, Massachusetts, and moved in 1842 to Albany, New York, where he spent eleven years as a public school principal (1842–53). Valentine served as superintendent of the Albany Orphan Asylum (1853–54) and moved to Brooklyn, New York, in 1855 where he was principal of Public School 19 until his death.

While in Albany, Valentine served as a city alderman (1852–54). He was active in teachers' organizations, calling and presiding over the first teachers' convention in Worcester (Massachusetts) County in 1838. At a meeting of the Albany County Teachers Association on March 29, 1845, Valentine initiated the organization of the New York State Teachers Association, the first permanent state teachers' organization in the United States. He served for two years as editor of the *New York Teacher*.

While president of the state association in 1857, Valentine and Daniel B. Hagar *(q.v.),* president of the Massachusetts Teachers Association, issued a call to educators and teachers' associations across the country to meet in Philadelphia on August 26, 1857, to organize the National Teachers' Association (later, National Education Association).

Valentine was active in the Baptist church and served as a lay preacher. He reported his activities in 1871 as consisting of operating a day school of seventeen hundred pupils, a five-day per week evening school, a Saturday evening singing class, and delivering three sermons a week.

REFERENCES: Thomas F. Finegan, *q.v., Free Schools* (Albany: University of the State of New York, 1921); D. Emma Wilber Hodge and Lamont Foster Hodge, *A Century of Service to Public Education: The Centennial History of the New York State Teachers Association* (Albany: The Association, 1945); Hyland C. Kirk, *A History of the New York State Teachers Association* (New York: E. L. Kellogg, 1883).

*John F. Ohles*


**VAN BOKKELEN, Libertus.** B. July 22, 1815, New York, New York, to Adrian H. and Deborah (Morris) Van Bokkelen. M. 1850 to Amelia D'Arcy. Ch. six. D. November 17, 1889, Buffalo, New York.

Libertus Van Bokkelen was educated in private schools. He established St. Paul's School at College Point, Long Island, New York, in 1836. In 1842 he entered the Protestant Episcopal priesthood.

Van Bokkelen established St. Timothy's Hall in Catonsville, Maryland, the first church-related military school in the country. He also was rector at St. Timothy's Church in Catonsville, Grace Church at Elk Ridge, and St. Peter's Church in Ellicott City. He was a school commissioner for Baltimore County, Maryland (1859–65), and was appointed Maryland state superintendent of public instruction in 1865. He was the first appointee in the post created under the state constitution adopted in 1864. In 1867 reaction to the new constitution led to another constitutional convention that abolished the office of state superintendent but maintained the free public system that had been established by Van Bokkelen. On the expiration of his term in 1867 Van Bokkelen moved to Mount Morris, New York, and to Buffalo, New York, where he was rector of Trinity Church.

Van Bokkelen was active in the National Teacher's Association (later, National Education Association), serving as director (1866), secretary (1868), and president (1869).

REFERENCES: *NCAB* (3:213); *NYT,* November 2, 1889, p. 5; Jim B. Pearsen and Edgar Fuller, *Education in the States: Historical Development and Outlook* (Washington, D.C.: National Education Association, 1969). *John F. Ohles*

**VAN DOREN, Mark.** B. June 13, 1894, Hope, Illinois, to Charles Lucius and Dora Anna (Butz) Van Doren. M. September 1, 1922, to Dorothy Graffe. Ch. two. D. December 10, 1972, Cornwall Hollow, Connecticut.

Mark Van Doren attended public schools in Urbana, Illinois, and was graduated from the University of Illinois with the A.B. (1914) and A.M. (1915) degrees. In 1915 he attended Columbia University, where his brother Carl was teaching, and received the Ph.D. degree in 1920, after serving in the United States Army during World War I.

Van Doren joined the Columbia University faculty in 1920 and continued as a teacher of English to 1959. He also lectured at St. John's College in Annapolis, Maryland (1937–57), and at the New School for Social Research and People's Institute in New York City. He was a participant in the radio program "Invitation to Learning" over the Columbia Broadcasting System (1940–42).

Van Doren was the author of many books of poetry, drama, and fiction. His nonfiction works include *Henry David Thoreau* (1916), *John Dryden* (1920), *American and British Literature Since 1890* (with Carl Van Doren, 1925), *Edwin Arlington Robinson* (1927), *Shakespeare* (1939), *Studies in Metaphysical Poetry* (with Theodore Spencer, 1939), *The New Invitation to Learning* (with others, 1942), *The Private Reader* (1942), *Liberal Education* (1943), *The Noble Voice* (1946), *Nathaniel Hawthorne* (1949), *Introduction to Poetry* (1951), *Man's Right to Knowledge and the Free Use Thereof* (1954), *Don Quixote's Profession* (1958), *The Happy Critic* (1961), *And Somebody Came* (1966), and *Commentaries in Thirty Days* (1968). He was literary editor of *The Nation* (1924–28) and edited many anthologies.

A member of the National Institute of Arts and Letters and the American Academy of Arts and Letters, Van Doren was the recipient of many honors, including the Pulitzer Prize for poetry (1940) and other awards. He received honorary degrees from nine colleges and universities.

REFERENCES: *CA* (1–4); *CB* (January-June 1940 and February 1973);

*NCAB* (D:48); *NYT,* December 12, 1972, p. 1; *WWW* (V); Dorothy Van Doren, *The Professor and I* (New York: Appleton-Century-Crofts, 1959); Mark Van Doren, *Autobiography* (New York: Harcourt, Brace, 1958).

*Joan Duff Kise*

**VAN DUSEN, Henry Pitney.** B. December 11, 1897, Philadelphia, Pennsylvania, to George Richstein and Katharine James (Pitney) Van Dusen. M. June 19, 1931, to Elizabeth Coghill Bartholomew. Ch. three. D. February 13, 1975, Belle Meade, New Jersey.

Henry P. Van Dusen was graduated from the William Penn Charter School in Philadelphia, Pennsylvania, in 1915 and attended Princeton (New Jersey) University where he received the A.B. degree (1919). He studied at the graduate level in Scotland at New College at Edinburgh and Edinburgh University (1921–22) and attended Union Theological Seminary in New York City (1922–24) from which he received the B.D. degree (1924). He returned to Edinburgh where he received the Ph.D. degree (1932).

Van Dusen worked with the Young Men's Christian Association in New York City with the student division (1924–26) and as an executive secretary (1927–28). He joined the faculty of Union Theological Seminary (1926), was dean of students (1932–39), and became Roosevelt Professor of Systematic Theology in 1936. He became president of the seminary and also president of Auburn (New York) Theological Seminary (1945). He also became president of the Union Settlement Association, which maintained a settlement house in New York City. Under Van Dusen the theological seminary came to include many Protestant denominations on its faculty and Roman Catholic priests and nuns as guest professors. He was active in the ecumenical movement and World Council of Churches.

Among the books Van Dusen wrote were *In Quest of Life's Meaning* (1926), *The Plain Man Seeks for God* (1933), *God in These Times* (1935), *For the Healing of the Nations* (1940), *Reality and Religion* (1940), *Methodism's World Mission* (1940), *What Is the Church Doing?* (1943), *East Indies Discoveries* (1944), *They Found the Church There* (1945), *World Christianity* (1947), *God in Education* (1951), *Life's Meaning* (1951), *Spirit, Son and Father* (1958), *One Great Ground of Hope* (1961), *The Vindication of Liberal Theology* (1963), *Christianity on the March* (1963) and *Dag Hammerskjold* (1967). He edited many other books and was on the editorial boards of *Religion in Life, Christianity and Crisis, Christendom, Presbyterian Tribune,* and *Ecumenical Review.*

A member of many religious organizations, Van Dusen was president of the United Board for Christian Colleges in China (1945) and the American Association of Theological Schools (1942–44) and was a delegate to many national and international conferences. He was a member of the boards of trustees of seven colleges and universities and of the Rockefeller Foundation, Fund for the Republic, and Freedom House. He received honorary degrees from more than fifteen colleges and universities.

REFERENCES: *CA* (1–4); *CB* (December 1950); *LE* (III); *NCAB* (H: 343); *NYT,* February 14, 1975, p. 40, February 26, 1975, p. 1; *WWAE* (XVI); *WWW* (VI).                                                                         *John F. Ohles*

**VAN DYKE, John Charles.** B. April 21, 1856, New Brunswick, New Jersey, to John and Mary Dix (Strong) Van Dyke. M. no. D. December 5, 1932, New York, New York.

In 1868 John Charles Van Dyke moved with his family to Minnesota where he was taught by tutors. He studied law at Columbia University and was admitted to the bar in 1877 but never practiced law. He spent many years in Europe studying art.

He became a librarian at Gardner A. Sage Library at New Brunswick (New Jersey) Theological Seminary (1886–1932) and was appointed a lecturer in art at Rutgers College (later, Rutgers, the State University) in 1889 and was professor of art history (1891–1929). He also lectured on art history at Columbia, Harvard, and Princeton universities.

Van Dyke traveled widely studying art. His books include *Books and How to Use Them* (1883), *Principles of Art* (1887), *How to Judge a Picture* (1888), *Notes on Sage Library* (1888), *Serious Art in America* (1890), *Art for Art's Sake* (1893), *History of Painting* (1894), *Nature for Its Own Sake* (1898), *The Desert* (1901), *The Meaning of Pictures* (1903), *The Opal Sea* (1906), *Studies in Pictures* (1907), *The Money God* (1908), *What Is Art?* (1910), *New Guides to Old Masters* (twelve volumes, 1914), *The Mountain* (1916), *American Art and Its Tradition* (1919), *Grand Canyon of the Colorado* (1920), *The Open Spaces* (1922), *Rembrandt and His School* (1923), *The Meadows* (1926), *The Rembrandt Drawings and Etchings* (1927), *In Java* (1929), *In Egypt* (1931), and *In the West Indies* (1932). He edited *A Text-book of the History of Painting* (1915), *History of American Art* (n.d.), *Autobiography of Andrew Carnegie* (1921), and was editor of journals, including *The Studio* (1883–84) and *Art Review* (1887–88).

Van Dyke was a member of professional organizations, including the National Institute of Arts and Letters and was a member of the New Jersey State Board of Education. He received two honorary degrees from Rutgers University.

REFERENCES: *AC; DAB; NCAB* (C:489); *NYT,* December 6, 1932, p. 21; *TC; WWW* (I).                                                                      *Roger H. Jones*

**VAN HISE, Charles Richard.** B. May 29, 1857, Fulton, Wisconsin, to William Henry and Mary (Goodrich) Van Hise. M. December 22, 1881, to Alice Bushnell Ring. Ch. none. D. November 19, 1918, Milwaukee, Wisconsin.

Charles Richard Van Hise attended the public schools at Fulton, Wisconsin, and Evansville (Wisconsin) Academy. He attended the University of Wisconsin and received the B.M.E. (1879), B.S. (1880), M.S. (1882), and Ph.D. (1892) degrees. He was the first to receive an earned Ph.D. degree from Wisconsin.

Although Van Hise spent his entire academic career at the University of Wisconsin (1879–1918), he also was a nonresident professor of structural geology at the University of Chicago (1892–1903). At Wisconsin he taught metallurgy and geology (1879–1903) and was president of the university from 1903 to his death.

While Van Hise was president, Wisconsin doubled the land holdings of the university, increased state appropriations almost fivefold, doubled student enrollment, and increased the faculty fourfold. He played a particularly significant role in the development of a university extension service as a means of providing services to its larger public constituency.

Van Hise was the author of a number of scientific publications, including *Archaean and Algonkian* (1892), *Principles of North American Pre-Cambrian Geology* (1896), *Some Principles Concerning the Deposition of Ores* (1900), *A Treatise on Metamorphism* (1904), *The Conservation of the Natural Resources of the United States* (1910), and *Concentration and Control* (1912). He was also joint author of several surveys of iron bearing areas of Michigan and Wisconsin and contributed many scientific and educational papers to professional and scholarly journals.

Van Hise was active in geological work, serving as a member of the United States Geological Survey (1893–1918) as geologist in charge of the survey's pre-Cambrian and metamorphic geology, and was consulting geologist of the Wisconsin Geological and Natural History Survey (1897–1903). He was chairman of the Wisconsin State Conservation Commission (1908–15) and State Board of Forestry (1905–18) and a trustee of the Carnegie Foundation for the Advancement of Teaching (1909–18). He was a member of many American and foreign professional and scientific associations, including the American Association for the Advancement of Science (vice-president of Section E, 1901), the Geological Society of America (president, 1907), and the Wisconsin Academy of Sciences, Arts and Letters (president, 1893–96). He was awarded honorary degrees by several American colleges and universities.

REFERENCES: *AC; DAB; DSB; NCAB* (19:19); *TC; WWW* (I); *NYT,* November 20, 1918, p. 15.                                          *John F. Ohles*

**VAN RENSSELAER, Martha.** B. June 21, 1864, Randolph, New York, to Henry Killian and Arvilla A. (Owen) Van Rensselaer. M. no. D. May 26, 1932, New York, New York.

Martha Van Rensselaer was graduated from Chamberlain Institute in

Randolph, New York (1884), and received the A.B. degree (1909) from Cornell University in Ithaca, New York.

Van Rensselaer taught in public schools in western New York and was elected commissioner of schools of Cattaraugus County, New York (1894–1900). She was an instructor at state teachers' institutes and secretary of the state summer school at Chautauqua, New York (1896–1903). In 1900 she joined the faculty of the New York State College of Agriculture at Cornell University as an extension lecturer and became professor of education and head of the home economics department (1910–20) and codirector of the school of home economics (1920–25) and the New York State College of Home Economics from 1925.

Editor of the homemaking department of *Delineator* (1921–26), she was compiler with others of *Manual of Home-Making* (1919) and coauthor of *Saving Steps* (1901), the first bulletin of the Farmers' Wives' Reading Course, which was distributed to over twenty thousand women. Some two hundred local study groups were organized.

Van Rensselaer was active in professional associations. She served as president of the American Home Economics Association (1914–16), state chairman of the Better Homes in America Association, and director of the Women's Farm and Garden Association and the New York state chapters of the Congress of Parents and Teachers and League of Women Voters. She was chairman of the home economics section of the Association of Land-Grant Colleges and Universities (1928–29). She was an assistant director of the White House Conference for Child Health and Protection (1929–31) and a participant in the President's Conference on Home Building and Home Ownership.

The home economics building at Cornell was named Martha Van Rensselaer Hall. She was awarded an honorary degree by the New York State College for Teachers at Albany (1930).

REFERENCES: *AC; DAB; LE* (I); *NAW; NCAB* (23:370); *NYT,* May 27, 1932, p. 21; *WWW* (I).                                              *Betty S. Harper*

**VAN TIL, William.** B. January 8, 1911, Corona, New York, to William Joseph and Florence Alberta (MacLean) Van Til. M. August 24, 1935, to Beatrice Barbara Blaha. Ch. three.

William Van Til received the B.A. degree (1933) from Columbia College of Columbia University and the M.A. degree (1935) from Teachers College at Columbia University. He received the Ph.D. degree (1946) from Ohio State University.

Van Til taught at the New York Training School for Boys in Warwick (1933–34) and was an assistant professor in the department of university schools of the college of education at Ohio State University (1936–43). He served as professor of education at the University of Illinois (1947–51) and became chairman of the division of curriculum and teaching at George Peabody College for Teachers in Nashville, Tennessee (1951–57). He was chairman of the department of secondary education at New York University (1957–66) and was head of the division of secondary and higher education (1966-67). In 1967 he went to Indiana State University at Terre Haute as Coffman Distinguished Professor of Education.

Among his many books are *The Danube Flows Through Fascism* (1938), *Foldboat Holiday* (1940), *Time on Your Hands* (1945), *Economic Roads for American Democracy* (1947), *Democracy Demands It: A Resource Unit in Intercultural Education for the High School* (1950), *The Making of a Modern Educator* (1961), *Modern Education for the Junior High School Years* (with others, 1961), *Education: A Beginning* (1971), *Curriculum Quest for Relevance* (1971), and *Education in American Life* (1972). He wrote hundreds of articles, reviews, bibliographies, and surveys in educational journals and other periodicals and contributed columns to *Educational Leadership, Contemporary Education,* and *Kappan.*

Van Til was director of publications and learning materials for the Bureau for Intercultural Education (1944–47), developing books and other materials to be used in American schools to contribute to better human relationships among Americans of varied races, religions, national backgrounds, and socio-economic statuses. He was editor and contributor to *Intercultural Attitudes in the Making,* a yearbook of the John Dewey Society (with William H. Kilpatrick, *q.v.,* 1946), and *Democratic Human Relations,* a yearbook for the National Council for the Social Studies (with Hilda Taba, *q.v.,* 1945) and was editor of *Forces Affecting Education,* the 1952 yearbook of the Association for Supervision and Curriculum Development.

Van Til was president of the John Dewey Society (1964–66), the Association for Supervision and Curriculum Development (1961–62), and the National Society of College Teachers of Education (1967–68) and a member of many other professional organizations. He was a member of the Illinois Interracial Commission (1948–51) and organized and presided over the first meetings in Nashville, Tennessee, planning the desegregation of the public schools (1955–57). He participated in a number of educational surveys and received awards from Ohio State University, the New Jersey Collegiate Press Association, and the New Jersey Association of Teachers of English.

REFERENCES: *CA* (25–28); *LE* (V); *WW* (XXXIX); *WWAE* (XXIII); *Who's Who in the Midwest,* 15th ed. (Chicago: Marquis, 1976).

*Robert C. Morris*

**VAWTER, Charles Erastus.** B. June 9, 1841, Monroe County, Virginia (later, West Virginia), to John Henderson and Clara (Peck) Vawter. M. July 1866 to Virginia Longley. Ch. seven. D. October 27, 1905, Albemarle County, Virginia.

Charles Vawter's education at Emory and Henry College in Emory, Virginia (1858–66), was interrupted by service in the Confederate army (1861–65) as a captain and by imprisonment in Fort Delaware. He also studied mathematics at the University of Virginia and was graduated in 1868.

Vawter taught school (1866–67) and was appointed professor of mathematics and teacher of Hebrew at Emory and Henry College (1868–78). He organized the Miller Manual Labor School in Albemarle County, Virginia, in 1878. It was supported by a bequest by Samuel Miller of over a million dollars in Virginia state certificates. The school enrolled orphan boys and girls of Albemarle County and was located on a farm with buildings and shops equipped to instruct students in manual skills as well as academic studies. The school served as a model for the South and established a national reputation among industrial educators. Vawter became an educational leader who greatly influenced the development of industrial education in public schools throughout the country.

Vawter served as a member of the Virginia state board of education, chairman of the board of trustees for the Normal and Industrial School for Girls at Farmville, the Normal and Industrial Institute for Negroes at Petersburg, and the state board of charities and corrections. He was a member of the board of visitors of Virginia Polytechnic Institute (later, Virginia Polytechnic Institute and State University) at Blacksburg. He helped organize the Conference of Education in the South in 1898 and was a trustee of Emory and Henry College. He assisted in the educational work of the Methodist Episcopal church and was president of the Virginia Sunday School Association and superintendent of Sunday schools in Albemarle County. He died at the Miller Manual Labor School.

REFERENCES: *DAB; WWW* (I); *Outlook* 81 (November 11, 1905): 586.                                                                    *Joel H. Magisos*

**VEBLEN, Oswald.** B. June 24, 1880, Decorah, Iowa, to Andrew Anderson and Kirsten (Hougen) Veblen. M. May 28, 1908, to Elizabeth Mary Dixon Richardson. Ch. none. D. August 10, 1960, Brooklin, Maine.

Oswald Veblen received the A.B. degree from the University of Iowa in 1898, a second A.B. degree from Harvard University in 1900, and the Ph.D. degree from the University of Chicago in 1903. He began his career at the University of Chicago in 1903 as an associate in mathematics. After two years he went to Princeton University as a preceptor in mathematics (1905–10), becoming professor of mathematics in 1910 and the first Fine Professor of Mathematics in 1926, holding the appointment until 1932. In 1932 he was appointed professor of mathematics at the Institute for Advanced Study at Princeton, retiring as professor emeritus in 1950.

His publications include *Cambridge Colloquium Lectures on Analysis-*

*Situs* (1922), which marked the starting point of the American school of topology, and books on quadratic differential forms and geometry. He coauthored with John W. Young volume 1 of *Projective Geometry* (1910) and volume 2 (1918) and with J. H. C. Whitehead *Foundations of Differential Geometry* (1932). The Veblen and Young books on projective geometry had a considerable effect on the subsequent development of abstract geometry and abstract algebra.

He held memberships in the National Academy of Sciences, the American Philosophical Society, the Mathematical Association of America, the American Mathematical Society (president, 1923–24), and foreign mathematical societies. He was a fellow of the American Academy of Arts and Sciences, the American Association for the Advancement of Science, and the American Physical Society. He presided at the International Congress of Mathematicians held at Harvard University in 1950. Veblen received honorary degrees from a number of foreign and American universities, including Oxford, Oslo, Hamburg, Chicago, Glasgow, and Princeton.

REFERENCES: *DSB; LE* (II); *NCAB* (F:330); *WWW* (IV); *NYT,* August 11, 1960, p. 27.                      *Katharine W. Hodgin*

**VENABLE, William Henry.** B. April 29, 1836, near Waynesville, Ohio, to William and Hannah (Baird) Venable. M. December 30, 1861, to Mary Ann Vater. Ch. seven, including Emerson Venable. D. July 6, 1920, Cincinnati, Ohio.

William Henry Venable moved with his parents to Ridgeville, Ohio, near Cincinnati in 1843 and attended the local district school. He was encouraged by his father to read the classics and was largely self-taught. After teaching for a period he was graduated from the South-Western Normal School (later, Lebanon Normal University) in Lebanon, Ohio, in 1860 and was one of the first teachers to receive a life teaching certificate from the newly established Ohio Board of Examiners. He received the A.M. degree (1864) from DePauw University in Greencastle, Indiana.

Venable began teaching at the age of seventeen in Sugar Grove, Ohio. He attended teachers' institutes at Miami University in Oxford, Ohio, during school vacation periods. He joined the faculty of the South-Western Normal School in 1856 and was principal of Jennings Academy in Vernon, Indiana (1860–61). He was professor of natural science (1862–81) and proprietor and principal (1881–86) of the Chickering Classical and Scientific Institute in Cincinnati. Venable gained a reputation as an educator and was a frequent lecturer at teachers' institutes and organizational meetings. He ended a period of retirement and renewed his teaching in Cincinnati as professor of English literature at Hughes High School (1889–95) and Walnut Hills High School (1895–1901).

Venable was the author of many books, including *June on the Miami and Other Poems* (1871), *A School History of the United States* (1872), *The School Stage* (1873), *The Teacher's Dream* (1880), *Melodies of the Heart* (1884), *Footprints of the Pioneer in the Ohio Valley* (1888), *Biography of William D. Gallagher* (1888), *Historical Sketch of Western Periodical Literature* (1888), *Down South Before the War* (1889), *Beginnings of Literary Culture in the Ohio Valley* (1891), *John Hancock, Educator* (1892), *The Last Flight* (1894), *Life and Poems of General W. H. Lytle* (1894), *Let Him First Be a Man* (1894), *Tales from Ohio History* (1896), *Selections from Burns, Byron and Wordsworth* (1898), *A Dream of Empire* (1901), *The Literature of Ohio* (1903), and *Saga of the Oak and Other Poems* (1903). He was editor for a time of the *Ohio Archaeological and Historical Quarterly*. *The Poems of William Henry Venable* was edited by Emerson Venable in 1925.

Active in many associations, Venable was the organizer and first president of the Cincinnati Society of Political Education (1880) and the first president of the Teachers' Club of Cincinnati (1891). He was president of the Western Association of Writers (1895). He received honorary degrees from DePauw and Ohio universities.

REFERENCES: *AC; DAB; NCAB* (19:364); *TC; WWW* (I).

*Charles M. Dye*

**VIGUERS, Ruth Hill.** B. July 24, 1903, Oakland, California, to Everett Merrill and Alfarsta (Kimball) Hill. M. June 2, 1937, to Richard Thomson Viguers. Ch. three. D. February 3, 1971, Boston, Massachusetts.

Ruth Hill Viguers received the B.A. degree (1924) from Willamette University in Salem, Oregon. She earned the B.S. degree in library science (1926) at the University of Washington.

After serving as children's librarian for one year at the Seattle (Washington) Public Library, Viguers joined the New York Public Library in 1927. She was the librarian for girls at the International Institute Library in Spain (1929–31) and a librarian for the American Library in Paris, France (1931–32). She returned to the New York Public Library (1932–36) and then became instructor of library science at the Boone Library School in Wuchang, China, in 1936. Upon returning to the United States she became assistant superintendent for children's work at the New York Public Library (1937–43). She taught children's literature at Simmons College in Boston (1949–71). She was a noted lecturer on children's literature.

From 1958 to 1967 Viguers edited the prestigious *Horn Book Magazine: About Children's Books and Reading*. She judged many important children's book awards, including the *New York Herald Tribune's* Spring Book Festival (1959), the Book World Spring Festival (1968), the *Boston Globe's* Children's Book Award (1967–68), and the Biennale Illustrated

Award (Bratislavia, 1967). She coauthored *Children's Books from Foreign Languages* (1936) and two basic children's literature reference books, *A Critical History of Children's Literature* (1953) and *Illustrators of Children's Books, 1946-1956* (1958). Her *Margin for Surprise* (1964), in which she shared her philosophy of children's literature, became a classic and was widely used in the United States and abroad.

Viguers was an active council member of the American Library Association and served on its Children's Services Division's board of directors. She was a delegate to the White House Conference on Children and Youth (1960). She received distinguished alumna awards from Willamette University and the University of Washington and the Constance Lindsay Skinner Award (1968). She received an honorary degree from Portia Law School (1965).

REFERENCES: *CA* (13–16); *NYT,* February 4, 1971, p. 38; *WWW* (V); Lee Ash, ed., *A Biographical Directory of Librarians in the United States and Canada,* 5th ed. (American Library Association, 1970); Anne Commire, *Something About the Authors* (Detroit: Gale Research, 1974), vol. 6.

*Jane M. Bingham*

**VINCENT, John Heyl.** B. February 23, 1832, Tuscaloosa, Alabama, to John Himrod and Mary (Rouer) Vincent. M. November 10, 1858, to Elizabeth Dusenbury. Ch. one, George Edgar Vincent, president, University of Minnesota. D. May 9, 1920, Chicago, Illinois.

John Heyl Vincent was born in Alabama and grew up in the Northumberland County area of Pennsylvania where he came under the influence of the English Unitarian Joseph Priestly. He became a circuit-riding preacher at the age of seventeen and was appointed to his first Methodist pastorate in North Belleville (later, Nutley), New Jersey, at the age of twenty-one. His formal education was limited; he studied at the Wesleyan Institute in Newark, New Jersey, and at nearby academies and seminaries as he moved from one church to another. He served other churches in Irvington, New Jersey (1855–57), and in Illinois at Joliet (1857–58), Mount Morris (1859), Galena, where Captain U. S. Grant was a member of his church (1860–61), and Rockford (1862–65).

In 1865 Vincent was placed in charge of Trinity Church in Chicago, Illinois, and, while forming the Northeast Sunday School Institute in Chicago, came into contact with Lewis Miller, a wealthy inventor and layman Sunday school teacher. Vincent and Miller organized the Chautauqua Assembly, at a Methodist camp meeting site on the Chautauqua Lake shore in Western New York state, as a residential summer institute for Sunday school teachers. It expanded into a wide diversity of educational activities including a teachers' retreat for public school teachers, the Teachers Reading Union, the nation's first organized book club, the first extension-lecture course (later called off-campus courses), and college degrees through study at home.

Vincent founded the Chautauqua Literary and Scientific Circle to offer carefully prepared correspondence courses to people who could not engage in full-time education. The original concept of Chautauqua was confused by a multitude of commercially motivated "tent Chautauqua" circuits, which had no relationship with the original Chautauqua. In many localities across the country, smaller editions of the summer institute were established and used Vincent's educational and religious programs. The original Chautauqua became known as Mother Chautauqua. In 1888 Vincent became a bishop of the Methodist church and he shared time between the Chautauqua movement and other duties.

Vincent was the author of several books, including *The Chautauqua Movement* (1886), *Outline History of Greece* (1888), *The Church School and the Sunday School Normal Guide* (1889), *Outline History of Rome* (1889), *To Old Bethlehem* (1890), *Studies in Young Life* (1890), *The Church at Home* (1898), *The Modern Sunday School* (1900), and *Family Worship for Every Day in the Year* (1905). He founded the *North-West Sunday School Quarterly* (1865) and *Sunday School Teacher* (1866). He was corresponding secretary of the Sunday School Union and editor of Sunday school publications (1868–84).

REFERENCES: *AC; DAB; NCAB* (24:378); *TC; WWW* (I); *NYT*, May 10, 1920, p. 13; Rebecca Richmond, *Chautauqua: An American Place* (New York: Duell, Sloan and Pearce, 1943).                    *James R. La Forest*

# W

**WADDEL, John Newton.** B. April 2, 1812, Willington, South Carolina, to Moses *(q.v.)* and Elizabeth Woodson (Pleasants) Waddel. M. November 27, 1832, to Martha Robertson. M. August 24, 1854, to Mary A. Werden. M. January 31, 1866, to Harriet (Godden) Snedecor. Ch. eight. D. January 9, 1895, Birmingham, Alabama.

John Newton Waddel was graduated from Franklin College (later, University of Georgia) with distinction in 1829 and taught for a time at Willington (South Carolina) Academy, an institution his father founded.

Waddel settled in Jasper County, Mississippi, as a farmer in 1840. He became a licensed minister of the Presbyterian church in 1841 and founded Montrose Academy in 1842, the first institution of higher learning for youth in Mississippi.

Waddel rode over two hundred miles on horseback to attend a meeting of the group that was establishing the University of Mississippi. He was appointed chairman of the committee to arrange a course of study for the institution. Waddel was elected professor of ancient languages at the University of Mississippi in 1847 and taught there until 1857, when he accepted the professorship of ancient languages at the Presbyterian Synodical College in La Grange, Tennessee. He served as president of the college from 1860 to 1862 when La Grange was occupied by the Union army.

In 1865 Waddel became chancellor of the University of Mississippi. He toured the leading colleges in the North and South to gather information and ideas to facilitate the reorganization of the university curriculum. Waddel's leadership was a significant factor in the university's survival during the Reconstruction period. In 1870 he issued an open letter threatening his and the faculty's resignations before they would allow Negro students to enter the university. In 1874 Waddel became secretary of education for the Southern Presbyterian church, and in 1879 he was appointed chancellor of the Southwestern Presbyterian University at Clarksville, Tennessee, where he served to 1888.

Waddel was an organizer of the first general assembly of the Southern Presbyterian church and served as its clerk (1861–65) and moderator (1868). He was the author of *Historical Discourse on the University of Mississippi* (1873). He received honorary degrees from the universities of Nashville (1851) and Georgia (1873).

REFERENCES: *AC; DAB; NCAB* (13:136); *TC; WWW* (H); J. A. Cabaniss, *A History of the University of Mississippi* (University, Miss.: University of Mississippi, 1950). *Robert E. Conner*
*Jeffrey Martin*

**WADDEL, Moses.** B. July 29, 1770, Rowan (later, Iredell) County, North Carolina, to William and Sarah (Morrow) Waddel. M. 1795 to Catherine Calhoun (sister of John C. Calhoun). M. 1800 to Elizabeth Woodson Pleasants. Ch. four, including John Newton Waddel *(q.v.).* D. July 21, 1840, Athens, Georgia.

Moses Waddel attended a local school in Rowan County, Georgia, and Clio's Nursery, an academy founded in 1778 by James Hall in Bethany, North Carolina. He was graduated from Hampden-Sydney (Virginia) College in 1791. He studied theology under Virginia clergymen and was licensed to preach in 1792.

Upon completion of his schooling at Clio's Nursery in 1784 Waddel taught local children in his home. In 1788 the family moved to Greene County, Georgia, where he opened a school. After serving churches in the Charleston, South Carolina, area, he moved to Columbia County, Georgia, where he opened a school near Appling. After his second marriage in 1800 he moved to Vienna, South Carolina, where he established another school.

In 1804 Waddel moved from Vienna to nearby Willington, where he conducted a well-known private school. Originally a two-room log cabin, by 1809 the school was conducted in four recitation rooms and a chapel. Waddel established a strict disciplinary system and employed a monitorial system of instruction. A traditional curriculum was instituted using highly structured instructional methods. From 1804 to 1819 Waddel taught over four thousand pupils, including many who became eminent public leaders.

Waddel wrote a theological work, *Memoirs of the Life of Miss Caroline Elizabeth Smelt* (1818). He was appointed president of Franklin College (later, part of the University of Georgia) in 1819. He served in the position for ten years, retiring in 1829. He was credited with increasing student enrollment and providing a stimulating religious program at Franklin College.

REFERENCES: *AC; DAB; NCAB* (9:179); *TC; WWW* (H).*Joe L. Green*

**WADSWORTH, James.** B. April 20, 1768, Durham, Connecticut, to John Noyes and Esther (Parsons) Wadsworth. M. October 1, 1804, to Naomi Wolcott. Ch. four. D. June 7, 1844, Geneseo, New York.

James Wadsworth was graduated from Yale College in 1787 and spent several winters teaching in Montreal, Canada. In 1790 he and his brother William settled in the present village of Geneseo, New York, and prospered as agriculturalists and land agents. Wadsworth developed two interests, business and public education. He sought to interest foreign capitalists in American investment and to apply scientific principles to improve agricultural methods.

As early as 1796 he perceived the need for improved public education. He believed this goal could be accomplished through the advancement and improvement of common schools and by the creation of normal schools and school district libraries. To advance the common schools, he paid newspapers to set aside space for the discussion of education; had essays on education printed and distributed throughout the state; assisted in the establishment of the *District School Journal* and *The Common School Assistant;* distributed large numbers of the *Report on the State of Public Instruction in Prussia* by Victor Cousins, the *School and the Schoolmaster* by Alonzo Potter *(q.v.)* and George B. Emerson *(q.v.),* and Samuel R. Hall's *(q.v.) Lectures on School-Keeping;* and provided funds to interest persons in preparing suitable textbooks.

Wadsworth advocated the establishment of schools devoted to teacher training and the diffusion of such schools throughout the state. He wanted the latest and most practical methods of school teaching disseminated. He favored the use of the Bell-Lancastrian monitorial system and urged the establishment of a school inspection system by which the standards of the common schools could be maintained. He was appointed to a county board of visitors whose duty it was to assess the quality of education in the schools.

He is credited with bringing about the legislative authorization for the establishment of the school district library system in New York State in 1835. He wanted libraries in every school district in the state and thought that support for libraries could be derived from taxes. Wadsworth donated land for the purpose of establishing a collegiate institution in Geneseo, the foundation for the present State University of New York College at Geneseo. He never ran for high office, but he was a behind-the-scenes force in politics, using this power to raise the level of the education of the people of New York state.

REFERENCES: *AC; DAB; TC; WWW* (H); Anthony M. Barraco, "The Wadsworth Family of Geneseo, New York: A Study of Their Activities Which Relate to Public Education in New York State and to the State University College of New York at Geneseo" (Ed. D. diss., State University of New York at Buffalo, 1967).                   *Norman J. Bauer*

**WAGNER, Jonathan Howard.** B. January 7, 1873, Columbia City, Indiana, to Simon Peter and Angeline (Thomas) Wagner. M. August 27, 1901, to Pearl Bickenstaff. Ch. five. D. December 16, 1953, Seattle, Washington.

Jonathan Wagner was graduated from high school in North Manchester, Indiana, in 1891. He was graduated from the State Normal School of Indiana (later, Indiana State University) at Terre Haute (1896) and received the A.B. degree (1900) from Manchester College in North Manchester, Indiana. He took additional courses at the universities of Michigan (1901), Chicago (1902), and Washington (1927–28 and 1930–31). In 1902 he was admitted to the bar in Auburn, Indiana.

Wagner was a cashier at the Savings Trust Company in Auburn, Indiana. He was a grade school principal at Silver Lake, Indiana (1893–95), and of Indiana high schools in North Manchester (1897–1901) and Alexandria (1901–05). He was superintendent of schools in New Mexico at Las Cruces (1905–09) and in Santa Fe (1909–14). He was elected superintendent of public instruction of New Mexico in 1914 and served in that office until 1920. He was superintendent of schools at Pueblo, Colorado (1920–21), and president of the New Mexico Normal University (later, New Mexico Highlands University) at Las Vegas (1921–23).

From 1923 to 1930 Wagner was chief of the Alaska division of the United States Office of Education with his office in Seattle, Washington. When the office was moved to Juneau, Alaska Territory, he resigned and accepted a position with the Seattle (Washington) public schools as a teacher at Roosevelt High School. He was principal of John Hay School and also in charge of the Children's Orthopedic School and Convalescent Home

School in Seattle (1935–42). He served as director of the Pacific School of Research and Genealogy.

Wagner was active in professional and educational organizations, serving as president and secretary of the New Mexico Educational Association and president of the Seattle (Washington) Principals' Association. He was the author of many articles and papers on native Alaskans. During World War I he was director of education and labor of the New Mexico Council for Defense and was an investigator for the United States Army from 1941 to 1947.

He was awarded the Hudson Bay Company Medal in 1924 for his services in rescuing twenty-three crewmen from the ship *Lady Kindersley,* which was crushed by ice.

REFERENCES: *WWW* (V); Charles F. Coan, *A History of New Mexico* (Chicago: American Historical Society, 1925), vol. 1; *Seattle Times,* June 13, 1942, December 17, 1953; Ralph E. Twitchell, *Old Santa Fe* (Santa Fe: New Mexican Publishing Corp., 1925).                              *E. A. Scholer*

**WAHLQUIST, John Thomas.** B. September 10, 1899, Heber, Utah, to Charles John and Elizabeth (Campbell) Wahlquist. M. August 30, 1923, to Grace Dorius. Ch. two.

John T. Wahlquist received the B.S. (1924) and M.S. (1926) degrees from the University of Utah and the Ph.D. (1930) degree from the University of Cincinnati.

Wahlquist was a member of the faculty at the University of Utah in Salt Lake City (1924-52)) and was dean of the school of education (1941–52). He assumed the presidency of San Jose (California) State College in 1952, retired in 1964, and continued to teach in the education department until his retirement in 1969. He was a visiting professor at many American universities.

Wahlquist played an influential role in the development of education in Utah. He was the author of books on education, including *The Philosophy of American Education* (1942), *An Introduction to American Education* (1947), *Lehrenals Anleitung zur Tätigkeit* (1950), *The Administration of American Education* (1951), *Administration of Public Education* (1952), *State Colleges and Universities* (with J. W. Thorton, 1964), *College Teaching as a Challenging Career* (1967), and *Innovations in the Preparation of College Teachers* (1970).

Engaged in professional activities, Wahlquist was a member of the Utah Textbook Commission (1941–52) and the Utah Course of Study Committee (1941–52), presided over the Utah Conference on Higher Education (1946), and served in the National Clinic in Teacher Education (1946), the White House Conference on Rural Education (1944), and the National Conference on the Education of Veterans (1946). He was a fellow of the

Utah Academy of Arts and Letters and a member of the National Council of Education and the National Education Association (director, 1941–48).
REFERENCES: *LE* (III); *WWAE* (XVI); *WW* (XXVIII).     *John F. Ohles*

**WAIT, Samuel.** B. December 19, 1789, White Creek, New York, to Joseph and Martha Wait. M. June 17, 1818, to Sarah Merriam. Ch. one. D. July 28, 1867, Wake Forest, North Carolina.

Samuel Wait, first president of Wake Forest (North Carolina) College, was educated in the local schools and Salem Academy (1813) in Washington County, New York. He studied theology in Philadelphia, Pennsylvania, and was ordained to the Baptist ministry in Sharon, Massachusetts, in 1818. One of the first students in 1821 at Columbian College (later, George Washington University) in Washington, D.C., he was graduated in 1822. He received the A.M. degree (1825) from Waterville (Maine) College (later, Colby College).

Wait served a church in Sharon, Massachusetts, and was a tutor at Columbian College (1822–26) and principal of its preparatory school (1822–25). He went to North Carolina to solicit funds for the college (1826–27) and accepted an appointment as Baptist minister to a church in New Bern, North Carolina. He organized a Baptist convention in Greenville, North Carolina, in 1830, served as its first corresponding secretary (1830–34), and organized churches throughout the state (1830–32).

Wait was instrumental in establishing a manual labor school in Wake Forest, North Carolina, and served as its first principal from 1834 to 1838, when the Wake Forest Manual Labour Institute was chartered as Wake Forest College. Wait was president (1838–46) and president of its board of trustees (1846–67). The manual training program had been abandoned at the institute; Wait established a solid foundation for the development of what eventually became Wake Forest University. Wait served as pastor of a church in Yanceyville, North Carolina (1846–51), and was president of Oxford (North Carolina) Female Seminary (1851–56).

The author of "Origin and History of Wake Forest College between 1850-60," which was published in the *Wake Forest Student,* Wait established the *Recorder* at Raleigh, the first Baptist periodical in North Carolina. He received honorary degrees from Waterville, Columbian, and Wake Forest colleges.

REFERENCES: *AC; DAB; NCAB* (21:254); *TC; WWW* (H). *John F. Ohles*

**WAIT, William Bell.** B. April 25, 1839, Amsterdam, New York, to Christopher Brown and Betsy Grinnell (Bell) Wait. M. October 27, 1863, to Phebe Jane Babcock. Ch. three. D. October 25, 1916, New York, New York.

William Bell Wait was graduated from Albany, New York, Normal College (later, State University of New York at Albany) in 1859 and taught at the New York Institute for the Education of the Blind. In 1862 he was admitted to the New York bar. While the first superintendent of schools of Kingston, New York, in 1863, he was appointed principal of the New York Institute for the Education of the Blind in New York City where he served until his retirement in 1905.

Wait invented the New York point system of printing for the blind and a form of tangible musical notation that received the approval of the American Association of Instructors of the Blind in 1872. He invented the kleidograph in 1894 for embossing the New York point system on paper and the stereograph for embossing metal plates, which are used in printing books, and developed an improved method of binding embossed books.

His writings include *The New York Tangible Point System of Literature* (1866), *The New York Tangible Point System of Music for the Blind* (1872), *The Normal Course of Piano Technique* (1887), *Harmonic Notation* (1888), with special reference to the instruction of the blind, *The Uniform Type Question* (1915), and *New Aspects of the Uniform Type Folly* (1916).

He was a founder of the American Association of Instructors of the Blind in 1871 and the Society for Providing Evangelical Religious Literature for the Blind in 1914. He received the Franklin Institute of Philadelphia John Scott Medal for his inventions for the blind.

REFERENCES: *DAB; NCAB* (2:451); *WWW* (I); *NYT,* October 26, 1916, p. 11.                                                        *John W. Schifani*

**WALD, Lillian D.** B. March 10, 1867, Cincinnati, Ohio, to Max D. and Minnie (Schwarz) Wald. M. no. D. September 1, 1940, Westport, Connecticut.

Lillian Wald attended Miss Cruttenden's English-French Boarding and Day School in Rochester, New York. At the age of sixteen she applied to Vassar College but was turned down because she was too young. She attended a course in nurses' training at New York Hospital (1889–91) and studied at Woman's Medical College in New York City. While attending medical school she accepted an offer to set up home nursing classes for immigrants on New York City's Lower East Side. When called upon to aid a sick woman in a tenement there, Wald's concern encouraged her to leave medical school and become a public health nurse. She organized the first visiting nurse service and in 1893 started the Henry Street Settlement House with a co-worker, Mary Brewster.

In 1902 Wald influenced the New York City Board of Health to establish the first public school nursing program in the United States. She was influential in the establishment of a nursing program for industrial policyholders of the Metropolitan Life Insurance Company and the introduction of a department of nursing and health at Teachers College, Columbia University. She successfully urged the establishment of special ungraded classes in the public schools, forerunners of special education services. She initiated the idea of a federal Children's Bureau, which was established in 1912, and supported many forms of social legislation.

Wald was the author of *The House on Henry Street* (1915) and *Windows on Henry Street* (1934). A pioneer in the movement to establish public playgrounds, she supported women's suffrage and the peace movement. In 1915 she became the first president of the American Union against Militarism. She served on many public boards and commissions and was a delegate to international conferences on children and women in Cannes, France, and Zurich, Switzerland, in 1919. She received awards from the National Institute of Social Sciences, Rotary Club, *Better Times,* and the city of New York, as well as honorary degrees from Mount Holyoke and Smith colleges.

REFERENCES: *DAB* (supp. 2); *EB; NAW; NCAB* (29:25); *NYT,* September 2, 1940, p. 15; *WWW* (I); George W. Alger, "Lillian D. Wald, The Memories of An Old Friend," *Survey* 29 (October 1940): 512–14; *American Journal of Public Health* 30 (November 1940): 1358–59; "Portrait," *Newsweek* 9 (March 20, 1937): 45; Clara Gruening Stillman, "Portrait of Lillian Wald," book review, *Nation* 147 (November 26, 1938). 569–70.

*Phyllis Appelbaum*

**WALKER, David Shelby.** B. May 2, 1815, Logan County, Kentucky, to David and Mary (Barbour) Walker. M. May 22, 1842, to Philoclea Alston. M. 1875 to Elizabeth Duncan. Ch. six. D. July 20, 1891, Tallahassee, Florida.

David S. Walker's father died when the boy was five years old and his mother died a year later. He lived with a sister in La Grange, Kentucky, and was educated in private schools in Kentucky and Tennessee. He studied law with his brother Henry in Tallahassee, Florida (1837–40). He was admitted to the bar and practiced law in Tallahassee.

Walker was elected to the first Florida state senate in 1845, and in 1848 he became mayor of Tallahassee and a member of the Florida house of representatives. He was instrumental in establishing one of the first free schools in the South in Tallahassee. He served as registrar of public lands (1851–59) and also as superintendent of public schools under a state law of 1849. Walker aggressively promoted the development of public education in Florida and was influential in legislation passed in 1853 that strengthened Florida public schools. Under his direction the number of common schools grew substantially, and he is credited as the Father of Florida Education.

An unsuccessful candidate for governor of Florida in 1856, he was associate justice of the Florida supreme court (1859–65) and was elected governor in 1865. As governor he sponsored legislation establishing schools for freedmen in Florida. Refusing to sign the loyalty oath passed by the United States Congress in 1867, Walker was removed from the office of governor and entered private law practice. He became a state judge in 1879 and served in that post to his death in 1891.

He was a trustee of Florida Agricultural and Mechanical College (later, University) and Southern Florida Seminary (later, Florida Southern College) at Lakeland. He donated a building for a public library in Tallahassee and was founder and president of the university library.

REFERENCES: *DAB; NCAB* (11:379); *TC; WWW* (H); N. K. Pyburn, *The History of the Development of a Single System of Education in Florida, 1822–1903* (Tallahassee: Florida State University, 1954); B.M. Watts, ed., *Florida Educators* (Tallahassee: Florida State University, 1959).

*Phil Constans, Jr.*

**WALKER, Francis Amasa.** B. July 2, 1840, Boston, Massachusetts, to Amasa and Hannah (Ambrose) Walker. M. August 16, 1865, to Exene Stoughton. Ch. seven. D. January 5, 1897, Boston, Massachusetts.

Francis Amasa Walker was graduated from Amherst (Massachusetts) College with the A.B. (1860) and A.M. (1863) degrees. He studied law in Worcester, Massachusetts, then joined the Union army and served in the Civil War (1861–65). He was wounded at Chancellorsville (1863) and captured at Reams's Station (1864).

Walker taught at Williston Seminary in Easthampton, Massachusetts (1865–68), and was editor of the *Springfield* (Massachusetts) *Republican*. He became head of the Bureau of Statistics of the United States Treasury (1869) and was superintendent of the 1870 United States Census. He was commissioner of Indian affairs (1871–73) and professor of political economy and history at Sheffield Scientific School at Yale College in 1873.

Walker became president of Massachusetts Institute of Technology in Cambridge, Massachusetts, in 1881. Under his leadership its enrollment increased nearly four times. He continued as president to his death in 1897. He was an advocate of mechanical training in the common school curriculum.

Walker was the author of many books, including *The Indian Question* (1874), *The Wages Question* (1876), *Money* (1878), *Money and Its Relation to Trade and Industry* (1879), *Political Economy* (1883), *Land and Its Rent* (1883), *History of the Second Army Corps in the Army of the Potomac* (1886), *The Life of General Hancock* (1894), *The Making of the Nation 1783-1817* (1895), and *International Bimetallism* (1896).

A member of the New Haven, Connecticut, school committee and Connecticut state board of education while at Yale, Walker also served on the Boston, Massachusetts, school committee (1885–88) and the Massachusetts board of education (1882–90). He was a member of professional and scholarly organizations and was a founder and president of the American Statistical Association (1882–97), president of the American Economic Society (1885–92), vice-president of the National Academy of Sciences (1890), and a fellow of the American Academy of Arts and Sciences. He was a trustee of Amherst College (1879–89) and the Boston Public Library (1896). He was decorated by the government of France and received many honorary degrees from American and foreign colleges and universities.

REFERENCES: *AC; DAB; NCAB* (5:401), *NYT,* January 6, 1897, p. 9; *TC; WWW* (H); Davis R. Dewey, "Francis A. Walker as a Public Man," *The Review of Reviews* (February 1897): 166-71; Charles F. Dunbar, "Career of Francis Amasa Walker," *Quarterly Journal of Economics* 11 (July 1897): 436-48; "General Francis A. Walker," *The Outlook* (January 16, 1897): 239-42; James Phinney Munroe, *A Life of Francis Amasa Walker* (New York: Henry Holt and Co., 1923); H. W. Tyler, "The Educational Work of Francis A. Walker," *Educational Review* (June 1897): 55-70.

*Robert H. Truman*

**WALLIN, John Edward Wallace.** B. January 21, 1876, Page County, Iowa, to Henry and Emma M. (Johnson) Wallin. M. June 21, 1913, to Frances Geraldine Tinsley. Ch. two. D. August 5, 1969, Wilmington, Delaware.

J. E. Wallace Wallin received the A.B. degree from Augustana College in Rock Island, Illinois (1897), and the M.A. (1899) and Ph.D. (1901) degrees from Yale University.

He was a research assistant in psychology at Clark University in Worcester, Massachusetts, in 1901 and an assistant in experimental psychology at the University of Michigan (1902–03). He served as a demonstrator in experimental psychology at Princeton University (1903–06) and vice-principal and head of the department of psychology and education at the State Teachers' College at East Stroudsburg, Pennsylvania (later, East Stroudsburg State College), from 1906 to 1909. He was head of the department of psychology and education at the Normal Training School at Cleveland, Ohio (1909–10). He was director of psychological research for the oral hygiene committee of the National Dental Association and director of the laboratory of clinical psychology at the New Jersey State Village for Epileptics (1910–11). He filled a dual role as professor of clinical psychology and director of the psychoeducational clinic at the University of Pittsburgh (1912–14).

Wallin was director of the psychoeducational clinic and special schools and instructor in the department of instruction of Harris Teachers' College in St. Louis, Missouri (1914-21). He was director of the psychoeducational clinic and professor of clinical psychology at Miami (Oxford, Ohio) University (1921–29), director of the division of special education for the

Baltimore (Maryland) department of education, and lecturer at Johns Hopkins University (1929–30). He was professor of psychology and director of the mental hygiene clinic at Atlantic University at Virginia Beach, Virginia (1930–32). His longest tenure was as director of the division of special education and mental hygiene for the Delaware State Department of Public Instruction (1932–47).

Wallin was the author of *Researches on the Rhythm of Speech* (1902), *Optical Illusions of Reversible Perceptive* (1905), *Spelling Efficiency in Relation to Age, Grade, and Sex* (1911), *Experimental Studies of Mental Defectives* (1912), *The Mental Health of the School Child* (1914), *Psycho-Motor Norms for Practical Diagnosis* (1916), *Problems of Subnormality* (1917), *The Achievement of Subnormal Children in Standardized Educational Tests* (1922), *Measurement of Mental Traits in Normal and Epileptic School Children* (1923), *The Education of Handicapped Children* (1924), *Studies of Mental Defects and Handicaps* (1925), *Clinical and Abnormal Psychology* (1927), *Personality Maladjustments and Mental Hygiene* (1935), *Minor Mental Maladjustments in Normal People* (1939), *Children with Mental and Physical Handicaps* (1949), *The Odyssey of a Psychologist* (1955), and *The Education of Mentally Handicapped Children* (1955). He was a cooperating editor of the *Journal of Applied Psychology* and the *Journal of Delinquency* and on the advisory board of the *Journal of Exceptional Children*. He was the coordinator for terms dealing with exceptional children for the *Dictionary of Education* (1940–45).

A member of numerous professional organizations, he served on many committees and was the founder (1919) of the department of special classes of the Missouri Teachers Association (chairman, 1920 and 1921), founder (1921) of the department of special education of the Ohio Education Association (president, 1922 and 1926–27), and founder (1934) of the department of special education and mental hygiene of the Delaware Education Association (chairman, 1934, 1937, 1943). He was secretary of the committee on special education for the White House Conference on Child Health and Protection (1929–30). He conducted surveys of handicapped children in Baltimore, Maryland, and for the state of Ohio. He held offices and served on boards of many associations: the National Association of State Directors and Supervisors of Special Education (secretary, 1941–47 and chairman, 1942–47), the Delaware State Society of Mental Hygiene (board of directors, 1942–46), the American Psychological Association (chairman, section on clinical psychology, 1917, 1918), and the International Council for Exceptional Children (member, board of directors, 1937–43 and 1946–47).

REFERENCES: *LE* (III); *WW* (XXII); *WWAE* (XVI); *WWW* (V); J. E. Wallace Wallin, *The Odyssey of a Psychologist* (Wilmington, Del.: The Author, 1955).                                    *Bruce D. Mattson*

**WANAMAKER, Pearl Anderson.** B. January 18, 1899, Mabana, Washington, to Nils and Johanna (Hellman) Anderson. M. June 4, 1927, to Lemuel A. Wanamaker. Ch. three.

Pearl Anderson Wanamaker attended Western Washington College of Education (later, Western Washington State College) in Bellingham and received the B.A. degree (1922) from the University of Washington. She served as a rural school teacher (1917–21), high school teacher (1922–23 and 1928–41), and superintendent of Island County (1923–27). Her father had been a legislator, and she won election to the state legislature in 1929 and the state senate in 1937.

Wanamaker fought successfully for education as Washington's superintendent of public instruction from 1941 to 1957. She persuaded governors and legislators to modernize the state's educational system. Under her leadership school districts were consolidated, teachers' salaries were increased, teacher certification standards were improved, special education facilities were expanded, and the superintendent's office assumed a greater responsibility in curriculum development. State aid to schools rose from 11 percent to 50 percent of school operating costs, leading to an extensive building program across the state, with modern school buildings replacing the one-room schools of rural Washington. Wanamaker suggested legislation in 1947 encouraging long-range master planning for local school districts, which prepared the state for the increases in pupil populations through the 1960s.

Wanamaker was active in several educational groups, serving as president of the National Education Association (1946–47) and the National Council of Chief State School Officers (1949–50), vice-president of the American Association of School Administrators (1951–52), second vice-president of the American Council on Education, and on the board of curators of the Washington State Historical Society. She served on many state and national advisory committees to private and governmental agencies. She was an adviser to the United States delegation to the United Nations Educational, Scientific, and Cultural Organization (UNESCO) Conference in Paris, France (1946), and a member of the United States National Commission for UNESCO. In 1946 Wanamaker was one of twenty-seven educators sent to Japan to advise General Douglas McArthur on rebuilding and modernizing the Japanese school system.

Awards and honors given to Wanamaker include the Distinguished Service Award from Altrusa International (1947), the American Education Award (1949), and the Achievement Award of the Women's National Press Club (1950). She received honorary degrees from Miami and Columbia universities and Mills and Smith colleges.

REFERENCES: *CB* (September 1946); *LE* (V); *WW* (XXXI); *WWAE* (XVI); Zita Lichtenberg, ed., *Washington Schools in the Good Old Days* (Olympia, Wash.: Office of Superintendent of Public Instruction, 1969);

"Fighting Lady," *Time* 67 (February 6, 1956): 60-61.

*Michael A. Balasa*

**WARD, Joseph.** B. May 5, 1838, Perry Center, New York, to Jabez and Aurilla (Tufts) Ward. M. August 12, 1868, to Sara F. Wood. Ch. five. D. December 11, 1889, Yankton, South Dakota.

Joseph Ward was graduated from Phillips Academy in Andover, Massachusetts, in 1861 and attended Brown University in Providence, Rhode Island (1861–62). He served with the Union army in 1862 and returned to Brown. He was graduated in 1862 and attended Andover (Massachusetts) Theological Seminary (1865–68).

Ward moved to South Dakota where he served a small mission church at Yankton in 1868 and was ordained to the ministry in 1869. He organized a private school that became Yankton Academy in 1872 and Yankton High School, the first in the territory. He was a founder of Yankton College in 1881 and served as first president and professor of mental and moral philosophy (1881–89).

Ward was active in the movement that led to the division of the Territory of Dakota and the admission of South Dakota to the Union. He was a major figure in the enactment of legislation providing for public schools in South Dakota. He selected the state motto "Under God the People Rule" and was a delegate to territorial and state constitutional conventions. He helped establish the Dakota Hospital for the Insane in 1879 and was a founder of the Citizens Constitutional Association. He received an honorary degree from Knox College in 1883.

REFERENCES: *DAB; NCAB* (23:150); *WWW* (H); G. H. Durand, *Joseph Ward of Dakota* (New York: Pilgrim Press, 1913); *Yankton Press and Dakotan*, December 19, 1889. *Lawrence S. Master*

**WARD, Lester Frank.** B. June 18, 1841, Joliet, Illinois, to Justus and Silence (Rolfe) Ward. M. August 13, 1862, to Elisabeth Carolyn Vought. M. March 6, 1873, to Rosamond Asenath Simons. Ch. one. D. April 18, 1913, Washington, D.C.

Considered by many the founder of modern systematic sociology, Lester Frank Ward exerted a great influence on American social and political thought of the twentieth century. Ward spent his youth in Illinois and Iowa. After studying at Susquehanna College in Selinsgrove, Pennsylvania, he was married for the first time and joined the Union army. Wounded at Chancellorsville, he went to Washington, D.C., in 1865 where he took a position with the Treasury Department. He served as chief of the Division of Navigation and Immigration and as librarian of the Bureau of Statistics. In 1871 he completed a law course at Columbian (later, George Washington) University. He also received the A.B. (1869) and A.M. (1873) degrees from the same institution.

About 1872 he took up the study of botany. In 1881 he became assistant geologist of the United States Geological Survey and seven years later was elevated to geologist, remaining in that position until the last few years of his life when he served as a professor at Brown University.

Among his published works were *Haeckel's Genesis of Man* (1879), *The Flora of Washington* (1881), *Dynamic Sociology* (1883), *Sketch of Paleontological Botany* (1885), *Synopsis of the Flora of the Laramie Group* (1886), *Types of the Laramie Flora* (1887), *Geographical Distribution of Fossil Plants* (1889), *The Psychic Factors of Civilization* (1893), *Outlines of Sociology* (1898), *Sociology and Economics* (1899), *Pure Sociology* (1903), *Applied Sociology* (1905), and *Glimpses of the Cosmos* (six volumes, 1913–18).

Ward applied the theory of evolution to human social behavior, stressing the group rather than the individual. He believed social improvement was preferable to mere survival for only the fittest few; he advocated a humane society with an emphasis on governmental elimination of poverty and fostering of education. He received an honorary degree from Columbia University.

REFERENCES: *AC; DAB; EB; NCAB* (13:112); *NYT,* April 19, 1913, p. 11; *TC; WWW* (I). *James M. Vosper*

**WARE, Edmund Asa.** B. December 22, 1837, North Wrentham, Massachusetts, to Asa Blake and Catharine (Slocum) Ware. M. November 10, 1869, to Sarah Jane Twichell. Ch. four, including Edward Twichell Ware, third president of Atlanta University. D. September 25, 1885, Atlanta, Georgia.

Edmund Asa Ware received his early education at North Wrentham, Massachusetts, and moved with his family to Norwich, Connecticut, where he attended the Norwich Free Academy. He was graduated from Yale College in 1863. He was licensed to preach by the Congregational church in 1866.

Ware taught at the Norwich Free Academy (1863–65) and moved to Nashville, Tennessee, in 1865 to assist in organizing the public schools. He moved to Atlanta, Georgia, with the support of the American Missionary Association to serve as superintendent of the Atlanta schools. Appointed Georgia state superintendent of schools by General Oliver O. Howard of the Freedmen's Bureau in 1867, Ware toured the state seeking to establish schools.

Ware was largely responsible for the issuance of a charter in 1867 to establish Atlanta University. First to be established was a preparatory school in 1869; three years later the normal and college departments were established. Ware served as the first president of Atlanta University from 1867 to his death. Atlanta was one of the earliest institutions of its type to develop a college level program for black students.

REFERENCES: *DAB; NCAB* (5:380); *WWW* (H); Robert C. Ogden, ed., *From Servitude to Service* (Boston: American Unitarian Assoc., 1905), pp. 170-73.                                                      *Walter C. Daniel*

**WARE, William Robert.** B. May 27, 1832, Cambridge, Massachusetts, to Henry and Mary Lovell (Prichard) Ware. M. no. D. June 10, 1915, Milton, Massachusetts.

William Robert Ware, founder of American architectural education, was educated in the Cambridge (Massachusetts) public schools and Phillips Academy in Exeter, New Hampshire. He was graduated from Harvard University with the A.B. degree (1852) and from Lawrence Scientific School at Harvard where he received the B.S. degree (1856). He worked in the office of Boston architect Edward Clarke Cabot and became one of the first pupils in the atelier established by Richard Hunt in his New York City office.

On completion of his studies with Hunt in 1860, he entered practice with E. S. Philbrick (1860–63) and with Henry Van Brunt. Ware and Van Brunt formed one of the major architectural firms and designed many notable buildings in New England. They opened an atelier for architectural students in their office and added systematic instruction in construction, theory, and history to the general instruction in design and drawing problems.

Appointed head of the proposed school of architecture at Massachusetts Institute of Technology (MIT) in 1865, Ware studied architectural education in France and England. On his return he organized the school on the Ecole de beaux arts system and invited the French instructor Eugène Létang to teach courses of design. In 1881 he moved to Columbia University to found a school of architecture, remaining there to his retirement in 1903. At MIT and Columbia, Ware developed a new system of architectural education based on the French model and adapted to American needs and conditions.

Ware was the author of *An Outline of a Course of Architectural Instruction* (1866), *Greek Ornament* (1878), *Modern Perspective* (1883), *The American Vignola* (two volumes, 1902–06), and *Shades and Shadows* (1912–13). He was a fellow of the American Academy of Arts and Sciences and a member of American and foreign professional associations. He was awarded an honorary degree by Harvard University (1869).

REFERENCES: *AC; DAB; NCAB* (8:440); *NYT,* June 10, 1915, p. 5; *WWW* (I).                                                      *Roger H. Jones*

**WARNER, William Everett.** B. August 22, 1897, Roanoke, Illinois, to Isaac Newton and Eva (Redmon) Warner. M. August 14, 1920, to Eleanor Todd. Ch. none. D. July 12, 1971, Columbus, Ohio.

William Everett Warner received the B.S. (1923) and M.S. (1924) degrees from the University of Wisconsin. He attended Columbia University, where he received the first Ph.D. degree (1928) awarded in the field of industrial arts education.

He was a teacher and principal in public and vocational schools (1917–24). In 1925 he joined the faculty of Ohio State University as an assistant professor of industrial arts and became professor in 1939; he continued there to his retirement in 1967. He initiated and directed the development of the Ohio Program of Industrial Arts in the late 1930s and early 1940s. The program included model programs of industrial arts development in Ohio and throughout the United States and several foreign nations.

During World War II he served as principal protection officer in the Facility Security Program of the United States Office of Civil Defense and later was on the staff of General Dwight D. Eisenhower in London charged with organizing civil defense programs for liberated European nations. He was sent to Belgium to organize and direct the civil and military passive defense programs in the American zone.

He was the author of *Pottery* (1953), *Industrial Arts for the General Shop* (1955), and *Woods and Wood-Working for Industrial Arts* (1958). He was editor of the Epsilon Pi Tau brochure series (1929–71) and Western Arts Association publications (1932–37) and consulting editor to the Arts and Industries Series.

He founded Epsilon Pi Tau, the international honorary fraternity in industrial arts and vocational-industrial education in 1929 with Alpha Chapter installed at Ohio State University. He served as the fraternity's executive secretary from its founding until his death. He was a fellow of the International Institute of Arts and Letters, a founder and first president of the American Industrial Arts Association (1939–41), president of the Advisory Committee for Industrial Safety (1948), and a member of other professional organizations. He was decorated by the government of Belgium and received awards from several universities.

REFERENCES: *WW* (XXXI); *WWAE* (XXII); *WWW* (V); Thomas G. Latimer, "William Everett Warner: Innovative Pioneer of Industrial Arts" (Ed. D. diss., North Carolina State University, 1974).     *Delmar W. Olson*

**WARREN, John.** B. July 27, 1753, Roxbury, Massachusetts, to Joseph and Mary (Stevens) Warren. M. November 4, 1777, to Abigail Collins. Ch. seventeen, including John Collins Warren *(q.v.).* D. April 4, 1815, Boston, Massachusetts.

John Warren was graduated from Harvard University in 1771 and studied medicine under his brother Joseph Warren (1771–73). He began to practice medicine in Salem, Massachusetts, in 1773. He served in the Revolutionary War at the battles of Lexington and Bunker Hill, where his brother General Joseph Warren was killed. He served as a hospital surgeon with the Revolutionary army to the end of the war.

Warren presented a course in dissection to the Boston Medical Association in 1781 and another in 1782 that was opened to Harvard students. He was asked to submit a plan for a school of medicine at Harvard and in 1783 became the first, and for twenty-three years only, professor of anatomy and surgery in the newly established school. In 1810 the school was moved from Cambridge to Boston.

Warren was a leading surgeon of his time. He was a pioneer in abdominal operations and amputation at the shoulder joint. He established a hospital for innoculations during the smallpox epidemic of 1778. He was the author of *A View of the Mercurial Practice in Febrile Diseases* (1813) and of many medical articles. He was the first president of the Massachusetts State Medical Association (1804–15) and president of the Humane Society and Agricultural Society and was a member of the American Academy of Arts and Sciences and founded the Boston Medical Society. He received an honorary M.D. degree (1786) from Harvard University.

REFERENCES: *AC; DAB; NCAB* (10:288); *TC; WWW* (H); G. Marks and W. K. Beatty, *The Story of Medicine in America* (New York: Scribners, 1973); *World Who's Who of Science,* 1st ed. (Chicago: Marquis, 1968).

*Paul Woodworth*

**WARREN, John Collins.** B. August 1, 1778, Boston, Massachusetts, to John *(q.v.)* and Abigail (Collins) Warren. M. November 17, 1803, to Susan Powell. M. October 1843 to Anne Winthrop. Ch. six. D. May 4, 1856, Boston, Massachusetts.

John Collins Warren received his early education at the Public Latin School in Boston, Massachusetts. He was graduated from Harvard University in 1797 as valedictorian of his class and was founder and president of the Hasty Pudding Club. He spent a year studying French with a private tutor and then became an apprentice in medicine at his father's office. He went to Europe and studied medicine in London, England; Edinburgh, Scotland; and Paris, France (1799–1802).

Warren returned to Boston in December 1802. In partnership with his father, he assisted in the anatomical dissections in preparation of the elder Warren's lectures at the Harvard Medical School. In 1808 he assisted in preparing a *Pharmacopoeia* for the Massachusetts Medical Society. Warren joined the faculty at Harvard Medical School in 1809. Upon the death of his father in 1815, Warren became a professor of anatomy and surgery and served to his retirement in 1847. He was dean of the medical school (1816–19).

A founder and surgeon at the Massachusetts General Hospital (1821–53), Warren performed amputations before the use of anesthesia, removed cataracts, and was the first surgeon in the United States to operate for strangulated hernia. He was first to operate on a patient under ether anesthesia in a public demonstration at the Massachusetts General Hospital (1846).

Warren was interested in geology and paleontology and owned the most complete mastodon skeleton in his day (later located in the American Museum of Natural History, New York City). His specimen collection formed the basis of the Warren Museum at Harvard. He promoted physical education, made many speeches on the subject, and was a leader in building a gymnasium in the city of Boston.

The author of numerous memoirs, essays, and books, the most important of Warren's books were *Cases of Organic Diseases of the Heart* (1809), *A Comparative View of the Sensorial and Nervous Systems in Men and Animals* (1822), *Surgical Observations on Tumors with Cases and Operations* (1837), *Physical Education and the Preservation of Health* (1845), *Etherization; with Surgical Remarks* (1848), *Mastodon Giganteus of North America* (1852), and *The Preservation of Health* (1854). He was a founder of the *New England Journal of Medicine and Surgery* (1811) and editor of the *Monthly Anthology* (1803).

He was president of the Massachusetts Temperance Society (1827–56) and the Society of Natural History and was a fellow of the American Academy of Arts and Sciences. He received an honorary M.D. degree from Harvard University (1819).

REFERENCES: *AC; DAB; NCAB* (6:426); *TC; WWW* (H).

*Richard M. Coger*

**WARREN, Samuel Edward.** B. October 29, 1831, West Newton, Massachusetts, to Samuel and Anne Catherine (Reed) Warren. M. November 18, 1884, to Margaret Miller. Ch. none. D. July 8, 1909, Newton, Massachusetts.

Samuel Edward Warren received his early education in a private school, at the elementary school of the West Newton (Massachusetts) State Normal School (later, Framingham State College), at Phillips Academy in Andover, Massachusetts, and at Putnam Free School in Newburyport, Massachusetts. He was graduated from Rensselaer Polytechnic Institute in Troy, New York, with the C.E. degree (1851).

Warren taught at Rensselaer Polytechnic Institute from 1851 and was professor of descriptive geometry and stereotomy (1854–72). He moved to Newton, Massachusetts, in 1872 and was a professor of descriptive geometry at Massachusetts Institute of Technology in Cambridge and lecturer at the Massachusetts Normal Art School (later, Massachusetts College of Art) from 1872 to 1875, when he engaged in private instruction and writing.

Warren was the author of *General Problems from the Orthographic*

*Projections of Descriptive Geometry* (1860), *Elementary Projection Draw-ing* (1861), *Elementary Linear Perspective* (1863), *Drafting Instruments and Operations* (1864), *Plane Problems in Elementary Geometry* (1866), *General Problems in Shades and Shadows* (1867), *Elements of Machine Construction and Drawing* (two volumes, 1870), *Elementary Freehand Geometrical Drawing* (1873), *Problems, Theorems and Examples in De-scriptive Geometry* (1874), *Problems in Stone Cutting* (1875), *Elements of Descriptive Geometry, Shadows and Perspectives* (1877), *A Primary Geometry* (1877), *The Sunday Question* (1890), and *Descriptive Geometry* (1904).

Warren was a member of scientific and scholarly organizations, includ-ing the American Association for the Advancement of Science and the New England Historic Genealogical Society. Drawings by Warren and his stu-dents won awards at the Centennial Exposition in Philadelphia (1876) and the Paris (France) Exposition (1878).

REFERENCES: *AC; NCAB* (4:199); *TC; WWW* (I); *Boston Evening Transcript,* July 9, 1909; "Samuel Edward Warren," *The New England Historical and Genealogical Register* 64 (April 1910 supplement): 63-65.

D. *Richard Bowles*

**WARREN, William Fairfield.** B. March 13, 1833, Williamsburg, Mas-sachusetts, to Mather and Anne Miller (Fairfield) Warren. M. April 14, 1861, to Harriet Cornelia Merrick. Ch. four. D. December 6, 1929, Brook-line, Massachusetts.

William Fairfield Warren was graduated with the A.B. degree from Wesleyan University in Middletown, Connecticut (1853). He also studied at Andover (Massachusetts) Theological Seminary, in Germany at the universities of Berlin and Halle, and at Ohio Wesleyan University.

Warren established a classical school in Mobile, Alabama, (1853). Or-dained in the Methodist ministry in 1855, he served churches at Wilbraham and Boston Massachusetts (1858–60). He was professor of systematic theology at the Mission Institute in Bremen, Germany, subsequently the Martin Institute at Frankfurt (1861–66). He returned to Boston in 1866 and was a founder and first president of the Boston Theological Seminary, which became Boston University. Warren was named the first president of Boston University in 1873 and served until 1903. He was professor of comparative theology and philosophy of religion from 1873 until his death at the age of ninety-six in 1929. He was also dean of the school of theology (1903–11).

Warren was an editorial contributor to several American and foreign journals. He was the author of *The True Key to Ancient Cosmology* (1882), *Paradise Found–The Cradle of the Human Race at the North Pole* (1885), *The Quest for the Perfect Religion* (1886), *In the Footsteps of Arminius*

(1888), *The Story of Gottlieb* (1892), *The Religions of the World and World-Religion* (1900), *Beginnings of Hebrew Monotheism* (1902), *The Earliest Cosmologies* (1909), *The Perfect Life* (1911), and *The Universe as Pictured in Milton's Paradise Lost* (1915).

Warren supported education for women; Boston University was first in America to open all professional schools to women. In 1878 the first Ph.D. degree awarded to a woman in the United States was given to Helen McGill, the wife of Andrew D. White *(q.v.).* An original member of the corporation of Wellesley College, Warren was president of the Massachusetts Society for the University Education of Women. His support for the admission of girls to the Boston Latin School contributed to the establishment of Girls' Latin School. He was active in many religious and church organizations. He received honorary degrees from Wesleyan, Boston, and Ohio Wesleyan universities.

REFERENCES: *AC; DAB; NCAB* (11:177); *TC; WWW* (I); *Boston Evening Transcript,* February 9, 1924, December 7, 1929; George Gary Bush, *History of Higher Education in Massachusetts* (Washington, D.C.: Government Printing Office, 1891). *Lawrence S. Master*

**WARSHAW, Jacob.** B. December 22, 1878, London, England, to Lewis and Sophia (Burston) Warshaw. M. August 3, 1920, to Hazel Marie Williams. Ch. none. D. September 30, 1944, Columbia, Missouri.

In a career as a professor, writer, and educator, Jacob Warshaw achieved fame through his labors in numerous organizations and publications with particular interest in Hispanic and Latin American culture. Warshaw's family left England in 1881 and settled at Quincy, Massachusetts, where young Warshaw attended the public schools. He earned the B.A. degree (1900) from Harvard University, the A.M. degree (1902) from the University of North Carolina, and a certificate from the University of Paris. He received the Ph.D. degree (1912) from the University of Missouri.

Warshaw spent six years in Puerto Rico where he was a teacher (1903–04), district superintendent of schools (1904–07), and associate editor of the *Puerto Rican Review* (1908). In 1909 he joined the faculty of the University of Missouri where he stayed until 1919, when he was named professor of modern languages at the University of Nebraska. In 1924 he returned to Missouri. In 1925 he was named chairman of the department of Romance languages and in 1926 became chairman of the Spanish department, a position he held until his death.

Warshaw was the author of *Spanish-American Composition Book* (1917), *The New Latin America* (1922), *Elements of Spanish* (1924), *Cosas, Cuentos y Chistes* (1931), and *Spanish Science and Invention* (1933). He was a joint author of Corman's and Gerson's Puerto Rican edition of *Geography Primer* (1917). He edited and translated several works from Spanish into English. He received the Santander Ateneo Prize for one translation. Warshaw was associate editor of *Hispania* (1938–40). He was a member of the American Association of Teachers of Spanish (vice-president, 1920 and 1934–36) and other American foreign language, professional, and social organizations. He was decorated by the Spanish government.

REFERENCES: *LE* (II); *NCAB* (42:183); *WWW* (II).   *James M. Vosper*

WASHBURN, Margaret Floy. B. July 25, 1871, New York, New York, to Francis and Elizabeth Floy (Davis) Washburn. M. no. D. October 29, 1939, Poughkeepsie, New York.

Margaret Floy Washburn attended Ulster Academy in Kingston, New York. She went to Vassar College in Poughkeepsie, New York, at the age of sixteen and received the A.B. (1891) and M.A. (1893) degrees. She was awarded the Ph.D. degree (1894) from Cornell University in Ithaca, New York, where she studied under E. B. Titchener *(q.v.).* She also studied with James McKeen Cattell *(q.v.)* for one year at Columbia University.

Washburn was professor of philosophy, psychology, and ethics at Wells College in Aurora, New York (1894-1900), and returned to Cornell as a warden of Sage College, a women's dormitory, and as a lecturer in psychology (1900–02). She was an assistant professor of psychology at the University of Cincinnati (1902–03) and joined the faculty of Vassar College in 1903 where she taught until her retirement in 1937. She first taught philosophy (1903–08) and was the first professor of psychology in 1908; she headed the department of psychology when it was established in 1912.

Washburn carried on considerable research and experimentation and was an extensive writer. Her complete bibliography consists of about two hundred entries. Seventy articles written with joint authorship were published from studies from the psychological laboratory of Vassar College. Washburn organized problems and the design of psychological research, which was then conducted by one or more advanced students; Washburn wrote the articles reporting on the research. Her most important publication was *The Animal Mind* (1908). She also wrote *Movement and Mental Imagery* (1916) and translated *Ethical Systems* (1901) and *Principles of Morality* (1901) by Wilhelm Wundt. She was cooperating editor (1903–25) and joint editor (1925–39) of the *American Journal of Psychology,* cooperating editor of the *Psychological Bulletin* (1909–30), associate editor of the *Journal of Comparative Psychology* (1921–35), advisory editor of the *Psychological Review* (1916–30), a member of the editorial board of the *Journal of American Behavior* (1911–17), and on the advisory board of the *Dictionary of Psychology* (1934).

In 1927 the *American Journal of Psychology* issued the Washburn com-

memorative volume containing articles by thirty-one psychologists in recognition of her thirty-three years of service in psychology. In 1931 she was
the second woman to be elected a member of the National Academy of
Sciences. Washburn was a member of the American Psychological Association (president, 1921), the Eastern Psychological Association (president, 1931), and other professional associations. She was awarded an
honorary degree by Wittenberg College in 1927.

She left her estate to Vassar College; it was combined with endowments
to found the Margaret Floy Washburn Fund for Promising Students in
Psychology.

REFERENCES: *DAB* (supp. 2); *LE* (I); *NAW; NCAB* (30:248); *WWW* (I);
*NYT,* October 30, 1939, p. 17; K. M. Dallenbach, ed., "Margaret Floy
Washburn," *The American Journal of Psychology* 53 (January 1940): 1-20;
C. Murchison *(q v ), A History of Psychology in Autobiography* (Worces-
ter, Mass.: Clark University Press, 1932), vol. 3, pp. 333-58.

*Betty S. Harper*

**WASHBURNE, Carleton Wolsey.** B. December 2, 1889, Chicago, Illinois,
to George Foote and Marion Guyon (Foster) Washburne. M. September
15, 1912, to Heluiz Bigelow Chandler. Ch. three. D. November 17, 1968,
Okemos, Michigan.

Carleton Washburne's mother was a child study lecturer with an interest
in education and was a personal friend of John Dewey *(q.v.)* and Francis
Parker *(q.v.).* Washburne attended schools directed by Dewey and Parker,
the University of Chicago (1908–10), and Hahnemann Medical School in
Chicago, Illinois (1910–11). He received the A.B. degree (1912) from
Stanford (California) University and the Ed.D. degree (1918) from the
University of California.

Washburne taught in a rural school near El Monte, California (1912–13),
and in Tulare, California (1913–14). He was head of the department of
science at San Francisco State Teachers College (later, State University)
from 1914 to 1919 under Frederic Burk *(q.v.).* He was superintendent of
schools at Winnetka, Illinois, where he gained a national reputation as an
educational innovator. Winnetka was the first school system to make
extensive use of programed instruction that was developed by the Winnetka staff during special in-service sessions or workshops. Individualized
teaching of reading and more accurate ability grading of children's books
were instituted. Washburne was influential in introducing early childhood
education for three- and four-year olds in public schools (1927), establishing the middle school in the 1920s, chartering the Winnetka Graduate
Teachers College, which led to M.A. degree programs in large universities,
and providing elementary school guidance programs in the 1930s that
included school psychologists, psychiatrists, and psychometrists on

school staffs. Educational materials were published by the local Winnetka Education Press. Washburne was chairman of the Winnetka Summer School for Teachers (1919–45) and the Winnetka Graduate Teachers College (1932–45).

Washburne worked in Italy with the United States Army, the United States Department of State, and the United Nations Educational, Scientific, and Cultural Organization in reorganizing the Italian public schools after World War II (1943–49). He was director of the graduate division and the teacher education program at Brooklyn College of the City University of New York (1949–60). He served as Distinguished Professor of Education at Michigan State University (1961–67).

A prolific writer, Washburne was the author of *New Schools in the Old World* (1926), *Results of Practical Experiments in Fitting Schools to Individuals* (with others, 1926), *Adjusting the School to the Child* (1932), *A Living Philosophy of Education* (1940), *What Is Progressive Education?* (1952), *The History and Significance of an Educational Experiment* (1963), and *Window to Understanding* (1968).

Washburne was active in professional organizations; he served as president of the International New Education Fellowship (1947–56) and the Progressive Education Association (1939–43), vice-president of the American Educational Research Association (1928), and yearbook chairman of the National Society for the Study of Education (1924 and 1937–39). He was decorated by the governments of Italy, France, and Cambodia and received an honorary degree from the University of Messina, Italy (1944).

REFERENCES: *LE* (III); *NYT,* November 28, 1968, p. 37; *WW* (XXXI); *WWAE* (VIII); Robert J. Havighurst *(q.v.),* ed., *Leaders in American Education* (Chicago: University of Chicago Press, 1971); Harold G. Shane, "Carleton W. Washburne: In Respectful Retrospect," *Phi Delta Kappan* 50 (February 1969): 320-21; George H. Thompson, "The Winnetka Superintendency: A Study in Educational Statemanship" (Ph.D. diss., Michigan State University, 1970); "Washburne of Winnetka," *Newsweek* 22 (November 29, 1943): 80-82.                    *Larry P. Donahue*

**WASHINGTON, Booker Taliaferro.** B. April 5, 1856, Hale's Ford, Franklin County, Virginia, to father n.a. and Jane Ferguson. M. 1882 to Fannie N. Smith. M. 1885 to Olivia A. Davidson. M. October 12, 1893, to Margaret James Murray. Ch. three. D. November 14, 1915, Tuskegee, Alabama.

Born in Virginia, Booker T. Washington moved with his mother and two other children to Malden, West Virginia. To help support his family, he began working at the age of nine in a salt furnace and later in a coal mine. Although it was impossible for him to attend school regularly, he was an avid reader and was largely self-educated. He enrolled at the Hampton

(Virginia) Normal and Agricultural Institute, (later, Hampton Institute). Working as a janitor to pay his expenses, Washington was graduated in 1875. He returned to Malden and taught children in a day school and adults in the evenings for two years. He studied at Wayland Seminary in Washington, D.C. (1878–79), before accepting a position to work with American Indians at Hampton Institute.

In 1881 he was appointed head of the recently established Tuskegee Normal and Industrial Institute in Alabama. Washington took charge of two buildings, without equipment or money, and built an institution that had over one hundred buildings, a faculty of 200 teachers, and an enrollment of over 1,500 students by 1915. For thirty-four years he taught, lectured, and traveled securing public support and financial assistance for Tuskegee. A most notable event was a speech delivered at the Cotton States and International Exposition at Atlanta, Georgia, on September 18, 1893, which resulted in the recognition of Washington as a leader of American Negroes. In educational circles, Washington's philosophy was in contrast with that of W. E. B. Du Bois (q.v.) and some other black intellectuals. Washington advocated industrial education, land ownership, productive farm management, desirable work habits, and high ethical and moral character. His ideas aroused considerable discussion and criticism from his intellectual peers.

Washington was the author of several books, including his autobiography, *Up from Slavery* (1901), which was an account of his struggles to overcome poverty and receive an education. A second autobiographical work, *My Larger Education,* was published in 1911. He also wrote *The Future of the American Negro* (1899) and *Sowing and Reaping* (1900), which reflected his basic philosophy, and *Character Building* (1902), *Working with the Hands* (1904), *Putting the Most into Life* (1906), *Frederick Douglass* (1907), *The Negro in Business* (1907), *The Story of the Negro* (1909), and *The Man Farthest Down* (with R. E. Park, 1912). He edited *Tuskegee and Its People* (1905). He received honorary degrees from Harvard University and Dartmouth College.

REFERENCES: *AC; DAB; EB; NCAB* (7:363); *TC; WWW* (1); *Afro-American Encyclopedia* (North Miami, Fla.: Educational Book Publishers, 1974), 9: 2746-61; *NYT,* November 15, 1915, p. 1; Louis R. Harlan, ed., *The Booker T. Washington Papers* (Urbana: University of Illinois Press, 1972); Booker T. Washington, *Up from Slavery* (New York: Doubleday & Co., 1913).                                    *Octavia B. Knight*

**WATERS, Henry Jackson.** B. November 23, 1865, Center, Missouri, to George Washington and Lavinia Jane (Smith) Waters. M. June 3, 1897, to Margaret Ward. Ch. one. D. October 26, 1925, Kansas City, Missouri.

Henry Jackson Waters' father was a farmer, author, lecturer, and editor of the St. Louis *Journal of Agriculture*. Waters was graduated from the University of Missouri with the B.S. degree in agriculture (1886). As a graduate student, he served as assistant secretary of the Missouri State Board of Agriculture (1886–88). He studied at the universities of Leipzig, Germany, and Zurich, Switzerland (1904–05).

Waters was professor of agriculture at Pennsylvania State College in 1892 and returned to the University of Missouri as professor of agriculture, dean of the college of agriculture, and director of the Agriculture Experiment Station (1895–1909). He was a lecturer on animal nutrition at the graduate school of agriculture at Ohio State University in 1902.

In 1909 Waters became president of Kansas State Agricultural College (later, Kansas State University) in Manhattan. The college grew and prospered under his leadership. He introduced engineering into the curriculum. He resigned in 1917 and became managing editor of the *Kansas City* (Missouri) *Weekly Star* until his death in 1925.

Waters conducted important studies in agriculture, including the effect of undernutrition on the growth of animals, and conducted research on the feeding of beef and swine.

Waters was the author of *Essentials of Agriculture* (1915), *Development of the Philippine Islands* (1915), *Laboratory Manual in Vocational Agriculture* (with J. D. Elliff, 1918), *Elementary Agriculture* (1923), *Essentials of the New Agriculture* (1924), and *Animal Husbandry* (with Franklin George King, 1925).

He was a commissioner for the United States and Philippine governments in 1914 reporting on educational and agricultural developments in the Philippines. He served on the Kansas state board of education (1909), the school book committee (1913–18), and the council of defense (1917–18). He was a member of the International Institute of Agriculture in Rome, Italy. He was president of the Kansas State Teachers' Association, the International Dry Farming Congress (1913–14), and the American Society for Promotion of Agricultural Science (1913–15). He was awarded honorary degrees by the New Hampshire State Agricultural College and the University of Missouri.

REFERENCES:*NCAB* (24:23); *WWW* (I); *NYT,* October 27, 1925, p. 23.

*S. E. Russell*

**WATSON, Fletcher Guard.** B. April 27, 1912, Baltimore, Maryland, to Fletcher Guard and Mabel Read (Jones) Watson. M. December 27, 1935, to Alice V. Hodson. Ch. four.

Fletcher Guard Watson received the A.B. degree (1933) from Pomona College in Claremont, California, and the A.M. (1935) and Ph.D. (1938) degrees from Harvard University.

Watson was an instructor in astronomy at Harvard University (1936–38) and research associate and executive secretary of the Harvard Observatory (1938–41). He served with the National Defense Corporation Radiation Laboratory at the Massachusetts Institute of Technology (1942–43) and was Loran officer with the United States Navy Hydrographic Office in Washington, D.C. (1943–46). He joined the faculty of the Harvard Graduate School of Education in 1946, becoming Henry Lee Shattuck Professor of Education in 1966. He was also James B. Conant Lecturer in Education (1954–57)). Watson was closely associated with James Bryant Conant's *(q.v.)* efforts to teach science to nonscientists. He gained wide recognition for his work in science education.

Watson was the author of *Between the Planets* (1955), *A Book of Methods for Teaching Science in the Secondary Schools* (1958), *Teaching Secondary School Teachers to Teach Science* (1966), *A Decade in Retrospect* (1968), *The Doctorate Program in Science Education* (1968), *Education Implications of Evaluation in a National Curriculum Project* (1969), and *Four-Year Follow-Up on Project Physics* (1973).

Active in professional associations, Watson was on the steering committees of the Biological Science Curriculum Study and Elementary Science Study and a committee member of the educational advisory group of the National Aeronautics and Space Administration. He was codirector of Harvard Project Physics (1964). He was a Ford Foundation consultant to Nigeria (1967) and a United Nations Educational, Social, and Cultural Organization consultant to Thailand (1972–73).

REFERENCES: *CA* (5–8); *LE* (V); *WW* (XXXVI); *WWAE* (XVI); *American Men and Women in Science,* 13th ed. (New York: R. R. Bowker Co., 1976).                                                      *Frances H. Nelson*

**WATSON, James Madison.** B. February 8, 1827, Onondaga Hill, New York, to Simeon and Sally Ann (Wilber) Watson. M. March 31, 1871, to Emma Hopper. Ch. one. D. September 29, 1900, Elizabeth, New Jersey.

James Madison Watson received his early education at the Onondaga Hill (New York) village school and from his father. In 1839 the family moved to Oswego County, New York. He attended Mexico (New York) Academy and Falley Seminary in Fulton, New York.

Watson worked on the family farm, sold books, and began teaching at the age of sixteen. He was a teacher in district schools, principal at the Howlett Hill Union School in Oswego, New York (1848–51), and an assistant teacher at the Chittenango (New York) Seminary (1851–52). He studied law in Syracuse and Albany, New York (1852–53), and was admitted to the bar in 1853.

Watson worked for A. S. Barnes and Company, publishers in New York City, to 1871. With Richard G. Parker *(q.v.)* he prepared the National Series of Readers (seven volumes, 1857–66). He also wrote *National*

*School Primer* (1855), *Handbook of Gymnastics* (1863), *Handbook of Calisthenics* (1863), Watson's Independent Readers (ten volumes, 1868–75), *Independent Child's Speller* (1874), *Independent Primary Reader* (1875), *Complete Speller* (1878), *Graphic Speller* (1884), *Pantography of My Life* (two volumes, n.d.), *Journal of My Travels in the U.S.* (n.d.), and many other works issued anonymously. He was editor of *Red Ribbon Record* (1885–90), a religious journal.

He was a member of the New Jersey Sanitation Association (president, 1882, and corresponding secretary, 1882–97). He was president of the Elizabeth (New Jersey) board of education (1881–82) and the Temperance Reform and Order Club.

REFERENCES: *AC; DAB; NCAB* (10: 194); *NYT,* September 30, 1900, p. 7; *WWW* (I).                                                    *James R. Layton*
                                                                *Mary Paula Phillips*


**WATSON, John Broadus.** B. January 9, 1878, near Greenville, South Carolina, to Pickins Butler and Emma K. (Roe) Watson. M. October 1, 1904, to Mary Ickes. M. December 31, 1920, to Rosalie Raynor. Ch. four. D. September 25, 1958, Woodbury, Connecticut.

John B. Watson attended the Greenville (South Carolina) public schools and was graduated with the A.M. degree (1900) from Furman University in Greenville. He studied psychology at the University of Chicago (1900–03) where he received the Ph.D. degree (1903).

Watson remained at Chicago as an assistant (1903–04) and instructor (1904–08) in experimental psychology. He became a professor of experimental and comparative psychology and director of the psychological laboratory at Johns Hopkins University in Baltimore, Maryland, in 1908. In 1920 he became a consulting psychologist and executive for advertising agencies in New York City and continued until his retirement in 1945. He also lectured at the New School for Social Research in New York City (1922–26). Watson was credited with founding the behaviorist school of psychology that emphasized the importance of the environment and the adaptability of humans and advocated limiting psychology to measurable behavior.

Watson was the author of *Animal Education* (1903), *Behavior* (1914), *Psychology from the Standpoint of a Behaviorist* (1914), *Homing and Related Activities of Birds* (1915), *Suggestions of Modern Science Concerning Education* (1917), *Behaviorism* (1925), *The Psychological Care of Infant and Child* (1928), and *The Ways of Behaviorism* (1928). He was the founder and editor of *Psychological Review* (1915–27), editor of the *Journal of Experimental Psychology* (1915–27), and joint editor of the *Journal of Animal Behavior* (1908–15).

Watson was a veteran of World War I. He was a fellow of the American

Academy of Arts and Sciences and president of the American Psychological Association (1915), which awarded him a citation in 1957. He received
an honorary degree from Furman University in 1919.

REFERENCES: *CB* (October 1942 and December 1958); *EB; NCAB*
(A:86, 48:578); *NYT*, September 26, 1958, p. 27; *WWAE* (VIII); *WWW*
(III); G. Bergmann, "The Contributions of John B. Watson," *Psychologi-
cal Review* 63 (July 1956): 265-76; B. F. Skinner (*q.v.*), "John Broadus
Watson, Behaviorist," *Science* 129 (January 23, 1959): 197-98; Robert I.
Watson, *The Great Psychologists* (Philadelphia: J. B. Lippincott Co.,
1971); R. S. Woodworth (*q.v.*), "John Broadus Watson: 1878-1958,"
*American Journal of Psychology* 72 (June 1959): 301-10.

*Michael L. Davis*

**WATTEVILLE, Henrietta Benigna Justina von Zinzendorf.** B. December
28, 1725, Berthelsdorf, Saxony, to Nicolaus Ludwig and Erdmuthe
Dorothea (von Reuss) von Zinzendorf. M. 1746 to Johann von (de) Watteville. Ch. four. D. May 11, 1789, Berthelsdorf, Saxony.

Benigna Watteville was the daughter of the founder of the Renewed
Moravian church. She accompanied her father to America in 1741 on a tour
of Moravian communities, most of which were located in Pennsylvania.
She opened a girls' boarding school in Germantown, Pennsylvania, in 1742;
the school is considered to be the first boarding school in the colonies. With
two assistants she taught reading, writing, household arts, and religion to
an enrollment of about twenty-five girls. The school moved to Bethlehem,
Pennsylvania, shortly after.

Returning to Europe in 1742 she married her father's secretary who was
consecrated a bishop in 1747. In 1748 the couple spent a year in America
inspecting church missions. Watteville became associated with the same
girls' school, which had been moved to Nazareth, Pennsylvania, in 1745.
The school was relocated in Bethlehem, consolidated with other Moravian
schools, and reopened in 1749 as the Seminary for Young Ladies.

Returning to Europe, the Wattevilles sailed for the colonies in 1783, were
shipwrecked in the West Indies, reached Bethlehem in 1784, and served
there to 1787. Benigna Watteville again became active in reorganizing the
school, which was opened to non-Moravians in 1785, incorporated as the
Moravian Seminary for Young Ladies (1863), became Moravian Seminary
and College for Women (1913), and part of the coeducational Moravian
College in 1953.

REFERENCES: *NAW;* J. Taylor Hamilton, *A History of the Church
Known as the Moravian Church* (Bethlehem, Pa.: Times Publishing Co.,
1900); Joseph M. Levering, *A History of Bethlehem, Pa., 1741-1892*
(Bethlehem, Pa.: Times Publishing Co., 1903); William C. Reichel, ed.,
*Memorials of the Moravian Church* (Philadelphia: J. B. Lippincott Co.,
1870). *M. Jane Dowd*

**WAYLAND, Francis.** B. March 11, 1796, New York, New York, to Francis and Sarah (Moore) Wayland. M. November 21, 1825, to Lucy Lane Lincoln. M. August 1, 1838, to Hepsy S. (Howard) Sage. Ch. three, including Francis Wayland, dean of Yale Law School. D. September 30, 1865, Providence, Rhode Island.

Francis Wayland was graduated from Union College in Schenectady, New York, with the A.B. (1813) and A.M. (1816) degrees. He studied medicine in Troy, New York, and attended medical lectures in New York City (1814–15). He went to Andover (Massachusetts) Theological Seminary (1816–17), where he studied under Moses Stuart.

Financially unable to continue his theological studies, he returned to Union College in 1817 as a tutor. In 1821 he became pastor of the First Baptist Church in Boston, where he developed a reputation as a preacher. One of his sermons, "The Moral Dignity of the Missionary Enterprise" (1823), was published and exerted an influence on religious thought in America and Europe.

He returned to Union College as professor of mathematics and natural philosophy (1826–27). In 1827 he became president of Brown University in Providence, Rhode Island, an office he held until 1855. At Brown he held that the classroom was not to be dependent on textbooks; the "analytic method" was substituted as a study technique. Courses in modern languages, history, economics, and the natural sciences were added. Nonresident professors were dismissed and a permanent and enlarged faculty was employed. The library was endowed and facilities for study were improved.

Wayland developed plans for organization of Providence, Rhode Island, schools and for a system of free public schools for the state (1828). He suggested a plan for a national university to be financed by the Smithsonian bequest (1838). He founded a free library in Wayland, Massachusetts, which resulted in legislation authorizing towns to levy taxes to support public libraries.

He was the author of many books, including *Elements of Moral Science* (1835), *Elements of Political Economy* (1837), *The Limitations of Human Responsibility* (1838), *Thoughts on the Present Collegiate System in the United States* (1842), *Domestic Slavery Considered as a Scriptural Institution* (1845), *Elements of Intellectual Philosophy* (1854), *Sermons to the Churches* (1858), and *Letters on the Ministry of the Gospel* (1863).

Wayland was the first president of the American Institute of Instruction (1830) and a member of the American Philosophical Society. He was a trustee of Butler Hospital and a member of the state prison board, where he proposed a program of prison reform. He received honorary degrees from Brown and Harvard universities and Union College.

REFERENCES: *AC; DAB; EB; NCAB* (8:22); *NYT* October 2, 1865, p. 5; *TC; WWW* (H).                                        *Albert S. Weston*

**WAYLAND, John Walter.** B. December 8, 1872, Shenandoah County, Virginia, to John Wesley and Anna (Kagey) Wayland. M. June 8, 1898, to Mattie V. Fry. Ch. two. D. January 10, 1962, Harrisonburg, Virginia.

John W. Wayland grew up on a farm and passed the teacher's examination at the age of eighteen. He attended Bridgewater (Virginia) College from which he received the A.B. degree (1899). He received the Ph.D. degree in history (1907) from the University of Virginia.

Wayland was a teacher in Shenandoah County (Virginia) public schools and the Jefferson School for Boys in Charlottesville, Virginia (1890–93). He taught history at Bridgewater College (1896–1906) and the University of Virginia (1906–09). In 1909 he joined the faculty of the newly opened State Normal School (later, Madison College) at Harrisonburg, Virginia. He served as professor and head of the history department until his retirement in 1931.

Wayland was the author of over thirty books, twenty pamphlets, and many articles. *A History of Virginia for Boys and Girls* (1920) was adopted as the official state text for the elementary grades. He also wrote *Paul, The Herald of the Cross* (1901), *The Twelve Apostles* (1905), *The German Element of the Shenandoah Valley of Virginia* (1907), *The Political Opinions of Thomas Jefferson* (1907), *Sidney Lanier at Rockingham Springs* (1912), *How to Teach American History* (1914), *History Stories for Primary Grades* (1919), *Christ as a Teacher* (1919), *History Helps* (1921), *Home and Nature Land* (with W. H. Ruebush, 1922), *Guide to the Shenandoah Valley* (1923), *Ethics and Citizenship* (1923), *Art Folio of the Shenandoah Valley* (1927), *Rambles in Europe* (1927), *Chapters in Church History* (1930), *Virginia Valley Records* (1930), *The Pathfinder of the Seas* (1930), *World History* (with others, 1932), *Colonel Samuel Washington* (1938), *Historic Homes of Northern Virginia* (1934), and *Stonewall Jackson's Way* (1940), and he edited several additional books.

Wayland was a founder of the Rockingham Historical Society and the Shenandoah Valley Civil War Roundtable. He was a member of many history and professional associations. He received an honorary degree from Bridgewater College (1936).

REFERENCES: *LE* (I); *NCAB* (A:394); *WWAE* (XVI); *Daily News Record* (Harrisonburg, Virginia), January 11, 1962; Raymond C. Dingledine, Jr., *Madison College, The First Fifty Years, 1908–1958* (Harrisonburg, Va.: Madison College, 1959). *Harold D. Lehman*

**WEBB, William Robert.** B. November 11, 1842, near Mount Tirzah, North Carolina, to Alexander Smith and Cornelia Adeline (Sanford) Webb. M. April 23, 1873, to Emma Clary. Ch. eight. D. December 19, 1926, Bellbuckle, Tennessee.

William Robert Webb attended the Bingham School in Oaks, North Carolina, and enrolled at the University of North Carolina in 1860. He enlisted in the Confederate army (1862), was wounded at the battle of Malverne Hill (Virginia), and returned to the university while recovering from his wounds. He returned to active military service in 1864 and was captured on April 3, 1865, three days before the surrender at Appomattox. On his release from prison in July 1865 he returned to North Carolina, where he was graduated by examination, receiving the A.B. (1868) and A.M. (1869) degrees.

Webb was an assistant teacher at Horner School in Oxford, North Carolina (1866–70). With his brother John Maurice Webb, he opened the Webb School at Culeoka, Tennessee. The school was moved to Bellbuckle, Tennessee, in 1886, and Webb continued as principal to 1908. The school became an outstanding private school in the South, called the first preparatory school west of the Allegheny Mountains.

He was active in the Methodist church as a lay member of the delegate assemblies of 1874 and 1902. He was a delegate to the 1896 convention of the Gold Democrats and served out the unexpired term as United States senator in 1913 after the death of Robert L. Taylor. Active in professional associations, he was a member of the Committee of Twelve on Latin in preparation for college of the National Education Association. He was active in the temperance movement and was a member of the national board of trustees of the Anti-Saloon League of America (1913–26).

REFERENCES: *DAB; NCAB* (37:199); *NYT,* December 20, 1926, p. 21; *WWW* (I).                                                              *John F. Ohles*

**WEBSTER, Horace.** B. September 21, 1794, Hartford, Vermont, to Laban and Lucy (Wright) Webster. M. to Sarah Maria Fowler. Ch. three. D. July 12, 1871, Geneva, New York.

Horace Webster was graduated from the United States Military Academy at West Point, New York, in 1818. He was assistant professor of mathematics at West Point (1818–25).

Webster resigned his commission in the army in 1825 and was professor of mathematics and natural philosophy at Geneva (New York) College (later, Hobart College) from 1825 to 1848. He was the first principal of the Free Academy in New York City, which had been authorized by the state legislature in 1847. He was principal of the academy to 1869. In 1866 the legislature authorized the institution to grant degrees as the College of the City of New York (CCNY), and Webster served as first president of the college from 1866 to his retirement to Geneva, New York, in 1869. He also served as professor of moral and intellectual philosophy (1851–52) and of moral, intellectual, and political philosophy (1852–69). He was primarily responsible for establishing a course of study and a system of discipline comparable to that at West Point. The college grew in size and recognition under Webster.

A close friend of Alden Partridge *(q.v.),* Webster was director (1851–70) and vice-president (1859–67) of Norwich University. He was awarded honorary degrees by the College of New Jersey (1824), Kenyon (1842), and Columbia (1849) colleges, and the University of Pennsylvania (1850).

REFERENCES: *AC; NCAB* (19:320); *NYT,* July 14, 1871, p. 2; *TC.*

*John F. Ohles*

**WEBSTER, Noah.** B. October 16, 1758, West Hartford, Connecticut, to Noah and Mercy (Steele) Webster. M. October 26, 1789, to Rebecca Greenleaf. Ch. eight. D. May 28, 1843, New Haven, Connecticut.

Noah Webster enrolled in Yale College at the age of sixteen, interrupted his studies to serve in the Revolutionary army under his father, and was graduated in 1778. He studied law and was admitted to the bar in 1781. In 1782 Webster taught school in Goshen, New York, where he wrote an elementary spelling book and the first of three parts of *A Grammatical Institute of the English Language. Grammatical Institute* was completed with the publication of a grammar in 1784 and a reader in 1785. The blue-backed speller was printed long after Webster's death, and eventually more than seventy million copies were sold. His other works in the field of study of English include *Dissertations on the English Language* (1789), from a series of lectures that had been delivered in 1785, and *A Philosophical and Practical Grammar of the English Language* (1807).

Webster wrote *Sketches of American Policy* (1785), which has been described as the first discussion of the principles of the American Constitution. Although a Philadelphia printer, John McCulloch, is credited with writing the first American history schoolbook, Webster was the author of a four-volume *Elements of Useful Knowledge* (1802–12), of which the first two volumes were a detailed history of the United States, the third volume a history of the world, and the last a biology text. In 1832 Webster wrote *History of the United States.*

Webster wrote frequently on the events of the day and founded in 1793 a New York City daily paper, the *American Minerva* (later, *Commercial Advertiser),* and the *Herald,* a semiweekly. To protect his copyright interests, particularly with his popular spelling book, he traveled extensively and campaigned successfully for the passage of state copyright laws.

Webster's most important contribution was as a lexicographer; his *Compendious Dictionary of the English Language* (1806) and the two-volume dictionary have remained the standard work in the United States.

In 1812 Webster moved to Amherst, Massachusetts, where he was a founder of Amherst College and a president of its board of trustees. He served in the Massachusetts legislature (he had previously done so in the Connecticut legislature). He returned to New Haven, Connecticut, in 1822 where he spent the rest of his life.

REFERENCES: *A C; DAB; EB; NCAB* (2:394); *TC; WWW* (H); Horace E. Scudder, *Noah Webster* (New York: Houghton Mifflin Co., c. 1881); Ervin C. Shoemaker, *Noah Webster, Pioneer of Learning* (New York: Columbia University Press, 1936); Harry Redcay Warfel, *Noah Webster, Schoolmaster to America* (New York: Macmillan, 1936).          *John F. Ohles*

**WEED, Ella.** B. January 27, 1853, Newburgh, New York, to Jonathan Noyes and Elizabeth Merritt (Goodsell) Weed. M. no. D. January 10, 1894, New York, New York.

Ella Weed grew up in Newburgh, New York, and attended Miss Mackay's School. She was graduated from Vassar College in Poughkeepsie, New York, in 1873. At Vassar she contributed to *Vassar Miscellany*, which gained a reputation as a quality college periodical.

In 1875 Weed accepted a teaching position at a girls' school in Springfield, Ohio. She returned to New York in 1882 as a teacher at Miss Mackay's School and became head of the day school at the Anne Brown School in New York City in 1884.

Successful in operating the day school, Weed was contacted by Annie Nathan Meyer for assistance in establishing an annex for women students at Columbia University. Weed was given the major credit for marshaling the support of influential New Yorkers to persuade the board of trustees of Columbia University to establish Barnard College in 1889. Weed served on the first board of trustees and assumed the duties of a dean. She served as college secretary and was involved with public relations, fund raising, and supervision of the physical plant. Rejecting the finishing school character of women's higher education, she advocated an education for women equal in demand to that for men.

Weed was the author of *A Foolish Virgin* (1883) and *Pearls Strung by Ella Weed* (1898). She served as a trustee of Barnard College, the Associate Alumnae of Vassar College, the Vassar Students' Aid Society, and the Associated Collegiate Alumnae.

REFERENCES: *NAW; NYT*, January 11, 1894, p. 8; "Friend of Education," *Outlook* 49 (January 27, 1894); 177.          *Betty S. Harper*


**WEEKS, Ila Delbert.** B. September 5, 1901, Scotia, Nebraska, to Fred C. and Blanche Laura (Pope) Weeks. M. June 11, 1926, to Virginia Shawkey. Ch. two.

Ila Delbert Weeks was graduated with the A.B. degree (1924) from Kearney (Nebraska) State Teachers College (later, State College) and received the M.A. degree (1925) from the University of Iowa. He studied at the University of Minnesota (1929–30).

Weeks was superintendent of schools at Riverdale, Nebraska (1921–23). He was professor of rural education at Northern State Teachers College (later, State College) in Aberdeen, South Dakota (1925–33), and state superintendent of public instruction for South Dakota (1933–35). In 1935 he became president of the University of South Dakota and served in that capacity to 1966. He was professor of education (1966–72).

Weeks contributed articles to numerous professional journals. He was president of the South Dakota Educational Association (1956–57), the South Dakota Association of Universities, and the National Association of State Universities (1950), trustee of Educational TV, Incorporated, and a board member of the Crippled Children's Hospital and School at Sioux Falls, the South Dakota Tuberculosis and Health Association (president), and the Wesley Foundation of Vermillion (president). He was state chairman of the Committee on Education Beyond the High School. He received an honorary degree from Dakota Wesleyan University.

REFERENCES: *LE* (III); *NCAB* (F:475); *WW* (XXXIX); *WWAE* (XVI); *Who's Who in the Midwest,* 10th ed. (Chicago: Marquis, 1967).

*Lawrence S. Master*

**WEEKS, Thomas Edwin.** B. May 5, 1853, Massillon, Ohio, to n.a. M. n.a. D. March 1, 1938, La Crosse, Wisconsin.

Thomas Edwin Weeks was educated in Mansfield (Ohio) public schools. He studied dentistry with W. F. Semple in Mount Vernon, Ohio (1873–76).

Weeks practiced dentistry in Council Bluffs, Iowa (1876–80), and moved to Minneapolis, Minnesota, in 1880, where he was a member of Bowman, Weeks and Jenison (1881–91). He established a private practice in 1891. In 1883 he organized the dental faculty of the Minnesota College Hospital and served on the faculty until it became the University of Minnesota school of dentistry in 1888. He was professor of operative dentistry (1888–91) and professor of operative dentistry and dental anatomy (1891–1901). He was dean of the school (1895–97) and taught at the Philadelphia (Pennsylvania) College of Dentistry (1907–12). He practiced dentistry in Argentina from 1912 to his retirement in 1922.

Weeks was credited with writing the first textbook of dental technic, *Weeks' Manual of Operative Technics* (1894). He was the first president of the Minnesota State Dental Association and the Minneapolis Dental Society and was a founder and vice-president of the National School of Dental Technics. He was an associate editor of *Dental Review.*

REFERENCES: *NCAB* (6:117); *Minnesota Daily,* March 4, 1938; E. B. Johnson, *Dictionary of the University of Minnesota* (Minneapolis: The University, 1908), pp. 205–06. *John F. Ohles*

**WEIGLE, Luther Allan.** B. September 11, 1880, Littlestown, Pennsylvania, to Elias Daniel and Hannah (Bream) Weigle. M. June 15, 1909, to Clara Rosetta Boxrud. Ch. four. D. September 2, 1976, New Haven, Connecticut.

Luther Allan Weigle received the B.A. (1900) and M.A. (1903) degrees from Gettysburg (Pennsylvania) College and attended the Lutheran Theological Seminary in Gettysburg (1900–02) and Yale University (1902–05); he received the Ph.D. degree (1905) from Yale. He was ordained to the Lutheran ministry in 1903 and transferred to the Congregational church in 1916.

Weigle was pastor of a church in Bridgeport, Connecticut (1903–04), and an assistant in psychology at Yale (1904–05). He joined the faculty of Carleton College in Northfield, Minnesota, as professor of philosophy (1905–16) and was dean of the college (1910–15). He became Horace Bushnell Professor of Christian Nurture at Yale University (1916–24), Sterling Professor of Religious Education (1924–49), and dean of the Yale Divinity School (1928–49). Under Weigle the Yale Divinity School experienced a period of growth and developed into a major theological seminary. Selective admission requirements were instituted, enrollment was limited, and the curriculum was revised.

Weigle was the author of *The Pupil and the Teacher* (1911), *Talks to Sunday School Teachers* (1920), *Training the Devotional Life* (with H. H. Tweedy, 1919), *Training Children in the Christian Family* (1921), *We Are Able* (1937), *Jesus and the Educational Method* (1939), *The Living Word* (1959), *A Bible Word Book* (with Ronald Bridges, 1959), *The New Testament Octapla* (1961), and *The Genesis Octapla* (1965), and he contributed to *American Idealism* (volume 10 in the Pageant of America set, 1928), *Religious Education* (with J. H. Oldham, volume 2 of Jerusalem Reports, 1928), and the autobiographical *The Religious Education of a Protestant* (volume 2 of Contemporary American Theology, 1939). In 1929 he was named chairman of a committee of twenty-two biblical scholars who translated the Revised Standard Version of the Bible, with publication of the *New Testament* (1946) and *Old Testament* (1952).

Active in professional associations, Weigle was president of the Conference of Theological Seminaries (1929), the Connecticut Council of Churches (1931–33), The Minnesota Educational Association (1913), and the Federal Council of Churches of Christ (1940–42). He was a member of the councils of the Religious Education Association and the World Council of Religious Education (chairman, 1928–58). He was president (1946–56) and trustee of Yale-in-China and trustee of Northfield School, Monson Academy, and Hazen Foundation, and a member of the board of founders of Nanking Theological Seminary. He was chairman of many groups, including the committee that planned the founding of the National Council of Churches (1941–50) and the Committee on Closer Cooperation of Interdenominational Agencies (1914–48), and he was a delegate to various international conferences. He received a number of awards, including the Gutenberg Award of the Chicago Bible Society (1959) and the Wilbur Cross

Medal of Yale University (1967) and was decorated Knight of St. Gregory the Great by Pope Paul VI. He received many honorary degrees from colleges and universities.

REFERENCES: *CB* (March 1946); *LE* (III); *NCAB* (F:142); *NYT,* September 3, 1976, p. 11; *WW* (XXVIII); *WWW* (VI).          *John F. Ohles*

**WEIR, Irene.** B. January 15, 1862, St. Louis, Missouri, to Walter and Annie Field (Andrews) Weir. M. no. D. March 22, 1944, Katonah, New York.

Irene Weir, granddaughter of Robert W. Weir, who established the art department at the United States Military Academy at West Point, attended Yale University where she received the B.F.A. degree (1906). After graduation from Yale, she studied with J. Alden Weir, an uncle, and later received the diplome (1923) from l'Ecole des beaux arts americaines in Fontainebleau, France. She traveled and studied in Paris, Italy, Spain, Holland, and England.

During her long career, Weir served as director of art instruction in New Haven, Connecticut (1887–90). She was director of the Slater Museum School of Art in Norwich, Connecticut (1890–93), director of art instruction in the Brookline (Massachusetts) public schools (1893–1905), and director of the art department of the Ethical Culture School in New York City (1905–17). She was founder and director (1917–29) of the School of Design and Liberal Arts in New York City.

Weir was probably best known for her portraits and paintings with a religious significance. Her religious subjects expressed in both paintings and murals include *Baptism, Crucifixion, Adoring Saints, Mother and Babe with Jesus, Nativity,* and others.

Although known primarily as an artist, Irene Weir was the author of *Greek Painter's Art* (1905) and *Robert W. Weir, Artist* (1947). She was a member of many art associations and was a director of the Art Alliance of America and the Salons of America.

REFERENCES: *NAW; WWW* (II); *NYT,* March 23, 1944, p. 19.
                                                            *Roger H. Jones*

**WELCH, Adonijah Strong.** B. April 12, 1821, Chatham, Connecticut, to Bliss and Elizabeth (Strong) Welch. M. to Eunice P. Buckingham. M. 1868 to Mary P. Beaumont Dudley. Ch. three. D. March 14, 1889, Pasadena, California.

Adonijah Welch was graduated with the B.A. degree (1846) with the first University of Michigan class and received the M.A. degree (1852) from Michigan. He studied law in the office of Judge Lothrop of Detroit, Michigan (1846), and was admitted to the bar in 1847.

Welch was a high school principal in Jonesboro, Michigan, for two years and moved to California. He returned to Michigan in 1851 and was principal of the State Normal School (later, Eastern Michigan University) at Ypsilanti (1851–65). He moved to Pensacola, Florida, in 1865 because of poor health and then to Jacksonville, where he was chairman of the Republican party state committee (1868). He served as United States senator from Florida on the readmission of the state to the Union (1868–69).

In 1869 Welch moved to Iowa where he was the first president of the State Agricultural College (later, Iowa State University of Science and Technology) at Ames (1869–83). He organized the course of study and opened the institution in 1869 and planned the campus. In 1884 he was sent to Europe by the United States government to inspect and report on the organization and management of agricultural schools. He resigned as president in 1883 but continued as professor of history of civilization and practical psychology to his death in 1889.

Welch was the author of *Analysis of the English Sentence* (1850), *Object Lessons* (1861), *Talks on Psychology* (1888), and *The Teachers' Psychology* (1888). He was an organizer and first president of the Michigan Teachers' Association (1851), a member of the board of trustees of the Michigan Agricultural College (later, State University), and the first president of the Michigan state board of education. He received two honorary degrees from the University of Michigan and one from the Iowa State Agricultural College.

REFERENCES: *AC; DAB; NCAB* (12:291); *TC; WWW* (H).

*Daniel L. Paul*

**WELCH, William Henry.** B. April 8, 1850, Norfolk, Connecticut, to William Wickham and Emeline (Collin) Welch. M. no. D. April 30, 1934, Baltimore, Maryland.

William Welch received the B.A. degree from Yale College in 1870. He taught in New York City for a year before he entered the College of Physicians and Surgeons of Columbia University to study medicine. After graduating in 1875, Welch studied in Europe for three years.

Returning to New York in 1878, Welch became a lecturer on pathology at Bellevue Hospital where he established the first pathological laboratory in the United States. He was appointed professor of pathology at Johns Hopkins University in Baltimore, Maryland (1883), and was the first dean when the medical school was organized in 1893. He recruited an outstanding faculty and applied high standards for admission. He resigned as dean in 1898 and continued to head the pathological department for many years. He spent increasingly more time with problems of public health, preventive medicine, and medical education.

Welch resigned as Baxley Professor of Pathology in 1916 to direct the organization of Johns Hopkins' School of Hygiene and Public Health, the first school of its kind. He was director of the school until 1926 and spent two years in Europe collecting a medical library, which was housed in 1929 in a building named for Welch. On his return from Europe, he assumed the chair of the history of medicine and directed the newly established Institute for the History of Medicine; he remained there until his retirement in 1931.

In 1896 Welch established the *Journal of Experimental Medicine,* a new type of medical publication; he served as its editor until 1906. He was the author of many medical papers and *General Pathology of Fever* (1888), *Biology of Bacteria, Infection and Immunity* (1894), *Bacteriology of Surgical Infection* (1895), and *Thrombosis and Embolism* (1899).

Welch was a founder and chairman of the board of scientific directors of the Rockefeller Institute for Medical Research from 1901 and served as a trustee of the Carnegie Institution (1906–34). He was president of the Maryland State Board of Health from 1898 to 1922. He was active in many scientific and medical associations and served as president of the Congress of American Physicians and Surgeons (1897), the Association of American Physicians (1901), the American Association for the Advancement of Science (1906), the Association of Pathologists and Bacteriologists (1906), the American Medical Association (1910), and the National Academy of Sciences (1913–16). He served with the surgeon general of the United States Army during World War I; in 1921 he was made a brigidier general. He was the recipient of many honorary degrees and fellowships and of a number of medals and decorations from institutions and governments around the world.

REFERENCES: *AC; DAB; LE* (I); *NCAB* (26:6); *WWW* (I); *NYT,* May 1, 1934, p. 23.                                                              *Paul Woodworth*
                                                                                      *John F. Ohles*


**WELLING, James Clarke.** B. July 14, 1825, Trenton, New Jersey, to William and Jane (Hill) Welling. M. 1850 to Genevieve H. Garnett. M. 1882 to Clementine Louise Dixon. Ch. three. D. September 4, 1894, Hartford, Connecticut.

James Clarke Welling was educated at Trenton (New Jersey) Academy and was graduated from the College of New Jersey (later, Princeton University) with the A.B. (1844) and A.M. (1847) degrees. He studied law in Providence, Rhode Island (1846–47), and was admitted to the bar.

He was a tutor in Virginia for two years and was associate principal of the New York Collegiate School in New York City (1848–50). He was literary editor (1850–56) and associate editor (1856–65) of the *National Intelligencer* in Washington, D.C. He was clerk of the United States court of claims in Washington (1866–67), president of St. Johns College in Annapolis, Maryland (1867–70), and professor of rhetoric and English literature at the College of New Jersey (1870–71).

He was president of Columbian College (later, George Washington University) from 1871 to 1894 and also taught philosophy of history and international law. The institution became Columbian University in 1873 and experienced significant growth, was moved to the center of Washington, D.C., and a school of graduate studies was established.

Welling was president of the board of trustees of the Corcoran Art Gallery (1881–94), a regent of the Smithsonian Institution (1884–94), and active in social and scholarly organizations. Welling's *Addresses, Lectures, and Other Papers* was published posthumously in 1903. He received an honorary degree from Columbian College in 1868.

REFERENCES: *AC; DAB; NCAB* (1:505); *NYT,* September 5, 1894, p. 5; *TC; WWW* (H).                                           *John F. Ohles*

**WELLS, Herman B.** B. June 7, 1902, Jamestown, Indiana, to Joseph Grandville and Anna Bernice (Harting) Wells. M. no.

Herman Wells attended public schools in Boone County, Indiana, and the University of Illinois where he received the B.S. degree (1924). He received the A.M. degree (1927) from Indiana University and studied at the University of Wisconsin (1927–28). He began his career as a banker, serving first as assistant cashier of the First Bank of Lebanon, Indiana, and then as an official in several state banking organizations.

In 1931 he became associated with Indiana University as an instructor of economics. He became dean of the school of business (1935–37); after serving a brief term as acting president of Indiana University, he became president in 1938. He retired as president in 1962 and became chancellor of the university.

During Wells's presidency enrollment more than doubled. He established several regional campuses and cooperative centers and led a rapid expansion of university facilities and the construction of a residence hall system.

In 1957 he was a delegate to the United Nations. He served on many advisory commissions on education around the world, was president of the Division of Higher Education of the National Education Association, vice-president of the International Association of Universities (1955–60), vice-chairman of the National Commission on the Humanities (1964–65), and president of the National Association of State Universities. He received many awards and honorary degrees.

REFERENCES: *CB* (April 1966); *LE* (III); *NCAB* (J:520); *WW* (XXXVI); *WWAE* (XVI).                                  *David Alan Gilman*

**WELLS, Webster.** B. September 4, 1851, Boston, Massachusetts, to Thomas and Sarah (Merrill) Wells. M. June 21, 1876, to Emily W. Langdon. Ch. none. D. May 23, 1916, Arlington, Massachusetts.

Webster Wells attended Nathaniel T. Allen's *(q.v.)* English and Classical School in West Newton, Massachusetts. He received the B.S. degree in civil engineering (1873) from Massachusetts Institute of Technology (MIT).

Wells spent his entire professional career as a teacher at MIT. Starting as an instructor in 1873, he became a professor in 1903. To his retirement in 1911 the only time he was away from MIT was when he took one year's leave of absence (1881–82).

Wells was noted as the author of many mathematics texts, including *Elementary Treatise on Logarithms* (1878), *University Algebra* (1880), *Plane and Spherical Trigonometry* (1883), *Academic Algebra* (1885), *Plane and Solid Geometry* (1887), *Essentials of Trigonometry* (1888), *Four-Place Logarithmic Tables* (1888), *Higher Algebra* (1889), *College Algebra* (1890), *Academic Arithmetic* (1892), *Revised Plane and Solid Geometry* (1894), *New Plane and Spherical Trigonometry* (1896), *Essentials of Algebra* (1897), *Essentials of Geometry* (1898), *New Higher Algebra* (1899), *Complete Trigonometry* (1900), *Advanced Course in Algebra* (1904), *Algebra for Secondary Schools* (1906), and *Text-Book in Algebra* (1906).

He was a member of several scholarly organizations. He was a pioneer member of the Appalachian Mountain Club and was a skilled mountain climber.

REFERENCES: *NCAB* (17:124); *NYT,* May 25, 1916, p. 13; *WWW* (I). *Robert McGinty*

**WELLS, William Harvey.** B. February 27, 1812, Tolland, Connecticut, to Harvey and Rhoda (Chapman) Wells. M. July 23, 1840, to Hannah Smith. M. May 8, 1843, to Tabitha Ordway. M. July 30, 1849, to Lydia Graves. Ch. eleven. D. January 21, 1885, Chicago, Illinois.

William Harvey Wells worked on his father's farm. He attended the local district school and academies in Vernon and Tolland, Connecticut. He attended Dartmouth College in Hanover, New Hampshire, but dropped out because of poor eyesight and taught in a grammar school in East Hartford, Connecticut. He studied at the teachers' seminary at Andover, Massachusetts (1843), and returned to the East Hartford grammar school as a teacher and principal.

Wells was an instructor of English and mathematics at the Andover teachers' seminary (1836–47). In 1848 he became principal of the Putnam Free School in Newburyport, Massachusetts. He was principal of the State Normal School at Westfield, Massachusetts, and became superintendent of the Chicago (Illinois) public schools. He founded the first high school in Chicago and admitted girls as well as boys. He established a centralized teacher-training program under the Chicago board of education and introduced a system of graded schools in the city. He resigned as superintendent at Chicago in 1864 to engage in writing and business enterprises.

Wells was the author of *Wells School Grammar* (1846), *The Graded Course of Study* (1861) for use in Chicago schools, *The Historical Authorship of English Grammar* (1878), and *A Shorter Course in English Grammar and Composition* (1880). Wells was an organizer and president (1851–53) of the Massachusetts Teachers' Association and one of the first editors of *Massachusetts Teacher*. He was a member of the Illinois state board of education and was president of the Illinois State Teachers' Association (1860) and the National Teachers' Association (later, National Education Association) in 1864.

REFERENCES: *AC; DAB; NCAB* (9:558); *NYT,* January 23, 1885, p. 5; *WWW* (H); Charles Northend *(q.v.),* "William Harvey Wells," *American Journal of Education* 8 (1860): 529.                          *Thomas Meighan*

**WENDELL, Barrett.** B. August 23, 1855, Boston, Massachusetts, to Jacob and Mary Betoldi (Barrett) Wendell. M. June 1, 1880, to Edith Greenough. Ch. four. D. February 8, 1921, Boston, Massachusetts.

Barrett Wendell attended a private school that emphasized the study of literature. He traveled and studied in Europe prior to attending Harvard University, from which he was graduated with the A.B. degree (1877).

Wendell became an instructor of English composition at Harvard in 1890 and continued there to his retirement in 1917 as professor emeritus. He advocated a systematic teaching and learning of good writing in his composition classes and was noted for his teaching of American literature. He was the first at Harvard to subject American literature to historical and critical study. He gave the Clark Lectures at Trinity College, Cambridge, England (1902–03), which were published as *The Temper of the Seventeenth Century in English Literature* (1904). He lectured at the Sorbonne and other French universities (1904–05), inaugurating an exchange program of professors between French institutions and Harvard University.

Wendell was the author of two novels, *The Duchess Emilia* (1885) and *Rankell's Remains* (1887), and also wrote *Cotton Mather* (1891), *English Composition* (1891), *Stelligeri and Other Essays Concerning America* (1893), *William Shakespeare: A Study in Elizabethan Literature* (1894), *A Literary History of America* (1900), *Raleigh in Guiana, Rosamond,* and *A Christmas Masque* (1902), *History of Literature in America* (with Chester N. Greenough, 1904), *Liberty, Union, and Democracy—The National Ideals of America* (1906), *The France of Today* (1907), *The Privileged Classes* (1908), *The Mystery of Education and Other Academic Performances* (1909), and *The Traditions of European Literature from Homer to Dante* (1920).

He was a fellow of the American Association for the Advancement of

Science and a member of the National Institute of Arts and Letters, the American Academy of Arts and Letters, and other professional organizations. He received honorary degrees from Columbia and Harvard universities and from the University of Strasbourg in 1920.

REFERENCES: *AC; DAB; NCAB* (9:207); *NYT,* February 9, 1921, p. 9; *TC; WWW* (I). *Earl W. Thomas*

**WENTWORTH, George Albert.** B. July 31, 1835, Wakefield, New Hampshire, to Edmund and Eliza (Lang) Wentworth. M. August 3, 1864, to Emily J. Hatch. Ch. three. D. May 24, 1906, Dover, New Hampshire.

George Wentworth studied at a district school and attended Phillips Academy in Exeter, New Hampshire. He was graduated in 1858 from Harvard University where he taught part-time in the neighborhood to help pay his expenses.

Wentworth was an instructor of ancient languages at Phillips Academy (1858–59) and became professor of mathematics in 1859 where he remained until his retirement in 1891. For more than thirty years he was chairman of the mathematics department. After retirement he was president of the Exeter (New Hampshire) Banking Company and a trustee of Phillips Academy.

Wentworth wrote over fifty books, including *Elements of Geometry* (1878), *Elements of Algebra* (1881), *Plane and Spherical Trigonometry* (1882), *Surveying and Navigation* (1882), *Five Place Tables of Logarithms* (1882), *Elements of Analytic Geometry* (1886), *School Algebra* (1887), *College Algebra* (1888), *Primary Arithmetic* (1890), *Higher Algebra* (1891), *Grammar School Arithmetic* (1891), *The First Steps in Numbers* (with E. M. Reed, 1891), and *Physics* (with G. A. Hill, 1898). He coauthored with G. A. Hill the Wentworth and Hill Series of exercise books in mathematics and physics (1884–87).

REFERENCES: *DAB; NCAB* (10:106); *WWW* (I); *A History of Mathematics Education* (Washington: National Council of Teachers of Mathematics, 1970). *Robert McGinty*

**WESLEY, Charles Harris.** B. December 2, 1891, Louisville, Kentucky, to Charles Snowden and Matilda (Harris) Wesley. M. November 25, 1915, to Louise Johnson. Ch. two.

Charles Harris Wesley attended Central High School in Louisville, Kentucky, and Fisk Preparatory School in Nashville, Tennessee. He received the B.A. degree (1911) from Fisk University and the M.A. degree (1913) from Yale University. He studied at the Guilde Internationale in Paris, France (1914), and attended Howard University Law School in Washington, D.C. (1915–16). He received the Ph.D. degree (1925) from Harvard University.

Wesley taught history at Howard University (1913–19), was professor and head of the history department (1919–37), acting dean (1937–38) and dean (1938–42) of the graduate school, and acting dean of the college of liberal arts (1938).

In 1942 Wesley became president of Wilberforce (Ohio) University, which included Wilberforce, an African Methodist-Episcopal (AME) university, Payne Theological Seminary, and the state-controlled Normal and Industrial Department. In 1947 the vocational division was separated from Wilberforce University and reorganized as the state-supported Central State University. Wesley built a new campus and instituted a program to enroll white students into an integrated institution. In 1965 he retired from Central State and became executive director of the Association for the Study of Negro Life and History.

Wesley was the author of *Negro Labor in the United States, 1850–1925* (1927), *Richard Allen: Apostle of Freedom* (1935), *The Collapse of the Confederacy* (1938), *A Manual of Research and Thesis Writing for Graduate Students* (1941), *The Story of the Negro Retold* (1959), *Negro Makers of History* (1959), *The Negro in Our History* (with C. G. Woodson, q.v., 1962), *Neglected History: Essays in Negro-American History by a College President* (1965), and *Negro Americans in the Civil War* (with P. W. Romero, 1967).

Active in Young Men's Christian Association work, Wesley was a presiding elder of the AME church (1918–37). He was a Guggenheim Fellow to England (1930–31). A member of professional organizations, he was general president of Alpha Phi Alpha (1931–40). A fellow of the American Geographical Society, he was president of the Inter-University Council of Ohio (1955–56), the Ohio College Association (1963–64), the Association of Ohio College Presidents and Deans (1954–55), and the Association for the Study of Negro Life and History. He received many honorary degrees and awards.

REFERENCES: *CB* (March 1944); *LE* (III); *WW* (XXXVI); *WWAE* (XVI); Wilhelmena S. Robinson, *International Library of Negro Life and History: Historical Negro Biographies* (New York: Publishers Co., 1967), pp. 258–59.                                                                  *John F. Ohles*

**WESLEY, Edgar Bruce.** B. December 5, 1891, Bethelridge, Kentucky, to Silas and Meania (Jones) Wesley. M. May 16, 1915, to Fay Medford. M. July 19, 1975, to Helen Case. Ch. five.

Edgar Bruce Wesley received the A.B. degree from Baldwin-Wallace College in Berea, Ohio (1914), and attended Yale University (1916–17) and the University of Wisconsin (1922). He received the A.M. (1925) and Ph.D. (1929) degrees from Washington University in St. Louis, Missouri.

Wesley taught in a rural school in Casey County, Kentucky (1910–11), and was a high school teacher of Latin and history and principal in Basil, Ohio (1914–16). He was an instructor of English and history at Jackson Academy in St. Louis, Missouri (1917–22). He taught social studies at the University High School at the University of Minnesota (1923–30). He was professor of social studies at the University of Minnesota (1930–51).

The author of a popular social studies textbook, *Teaching the Social Studies in High Schools* (1937), Wesley also wrote *Social Problems of Today* (with G. S. Dow, 1925), *Principles of Social Science* (with T. R. Williamson, 1932), *World Civilization* (with H. Webster, 1934), *Guarding the Frontier* (1935), *Proposed—The University of the United States* (1936), *America's Road to Now* (1939), *Reading Guide for Social Studies' Teachers* (1941), *American History in Schools and Colleges* (1944), *Teaching Social Studies in Elementary Schools* (1946), *Contemporary Problems* (with others, 1947), *History of the United States* (1948), *NEA: The First Hundred Years* (1957), and *Too Short the Days* (1966). He was editor of the Heath's Correlated Social Studies (with William Hamm, 1938–40), Wesley Social Studies Maps (1948–49), and the Our America Series.

Active in professional organizations, Wesley served as the centennial historian for the National Education Association (1957), was president of the National Council for the Social Studies (1935), and was a member of the Minnesota Resources Committee (1936–42). He directed the Program of Information on World Affairs for the *Minneapolis Tribune*. He was awarded honorary degrees by Baldwin Wallace College (1945) and Union College (1943).

REFERENCES: *LE* (IV); *WW* (XXXV); George D. Heiss, "Edgar Bruce Wesley and the Social Studies" (Ed. D. diss., Rutgers University, 1967). *Wayne Mahood*

**WEST, Charles Edwin.** B. February 23, 1809, Washington, Massachusetts, to Abel West and his wife n.a. M. April 24, 1835, to Antoinette Gregory. M. 1843 to Elizabeth Green Giles. Ch. six. D. March 9, 1900, Brooklyn, New York.

Charles Edwin West received his early education in the public schools of Pittsfield, Massachusetts, where he also engaged in his first teaching. He attended Union College in Schenectady, New York, graduating in 1832.

West went to Albany, New York, to study law but became involved in private teaching. Recruiting a class of fifty boys, he organized the Albany Classical School, which he conducted for three years (1832–35). He became principal of the newly incorporated Rutgers Female Institute in New York City (1839–51). He left that institution to take charge of the Buffalo Female Academy (1852–60) and succeeded Alonzo Gray, the founder of Brooklyn Heights Seminary, as principal in 1860. For the next twenty-nine years he was highly successful in conducting the seminary, from which he retired in 1889.

West was recognized for his work in providing education for women. He believed that women should have adequate educational facilities and be permitted to study any academic area in which they were competent. While at Rutgers Institute, he established a college course for the women students and included the study of chemistry, astronomy, and higher mathematics in the curriculum.

West was a member of many learned societies and delivered many public addresses. He was awarded honorary degrees by Columbia and Rutgers colleges, and the State University of New York instituted a doctor of pedagogy degree to award him (1890).

REFERENCES: *NCAB* (8:235); *NYT,* March 10, 1900, p. 9; *WWW* (I).

*Karen H. Westerman*

**WEST, Willis Mason.** B. November 15, 1857, St. Cloud, Minnesota, to Joseph E. and Alcetta M. West. M. January 1883 to Melissa Mott. M. December 1902 to Elizabeth Beach. Ch. fourteen. D. May 2, 1931, Minneapolis, Minnesota.

Willis Mason West, educator and prolific author of history textbooks, attended the St. Cloud (Minnesota) public schools and received the A.B. (1879) and A.M. (1881) degrees from the University of Minnesota.

West began his career as superintendent of schools in Duluth, Minnesota (1881–84), and Faribault, Minnesota (1884–91). He became a professor of history at the University of North Dakota (1891–92) and joined the faculty of the University of Minnesota in 1892, remaining until 1912. He retired at the age of fifty-five to become a farmer and writer.

West was the author of *Ancient History to Charlemagne* (1902), *Modern History* (1904), *The Ancient World* (1904), *American History and Government* (1913), *A Source Book in American History to 1790* (1913), *Modern World* (1915), *History of the American People* (1918), *German Plots and Intrigue* (1918), *The War and the New Age* (1919), *Story of Modern Progress* (1919), *Story of Man's Early Progress* (1920), *Story of American Democracy* (1922), *Short History of Early Peoples* (1921), *Short History of Modern Peoples* (1923), *World Progress* (with Ruth West, 1923), *The Story of Our Country* (1926), and *History of the American Nation* (1929). He wrote a United States Bureau of Education circular, *History of the University of Minnesota* (1902). During World War I West served on the Committee on Public Information in Washington, D.C.

REFERENCES: *NCAB* (5:122); *WWW* (I); *Minneapolis* (Minnesota) *Tribune,* May 4, 1931.                                     *Joan Duff Kise*

**WHEATLEY, William Alonzo.** B. February 28, 1869, Verona, New York, to William and Lottie (Fry) Wheatley. M. August 8, 1901, to Mabel Ballantine. Ch. three. D. May 3, 1955, Los Angeles, California.

William Alonzo Wheatley received his college education at Syracuse (New York) University, from which he was graduated in 1894, and at Yale University, where he completed the A.M. degree in 1897. He also studied at Yale in 1904–05 and 1911–12.

Wheatley was employed in New York as principal of the Minoa Grammar School (1894), vice-principal of the East Syracuse High School (1895), and principal of schools at Andes (1896–97), and the preparatory schools at Syracuse University (1898–99) and at Chester (1900–04). Moving to Connecticut, he served as superintendent of schools at Fairchild (1905), Branford, and Westport (1906–10). He was principal of City High School and superintendent of schools at Middletown, Connecticut (1910–17), and a teacher at Hartford (Connecticut) High School (1921–23).

In 1923 he became the head of the education department at Edinboro (Pennsylvania) State Teachers College (later, State College) and served as dean of instruction (1936–39). He joined United Air Lines in 1940 and moved to Los Angeles, California, where he remained to his death.

Wheatley was active in promoting the guidance movement and is credited with being the first to organize an occupational information course in 1904. He wrote *German Declension Made Easy for Beginners* (1895), *Occupations, a Textbook in Vocational Guidance* (with Enoch B. Gowin, 1916), *The Good Citizen, Sticking to the Main Issue* (1920), *Teaching Aptitude Tests* (1927), *Building Character and Personality, A Textbook in Orientation* (with Royce R. Mallory, 1936), and *Teachers Manual of Aviation* (1940).

Active in professional organizations, Wheatley was a member of the social studies committee of the Commission on the Reorganization of Secondary Education of the National Education Association (1913–19) and president of the Connecticut Teachers Association and several local teacher associations.

REFERENCES: *LE* (III); *WWAE* (XVI); *WWW* (V).      *Gary M. Miller*

**WHEELER, Anna Johnson Pell.** B. May 5, 1883, Hawarden, Iowa, to Andrew Gustav and Amelia (Frieberg) Johnson. M. July 19, 1907, to Alexander Pell. M. July 6, 1925, to Arthur L. Wheeler. Ch. none. D. March 26, 1966, Bryn Mawr, Pennsylvania.

Anna Johnson Pell Wheeler studied at the University of South Dakota in Vermillion, where she received the A.B. degree (1903); she received the master's degree from the University of Iowa (1904) and Radcliffe College in Cambridge, Massachusetts (1905). She was awarded the Alice Freeman Palmer Fellowship from Wellesley College and studied in Göttingen, Germany, the foremost mathematical center in Europe. She completed her graduate work at the University of Chicago, where she obtained the Ph.D. degree in 1910.

Wheeler began her teaching career at Mount Holyoke College in South Hadley, Massachusetts (1911–18), and she joined the faculty of Bryn Mawr (Pennsylvania) College and remained there from 1918 to 1925 and from 1932 to her retirement in 1948. She also taught at Princeton University (1927–32).

During her years as head of the mathematics department at Bryn Mawr College, she encouraged research by giving younger faculty members light teaching loads and improving and expanding the mathematical library. She built up the graduate program and established an exchange program with the University of Pennsylvania. In 1927 she was the first woman asked by the American Mathematical Society to deliver the Colloquium Lectures at the Madison meetings of the society. She was awarded honorary degrees by the New Jersey College for Women, Mount Holyoke College, and Rutgers University.

REFERENCES: *LE* (II); *NYT*, April 1, 1966, p. 35; *WW* (XXI); *Bryn Mawr Alumnae Bulletin* (Summer 1966); *Evening Bulletin* (Philadelphia, Pennsylvania), March 29, 1966, p. 70.                    *Christine W. Ayoub*

**WHEELER, Benjamin Ide.** B. July 15, 1854, Randolph, Massachusetts, to Benjamin and Mary E. (Ide) Wheeler. M. June 27, 1881, to Amey Webb. Ch. one. D. May 2, 1927, Vienna, Austria.

After graduating from Colby Academy in New London, New Hampshire (1871), Benjamin Ide Wheeler matriculated at Brown University in Providence, Rhode Island, from which he was graduated with distinction in 1875. While teaching in the classical department at Providence (Rhode Island) High School (1875–79), he pursued graduate studies at Brown University and received the A.M. degree in 1879. He taught classics at Brown until 1881. From 1881 to 1885 he studied in Germany at the universities of Leipzig, Jena, Berlin, and Heidelberg, receiving the Ph.D. degree summa cum laude (1885) in comparative philology from Heidelberg.

Upon returning to the United States, Wheeler taught Latin, Greek, and comparative philology at Harvard (1885–86) and Cornell (1886–99) universities. He was director of the American School of Classical Studies at Athens, Greece (1895–96). He became president of the University of California in 1899. For the next twenty years he guided the development of the university. During his administration the student body nearly tripled in size. Recognizing the importance of research and the necessity of expanding library and laboratory facilities in the interest of scholarship, he attracted authorities of international reputation as well as young scholars of promise to Berkeley. He helped found the university press and expanded the graduate division, extension studies, summer sessions, and the college of agriculture.

Wheeler served as Theodore Roosevelt Professor at the University of

Berlin (1909–10). His lectures at Berlin were published in 1910 as *Unterricht und Demokratie in Amerika*. He also wrote *The Greek Noun-Accent* (1885), *Analogy in Language* (1887), *Introduction to the Study of the History of Language* (with others, 1891), *Organization of Higher Education in the United States* (1896), *Dionysos and Immortality* (1899), and *Life of Alexander the Great* (1900).

Wheeler was a corresponding member of the Kaiserliches Archaeologisches Institut in Germany and received honorary degrees from many colleges and universities.

REFERENCES: *AC; DAB; NCAB* (4:480); *NYT,* May 4, 1927, p. 25; *TC; WWW* (I); Monroe E. Deutsch, ed., *The Abundant Life* by Benjamin Ide Wheeler (Berkeley: University of California Press, 1926); William Warren Ferrior, *Origin and Development of the University of California* (Berkeley: The Sather Gate Book Shop, 1930); Verne A. Stadtman, *The University of California, 1868–1968* (New York:McGraw-Hill Book Co., 1970). *Patrick Joseph Foley*

**WHEELER, Raymond Holder.** B. March 9, 1892, Berlin, Massachusetts, to Henry Arthur and Nellie F. (Reed) Wheeler. M. August 14, 1915, to Ruth Dunlop. Ch. one. D. August 24, 1961, Wellesley, Massachusetts.

Raymond Holder Wheeler received the A.B. (1912), A.M. (1913), and Ph.D. (1915) degrees from Clark University in Worcester, Massachusetts. He served as a graduate fellow and research assistant at Clark (1912–15).

Wheeler was a member of the faculty of the University of Oregon (1915–25) and was director of the psychology laboratories (1920–25). He was professor of psychology at the University of Kansas (1925–47) and at Erskine College in Due West, South Carolina (1947–48). He was on the faculty of the Babson Institute of Business Administration at Wellesley, Massachusetts (1948–61).

Wheeler was a gestalt psychologist who was identified with organismic theories of learning. His theories were contained in several books, including *The Science of Psychology* (1929), *Readings in Psychology* (1930), *Laws of Human Nature* (1931), and *Principles of Mental Development* (with F. T. Perkins, 1932). He was editor of the *Journal of General Psychology* (1927–61) and founder and editor of the *Journal of Human Ecology* (1951–61).

He served in World War I as a member of a committee constructing intelligence tests for the Surgeon General's Office and was on the staff of the School of Military Psychology at Camp Greenleaf, Georgia, and chief of psychological services at Camp Bowie, Texas. He was a fellow of the American Geographical Society and a member of several professional associations.

REFERENCES: *LE* (III); *WW* (XXII); *WWW* (IV). *John F. Ohles*

**WHEELOCK, Eleazar.** B. April 22, 1711, Windham, Connecticut, to Ralph and Ruth (Huntington) Wheelock. M. April 29, 1735, to Sarah (Davenport) Maltby. M. November 21, 1747, to Mary Brinsmead. Ch. eleven, including John Wheelock *(q.v.),* president of Dartmouth College. D. April 24, 1779, Hanover, New Hampshire.

Eleazar Wheelock was graduated from Yale College in New Haven, Connecticut, with the A.B. (1733) and A.M. (1736) degrees. He studied theology and was ordained to the Congregational ministry in 1735 and served at the Second Congregational Church in Lebanon Crank (later, Columbia), Connecticut (1735–70).

In 1743, seeking to supplement his low salary, Wheelock tutored in his home Samuel Occum, a Mohican Indian who became a prominent Presbyterian clergyman among the Indians. In 1754 he opened a school for Indians in Lebanon, Connecticut, on land donated by Joshua Moor. Unable to obtain a charter for Moor's Indian Charity School, Wheelock received support from a board of trustees organized in England headed by William Legge, earl of Dartmouth. Seeking to expand the school by adding a program for English men, Wheelock moved to Dresden (later, Hanover), New Hampshire, where he was assured of the granting of a charter. In 1769 the charter was granted and the renamed Dartmouth College was established in New Hampshire in the fall of 1770; the first class was graduated in 1771. Wheelock served as president of Dartmouth to his death in 1779 when his son John Wheelock succeeded him.

Wheelock was the author of *Narrative of the Indian School at Lebanon* (1762–75) and received an honorary degree from Edinburgh (Scotland) University in 1767.

REFERENCES: *AC; DAB; EB; NCAB* (9:85); *TC; WWW* (H); F. Gardiner F. Bridge, "Eleazar Wheelock: A Voice in the Wilderness," *Connecticut Teacher* 33 (February 1966): 8–12.                                   *Norman E. Delisle*

**WHEELOCK, John.** B. January 28, 1754, Lebanon, Connecticut, to Eleazar *(q.v.)* and Mary (Brinsmead) Wheelock. M. November 29, 1786, to Maria Suhm. Ch. one. D. April 4, 1817, Hanover, New Hampshire.

John Wheelock transferred from Yale College in New Haven, Connecticut, to be in the first graduating class (1771) of Dartmouth College in Dresden (later, Hanover), New Hampshire, where his father was president. He was a tutor at the college, served in the New Hampshire Assembly (1775), and joined the Continental Army in 1777, rising to the rank of lieutenant colonel.

Wheelock abided by his father's will and became Dartmouth's second president and head of Moor's Charity School in 1779. He visited Europe in 1783 soliciting funds for the debt-ridden college and collecting books, but the money and his personal papers were lost in a shipwreck. He received support from the state legislature and established professorships and constructed two buildings with funds obtained from the legislature, a lottery, several small donations, and the sale of land. Enrollment increased to over one hundred pupils, and the medical school was founded (1798). In addition to administrative duties, Wheelock lectured and conducted prayer services.

Wheelock came into conflict with the board of trustees and was removed from office in 1815. He appealed to the state legislature, which revoked the charter and reorganized the college. Wheelock was reinstated as president but died shortly after. The trustees of the college carried their case to the courts, and the United States Supreme Court ruled in 1820 against the state's revocation of the charter in the famous Dartmouth College case.

Wheelock was the author of *Essay on Painting, Music and Poetry* (1774), *Eulogy on Dr. John Smith* (1810), and *Sketches of the History of Dartmouth College* (1816). He was awarded an honorary degree by Dartmouth College (1789).

REFERENCES: *AC; DAB; NCAB* (9:86); *TC; WWW* (H); Samuel Colcord Bartlett, "Dr. John Wheelock," *Proceedings of the New Hampshire Historical Society* 2 (June 1888–June 1895); 408–26; Leon Burr Richardson (*q.v.*), *History of Dartmouth College* (Hanover: Dartmouth College Publications, 1932), vol. 1. *David Delahanty*

**WHEELOCK, Lucy.** B. February 1, 1857, Cambridge, Vermont, to Edwin and Laura (Pierce) Wheelock. M. no. D. October 2, 1946, Boston, Massachusetts.

Lucy Wheelock left Underhill (Vermont) Academy after one year and lived with friends so that she could attend the Reading (Massachusetts) public high school, where she was graduated in 1874. She taught briefly in Cambridge, Vermont, then entered Chauncy Hall School in Boston (1876), intending to prepare for Wellesley College. She became interested in the school's kindergarten, and enrolled in Mrs. Ella S. Hatch's Kindergarten Training School in Boston in 1878. She received a diploma in 1879.

Wheelock taught at Chauncy Hall's kindergarten for ten years (1879–89). When kindergartens were introduced into the Boston public schools in 1888, Chauncy Hall established a one-year teacher-training course under Wheelock's direction. The course attracted students nationally and was lengthened to two years in 1893.

In 1896 Wheelock left Chauncy Hall to open Wheelock Kindergarten Training School, which she owned and directed until her retirement in 1939, when it was incorporated as a nonprofit institution. It became Wheelock College in 1941. The school was immediately successful; Wheelock added teacher training for primary grades to the curriculum in 1899 and preparation for teaching nursery school in 1926. The first permanent building was erected in 1914.

Wheelock traveled on a "Mothers' Crusade" to promote the kindergarten movement in eight southern states in 1916. In Boston she was active in providing kindergartens for the poor in churches and schools. She was a member of the board of the Ruggles Street Neighborhood House in Roxbury and the House of Good Will in East Boston. She was coauthor with Elizabeth Colson of *Talks to Teachers* (1920) and edited *Pioneers of Kindergartens in America* (1923). She contributed a weekly column, "Hints to Teachers," in the *Congregationalist* and wrote numerous articles in educational journals. She translated several German publications for *Barnard's Journal of Education* and compiled in translation several of Johanna Spyri's stories for children in *Red Letter Tales* (1884) and *Swiss Stories for Children* (1887).

In 1892 Wheelock helped organize the International Kindergarten Union, becoming its second president (1895–99). She was chairman (1905–09) of the Committee of Nineteen, which studied dissension in the kindergarten movement over teaching methods and helped edit the final report, *The Kindergarten* (1913). She chaired the National Congress of Mothers (1908) and committees on cooperation between the National Congress of Mothers and the International Kindergarten Union (1916) and the Kindergarten Union and the National Education Association (1913–18). In 1929 she served on the educational committee of the League of Nations.

REFERENCES: *DAB* (supp. 4); *LE* (II); *NAW; NCAB* (39:119); *WC; WWW* (II); *NYT,* October 3, 1946, p. 27; *Childhood Education* 23 (January 1947): 247; *School and Society* 64 (October 12, 1946): 260.

*M. Jane Dowd*

**WHIPPLE, Guy Montrose.** B. June 12, 1876, Danvers, Massachusetts, to John Francis and Cornelia Eliza (Hood) Whipple. M. September 4, 1901, to Clarice Johnson Rogers. M. October 13, 1925, to Helen Davis. Ch. four. D. August 1, 1941, Clifton, Massachusetts.

Guy Montrose Whipple received the A.B. degree (1897) from Brown University in Providence, Rhode Island. He was an assistant in psychology at Clark University in Worcester, Massachusetts (1897–98), and studied at Cornell University in Ithaca, New York (1898–1900), from which he received the Ph.D. degree (1900).

Whipple joined the faculty at Cornell University in 1898 as an assistant in psychology and continued there to 1904 when he moved to the University of Illinois. In 1919 he was appointed professor of experimental education at the University of Michigan (1919–25). He also was the acting director of the bureau of salesmanship research and professor of applied psychology at the Carnegie Institute of Technology (later, Carnegie-Mellon University) in Pittsburgh, Pennsylvania (1917–19). He was a temporary lecturer at Harvard University (1924–25). He was editor of elementary school textbooks for D. C. Heath & Company (1928–37).

Whipple was the author of *Guide to High School Observation* (1908), *Questions in General and Educational Psychology* (1908), *Questions in School Hygiene* (1909), *Manual of Mental and Physical Tests* (1910), *How to Study Effectively* (1916), *Classes for Gifted Children* (1919), *Problems in Educational Psychology* (1922), and *Problems in Mental Testing* (with Helen D. Whipple, 1925). He translated *Mental Fatigue* by M. Offner (1911) and *The Psychological Methods of Testing Intelligence* by W. Stern (1914). He was cooperating editor of the *Journal of Applied Psychology*, coeditor of the *Journal of Educational Research,* and a founder of the *Journal of Educational Psychology*.

During World War I Whipple was on the committee for the psychological examination of recruits for the United States Army. He was a member of the board of directors of the American Psychological Association (1914–16), vice-president of the American Association for the Advancement of Science (chairman of the education section, 1922), and director of the National Intelligence Tests of the National Research Council (1921–24).

REFERENCES: *LE* (I); *NCAB* (31:226); *NYT,* August 3, 1941, p. 35; *WWW* (I); *School and Society* 54 (August 9, 1941): 91. *Joseph P. Cangemi*
*Thomas E. Kesler*

**WHITAKER, Ozi William.** B. May 10, 1830, New Salem, Massachusetts, to Ira and Chloe (Wood) Whitaker. M. November 25, 1857, to Elizabeth A Richardson. M. August 31, 1865, to Julia Chester. Ch. none. D. February 9, 1911, Philadelphia, Pennsylvania.

Ozi William Whitaker received his early education at New Salem (Massachusetts) Academy to 1836 and at Brattleboro (Vermont) Academy. He enrolled in Amherst (Massachusetts) College in 1851 but left in the sophomore year to accept a position as a teacher in the New Salem Academy. He taught and attended classes part-time at Middlebury (Vermont) College where he received the A.B. degree (1856). He attended the General Theological Seminary in New York City, was graduated in 1863, and was ordained a deacon in the Episcopal church. Ordained to the priesthood in 1863, he traveled to Nevada where he served St. John's parish in Gold Hill and a mission in Dayton.

Whitaker was principal of the high school at North Brookfield, Massachusetts (1856–60). He returned to the East from Nevada in 1865 and served St. Paul's Church in Englewood, New Jersey, to 1867. He moved back to Nevada in 1867 and served as rector of St. Paul's Church in Virginia City (1867–69). Elected missionary bishop of Nevada and Arizona, he established the Church School for Girls at Reno, Nevada, a pioneer girls' school in the region.

At a special convention held in St. Luke's Church in Philadelphia in June 1886, Whitaker was elected assistant bishop of Pennsylvania and became bishop of Pennsylvania in 1877. He received an honorary degree from Kenyon College in 1868.

REFERENCES: *AC; NCAB* (3:471); *TC; WWW* (I); *NYT*, February 10, 1911, p. 9.                                                  *Joan Duff Kise*

**WHITE, Andrew Dickson.** B. November 7, 1832, Homer, New York, to Horace and Clara (Dickson) White. M. September 24, 1857, to Mary A. Outwater. M. September 10, 1890, to Helen Magill. Ch. three. D. November 4, 1918, Ithaca, New York.

Andrew Dickson White received his early education at public and private schools in Syracuse, New York. After some parental opposition, he entered Yale College from which he was graduated with the A.B. (1853) and A.M. (1856) degrees. He studied at the Sorbonne Collège de France in Paris, as well as at the University of Berlin (1853–54), and was appointed attaché to the United States legation at St. Petersburg, Russia (1854). He returned to Yale in 1856 for another year of graduate study. He was professor of history and English literature at the University of Michigan (1857–64).

White was elected a member of the New York State Senate from Syracuse in 1864 and became chairman of the Senate committee on education. With a long-time interest in establishing a university similar to the European universities he had attended, he supported the proposal of Senator Ezra Cornell of Ithaca to found a new agricultural college in New York. Cornell sought the state land grant provided for under the Morrill Act of 1862 and pledged a cash endowment of a half-million dollars, a campus, and a farm for the institution. His proposal was accepted, and the charter for the new college was granted in April 1865.

Cornell insisted that White should be the first president; White accepted and held the post until 1885 when poor health prompted him to resign. He personally contributed three hundred thousand dollars, founded the Andrew Dickson White School of History and Political Science, donated his historical library of over forty thousand volumes, and guided Cornell through its early years. He resumed teaching in 1889 and gave courses at many university centers in the United States.

White was the author of many published works, among them *Relations of the National and State Governments to Advanced Education* (1874), *Paper Money Inflation in France* (1876), *Battlefields of Science* (1876), *The New Germany* (1882), *Message of the 19th Century to the 20th* (1883), *The Teaching of History in Our Public Schools* (1890), *Democracy and Education* (1891), *A History of the Warfare of Science with Theology in Christiandom* (1896), *Erasmus in the Library of the World's Best Literature* (1896), *The Warfare of Humanity with Unreason* (1903), *Autobiography of Andrew Dickson White* (1905), *The Work of Benjamin Hale*

*(1911), and Seven Great Statesmen in the Warfare of Humanity with Unreason* (1910), and he published several outlines of university lectures.

White's governmental experiences included serving as United States commissioner to Santo Domingo (1871), chairman of the Jury of Public Instruction at the Centennial Exposition in Philadelphia (1882), United States minister to Germany (1879–81), honorary United States commissioner to the Paris Exposition (1878), United States minister to Russia (1892–94), member of the Venezuela Commission (1896–1902), and president of the Peace Commission at the Hague (1899).

White was a member of the board of trustees of Hobart College (1866–77), Cornell University (1866–1918), Carnegie Institution for Research, and the Carnegie Peace Endowment in Washington, D.C., and he was a regent of the Smithsonian Institution. He received many honorary degrees and was an honorary member of the Royal Academy of Sciences in Berlin. He was an organizer and first president of the American Historical Association (1884–85), president of the American Social Sciences Association and American Philosophical Society, and a member of the American Academy of Arts and Letters. He was an officier of the Legion of Honor, France, and received the Royal Gold Medal of Prussia for Arts and Sciences in 1902.

REFERENCES: *AC; DAB; EB; NCAB* (4:476); *TC; WWW* (1); *NYT*, November 5, 1918, p. 13; Andrew D. White, *Autobiography of Andrew Dickson White* (New York: Century Co., 1905); Karl G. Peterson, "Andrew Dickson White's Educational Principles: Their Sources, Development, Consequence" (Doct. diss., Stanford University, 1950).

*J. Franklin Hunt*

**WHITE, Emerson Elbridge.** B. January 10, 1829, Mantua, Ohio, to Jonas and Sarah (McGregory) White. M. July 26, 1853, to Mary Ann Sabin. Ch. none. D. October 21, 1902, Columbus, Ohio.

After attending Twinsburg (Ohio) Academy, E. E. White studied at Cleveland (Ohio) University (1848–51). He had taught in a district school at the age of seventeen and left Cleveland University in the senior year to become principal of a Cleveland elementary school (1851). After four years he was principal of Central High School in Cleveland (1855–56). He was superintendent of Portsmouth (Ohio) schools (1856–61) and moved to Columbus, Ohio, where he was owner and editor of *Ohio Educational Monthly* (1861–76).

White was Ohio state commissioner of common schools (1863–65) and codified the state school laws, established the state board of examiners, and was able to obtain state support for teachers' institutes. White was president of the newly established Purdue University in Lafayette, Indiana (1876–83). He became superintendent of the Cincinnati (Ohio) public schools (1886–89).

White was an influential educator during the last half of the nineteenth century. Widely known for his textbooks on mathematics and pedagogy, he was the author of *New Complete Arithmetic* (1883), *Oral Lessons in Number* (1884), *School Records* (1886), *Elements of Pedagogy* (1886), *First Book of Arithmetic* (1890), *School Management* (1893), *Elements of Geometry* (1895), *School Algebra* (1896), and *The Art of Teaching* (1901). He also wrote Series of Mathematical Text Books (1870–86).

An organizer and president (1872) of the National Teachers' Association (later, National Education Association), White was president of the Ohio Teachers' Association (1863), the National Superintendents Association (1886), and the National Council of Education (1884). He was instrumental in founding the United States Bureau of Education and was credited with writing the bill that created the agency. White was the recipient of honorary degrees from Indiana State University and Western Reserve and Marietta colleges.

REFERENCES: *AC; DAB; NCAB* (13:40); *TC; WWW* (I); "Emerson E. White," *Educational Review* 25 (February, 1903): 200–05; *Report of the Commissioner of Education, 1892–93* (Washington, D.C.: Government Printing Office, 1894): 1288–91.                        *Charles C. Chandler*

**WHITE, John Stuart.** B. February 3, 1847, Wrentham, Massachusetts, to John S. and Anna (Richardson) White. M. February 28, 1871, to Georgia R. Read. Ch. two. D. October 5, 1922, Bath, New York.

John Stuart White was educated in public schools in Boston, Massachusetts. He attended Harvard University on a Thayer scholarship and was graduated with honors in 1870. He was selected to deliver the Latin oration of welcome at Charles W. Eliot's *(q.v.)* inauguration as president of Harvard (1869).

He was master of Boston Latin School (1870–74). In 1874 he opened Brooks School, a preparatory school for boys in Cleveland, Ohio, where the curriculum included military drill and calisthenics. In 1880 he moved to New York City where he founded the Berkeley School, which grew to be one of the most highly respected preparatory schools in the country. He served as principal of Berkeley School for over twenty-two years. In 1903 he established another preparatory school, the Phillips Brooks School, in Philadelphia, Pennsylvania, and served as headmaster to 1908. From 1908 to 1912, he was in Europe and, on his return to the United States, founded and conducted the Thomas Arnold School in Chicago, Illinois (1912–17).

He was the winner of the bronze medal at the Paris Exposition (1889) for the educational exhibit of the Berkeley School.

White authored *Plutarch's Lives for Boys* (1884), *The Boys' and Girls' Herodotus* (1885), *The Boys' and Girls' Pliny* (1886), and *The Viking Ship* (1891). During his stay in Europe he was a special correspondent of the

*Boston Daily Advertiser, St. Paul Dispatch,* and other newspapers. He served as a member of the editorial staff of *Cosmopolitan* magazine. He received an honorary degree from Trinity College (1879).

REFERENCES: *AC; NCAB* (2:335); *WWW* (I); *NYT,* October 6, 1922, p. 23.                                                          *Michael R. Cioffi*

**WHITE, Leonard Dupee.** B. January 17, 1891, Acton, Massachusetts, to John Sidney and Bertha Howard (Dupee) White. M. June 17, 1916, to Una Lucille Holden. Ch. one. D. February 23, 1958, Chicago, Illinois.

Leonard Dupee White was graduated with the B.S. (1914) and M.A. (1915) degrees from Dartmouth College in Hanover, New Hampshire. He received the Ph.D. degree (1921) from the University of Chicago. White studied at Harvard University (summer 1917) and Clark University (1916–18).

White taught political science at Clark University (1915–18). He was on the Dartmouth College faculty (1918–20) and moved to the University of Chicago where he taught from 1918 to his retirement in 1956; he served as chairman of the political science department from 1940 to 1948.

White authored many books, including *Introduction to the Study of Public Administration* (1926), *The City Manager* (1927), *Trends in Public Administration* (1933), *Introduction to the Study of Public Administration* (1939), *The States and the Nation* (1953), *The Federalists* (1948), *The Jeffersonians* (1951), *The Jacksonians* (1954), and *The Republican Era: 1896–1901* (1958). He was a founder and the first editor-in-chief (1940–41) of the *Public Administration Review.* He also served on the editorial boards of the *American Political Science Review, Public Management,* and *Revue internationale des sciences administratives.*

White was a frequent member of local and federal committees and commissions, including the Chicago Civil Service Commission (1929–31), the United States Civil Service Commission and Central Statistical Board (1934–37), and the President's Committee on Civil Service Improvement (1939–41), and he participated in the first and second Hoover commissions (1948–49 and 1953–55). He was a Guggenheim Fellow (1927–29). He was vice-president (1927) and chairman of the United States delegation (1936) to the International Congress of the Administrative Sciences. He participated in the planning for the Littauer School of Public Administration at Harvard University.

He was active in professional associations, including the Institute international des sciences administratives (vice-president, 1936–47, and honorary vice-president from 1947), the Political Science Association (president, 1944), and the American Society for Public Administration (president, 1947). He received a number of honors, including honorary degrees, the Bancroft Prize for *The Jacksonians,* the Woodrow Wilson Award for *The*

*Federalists*, and the Pulitzer Prize in history (1959) for *The Republican Era: 1896–1901* (1959).

REFERENCES: *NCAB* (44:242); *WWW* (III); *NYT,* February 24, 1958, p. 19; *National Municipal Review* 47 (April 1958): 154.

*Thomas Meighan*

**WHITE, Samuel Holmes.** B. October 7, 1830, Lockport, New York, to Samuel and Amanda (Holmes) White. M. August 17, 1860, to Mary Jane Babcock. M. July 20, 1865, to Jennie E. McLaren. Ch. five. D. March 9, 1882, Mapleton, Iowa.

Samuel H. White moved at the age of three with his parents to Michigan. He was graduated from the University of Michigan with the A.B. degree (1856) and attended Albany (New York) Law College from which he received the LL.B. degree (1859).

White was a teacher at the age of sixteen and taught and farmed to finance his education. He taught at the Lockport (New York) high school (1856–58). He was principal of public schools in Chicago, Illinois (1859–68) and was organizer and principal of the Peoria (Illinois) Normal School (1868–79). White was an advocate of providing teachers with security and a feeling of permanence in their jobs. He supported extension of the school to the kindergarten.

Active in professional associations, White participated in the Principals' Association of Chicago and was president of the Illinois State Teachers' Association (1865–66) and the National Teachers' Association (later, National Education Association) in 1873–74 and served as secretary (1866 and 1872–73). He was editor of the *Illinois Teacher* (1863–71).

REFERENCES: *NCAB* (13:101); *Report of the Commissioner of Education for the Year 1882–83* (Washington, D.C.: Government Printing Office, 1884), p. 60.                                              *Abdul Samad*

**WHITFIELD, Henry Lewis.** B. June 20, 1868, Rankin County, Mississippi, to Robert Allen and Mary Ann (Fitzhugh) Whitfield. M. August 25, 1897, to Mary White. Ch. four. D. March 18, 1927, Jackson, Mississippi.

Henry Lewis Whitfield attended school in Fannin, Mississippi, and worked on the family farm. At the age of sixteen he was licensed to teach and at seventeen was employed as a teacher in Simpson County. He attended Mississippi College in Clinton on a part-time basis and received the B.A. degree (1895). He later studied law at Millsaps College in Jackson, Mississippi, and the University of Mississippi.

Whitfield was a high school principal at Westville, Steen's Creek, and Florence, Mississippi. He gained a reputation as an educator and a disciplinarian. In 1897 Whitfield was appointed to fill an unexpired term as state superintendent of education and was elected to the office in 1899 and 1903.

He was successful in having the state and county appropriations for education increased. Under his leadership there were improvements in teacher training, the organizing of normal schools, and the establishment of agricultural high schools. He introduced physical education in the public schools and was instrumental in upgrading school buildings and the qualifications for county superintendents. He was influential in the establishing of a textile school at Mississippi A&M College.

Whitfield did not run for reelection in order to accept the presidency of Mississippi Industrial Institute & College (later, Mississippi State College for Women) in Columbus in 1907. He instituted a department of physical education in the college, organized courses for teachers, raised entrance requirements, and expanded the curriculum. He was dismissed as president of the college in 1920 for apparently political reasons and became superintendent of the B. B. Jones Masonic Boys' School, near Columbus, Mississippi. He was the author of numerous articles and *Know Mississippi* (1925).

In 1924 he was elected governor of the state. During his term he instituted numerous reforms that were beneficial to industry and agriculture. He died in office.

REFERENCES: *NCAB* (21:481); *NYT*, March 19, 1927, p. 17; *WWW* (I); Bill R. Baker, *Catch the Vision: The Life of Henry L. Whitfield of Mississippi* (Jackson: University Press of Mississippi, 1974).          *S. S. Britt, Jr.*

**WHITFORD, William Clarke.** B. May 5, 1828, West Edmeston, New York, to Samuel and Sophia (Clarke) Whitford. M. to Elmina Coon. M. March 23, 1852, to Ruth Hemphill. Ch. one. D. May 20, 1902, Milton, Wisconsin.

William Clarke Whitford was graduated from De Ruyter (New York) Institute (1850), Union College in Schenectady, New York (1853), and Union Theological Seminary (1856), and he received the M.A. degree there in 1858.

He moved from New York to Milton, Wisconsin, in 1850, where he taught for one year at Milton Academy. Returning to the East in 1851, he was principal of Union Academy in Shiloh, New Jersey (1851–53), where he prepared for publication an elaborate map of several towns in Madison County, New York. In April 1856 he was ordained to the ministry of the Seventh-Day Baptist Church, at New Market, New Jersey, and accepted a pastorate at Milton, Wisconsin, where he remained for three years.

In 1858 Whitford became principal of Milton Academy. During the Civil War, over three hundred of his students fought with the Union army. The academy was incorporated by the state as a college in 1869. Whitford was elected president, serving until his death at the college in 1902.

Whitford was Wisconsin state superintendent of public instruction

(1878–82) and was a member of the Wisconsin State Assembly in 1868. As state superintendent, he sought to improve the rural schools. The United States Commissioner of Education adopted many of his suggestions for improved heat, light, seats, and ventilation of rural schools. He introduced a graded system in Wisconsin's rural schools.

Whitford authored *History of Education in Wisconsin* (1876), *Historical Sketch of Milton College* (1876), *Plans and Specifications for School Houses* (1882), and numerous addresses and articles on Wisconsin history and education. He was a corresponding editor of the *Wisconsin Journal of Education* (1878–81), the *Seventh-Day Baptist Quarterly* (1884), and *Sabbath Recorder* (1887).

Whitford was president of the Wisconsin Teachers' Association (1865) and a member of the state board of normal school regents (1867–75) and 1878–82). He was active in the Seventh-Day Baptist church and was in charge of its exhibit at the Chicago World's Fair in 1893. For many years he was corresponding secretary of the church's education society.

REFERENCES: *NCAB* (6:119); *WWW* (I); *Dictionary of Wisconsin Biography* (Milwaukee: State Historical Society of Wisconsin, 1960); *Milwaukee Sentinel,* May 21, 1902.                              *Lawrence S. Master*

**WHITTLESEY, Derwent Stainthorpe.** B. November 11, 1890, Pecatonica, Illinois, to Joseph Henry and Sophia Jane (Derwent) Whittlesey. M. no. D. November 25, 1956, Boston, Massachusetts.

Derwent Whittlesey attended a rural school and Rockford (Illinois) public schools. He studied at the University of Chicago where he received the Ph.B. (1914), M.A. (1915), and Ph.D. (1920) degrees. He served as assistant professor of history for one year (1915–16) at Denison University in Granville, Ohio, before joining the United States Army Ordnance Corps. After World War I he returned to the University of Chicago as an instructor of geography and remained there from 1919 to 1928. He left Chicago to join the faculty of Harvard University (1928–56).

Whittlesey was editor of the *Annals of the Association of American Geographers* (1930–42). He contributed to a number of journals, encyclopedias, and atlases. His major published works include *Major Geographic Regions of North America* (with Mabel C. Stark, 1923), *Introduction to Economic Geography* (with Wellington D. Jones, 1925), *The Earth and the State* (1939), *German Strategy of World Conquest* (with others, 1942), *Geografia Politica* (1948), *Environmental Foundations of European History* (1949), *Wall Map of Agricultural Regions of the World* (1951), and *Regional Study with Special Reference to Geography* (1952).

Whittlesey served in several consulting positions for the federal government. He was committee chairman of the geology and geography division of the National Research Council (1937–43 and 1948–53), worked with the departments of State, War, and Navy and the Office of Strategic Services (1940–46), and was consultant to the Department of Defense (1948–53). He was a Fulbright research scholar in Africa in 1951.

Whittlesey was a member of professional organizations, including the American Association for the Advancement of Science and the Association of American Geographers (president, 1944, and first honorary president, 1954), and he was an honorary member and gold medalist of the Chicago Geographic Society. He received two honorary degrees.

REFERENCES: *NCAB* (42:467); *WWAE* (XVI); *WWW* (III); *NYT*, November 26, 1956, p. 27; *Geographical Journal* 123 (March 1957); 132–33; *Geographical Review* 47 (July 1957): 443–45.    *Vincent Giardina*

**WHITWORTH, George Frederic.** B. March 15, 1816, Boston, England, to n.a. M. July 17, 1838, to Mary Elizabeth Thomson. Ch. five. D. October 6, 1907, Seattle, Washington.

George Frederic Whitworth was graduated from Hanover (Indiana) College (1838) and studied law in Lancaster, Ohio, and Greenburg, Indiana. He was admitted to the bar in 1843 and practiced for a short time. He attended New Albany (Indiana) Theological Seminary (later, McCormick Theological Seminary in Chicago, Illinois) and was graduated in 1847.

Whitworth served churches at Corydon and Cannelton, Indiana, und Hawesville, Kentucky (1847–53). He moved by ox team with a group of colonizers who settled at Puget Sound. He helped organize the area's first Presbyterian church in Portland, Oregon (1853), and churches in Olympia, Washington (1854), and Claquato and Grand Mound, Washington (1855). He served as the first moderator of the presbytery of Puget Sound (1858) and the synods of Columbia (1876) and Washington (1890). Whitworth and his wife established and taught in a boarding school in Olympia, Washington (1855), and in a school in their home in Seattle, Washington (1869).

Resigning from his missionary duties in 1856, Whitworth served in civil posts to 1865 and was engaged in the coal business from 1866. He served on a committee that drafted the first territorial school laws (1877) and was credited as a major influence in enactment of school laws. He was elected county superintendent of public instruction in Thurston County, Washington (1854 and 1857), and King County, Washington (1868 and 1873). While in Thurston and King counties he was active in the organizing of fifteen Presbyterian churches in the Puget Sound area.

Whitworth became president of the Territorial University (later, University of Washington) in Seattle (1866–67 and 1875–76). He established Sumner (Washington) Academy (1883) and served as president of the board of trustees. Incorporated as a college in 1890, it was moved to Tacoma, Washington, in 1899, was renamed Whitworth College, and was later located in Spokane, Washington.

REFERENCES: *DAB; NCAB* (2:126); Clifford M. Drury, "George Frederic Whitworth, Father of Presbyterianism in Washington," *Journal of the Presbyterian Historical Society* 26 (March 1948): 1–10; Alfred O. Gray, *Not By Might* (Spokane, Wash.: Whitworth College, 1965); *Seattle Post-Intelligencer,* October 7, 1907, p. 1.                    Michael A. Balasa

**WICKERSHAM, James Pyle.** B. March 5, 1825, Chester County, Pennsylvania, to Caleb and Abigail Swayne (Pyle) Wickersham. M. December 24, 1847, to Emerine Isaac Taylor. Ch. four. D. March 25, 1891, Lancaster, Pennsylvania.

James P. Wickersham attended local Chester County district schools and the nearby Unionville Academy under Jonathan Gause. He taught in three district schools in Chester County and in 1845 became principal of the Susquehanna Institute in Marietta, Pennsylvania. He was the first superintendent of Lancaster County (Pennsylvania) schools (1854–56) and established a teacher-training program in 1855 at Lancaster County Normal School at Millersville (later, Millersville State College).

In 1856 Wickersham became principal of the normal school that became Pennsylvania's first state normal school in 1859. He promoted the idea of a state system of normal schools and was instrumental in drafting the state normal school law of 1857. In 1862 he organized a regiment of the Lancaster County teachers and served as commanding colonel of the Forty-seventh Regiment of the Pennsylvania Volunteer Emergency Militia. In 1866 he became Pennsylvania state superintendent of public instruction and served in the office to 1881. Under Wickersham schools were organized in every county in the state. The schools were better organized and supervised and provisions were made to improve the qualifications of teachers. He drafted articles on education for the state constitution of 1874 and made the state education department one of the five major governmental departments.

Editor of the *Pennsylvania School Journal* (1870–81), Wickersham was the author of *School Economy* (1864), *Methods of Instruction* (1865), *Education and Crime* (1881), and *History of Education in Pennsylvania* (1886), which was a significant work in the historiography of American education.

Wickersham was a founder of the Lancaster County Educational Association in 1851 (president, 1863), the Pennsylvania State Teachers Association in 1852 (president, 1855), and the National Teachers' Association (later, National Education Association), which he served as president in 1865. He helped establish in 1864 the Soldiers' Orphans Homes for children orphaned by the Civil War. He served as United States minister to Denmark (1882). He was awarded medals for educational exhibits by the governments of France and Chile and received honorary degrees from Washington and Jefferson College and Lafayette College.

REFERENCES: *AC; DAB; NCAB* (12:239); *NYT*, March 26, 1891, p. 5; *WWW* (H); A. E. Winship *(q.v.)*, *Great American Educators* (New York: American Book, 1900), pp. 163–73. *William W. Brickman*

**WIENER, Leo.** B. July 26, 1862, Bialystok, Poland, to Solomon and Frieda (Rabinowicz) Wiener. M. 1893 to Bertha Kahn. Ch. four. D. December 12, 1939, Belmont, Massachusetts.

Leo Wiener developed an extraordinary aptitude for languages in his youth. He was educated in Poland at the gymnasia of Minsk and Warsaw, entered the University of Warsaw as a medical student in 1880, and studied at the Berlin Polytechnicum (1881). Discontinuing his medical studies, he failed in an attempt to found a socialist and vegetarian community in Central America. He arrived in New Orleans, Louisiana, in 1882, supporting himself with menial jobs.

Wiener spent a year teaching in a country school in Odessa, Missouri (1883–84), and taught Greek, Latin, and mathematics in a Kansas City high school (1884–92). He was assistant professor of Germanic and Romance languages at the University of Missouri (1892–95). Wiener went to Boston where he taught languages at the New England Conservatory of Music (1895–96), and became associated with Francis Child of Harvard University with whom he researched Scottish ballads through the south Slavic area. Wiener was appointed an instructor of Slavic languages and literature at Harvard in 1896, the first post of its type in the United States. He taught Russian, Polish, and Old Church Slavonic at Harvard until his retirement as professor emeritus in 1930.

Wiener was editor of *Anthology of Russian Literature* (two volumes, 1902–03) and *The Complete Works of Leo N. Tolstoy* (twenty-four volumes, 1904–05) and wrote *History of Yiddish Literature in the Nineteenth Century* (1899) and *Interpretation of the Russian People* (1915). He contributed etymologies to the Merriam-Webster Dictionary. With his strong opposition to the communist regime in the U.S.S.R., his interest in the Slavic field waned, and he began to study Arabic, German, African, and American Indian cultures. From those studies he wrote *Commentary to the Germanic Laws and Mediaeval Documents* (1915), *Contributions Toward a History of Arabic Gothic Culture* (four volumes, 1917), *Africa and the Discovery of America* (three volumes, 1919), and *Mayan and Mexican Origins* (1936).

REFERENCES: *DAB* (supp. 2); *NYT*, December 14, 1939, p. 27; *WWW* (I). *Kenneth Sipser*

**WIER, Jeanne Elizabeth.** B. April 8, 1870, Grinnell, Iowa, to Adolphus William and Elizabeth (Greenside) Wier. M. no. D. April 7, 1950, Reno, Nevada.

Jeanne Wier was educated in the public schools of Grinnell, Rockwell, and Clear Lake, Iowa. She was graduated from Iowa State Teachers College (1893) and received the B.A. degree (1901) from Stanford (California) University.

Her first professional positions were as a teacher in Iowa public schools (1889–92). She was an assistant principal at the high school in Heppner, Oregon (1893–95). She joined the faculty of the University of Nevada in 1895 and was head of the department of history and political science (1901–40).

Wier was a contributor to the *Dictionary of American Biography,* the *Dictionary of American History,* and wrote a chapter, "Nevada Politics," for *Rocky Mountain Politics* (1940). She wrote articles on Nevada for the *Encyclopaedia Britannica.* She was commissioned by the Nevada legislature in 1919 to write a wartime history of the state. She was in charge of the preparation of a WPA publication, *Historical Records Survey in Nevada,* and *Nevada, A Guide to the Silver State.*

In 1911 she called the first meeting of woman suffragettes in Nevada. She belonged to many professional organizations, including the American Historical Association (vice-president of the Pacific Coast branch 1915–16). She founded the Nevada State Historical Society (1904) and served as secretary. She was compiler and editor of its publications. She received an honorary degree from the University of Nevada in 1924.

REFERENCES: *LE* (II); *NCAB* (A:466, 51:665); *WWAE* (VIII); *WWW* (III).                                                                 *Joan Duff Kise*

**WIGGIN, Kate Douglas.** B. September 28, 1856, Philadelphia, Pennsylvania, to Robert Noah and Helene Elizabeth (Dyer) Smith. M. December 28, 1881, to Samuel Bradley Wiggin. M. March 30, 1895, to George Christopher Riggs. Ch. none. D. August 24, 1923, Harrow-on-Hill, England.

After the death of her father, Kate Douglas Wiggin moved to Maine with her sister and mother. Her mother remarried and the family moved to rural Hollis, Maine, where she was educated by her stepfather. She attended Gorham (Maine) Female Seminary, Morison Academy in Baltimore, Maryland, and Abbott Academy in Andover, Massachusetts. In 1873 the family moved to Santa Barbara, California, and shortly thereafter her stepfather died, leaving the family in financial difficulties. She wrote "Half a Dozen Housekeepers," which appeared in *St. Nicholas Magazine,* to raise money.

In 1887 Wiggin began to study kindergarten methods under Emma Marwedel (*q.v.*), a pupil of Friedrich Froebel's widow. She organized the Silver Street Kindergarten in 1878 in a slum area of San Francisco. It was the first free kindergarten west of the Rocky Mountains, where little was known about kindergartens. She worked and studied with Susan Blow (*q.v.*) and Elizabeth Peabody (*q.v.*) and returned to Silver Street. With the assistance of Sarah B. Cooper (*q.v.*) and Wiggin's sister, Nora Archibald Smith, she organized the California Kindergarten Teacher Training School in 1880. The Silver Street School was a model for the organization of sixty kindergartens on the Pacific Coast.

After the death of her first husband, Wiggin traveled abroad and gathered ideas for the stories she wrote. She was married to George C. Riggs in 1895 and resided in New York City, where she engaged in the social life of the city and in writing stories for children. She traveled to England in 1923 as a delegate to the Dickens Fellowship.

Wiggin wrote independently and in collaboration with her sister. Her many books include *The Birds' Christmas Carol* (1888), *The Story of Patsy* (1889), *A Book of Nursery Logic* (1892), *A Cathedral Courtship* (1893), *The Republic of Childhood* (three volumes 1895–96), *Golden Numbers: A Book of Verse for Youth* (1902), *Rebecca of Sunnybrook Farm* (1903), *Mother Carey's Chickens* (1911), *New Chronicles of Rebecca* (1911), *A Child's Journey with Dickens* (1912), and *My Garden of Memory* (1923), an autobiography completed just before her death. Her *Collected Works* was published in 1917.

Among the books she wrote with Nora Archibald Smith were *Children's Rights* (1892), *Froebel's Gifts* (1895), *Froebel's Occupations* (1896), *Kindergarten Principles and Practices* (1896) and *Magic Casements* (1909). She received an honorary degree from Bowdoin College (1906).

REFERENCES: *DAB; EB; NAW; NCAB* (6:207); *TC* (under Riggs); *WC; WWW* (I); *NYT*, August 25, 1923, p. 7; Nora Archibald Smith, *Kate Douglas Wiggin* (Boston: Houghton Mifflin, 1925).

*Barbara Ruth Peltzman*


**WIGGLESWORTH, Edward.** B. 1693, Malden, Massachusetts, to Michael and Sybil (Sparhawk) Avery Wigglesworth. M. June 15, 1726, to Sarah Leverett. M. September 10, 1729, to Rebecca Coolidge. Ch. four, including Edward Wigglesworth, Harvard College professor. D. January 16, 1765, Cambridge, Massachusetts.

Edward Wigglesworth attended the Boston Latin Grammar School where he was also an usher (assistant teacher). He was graduated with the A.B. (1710) and A.M. (1713) degrees and studied theology at Harvard College. On completion of his studies, Wigglesworth served various churches in New England. In 1721 Thomas Hollis of London, England, established a professorship of theology at Harvard, and Wigglesworth served in the chair from 1722 to his death.

Wigglesworth was the author of a number of theology works, including *Sober Remarks on a Modest Proof of the Order and Government Settled by Christ and His Apostles in the Church* (1724), *A Discourse Concerning the Duration of the Punishment of the Wicked* (1729), *The Blessedness of the Dead Who Die in the Lord* (1731), *A Seasoned Caveat Against Believing Every Spirit* (1735), *An Inquiry into the Truth of the Imputation of Adam's First Sin to his Posterity* (1738), *The Sovereignty of God in the Exercise of His Mercy* (1741), *An Answer to Mr. Whitefield's Reply to the College Testimony* (1745), *Some Evidences of the Divine Inspiration* (1755), *Some Thoughts on the Spirit of Infallibility Claimed by the Church of Rome* (1757), and *The Doctrine of Reprobation Briefly Considered* (1763).

Wigglesworth was commissioner of the London Society for Propagating the Gospel Among the Indians to 1755. He was a fellow of Harvard College (1724–65) and received an honorary degree from the University of Edinburgh, Scotland (1730).

REFERENCES: *AC; DAB; NCAB* (9:237); *TC.*          David Delahanty

**WILBUR, Hervey Backus.** B. August 18, 1820, Wendell, Massachusetts, to Hervey and Ann (Toppan) Wilbur. M. May 12, 1847, to Harriet Holden. M. August 13, 1874, to Emily Petheram. Ch. four. D. May 1, 1883, Syracuse, New York.

Hervey Backus Wilbur attended Dartmouth College in Hanover, New Hampshire (1834–36), and was graduated from Amherst (Massachusetts) College with the B.A. (1838) and M.A. (1841) degrees. He was graduated from the Berkshire Medical Institution in Pittsfield, Massachusetts, in 1843 and practiced medicine in Lowell, Dana, and Barre, Massachusetts (1843–48).

Wilbur became interested in the work of the French educator Edward Sequin to educate the mentally retarded and opened a private school for the feebleminded in Barre in 1848, the first school of its kind in the United States. He developed a successful program in educating his pupils and gained widespread attention. Frederick F. Backus, a New York state legislator, sponsored a law that established a similar school on an experimental basis in Albany, New York, in 1851 with Wilbur as head. In 1854 the New York State Asylum for Idiots was moved to Syracuse, New York, where Wilbur headed the school to his death. Wilbur's system of training was adopted by similar institutions in the United States and foreign countries, and he also became a leader in the movement to improve the care of the insane.

Wilbur was the author of *Report on Management of the Insane in Great Britain* (1876) and the pamphlet *Aphasia* (1867). He was a founder of Syracuse (New York) University and lectured there on mental diseases. He served as a director of an institution in Newark, New Jersey. He served as president of the National Association for the Protection of the Insane and the Prevention of Insanity.

REFERENCES: *AC; DAB; NCAB* (10:450); *WWW* (H).

*David E. Koontz*

**WILBUR, Ray Lyman.** B. April 13, 1875, Boonesboro, Iowa, to Dwight Locke and Edna Maria (Lyman) Wilbur. M. December 5, 1898, to Marguerite May Blake. Ch. five. D. June 26, 1949, Palo Alto, California.

Ray Lyman Wilbur moved with his family to Riverside, California, at the age of twelve. He was graduated from the Riverside High School and Stanford (California) University, from which he received the A.B. (1896) and A.M. (1897) degrees. He was graduated with the M.D. degree (1899) from Cooper Medical College. He studied in Europe at Frankfurt am Main, Germany, and London, England (1903–04), and at the universities of Munich, Germany, and Vienna, Austria (1909–10).

Wilbur began the practice of medicine in Palo Alto, California, in 1900 and also taught physiology at Stanford from 1894. In 1908 the Cooper Medical College became part of Stanford University. In 1909 Wilbur joined the faculty as professor of medicine and served as dean of the renamed Stanford School of Medicine (1911–16). Wilbur was elected president of Stanford in 1916 and served to his retirement in 1943. He also was named chancellor in 1940 and held that post to his death.

During Wilbur's tenure as president of Stanford the campus was enlarged, enrollment doubled, and the graduate and engineering schools were established in 1925. He was granted leaves of absence to assist Herbert Hoover during World War I in the United States Food Administration and to serve as secretary of the interior (1929–33). During his term as secretary he served on the Federal Oil Conservation Board (1929–33), reorganized the Bureau of Indian Affairs, and was chairman of the National Advisory Commission on Illiteracy (1930–31).

He wrote *Conservation* (with W.A. de Puy, 1931), *Hoover Dam Contracts* (with Elwood Mead, 1935), *Construction of Hoover Dam* (with Elwood Mead, 1935), *Stanford Horizons* (1936), *Hoover Policies* (with A.M. Hyde, 1937), *March of Medicine* (1938), and *Human Hopes* (1940).

A member of many organizations, Wilbur was a fellow of the American Association for the Advancement of Science and president of the American Academy of Medicine (1912–13), the California Academy of Medicine (1917–18), the American Medical Association (1923–24), and the American Social Hygiene Association (1936–48). He organized the National Advisory Committee on Education (1929) and the California Physicians Service (1939, president, 1939–45). He was chairman of the White House Conference on Child Care and Protection (1929–31), the Institute of Pacific Relations (1925, 1927), and the World Citizens' Association (1938). He served on the Commission on the Reorganization of the Executive Branch of the Government (1947–49). Wilbur was the recipient of many honorary degrees and was decorated by the governments of France and Belgium.

REFERENCES: *CB* (November 1947 and September 1949); *DAB* (supp. 4); *LE* (III); *NCAB* (15:353, 54:337); *NYT*, June 27, 1949, p. 27; *WWAE* (VIII); *WWW* (II).                                        *John F. Ohles*

**WILES, Kimball.** B. October 17, 1913, Ripley, Ohio, to M. K. and Ethel (Griffith) Wiles. M. June 6, 1936, to Hilda Long. Ch. four. D. February 2, 1968, near Gainesville, Florida.

Kimball Wiles was a leader in educational curriculum and supervision. He received the B.S. degree in education (1934) from Miami University (Oxford, Ohio) and the M.A. (1938) and Ph.D. (1940) degrees from Ohio State University. He attended Ohio State during the years that the staff of the Eight Year Study of the Progressive Education Association (PEA) was housed there. His association with PEA evaluators influenced his educational theories and the direction of his professional life.

He taught in public schools in Liberty Township (1934–35) and Hamilton (1935–37), Ohio. He taught education at the University of Alabama (1939–42). He was training coordinator at Sperry Gyroscope Company (1942–44) and directed the school and college division of the National Safety Council (1944–46). He taught education at New York University (1946–50) and the University of Florida (1950–68), where he was dean of the college of education from 1964 to 1968.

Wiles was the author of several books, including the influential *Supervision for Better Schools* (1955), in which he investigated human dynamics and group processes as bases for instructional supervision. He also wrote *Teaching for Better Schools* (1952), *Supervision in Physical Education* (with others, 1956), *The High School We Need* (with Franklin Paterson, 1959), and *The Changing Curriculum of the American High School* (1963). He edited *Toward Better Teaching* (with Alice Miel, 1949), *Readings in Curriculum* (with Glen Hass, 1965), and *Readings in Secondary Education* (with others, 1970). He also wrote many articles published in the professional literature. Wiles was president of the Association for Supervision and Curriculum Development (1963–64).

REFERENCES: *CA* (5–8); *NYT*, February 3, 1968, p. 23; *WWAE* (XV); *WWW* (V); Jesse Merrell Hansen, "Kimball Wiles' Contributions to Curriculum and Instruction: An Analysis within an Historical Context" (Ph.D. diss., University of Texas at Austin, 1971).                     *Gerald A. Ponder*

**WILEY, Calvin Henderson.** B. February 3, 1819, Guilford County, North Carolina, to David L. and Anne (Woodburn) Wiley. M. February 25, 1862, to Mittie Towles. Ch. seven. D. January 11, 1887, Winston-Salem, North Carolina.

Calvin H. Wiley attended Caldwell Institute in Greensboro, North

Carolina, and was graduated with high honors from the University of North Carolina at Chapel Hill in 1840. He was admitted to the bar in 1841 and settled in Oxford, North Carolina. He served in the North Carolina legislature (1850–52) when the law establishing the office of state superintendent of the common schools was passed.

Wiley was elected state superintendent of the common schools in 1852, serving from January 1, 1853, until April 26, 1865, when all state offices were declared vacant after the surrender of the Confederacy. During his tenure as chief school officer he established and edited the *Common School Journal* (later, *North Carolina Education*), organized the state education association, cooperated with Braxton Craven *(q.v.)* to begin teacher-training institutes, established standards and examining boards for teachers, required annual certification of teachers, organized county school units giving instruction to county superintendents and school committeemen, and began plans to prescribe and distribute uniform textbooks. He promoted universal education, advocating acceptance and support of the common schools. During the Civil War Wiley urged the governor not to divert school funds to the war effort; Governor John W. Ellis supported Wiley's position and the schools were kept open.

Wiley was licensed to preach by the Presbyterian church in 1855 and was ordained in 1866. He was general agent of the American Bible Society for Eastern and Middle Tennessee (1869–74) and was transferred to a similar position in North Carolina in 1874. The family moved to Winston-Salem where he helped establish the local public school system.

Wiley was the author of *Alamance or the Great and Final Experiment* (1847), *Roanoke or Where Is Utopia?* (1849), *The North Carolina Reader* (1851), *Adventures of Old Dan Tucker* (1851), *Utopia: A Picture of Early Life in the South* (1852), *Life in the South* (1852), and *Scriptural Views of National Trials* (1863). He was a founder of the *Southern Weekly Post* at Raleigh, North Carolina, edited and published the Oxford, South Carolina, *Mercury* (1841–43), and was one of the founders of the *North Carolina Presbyterian.*

REFERENCES: *AC; DAB; WWW* (H); Samuel A. Ashe, ed., *Biographical History of North Carolina* (Greensboro, N.C.: Charles L. Van Noppen, 1905), 2: 427–41; William K. Boyd, *History of North Carolina* (Spartanburg, S.C.: The Reprint Co., 1973), vol. 2.          *Barbara M. Parramore*

**WILKINSON, Robert Shaw.** B. February 18, 1865, Charleston, South Carolina, to Charles H. and Lavinia (Brown) Wilkinson. M. June 29, 1897, to Marion Raven Birnie. Ch. four. D. March 13, 1932, Charleston, South Carolina.

Robert Shaw Wilkinson, black educator and college president, was named for Robert Gould Shaw, commander of the black Fifty-fourth Massachusetts Regiment during the Civil War. He attended Shaw Memorial School and Avery Institute. He was appointed to the United States Military Academy at West Point, New York, in 1883. He attended the academy (1884–85) and the Oberlin (Ohio) Academy in 1887. He received the A.B. degree (1891) from Oberlin (Ohio) College and the Ph.D degree (1904) from Columbia University.

Wilkinson was professor of Greek and Latin at the State University of Kentucky in Louisville (later, Kentucky State College at Frankfort), Kentucky's black institution of higher education (1891–95). He joined the faculty of State Agricultural and Mechanical College (later, South Carolina State College) at Orangeburg, South Carolina. He became president of the college in 1911 and continued to his death. During his administration the enrollment tripled and state financial support was greatly increased. He emphasized both academic and vocational instruction.

Wilkinson was a member of the general advisory committee of the land grant college survey conducted by the federal Bureau of Education, the advisory committee for the Lincoln Scholarship Fund, and president of the South Carolina Business League. He was a director of the Mutual Savings Bank. Wilkinson received four honorary degrees.

REFERENCES: *DAB; LE* (I); *NYT,* March 14, 1932, p. 17; *WWW* (I).

*Don C. Locke*

**WILLARD, Emma Hart.** B. February 3, 1787, Berlin, Connecticut, to Samuel and Lydia (Hinsdale) Hart. M. August 10, 1809, to John Willard. M. September 17, 1838, to Christopher C. Yates. Ch. one, John Hart Willard, educator. D. April 15, 1870, Troy, New York.

Emma Hart Willard was self-taught and attended the local district school and Berlin Academy in Worthington Center, Connecticut. She began to teach at the age of seventeen in Westfield, Massachusetts, and was placed in charge of a female academy in Middlebury, Vermont (1807–09).

She was married in 1809 and, because of financial difficulties, opened a boarding school for girls in Middlebury in 1814. The school was successful and became well known. In 1818 Willard sought support from New York Governor De Witt Clinton *(q.v.)* and the New York state legislature for a girls' academy in Waterford, New York. Funds were authorized for the initial term under the first law passed for the specific improvement of education of women. In an unsuccessful effort to obtain permanent funding Willard wrote *An Address to the Public: Particularly to the Members of the Legislature of New York, Proposing a Plan for Female Education* (1819).

Willard accepted an offer of financial backing for a school in Troy, New York, and opened the Troy Seminary in 1821. At the seminary she developed new teaching methods, initiated new programs, and wrote geography and history textbooks. At the time of her second marriage in 1838, she gave up the direction of the school to her son, John Hart Willard, and his wife. After her divorce from Christopher Yates in 1843 she resumed the use of the name Willard. She moved to Kensington, Connecticut, where she supported the efforts of Henry Barnard *(q.v.)* to reform education. From 1845 to 1847 she traveled and lectured in the southern and western United States. She spent her last years in residence at the Troy Female Seminary, which was renamed the Emma Willard School in 1910.

Willard was the author of a book of poems that included "Rocked in the Cradle of the Deep" and *System of Universal Geography* (with W. C. Woodbridge, *q.v.*, 1824), *Geography for Beginners* (1826), *History of the United States* (1828); *Journals and Letters from France and Great Britain* (1833), *Universal History in Perspective* (1837), *Treatise on the Circulation of the Blood* (1846), *Abridged History of the United States* (1846), *Historic Guide* (1849), *Respiration and Its Effects* (1849), *Last Leaves of American History* (1849), *Astronomy* (1853), and *Morals for the Young* (1857).

Willard was elected superintendent of the Kensington (Connecticut) schools in 1840, probably the first woman to serve in that post. With Henry Barnard she represented the United States at the World's Educational Convention in London, England, in 1854. In 1905 Willard was elected to the Hall of Fame for Great Americans at New York University. She was a sister of Almira Hart Lincoln Phelps *(q.v.)*.

REFERENCES: *AC; DAB; EB; NAW; NCAB* (1:244); *NYT,* April 19, 1870, p. 8; *TC; WC; WWW* (H); Alice Fleming, *Great Women Teachers* (Philadelphia: J. B. Lippincott Co., 1965); Alma Lutz, *Emma Willard, Pioneer Educator of American Women* (Boston: Beacon Press, 1964).

*Joanne L. Schweik*

**WILLARD, Frances Elizabeth Caroline.** B. September 28, 1839, Churchville, New York, to Josiah Flint and Mary Thompson (Hill) Willard. M. no. D. February 18, 1898, New York, New York.

Frances E. Willard moved with her family to a farm near Janesville, Wisconsin, where she grew up and was largely educated by her mother. At the age of seventeen she attended Milwaukee (Wisconsin) Female College (later part of Lawrence University in Appleton, Wisconsin) and a year later went to Northwestern Female College in Evanston, Illinois, from which she was graduated in 1859.

Willard taught in Illinois in a district school (1858) and at Evanston and Harlem (1859–60). She taught at Kankakee Academy (1861–62), Northwestern Female College (1862), Pittsburgh (Pennsylvania) Female College (1863–64), and the Grove School in Evanston (1864–65) and was secretary of the American Methodist Ladies Centennial Association (1865–66). She was preceptress of the Genesee Wesleyan Seminary in Lima, New York

(1866–67). In the winter of 1867–68 she nursed her father in his final illness.

She traveled and studied in Europe and the Middle East (1868–70) and was appointed president in 1871 of the newly organized successor to the Northwestern Female College, the Evanston College for Ladies. Willard was the first woman college president to award degrees to graduates. The college merged with Northwestern University in 1873, and Willard served as dean of women and professor of English and art to 1874 when she resigned to become president of the Chicago Temperance Union.

In 1874 Willard was a delegate to the Cleveland, Ohio, convention that organized the Women's Christian Temperance Union (WCTU) and served as corresponding secretary (1874–79). She served as president of the WCTU from 1879 to her death in 1898 and organized and was first president of the World's Women's Christian Temperance Union in 1883.

Willard was the author of a biography of her sister, *Nineteen Beautiful Years* (1864), *Women and Temperance* (1883), *How to Win* (1886), *Glimpses of Fifty Years* (1889), *A Classic Town* (1892), *A Wheel Within a Wheel* (1895), and *Occupations for Women* (1897). She edited *A Woman of the Century* (with Mary H. Livermore, 1893).

A founder of the Association for the Advancement of Women (1873) and the General Federation of Women's Clubs, she was first president of the National Council of Women (1889–90) and vice-president of the Universal Peace Union (1888). In 1887 she was one of the group of five women to be elected as delegates to the Methodist General Conference; they were excluded as women from the conference by Bishop Charles H. Fowler. Willard was the first woman to be represented in the statuary hall in the United States Capitol in Washington, D.C., and was elected to the Hall of Fame at New York University in 1910.

REFERENCES: *AC; DAB; EB; NAW; NCAB* (1:376); *NYT,* February 18, 1898, p. 1; *TC; WC; WWW* (H); Lydia Jones Trowbridge, *Frances Willard of Evanston* (Chicago: Willett, Clark and Co., 1938). *Darlene E. Fisher*

**WILLIAMS, Jesse Feiring.** B. February 12, 1886, Kenton, Ohio, to Ora Otis and Ida May (Feiring) Williams. M. August 21, 1912, to Gertrude Carey Finney. Ch. two. D. August 5, 1966, Carmel, California.

Jesse Feiring Williams was one of those prominent men in physical education who used the M.D. degree as the route for establishing physical education, health, recreation, and hygiene with full academic status in the colleges and universities of the United States. He received a diploma from the Chautauqua School of Physical Education in 1907 and the A.B. degree from Oberlin (Ohio) College in 1909. During his education at Oberlin he was influenced by Delphine Hanna *(q.v.),* who administered the physical education and health program there from 1885 to 1920. Williams received the Sc.D. degree from Rollins College (Winter Park, Florida) in 1912 and the

M.D. from the College of Physicians and Surgeons, Columbia University, in 1915.

His long career at Columbia University began in 1911 where he served as assistant professor until 1916. He served in the medical corps of the United States Army (1918–19) and as a major in the Red Cross during 1919 in charge of recreation in the hospitals of the Atlantic Division. He returned to Columbia in 1919 where his peers included John Dewey *(q.v.)*, William H. Kilpatrick *(q.v.)*, E. L. Thorndike *(q.v.)*, Thomas D. Wood *(q.v.)*, and Clark W. Hetherington *(q.v.)*. He adapted the educational philosophy of Dewey and Kilpatrick to the profession of physical education.

Williams was the author of at least twenty-four volumes dealing with health education, physical education, narcotics, alcohol, hygiene, athletics, anatomy, and physiology, and over twenty revisions of these texts between the years 1919 and 1951. Among these were *Healthful Living* (1919), *Organization and Administration of Physical Education* (1922), *Personal Hygiene Applied* (1922), *Textbook of Anatomy and Physiology* (1923), *Hygiene and Sanitation* (1927), *Principles of Physical Education* (1927), *The Business Man and His Health* (1933), *Narcotics* (1953), *Alcohol* (1953), and many other publications coauthored with colleagues.

Williams was named to the American Public Health Association in 1925. He was elected president (1932–33) of the American Physical Education Association (later, the American Alliance for Health, Physical Education, and Recreation) and president (1935–36) of the Society of Directors of Physical Education in Colleges. He acted as Carnegie Visiting Professor in Latin American universities (1935–36), and served as United States delegate to the International Congress of Sports Medicine held in Berlin, Germany, during the Olympic year of 1936.

Williams received the AAHPER's coveted Gulick Medal in 1939. He received honorary degrees from Oberlin College and Rollins College. He died in a community hospital he had helped establish in Carmel, California. At the time of his death he was considered by many to have made more contributions to the profession of physical education than any other person.

REFERENCES: *LE* (II); *WWW* (IV); C. W. Hackensmith, *History of Physical Education* (New York: Harper & Row, 1966); *Journal of HPER* 57 (November 1966): 79; *NYT*, August 7, 1966, p. 80; Deobold B. Van Dalen and Bruce L. Bennett, *A World History of Physical Education, Cultural, Philosophical, Comparative,* 2d ed. (Englewood Cliffs, N.J.: Prentice-Hall, 1971).                                            *Curtis C. Stone*

**WILLIAMS, Walter.** B. July 2, 1864, Boonville, Missouri, to Marcus and Mary Jane (Littlepage) Williams. M. June 30, 1892, to Hulda Harned. M. October 22, 1927, to Sarah Lawrence Lockwood. Ch. three. D. July 29, 1935, Columbia, Missouri.

Walter Williams completed high school at the age of fourteen in Boonville, Missouri. He worked for the *Boonville Topic* newspaper for six years to learn the printing trade; he then bought an interest in the *Boonville Advertiser* and became its editor (1884–89). In 1889 Williams left newspaper work and was a bookkeeper in the state penitentiary for eight months. He then became editorial manager of the *Columbia* (Missouri) *Herald* (1890–98) and began publishing the *Country Editor* in 1895. In 1897 Williams assumed editorship of the *St. Louis* (Missouri) *Presbyterian* and was editor for the Jefferson City, Missouri, *State-Tribune* (1898).

Williams organized the world's first school of journalism at the University of Missouri in Columbia and served as dean (1908–31). Between June and December 1930 he was acting president of the University of Missouri and served as president from 1931 to 1934, when he resigned because of ill health.

Williams was the author of *How the Cap'n Saved the Day* (1901), *Some Saints and Sinners in the Holy Land* (1902), *The State of Missouri* (1904), *Civil Government: Local, State, and National* (with Isidor Loeb, 1907), *History of Missouri* (1908), *Missouri Since the Civil War* (1909), *From Missouri to the Isle of Mull* (1909), *Eloquent Sons of the South* (1909), *Law in Shakespeare* (with F. L. Martin, 1910), *Legal Antiquities* (1911), *The Practice of Journalism* (1911), *History of Northeast Missouri* (1914), *History of Northwest Missouri* (1915), *The World's Journalism* (1915), *Journalism–The Newest Weapon for Democracy* (1919), *The Press Congress of the World in Hawaii* (1922), *The Press Congress of the World in Switzerland* (1928), and *Missouri, Mother of the West* (with F. C. Shoemaker, 1930).

He was president of the Missouri Press Association (1889) and the National Editorial Association (1895) and president for North America of the International Press Congress (1902) in Berne, Switzerland. He organized and was secretary of the World's Press Parliament (1904) in St. Louis and was the first president of the Press Congress of the World (1915–25) and the American Association of Schools and Departments of Journalism (1916). He received awards from several foreign universities and was awarded honorary degrees by Missouri Valley College (1906), Kansas State Agricultural College (1909), and Washington University (1926).

REFERENCES: *DAB* (supp. 1); *LE* (I); *NCAB* (C:522, 28:187); *NYT*, July 30, 1935, p. 19; *WWAE* (VI); *WWW* (I); *School and Society* 42 (August 3, 1935): 137–43; Floyd Calvin Shoemaker, *Missouri and Missourians* (Chicago: Lewis Publishing Co., 1943), 2: 741–45.      *James R. Layton*
*Mary Paula Phillips*


**WILLIAMSON, Charles Clarence.** B. January 26, 1877, Salem, Ohio, to Clarence and Lizzie K. (Mather) Williamson. M. June 22, 1907, to Bertha

Louise Torrey. M. August 28, 1940, to Genevieve Austen Hodge. Ch. one. D. January 11, 1965, Wethersfield, Connecticut.

Charles Clarence Williamson studied at Ohio Wesleyan University in Delaware, Ohio (1897–98). He attended Western Reserve University (later, Case Western Reserve University) in Cleveland, Ohio, where he received the B.A. degree (1904). He studied at the University of Wisconsin (1904–06) and at Columbia University where he earned the Ph.D. degree in economics (1907).

Williamson taught in the Salem (Ohio) public schools (1898–1900). He headed the economics department at Bryn Mawr (Pennsylvania) College (1907–11). He changed from teacher to librarian in 1911 when he became chief of the economics division of the New York Public Library. He was a librarian at the New York Municipal Reference Library (1914–18) and a statistician with the Carnegie Corporation (1918–19). He returned to the New York Public Library for two years (1919–21) and was director of the information service at the Rockefeller Foundation (1921–26).

In 1926 Williamson assumed dual roles at Columbia University as director of libraries and director of the school of library service. The new school was the result of the merger of the New York State Library School, formerly located at Albany, and the school of the New York Public Library. Under his direction the school increased its enrollment, diversified its program, and expanded its faculty, resources, and physical facilities. The university libraries doubled their book collections and expanded services to users. When Williamson retired in 1943, Columbia had nearly two million volumes, ranking third behind the collections at Harvard and Yale universities.

Williamson's most important contribution to the field of librarianship was his *Training for Library Service* (1923), commissioned by the Carnegie Corporation. The report had a great impact on library schools. It defined the library profession, described existing weak areas in library education, and pointed out possibilities for the improvement and future development of library schools. The recommendations prompted widespread revisions in the professional training of librarians. He also wrote *Finances of Cleveland* (1907) and *Training for Library Service* (1923) and edited *Who's Who in Library Service* (1933 and 1943).

Williamson was a member of professional associations, a knight of the Legion of Honor of France (1929), and a recipient of an honorary degree from Columbia University.

REFERENCES: *LE* (III); *WWW* (IV); *Encyclopedia of Library and Information Science* (New York: M. Dekker, 1968), 7: 422–23; *NYT*, January 13, 1965, p. 25.                                                        *Gary D. Barber*

**WILLIAMSON, Edmund Griffith.** B. August 14, 1900, Rossville, Illinois, to Oliver and Anabelle (Fred) Williamson. M. August 12, 1928, to Lorraine

Elizabeth Fitch. Ch. four.

After graduating from the University of Illinois in 1925, E. G. Williamson moved to Minneapolis to begin a lifelong career at the University of Minnesota. He received the Ph.D. degree in psychology (1931) at Minnesota while teaching in that department. He was director of the Testing and Counseling Bureau (1932–38), coordinator of student personnel services (1938–41), and professor of psychology and dean of students from 1941 until his retirement in 1969.

A researcher and innovator in the developing fields of counseling and student personnel work, his ideas influenced practitioners in both fields. He was interested in the applications of psychology to college student problems and in program administration and college-student relationships. Williamson's student personnel program at Minnesota became the model for similar programs throughout the United States.

He was chairman of the American Council on Education's student personnel monograph series, for which he wrote *The Student Personnel Point of View* (1937). He was the author of *Students and Occupations* (1937), *Student Personnel Work* (with J. G. Darley, 1937), *Student Guidance Techniques* (with D. G. Paterson and G. Schneidler, 1938), *How to Counsel Students* (1939), *Introduction to High School Counseling* (with M. E. Hahn, 1940), *Trends in Student Personnel Work* (1949), *Counseling and Discipline* (with J. D. Foley, 1949), *Counseling Adolescents* (1950), *Student Personnel Services in Colleges and Universities* (1961), *Vocational Counseling* (1965), *The American Student's Freedom of Expression* (1966), and *Student Personnel Work* (with D. A. Biggs, 1975). He was a consulting editor of the *Journal of Counseling Psychology.*

Williamson was a lecturer and consultant to government and higher education. He was president of the American College Personnel Association (1940–44), division seventeen of the American Psychological Association (1945–47), and the American Personnel and Guidance Association. He was vice-president of the National Association of Student Personnel Administrators (1953–54) and on the advisory council of the National Students Association. He received the Research Award from the American Personnel and Guidance Association (1953).

REFERENCES: *LE* (III); *WW* (XXXIV); *WWAE* (XI); *American Men and Women of Science,* 12th ed. (New York: Jacques Cattell Press/R. R. Bowker Co., 1973); "E. G. Williamson Presented 1962 Nancy C. Wimmer Award," *The Personnel and Guidance Journal* 41 (September 1962): 95; W. H. Van Hoose and J. J. Pietrofesa, eds., *Counseling and Guidance in the Twentieth Century* (Boston: Houghton Mifflin Co., 1970), pp. 307–16.

*Paul A. Bloland*

**WILLISTON, Arthur Lyman.** B. October 11, 1868, Cambridge, Massachusetts, to Lyman Richards and Anne E. (Gale) Williston. M. June 21,

1893, to Irene L. Simmons. M. December 9, 1925, to Mary deForest Denny. Ch. none. D. November 16, 1956, Dedham, Massachusetts.

Arthur Lyman Williston, educator and engineer, was educated in the public schools of Cambridge, Massachusetts, and at the Massachusetts Institute of Technology (MIT) where he was awarded the B.S. degree (1889). He remained at MIT for an additional year of graduate study (1890).

Williston worked as an engineer in maintaining railroad lines and bridges (1890–91). He began teaching engineering at MIT (1891–92) and was a power plant engineer (1892–93). He was professor of applied mechanics and machine design and director of the department of industrial arts at Ohio State University (1893–95) and secretary to the college of engineering (1895–98). Williston was director of the school of science and technology at Pratt Institute in New York City (1898–1910). In 1910 he left Pratt to become the principal of Wentworth Institute in Boston, Massachusetts, where he served to his retirement in 1924. Under his leadership Wentworth established a reputation for the quality of its scientific and industrial programs. He was a founder of the Boston School of Occupational Therapy in 1918 and served on the board of trustees.

Williston contributed articles to professional journals and was the author of *Beyond the Horizon in Science* (1944). He was awarded the James H. McGraw Award in Technical Institution Education (1925). He established the Arthur L. Williston Medal and Award for mechanical engineers (1927). Williston traveled to Scotland (1925) and Denmark (1926) to represent the United States at international education conferences. He carried out important research work for the American Council on Education and the Hawkes Committee on Personnel Research (1927–32). He was an active member of many professional associations and did consultative work for many organizations and institutions.

REFERENCES: *LE* (I); *NCAB* (46:165); *WWAE* (XIV); *WWW* (V).

*Thomas L. Bernard*

**WILSON, Atwood Sylvester.** B. March 29, 1895, Louisville, Kentucky, to Allen and Mary (Mukes) Wilson. M. July 1, 1918, to Essel Schaefer. M. 1942 to Eunice Singleton. Ch. five. D. March 25, 1967, Louisville, Kentucky.

Atwood S. Wilson, black educational leader in Kentucky, grew up in Louisville, Kentucky, and received his schooling in the Louisville elementary schools and Central High School (1910). He was graduated from Fisk University in Nashville, Tennessee (1915), and received the B.S. (1920) and M.A. (1934) degrees from the University of Chicago. He attended twenty-six summer terms at the University of Chicago and six summer terms at the University of Colorado following his graduation from Fisk.

Wilson taught science and arts in the State Street High School in Bowling
Green, Kentucky (1915–17). He was a veteran of World War I, serving as a
research chemist in the American University Experiment Station in
Washington, D.C. He spent the rest of his career in Louisville, Kentucky,
as a teacher of chemistry at Central High School and as a principal at
Madison Street Junior High School (1928–34) and Central High School
(1934–63). He was an instructor of evening classes for Louisville Municipal
College for about twenty years.

Wilson was a joint author of a handbook, *Group Guidance in the Senior
High Schools* (n.d.), and contributed articles to educational journals, including the *School Review*. He was active in educational organizations,
serving as secretary-treasurer (1922–42) of the Kentucky Negro Education
Association (later, Kentucky Teachers Association). He was chairman of
the merger committee of the Kentucky Teachers Association to unite with
the white Kentucky Education Association (1957). He was elected to the
University of Chicago chapter of Phi Delta Kappa in 1935, one of the first
blacks in the country to become a member of that educational fraternity.
He served on a state curriculum revision committee (1960–61).

Wilson participated in civic affairs as a member of the executive commit-
tee of the National Youth Administration for Kentucky, a trustee of the
Louisville Free Public Libraries, (1943–53), and a member of the advisory
board to the mayor of Louisville. He was awarded the Silver Beaver by
President Herbert Hoover for his service to youth (1933). He received the
Lincoln Institute Key Award for service to the education of blacks in
Kentucky and was awarded an honorary degree by Simmons University of
Louisville. The Kentucky Education Association initiated the Lucy Harth
Smith-Atwood S. Wilson Award for Civil and Human Rights in Education
in 1974.

REFERENCES: *LE* (III).                                    *John F. Ohles*

**WILSON, Guy Mitchell.** B. November 10, 1876, Frankfort, Indiana, to
Edward and Mary (Norris) Wilson. M. August 28, 1897, to Ina Hieatte. M.
June 10, 1922, to Dorothy Marston Waters. Ch. three. D. June 1, 1965,
Newton, Massachusetts.

Guy Wilson's father was a farmer and part-time schoolteacher. Wilson
was graduated from Indiana State Normal School (later, Indiana State
University) at Terre Haute (1896); he received the B.A. (1900) and M.A.
(1908) degrees from Indiana University and the Ph.D. degree (1918) from
Columbia University. His special interest was the teaching of arithmetic to
children.

Wilson served Indiana schools as a teacher in a rural school in Clinton
County (1892–94) and a high school in Alexandria (1896–97), as superintendent in Chalmers (1899–1900), and as county superintendent in Hen-

dricks County (1903–12). He was professor of vocational education at Iowa State College (later, Iowa State University of Science and Technology) in Ames (1913–22) and a professor at Boston University (1922–43), where he retired as professor emeritus.

His writings were primarily concerned with instruction in arithmetic. Among his books were *Course of Study in Arithmetic* (1912), *The Motivation of School Work,* (with Harry Wilson, 1916), *A Survey of the Social and Business Usage of Arithmetic* (1919), *How to Measure* (with K. Hoke 1920), *Course of Study in Mathematics for the Elementary Grades* (1922), *Standardized Tests in Language* (1923), *What Is Americanism?* (1924), *The Motivation of Arithmetic* (1925), *Inventory and Diagnostic Tests in Arithmetic* (1925), *What Arithmetic Shall We Teach?* (1926), and *Teaching the New Arithmetic* (1939). He was a contributing editor for the *Journal of Experimental Education.*

Wilson was influential in determining the content of arithmetic taught to children. He believed children should be motivated to learn arithmetic and instruction should relate to their needs. He lobbied against the adoption of the metric system. He belonged to many professional associations and was secretary of the Society of College Teachers of Education (1916–21).

REFERENCES: *LE* (III); *NCAB* (51:250); *WWW* (IV).

*Robert McGinty*

**WILSON, Howard Eugene.** B. October 10, 1901, Bluffs, Illinois, to Joseph and Della (Vandeventer) Wilson. M. August 7, 1926, to Florence Heden. Ch. two. D. August 12, 1966, Los Angeles, California.

Howard Eugene Wilson attended Illinois College in Jacksonville, Illinois, and was graduated from the University of Chicago with the Ph.B., (1923) and M.A. (1928) degrees. He completed the Ed.D. degree at Harvard University in 1931. He was a teacher in Stevens Point, Wisconsin, from 1923 to 1925 and at the University of Chicago High School from 1925 to 1928. Wilson became an instructor at the Harvard Graduate School of Education while working on his doctorate and remained there as an assistant and then associate professor until 1945.

Wilson became assistant director of the Division of Education for the Carnegie Endowment for International Peace (1945) and he was selected as a representative to the Preparation Commission of the United Nations Educational, Social, and Cultural Organization (1946). He was executive associate in charge of education for the Carnegie Endowment (1947–55) and became secretary of the Educational Policies Commission of the National Education Association (1953). He served as a member of the United States National Commission for UNESCO (1947–51 and 1957–59). In 1957 Wilson was appointed dean of the school of education at the University of California, Los Angeles, where he stayed until his death.

Wilson believed that international understanding could be improved through education and was a critic of the nationalistic bias in school textbooks and curriculum. His studies in the 1940s of bias in school materials found distorted and inaccurate information presented about other countries and peoples.

His publications include *Mary McDowell, Neighbor* (1929), *Fusion of Social Studies in Junior High School* (1933), *The United States National Commission for UNESCO* (1948), *Universities and World Affairs* (1951), *College Life as Education in World Outlook* (1956), and *American Higher Education and World Affairs* (with Florence H. Wilson, 1963). He was editor of the *Harvard Educational Review* (1937–45).

Wilson was active in many professional organizations. He was president of the National Council for the Social Studies (1934), directed the civil education section of the New York State Regents Inquiry into the Character and Content of Education (1936–38), chaired the Committee on Asiatic Studies for the American Council on Education (1941–47), and was chairman of the Education Committee of the National Conference of Christians and Jews (1943–47). He received an honorary degree from Illinois College in 1954.

REFERENCES: *LE* (III); *WWW* (IV); *NYT,* August 13, 1966, p. 25; *Social Education* 30 (November 1966):555.                                        *Jack L. Nelson*

**WILSON, Louis Round.** B. December 27, 1876, Lenoir, North Carolina, to Jethro Reuben and Louisa Jane (Round) Wilson. M. June 10, 1909, to Penelope Bryan Wright. Ch. four.

Louis Round Wilson, dean of American university librarianship, attended Haverford (Pennsylvania) College from 1895 to 1898 and transferred to the University of North Carolina in his senior year. He received the A.B. (1899), A.M. (1902), and Ph.D. (1905) degrees from North Carolina, where he also served as librarian from 1901 to 1932.

During his tenure as librarian at North Carolina, Wilson was also associate professor of library administration (1907–12), professor (1912–20), Kenan Professor (1920–32), and the first director of the school of library science (1931–32). He was director of the university's bureau of extension (1912–21) and of the university press (1922–32).

Wilson took over the University of Chicago graduate library school in 1932; the school expanded its program and became one of the most pretigious library schools in the country. He established a curriculum that provided training in administrative skills for all types of libraries and helped establish librarianship as a recognized profession. Wilson retired in 1942 and was named dean emeritus of the University of Chicago graduate library school. From 1942 to 1947 he served as professor of library administration at the University of North Carolina.

Basically an educator, Wilson saw librarianship as a way to help people at all societal levels to gain knowledge and a better life, particularly in the South. Wilson championed equal opportunity for blacks to extend their educational background through the use of libraries. He felt that training black librarians was one way to expand library service. In 1925 he visited southern black colleges for the American Library Association to determine where the Carnegie Corporation of New York should finance a library school for blacks; Hampton Institute in Hampton, Virginia, was chosen. The institute did significant work in training able librarians. The program was discontinued in 1939, but in 1957 Hampton Institute began a successful program for training school librarians.

Wilson was the author of *Chaucer's Relative Constructions* (1906), *The Geography of Reading* (1938), and *Library Planning* (1944). He coauthored *County Library Service in the South* (1935) and *The University Library: Its Organization, Administration and Functions* (1945).

Wilson participated in library surveys at the universities of Georgia, Florida, South Carolina, Stanford, and Cornell. He was chairman of the North Carolina Library Commission (1909–16), president of the American Library Association (1935–36) and the Southeastern Library Association (1924–26), and a member of executive committees of the American Council on Education (1936–39) and the Tennessee Valley Library Council (1946–49). He received several honorary degrees.

REFERENCES: *LE* (III); *WWAE* (XIV); *WWW* (V); Maurice Tauber, *L. R. Wilson: Librarian and Administrator* (New York, Columbia University Press, 1967). *Gary D. Barber*

**WILSON, Lucy Langdon Williams.** B. August 18, 1864, Saint Albans, Vermont, to Samuel and Lucy E. (Crampton) Williams. M. July 17, 1893, to William Powell Wilson. Ch. one. D. September 3, 1937, Lake Placid, New York.

Lucy L. W. Wilson was graduated from the Philadelphia Normal School (1881) and studied at the University of Pennsylvania, from which she received the Ph.D. degree (1897). She also studied at Cornell and Harvard universities and the Marine Biological Laboratory at Woods Hole, Massachusetts.

Wilson was a teacher at Bolivar, Tennessee (1882–84), and returned to Philadelphia where she was a teacher at the Girls' High School (1884–88) and teacher-principal at Rugby Academy (1888–92). She returned to teach at the Girls' High School (1892–1915) and was also chairman of the biology department of the Philadelphia Normal School (1893–1916) and principal of the Evening High School for Women (1900–15). From 1916 to 1934 she was principal of the South Philadelphia High School for Girls. She was a lecturer at Temple University in Philadelphia (1934–36). An internationally recognized advocate of education for women and of individualized laboratory methods of instruction, she lectured and was a consultant in the United States, Europe, and South America.

Wilson was the author of *A Too Short Vacation* (1891), *Nature Study, A Manual for Teachers* (1897), *Nature Study, A Reader* (1897), *A History Reader* (1898), *History in Elementary Schools* (1899), *Domestic Economy and Household Arts* (1900), *Domestic Economy in Grammar Schools* (1900), *Picture Study* (1900), *Domestic Science* (1906), *Geography Visualized by the Stereoscope* (1909), *The New Schools of New Russia* (1928), and *History Reader for Elementary Schools* (1929). She edited *Everyday Manners for Boys and Girls* (1922) and *Education for Responsibility* (1926).

A member of professional associations, she was the president of the Philadelphia Teachers Association (1918–20). She was the first woman recipient of the Bok Award for service to the city of Philadelphia (1934).

REFERENCES: *LE* (I); *NCAB* (29:206); *NYT,* September 4, 1937, p. 15; *WWAE* (I); *WWW* (I); "Two More Colleagues Depart," *Clearing House* 12 (December 1937): 243; *School and Society* 46 (November 6, 1937): 592–94.

*Sylvester Kohut, Jr.*

**WILSON, Peter.** B. November 23, 1746, Ordiquhill, Scotland, to n.a. M. to n.a. M. to Catherine Duryea. Ch. seven. D. August 1, 1825, New Barbadoes, New Jersey.

Peter Wilson's enthusiasm for Greek and Latin studies began under the tutelage of a local clergyman and continued later at Aberdeen (Scotland) University. He emigrated to America in 1763 and taught in New York City where his reputation led to his being named principal of Hackensack Academy in New Jersey.

He declined a teaching position at Queen's (later, Rutgers) College in 1783 and 1786 and accepted an invitation to be professor of classics at Columbia College in 1789. He resigned in 1792 to become principal of Erasmus Hall Academy in Flatbush, Long Island, New York, but rejoined Columbia College in 1797 as professor of Greek and Latin languages and antiquities. Except for administrative duties in 1800–01 while the college was choosing a president, Wilson's chief activities were those of a scholar and a teacher.

Wilson's most widely used work, *Introduction to Greek Prosody* (1811), was written because "the candidates for the freshman class at Columbia College were enjoined to render themselves masters of Greek prosody, previous to admission." His other textbooks were *Rules of Latin Prosody for the Use of Schools* (1810) and *Compendium of Greek Prosody* (1817). He also edited Sallust's *Cataline and Jugurtha* (1808), Zacharias Pearce's Greek text of *Longinus on the Sublime* (1812), Alexander Adam's *Roman*

*Antiquities* (1819), and a Greek text of the *New Testament* (1822).

He represented Bergen County in the New Jersey legislature from 1777 to 1781 and again in 1787. He was selected in 1783 to revise and codify the laws of New Jersey. He received honorary degrees from Brown University (1786) and Union College (1798). He retired from Columbia College in 1820.

REFERENCES: *AC; DAB; NCAB* (6:276); *WWW* (H).    *David Delahanty*

**WILSON, Thomas Woodrow.** B. December 28, 1856, Staunton, Virginia, to Joseph Ruggles and Janet (Woodrow) Wilson. M. June 24, 1885, to Ellen Louise Axson. M. December 18, 1915, to Edith (Bolling) Galt. Ch. three. D. February 3, 1924, Washington, D.C.

Woodrow Wilson moved with his family to Augusta, Georgia, in 1858 and to Columbia, South Carolina, in 1870. After being informally taught by his father and selected tutors, he enrolled at Davidson (North Carolina) College in 1874. He studied at the College of New Jersey (later, Princeton University) in 1875 and received the A.B. degree (1879). He chose to practice law and studied at the University of Virginia Law School in Charlottesville. After one year of study, he withdrew for health reasons and completed his legal studies by correspondence. He was admitted to the Georgia bar in 1882 and opened a law office in Atlanta, Georgia. Dissatisfied with law, he decided to become a college teacher and studied history at the Johns Hopkins University in Baltimore, Maryland, from which he received the Ph.D. degree (1886).

Wilson taught at the newly opened Bryn Mawr (Pennsylvania) College (1885–88) and Wesleyan University in Middletown, Connecticut (1888–90). He joined the faculty of the College of New Jersey in 1890 and became professor of jurisprudence. On August 1, 1902, he was appointed president of Princeton University and resigned the post in 1910. He established the preceptorial system, which sought to provide stimulating contacts between students and teachers, and reorganized the undergraduate curriculum. He contributed to the development of the role of university administration. He gained a national reputation by his speeches and writings on political questions and was elected governor of New Jersey in 1910. His reputation grew, and in 1912 he was nominated as the Democratic candidate for president of the United States. He was elected in 1912 and reelected in 1916, serving as president during World War I.

A prolific writer, Wilson wrote many articles and books, including *Congressional Government, A Study in American Politics* (1885), *The State—Elements of Historical and Practical Politics* (1889), *Division and Reunion (1829–1889)* (1893), *An Old Master and Other Political Essays* (1893), *Mere Literature and Other Essays* (1893), *George Washington* (1896), *A History of the American People* (1902), *Constitutional Government in the United States* (1908), *Free Life* (1913), *The New Freedom*

(1913), *When a Man Comes to Himself* (1915), *On Being Human* (1916), and *International Ideals* (1919).

He belonged to many professional associations and was awarded many honorary degrees from American and foreign universities. He was awarded the Nobel Prize for Peace (1920).

REFERENCES: *AC; DAB; EB; NCAB* (19:1) *NYT,* February 4, 1924, p. 1; *TC; WWW* (I); Henry Wilkinson Bragdon, *Woodrow Wilson: The Academic Years* (Cambridge, Mass.: Harvard University Press, 1967); George C. Osborn, *Woodrow Wilson: The Early Years* (Baton Rouge: Louisiana State University Press, 1968); Arthur Walworth, *Woodrow Wilson* (Boston: Houghton Mifflin Co., 1965).          *Richard J. Frankie*

**WILSON, William Dexter.** B. February 28, 1816, Stoddard, New Hampshire, to William and Rhoda Lane (Gould) Wilson. M. November 25, 1846, to Susan Whipple Trowbridge. Ch. none. D. July 30, 1900, Syracuse, New York.

William Dexter Wilson attended an academy at Walpole, New Hampshire, and studied for the ministry at the Harvard Divinity School. He was graduated in 1838 and served as a Unitarian minister (1838–42). He joined the Protestant Episcopal church and served as rector of a church in Sherburne, New York (1842–50).

In 1850 Wilson became an instructor in moral and mental philosophy at Geneva (New York) Divinity School (later, Hobart College) and served as acting president (1867–68). He became a professor of moral and mental philosophy at Cornell University in Ithaca, New York, on its establishment in 1868. On his retirement from Cornell in 1886 he was dean of St. Andrew's Divinity School in Syracuse, New York, to his death.

A prolific writer, Wilson was the author of *The Church Identified by a Reference to the History of its Origin, Perpetuation, and Extension into the United States* (1848), *An Explanation of the Rubrics in the Book of Common Prayer* (1854), *An Elementary Treatise on Logic* (1856), *Attainder of Treason and Confiscation of the Property of Rebels* (1863), *The Closing Scenes of the Life of Christ, a Harmonized Combination of the Gospels* (1869), *Lectures on the Psychology of Thought and Action, Comparative and Human* (1871), *Logic, Theoretical and Practical, a Textbook* (1872), *Fancy and Philosophy, an Introduction to the Study of Metaphysics and the History of Philosophy* (1872), *The Nature of Differentials and the Methods of Finding Them* (1873), *Positive and Negative Terms in Mathematics* (1874), *First Principles of Political Economy* (1875), *Order of Instruction in Mathematics* (1876), *The Influence of Language on Thought* (1879), *Live Questions in Psychology and Metaphysics* (1877), *The Papal Supremacy and the Canon Law of the Ancient Church* (1889), and *Theories of Knowledge Historically Considered with Special Reference to Skepticism and Belief* (1889).

In addition to his scholarship in philosophy, Wilson was a remarkable linguist; he was conversant in Greek, Latin, Arabic, Syriac, French, German, Italian, and ancient Chaldean. Wilson received honorary degrees from Geneva College, Bedford University, and the regents of the University of the State of New York.

REFERENCES: *AC; DAB; NCAB* (12:510). *J. Franklin Hunt*

**WINCHELL, Alexander.** B. December 31, 1824, North East, New York, to Horace and Caroline (McAllister) Winchell. M. December 5, 1849, to Julia F. Lines. Ch. six. D. February 19, 1891, Ann Arbor, Michigan.

Alexander Winchell attended the local North East, New York, district school and one in South Lee, Massachusetts. He was a student at Stockbridge (Massachusetts) Academy and Amenia (New York) Seminary. He was graduated from Wesleyan University in Middletown, Connecticut, with the A.B. (1847) and A.M. (1850) degrees.

Winchell taught in a district school near his home while attending Amenia Seminary and Pennington (New Jersey) Male Seminary (1847–48). He taught natural sciences at Amenia Seminary (1848–50). He moved to Alabama, where he headed Newbern Academy (1850–51) and Mesopotamia Academy at Eutaw (1851–53) and was president of Masonic University at Selma (1853). There was an outbreak of yellow fever at Selma, and he accepted an offer to teach physics and civil engineering at the University of Michigan (1853–55); he became professor of geology, zoology, and botany in 1855. He continued at Michigan to 1873 and also held a similar position at the University of Kentucky (1866–69).

Winchell was chancellor of Syracuse (New York) University (1873–74) and professor of geology to 1878 and also was professor of geology, zoology, and botany at Vanderbilt University in Nashville, Tennessee (1873–78). His views on evolution brought him into conflict at Vanderbilt. When he refused to resign from the professorship at Vanderbilt, the trustees abolished the position in 1878 for alleged economic reasons. He returned to the University of Michigan as professor of geology and paleontology in 1879 and continued there to his death.

Credited with organizing geology as a science in America, Winchell was a major scholar in the field; he described seven new genera and 304 new species of primarily fossil organs. He established the Marshall group in American geology and sought to resolve the conflict between science and religion. He conducted a number of major geological surveys.

In addition to geological reports, Winchell was the author of *Theological Geology* (1857), *Sketches of Creation* (1870), *A Geological Chart* (1870), *The Geology of the Stars* (1873), *The Doctrine of Evolution* (1874), *Reconciliation of Science and Religion* (1877), *Preadamites* (1880), *Sparks from a Geologist's Hammer* (1881), *World Life* (1883), *Geological Excursions* (1884), *Geological Studies* (1886), and *Walks and Talks in the Geological*

*Field* (1886). He was one of the founders of the *American Geologist* (1888).

Winchell was a fellow and vice-president of the American Association for the Advancement of Science, vice-president of the Geological Society of America, and a member of many American and foreign organizations. He was awarded an honorary degree by Wesleyan University in 1867.

REFERENCES: *AC; DAB; DSB; NCAB* (16:119); *NYT,* February 20, 1891, p. 5; *TC; WWW* (H).                                        *Robert C. Morris*

**WINSHIP, Albert Edward.** B. February 24, 1845, West Bridgewater, Massachusetts, to Isaac and Drusilla (Lothrop) Winship. M. August 24, 1870, to Ella Rebecca Parker. Ch. six. D. February 18, 1933, Cambridge, Massachusetts.

Albert E. Winship, dean of educational journalists, attended school in a neighbor's kitchen and East Greenwich (Rhode Island) Academy.

Winship served in the Civil War (1864–65) and was a teacher in a rural school and principal of a grammar school in Newton, Massachusetts (1865–68). He was a teacher at Bridgewater (Massachusetts) State Normal School (later, Bridgewater State College) from 1868 to 1871 and, after a business venture that was destroyed in the Boston fire of 1872, studied at Andover (Massachusetts) Theological Seminary to 1876. He was pastor of the Prospect Hill Congregational Church in Somerville, Massachusetts (1872–83), where he also organized and taught evening classes for workers. The classes were considered to be one of the first adult education programs in the country.

Secretary to the New West Education Commission (1883–86), Winship was editor of the *Journal of Education* in Boston (1886–1933). He became an influential figure in school finance and the improvement of education. He supported the concept of the school as a community center and the teaching of agriculture, music, art, health, and physical education. Winship was the author of *The Shop* (1889), *Life of Horace Mann* (1896), *Great American Educators* (1900), *Jukes-Edwards, a Study in Education and Heredity* (1900), *Danger Signals of Teachers* (1919), *Educational Preparedness* (1919), *Heredity* (1919), *Fifty Famous Farmers* (with L. S. Ivins, 1924), and *Educational History* (1929). He was editor-in-chief of the *Boston Traveller* (1891).

Elected honorary life president of the National Education Association in 1932, Winship was active in many organizations and was president of the National Educational Press Association (1895) and the American Institute of Instruction (1896). He was Massachusetts representative to the Editorial Association (1899–1906) and a member of school committees of Bridgewater, Somerville, and Reading, Massachusetts, and the Massachusetts State Board of Education (1903–09). He was a member of the National Advisory Commission on Illiteracy appointed by President Herbert Hoover. He was the recipient of honorary degrees by the universities of Nashville and Vermont, New York State College for Teachers, Andover Theological Seminary, and the College of William and Mary.

REFERENCES: *DAB; LE* (I); *NCAB* (2:119); *NYT*, February 18, 1933, p. 15; *WWAE* (II); *WWW* (I); J. W. Crabtree *(q.v.)*, "Albert E. Winship," *School and Society* 38 (July 29, 1933):149–50.                *Robert Emans*

**WINSLOW, Charles-Edward Amory.** B. February 4, 1877, Boston, Massachusetts, to Erving and Catherine Mary (Reignolds) Winslow. M. May 19, 1907, to Anne Fuller Rogers. Ch. one. D. January 8, 1957, New Haven, Connecticut.

Charles-Edward Amory Winslow received the B.S. (1898) and M.S. (1899) degrees from Massachusetts Institute of Technology (MIT), the A.M. degree from Yale University in 1916, and the D.P.H. degree from New York University in 1908.

Winslow served as a research assistant and instructor at MIT in sanitary bacteriology and sanitary biology from 1900 to 1910. He was associate professor of biology at City College of New York (1910–14) and curator of public health at the American Museum of Natural History in New York (1910–22). He was director of the Division of Public Health Education of the New York State Department of Health (1914–15). In New York, he gained prominence in public health administration. Winslow was Anna M. R. Lauder Professor of Public Health at Yale Medical School and founder and first chairman of the department of public health from 1915 to 1945. He was director of the John B. Pierce Laboratory of Hygiene (1932–47).

He was the author and coauthor of many books on sanitation and health, including *Elements of Water Bacteriology* (with Samuel C. Prescott, 1904), *Elements of Industrial Microscopy* (1905), *Healthy Living* (1917), *The Land of Health* (with Grace T. Hallock, 1922), *Nursing and Nursing Education in the United States* (1923), *The Laws of Health and How to Learn Them* (with Pauline B. Williamson, 1925), *Fresh Air and Ventilation* (1926), *The Road to Health* (1929), and *Health on the Farm and in the Village* (1931). He edited the *American Journal of Public Health* and was first editor of the *Journal of Bacteriology* (1916–44).

Winslow was active in many professional organizations; he was a fellow of the American Association for the Advancement of Science and a member of the American Public Health Association (president, 1925–26) and the Society of American Bacteriologists (president, 1913–14). He was a member of the Public Health Council of Connecticut and the advisory council of the National Institute of Health. He received the Leon Bernard Foundation Award (1952) and William T. Sedgwick Medal and was awarded honorary degrees by Yale and New York universities.

REFERENCES: *NCAB* (D:443); *NYT*, January 9, 1957, p. 31; *WWW* (III);

*American Journal of Public Health* 42 (December 1952): 1616; Reginald M. Atwater, "C-E. A. Winslow, An Appreciation of a Great Statesman," *American Journal of Public Health* 47 (September 1957): 1065–70; John F. Fulton, "C-E. A. Winslow, Leader in Public Health," *Science* 125 (June 21, 1957): 1236; Ira V. Hiscock, "Charles-Edward Amory Winslow," *Journal of Bacteriology* 73 (March 1957): 295–96.    *Jerry L. Ainsworth*
*Karen Ann Hayward*

**WINTHROP, John.** B. December 19, 1714, Boston, Massachusetts, to Adam and Anne (Wainwright) Winthrop. M. July 1, 1746, to Rebecca Townsend. M. March 24, 1756, to Hannah (Fayerweather) Tolman. Ch. five. D. May 3, 1779, Cambridge, Massachusetts.

John Winthrop, America's first astronomer and founder of seismology, was credited with an important role in establishing science in the colonies. He was graduated from Harvard College with the A.B. degree (1732) and continued in private scientific study (1732–38).

Winthrop became professor of mathematics and natural science at Harvard in 1738 and served to his death. The foremost teacher of science in the eighteenth century, he was credited with influencing Benjamin Franklin *(q.v.),* Benjamin Thompson, and others to scientific endeavors. He introduced the study of calculus to the Harvard curriculum. Winthrop gained international recognition for astronomical observations, including the first transit of the century of Venus in 1740 and the second transit (1761) in Newfoundland on an expedition financed by the Massachusetts colonial government, believed to be the first sent out by an American government. He was the first to apply computations to earthquakes when he observed the November 18, 1775, quake that struck New England and is thus credited with establishing the science of seismology.

Winthrop was the author of *Lecture on Earthquakes* (1755), *Answer to Mr. Prince's Letter on Earthquakes* (1756), *Account of Some Fiery Meteors* (1765), and *Two Lectures on the Parallax* (1769). He served as probate judge of Middlesex County, Massachusetts, and a member of the Massachusetts Governor's Council (1773–74). A fellow of the Royal Society and member of the American Philosophical Society, he was awarded honorary degrees by the University of Edinburgh, Scotland (1771), and Harvard College (1773).

REFERENCES: *AC; DAB; DSB; NCAB* (7:165); *WWW* (H).
*D. Richard Bowles*

**WIRT, William Albert.** B. January 21, 1874, near Markle, Indiana, to Emanuel and Mary (Elick) Wirt. M. August 15, 1900, to Bertha Ann Koch. M. July 10, 1919, to Martha Ruth Jacques. M. to Mildred Harter. Ch. three. D. March 11, 1938, Gary, Indiana.

William Albert Wirt was graduated from DePauw University in Greencastle, Indiana, with the Ph.B. (1898) and Pd.D. (1916) degrees. He studied at the postgraduate level at DePauw and at the University of Chicago and studied educational methods in England, Belgium, France, and Germany.

Wirt was superintendent of schools at Redkey, Indiana (1895–97), and taught high school mathematics at Greencastle, Indiana (1897–99). Superintendent of the Bluffton (Indiana) public schools (1899–1907), Wirt gained national recognition with his innovative educational methods. In 1907 Wirt became superintendent of the Gary (Indiana) public schools, where he remained to his death in 1938.

Wirt developed the Gary, platoon, or work-study-play system in which students were assigned to two groups or platoons. While one platoon studied basic subjects, the other was engaged in activity subjects, such as physical education, in special rooms. By alternating classes, the capacity of a school was increased 40 percent and the children's school day was 20 percent longer than the schoolteachers', without hiring additional staff. Wirt was hired by the New York City board of education in 1914 to establish the system in New York schools. A report of a study of the system by the General Education Board was published in 1918.

Wirt attracted national attention in April 1935 by making charges that President Franklin D. Roosevelt was a potential "Kerensky" and his brain trust was engaged in revolutionary activities. He suggested that the schools were being used to spread communist propaganda. A congressional investigation was made and found no evidence to support the charges.

Wirt received an honorary degree from DePauw University in 1916.

REFERENCES: *DAB* (supp. 2); *LE* (I); *NCAB* (A:138); *NYT,* March 12, 1938, p. 17; *WWW* (I).                                          *Dolores Michalski*

**WISE, Isaac Mayer.** B. March 29, 1819, Steingrub, Bohemia, to Leo and Regina (Weis) Weis. M. May 26, 1844, to Therese Bloch. M. April 25, 1876, to Selma Bondi. Ch. fourteen. D. March 26, 1900, Cincinnati, Ohio.

Isaac Mayer Wise lived in Prague, Bohemia (later, Czechoslovakia), and Vienna, Austria, where he studied at various rabbinical schools, a gymnasium at Prague, and the University of Prague and the University of Vienna. He became a rabbi at the age of twenty-three and served a congregation at Radnitz, Bohemia (1843–46). About 1846 he changed his name from Weis to Wise.

Wise emigrated to the United States in 1846 and served as a rabbi to the Congregation Beth El in Albany, New York, where he introduced reforms, including equal rights for women in the synagogue, family pews, choral singing, confirmation, and sermons in the vernacular. In 1847 he proposed a single ritual for American Jews and called a meeting in 1848 seeking a union of congregations. Unsuccessful, he continued to seek unity in the Jewish community.

In 1854 Wise moved to Cincinnati, Ohio, where he served to his death as rabbi of Congregation B'nai Jeshurun. In 1854 he established the short-lived Zion College. He called a conference in Cleveland, Ohio, seeking establishment of a synod that would constitute the authority for American Judaism. The synod did not materialize, but Wise carried out other projects discussed at Cleveland. With others he edited *Menhag America* (1855), the first successful American Hebrew prayer book to provide a common text and uniform ritual. He was credited with organizing the Union of American Hebrew Congregations (1873) and helped organize and was first president (1889–1900) of the Central Conference of American Rabbis. He helped establish the Hebrew Union College and served as first president from 1875 to his death in 1900.

Among the books Wise wrote were *History of the Israelitish Nation* (1854), *Essence of Judaism* (1860), *Judaism: Its Doctrines and Duties* (1862), *The Martyrdom of Jesus of Nazareth* (1874), *The Cosmic God* (1876), *History of the Hebrews' Second Commonwealth* (1880), and *Pronaos to Holy Writ* (1891). His *Reminiscences* (1901) was published posthumously. He was publisher of the *Israelite* (later, *American Israelite*) from 1854 to 1900 and of the German language supplement, *Die Deborah* (from 1854). He wrote novels in English and German and two plays.

Wise was active in secular education and served as an examiner of teachers applying for positions in the Cincinnati public schools. He was on the board of directors of the University of Cincinnati.

REFERENCES: *AC; DAB; EB; NCAB* (10:116); *NYT,* March 27, 1900, p. 1; *WWW* (H); Bernard J. Bamberger, *The Story of Judaism* (New York; Schocken Books, 1957); *Encyclopaedia Judaica* (New York: Macmillan, 1971); Bernard Martin, *A History of Judaism* (New York: Basic Books, 1974), vol. 2; Simon Noveck, *Great Jewish Thinkers of the Twentieth Century* (New York: B'nai B'rith Department of Adult Jewish Education, 1963); David Philipson, *The Reform Movement in Judaism* (New York: Macmillan, 1931).                                        *David E. Kapel*

**WIST, Benjamin Othello.** B. August 7, 1889, St. Paul, Minnesota, to Johannes Benjamin and Josephine (Aasve) Wist. M. December 18, 1912, to Blanche Carmen Canario. Ch. three. D. October 26, 1951, Washington, D.C.

Benjamin Othello Wist studied at Luther College in Decorah, Iowa (1906–09), and received the A.B. degree (1911) from Spokane (Washington) College. He received the M.A. (1924) and the Ph.D. (1937) degrees from Yale University. He studied at the University of California in 1911.

Wist was a high school teacher in Almira, Washington (1910–11), and principal of elementary schools in Hawaii at Kaiwiki (1911–12), Pahala

(1912–14), and Honokaa (1914–15). He served as principal of the Kamehameha III School on Maui Island (1915–21).

Wist was president of the Territorial Normal School in Honolulu (1921–31) and dean of the teachers' college of the University of Hawaii (1931–48). He developed a five-year teacher education program at Hawaii, established laboratory schools, and initiated planning for a university school, which was established after his retirement. A friend and associate of Governor Oren E. Long *(q.v.),* Wist was active in the movement for statehood for Hawaii and suffered a fatal heart attack in Washington, D.C., while on a statehood mission.

Wist was the author of *A Century of Public Education in Hawaii* (1940). He was chairman of the Survey Commission to American Samoa (1932–33), director of the Honolulu Education Council, and president of the Hawaii Education Association (1925). A regent of the University of Hawaii, he was a delegate to the Hawaii State Constitutional Convention of 1950 and was vice-chairman of the Hawaii Statehood Commission.

REFERENCES: *LE*(III); *WWW* (III); *Hawaii Advertiser,* October 27, 1951, p. 1, October 28, 1951.                                    *John F. Ohles*

**WITHERSPOON, John.** B. February 5, 1722, Gifford (sometimes given as Yester), Haddingtonshire, Scotland, to James and Anne (Walker) Witherspoon. M. September 12, 1748, to Elizabeth Montgomery. M. May 30, 1791, to Ann Dill. Ch. twelve. D. September 15, 1794, near Princeton, New Jersey.

John Witherspoon attended the Haddington (Scotland) Grammar School and was graduated from the University of Edinburgh (Scotland) with the master of arts (1739) and divinity (1743) degrees. He was ordained to the ministry in Beith (1745) and Paisley (1757), Scotland.

Declining the presidency of the College of New Jersey (later, Princeton University) in 1766, Witherspoon accepted a second offer in 1768 and moved to Princeton, New Jersey, bringing with him three hundred volumes for the college library. He toured the colonies soliciting financial support for the college. He taught theology at the college, enlarged the study of philosophy to include political science and international law, and introduced instruction in Hebrew and French and the use of the lecture method of instruction. He served as president to his death.

Witherspoon was a leader of Presbyterian support for the revolutionary forces in the colonies and was a signer of the Declaration of Independence. He was a member of the New Jersey Committee of Correspondence (1775) and the New Jersey Provincial Congress (1776), was a delegate from New Jersey to the Continental Congress (1776–82), and was a member of the board of war and committee of finance. He was chairman of the committee to organize the church government by the Presbyterian church in America (1785–89).

Witherspoon was the author of *Ecclesiastical Characteristics* (1753), *Essay on Justification* (1756), *Regeneration* (three volumes, 1764), *Sermons on Practical Subjects* (1768), *Practical Discourses* (1768), and *The Dominion of the Providence over the Passions of Men* (1776). He was awarded an honorary degree by the University of Aberdeen, Scotland (1764).

REFERENCES: *AC; DAB; EB; NCAB* (5:466); *TC; WWW* (H); Willard Thorp, ed., *The Lives of Eighteen From Princeton* (Princeton, N.J.: Princeton University Press, 1946); Martha L. Lemmon Stohlman, *John Witherspoon* (Philadelphia: Westminster Press, 1976).

*Michael R. Cioffi*

**WITHERSPOON, John Alexander.** B. September 13, 1864, Columbia, Tennessee, to John McDowell and Mary (Hanks) Witherspoon. M. November 8, 1888, to Cornelia Dixon. Ch. four. D. April 26, 1929, Nashville, Tennessee.

John Alexander Witherspoon received his formal education in local Maury County (Tennessee) schools and at Austin College in Sherman, Texas. He returned to Maury County, studied medicine for two years with a local physician, and attended the Medical School of the University of Pennsylvania from which he received the M.D. degree (1887). He engaged in postgraduate study in New York City, Germany, France, Scotland, and England.

Witherspoon practiced medicine briefly in Columbia, Tennessee. He joined the medical faculty of the University of Tennessee as a professor of physiology and became professor of medicine in 1891. Moving to Vanderbilt University in Nashville, Tennessee, in 1895, he assisted in reorganizing the medical department. He visited Europe to study its better medical schools and to obtain supplies for the department. He served as professor of medicine and clinical medicine at Vanderbilt to his death. He worked to raise the standards of medical education and practice.

The author of articles on medical practice and standards and on treatment of diseases, Witherspoon helped found the *Southern Medical Journal* and was its first editor (1908–09) and associate editor (1911–15). He was president of the American Medical Association (1913–14) and a member of its council on medical education (1904–13). He was also president of the Association of American Medical Colleges (1909), the Southern Medical Association, the Tennessee State Medical Association, the Nashville Academy of Medicine, and the Mississippi Valley Medical Association (1909–10). He was a delegate to the International Medical Congress in London, England, and served as a member of the house of delegates of the congress for eight years.

REFERENCES: *DAB; NYT,* April 27, 1929, p. 19; *WWW* (I); Morris

Fishbein, *History of the American Medical Association, 1847–1947* (Philadelphia: W. B. Saunders, 1947), p. 724; John Trotwood Moore and Austin P. Foster, *Tennessee, The Volunteer State* (Nashville: S. J. Clarke Publishing Co., 1923), 2: 644–45; *Southern Practitioner* 34 (July 1912): 315–16.                                                                *Leon W. Brownlee*

**WITTKOWER, Rudolf.** B. June 22, 1901, Berlin, Germany, to Henry and Gertrude (Ansbach) Wittkower. M. December 31, 1923, to Margot Holzmann. Ch. one. D. October 11, 1971, Scarsdale, New York.

Rudolf Wittkower received the Ph.D. degree from the University of Berlin in 1923 at the age of twenty-two. He went to Rome where he was an assistant and research fellow at the Bibliotheca Hertziana (1923–32). He returned to Germany, where he was a lecturer at the University of Cologne (1932–33). He continued teaching at the Warburg Institute of the University of London (1934–56).

He was at Columbia University as chairman of art history and archaeology (1956–69), where he built a world-famous school of art history. He was Kress Professor at the National Gallery of Art in Washington, D.C. (1969–71), and Slade Professor of Fine Arts at Cambridge University in England (1970–71).

Wittkower was the author of *British Art and the Mediterranean* (1948), *Architectural Principles in the Age of Humanism* (1949), *Gianlorenzo Bernini* (1955), *Born under Saturn* (1963), *The Divine Michelangelo* (1964), *La Cupola di San Pietro di Michelangelo* (1964), and *Art and Architecture in Italy, 1600–1750* (1958).

He was an honorary trustee of the Metropolitan Museum of Art, a Guggenheim Fellow (1961–62), a fellow of the British Academy, the Warburg Institute, and the American Academy of Arts and Sciences, an honorary fellow in the American Philosophical Society and the Royal Institute of British Architects, and a member of the Archaeological Institute of Great Britain and Ireland and many other American and foreign scholarly and professional associations. He was awarded honorary degrees by Duke, Columbia, and Leeds (England) universities.

REFERENCES: *WWW* (V); *NYT,* October 12, 1971, p. 47; "Rudolf Wittkower," *Architectural Review* 151 (January 1972): 63; Milton J. Lewine, "Rudolf Wittkower, 1901–1971," *Art Journal* 31 (Winter 1971–72); 236–37; Howard Hibbard, "Rudolf Wittkower," *Burlington Magazine* 114 (March 1972): 173–77.                     *Roy V. Schoenborn*

**WITTY, Paul Andrew.** B. July 23, 1898, Terre Haute, Indiana, to William L. and Margaret (Kerr) Witty. M. no. D. February 11, 1976, Chicago, Illinois.

Paul Andrew Witty received the A.B. degree (1920) from Indiana State

Teachers College (later, Indiana State University) in Terre Haute and studied at the University of Chicago (1920–22). He received the M.A. (1923) and Ph.D. (1931) degrees from Columbia University.

Witty served as school psychologist at Scarborough-on-Hudson, New York (1922), and was associate professor of educational psychology at the University of Kansas at Lawrence (1924–25). He became professor of education and director of the Psycho-Educational Clinic at Northwestern University in Evanston, Illinois (1930–66).

Witty's first interest was in the development of children. Later he was concerned with the process of learning to read, which led to programs to assist teachers in the teaching of reading and self-help pamphlets and books for children and adults who wished to improve their reading. He conducted significant research in the area of reading and child development. His studies of children's responses to television (distributed through the Television Information Office in 1960) were some of the first attempts at determining the influence of this medium.

Witty was chief educational consultant to D. C. Heath and Company and Western Publishing Company, advisory editor of *My Weekly Reader,* associate editor of *Highlights for Teachers* and *Highlights for Children,* and on the editorial boards of *Exceptional Children* and *Parent Teachers Magazine.* His publications include *The Psychology of Play Activities* (with H. C. Lehman, 1927), *Causation and Diagnosis of Reading Disability* (with David Kopel, 1936), *Mental Hygiene in Modern Education* (1939), *Reading and the Educative Process* (with David Kopel, 1939), *You and the Constitution of the United States* (with Julilly Kohler, 1948), *Reading in Modern Education* (1949), *Helping the Gifted Child* (1952), *Salome Goes to the Fair* (with Anne Coomer, 1953), *How to Become a Better Reader* (1953), *How to Improve Your Reading* (1956), *Developing Your Vocabulary* (with Edith Grotberg, 1960), and *The Teaching of Reading* (with others, 1966). He edited *The Gifted Child* (1951), *The Educationally Retarded and Disadvantaged* (1967), and *Reading for the Gifted and Creative Student* (1971). He wrote the Reading Roundup Series (with others, 1954) and Reading Caravan (seven volumes, with others, 1965).

Witty was a fellow of the American Association for the Advancement of Science and American Psychological Association, director of the National Society for the Study of Education, and president (1954) of the International Council for the Improvement of Reading Instruction, and a member of other professional associations.

REFERENCES: *LE* (III); *NYT,* February 14, 1976, p. 28; *WW* (XXXVIII); *WWAE* (XVI); *WWW* (VI); *Publisher's Weekly* 209 (March 22, 1976): 22.                                                   *Darlene E. Fisher*

**WOLFE, Harry Kirke.** B. November 10, 1858, Bloomington, Illinois, to Jacob Vance and Ellen (Batterton) Wolfe. M. December 19, 1888, to Katherine H. Brandt. Ch. three. D. July 31, 1918, Wheatlands, Wyoming.

Harry Kirke Wolfe moved from Illinois to Lincoln, Nebraska, in 1871. He earned the A.B. degree (1880) from the University of Nebraska. He studied at the University of Berlin, Germany (1883–84), and then spent two years in further study and research at the University of Leipzig, Germany, under Wilhelm Wundt (1884–86). He received the A.M. and Ph.D. degrees in 1886 from the University of Leipzig.

He taught for three years in Nebraska at schools in Edgar, Ponca, and Lincoln. In 1889 Wolfe became the founder and first chairman of the department of philosophy at the University of Nebraska. Interested in pedagogy, he offered several courses in the subject in the philosophy department and established one of the first psychological laboratories in the country. A department of pedagogy was established in 1895. From 1897 to 1901 Wolfe served as superintendent of the South Omaha public schools, leaving that position to serve as principal of Lincoln (Nebraska) High School (1902–05).

Wolfe was professor of education and philosophy at the University of Montana (1905–06) and returned to Nebraska as professor of educational psychology (1906–09). He was head of the department of educational psychology when the university's teachers' college was established in 1908. He continued in that position until 1918, when he was forced to leave when suspicions were raised because of his record of study at German universities. Wolfe was a charter member of the American Psychological Association and wrote a number of articles for professional journals.

REFERENCES: *DAB; NCAB* (18:252); *WWW* (I); Erwin H. Goldenstein, *The First Fifty Years* (Lincoln: University of Nebraska, 1958); *Science* 48 (September 17, 1918): 312–13. *Erwin H. Goldenstein*

**WOLFF, Mary Evaline.** See **MADELEVA, Sister Mary.**

**WOOD, De Volson.** B. June 1, 1832, Smyrna, New York, to Julius and Amanda (Billings) Wood. M. 1859 to Cordera E. Crane. M. 1868 to Frances Hartson. Ch. seven. D. June 27, 1897. Hoboken, New Jersey.

De Volson Wood was limited in his early educational opportunities, but taught in a public school at the age of seventeen. He studied at Cazenovia and Albany, New York, and at the Rensselaer Polytechnic Institute in Troy, New York, where he was graduated in 1857.

He was a professor of civil engineering at the University of Michigan (1857–72). In 1872 he was appointed to the chair of mathematics and mechanics at Stevens Institute in Hoboken, New Jersey, and was given the chair of engineering in 1885, which he held to his death.

Wood invented an air compressor, a steam pump, and a steam rock drill. He contributed many articles to technical journals, and he wrote several books, including *A Treatise on the Resistance of Materials and an Appendix on the Preservation of Timber* (1871), *A Treatise on the Theory of the Construction of Bridges and Roofs* (1873), *The Elements of Analytical Mechanics* (1876), *Principles of Elementary Mechanics* (1878), *The Elements of Co-ordinate Geometry* (1879), *The Mechanics of Fluids* (1884), *Trigonometry, Analytical, Plane, and Spherical* (1885), *The Luminiferous Aether* (1886), *Thermodynamics* (1887), and *Theory of Turbines* (1895).

He was a fellow of the American Association for the Advancement of Science, a corresponding member of the Society of Architects, and a member of the American Society of Civil Engineers and the Society of Mechanical Engineers. He received honorary degrees from Hamilton College and the University of Michigan.

REFERENCES: *A C; NCAB* (13:351); *NYT,* June 28, 1897, p. 7; *WWW* (H); R. S. Woodward, "De Volson Wood," *Science* 6 (August 6, 1897): 204–06.

*Robert H. Truman*

**WOOD, George Bacon.** B. March 12, 1797, Greenwich, New Jersey, to Richard and Elizabeth (Bacon) Wood. M. April 2, 1823 to Caroline Hahn. Ch. none. D. March 30, 1879, Philadelphia, Pennsylvania.

George Bacon Wood was educated in New York City and attended the University of Pennsylvania where he received the A.B. (1815) and M.D. (1818) degrees.

After graduation he practiced medicine in Philadelphia. He was a professor of chemistry (1822–31) and professor of materia medica (1831–35) at the Philadelphia College of Pharmacy. He became professor of materia medica and pharmacy at the University of Pennsylvania (1835–50) and professor of the theory and practice of medicine (1850–60). He was an attending physician at the Pennsylvania Hospital (1835–59). In 1865 he endowed an auxiliary faculty of medicine of five academic chairs.

Wood was the author of *The History of the University of Pennsylvania* (1834), *The Dispensatory of the United States* (with Franklin Bache, 1833), *Treatise on the Practice of Medicine* (two volumes 1847), and *Treatise on Therapeutics and Pharmacology, or Materia Medica* (two volumes, 1856).

Wood was elected president of the College of Physicians of Philadelphia in 1848 and continued in that position until his death, the longest administration in the history of the organization. He was president of the American Medical Association (1855–56) and the American Philosophical Society (1859–79) and chaired the National Committee for the Revision of the United States Pharmacopeia (1850–60). From 1863 until his death, he was a

trustee of the University of Pennsylvania.
REFERENCES: *AC; DAB; NCAB* (5:346); *WWW* (H).

*Richard M. Coger*

**WOOD, Thomas Denison.** B. August 2, 1865, Sycamore, Illinois, to Thomas H. and Katharine Hannah (Allen) Wood. M. June 25, 1891, to Abbie W. Alden. Ch. none. D. March 20, 1951, New York, New York.

Thomas D. Wood attended Oberlin (Ohio) College from which he received the A.B. (1888) and A.M. (1891) degrees. After his sophomore year he studied with Dudley Sargent *(q.v.)* at the Normal School of Physical Training in Boston, Massachusetts, and during the summer of 1889 worked with Robert J. Roberts *(q.v.)* at the Boston Young Men's Christian Association. He studied medicine at the College of Physicians and Surgeons at Columbia University and received the M.D. degree (1891).

Wood went to the newly established Stanford (California) University in 1891 as professor of hygiene and physical training, director of physical education, and college physician. He established a program that was the first in the United States to award credit for physical education. He organized a summer school for teachers at Pacific Grove, California.

In 1901 Wood returned to Columbia University to organize a department of physical education and to improve the student health services program. Remaining at Columbia to his retirement in 1931, Wood became the first professor of health education (1927) in the United States, initiated the first school health program, and established the first graduate programs in the field. Called the Father of the Natural Idea of Play, he developed purposes, content, and methods for school and college physical education programs centering on games, sports, dancing, outdoor activities, and general skills. He was among the first to emphasize health as a fundamental condition to meet the aims of education.

Wood was chairman of the committee that produced *Health and Education,* the ninth yearbook of the Society for the Study of Education (1910), and also wrote *Healthful Schools* (with others, 1910), *The Child in School* (1924), *Course of Study in Health Education* (with Ruth Strang, *q.v.,* 1925), *Byways to Health* (with Theresa Dansdill, 1925), *Source Book in Health and Physical Education* (with C. L. Brownell, 1925), *Health Through Prevention and Control of Disease* (with H. G. Rowell, 1927), *Health Supervision and Medical Inspection of Schools* (with H. G. Rowell, 1927), *Ventilation and Health* (with E. M. Hendriksen, 1927), *The New Physical Education* (with Rosalind Cassidy, *q.v.,* 1927), *Health Behavior* (with M. O. Lerrigo, 1928), and *Teaching How to Get and Use Human Energy* (with M. O. Lerrigo, 1928). He was coauthor of the Adventures in Living Series (1936).

Active in professional associations, Wood was chairman of the joint committee on health problems in education for the American Medical Association and the National Education Association (1911–38), the Commission on the Welfare of Teachers of the New York State Teachers Association (1913–16), the health section of the International Federation of Home and School (1928–36), and the committee on the schoolchild of the White House Conference on Child Health and Protection (1930). He was a fellow of the American Academy of Medicine, the American Academy of Physical Education, and the American Association for the Advancement of Science. He received an award from the American Academy of Physical Education and received the Gulick Award for distinguished professional service three times.

REFERENCES: *LE* (III); *NCAB* (E:485); *NYT,* March 21, 1951, p. 33; *WWW* (III); Ellen W. Gerber, *Innovators and Institutions in Physical Education* (Philadelphia: Lea and Febiger, 1971); Dorothy La Salle, "Thomas Denison Wood," *Journal of Health, Physical Education and Recreation* 31 (April 1960): 61; *School and Society* 73 (March 31, 1951): 204; Deobold Van Dalen, Elmer D. Mitchell *(q.v.),* and Bruce L. Bennett, *A World History of Physical Education* (New York: Prentice-Hall, 1953); Arthur Weston, *The Making of American Physical Education* (New York: Appleton-Century-Crofts, 1962).                                  *Adelaide M. Cole*
                                                                          *Richard B. Morland*

**WOOD, William Christopher.** B. December 10, 1880, Elmira, California, to Emerson and Martha Jane (Turner) Wood. M. July 12, 1905, to Agnes Kerr. Ch. one. D. May 15, 1939, Piedmont, California.

Will Christopher Wood began his career teaching in a country school for two years. Following a year of study at Stanford (California) University, he became principal of his hometown school in Elmira, California, and then of a school in Fairfield, California, where he remained for five years. He also served as head of the Solano County Board of Education. Wood accepted a principalship at Wilson School in Alameda (1906–09) and served as superintendent of Alameda schools (1909–14).

In 1914 at the age of thirty-three, Wood became the first California State Commissioner of Secondary Schools. He took over the post of California State Superintendent of Public Instruction in 1919 and served in that position until 1927. Through the years Wood attended the University of California and University of Southern California, from which he received the M.A. degree in 1919.

He served as secretary of the California Teachers Association (1908–09), a member of the Board of Regents of the University of California (1919–1927), and president of the National Council of State Departments of Education (1919–20). He was a contributor of articles to various journals and was coeditor with Alice C. Cooper and Frederick A. Rice of a high school textbook, *America's Message* (1925), which included selections from American literature.

In 1927 Wood accepted an appointment by Governor Clement C. Young as State Superintendent of Banks. Later, he was vice-president and manager of the main office of the Bank of America in Oakland, California. Ill health forced his retirement at the age of fifty-four; he died five years later.

REFERENCES: *NCAB* (29:470); *WWW* (I); Roy W. Cloud, *Education in California* (Stanford, Cal.: Stanford University Press, 1952); Jeannette A. Vanderpol, "Will C. Wood, Chief of Schools" (Doct. diss., University of Southern California, 1953). *Dana T. Elmore*

**WOODBRIDGE, Frederick James Eugene.** B. March 26, 1867, Windsor, Ontario, Canada, to James and Melissa Ella (Bingham) Woodbridge. M. June 25, 1895, to Helena Belle Adams. Ch. four. D. June 1, 1940, New York, New York.

F. J. E. Woodbridge moved with his family to Kalamazoo, Michigan, in 1868 where he grew up and attended school. He received the A.B. (1889) and A.M. (1898) degrees from Amherst (Massachusetts) College where he was attracted to the study of philosophy and religion. He was graduated from Union Theological Seminary in 1892. From 1892 to 1894 he studied philosophy in Berlin, Germany.

Woodbridge returned from Germany and taught philosophy at the University of Minnesota (1894–1902). He moved to Columbia University in 1902 and assumed the professorship of philosophy that had been held by Nicholas Murray Butler *(q.v.)*. He became Johnsonian Professor of Philosophy in 1904 and was dean of the graduate faculties (1912–29); he reorganized graduate education at Columbia. He served as Mills Professor of Philosophy at the University of California (1916–17) and was Roosevelt Exchange Professor of American History at Berlin, Germany (1931–32).

A scholar of Plato and Aristotle, Woodbridge taught a yearly seminar on Aristotle's writings. He was a leader of the American realist movement in philosophy. He was a founder with James M. Cattell *(q.v.)* of the *Journal of Philosophy* and served as editor (1904–40). He was the author of *The Philosophy of Hobbes* (1903), *The Purpose of History* (1916), *The Realm of Mind* (1926), *Contrasts in Education* (1929), *Son of Apollo* (1929), and *Nature and Mind* (1937).

He was a fellow in the American Psychological Association, the American Association for the Advancement of Science, and the New York Academy of Sciences and served as president of the American Philosophical Association (1912). He was elected an Amherst College trustee in 1920 and also served for some time as chairman of the board of education in Montrose, New York. He received honorary degrees from six colleges and universities in the United States, Canada, and Germany.

REFERENCES: *DAB* (supp. 2); *LE* (I); *NCAB* (D:301); *NYT*, June 2, 1940, p. 45; *WWW* (I); Paul A. Wolfe, "Conversations with the Old Man," *American Scholar* 14 (Winter 1944): 33–44.        *Erwin H. Goldenstein*

**WOODBRIDGE, William Channing.** B. December 18, 1794, Medford, Massachusetts, to William and Ann Nancy (Channing) Woodbridge. M. November 27, 1832, to Lucy Ann Reed. Ch. two. D. November 9, 1845, Boston, Massachusetts.

William Channing Woodbridge was graduated from Yale College in 1811 at the age of sixteen. He studied in Philadelphia for nearly a year and studied theology at Yale and the College of New Jersey (later, Princeton University).

He was principal of an academy at Burlington, New Jersey (1812–14). He joined Thomas Gallaudet (*q.v.*) at the new Asylum for the Deaf and Dumb at Hartford, Connecticut (1817–20). Failing health ended Woodbridge's teaching career by 1820. He followed the advice of his physician to travel in southern Europe, where he gathered geographic data and visited schools. The rest of his life he traveled in Europe and published books in the United States. Woodbridge observed the application of Johann Heinrich Pestalozzi's ideas in schools he visited and became personally acquainted with Pestalozzi.

During his travels Woodbridge gathered material for his geographies, which included *Rudiments of Geography* (1821), *Universal Geography, Ancient and Modern* (with Emma Willard, *q.v.*, 1824), *Woodbridge's Geography* (1827), *Preparatory Lessons for Beginners* (1831), and *Modern School Geography* (1844). These texts introduced the concept of the teaching of geography by comparison and classification, rather than by question and answer. He bought the *American Journal of Education* in 1831 and changed the title to *American Annals of Education and Instruction*. He served as editor from 1831 to 1837.

REFERENCES: *AC; DAB; NCAB* (11:214); *WWW* (H); William A. Alcott (*q.v.*), "Memoir of William C. Woodbridge," *American Journal of Education* 5 (June 1858); 51–64; F. B. Dexter, *Biographical Sketches of Graduates of Yale College* (New York: Henry Holt and Co., 1885), 6: 429–32.        *D. Richard Bowles*

**WOODHOUSE, James.** B. November 17, 1770, Philadelphia, Pennsylvania, to William and Anne (Martin) Woodhouse. M. no. D. June 4, 1809, Philadelphia, Pennsylvania.

James Woodhouse was a pioneer in chemical education. He spent his academic career at the University of Pennsylvania where he received the B.A. (1787), M.A. (1790), and M.D. (1792) degrees. In 1795 he succeeded his former professor, Benjamin Rush (*q.v.*), to the chair of chemistry at the

University of Pennsylvania, a position he held until his death in 1809. His students included Robert Hare (inventor of the oxy-hydrogen blowtorch) and Benjamin Silliman *(q.v.),* the first professor of chemistry at Yale University and founder of the *American Journal of Science and Art.*

Woodhouse was a disciple of the new chemistry of Antoine Laurent Lavoisier. He accepted the theory that combustion takes place when combustible material combines with oxygen. He helped establish Lavoisier's concepts in the United States. An avid experimenter, Woodhouse devoted much of his research to the chemistry of plants and plant products and was credited with being the first to demonstrate the superiority of Lehigh anthracite coal over bituminous coal for heating; he conducted other significant research. He was a pioneer in the use of laboratory methods in the instruction of chemistry.

Woodhouse was the author of *The Young Chemist's Pocket Companion,* (1797), the first publication of chemical experiments for students in the United States. He also wrote *Observations on the Combinations of Acids, Bitters, and Astringents* (1793), *Answer to Dr. J. Priestley's Considerations on the Doctrine of Phlogiston and the Decomposition of Water* (1794), and *Experiments and Observations in the Vegetation of Plants* (1802), and he edited James Parkinson's *Chemical Pocket-Book* (1802) and *Elements of Chemistry* by J. A. C. Chaptal (two volumes, 1807).

Woodhouse served as a surgeon in the expedition against western Indians by General Arthur St. Clair in 1791. He founded the Chemical Society of Philadelphia, one of the first in the world, in 1792. He was president of the society for seventeen years.

REFERENCES: *AC; DAB; WWW* (H).                    *B. Richard Siebring*

**WOODRUFF, Caroline Salome.** B. July 15, 1866, West Burke, Vermont, to George and Octavia (Bemis) Woodruff. M. no. D. July 13, 1949, Castleton, Vermont.

Caroline Salome Woodruff attended local public schools and St. Johnsbury (Vermont) Academy. She was graduated from the State Normal School (later, Johnson State College) at Johnson, Vermont, and studied at Teachers College, Columbia University.

Woodruff began her teaching career in a small Vermont rural school around 1885 while completing her high school and academy courses and was principal and teacher at Union Graded School in St. Johnsbury (1886–1914). She was with the Vermont state department of education (1915–17) and was district superintendent of schools in Essex County, Vermont (1917–18), being responsible for the schools in Concord and surrounding towns. She was principal of the junior high school at the State Normal School at Johnson (1918–20).

Woodruff was invited to become principal of the Castleton (Vermont)

Normal School (later, Castleton State College) in 1921. Although the school had been closed for a year, by the end of her first year in office, the school had thirty students. During the time she headed the school (1921–40), the Castleton school survived and prospered while other normal schools were closed in favor of high school training courses for teachers. The one-year training program was increased to a four-year degree program.

Woodruff was active in professional associations, including the National Education Association (member of the executive committee, director, vice-president, and president, 1937–38), the National Council of Administrative Women in Education (president, 1927–29), the New England Normal School Association (president, 1936), and the Vermont State Teachers Association (first woman president, 1914–15). She was a delegate to the World Federation of Education Associations seven times (1923–35) and was chairman of the board of managers of the Vermont State Teachers Retirement Fund.

Woodruff was the author of *A Textbook on Vermont Taxes* (1915) and *My Trust and Other Verse* (1928). She received honorary degrees from Middlebury College and Norwich University, the first woman to be so honored by the military college.

REFERENCES: *WWW* (II); *American Women: The Official Who's Who Among the Women of the Nation* (Los Angeles: American Publications, 1937); *New York Herald Tribune*, July 15, 1949; *NYT*, July 16, 1949, p. 13; *Rutland* (Vermont) *Herald*, July 15, 1949.                    *John F. Ohles*

**WOODS, Albert Fred.** B. December 25, 1866, near Belvidere, Illinois, to Fred Moffit and Eliza Olivia (Eddy) Woods. M. June 1, 1898, to Bertha Gerneaux Davis. Ch. four. D. April 12, 1948, Hyattsville, Maryland.

Albert Fred Woods was graduated from the University of Nebraska with the B.Sc. (1890) and M.A. (1892) degrees and worked there as an assistant botanist (1890–93).

Woods worked for the United States Department of Agriculture, as a pathologist in the Division of Vegetable Physiology and Pathology (1893–1900) and in the Bureau of Plant Industry (1900–10). In 1910 Woods became dean of the Minnesota State Agricultural College and director of the Experimental Station. He reorganized the agricultural curriculum into groups of related subjects and abolished the various divisions within the school. His success led to an offer of the presidency of the Maryland State College in 1917.

Woods went to Maryland during World War I, and the school became a virtual military camp as a center for military programs. He raised standards, increased programs, and built new physical facilities. When the war ended, enrollment rapidly increased, and Woods successfully fought for increased state funds. He lobbied with the legislature to make the school an institution of higher education that did not specialize solely in agriculture. In 1919 seven schools were established within the college (agriculture, engineering, arts and sciences, chemistry, education, home economics, and graduate school). The liberal arts were established as a basic part of the curriculum. Maryland State College merged with the University of Maryland in 1920.

Woods remained as president of the university. He recruited outstanding educators and set up a committee to evaluate programs and raise standards. The enrollment and prestige of the university increased. In 1920 the University of Maryland awarded its first M.A. degree in a field other than agriculture and its first Ph.D.; in 1925 it was accredited by the Association of American Universities.

Woods resigned in 1926 and returned to the Department of Agriculture where he served as director of scientific work (1926–34), as director of its graduate school (1926–41), and as an educational adviser (1941–47). As director of the graduate school he implemented a better system of continuing education that improved the overall qualities of the personnel of the Department of Agriculture.

Woods was active in professional organizations and published many articles and reports, primarily in scientific journals. He was president of the American Horticultural Society (1921–23) and Land Grant Colleges Association (1925). A fellow of the American Association for the Advancement of Science, he was president of the first Inter-American Conference on Agriculture, Forestry and Animal Husbandry (1930). He received several honorary degrees.

REFERENCES: *NCAB* (B:467, 46:457); *WWW* (II); Gladys L. Baker et al., *Century of Service: The First 100 Years of the United States Department of Agriculture* (Washington, D.C.: Government Printing Office, 1963); George H. Callcott, *A History of the University of Maryland* (Baltimore: Maryland Historical Society, 1966); *NYT,* April 13, 1948, p. 27; *School and Society* 67 (April 24, 1948); 312.                                 *Richard J. Cox*

**WOODS, Leonard.** B. November 24, 1807, Newbury, Massachusetts, to Leonard and Abigail (Wheeler) Woods. M. no. D. December 24, 1878, Boston, Massachusetts.

Leonard Woods, son of the eminent theologian Leonard Woods, attended Phillips Academy at Andover, Massachusetts (1815–23), and Dartmouth College in Hanover, New Hampshire (1823–24). He was graduated from Union College in Schenectady, New York, with the A.B. degree (1827). He was graduated from Andover (Massachusetts) Theological Seminary in 1827 and was a resident postgraduate student (1831–33). He was licensed to preach and was ordained in the Presbyterian ministry (1833).

Woods was an assistant instructor in Hebrew at Andover Theological Seminary (1830–31) and was an acting pastor and editor of *Literary and Theological Review* in New York City (1833–36). He was professor of sacred literature at Bangor (Maine) Theological Seminary (1836–39) and president of Bowdoin College in Brunswick, Maine (1839–66). He replaced the formal system of discipline with the honor system and was responsible for the construction of the King Chapel. In 1866 he traveled to Europe for the state of Maine to collect materials about the early history of the state.

Woods wrote *Discovery of Maine* (1868) and translated *Lectures on Christian Theology* by G. C. Knapp (two volumes, 1831–33). He was a member of the state historical societies of Maine, Massachusetts, and New York. He received honorary degrees from Harvard University and Colby and Bowdoin colleges.

REFERENCES: *AC; DAB; NCAB* (1:418); *TC; WWW* (H).   *John F. Ohles*

**WOODSON, Carter Godwin.** B. December 19, 1875, New Canton, Virginia, to James Henry and Anne Eliza (Riddle) Woodson. M. no. D. April 3, 1950, Washington, D.C.

Carter Godwin (sometimes, Goodwin) Woodson was self-educated as a boy and attended the Douglas High School in Huntington, West Virginia, while working in a coal mine. He was graduated from high school in 1896 and enrolled in Berea (Kentucky) College (1896–98 and 1901–02), where he received the LL.B. degree (1903). He attended the University of Chicago during the summers of 1900–03 and 1907–08 and received the A.B. (1907) and M.A. (1908) degrees. He was a student in residence (1908–09) and received the Ph.D. degree (1912) from Harvard University. He also traveled and studied in Europe, Asia, and Egypt, including one semester in the Sorbonne in Paris, France (1906–07).

Woodson taught school in Winona, West Virginia (1898–1900), and was principal (1900–03) of Douglas High School. He was a supervisor of schools in the Philippine Islands (1903–06), a high school teacher in Washington, D.C. (1909–18), and principal of Washington's Armstrong Manual Training High School (1918–19). He was also an instructor in Miner Normal School (later, District of Columbia Teachers College) in Washington (1918–19) and served as professor of history and dean of the school of liberal arts at Howard University (1920–22) and dean of West Virginia Collegiate Institute (later, State College) at Institute (1922–24). He organized and served as executive director of the Association for Study of Negro Life and History (1916–50), and founded and served as president of Associated Publishers (1921–50), a publishing company to produce books by blacks not generally accepted by commercial publishers.

A major author of books on blacks and black culture, Woodson wrote *The Education of the Negro Prior to 1861* (1915), *A Century of Negro*

*Migration* (1918), *History of the Negro Church* (1921), *The Negro in Our History* (1922), *Negro Orators and their Orations* (1925), *Free Negro Owners of Slaves in the United States in 1830* (1925), *The Mind of the Negro* (1925), *Negro Makers of History* (1928), *African Myths* (1928), *The Rural Negro* (1930) *The Negro Professional Man and the Community* (1934), *The Story of the Negro Retold* (1935), *The African Background Outlived* (1936), and *African Heroes and Heroines,* (1939). He edited *The Works of Francis J. Grimké* (1942) and was founder and editor of *The Journal of Negro History* (1916–50) and *Negro History Bulletin* (1937–50).

In 1926 Woodson promoted observance of the annual Negro History Week in the schools. He received the Spingarn Medal of the National Association for the Advancement of Colored People (1926) and an honorary degree from Virginia State College (1939).

REFERENCES: *CB* (February 1944); *DAB* (supp. 4); *NCAB* (38:367); *NYT,* April 5, 1950, p. 31; *WWW* (III); Wade Barkin and Richard N. Runes, *Dictionary of Black Culture* (New York: Philosophical Library, 1973); L. H. Reddich, "Carter Woodson (1875–1950), An Appreciation," *Phylon* 10 (June 1950): 177–79; Charles H. Wesley *(q.v.),* "Carter G. Woodson, As a Scholar," *Journal of Negro History* 36 (January 1951); 12–24.                                                              *John F. Ohles*

**WOODWARD, Calvin Milton.** B. August 25, 1837, Fitchburg, Massachusetts, to Isaac Burnap and Eliza (Wetherbee) Woodward. M. September 30, 1863, to Fanny Stone Balch. Ch. nine. D. January 12, 1914, St. Louis, Missouri.

Calvin M. Woodward received the A.B. degree (1860) from Harvard University. In 1861 he became principal of Brown High School in Newburyport, Massachusetts, a post he left for a year to join the Forty-eighth Regiment of the Massachusetts Volunteers as a lieutenant (1862–63). He returned to Newburyport in 1863 and served as principal of Brown High School until 1865 when he became vice-principal and teacher of mathematics at the Smith Academy in St. Louis, Missouri, the academy of the newly established Washington University. In 1870 he became Thayer Professor of Mathematics and Applied Mechanics at Washington University and became dean of the university's polytechnic school in 1871. He was dean of the reorganized school of engineering and architecture in 1901 and held that position until his retirement in 1910.

Woodward became concerned about the inability of his university students to perform elementary toolwork and came to believe that the problem lay in inadequate preparation in the public schools. He studied manual training programs developed in Russia and by John D. Runkle *(q.v.)* of the Massachusetts Institute of Technology. He developed a high school program that combined toolwork and science, mathematics, modern language, and literature. Woodward persuaded the university to establish the St. Louis Manual Training High School as a separate preparatory branch of Washington University. The school opened in 1879 with Woodward as its director; he gained national recognition for his work with the school. He became a popular speaker at educational meetings and traveled to Great Britain promoting manual training.

He was the author of *A History of the St. Louis Bridge* (1881), *The Manual Training School* (1887), *Manual Training in Education* (1890), and *Rational and Applied Mechanics* (1912).

Woodward was active in educational and engineering organizations and was a member (1877–79 and 1897–1914) and president (1899–1900 and 1903–04) of the St. Louis Board of Education. He was a member of the board of curators of the University of Missouri (1891–97 and president, 1894–97). He was president of the American Association for the Advancement of Science (1905–06), the St. Louis Academy of Science (1907–08), and the North Central Association of Colleges and Secondary Schools (1909–10).

REFERENCES: *DAB; NCAB* (9:469); *WWW* (I); Charles P. Coates, *History of the Manual Training School of Washington University* (Washington, D.C.: United States Bureau of Education Bulletin, no. 3, 1923); *Washington University Record* 9 (January 1914).

*B. Edward McClellan*


**WOODWORTH, Robert Sessions.** B. October 17, 1869, Belchertown, Massachusetts, to William Walter and Lydia Ames (Sessions) Woodworth. M. April 23, 1903, to Gabrielle Marie Schjöth. Ch. four. D. July 4, 1962, New York, New York.

Robert S. Woodworth was graduated from Amherst (Massachusetts) College in 1891 and then taught for two years at the high school in Watertown, New York. From 1893 to 1895 he was an instructor in mathematics at Washburn College in Topeka, Kansas. He attended Harvard University from which he was graduated with the A.B. (1896) and A.M. (1897) degrees. He was an assistant in physiology at the Harvard Medical School (1897–98) before attending Columbia University, from which he received the Ph.D. degree (1899).

Woodsworth was an instructor in physiology at the University and Bellevue Hospital Medical College in New York City (1899–1902). He was a Johnson Fellow and demonstrator of physiology at the University of Liverpool, England (1902–03). Returning to Columbia in 1903, he began his distinguished and long career in psychology, retiring as professor emeritus in 1942. He continued to lecture in Columbia's school of general studies until 1958.

Woodworth's first psychological studies were concerned with the speed of dreaming. He became an expert on the voluntary control of movements, tests and measurements, race differences, and physiological psychology. Of particular importance were his questionnaires to test emotional fitness of World War I draftees, his advocacy in 1924 that immigration tests should be based solely on the physical and mental merits of the individuals, and his development of aptitude tests for specific job categories in the early 1930s.

His books in the fields of psychology and physiology include *Le Mouvement* (1903), *Elements of Physiological Psychology* (with G. T. Ladd, *q.v.*, 1911), *The Care of the Body* (1912), *Dynamic Psychology* (1918), *Psychology: A Study of Mental Life* (1921), *Contemporary Schools of Psychology* (1931), *Adjustment and Mastery* (1933), *Experimental Psychology* (1938), *Psychological Issues* (1939), *Heredity and Environment* (1941), *First Course in Psychology* (with Mary R. Sheehan, 1944), and *Dynamics and Behavior* (1958). In addition to contributing many articles to journals in these fields he was editor of *Archives of Psychology* (1906–45).

Woodworth was a fellow of the American Association for the Advancement of Science (vice-president, 1909, 1924), and he held memberships in many other professional and scholarly associations, including the American Psychological Association (president, 1914) and the Social Science Research Council (president, 1931–32). He was awarded the first gold medal of the American Psychological Foundation in 1956 and five honorary degrees from American colleges and universities.

REFERENCES: *LE* (III); *NCAB* (A.24, 48:546); *NYT*, July 5, 1962, p. 25; *WWAE* (XVI); *WWW* (IV); H. J. Eyseneck, W. Arnold, and R. Meili, eds., *Encyclopedia of Psychology* (New York: Herder and Herder, 1972).

*Robert H. Truman*

**WOODY, Clifford.** B. June 2, 1884, Thorntown, Indiana, to Thomas and Susanna (Beesley) Woody. M. August 29, 1917, to Alice May Woody. Ch. none. D. November 19, 1948, Ann Arbor, Michigan.

Clifford Woody spent his early life on a farm and attended public schools in Thorntown, Indiana. He received the B.A. (1908) and M.A. (1913) degrees from Indiana University and the Ph.D. degree (1916) from Columbia University.

Woody taught high school and was superintendent of schools in Gaston, Indiana (1908–12), and he taught high school in Bloomington, Indiana (1912). He went to the University of Washington in 1916, remaining to 1921 as professor of education. From 1921 to 1948 he was professor of education and director of the Bureau of Education and Research at the University of Michigan. He was a specialist in the training of elementary teachers and worked in the area of educational measurement.

Among Woody's writings were *Measurements of Some Achievements in Arithmetic* (1916), *Woody Arithmetic Scales—How to Use Them* (1920),

*Problems of Elementary School Instruction* (1923), *Brown Woody Civic Test* (1925), *Sangren Woody Reading Test* (1927), *New Problems in Elementary School Instruction* (1932), *Adventures in Dictionary Lands* (books 1–3, 1932), *Administration of Testing Programs* (1932), *Child Life Arithmetics* (1935), and *Modern Life Speller* (1936). He edited the twenty-eighth and twenty-ninth yearbooks of the National Society of College Teachers of Education. He was a member of the editorial board of the *Journal of Educational Research* and wrote numerous journal articles.

Woody was a fellow of the American Association for the Advancement of Science, secretary-treasurer of the National Society of College Teachers of Education (1940–47), president of the American Educational Research Association (1923–24), and a member of many other professional associations.

REFERENCES: *LE* (III); *NCAB* (37:487); *WWAE* (XIII); *WWW* (II); *NYT,* November 21, 1948, p. 88.                                    *Robert McGinty*

**WOOLLEY, Helen Bradford Thompson.** B. November 6, 1874, Chicago, Illinois, to David W. and Isabella P. (Faxon) Thompson. M. August 8, 1905, to Paul Gerhardt Woolley. Ch. two. D. December 24, 1947, Havertown, Pennsylvania.

Helen Bradford Thompson Woolley received the Ph.B. (1897) and Ph.D. (1900) degrees from the University of Chicago. She studied in Paris, France, and Berlin, Germany (1900–01), and then joined the faculty of Mount Holyoke College in South Hadley, Massachusetts, becoming director of the psychological laboratory and professor of psychology.

Woolley went to Japan in 1905 and worked in Manila, Philippine Islands, as a psychologist, returning to the United States where she joined the faculty of the University of Cincinnati (1909–11). She founded the Cincinnati Vocational Bureau and conducted research about students leaving school. Her findings were reported in national publications and at national meetings and were published in 1926 as *An Experimental Study of Children at Work and in School between the Ages of Fourteen and Eighteen Years.* She was active in the passage of a revised compulsory school attendance and child labor law for Ohio.

The Woolleys moved to Detroit, Michigan, in 1921. She was a psychologist and became associate director (1922) of the Merrill-Palmer School. She established one of the first nursery schools in the country for the study of child development and teacher education. She worked with Elizabeth Cleveland to develop the Merrill-Palmer Scale of Mental Tests.

In 1925 Woolley became professor of education at Teachers College, Columbia University, and director of the Institute of Child Welfare Research. She remained there until 1930 when she was forced to resign because of ill health and personal problems. She spent the remaining years of her life with her daughter in Havertown, Pennsylvania.

In addition to her professional contributions, Woolley was active as a community leader. She had many publications to her credit that reflect her interdisciplinary approach to the study of children where she tried to bring to bear research in many disciplines to focus on the whole child. Among these are *The Mental Traits of Sex* (1903), *Mental and Physical Measurements of Working Children* (1914), *Diagnosis and Treatment of Young School Failures* (1922), *An Experimental Study of Children* (1926), and *Education and the Pre-School Child* (1930). She also contributed numerous papers to journals and conferences.

Woolley was a fellow of the American Association for the Advancement of Science and a member of other professional associations. She was a delegate to the Ninth International Congress of Psychology at Yale University (1930), Third Conference of Nursery School Workers in Chicago (1929), White House Conference on Child Health and Protection (1930), and the First International Conference on Mental Hygiene in Washington (1930).

REFERENCES: *LE* (II); *NAW; WWW* (III).          *Sally H. Wertheim*

**WOOLLEY, Mary Emma.** B. July 13, 1863, South Norwalk, Connecticut, to Joseph J. and Mary A. (Ferris) Woolley. M. no. D. September 5, 1947, Westport, New York.

Mary Emma Woolley was educated in elementary and secondary schools in Connecticut and Rhode Island. She was graduated from Wheaton Seminary (1884) in Norton, Massachusetts, and taught at Wheaton from 1886 to 1891. In 1891 Woolley was the first woman to enroll at Brown University in Providence, Rhode Island, where she was one of the first two women to receive the A.B. degree (1894). She received the M.A. degree from Brown in 1895.

Woolley was a member of the biblical history and literature department at Wellesley (Massachusetts) College (1895–1900) and served as head of the department (1899–1900). In 1900 she was appointed president of Mount Holyoke College in South Hadley, Massachusetts, where she served to her retirement in 1937. As president of Mount Holyoke College for thirty-seven years, Woolley won national recognition for her administration of the college. She raised academic standards, built a strong faculty, strengthened the undergraduate liberal arts program, and created an innovative graduate program. Sixteen major buildings were added to the physical plant, and the endowment was increased to nearly $5 million.

Woolley was the author of several historical monographs, a contributor to the *Encyclopaedia Britannica,* and a writer of articles on education. She was a senator of Phi Beta Kappa, chairman of the College Entrance Examination Board (1924–27), president (1927–33) and chairman of the committee on international relations (1933–39) of the American Association of University Women, and a director of the World Alliance for Promoting International Friendship through the Churches.

Woolley was associated with many organizations. She was the only woman member of the Commission on Christian Education to China (1922) and the first woman delegate to the Geneva Conference for Reduction and Limitation of Armaments (1932). She was named one of the twelve greatest American women in 1932.

She received the Susan Rosenberger Award from Brown University (1937), the Kassavo Medal of the Royal Red Cross of Yugoslavia (1931), and the Christobol Colon Medal (1940) and was honored by the Women's Centennial Congress (1940) and the Federation of Women's Clubs (1941). She received seventeen honorary degrees from American colleges and universities.

REFERENCES: *CB* (March 1942); *DAB* (supp. 4); *EB; LE* (II); *NAW; NCAB* (D:58, 37:70); *WWAE* (XI); *WWW* (II); *N YT*, September 6, 1947, p. 17; "America's Twelve Greatest Women: Mary E. Woolley," *Good Housekeeping* 92 (March 1931): 34.

*Marie Della Bella*

**WOOLMAN, Mary Raphael Schenck.** B. April 26, 1860, Camden, New Jersey, to John Voorhees and Martha (McKeen) Schenck. M. October 18, 1883, to Franklin Conrad Woolman. Ch. none. D. August 1, 1940, Newton Highlands, Massachusetts.

Mary Schenck Woolman attended a private Quaker school in Philadelphia run by Mary Anna Longstreth and was graduated in 1878. She studied languages and history at the University of Pennsylvania (1883–84). She received a diploma in 1895 and the B.S. degree (1897) from Teachers College, Columbia University.

After the death of Woolman's father and the illness of her husband in 1891, the family moved from New Jersey to New York City where she was appointed an instructor in sewing at Teachers College in 1892. She was an adjunct professor of household arts education and was one of the first women to hold the title of professor at Columbia in 1903.

Woolman took a half-time leave from Teachers College (1901–10) to help organize and direct the establishment in 1902 of the first trade school for girls in the United States, the Manhattan Trade School for Girls. In 1912 she became acting head of the home economics department of Simmons College in Boston, Massachusetts, where she remained to her retirement in 1914 to write, lecture, and lobby to upgrade the education and employment of women and promote vocational education.

Woolman wrote a number of books on domestic and consumer education, including *A Sewing Course for Girls* (1900), *A Sewing Course for Teachers* (1907), *The Making of a Trade School* (1910), *Textiles: A Handbook for Student and Consumer* (with Ellen McGowan, 1917), *Clothing,*

*Choice, Care and Cost* (1920), and *Textile Problems for the Consumer* (with Ellen McGowan and Thomas Carver, 1935).

A vice-president of the National Education Association (1917–18), Woolman was a founding member of the American Home Economics Association and was president of the Women's Educational and Industrial Union (1912–14). She served on school survey committees for the National Society for Vocational Education (later, American Vocational Association) from 1915 to 1917 and helped promote the passage of the Smith-Hughes Act for vocational education in 1917. She was awarded a gold medal by the National Institute of Social Sciences (1926).

REFERENCES: *NAW; NCAB* (A:543); *WWAE* (I); *WWW* (IV); Anna M. Cooley, "Mary Schenck Woolman, Personality and Interests," *Journal of Home Economics* 32 (November 1940): 585–88; Ellen Beers McGowan, "Mary Schenck Woolman, Contributions to the Teaching of Textiles and Clothing," *Journal of Home Economics* 32 (November 1940): 588–89; *School and Society* 52 (August 24, 1940): 124.        *Phyllis Appelbaum*

**WOOLSEY, Theodore Dwight.** B. October 31, 1801, New York, New York, to William Walton and Elizabeth (Dwight) Woolsey. M. September 5, 1833, to Elizabeth Martha Salisbury. M. September 6, 1854, to Sarah Sears Prichard. Ch. thirteen, including Theodore Dwight Woolsey, jurist and Yale University professor of law. D. July 1, 1889, New Haven, Connecticut.

Theodore Dwight Woolsey was graduated from Yale College as valedictorian of his class in 1820. He studied law for a year before entering Princeton (New Jersey) Theological Seminary but left in 1823 to return to Yale as a tutor. He completed his theological studies at Yale. Deciding against a career in the ministry he went abroad in 1827 for further study. He spent his first winter in Paris, France, studying Arabic and studied Greek language and literature at Leipzig, Bonn, and Berlin, Germany (1828–30).

He became professor of Greek at Yale in 1831 and taught for fifteen years before becoming the college's tenth president on October 21, 1846. He was ordained to the ministry on the same day. While he was president, he taught history, political science, and international law. Yale made great strides under Woolsey's leadership. The faculty was enlarged, the curriculum was expanded, and standards were significantly improved. The Sheffield Scientific School and the first college school of fine arts were established, the first American doctor of philosophy degree was awarded (1861), and the corporation of the university was reorganized to include alumni representation (1871).

Woolsey wrote a number of Greek textbooks, including *The Alcestis of Euripides* (1834), *The Antigone of Sophocles* (1835), *The Prometheus of Aeschylus* (1837), *The Electra of Sophocles* (1837), and *The Gorgias of*

*Plato, Chiefly According to Stallbaun's Text with Notes* (1842). His *Introduction to the Study of International Law* (1860) was a major contribution to the field and, with his *Essay on Divorce and Divorce Legislation* (1869), went through many editions. Among his other numerous publications were *The Religion of the Present and of the Future* (1871), *Helpful Thoughts for Young Men* (1874), *Political Science* (1878), and *Communism and Socialism* (1880). He was editor of the *New Englander* for a number of years.

Woolsey received honorary degrees from Wesleyan and Harvard universities.

REFERENCES: *A C; DAB; EB; NCAB* (1:170); *TC; WWW* (H); *NYT,* July 2, 1889, p. 4.                                                      *Robert H. Truman*

**WORCESTER, Joseph Emerson.** B. August 24, 1784, Bedford, New Hampshire, to Jesse and Sarah (Parker) Worcester. M. June 29, 1841, to Amy Elizabeth McKean. Ch. none. D. October 27, 1865, Cambridge, Massachusetts.

Joseph Emerson Worcester left the family farm to prepare for college at Boscawen and Salisbury, New Hampshire, and at Phillips Academy in Andover, Massachusetts. He was graduated from Yale College in New Haven, Connecticut, with the A.B. (1811) and A.M. (1814) degrees.

Worcester taught at Salem, Massachusetts (1811–16). He lived in Andover, Massachusetts (1817–18), and spent the rest of his life in Cambridge, Massachusetts. He was a major lexicographer and writer of textbooks, including the *Geographical Dictionary, or Universal Gazeteer, Ancient and Modern* (two volumes, 1817), *A Gazetteer of the United States* (1818), *Elements of Geography, Ancient and Modern* (1819), *Sketches of the Earth and Its Inhabitants* (1823), *Elements of History, Ancient and Modern* (1826), *Epitome of History* (1827), and *Outlines of Scriptural Geography* (1828). He edited Samuel Johnson's *Dictionary* (1828) and an abridgement of Noah Webster's *(q.v.) American Dictionary* (1829) and compiled the *Comprehensive Pronouncing and Explanatory English Dictionary* (1830), *Universal and Critical Dictionary of the English Language* (1846), and *Dictionary of the English Language* (1860), the first to use illustrations.

Worcester was a fellow of the American Academy of Arts and Sciences and a member of the Massachusetts Historical Society and other groups. He received honorary degrees from Harvard (1820) and Brown (1847) universities and Dartmouth College (1856).

REFERENCES: *AC; DAB; NCAB* (6:50); *NYT,* October 30, 1865, p. 8; *TC; WWW* (H); F. B. Dexter, *Biographical Sketches of Graduates of Yale College* (New York: H. Holt and Co., 1912), 6: 432–37; G. P. Krapp, *The English Language in America* (New York: Century Co., 1925), pp. 370–72;

William Newell, "Memoir of J. E. Worcester, LL.D.," *Proceedings of the Massachusetts Historical Society* 18 (1881): 169–73.

*Stephen J. Clarke*

**WRENN, Charles Gilbert.** B. April 2, 1902, New Paris, Ohio, to Charles C. and Flora (Parker) Wrenn. M. June 15, 1926, to Kathleen LaRaut. Ch. one.

C. Gilbert Wrenn, a leader in the guidance movement, was a student at Tennessee Wesleyan College in Athens (1921–23) and earned the A.B. degree (1927) from Willamette University in Salem, Oregon. He received the A.M. (1929) and Ph.D. (1932) degrees from Stanford (California) University.

Wrenn was vice-principal at Raymond (Washington) High School (1926–27) and director of the training center at Oregon Normal College (later, Oregon College of Education) in Monmouth (1927–28). He was a vocational counselor and assistant professor of education at Stanford University (1932–36). He joined the faculty of the University of Minnesota in 1936 and was professor of educational psychology for twenty-seven years (1937–64). He was professor of educational psychology at Arizona State University (1964–68), visiting professor at Arizona State, and Distinguished Professor at Macalester College in St. Paul, Minnesota.

Wrenn was the author or coauthor of more than 350 books, chapters in textbooks, and articles in journals, encyclopedias, monographs, and yearbooks. His books include *Reading Rapidly and Effectively* (1935), *Time on Their Hands* (1941), *Studying Effectively* (1942), *Student Personnel Problems* (1942), *Building Self-Confidence* (1948), *Guidance Procedures in High School* (1950), *Student Personnel Work in Colleges* (1951), *How to Develop Self Confidence* (1953), *Learning to Study* (1960), *The Counselor in a Changing World* (1962), and *The World of the Contemporary Counselor* (1973). He was editor of the *Journal of Counseling Psychology* (1952–63) and an editorial adviser for Houghton Mifflin Company.

Wrenn served in the United States Navy during World War II. He received the Fulbright Distinguished Scholar Award, England (1965–66), the United States Department of Labor Distinguished Service Award, the Nancy C. Wimmer Award of the American Personnel and Guidance Association (1964), and the Eminent Career Award from the National Vocational Guidance Association (1975). He was a trustee of the American Board of Examiners of Professional Psychology (1951–57), a fellow of the American Psychological Association (president of the division of counseling psychology, 1950–51), president of the American College Personnel Association, president and trustee of the National Vocational Guidance Association, and vice-president and trustee of the Council of Guidance and Personnel Associations. He was a trustee of the Wesley Foundation and of Macalester College.

REFERENCES: *LE* (III); *WW* (XXXVI); *WWAE* (XVI); "C. Gilbert Wrenn Presented Nancy C. Wimmer Award," *Personnel and Guidance Journal* (May 1964): 945–46.                                    *Vernon Lee Sheeley*

**WRIGHT, Arthur Davis.** B. March 24, 1885, Boston, Massachusetts, to John and Margaret Ella (Snell) Wright. M. October 25, 1910, to Mary Morris Rowe. Ch. two. D. May 10, 1947, Washington, D.C.

Arthur D. Wright received the A.B. and A.M. degrees (1904) from the College of William and Mary in Williamsburg, Virginia, and the Ed.M. degree (1922) from Harvard University.

Wright was a teacher in the Hampton, Virginia, high school (1904–06), principal of Baker School in Richmond, Virginia (1906–09), and superintendent of schools in Fredericksburg, Virginia (1909–10), and Henrico (Virginia) County (1910–15). He was Virginia state supervisor of Negro schools (1915–20). He was an educational consultant to the United States Army (1920–21).

Wright was a member of the faculty of Dartmouth College (1921–31) and became president of the Anna T. Jeanes Negro Rural Fund and the John F. Slater Fund (1931–37). The two funds were consolidated into the Southern Education Foundation in 1937 with Wright as president.

Among Wright's books were *Readings in American College Education* (with J. G. Stevens, 1924), *Readings in the Principles of Guidance* (with J. G. Stevens, 1924), and *The Negro Rural School Fund 1907–33* (1933). He edited with G. E. Gardner *Hall's Lectures on School Keeping* (1928). He was a member of state survey teams for Virginia (1919) and Florida (1928). He was president of the New England Association of College Teachers of Education (1928–29) and founder (1922) and national secretary of Kappa Phi Kappa. He was awarded an honorary degree by Dartmouth College.

REFERENCES: *LE* (I); *NCAB* (37:226); *NYT,* May 11, 1947, p. 62; *WWAE* (XI); *WWW* (II); Lance Jones, *The Jeanes Teacher in the United States* (Chapel Hill: University of North Carolina, 1937); *Journal of Negro History* 32 (July 1947): 403–05.                                    *Earl W. Thomas*

**WRIGHT, John Calvin.** B. June 24, 1876, Elkhart County, Indiana, to John J. and Hannah (Postma) Wright. M. June 4, 1903, to Cordelia D. Bennett. Ch. three. D. April 4, 1955, Bamberg, South Carolina.

J. C. Wright attended a country school and was graduated from the Lawrence (Kansas) Business School. He attended the Kansas State Normal School (later, Emporia Kansas State College) in Emporia. He was graduated from the University of Missouri with the B.S. (1918) and A.M. (1919) degrees.

Wright taught in one-room schools in Douglas County, Nebraska (1895–98). He was a teacher, principal, and superintendent of schools in

Belleville, Kansas (1900–04), and a teacher at Central High School in Kansas City, Missouri (1904–12). He was a high school vice-principal and director of vocational education for the Kansas City public schools (1913–17).

When the Smith-Hughes Act was passed and the Federal Board for Vocational Education was established in 1917, Wright was invited to be a field agent for the board and was chief of the trade and industrial division (1917–22). From 1922 to 1934 he was director of the board and became assistant commissioner for vocational education at the United States Office of Education in Washington, D.C. (1934–46).

Wright was the author of many articles and was the coauthor of books, including four professional works with Charles R. Allen *(q.v.)*: *Administration of Vocational Education* (1926), *Supervision of Vocational Education* (1926), *Efficiency in Education* (1929), and *Efficiency in Vocational Education* (1929). He also coauthored four automotive repair manuals (1921) and *Automotive Construction and Operation* (with Fred O. Smith, 1924). He was editor of the Trade and Industrial Education Series.

Wright was a member of professional organizations. He was chairman of the United States delegation to the Second Inter-American Conference in Education held in Santiago, Chile (1934), and a delegate to the Second Inter-American Conference on Agriculture in Mexico City, Mexico (1942), and he made a survey of technical education in Mexico City (1942). He was chairman of the United States Commission to study vocational education in Mexico (1945) and a member of the United States Commission on Life Adjustment Education for Youth (1947–50). He received an honorary degree from Stout Institute (1926).

REFERENCES: *LE* (III); *WWW*(V). *Ming H. Land*

**WRIGHT, Richard Robert.** B. May 16, 1853, Whitfield, County, Georgia, to Robert and Harriett Waddell. M. June 7, 1876, to Lydia Elizabeth Howard. Ch. none. D. July 2, 1947, Philadelphia, Pennsylvania.

Richard R. Wright took the surname of his stepfather, Alexander Wright. Hearing about a Freedman's Bureau school for Negroes that had been opened in Atlanta, Georgia, his mother took her three children there, where she opened a boardinghouse. Wright entered Starr's School operated by the American Missionary Association (it has been memorialized in John Greenleaf Whittier's 1869 poem, "Howard at Atlanta"). Wright entered the preparatory department of Atlanta University in 1869, graduating as valedictorian of that institution's first class with the A.B. (1876) and A.M. (1879) degrees.

Wright's first job was as principal of an elementary school in Cuthbert, Georgia, where he helped farmers devise methods of marketing their own produce and helped conduct the first Negro county fair in the state. In 1880

Wright was invited to Augusta, Georgia, to establish and head Ware High School, the state's first public high school for blacks.

When the State Industrial College for Negroes (later, Savannah State College) was established at Savannah in 1891 under the authority of the Morrill Act of 1890, Wright was appointed president and remained until his retirement in 1921. After retiring from public education, Wright moved to Philadelphia to establish the successful Citizens and Southern Bank.

Wright was the author of *A Brief Historical Sketch of Negro Education in Georgia* (1894). In 1878 he called the first convention of Negro teachers in the state and served as first president of the Georgia State Teachers' Association. He began publishing the *Weekly Journal of Progress,* first as an association organ and later as the *Weekly Sentinel,* a general newspaper.

He was a founder and president of the Georgia State Agricultural and Industrial Association and trustee of Atlanta University (1880–98). He was president of the National Association of Presidents of A&M Colleges for Negroes (1900–06), the National Association of Teachers in Colored Schools (1908–12), and the Negro Bankers Association. He served on many state commissions and was the founder (1941) of National Freedom Day. He received the Muriel Dobbins Pioneers of Industry Award (1946) and an honorary degree from Wilberforce University.

REFERENCES: *DAB* (supp. 4); *WWW* (II); Horace Mann Bond (*q.v.*), *Black American Scholars—A Study of Their Beginnings* (Detroit, Mich.: Balamp, 1972); Rayford W. Logan, *The Betrayal of the Negro* (New York: Collier Books, 1965); *NYT,* July 3, 1947, p. 21.          *Walter C. Daniel*

**WRISTON, Henry Merritt.** B. July 4, 1889, Laramie, Wyoming, to Henry Lincoln and Jennie Amelia (Atcheson) Wriston. M. June 6, 1914, to Ruth Colton Bigelow. M. June 28, 1947, to Marguerite Woodworth. Ch. two.

Henry Merritt Wriston attended Wesleyan University in Middletown, Connecticut, from which he received the A.B. (1911) and A.M. (1912) degrees. He studied at Harvard University (1911–14), was an Austin Teaching Fellow (1912–14), and was awarded the Ph.D. degree (1922).

Wriston taught history at Wesleyan University (1911–25). He was president of Lawrence College (later, University) in Appleton, Wisconsin (1925–37), and also was director of the Institute of Paper Chemistry in Appleton (1929–37). He was president of Brown University in Providence, Rhode Island (1937–55). He doubled Brown's endowment funds, increased the enrollment, built the Metcalf Research Laboratory, and set up a new infirmary and health center. Wriston was executive director (1955–58), president (1958–62), and chairman (1962–65) of the American Assembly.

Wriston was the author of *War Chest Practice* (1918), *Report of Connecticut State Council of Defense* (1919), *Executive Agent in Foreign Relations* (1929), *The Nature of a Liberal College* (1937), *Prepare for Peace*

(1941), *Challenge to Freedom* (1943), *Strategy of Peace* (1944), *Diplomacy in a Democracy* (1956), *Wriston Speaking* (1957), *Academic Procession* (1959), and *Perspectives on Policy* (1963).

A member of many organizations, Wriston was president of the North Central Association of Colleges and Secondary Schools (1933–34), the Educational Association of the Methodist-Episcopal Church (1933–34), the Association of American Colleges (1935–36), the Association of American Universities (1948–50), and the Council on Foreign Relations (1951), and he was vice-president of the American Association for Adult Education (1937–43). He was public governor of the New York Stock Exchange (1950–52), chairman of the Secretary of State's Public Committee on Personnel (1954), and trustee of the Carnegie Foundation for the Advancement of Teaching (1933–55), the American Federation of the Arts (1933–38 and 1940–41), the Educational Records Bureau (1939–54), the World Peace Foundation (1939–52), and the Carnegie Endowment for International Peace (1943–54). He was a fellow of the American Academy of Arts and Sciences, a delegate to the International Studies Conference in Bergen, Norway (1939), and a member of the executive committees of the American Council on Education (1941–44) and the Council on Financial Aid to Education (1953–56). He was the recipient of many honorary degrees from American and foreign colleges and universities.

REFERENCES: *CB* (May 1952); *LE* (III); *NCAB* (F:340); *WW* (XXXI); *WWAF* (XVI); "How to Live Dangerously," *Time* 65 (April 11, 1955): 46.                                                                *John F. Ohles*

**WULLING, Frederick John.** B. December 24, 1866, Brooklyn, New York, to John C. and Louise C. (Muns) Wulling. M. September 15, 1897, to Lucile Truth Gissel. Ch. one. D. October 21, 1947, Excelsior, Minnesota.

Frederick John Wulling was graduated from Bryant and Stratton Business College in New York City (1884). He studied medicine and turned to pharmacy, graduating from the Columbia University College of Pharmacy (1887). He received the Pharm.D. degree (1894) from the University of Minnesota and also studied law there, receiving the LL.B. (1896) and LL.M. (1898) degrees. He made study trips to Europe in 1887, 1889, 1894, 1897, and 1911.

Wulling taught inorganic pharmaco-diagnosis at the Brooklyn (New York) College of Pharmacy (1891–92) and spent the rest of his professional career at the University of Minnesota, where he established the college of pharmacy. He served as dean of the college and professor of pharmacology (1892–1936). He established the first medicinal plant garden at an American university at Minnesota and served as its director (1911–36). The Minnesota school developed into one of the leading institutions of its kind in the country.

Wulling was the author of a number of books, including *Evolution of Botany* (1891), *Medicinal and Pharmaceutical Chemistry* (1894), *Chemistry of the Carbon Compounds* (1900), *A Course in Law* (1908), *The Pharmacist's Relation to the Public* (1931), *Charles F. Chandler: A Retrospect* (1944), *Peter Wendover Bedford: A Retrospect* (1945), and *The First Four Melendy Memorial Lectures* (1946). He served as editor of *Pharmaceutical Record* (1887–91).

Wulling was active in professional affairs. He was a fellow of the American Association for the Advancement of Science and founder of the American Association of Colleges of Pharmacy (president, 1914–15). He was a member of the American Pharmaceutical Association (president, 1916–17) and a trustee of the United States Pharmacopaeial Convention (1920–30). He was chairman of the Minnesota Academy of Science (1910–30). He received honorary degrees from the Philadelphia College of Pharmacy and Columbia University. The college of pharmacy building at the University of Minnesota was named in his honor.

REFERENCES: *LE* (II); *NCAB* (E:131); *WWAE* (VIII); *WWW* (II).

B. Richard Siebring


**WYLIE, Andrew.** B. April 12,1789, Washington, Pennsylvania, to Adam Wylie and his wife n.a. M. May 1813 to Margaret Ritchie. Ch. none. D. November 11, 1851, Bloomington, Indiana.

Andrew Wylie received his early education at home and in local schools before entering Jefferson College (later, Washington and Jefferson College in Washington, Pennsylvania) in Canonsburg, Pennsylvania, at the age of fifteen. He studied theology, was licensed to preach in 1812, and was ordained in the Presbyterian ministry in 1813. Eventually dissatisfied with the Presbyterian church he was ordained a deacon (1841) and priest (1842) in the Protestant Episcopal church.

Wylie was a tutor at Jefferson College in 1811 and served a church at Miller's Run, Pennsylvania (1813–16). He was president of Jefferson College (1812–16) and of Washington (Pennsylvania) College (later, Washington and Jefferson College) in 1817–28. He also was a pastor at Ten Mile and West Liberty, Pennsylvania (1817–28).

In 1828 Wylie became the first president of Indiana College, which became Indiana University in 1838. Serving as president to his death in 1851, he led the university to a steady growth. He introduced the rotation system of instruction in which a student mastered one subject before studying another. In 1840 a school of law was established at Indiana.

Wylie was the author of *English Grammar* (1822), *The Use of History* (1831), *Eulogy of General Lafayette* (1834), *Latin and Roman Classics* (1838), and *Sectarianism Is Heresy* (1840). He received an honorary degree from Union College in 1825.

REFERENCES: *AC; DAB; NCAB* (13:116); *TC; WWW* (H).

*Robert H. Truman*

**WYTHE, George.** B. 1726, Elizabeth City, Virginia, to Thomas and Margaret (Walker) Wythe. M. December 1747 to Ann Lewis. M. 1755 to Elizabeth Taliafero. Ch. one. D. June 8, 1806, Richmond, Virginia.

George Wythe was tutored by his mother and attended the College of William and Mary in Williamsburg, Virginia. He studied law under John Lewis and was admitted to the bar in 1757.

Wythe was active in politics serving as a member of the House of Burgesses (1758–75). He was a member of the committee that petitioned the king in 1775 for relief from the Stamp Act, was a delegate from Virginia to the Continental Congress (1775), and signed the Declaration of Independence (1776). He was appointed to a committee and with Thomas Jefferson (*q.v.*) and Edmund Pendleton revised the laws of Virginia and was speaker of the House of Delegates (1777). He was a member of the United States Constitutional Convention in 1786. Wythe was selected in 1777 as one of the judges of the chancery court of Virginia and served in the post for twenty years. In a notable decision he ruled that legal claims between British and American merchants were recoverable. He was one of the first judges to hold that a court could rule that a law in conflict with the Constitution is void.

Wythe was the first professor of law in the country; he was appointed professor of law and police at the College of William and Mary (1779–89) and opened a small law school in Richmond, Virginia, when his duties forced him to move from Williamsburg in 1789. Among his law students were Thomas Jefferson, John Marshall, and Henry Clay.

The author of *Decisions in Virginia by the High Court of Chancery* (1795), Wythe was awarded an honorary degree (1790) by the College of William and Mary. He was alleged to have died from poison administered by his nephew George Wythe Sweeney, who was tried and acquitted of the charges.

REFERENCES. *AC; DAB; ED, NCAB* (3.308), *TC; WWW* (H).

*Ronald Iannarone*

# ___ Y ___

**YALE, Caroline Ardelia.** B. September 29, 1848, Charlotte, Vermont, to William Lyman and Ardelia (Strong) Yale. M. no. D. July 2, 1933, Northampton, Massachusetts.

Caroline Ardelia Yale, educator of the deaf, received her early education at home. She attended Williston (Vermont) Academy and Mount Holyoke Seminary (later, College) in South Hadley, Massachusetts.

After two years of teaching in Williston and Brandon, Vermont, she joined the faculty of the Clarke Institution for Deaf Mutes (later, Clarke School for the Deaf) in Northampton, Massachusetts, in 1870, three years after its founding by Harriet B. Rogers *(q.v.)* as the pioneer school in the United States for teaching deaf children by the oral method. In 1873 she became associate principal and succeeded Rogers as principal in 1886. She retired in 1922 with the title of principal emeritus but continued as director of the teacher-training program.

She established the teacher-training program in 1889. Clarke School had been designated the official training center by the American Association for the Promotion of Teaching Speech to the Deaf, an association founded by Alexander Graham Bell *(q.v.)*. During more than fifty years at Clarke School, Yale advocated the oral method and also developed methods that revolutionized the instruction of the deaf by bringing speech and an understanding of speech to deaf children. With Alice C. Worcester, she developed the Northampton speech charts that were widely used as an aid in teaching articulation. She introduced sense training as an aid to teaching deaf children. She believed that children should be regarded as individuals and taught in accordance with their specific skills, abilities, and aptitudes.

She authored *Formation and Development of Elementary English Sounds* (1892) and *Years of Building: Memories of a Pioneer in a Special Field of Education* (1931). She lectured at Smith College, was a member of the Northampton school board, served as trustee of Clarke School (1918–33) and the Northampton State Hospital for the Insane, and was a member of the board of the Massachusetts School for the Feebleminded and a director of the American Association to Promote the Teaching of Speech to the Deaf. She received honorary degrees from Illinois Wesleyan University, Mount Holyoke College, and Smith College.

REFERENCES: *DAB; EB; LE* (I); *NCAB* (31:265); *NYT,* July 3, 1933, p. 11; *WWW* (I); Caroline A. Yale, *Years of Building* (New York: Dial Press, 1931).                                                                *J. Franklin Hunt*

**YOUMANS, Edward Livingston.** B. June 3, 1821, Albany County, New York to Vincent and Catherine (Scofield) Youmans. M. 1861 to Catherine E. (Newton) Lee. Ch. none. D. January 18, 1887, New York, New York.

Edward Livingston Youmans developed an early interest in science. He attended local district schools, but at the age of thirteen, he suffered an eye infection that caused alternating periods of total and near blindness and hindered his scientific interests. In the summer of 1838 he attended an academy in Galway, New York. His sister Eliza Ann read to him and conducted chemical experiments for him. In spite of his ailment, he invented a chemical chart that showed important principles and laws of chemistry by the use of colored diagrams.

Youmans's health improved, and his career as a lecturer on science and as a writer began at the age of thirty. He was active on the lyceum circuit from 1852 to 1869, speaking on chemistry, evolution, and other scientific and educational subjects. He lectured at Antioch College in Yellow Springs, Ohio, in 1866.

Youmans was the author of *A Class-Book of Chemistry* (1851), *Alcohol and the Constitution of Man* (1853), *Chemical Atlas: On the Chemistry of Familiar Objects* (1854), and *Handbook of Household Science* (1854), a text in domestic science. He edited several volumes of the writings of Herbert Spencer and *Correlation and Conservation of Forces* (1864) and *The Culture Demanded by Modern Life* (1867).

He founded the International Scientific Series of more than sixty volumes that were contributed by distinguished scientists, such as Charles Darwin, Hermann von Helmholtz, and Thomas Huxley. He founded *Popular Science Monthly* (later, *Scientific Monthly*) in 1872.

REFERENCES: *AC; DAB; NCAB* (2:466); *TC; WWW* (H); *NYT,* January 19, 1887, p. 8; John Fiske, *Edward Livingston Youmans: Interpreter for the People* (New York. D. Appleton, 1894). *Robert F. Smith*

**YOUNG, Andrew White.** B. March 2, 1802, Carlisle, New York, to n.a. M. October 4, 1827, to Eliza Webster. Ch. five. D. February 17, 1877, Warsaw, New York.

Andrew W. Young was educated in the local common schools and had already taught school for a year by his fourteenth birthday. He moved to Warsaw, New York, in 1816, alternately teaching and working on the family farm. He engaged in the mercantile business for several years. He began publication of the *Warsaw Sentinel* (1830), acquired the *Republican Advocate,* published in Batavia in 1832, and merged the two papers under the *Advocate* title. In 1836 Young published and edited a paper called the *American Citizen.* He represented Wyoming County in the legislature (1845–46) and in the New York State constitutional convention (1846).

In 1856 Young moved to Ripley, New York. His family went to Red Wing, Minnesota, in 1867. He remained behind to complete an unfinished work and joined his family the following year. When his wife died in Red Wing, he moved to Warsaw, New York, in 1876.

After about five years as a newspaper editor, Young had, according to his account, "directed his attention to what has been the principal business of his life": the writing of school texts, particularly in the field of government. Among his books were *Introduction to the Science of Government* (1835), *First Lessons in Civil Government* (1843, followed by a revised edition for use in Ohio, 1847), *Citizens' Manual of Government and Law* (1851), *The American Statesman: A Political History of the United States* (1855), *Government Class Report* (1859), *National Economy: A History of the American Protective System* (1860), and *First Book on Civil Government* (1867). He wrote local histories of Wayne County (Indiana), Chautauqua County (New York), and Warsaw, New York.

REFERENCES: *AC;* Thomas E. Finegan *(q.v.), Free Schools: A Documentary History of the Free School Movement in New York State* (Albany: University of the State of New York, 1921), pp. 120–21; Andrew W. Young, *History of Chautauqua County from Its First Settlement to the Present Time* (Buffalo, N.Y.: Matthews and Warren, 1875), pp. 529–30.

*Jo Ann Kaufman*

**YOUNG, Charles Augustus.** B. December 15, 1834, Hanover, New Hampshire, to Ira and Eliza Minot (Adams) Young. M. August 26, 1857, to Augusta Spring Mixer. Ch. three. D. January 3, 1908, Hanover, New Hampshire.

Charles Augustus Young entered Dartmouth College in Hanover, New Hampshire, at the age of fourteen and was graduated first in his class in 1853. He studied at Andover (Massachusetts) Theological Seminary (1855–56). He accompanied his father, who was professor of natural science and astronomy at Dartmouth, to Europe seeking instruments to equip the Shattuck Observatory being constructed at the college.

Young taught classics at Phillips Academy in Andover, Massachusetts (1853–56), and accepted a position in January 1857 at Western Reserve College at Hudson, Ohio (later, Case Western Reserve University in Cleveland, Ohio). He spent four months in 1862 as a captain of Company B, Eighty-fifth Regiment of the Ohio Volunteers. In 1866 he succeeded his father and grandfather as Appleton Professor of Mathematics, Natural Philosophy, and Astronomy at Dartmouth. He moved to the College of New Jersey (later, Princeton University) where he was professor of astronomy to his retirement in 1905. Under Young, the Princeton Astronomical Observatory became the foremost observatory in the country. He was a participant or organizer of many expeditions to engage in astronomical observations and made significant contributions to the science. He participated in scientific expeditions to Jerez, Spain, in 1870 and Peking, China, in 1874.

Young designed an automatic spectroscope and contributed many articles to popular and scientific publications. He was the author of *The Sun* (1884), *A General Astronomy* (1888), *Elements of Astronomy* (1890), *Lessons in Astronomy* (1891), and *Manual of Astronomy* (1902). A member of professional and scientific organizations, Young was president of the American Association for the Advancement of Science (1883) and a fellow of the National Academy of Sciences. He was the recipient of the Janssen Medal of the French academie des sciences and several honorary degrees from American colleges and universities.

REFERENCES: *AC; DAB; DSB; NCAB* (6:325); *NYT,* January 5, 1908, p. 11; *TC; WWW* (I).                                      *Joseph P. Cangemi*
*Thomas E. Kesler*

**YOUNG, Clark Montgomery.** B. September 3, 1856, Hiram, Ohio, to Erastus Montgomery and Chestina (Allyn) Young. M. August 1, 1883, to Loretta F. Murray. Ch. four. D. February 28, 1908, Vermillion, South Dakota.

Clark Montgomery Young attended a local district school and the preparatory department of Hiram (Ohio) College (1875–78). He taught in the public schools of Kenton, Ohio, and then returned to study at Hiram College in 1880, where he received the Ph.B. degree (1883).

A brother, Sutton E. Young, who had settled in Dakota Territory, encouraged Young to move to the territory, where Young became a principal in the public schools of Scotland. He was superintendent of schools at Mitchell (1884) and at Tyndall (1885), where he also became the publisher of a weekly newspaper, the *Tyndall Tribune.* He was both an educator and a newspaper publisher and editor until 1892.

Young was appointed a member of the territorial board of education in 1889 and became secretary of the South Dakota state board of education later in 1889, serving to 1890. He was professor of history and political science at the University of South Dakota in Vermillion (1892–1901). In 1901 the university was organized into colleges. Young became the first dean of the college of arts and sciences and held this position from 1902 until his death.

Young was the author of *The State and the Nation* (with G. M. Smith, 1895), *The Elements of Pedagogy* (1898), and *History and Government of South Dakota* (1898).

Young served as president of the South Dakota Educational Association (1892–93), was editor of the *South Dakota Educator* from 1900, and helped draft school laws for the state (1901). He served as chairman of the committee that planned the reorganization of the high schools and revised the courses of study for the schools (1905–06).

REFERENCES: *DAB; WWW* (I); *Dakota Republican* (Vermillion, South Dakota), March 5, 1908; *Volante* (University of South Dakota), March 10, 1908.                                      *Lawrence S. Master*

**YOUNG, Ella Flagg.** B. January 15, 1845, Buffalo, New York, to Theodore and Jane (Reed) Flagg. M. 1868 to William Young. Ch. none. D. October 26, 1918, Washington, D.C.

Because of frail health, Ella Flagg Young did not attend school until she was ten years old. The family moved to Chicago, Illinois, in 1858, and she attended the Chicago High School, was admitted to the Chicago Normal School at the age of fifteen, and was graduated in 1862. She later studied at the University of Chicago under John Dewey *(q.v.)* and was awarded the Ph.D. degree in 1900.

Young taught in Chicago at the Foster School (1862–63) and became head assistant at the Brown School (1863–65). She was practice school principal at the Chicago Normal School (1865–71), taught high school classes at Haven School (1871–72), and returned to the normal school as teacher of mathematics (1872–76). She was principal of Scammon School (1876–79) and Skinner School (1879–87) and became assistant superintendent of the Chicago public schools (1887–99). She was professor of education at the University of Chicago (1899–1904) and traveled in Europe for a year before serving as principal of the Chicago Normal School from 1905 to 1909 when she was appointed superintendent of the Chicago public schools, the first woman in the country to head a large city school system.

Under Young a conflict between the teachers' federation and the board of education was resolved, instruction in sex hygiene was instituted, and bright students were accelerated in promotion through the grades. She retired at the end of 1915 and was chairman of the Woman's Liberty Loan Committee in 1917.

Young was the author of many educational papers, including three of the six monographs of the University of Chicago Contributions to Education Series (1901–02) in which she collaborated with John Dewey. She was the author of *Isolation in the School* (1901), *Ethics in the School* (1902), and *Some Types of Modern Educational Theory* (1902). She edited *The Educational Bi-Monthly* (1906–09).

A member of the Illinois state board of education (1888–1912), Young was president of the Illinois State Teachers' Association (1910) and the National Education Association (1910–11). She received an honorary degree from the University of Illinois (1910).

REFERENCES: *DAB; NAW; NCAB* (19:26); *NYT,* October 27, 1918, p. 17; *WWW* (I); *Chicago Tribune,* October 27, 1918, p. 8; Mildred Sandison Fenner and Eleanor C. Fishburn, *Pioneer American Educators* (Port Washington, N.Y.: Kennikat Press, 1944) pp. 129–36; Alice Fleming, *Great Women Teachers* (Philadelphia: J. B. Lippincott Co., 1965), pp. 101–14; John T. McManis, *Ella Flagg Young and a Half Century of the Chicago Schools* (Chicago: A. C. McClurg and Co., 1916).

*Joanne L. Schweik*

**YOUNG, Jacob William Albert.** B. December 28, 1865, York, Pennsylvania, to Jacob and Mary (Lentz) Young. M. 1896 to Dora Louise van Hees. Ch. none. D. October 25, 1948, New York, New York.

Jacob William Albert Young received the A.B. (1887) and A.M. (1890) degrees from Bucknell University in Lewisburg, Pennsylvania. He attended the University of Berlin, Germany (1888–89), and received the Ph.D. degree (1892) from Clark University in Worcester, Massachusetts. He studied methods of teaching mathematics in Germany (1897–98), France (1901 and 1904–05), England (1904–05), Austria (1906), and Italy (1908).

Young was an instructor of mathematics at Bucknell Academy in Lewisburg, Pennsylvania (1887–88), and became a member of the faculty of the University of Chicago, where he taught mathematics until his retirement in 1926. He was the author of *Differential and Integral Calculus* (with C. E. Linebarger, 1900), *The Teaching of Mathematics in Prussia* (1900), *Arithmetic* (three volumes, with L. L. Jackson, 1904 and 1905), *The Teaching of Mathematics* (1907), *Algebra* (1908), *Second Course in Algebra* (with L. L. Jackson, 1910), and *High School Algebra* (with L. L. Jackson, 1913). He wrote the Appleton Arithmetic Series with L. L. Jackson (1909) and was editor and joint author of Monographs on Modern Mathematics (1911).

Young was active in professional organizations and was a member of the International Commission on the Teaching of Mathematics.

REFERENCES: *LE* (III); *NYT*, October 27, 1948, p. 28; *WWW* (II).

*John R. O'Donnell*

**YOUNG, John Clarke.** B. August 12, 1803, Greencastle, Pennsylvania, to John and Mary (Clarke) Young. M. November 3, 1829, to Frances Breckinridge. M. 1839 to Cornelia Crittenden. Ch. ten. D. June 23, 1857, Danville, Kentucky.

John Clarke Young studied in New York City under John Borland, attended Columbia College for three years, and was graduated with the A.B. (1823) and A.M. (1826) degrees from Dickinson College in Carlisle, Pennsylvania. He was graduated from the Princeton (New Jersey) Theological Seminary in 1827.

Young was a tutor at the College of New Jersey (later, Princeton University) from 1826 to 1828. Licensed to preach in 1827 and ordained in 1828, he served a church in Lexington, Kentucky (1828–30). He was president of Centre College in Danville, Kentucky (1830–57). He increased the student body and built the endowment fund of the college. He also served as pastor of the Presbyterian church in Danville from 1834 and organized the Second Presbyterian Church in Danville in 1852.

He was the author of papers on slavery and was moderator of the synod of Kentucky twice and of the general assembly of the Presbyterian church (1853). He received an honorary degree from the College of New Jersey (1839).

REFERENCES: *AC; DAB; TC; WWW* (H).          *Marie V. Stephenson*

**YOUNG, John Wesley.** B. November 17, 1879, Columbus, Ohio, to William Henry and Marie Louise (Widenhorn) Young. M. July 20, 1907, to Mary Louise Aston. Ch. one. D. February 17, 1932, Hanover, New Hampshire.

John Wesley Young grew up in Ohio and Germany where his father was United States consul in Karlsruhe. He was graduated from the gymnasium in Baden-Baden, Germany (1895), and Ohio State University, from which he received the Ph.B. degree (1899). He received the A.M. (1901) and Ph.D. (1904) degrees from Cornell University in Ithaca, New York.

Young taught mathematics at Northwestern University in Evanston, Illinois (1903–05), Princeton University (1905–08), and the University of Illinois (1908–10). He was head of the mathematics department at the University of Kansas (1910–11) and professor of mathematics at Dartmouth College in Hanover, New Hampshire, from 1911 to his death. He modernized the teaching of mathematics at Dartmouth and was a leading mathematics educator.

Chief examiner in geometry for the College Entrance Examination Board (1915–17), Young wrote books that influenced the content and method of mathematical instruction, including *Projective Geometry* (two volumes, with Oswald Veblen, *q.v.*, 1910–18), *Lectures on Fundamental Concepts of Algebra and Geometry* (1911), *Plane Geometry* (with A. S. Schwartz, 1915), *Elementary Mathematical Analysis* (with F. M. Morgan, 1917), *Plane Trigonometry* (with F. M. Morgan, 1919), and *Projective Geometry* (1929). He was editor of *Mathematics Teacher, Bulletin* (1907–25) and Colloquium Publications of the American Mathematical Society and of Carus Mathematical Monographs.

Young was a member of many mathematic societies. He helped found the Mathematical Association of America (vice-president, 1918, and president, 1929–31). He was active in the American Mathematical Society (council member, 1907–25 and vice-president, 1928–30). He was chairman of the Committee on College Requirements in Mathematics (1916–24) and edited the committee report, *The Reorganization of Mathematics in Secondary Education* (1923).

REFERENCES: *DAB; DSB; NCAB* (23:279); *WWW* (I); V. Sanford, "John Wesley Young," *Mathematics Teacher* 25 (April 1932): 232–34.

*Robert McGinty*

# Z

**ZACHOS, John Celivergos.** B. December 20, 1820, Constantinople, Turkey, to Nicholas and Euphrosyne Zachos. M. July 26, 1849, to Harriet Tomkins Canfield. Ch. six. D. March 20, 1898, New York, New York.

John Celivergos Zachos was four years old when his father, a general in the Greek army during the Grecian Revolution, died in battle. Samuel Gridley Howe *(q.v.)* brought him to America as a boy. He attended preparatory school in Amherst, Massachusetts, and Kenyon College in Gambier, Ohio, from which he received the B.A. degree (1840). He studied at the Medical School of Miami University in Oxford, Ohio, for three years, but did not receive a degree. He later studied theology and was ordained to the Unitarian ministry in 1865.

Zachos was associate principal of the Cooper Female Seminary in Dayton, Ohio (1851–54). He was principal and teacher of literature of the grammar school of Antioch College in Yellow Springs, Ohio (1854–57), where he worked with Horace Mann *(q.v.)*. He served as an assistant surgeon in the Union army during the Civil War. He served a church in Meadville, Pennsylvania, and taught in the Meadville Theological School (1866–67). In 1871 he moved to New York City where he was associated with the Cooper Union as a teacher and curator until his death in 1898.

A prolific writer, Zachos was the author of *The New American Speaker* (1851), *Analytic Elocution* (1861), *A New System of Phonic Reading Without Changing the Orthography* (1863), *Phonic Primer and Reader* (1864), *The Phonic Text* (1865), *A Sketch of the Life and Opinions of Mr. Peter Cooper* (1867), *The Political and Financial Opinions of Peter Cooper* (1877), *Our Financial Revolution* (1878), and *The Fiscal Problems of All Civilized Nations* (1881). He was editor of the *Ohio Journal of Education* (1852–53). He patented a machine for printing a legible English text at a high reporting speed in 1876.

REFERENCES: *AC; DAB; NYT,* March 21, 1898, p. 7; *WWW* (H).

*Sara Throop*

**ZEISBERGER, David.** B. April 11, 1721, Zauchental, Moravia, to David and Rosina Zeisberger. M. June 4, 1781, to Susan Lecron. Ch. none. D. November 17, 1808, Goshen, Ohio.

David Zeisberger was born in Moravia and lived in Holland and London, England. In 1739 he joined a Moravian colony in Savannah, Georgia, and moved with the group to Pennsylvania in 1740. He became a missionary in 1743 and worked with the Iroquois and Delaware Indians at Onondaga, New York, and at Shamokin and in the Wyoming Valley of Pennsylvania from 1745. In 1765 he assisted in moving Christian converts among the Indians near Bethlehem, Pennsylvania, to Bradford County in western Pennsylvania.

When the Delawares entered Ohio in 1771, Zeisberger established a Christian Indian settlement at Schoenbrunn in the Tuscarawas Valley and, later, at Gnadenhuetten. He established the first school in the colonies west of the Allegheny Mountains. The village of Liehtenau was established and became the center of the Christian Indians when Schoenbrunn was destroyed and Gnadenhuetten abandoned during the Revolutionary War. Zeisberger moved with the Indians to Michigan, back to Ohio, to Canada, and finally to congressional land grants in the Tuscarawas Valley in Ohio. He settled in the new town of Goshen in 1798 where he spent the rest of his life ministering to the Indians.

Zeisberger was credited with writing the first schoolbook for use in Ohio, *A Delaware Indian and English Spelling Book for Use in the Schools of the Christian Indians on the Muskingum River* (1776). He also wrote *A Collection of Hymns for the Christian Indians* (1803) and *Sermons for Children* (1803). He left seven volumes of manuscripts, of which *Dictionary in German and Delaware* (1887) and *Essay Toward an Onondaga Grammar* (1888) were later published.

REFERENCES: *AC; DAB; NCAB* (2:250); *WWW* (H); Simeon D. Fess, ed., *Ohio: A Four-Volume Reference Library* (Chicago: Lewis, 1937), 4: 7–9.								*Richard J. Nichols*

**ZIRBES, Laura.** B. April 26, 1884, Buffalo, New York, to William J. and Louisa (Volk) Zirbes. M. no. D. June 9, 1967, Columbus, Ohio.

Laura Zirbes received the B.S. (1925), A.M. (1926), and Ph.D. (1928) degrees from Columbia University.

Zirbes was an elementary school teacher in Cleveland, Ohio (1903–19). She conducted research in reading at Lincoln School of Teachers College, Columbia University (1920–25), and was a lecturer at Teachers College (1922–28). She became a consultant in education for the Ohio state department of education (1928–31), joined the faculty of Ohio State University in 1928, and continued there to her retirement in 1954. She was director of the Ohio State summer demonstration school (1929–38).

Zirbes was the author of *Curriculum Trends* (1933), *Teachers for Today's Schools* (1952), *Spurs to Creative Teaching* (1959), *Focus on Values in Elementary Education* (1960), and *Guidelines to Developmental Teaching* (1961). She was chairman of the editorial board of *Childhood Education* (1947–49) and assistant editor of the *Journal of Educational Psychology* (1921–25) and *Journal of Educational Research* (1926–28).

Active in professional associations, Zirbes was a member of the staff of the Educational Policies Commission of the National Education Association (1946) and consultant to the Commission on Crowding in the Schools for the Association of Supervision and Curriculum Development (ASCD) in 1954, the Commission for Teacher Education of the Association for Childhood Education International (ACEI) in 1955, and the Tennessee Valley Authority (1945–50). She was chairman of the National Education Commission of the American Association of University Women (1941–47). She was chairman of the National Commission on Cooperative Research for the ACEI, a member of the research board of the ASCD (1952–54), secretary-treasurer of the American Educational Research Association (1926–29), and on the executive committee of the Educational Policies Commission (1938–42). She received an achievement award in education from the National Women's Press Club (1948).

REFERENCES: *LE* (I); *WWAE* (XXII); L. B. Jacobs, "Dedication to Laura Zirbes," *Childhood Education* 44 (December 1967): 210–11; "Laura Zirbes: A Creative Person," *Childhood Education* 44 (December 1967): 216–17.                                                                  *John F. Ohles*

**ZOOK, George Frederick.** B. April 22, 1885, Fort Scott, Kansas, to Douglas and Helen (Follenius) Zook. M. August 21, 1911, to Susie Gant. Ch. none. D. August 17, 1951, Washington, D.C.

George Frederick Zook attended the University of Kansas after graduation from Fort Scott (Kansas) High School. He received the B.A. (1906) and M.A. (1907) degrees and pursued graduate study at Cornell University in Ithaca, New York, where he received the Ph.D. degree (1913).

Zook taught European history at Pennsylvania State College (later, University) in 1906–07, 1909–11, and 1912–20. He was chief of the Division of Higher Education, United States Bureau of Education (1920–25), and president of the University of Akron (Ohio) (1926–33). He resigned that post in 1933 to become United States commissioner of education. He served as president of the American Council on Education (1934–50), where he played an influential role in the development of American education.

Zook was a member of the National Advisory Committee on Education (1929–31) and served as secretary of the Commission on Higher Institutions of the North Central Association of Colleges and Secondary Schools (1926–31). He was appointed chairman of the President's Commission on Higher Education (1946–47) and was active in the United Nations Educational, Scientific, and Cultural Organization from 1946.

Zook was the author of *The Royal Adventures Trading into Africa* (1919), *Principles of Accrediting Higher Institutions* (with M. E. Haggerty, 1936), and *The Role of the Federal Government in Education* (1945). He received honorary degrees from eleven American colleges and universities.

REFERENCES: *CB* (February 1946); *LE* (III); *NCAB* (38:563); *WWAE* (VIII); *WWW* (III); *NYT*, August 19, 1951, p. 84; B. P. Brodinsky (ed.), "Valedictory of President of American Council," *Nation's Schools* 45 (June 1950): 24–27; R. E. Himstead, "George Frederick Zook: College Teacher and Educational Administrator," *American Association of University Professors Bulletin* 37 (September 1951): 423–26.

*John F. Ohles*

# APPENDIX A:
## PLACE OF BIRTH

### ALABAMA

| | |
|---|---|
| Abercrombie, John William | Kelly's Creek |
| Carmichael, Oliver Cromwell | Goodwater |
| Carmichael, Omer | Hollins |
| Fleming, Walter Lynwood | Pike County |
| Hollingsworth, Orlando Newton | Calhoun County |
| Manly, John Matthews | Sumter County |
| Murphree, Albert Alexander | Murphree Valley |
| Petrie, George | Montgomery |
| Powers, James Knox | Lauderdale County |
| Tutwiler, Julia Strudwick | Tuscaloosa |
| Vincent, John Heyl | Tuscaloosa |

### ARKANSAS

| | |
|---|---|
| Adler, Cyrus | Van Buren |
| Armstrong, Wesley Earl | Fulton County |
| Gammage, Grady | Prescott |
| Shinn, Josiah Hazen | Russellville |
| Sutton, William Seneca | Fayetteville |

### CALIFORNIA

| | |
|---|---|
| Foshay, Arthur Wellesley | Oakland |
| Keppel, Mark | Butte County |
| Leonard, Robert Josselyn | San Jose |
| Leonard, Sterling Andrus | National City |
| Mezes, Sidney Edward | Belmont |
| Reinhardt, Aurelia Isabel Henry | San Francisco |
| Scates, Douglas Edgar | San Diego |
| Simpson, Roy E. | Santa Rosa |
| Snedden, David Samuel | Kavilah |
| Sproul, Robert Gordon | San Francisco |
| Sturtevant, Sarah Martha | Sonora |
| Suzzallo, Henry | San Jose |
| Viguers, Ruth Hill | Oakland |
| Wood, William Christopher | Elmira |

### COLORADO

| | |
|---|---|
| Espinosa, Aurelio Macedonio | Carneo |
| Proctor, William Martin | Denver |
| Sabin, Florence Rena | Central City |

### CONNECTICUT

| | |
|---|---|
| Alcott, Amos Bronson | near Wolcott |
| Alcott, William Andrus | Wolcott |

| | |
|---|---|
| Allyn, Harriet May | New London |
| Allyn, Robert | Ledyard |
| Andrews, Charles McLean | Wethersfield |
| Andrews, Ethan Allen | New Britain |
| Andrews, Lorrin | East Windsor |
| Atwater, Lyman Hotchkiss | New Haven |
| Ayres, Leonard Porter | Niantic |
| Baldwin, Theron | Goshen |
| Banister, Zilpah Polly Grant | Norfolk |
| Barnard, Henry | Hartford |
| Benedict, Erastus Cornelius | Branford |
| Bingham, Caleb | Salisbury |
| Bulkley, John Williams | Fairfield |
| Calkins, Mary Whiton | Hartford |
| Camp, David Nelson | Durham |
| Chapin, Aaron Lucius | Hartford |
| Chittenden, Russell Henry | New Haven |
| Collar, William Coe | Ashford |
| Comstock, John Lee | Lynne |
| Crary, Isaac Edwin | Preston |
| Cross, Wilbur Lucius | Mansfield |
| Daboll, Nathan | Groton |
| Davenport, Charles Benedict | Stamford |
| Davies, Charles | Washington |
| Day, Henry Noble | New Preston |
| Day, Jeremiah | New Preston |
| Dwight, Timothy (1828–1916) | Norwich |
| Ely, Charles Wright | Madison |
| Engelhardt, Fred | Naugatuck |
| Engelhardt, Nickolaus Louis | Naugatuck |
| Fillmore, John Comfort | Franklin |
| Finney, Charles Grandison | Warren |
| Gallaudet, Edward Miner | Hartford |
| Giddings, Franklin Henry | Sherman |
| Gilbert, Eliphalet Wheeler | New Lebanon |
| Gilman, Daniel Coit | Norwich |
| Goodrich, Chauncey Allen | New Haven |
| Goodrich, Samuel Griswold | Ridgefield |
| Gould, James | Branford |
| Gruhn, William Theodore | Bridgeport |
| Gulliver, Julia Henrietta | Norwich |
| Gunn, Frederick William | Washington |
| Hadley, Arthur Twining | New Haven |
| Harris, William Torrey | North Killingly |
| Hawley, Gideon | Huntington |
| Hayden, Horace H. | Windsor |
| Holbrook, Alfred | Derby |
| Holbrook, Josiah | Derby |
| Holley, Horace | Salisbury |
| Hunt, Mary Hannah Hanchet | South Canaan |
| Inglis, Alexander James | Middletown |

| | |
|---|---|
| Johnson, Samuel | Guilford |
| Kingsbury, John | South Coventry |
| Kingsley, James Luce | Scotland |
| Lanman, Charles Rockwell | Norwich |
| Lord, Livingston Chester | Killingworth |
| Mather, Frank Jewett, Jr. | Deep River |
| Mitchell, Samuel Augustus | Bristol |
| Morse, Jedidiah | Woodstock |
| North, Edward | Berlin |
| Northrop, Birdsey Grant | Kent |
| Northrop, Cyrus | Ridgefield |
| Nott, Eliphalet | Ashford |
| Olmsted, Denison | East Hartford |
| Olney, Jesse | Union |
| Osborn, Henry Fairfield | Fairfield |
| Peck, William Guy | Litchfield |
| Peet, Harvey Prindle | Bethlehem |
| Peet, Isaac Lewis | Hartford |
| Phelps, Almira Hart Lincoln | Berlin |
| Phelps, William Lyon | New Haven |
| Picket, Albert | n.a. |
| Pierce, Sarah | Litchfield |
| Pierpont, John | Litchfield |
| Pinney, Norman | Simsbury |
| Porter, Arthur Kingsley | Stamford |
| Porter, Noah | Farmington |
| Porter, Sarah | Farmington |
| Sanford, Maria Louise | Saybrook |
| Seelye, Julius Hawley | Bethel |
| Seelye, Laurenus Clark | Bethel |
| Sill, Edward Rowland | Windsor |
| Silliman, Benjamin | Trumbull |
| Silliman, Benjamin, Jr. | New Haven |
| Snyder, Franklyn Bliss | Middletown |
| Sparks, Jared | Willington |
| Stiles, Ezra | North Haven |
| Sturtevant, Julian Monson | Warren |
| Thompson, Charles Oliver | East Windsor Hills |
| True, Alfred Charles | Middletown |
| Tucker, William Jewett | Griswold |
| Tyler, Moses Coit | Griswold |
| Wadsworth, James | Durham |
| Webster, Noah | West Hartford |
| Welch, Adonijah Strong | Chatham |
| Welch, William Henry | Norfolk |
| Wells, William Harvey | Tolland |
| Wheelock, Eleazar | Windham |
| Wheelock, John | Lebanon |

Willard, Emma Hart                          Berlin
Woolley, Mary Emma                          South Norwalk

## DELAWARE

Groves, James Henry                         Red Lion
Kent, Roland Grubb                          Wilmington

## DISTRICT OF COLUMBIA

Coppin, Fanny Marion Jackson
Ewell, Benjamin Stoddert
Holzinger, Karl John
Hullfish, Henry Gordon
Hyatt, Alpheus
Powell, Lawrence Clark

## FLORIDA

English, John Colin                         Alva
Kirby-Smith, Edmund                         St. Augustine
Pace, Edward Aloysius                       Starke
Smith, Bunnie Othanel                       Clarksville

## GEORGIA

Aderhold, Omer Clyde                        Lavonia
Andrews, Eliza Frances                      Haywood
Barrett, Janie Porter                       Athens
Battle, Archibald John                      Powelton
Berry, Martha McChesney                     near Rome
Brittain, Marion Luther                     Wilkes County
Bruce, William Herschel                     Troup County
Collins, Mauney Douglass                    Choestoe
Coppée, Henry                               Savannah
Curry, Jabez Lamar Monroe                   Lincoln County
Davis, John Warren                          Milledgeville
De Vane, William Clyde                      Savannah
Evans, Lawton Bryan                         Lumpkin
Glenn, Gustavus Richard                     Jackson County
Hale, William Gardner                       Savannah
Haygood, Atticus Green                      Walkinsville
Hope, John                                  Augusta
Hunt, Henry Alexander                       Sparta
Hyer, Robert Stewart                        Oxford
Johnston, Richard Malcolm                   Hancock County
Kilpatrick, William Heard                   White Plains
Laney, Lucy Craft                           Macon
Odum, Howard Washington                     Bethlehem
Perry, William Flake                        Jackson County
Scarborough, William Sanders                Macon
Sheats, William Nicholas                    Auburn
Stewart, Joseph Spencer                     Oxford

| | |
|---|---|
| Thach, Charles Coleman | Athens |
| Wright, Richard Robert | Whitfield County |

HAWAII

| | |
|---|---|
| Armstrong, Samuel Chapman | Maui |
| Gulick, Luther Halsey | Honolulu |

ILLINOIS

| | |
|---|---|
| Ainsworth, Dorothy Sears | Moline |
| Atwood, Wallace Walter | Chicago |
| Baker, Edna Dean | Normal |
| Bestor, Arthur Eugene | Dixon |
| Bloomfield, Leonard | Chicago |
| Bode, Boyd Henry | Ridott |
| Bonser, Frederick Gordon | Tower Hill |
| Breasted, James Henry | Rockford |
| Brueckner, Leo John | Streator |
| Bryant, Ralph Clement | Princeton |
| Butcher, Thomas Walter | Industry |
| Butts, Robert Freeman | Springfield |
| Cady, Calvin Brainerd | Barry |
| Case, Charles Orlando | near Rock Island |
| Cassidy, Rosalind | Quincy |
| Cottingham, Harold Fred | Charleston |
| Davis, Jesse Buttrick | Chicago |
| De Boer, John James | Chicago |
| Elliott, Edward Charles | Chicago |
| Finley, John Huston | near Grand Ridge |
| Gilman, Arthur | Alton |
| Gray, William Scott | Coatsburg |
| Greenlaw, Edwin Almiron | Flora |
| Greenwood, James Mickleborough | Sangamon County |
| Haley, Margaret Angela | Joliet |
| Hand, Harold Curtis | Piper City |
| Hibben, John Grier | Peoria |
| Hilgard, Ernest Ropriequet | Belleville |
| Hills, Elijah Clarence | Arlington |
| Hosic, James Fleming | Henry |
| Hunt, Thomas Forsyth | Ridott |
| Huntington, Ellsworth | Galesburg |
| James, Edmund Janes | Jacksonville |
| Kirk, John Robert | n.a. |
| Koos, Leonard Vincent | Chicago |
| Lloyd-Jones, Esther McDonald | Lockport |
| McConnell, Wallace Robert | Mount Sterling |
| McKown, Harry Charles | Peoria |
| Miller, Edwin Lillie | Aurora |
| Millikan, Robert Andrews | Morrison |
| Myers, George William | Champaign County |
| Nevins, Allan | Camp Point |
| O'Harra, Cleophas Cisney | Bentley |
| Putnam, Alice Harvey Whiting | Chicago |

| | |
|---|---|
| Raymond, George Lansing | Chicago |
| Rice, James Edward | Aurora |
| Robinson, James Harvey | Bloomington |
| Rogers, Carl Ransom | Oak Park |
| Scott, Walter Dill | Cooksville |
| Sharp, Katharine Lucinda | Elgin |
| Smith, Eleanor | Atlanta |
| Steinhaus, Arthur H. | Chicago |
| Stone, John Charles | Albion |
| Sunderland, Eliza Jane Read | Huntsville |
| Temple, Alice | Chicago |
| Thomas, Augustus Orloff | Mercer County |
| Thurstone, Louis Leon | Chicago |
| Tompkins, Arnold | Paris |
| Tyler, Ralph Winfred | Chicago |
| Van Doren, Mark | Hope |
| Ward, Lester Frank | Joliet |
| Warner, William Everett | Roanoke |
| Washburne, Carleton Wolsey | Chicago |
| Whittlesey, Derwent Stainthorpe | Pecatonica |
| Williamson, Edmund Griffith | Rossville |
| Wilson, Howard Eugene | Bluffs |
| Wolfe, Harry Kirke | Bloomington |
| Wood, Thomas Denison | Sycamore |
| Woods, Albert Fred | near Belvidere |
| Woolley, Helen Bradford Thompson | Chicago |

INDIANA

| | |
|---|---|
| Ahern, Mary Eileen | Marion County |
| Allport, Gordon Willard | Montezuma |
| Aydelotte, Frank | Sullivan |
| Baldwin, James | Hamilton County |
| Barr, Arvil Sylvester | Selvin |
| Beadle, William Henry Harrison | Parke County |
| Beard, Charles Austin | near Knightstown |
| Blackburn, William Maxwell | Carlisle |
| Bobbitt, John Franklin | English |
| Bogue, Benjamin Nathaniel | Wabash County |
| Bryan, Enoch Albert | Bloomington |
| Bryan, William Lowe | Bloomington |
| Burchenal, Elizabeth | Richmond |
| Burns, James Aloysius | Michigan City |
| Caldwell, Otis William | Lebanon |
| Chase, William Merritt | Williamsburg |
| Coffman, Lotus Delta | near Salem |
| Cotton, Fassett Allen | Ninevah |
| Craig, Oscar John | Madison |
| Cubberly, Elwood Patterson | Antioch |
| Curme, George Oliver | Richmond |
| DuShane, Donald | South Bend |
| Givens, Willard Earl | Anderson |
| Hart, Joseph Kinmont | near Columbia City |

| | |
|---|---|
| Hedrick, Earle Raymond | Union City |
| Hodgin, Charles Elkanah | Lynn |
| Holland, Ernest Otto | Bennington |
| Jessup, Walter Albert | Richmond |
| Kitson, Harry Dexter | Mishawaka |
| Lindley, Ernest Hiram | Paoli |
| Luckey, George Washington Andrew | Decatur |
| Mace, William Harrison | near Lexington |
| McMurry, Charles Alexander | Crawfordsville |
| McMurry, Frank Morton | Crawfordsville |
| Monroe, Paul | North Madison |
| Morgan, Thomas Jefferson | Franklin |
| Morphet, Edgar Leroy | Grass Creek |
| Newlon, Jesse Homer | Salem |
| Prosser, Charles Allen | New Albany |
| Reavis, William Claude | Francisco |
| Reeve, William David | Edwardsport |
| Rice, Thurman Brooks | Landers |
| Ridpath, John Clark | Putnam County |
| Schelling, Felix Emanuel | New Albany |
| Schorling, Raleigh | Batesville |
| Seerley, Homer Horatio | near Indianapolis |
| Smith, Henry Lester | Bloomington |
| Swain, Joseph | Pendleton |
| Terman, Lewis Madison | Johnson County |
| Thomas, Frank Waters | Danville |
| Trabue, Marion Rex | Kokomo |
| Trueblood, Thomas Clarkson | Salem |
| Wagner, Jonathan Howard | Columbia City |
| Wells, Herman B. | Jamestown |
| Wilson, Guy Mitchell | Frankfort |
| Wirt, William Albert | near Markle |
| Witty, Paul Andrew | Terre Haute |
| Woody, Clifford | Thorntown |
| Wright, John Calvin | Elkhart County |

## IOWA

| | |
|---|---|
| Arbuthnot, May Hill | Mason City |
| Axline, George Andrew | Fairfield |
| Becker, Carl Lotus | Black Hawk County |
| Betts, Emmett Albert | Elkhart |
| Betts, George Herbert | Clarkesville |
| Brandenburg, William Aaron | Clayton County |
| Cocking, Walter Dewey | Manchester |
| Cooley, Edwin Gilbert | Strawberry Point |
| Deyoe, George Percy | Mason City |
| Dobbs, Ella Victoria | Cedar Rapids |
| Hanna, Paul Robert | Sioux City |
| Hebard, Grace Raymond | Clinton |
| Henderson, Lester Dale | Lenox |

Irwin, Robert Benjamin                  Rockford
Jersild, Arthur Thomas                  Elk Horn
Johnson, Earl Shepard                   Stratford
Johnson, Palmer Oliver                  Eagle Grove
Jones, Arthur Julius                    Grinnell
Kent, Raymond Asa                       Plymouth
Kirkpatrick, Edwin Asbury               Peoria
Lee, Mabel                              Clearfield
Lindquist, Everet Franklin              Gowrie
McConnell, Thomas Raymond               Mediapolis
Merriam, Charles Edward                 Hopkinton
Merriam, John Campbell                  Hopkinton
Noyes, William Albert                   Independence
Pillsbury, Walter Bowers                Burlington
Studebaker, John Ward                   McGregor
Veblen, Oswald                          Decorah
Wallin, John Edward Wallace             Page County
Wheeler, Anna Johnson Pell              Hawarden
Wier, Jeanne Elizabeth                  Grinnell
Wilbur, Ray Lyman                       Boonesboro

## KANSAS

Benne, Kenneth Dean                     Morrowville
Carpenter, William Weston               Lawrence
Caswell, Hollis Leland                  Woodruff
Counts, George Sylvester                Baldwin City
Eisenhower, Milton Stover               Abilene
Haydon, Glen                            Inman
Henderson, Algo Donmyer                 Solomon
Long, Oren Ethelbirt                    Altoona
Maddy, Joseph Edgar                     near Wellington
Marlatt, Abby Lillian                   Manhattan
Monroe, Walter Scott                    Chase
Renner, George Thomas, Jr.              Winfield
Traxler, Arthur Edwin                   Irving
Zook, George Frederick                  Fort Scott

## KENTUCKY

Bernard, Luther Lee                     Russell County
Bowman, John Bryan                      Mercer County
Breckinridge, Robert Jefferson          Cabell's Dale
Breckinridge, Sophonisba Preston        Lexington
Bryan, Anna E.                          Louisville
Cherry, Henry Hardin                    near Bowling Green
Dinwiddie, Albert Bledsoe               Lexington
Duveneck, Frank                         Covington
Ellis, Alston                           Kenton County

| | |
|---|---|
| Flexner, Abraham | Louisville |
| Gates, Noah Putnam | near Princeton |
| Green, Lewis Warner | Boyle County |
| Harrison, Elizabeth | Athens |
| Henderson, Howard Andrew Millet | Paris |
| Hill, Patty Smith | Louisville |
| Lessenberry, David Daniel | Barren County |
| McConathy, Osbourne | Bullitt County |
| Morgan, William Henry | Logan County |
| Pettit, Katherine Rhoda | near Lexington |
| Roark, Ruric Nevel | Greenville |
| Roemer, Joseph | Sugar Grove |
| Shaler, Nathaniel Southgate | near Newport |
| Smith, Zachariah Frederick | Henry County |
| Spalding, John Lancaster | Lebanon |
| Stewart, Cora Wilson | Farmers |
| Taylor, William Septimus | Beaver Dam |
| Walker, David Shelby | Logan County |
| Wesley, Charles Harris | Louisville |
| Wesley, Edgar Bruce | Bethelridge |
| Wilson, Atwood Sylvester | Louisville |

## LOUISIANA

| | |
|---|---|
| Aswell, James Benjamin | Jackson Parish |
| Chambers, Henry Edward | New Orleans |
| Dimitry, Alexander | New Orleans |
| Matthews, James Brander | New Orleans |

## MAINE

| | |
|---|---|
| Abbott, Gorham Dummer | Brunswick |
| Abbott, Jacob | Hallowell |
| Anderson, Martin Brewer | Brunswick |
| Archer, Gleason Leonard | Great Pond |
| Bailey, Rufus William | North Yarmouth |
| Baker, James Hutchins | Harmony |
| Barrows, Anna | Fryeburg |
| Bradbury, William Batchelder | York |
| Bradley, Amy Morris | East Vassalboro |
| Chadbourne, Paul Ansel | North Berwick |
| Chamberlain, Joshua Lawrence | Brewster |
| Cummings, Joseph | Falmouth |
| Cutler, Elliott Carr | Bangor |
| Day, James Roscoe | Whitneyville |
| Dexter, Edwin Grant | Calais |
| Dix, Dorothea Lynde | Hampden |
| Emerson, George Barrell | Wells |
| Fernald, Charles Henry | Mt. Desert |

| | |
|---|---|
| Fisher, Ebenezer | Charlotte |
| Frost, John | Kennebunk |
| Frye, Alexis Everett | North Haven |
| Goddard, Henry Herbert | Vassalboro |
| Goodale, George Lincoln | Saco |
| Hamlin, Cyrus | Waterford |
| Harris, Samuel | East Machias |
| Hill, Frank Alpine | Biddeford |
| Hillard, George Stillman | Machias |
| Homans, Amy Morris | Vassalboro |
| Larrabee, William Clark | Cape Elizabeth |
| Leigh, Edwin | South Berwick |
| Lord, Nathan | South Berwick |
| McCurdy, James Huff | Princeton |
| Marble, Albert Prescott | Vassalboro |
| Mason, Luther Whiting | Turner |
| Merrill, George Arthur | South Portland |
| Morrison, Henry Clinton | Oldtown |
| Packard, Alpheus Spring, Jr. | Brunswick |
| Paine, John Knowles | Portland |
| Richardson, Charles Francis | Hallowell |
| Ricker, Nathan Clifford | Acton |
| Sargent, Dudley Allen | Belfast |
| Small, Albion Woodbury | Buckfield |
| Smith, Payson | Portland |
| Smyth, William | Pittstown |
| Stetson, William Wallace | Greene |
| Thwing, Charles Franklin | New Sharon |

## MARYLAND

| | |
|---|---|
| Browne, William Hand | Baltimore |
| Butler, Edward Mann | Baltimore |
| Fischer, John Henry | Baltimore |
| Frazier, Edward Franklin | Baltimore |
| Gibson, William | Baltimore |
| Gordy, John Pancoast | near Salisbury |
| Gordy, Wilbur Fisk | Salisbury |
| Hardey, Mary Aloysia | Piscataway |
| Howison, George Holmes | Montgomery County |
| Kefauver, Grayson Neikirk | Middletown |
| Quillen, Isaac James | Bishop |
| Sachs, Julius | Baltimore |
| Snavely, Guy Everett | Antietam |
| Spalding, Catherine | Charles County |
| Tall, Lida Lee | Dorchester County |
| Thomas, Martha Carey | Baltimore |
| Valentine, Milton | Uniontown |
| Watson, Fletcher Guard | Baltimore |

## MASSACHUSETTS

| | |
|---|---|
| Abbot, Benjamin | Andover |
| Adams, Daniel | Townsend |
| Adams, Henry Brooks | Boston |
| Adams, Herbert Baxter | Shutesbury |
| Agassiz, Elizabeth Cabot Cary | Boston |
| Allen, Charles Ricketson | New Bedford |
| Allen, Edward Ellis | West Newton |
| Allen, Nathaniel Topliffe | Medfield |
| Alvord, Henry Elijah | Greenfield |
| Ames, James Barr | Boston |
| Andrews, Jane | Newburyport |
| Atherton, George Washington | Boxford |
| Atkinson, George Henry | Newburyport |
| Bailey, Ebenezer | West Newbury |
| Bailey, Henry Turner | Scituate |
| Baker, Benjamin Franklin | Wenham |
| Baldwin, Maria Louise | Cambridge |
| Bardeen, Charles William | Groton |
| Barnard, Frederick Augustus Porter | Sheffield |
| Barrows, Alice Prentice | Lowell |
| Bartholomew, William Nelson | Boston |
| Bates, Katharine Lee | Falmouth |
| Bennett, Charles Alpheus | Holden |
| Bigelow, Harry Augustus | Norwood |
| Birge, Edward Bailey | Northampton |
| Bowditch, Henry Pickering | Boston |
| Boyden, Albert Gardner | South Walpole |
| Boyden, Frank Learoyd | Foxboro |
| Brackett, Anna Callender | Boston |
| Brackett, Jeffrey Richardson | Quincy |
| Bradford, Edward Hickling | Roxbury |
| Brattle, William | Boston |
| Brooks, Charles | Medford |
| Brownell, Thomas Church | Westport |
| Brubacher, John Seiler | Easthampton |
| Cady, Sarah Louise Ensign | Northampton |
| Capen, Elmer Hewitt | Stoughton |
| Carter, James Gordon | Leominster |
| Chadwick, George Whitfield | Lowell |
| Clap, Thomas | Scituate |
| Clapp, Cornelia Maria | Montague |
| Cleaveland, Parker | Rowley |
| Cobb, Lyman | Lenox |
| Cobb, Stanwood | Newton |
| Colburn, Dana Pond | West Dedham |
| Colburn, Warren | Dedham |

| | |
|---|---|
| Conant, James Bryant | Boston |
| Cooke, Josiah Parsons | Boston |
| Coolidge, Julian Lowell | Brookline |
| Cooper, Hermann | Wilbraham |
| Corson, Juliet | Mt. Pleasant, Roxbury |
| Crocker, Lucretia | Barnstable |
| Cross, Anson Kent | Lawrence |
| Currier, Enoch Henry | Newburyport |
| Cushman, Frank | Boston |
| Dalton, John Call | Chelmsford |
| Davidson, Hannah Amelia Noyes | Campello |
| Dewey, Chester | Sheffield |
| Dickinson, John Woodbridge | Chester |
| Dodge, Ebenezer | Salem |
| Dodge, Richard Elwood | Wenham |
| Dow, Arthur Wesley | Ipswich |
| Downing, Elliot Rowland | Boston |
| Du Bois, William Edward Burghardt | Great Barrington |
| Durant, Henry | Acton |
| Dwight, Francis | Springfield |
| Dwight, Timothy (1752–1817) | Northampton |
| Eells, Cushing | Blandford |
| Eliot, Charles William | Boston |
| Elson, Louis Charles | Boston |
| Fairchild, James Harris | Stockbridge |
| Fairchild, Mary Salome Cutler | Dalton |
| Farmer, Fannie Merritt | Boston |
| Farnum, Royal Bailey | Somerville |
| Farrar, John | Lincoln |
| Fiske, George Walter | Holliston |
| Fitton, James | Boston |
| Flint, Austin | Petersham |
| Ford, Jeremiah Denis Matthias | Cambridge |
| Foster, William Trufant | Boston |
| Fowle, William Bentley | Boston |
| Franklin, Benjamin | Boston |
| Frieze, Henry Simmons | Boston |
| Fuller, Sarah | Weston |
| Goodwin, William Watson | Concord |
| Gould, Benjamin Apthorp | Lancaster |
| Grandgent, Charles Hall | Dorchester |
| Green, Samuel Bowdlear | Chelsea |
| Greene, Samuel Stillman | Belchertown |
| Greenleaf, Benjamin | Haverhill |
| Greenleaf, Simon | Newburyport |
| Greenwood, Isaac | Boston |
| Guilford, Nathan | Spencer |

| | |
|---|---|
| Hagar, Daniel Barnard | Newton Lower Falls |
| Hale, Benjamin | Newburyport |
| Hale, Florence Maria | Athol |
| Hall, Granville Stanley | Ashfield |
| Hall, Willard | Westford |
| Harkness, Albert | Mendon |
| Hart, John Seely | Stockbridge |
| Hedges, Cornelius | Westfield |
| Henderson, Lawrence Joseph | Lynn |
| Hitchcock, Edward (1793–1864) | Deerfield |
| Hitchcock, Edward (1828–1911) | Amherst |
| Hooker, Worthington | Springfield |
| Hopkins, Mark | Stockbridge |
| Howe, Samuel Gridley | Boston |
| Hyde, William DeWitt | Winchedon |
| Jefferson, Mark Sylvester William | Melrose |
| Johnson, Joseph French | Hardwick |
| Leach, Daniel Dyer | Bridgewater |
| Leonard, Levi Washburn | Bridgewater |
| Lewis, Samuel | Falmouth |
| Lowell, Abbott Lawrence | Boston |
| Lyon, Mary Mason | Buckland |
| Mahoney, John Joseph | Lawrence |
| Mann, Horace | Franklin |
| March, Francis Andrew | Sutton (later, Millbury) |
| Mason, Lowell | Medfield |
| Mason, William | Boston |
| Mather, Increase | Dorchester |
| Maxcy, Jonathan | Attleboro |
| Mayo, Amory Dwight | Warwick |
| Meserve, Charles Francis | North Abington |
| Messer, Asa | Methuen |
| Minot, Charles Sedgwick | West Roxbury |
| Mitchell, Maria | Nantucket Island |
| Mowry, William Augustus | Uxbridge |
| Muzzey, David Saville | Lexington |
| Newman, Samuel Phillips | Andover |
| Northend, Charles | Newbury (later, Newburyport) |
| Norton, Charles Eliot | Cambridge |
| Norton, Mary Alice Peloubet | Lanesville |
| O'Gorman, Thomas | Boston |
| Packard, Silas Sadler | Cummington |
| Packard, Sophia B. | New Salem |
| Palmer, George Herbert | Boston |
| Parker, Horatio William | Auburndale |
| Parker, Richard Green | Boston |
| Peabody, Elizabeth Palmer | Billerica |

| | |
|---|---|
| Peabody, Endicott | Salem |
| Pearson, Eliphalet | Newbury |
| Peirce, Benjamin | Salem |
| Peirce, Charles (Santiago) Sanders | Cambridge |
| Peirce, Cyrus | Waltham |
| Peirce, James Mills | Cambridge |
| Perrin, Ethel | Needham |
| Phillips, John | Andover |
| Pickard, Josiah Little | Rowley |
| Pickering, Edward Charles | Boston |
| Quincy, Josiah | Boston |
| Rice, William North | Marblehead |
| Richards, Charles Russell | Boston |
| Richards, Ellen Henrietta Swallow | Dunstable |
| Richards, William | Plainfield |
| Richards, Zalmon | Cummington |
| Robinson, Ezekiel Gilman | Attleboro |
| Rogers, Harriet Burbank | North Billerica |
| Root, George Frederick | Sheffield |
| Rugg, Harold Ordway | Fitchburg |
| Sargent, Epes | Gloucester |
| Sargent, Walter | Worcester |
| Sears, Barnas | Sandisfield |
| Shedd, William Greenough Thayer | Acton |
| Sibley, Frederick Hubbard | Oxford |
| Sinnott, Edmund Ware | Cambridge |
| Smith, Harold Babbitt | Barre |
| Smith, John | Rowley |
| Smith, Nathan | Rehoboth |
| Sprague, Homer Baxter | Sutton |
| Stearns, Eben Sperry | Bedford |
| Stevens, Georgia Lydia | Boston |
| Stimson, Rufus Whittaker | Palmer |
| Story, Joseph | Marblehead |
| Stowe, Calvin Ellis | Natick |
| Symonds, Percival Mallon | Newtonville |
| Tappan, Eva March | Blackstone |
| Tapper, Thomas | Canton |
| Tarr, Ralph Stockman | Gloucester |
| Thayer, Gideon French | Watertown |
| Thayer, Sylvanus | Braintree |
| Thorndike, Edward Lee | Williamsburg |
| Ticknor, George | Boston |
| Town, Salem | Belchertown |
| Trowbridge, John | Boston |
| Turner, Jonathan Baldwin | Templeton |
| Valentine, Thomas Weston | Northboro |

| | |
|---|---|
| Walker, Francis Amasa | Boston |
| Ware, Edmund Asa | North Wrentham |
| Ware, William Robert | Cambridge |
| Warren, John | Roxbury |
| Warren, John Collins | Boston |
| Warren, Samuel Edward | West Newton |
| Warren, William Fairfield | Williamsburg |
| Wells, Webster | Boston |
| Wendell, Barrett | Boston |
| West, Charles Edwin | Washington |
| Wheeler, Benjamin Ide | Randolph |
| Wheeler, Raymond Holder | Berlin |
| Whipple, Guy Montrose | Danvers |
| Whitaker, Ozi William | New Salem |
| White, John Stuart | Wrentham |
| White, Leonard Dupee | Acton |
| Wigglesworth, Edward | Malden |
| Wilbur, Hervey Backus | Wendell |
| Williston, Arthur Lyman | Cambridge |
| Winship, Albert Edward | West Bridgewater |
| Winslow, Charles-Edward Amory | Boston |
| Winthrop, John | Boston |
| Woodbridge, William Channing | Medford |
| Woods, Leonard | Newbury |
| Woodward, Calvin Milton | Fitchburg |
| Woodworth, Robert Sessions | Belchertown |
| Wright, Arthur Davis | Boston |

## MICHIGAN

| | |
|---|---|
| Anderson, William Gilbert | St. Joseph |
| Avery, Elroy McKendree | Erie |
| Bagley, William Chandler | Detroit |
| Bailey, Liberty Hyde | South Haven |
| Birkhoff, George David | Overisel |
| Bowen, Wilbur Pardon | Lima |
| Brownson, Josephine Van Dyke | Detroit |
| Butterfield, Kenyon Leech | Lapeer |
| Campbell, Douglas Houghton | Detroit |
| Courtis, Stuart Appleton | Wyandotte |
| Davenport, Eugene | Woodland |
| Davis, Calvin Olin | Macomb |
| Dewey, Henry Bingham | Niles |
| Dykema, Peter William | Grand Rapids |
| Eurich, Alvin Christian | Bay City |
| Immel, Ray Keeslar | West Gilead |
| Kelley, Truman Lee | Whitehall |
| Mitchell, Elmer Dayton | Negaunee |

| | |
|---|---|
| Mort, Paul R. | Elsie |
| Mumford, Frederick Blackman | Moscow |
| Parkins, Almon Ernest | Marysville |
| Smith, Nila Banton | Altoona |
| Thomas, Calvin | near Lapeer |

## MINNESOTA

| | |
|---|---|
| Bancroft, Jessie Hubbell | Winona |
| Comstock, Ada Louise | Moorhead |
| Dale, Edgar | Benson |
| Dickinson, George Sherman | St. Paul |
| Gates, Arthur Irving | Red Wing |
| Goode, John Paul | Stewartville |
| Gowan, Mary Olivia | Stillwater |
| Grace, Alonzo Gaskell | Morris |
| Hamrin, Shirley Austin | St. Paul |
| Hetherington, Clark Wilson | Lanesboro |
| Johnson, Marietta Louise Pierce | St. Paul |
| Laird, Warren Powers | Winona |
| Lancour, Adlore Harold | Duluth |
| Melby, Ernest Oscar | Lake Park |
| Preston, Josephine Corliss | Fergus Falls |
| Rosskopf, Myron Frederick | Fairmont |
| Schlesinger, Hermann Irving | Minneapolis |
| Schweickhard, Dean Merrill | Mankato |
| Shields, Thomas Edward | Mendota |
| Silvius, George Harold | Virdi |
| Smith, Dora Valentine | Minneapolis |
| West, Willis Mason | St. Cloud |
| Wist, Benjamin Othello | St. Paul |

## MISSISSIPPI

| | |
|---|---|
| Brigance, William Norwood | Olive Branch |
| Humphrey, George Duke | Dumas |
| Mitchell, Samuel Chiles | Coffeeville |
| Pittman, Marvin Summers | Eupora |
| Whitfield, Henry Lewis | Rankin County |

## MISSOURI

| | |
|---|---|
| Almack, John Conrad | Texas County |
| Baker, Samuel Aaron | Patterson |
| Blow, Susan Elizabeth | Carondelet |
| Brooks, Stratton Duluth | Everett |
| Campbell, Prince Lucien | Newmarket |
| Carrington, William Thomas | Calloway County |
| Case, Adelaide Teague | St. Louis |
| Chapman, Paul Wilber | Brookfield |

| | |
|---|---|
| Douglass, Harl Roy | Richmond |
| Fretwell, Elbert Kirtley | Williamstown |
| Gillette, John Morris | near Maryville |
| Goldstein, Max Aaron | St. Louis |
| Hewett, Waterman Thomas | Miami |
| Hill, Clyde Milton | West Plains |
| Hill, Howard Copeland | St. Louis |
| Hodge, Oliver | Exeter |
| Hunter, Frederick Maurice | Savannah |
| Jones, Lawrence Clifton | St. Joseph |
| Lange, Alexis Frederick | Lafayette County |
| Linville, Henry Richardson | St. Joseph |
| Lomax, Paul Sanford | Laclede |
| Patterson, Edwin Wilhite | Kansas City |
| Pritchett, Henry Smith | Fayette |
| Sachar, Abram Leon | St. Louis |
| Selvidge, Robert Washington | Moundview |
| Taussig, Frank William | St. Louis |
| Tippett, James Sterling | Memphis |
| Waters, Henry Jackson | Center |
| Weir, Irene | St. Louis |
| Williams, Walter | Boonville |

## MONTANA

| | |
|---|---|
| Henzlik, Frank Ernest | Great Falls |

## NEBRASKA

| | |
|---|---|
| Alexander, Hartley Burr | Lincoln |
| Arny, Clara Maude Brown | Grand Island |
| Bryson, Lyman Lloyd | Valentine |
| Cartwright, Morse Adams | Omaha |
| Cloud, Henry Roe | Winnebago |
| Curti, Merle Eugene | Papillion |
| Hamerschlag, Arthur Acton | Omaha |
| Hanson, Howard Harold | Wahoo |
| Hollingworth, Leta Anna Stetter | Chadron |
| Hughes, William Leonard | Edgar |
| Johnson, Alvin Saunders | near Homer |
| Leigh, Robert Devore | Nelson |
| McHugh, Anna (Antonia) | Omaha |
| Pound, Louise | Lincoln |
| Pound, Roscoe | Lincoln |
| Saylor, John Galen | Carleton |
| Showalter, Noah David | Cass County |
| Weeks, Ila Delbert | Scotia |

## NEW HAMPSHIRE

| | |
|---|---|
| Adams, Ebenezer | New Ipswich |
| Andrews, Elisha Benjamin | Hinsdale |
| Bancroft, Cecil Franklin Patch | New Ipswich |
| Brown, Alice Van Vechten | Hanover |
| Burnham, William Henry | Dunbarton |
| Burton, Warren | Wilton |
| Crosby, Alpheus | Sandwich |
| Cutter, Calvin | Jaffrey |
| Dutton, Samuel Train | Hillsboro |
| Eaton, John | Sutton |
| Emerson, Joseph | Hollis |
| Gardner, Helen | Manchester |
| Gove, Aaron Estellus | Hampton Falls |
| Haddock, Charles Brickett | Salisbury |
| Hale, Horace Morrison | Hollis |
| Hall, Samuel Read | Croyden |
| Hartwell, Edward Mussey | Exeter |
| Harvey, Lorenzo Dow | Deerfield |
| Harvey, Thomas Wadleigh | New London |
| Hopkins, Ernest Martin | Dunbarton |
| Howard, Ada Lydia | Temple |
| King, Charles Francis | Wilton |
| Ladd, Azel Parkhurst | Haverhill |
| Langdell, Christopher Columbus | New Boston |
| Mills, Caleb | Dunbarton |
| Orcutt, Hiram | Acworth |
| Page, David Perkins | Epping |
| Parker, Francis Wayland | Piscatoquog |
| Pattee, Fred Lewis | Bristol |
| Patterson, James Willis | Henniker |
| Philbrick, John Dudley | Deerfield |
| Pierce, John Davis | Chesterfield |
| Pike, Nicholas | Somersworth |
| Poland, William Carey | Goffstown Center (later, Grasmere) |
| Poor, John | Plaistow |
| Richardson, Leon Burr | Lebanon |
| Shahan, Thomas Joseph | Manchester |
| Shattuck, Joseph Cummings | Marlborough |
| Sherwin, Thomas | Westmoreland |
| Smart, James Henry | Center Harbor |
| Spaulding, Frank Ellsworth | Dublin |
| Swett, John | Pittsfield |
| Taylor, Samuel Harvey | Londonderry |
| Wentworth, George Albert | Wakefield |
| Wilson, William Dexter | Stoddard |

| | |
|---|---|
| Worcester, Joseph Emerson | Bedford |
| Young, Charles Augustus | Hanover |

## NEW JERSEY

| | |
|---|---|
| Anderson, Archibald Watson | Hammond |
| Apgar, Ellis A. | Peapack |
| Bard, Samuel | Burlington |
| Bateman, Newton | Fairfield |
| Bishop, John Remsen | New Brunswick |
| Boynton, Percy Holmes | Newark |
| Butler, Nicholas Murray | Elizabeth |
| Caldwell, Joseph | Lammington |
| Clapp, Margaret | East Orange |
| Cook, Albert Stanburrough | Montville |
| Dod, Thaddeus | Newark |
| Douglass, Mabel Smith | Jersey City |
| Drake, Daniel | near Plainfield |
| Fay, Edward Allen | Morristown |
| Fitz-Gerald, John Driscoll, II | Newark |
| Frelinghuysen, Theodore | Millstone |
| Goetschius, Percy | Paterson |
| Goodrich, Annie Warburton | New Brunswick |
| Griscom, John | Hancock's Bridge |
| Griswold, Alfred Whitney | Morristown |
| Halsted, George Bruce | Newark |
| Hill, Thomas | New Brunswick |
| Lindsley, John Berrien | Princeton |
| Lindsley, Philip | near Morristown |
| Lozier, Clemence Sophia Harned | Plainfield |
| Maclean, John (1800–1886) | Princeton |
| Manning, James | Piscataway |
| Merrill, Helen Abbot | Orange |
| Parsons, Frank | Mount Holly |
| Rickoff, Andrew Jackson | near New Hope |
| Rusby, Henry Hurd | Franklin |
| Seeley, Levi | Harpersfield |
| Seybolt, Robert Francis | Kearny |
| Shafer, Helen Almira | Newark |
| Stimson, John Ward | Paterson |
| Strang, Ruth May | Chatham |
| Sumner, William Graham | Paterson |
| Taylor, John Orville | Charleton |
| Van Dyke, John Charles | New Brunswick |
| Welling, James Clarke | Trenton |
| Wood, George Bacon | Greenwich |
| Woolman, Mary Raphael Schenck | Camden |

## NEW MEXICO

Sanchez, George Isidore                    Barela

## NEW YORK

| | |
|---|---|
| Alberty, Harold Bernard | Lockport |
| Alden, Joseph | Cairo |
| Anderson, John Jacob | New York |
| Anthon, Charles | New York |
| Atwater, Wilbur Olin | Johnsburg |
| Barnes, Earl | Martville |
| Barnes, Harry Elmer | Auburn |
| Barnes, Mary Downing Sheldon | Oswego |
| Bascom, John | Genoa |
| Beberman, Max | New York |
| Beecher, Catharine Esther | East Hampton |
| Benedict, Ruth Fulton | New York |
| Birge, Edward Asahiel | Troy |
| Bradford, Mary Carroll Craig | New York |
| Brickman, William Wolfgang | New York |
| Brigham, Albert Perry | Perry |
| Brooks, Edward | Stony Point |
| Brown, Elmer Ellsworth | Kiantone |
| Brownell, Herbert | Madison |
| Burgess, Theodore Chalon | Little Valley |
| Butler, Howard Crosby | Croton Falls |
| Buttrick, Wallace | Potsdam |
| Calderone, Mary Steichen | New York |
| Calkins, Norman Allison | Gainesville |
| Clinton, De Witt | Little Britain |
| Cochran, David Henry | Springville |
| Coe, George Albert | Monroe County |
| Comfort, George Fisk | Berkshire |
| Comstock, Anna Botsford | Otto |
| Cook, John Williston | near Oneida |
| Cooley, LeRoy Clark | Point Peninsula |
| Cooper, Sarah Brown Ingersoll | Cazenovia |
| Crane, Julia Ettie | Hewittville |
| Crane, Thomas Frederick | New York |
| Dana, James Dwight | Utica |
| Davis, Henry | East Hampton |
| Davis, Nathan Smith | Greene |
| Dewey, Melvil | Adams Center |
| Dodge, Grace Hoadley | New York |
| Dorsey, Susan Almira Miller | Penn Yan |
| Draper, Andrew Sloan | Westford |
| Drisler, Henry | Staten Island |
| Duer, William Alexander | Rhinebeck |

| | |
|---|---|
| Duggan, Stephen Pierce | New York |
| Dwight, Theodore William | Catskill |
| Eaton, Amos | Chatham |
| Ely, Richard Theodore | Ripley |
| Erskine, John | New York |
| Finegan, Thomas Edward | West Fulton |
| Fisher, Irving | Saugerties |
| Fitzpatrick, Edward Augustus | New York |
| Folwell, William Watts | Romulus |
| Forbes, John Franklin | Middlesex |
| Frank, Michael | Virgil |
| Frissell, Hollis Burke | South Amenia |
| Frost, William Goodell | LeRoy |
| Gale, George Washington | Stamford |
| Gildersleeve, Virginia Crocheron | New York |
| Graves, Frank Pierrepont | Brooklyn |
| Gray, Asa | Sauquoit |
| Gregory, John Milton | Sand Lake |
| Hadley, James | Fairfield |
| Halleck, Reuben Post | Rocky Point, Long Island |
| Halsted, William Stewart | New York |
| Hanchett, Henry Granger | Syracuse |
| Harris, Chapin Aaron | Pompey |
| Hayes, Carlton Joseph Huntley | Afton |
| Haynes, Benjamin Rudolph | Plattsburgh |
| Heald, Henry Townley | Chancellor |
| Hook, Sidney | New York |
| Howland, Emily | Sherwood |
| Hull, Clark Leonard | Akron |
| Hutchins, Robert Maynard | Brooklyn |
| Jackson, Sheldon | Minaville |
| James, William | New York |
| Johnson, William Woolsey | near Owego |
| Jordan, David Starr | Gainesville |
| Judson, Harry Pratt | Jamestown |
| Kellas, Eliza | Mooers Forks |
| Kendall, Calvin Noyes | Augusta |
| Keppel, Frederick Paul | Staten Island |
| Kiehle, David Litchard | Danville |
| Kingsley, Clarence Darwin | Syracuse |
| Kirkland, John Thornton | Little Falls |
| Knapp, Seaman Asahel | Schroon Lake |
| Lathrop, John Hiram | Sherburne |
| Lee, James Melvin | Port Crane |
| Levy, Florence Nightingale | New York |
| Lewis, Dioclesian | near Auburn |
| Lord, Asa Dearborn | Madrid |

| | |
|---|---|
| MacDonald, Arthur | Caledonia |
| McGrath, Earl James | Buffalo |
| McMaster, John Bach | Brooklyn |
| McMynn, John Gibson | Palatine Ridge |
| McQuaid, Bernard John | New York |
| Mahan, Asa | Vernon |
| Mahan, Dennis Hart | New York |
| Mannes, David | New York |
| Maslow, Abraham Harold | Brooklyn |
| Mason, John Mitchell | New York |
| Mechem, Floyd Russell | Nunda |
| Meyer, Adolphe Erich | New York |
| Miles, Manly | Homer |
| Miner, Myrtilla | Brookfield |
| Morgan, Lewis Henry | near Aurora |
| Myers, Phillip Van Ness | Tribes Hill |
| Nichols, Frederick George | Avon |
| Norsworthy, Naomi | New York |
| Norton, John Pitkin | Albany |
| Oppenheimer, J. Robert | New York |
| Orton, Edward, Jr. | Chester |
| Orton, Edward Francis Baxter | Deposit |
| Orton, James | Seneca Falls |
| O'Shea, Michael Vincent | LeRoy |
| Palmer, Alice Elvira Freeman | Colesville |
| Palmer, Horatio Richmond | Sherburne |
| Payne, William Harold | Farmington |
| Penny, George Barlow | Haverstraw-on-Hudson |
| Phelps, William Franklin | Auburn |
| Pierson, Abraham | Southampton, Long Island |
| Pirsson, Louis Valentine | Fordham |
| Potter, Alonzo | Beekman |
| Powell, William Bramwell | Castile |
| Prang, Mary Amelia Dana Hicks | Syracuse |
| Pratt, Caroline | Fayetteville |
| Pratt, Orson | Hartford |
| Pratt, Richard Henry | Rushford |
| Pressey, Sidney Leavitt | Brooklyn |
| Quackenbos, George Payn | New York |
| Quackenbos, John Duncan | New York |
| Rambaut, Mary Lucinda Bonney | Hamilton |
| Randall, Samuel Sidwell | Norwich |
| Raymond, John Howard | New York |
| Reed, David Allen | Troy |
| Reeve, Tapping | Brookhaven |
| Remsen, Ira | New York |
| Rice, Victor Moreau | Mayville |

| | |
|---|---|
| Richards, Linda (Melinda Ann) Judson | near Potsdam |
| Richman, Julia | New York |
| Rivlin, Harry N. | New York |
| Robertson, William Schenck | Huntington |
| Robinson, Frederick Bertrand | Brooklyn |
| Rogers, Henry Wade | Holland Patent |
| Runkle, John Daniel | Root |
| Russell, James Earl | Hamden |
| Russell, William Fletcher | Delhi |
| Ryan, Will Carson, Jr. | New York |
| Sammartino, Peter | New York |
| Sanders, Charles Walton | Newport |
| Seton, Elizabeth Ann Bayley | New York |
| Sheldon, Edward Austin | near Perry Center |
| Shores, Louis | Buffalo |
| Sill, Anna Peck | Burlington |
| Skinner, Charles Rufus | Union Square |
| Smith, David Eugene | Cortland |
| Soulé, George | Barrington |
| Spencer, Platt Rogers | East Fishkill |
| Steele, Joel Dorman | Lima |
| Stoddard, John Fair | Greenfield |
| Stowell, Thomas Blanchard | Perry |
| Strong, Edward Kellogg, Jr. | Syracuse |
| Strong, Frank | Venice |
| Stryker, Melancthon Woolsey | Vernon |
| Tappan, Henry Philip | Rhinebeck on the Hudson |
| Tonne, Herbert Arthur | New York |
| Van Bokkelen, Libertus | New York |
| Van Rensselaer, Martha | Randolph |
| Van Til, William | Corona |
| Wait, Samuel | White Creek |
| Wait, William Bell | Amsterdam |
| Ward, Joseph | Perry Center |
| Washburn, Margaret Floy | New York |
| Watson, James Madison | Onondaga Hill |
| Wayland, Francis | New York |
| Weed, Ella | Newburgh |
| Wheatley, William Alonzo | Verona |
| White, Andrew Dickson | Homer |
| White, Samuel Holmes | Lockport |
| Whitford, William Clarke | West Edmeston |
| Willard, Frances Elizabeth Caroline | Churchville |
| Winchell, Alexander | North East |
| Wood, De Volson | Smyrna |
| Woolsey, Theodore Dwight | New York |
| Wulling, Frederick John | Brooklyn |

| | |
|---|---|
| Youmans, Edward Livingston | Albany County |
| Young, Andrew White | Carlisle |
| Young, Ella Flagg | Buffalo |
| Zirbes, Laura | Buffalo |

## NORTH CAROLINA

| | |
|---|---|
| Alderman, Edwin Anderson | Wilmington |
| Allen, Arch Turner | Hiddenite |
| Aycock, Charles Brantley | Wayne County |
| Briggs, Thomas Henry | Raleigh |
| Brooks, Eugene Clyde | Greene County |
| Brown, Charlotte Hawkins | Henderson |
| Cain, William | Hillsboro |
| Clement, Rufus Early | Salisbury |
| Councill, William Hooper | Fayetteville |
| Craven, Braxton | Randolph County |
| Dougherty, Blanford Barnard | Boone |
| Dudley, James Benson | Wilmington |
| Edwards, Newton | Carthage |
| Elliott, Aaron Marshall | Wilmington |
| Foust, Julius Isaac | Graham |
| Graham, Edward Kidder | Charlotte |
| Graham, Frank Porter | Fayetteville |
| Horne, Herman Harrell | Clayton |
| Joyner, James Yadkin | Davidson County |
| Knight, Edgar Wallace | Northampton County |
| McIver, Charles Duncan | Moore County |
| Murchison, Carl Allanmore | Hickory |
| Payne, Bruce Ryburn | near Morganston |
| Poteat, William Louis | Caswell County |
| Revels, Hiram Rhodes | Fayetteville |
| Shepard, James Edward | Raleigh |
| Smith, Charles Alfonso | Greensboro |
| Smith, Henry Louis | Greensboro |
| Swain, David Lowry | Asheville |
| Waddel, Moses | **Rowan (later, Iredell) County** |
| Webb, William Robert | near Mount Tirzah |
| Wiley, Calvin Henderson | Guilford County |
| Wilson, Louis Round | Lenoir |

## NORTH DAKOTA

| | |
|---|---|
| Kirk, Samuel Alexander | Rugby |
| Squires, James Duane | Grand Forks |

## OHIO

| | |
|---|---|
| Andrews, Lorin | Ashland |
| Babbitt, Irving | Dayton |
| Bawden, William Thomas | Oberlin |

| | |
|---|---|
| Bessey, Charles Edwin | Wayne County |
| Bevier, Isabel | near Plymouth |
| Bodley, Rachel Littler | Cincinnati |
| Boyd, David Ross | Coshocton |
| Brown, LeRoy Decatur | Noble County |
| Chambers, Merritt Madison | Knox County |
| Compton, Arthur Holly | Wooster |
| Compton, Karl Taylor | Wooster |
| Corbin, Joseph Carter | Chillicothe |
| Crabbe, John Grant | Mt. Sterling |
| Crabtree, James William | Crabtree |
| Davidson, Charles | Streetsboro |
| Dickey, Sarah Ann | near Dayton |
| Dyer, Franklin Benjamin | Warren County |
| Earhart, Will | Franklin |
| Elson, William Harris | Carroll County |
| Fairchild, Edward Thomson | Doylestown |
| Fairchild, George Thompson | Brownhelm |
| Fess, Simeon Davidson | Harrod |
| Gage, Lucy | Portsmouth |
| Gault, Franklin Benjamin | Wooster |
| Gehrkens, Karl Wilson | Kelleys Island |
| Griffith, Emily | Cincinnati |
| Hadley, Hiram | Wilmington |
| Hancock, John | near Point Pleasant |
| Harper, William Rainey | New Concord |
| Harrington, Harry Franklin | Logan |
| Henri, Robert | Cincinnati |
| Hinsdale, Burke Aaron | Wadsworth |
| Hocking, William Ernest | Cleveland |
| Hoyt, John Wesley | near Worthington |
| Jackman, Wilbur Samuel | Mechanicstown |
| Johnson, Franklin | Frankfort |
| Kauffman, Treva Erdine | Osborn |
| King, William Fletcher | near Zanesville |
| Ladd, George Trumbull | Painesville |
| McCloy, Charles Harold | Marietta |
| MacCracken, Henry Mitchell | Oxford |
| McVey, Frank LeRond | Wilmington |
| Marshall, Leon Carroll | Zanesville |
| Meriam, Junius Lathrop | Randolph |
| Molloy, Mary Aloysius | Sandusky |
| Moore, Ernest Carroll | Youngstown |
| Morgan, Arthur Ernest | Cincinnati |
| Murlin, Lemuel Herbert | Convoy |
| Nash, Jay Bryan | New Baltimore |
| Owen, William Bishop | Union Station |

| | |
|---|---|
| Park, John Rocky | Tiffin |
| Paterson, Donald Gildersleeve | Columbus |
| Read, Daniel | near Marietta |
| Read, Gerald Howard | Akron |
| Rice, Fenelon Bird | Greensburg |
| Rose, Mary Davies Swartz | Newark |
| Schevill, Rudolph | Cincinnati |
| Shera, Jesse Hauk | Oxford |
| Sloane, William Milligan | Richmond |
| Stubbs, Joseph Edward | Ashland |
| Taft, Horace Dutton | Cincinnati |
| Tappan, Eli Todd | Steubenville |
| Thompson, William Oxley | Cambridge |
| Vaile, Edwin Orlando | Piqua |
| Venable, William Henry | near Waynesville |
| Wald, Lillian D. | Cincinnati |
| Weeks, Thomas Edwin | Massillon |
| White, Emerson Elbridge | Mantua |
| Wiles, Kimball | Ripley |
| Williams, Jesse Feiring | Kenton |
| Williamson, Charles Clarence | Salem |
| Wrenn, Charles Gilbert | New Paris |
| Young, Clark Montgomery | Hiram |
| Young, John Wesley | Columbus |

## OKLAHOMA

| | |
|---|---|
| Colton, Elizabeth Avery | Choctaw Nation |

## OREGON

| | |
|---|---|
| Hyde, Grant Milnor | The Dalles |
| Oberteuffer, Delbert | Portland |

## PENNSYLVANIA

| | |
|---|---|
| Agnew, David Hayes | Lancaster County |
| Apple, Thomas Gilmore | Easton |
| Armstrong, Richard | McEwensville |
| Bache, Alexander Dallas | Philadelphia |
| Baldwin, Joseph | New Castle |
| Balliet, Thomas Minard | New Mahoning |
| Barton, Benjamin Smith | Lancaster |
| Belfield, Henry Holmes | Philadelphia |
| Blaker, Eliza Ann Cooper | Philadelphia |
| Blunt, Katharine | Philadelphia |
| Bogle, Sarah Comly Norris | Milton |
| Bonnell, John Mitchell | Bucks County |
| Boring, Edwin Garrigues | Philadelphia |
| Brown, Hallie Quinn | Pittsburgh |

| | |
|---|---|
| Brownell, William Arthur | Smethport |
| Brubacher, Abram Royer | Lebanon |
| Brumbaugh, Martin Grove | Huntingdon County |
| Bunnell, Charles Ernest | Dimock |
| Burrowes, Thomas Henry | Strasburg |
| Butler, Noble | Chester County |
| Byerly, William Elwood | Philadelphia |
| Caldwell, David | Lancaster County |
| Carmichael, Leonard | Philadelphia |
| Carrick, Samuel | York (later, Adams) County |
| Cattell, James McKeen | Easton |
| Chauvenet, William | Milford |
| Cheyney, Edward Potts | Wallingford |
| Commager, Henry Steele | Pittsburgh |
| Cook, Albert Samuel | Greencastle |
| Crawford, James Pyle Wickersham | Lancaster |
| Dann, Hollis Ellsworth | Canton |
| Davis, Noah Knowles | Philadelphia |
| Davis, William Morris | Philadelphia |
| Dodds, Harold Willis | Utica |
| Downey, John | Germantown |
| Eakins, Thomas | Philadelphia |
| Eisenhart, Luther Pfahler | York |
| Feder, Daniel Dunn | Philadelphia |
| Foster, Thomas Jefferson | Pottsville |
| Gallaudet, Thomas Hopkins | Philadelphia |
| Galloway, Samuel | Gettysburg |
| Garrett, Emma | Philadelphia |
| Gibbs, Jonathan C. | Philadelphia |
| Gillespie, Eliza Maria (Mother Angela) | Brownsville |
| Goff, Milton Browning | Pittsburgh |
| Good, Harry Gehman | Lancaster |
| Goucher, John Franklin | Waynesburg |
| Gratz, Rebecca | Philadelphia |
| Green, Jacob | Philadelphia |
| Grillis, William Elliot | Philadelphia |
| Grimké, Charlotte L. Forten | Philadelphia |
| Gross, Samuel David | near Easton |
| Gummere, John | Willow Grove |
| Haldeman, Samuel Stehman | Locust Grove |
| Hallowell, Anna | Philadelphia |
| Hart, Albert Bushnell | Clarksville |
| Hart, William Richard | Greene County |
| Hartranft, Chester David | Frederick |
| Heathcote, Charles William | Glen Rock |
| Henry, David Dodds | East McKeesport |
| Himes, Charles Francis | Lancaster County |

| | |
|---|---|
| Jacoby, Henry Sylvester | Springtown |
| Junkin, George | near Carlisle |
| Keen, William Williams | Philadelphia |
| Kerr, Clark | Stony Creek |
| Laubach, Frank Charles | Benton |
| Leidy, Joseph | Philadelphia |
| Lewis, Enoch | Radnor |
| Locke, Alain LeRoy | Philadelphia |
| Lodge, Gonzalez | Fort Littleton |
| Lyte, Eliphalet Oram | Bird-in-Hand |
| McClellan, Henry Brainerd | Philadelphia |
| McCorkle, Samuel Eusebius | near Harris's Ferry |
| McCormick, Samuel Black | Irwin |
| McGuffey, William Holmes | Washington County |
| Magill, Edward Hicks | Bucks County |
| Marshall, Charles | Philadelphia |
| Marvin, John Gage | La Raysville |
| Mearns, William Hughes | Philadelphia |
| Monroe, Will Seymour | Hunlock |
| Morgan, John | Philadelphia |
| Morrison, John Irwin | near Chambersburg |
| Murray, Lindley | Swetara |
| Myers, Garry Cleveland | Sylvan |
| Neill, Edward Duffield | Philadelphia |
| Ogden, Robert Curtis | Philadelphia |
| Parrish, Edward | Philadelphia |
| Pepper, William | Philadelphia |
| Physick, Philip Syng | Philadelphia |
| Priestley, James | n.a. (or Virginia) |
| Pugh, Evan | Oxford |
| Raub, Albert Newton | Leesburg |
| Rice, Joseph Mayer | Philadelphia |
| Riesman, David | Philadelphia |
| Rogers, William Barton | Philadelphia |
| Rorer, Sarah Tyson Heston | Richboro |
| Rush, Benjamin | Philadelphia |
| Sartain, Emily | Philadelphia |
| Schaeffer, Nathan Christ | near Kutztown |
| Schneider, Herman | Summit Hill |
| Scott, John Work | York County |
| Shippen, William, Jr. | Philadelphia |
| Skinner, Burrhus Frederic | Susquehanna |
| Slagle, Robert Lincoln | Hanover |
| Smith, Daniel B. | Philadelphia |
| Smith, Samuel Stanhope | Pequea |
| Smith, Thomas | Lancaster |
| Stillé, Charles Janeway | Philadelphia |

| | |
|---|---|
| Stoddard, George Dinsmore | Carbondale |
| Strayer, George Drayton | Wayne |
| Suhrie, Ambrose Leo | New Baltimore |
| Taylor, Joseph Schimmel | Passer |
| Thompson, Samuel Rankin | South Shenango |
| Tyler, William Seymour | Harford |
| Van Dusen, Henry Pitney | Philadelphia |
| Weigle, Luther Allan | Littlestown |
| Wickersham, James Pyle | Chester County |
| Wiggin, Kate Douglas | Philadelphia |
| Woodhouse, James | Philadelphia |
| Wylie, Andrew | Washington |
| Young, Jacob William Albert | York |
| Young, John Clarke | Greencastle |

## PUERTO RICO

| | |
|---|---|
| Cordero y Molina, Rafael | San Juan |
| Fuertes, Estevan Antonio | San Juan |
| Hostos, Eugenio Maria de | Rio Cañas, Mayaguez |
| Osuna, Juan Jóse | Caguas |

## RHODE ISLAND

| | |
|---|---|
| Angell, James Burrill | Scituate |
| Ashley, Samuel Stanford | Cumberland |
| Baker, George Pierce | Providence |
| Bennett, Charles Edwin | Providence |
| Bicknell, Thomas Williams | Barrington |
| Brown, Goold | Providence |
| Bushee, James | Smithfield |
| Channing, Edward Tyrrell | Newport |
| Colvin, Stephen Sheldon | Phenix |
| Craig, Clara Elizabeth | Providence |
| Crandall, Prudence | Hopkinton |
| Hammond, William Gardiner | Newport |
| Hazard, Caroline | Peace Dale |
| Howland, John | Newport |
| Pendleton, Ellen Fitz | Westerly |
| Potter, Elisha Reynolds, Jr. | South Kingston |
| Stanley, Albert Augustus | Manville |
| Thurston, Robert Henry | Providence |
| Tourjée, Eben | Warwick |

## SOUTH CAROLINA

| | |
|---|---|
| Bailey, Thomas David | Lugoff |
| Baldwin, James Mark | Columbia |
| Bethune, Mary McLeod | Mayville |

| | |
|---|---|
| Brawley, Benjamin Griffith | Columbia |
| Few, William Preston | Greenville |
| Gildersleeve, Basil Lanneau | Charleston |
| Hill, Daniel Harvey | Hill's Iron Works, York District |
| | |
| Jones, Gilbert Haven | Fort Mott |
| Kirkland, James Hampton | Spartanburg |
| Lee, Stephen Dill | Charleston |
| Loughridge, Robert McGill | Laurensville |
| McCrorey, Henry Lawrence | Fairfield County |
| Mays, Benjamin Elijah | Epworth |
| Miller, Kelly | Winnsboro |
| Orr, Gustavus John | Orrville |
| Payne, Daniel Alexander | Charleston |
| Rice, John Andrew | Lynchburg |
| Roberts, Oran Milo | Laurens County |
| Sanders, Daniel Jackson | Winnsboro |
| Thompson, Hugh Smith | Charleston |
| Toland, Hugh Huger | Guilder's Creek |
| Waddel, John Newton | Willington |
| Watson, John Broadus | near Greenville |
| Wilkinson, Robert Shaw | Charleston |

SOUTH DAKOTA

| | |
|---|---|
| MacCaughey, Vaughan | Huron |
| Putnam, Rex | Buffalo Gap |

TENNESSEE

| | |
|---|---|
| Benton, Thomas Hart | Williamson County |
| Bond, Horace Mann | Nashville |
| Burgess, John William | Giles County |
| Claxton, Philander Priestley | near Shelbyville |
| Fanning, Tolbert | Cannon County |
| Hill, David Spence | Nashville |
| Johnson, David Bancroft | LaGrange |
| Johnson, Mordecai Wyatt | Paris |
| Redway, Jacques Wardlaw | near Murfreesboro |
| Tigert, John James | Nashville |
| Witherspoon, John Alexander | Columbia |

TEXAS

| | |
|---|---|
| Axtelle, George Edward | Crandale |
| Blanton, Annie Webb | Houston |
| Bralley, Francis Marion | Honey Grove |
| Burton, William Henry | Fort Worth |
| Coleman, Satis Narrona Barton | Tyler |
| Cooper, Oscar Henry | near Carthage |

London, Hoyt Hobson — Fannin County
Nash, Mell Achilles — Tryon
Osborne, Estelle Massey Riddle — Palestine
Samaroff, Olga — San Antonio

## UTAH

Bennion, Milton — Taylorsville
Cowles, LeRoy Eugene — Chester
Harris, Franklin Stewart — Benjamin
Kerr, William Jasper — Richmond
McMurrin, Sterling Moss — Woods Cross
Stewart, William Mitton — Draper
Wahlquist, John Thomas — Heber

## VERMONT

Adams, Charles Kendall — Derby
Angell, James Rowland — Burlington
Bishop, Harriet E. — Panton
Dewey, John — Burlington
Fisk, Wilbur — Brattleboro
Goodnow, Isaac Tichenor — Whitingham
Gregory, Samuel — Guilford
Hine, Charles Daniel — Fair Haven
Hovey, Charles Edward — Thetford
Hughes, Ray Osgood — Saxtons River
Hunt, William Morris — Brattleboro
Jenne, James Nathaniel — Berkshire
Jewett, Milo Parker — St. Johnsbury
Kendrick, Asahel Clark — Poultney
Merrifield, Webster — Williamsville
Miller, Leslie William — Brattleboro
Mills, Susan Lincoln Tolman — Enosburg
Olin, Stephen — Leicester
Partridge, Alden — Norwich
Peabody, Selim Hobart — Rockingham
Perrin, Porter Gale — Williamstown
Robinson, Stillman Williams — Reading
Safford, Anson Peacely-Killen — Hyde Park
Sheldon, William Evarts — Dorset
Stoddard, Francis Hovey — Middlebury
Stone, Lucinda Hinsdale — Hinesburg
Strong, James Woodward — Brownington
Thomson, James Bates — Springfield
Webster, Horace — Hartford
Wheelock, Lucy — Cambridge
Wilson, Lucy Langdon Williams — Saint Albans
Woodruff, Caroline Salome — West Burke

Yale, Caroline Ardelia                    Charlotte

VIRGINIA

| | |
|---|---|
| Barr, Frank Stringfellow | Suffolk |
| Boyd, David French | Wytheville |
| Boyd, Thomas Duckett | Wytheville |
| Caliver, Ambrose | Saltville |
| Chapman, John Gadsby | Alexandria |
| Chavis, John | Mecklenburg County |
| Dabney, Charles William | Hampden-Sydney |
| Dearmont, Washington Strother | Clark County |
| Dillard, James Hardy | Nansemond County |
| Doak, Samuel | Augusta County |
| Doyne, John James | Farmville |
| Eggleston, Joseph Dupuy, Jr. | Prince Edward County |
| Garland, Landon Cabell | Nelson County |
| Garrett, William Robertson | Williamsburg |
| Good, Carter Victor | Dayton |
| Hatcher, Orie Latham | Petersburg |
| Houston, Edwin James | Alexandria |
| Jefferson, Thomas | Shadwell |
| Jesse, Richard Henry | Epping Forest |
| Johnson, Charles Spurgeon | Bristol |
| Joynes, Edward Southey | Accomack County |
| Langston, John Mercer | Louisa County |
| Laws, Samuel Spahr | Ohio County |
| Magruder, Frank Abbott | Woodstock |
| Markham, Walter Tipton | Ewing |
| Maupin, Socrates | Albemarle County |
| Minor, John Barbee | Louisa County |
| Moore, James | n.a. |
| Moten, Lucy Ella | near White Sulphur Springs |
| Moton, Robert Russa | Amelia County |
| Munford, Mary Cooke Branch | Richmond |
| Newcomb, John Lloyd | Sassafras |
| Page, Inman Edwards | Warrenton |
| Painter, Franklin Verzelius Newton | Hampshire County |
| Parrish, Celestia Susannah | Swansonville |
| Peers, Benjamin Orr | Loudoun County |
| Pendleton, William Kimbrough | Yanceyville |
| Penniman, James Hosmer | Alexandria |
| Priestley, James | n.a. (or Pennsylvania) |
| Reid, Ira de Augustine | Clifton Forge |
| Ruffner, Henry | Shenandoah County |
| Ruffner, William Henry | Lexington |
| Russell, Albert Jonathan | Petersburg |
| Sanford, Robert Nevitt | Chatham |

| | |
|---|---|
| Smith, Francis Henney | Norfolk |
| Trent, William Peterfield | Richmond |
| Tutwiler, Henry | Harrisonburg |
| Vawter, Charles Erastus | Monroe County |
| Washington, Booker Taliaferro | Hale's Ford |
| Wayland, John Walter | Shenandoah County |
| Wilson, Thomas Woodrow | Staunton |
| Woodson, Carter Godwin | New Canton |
| Wythe, George | Elizabeth City |

## WASHINGTON

| | |
|---|---|
| Chandler, Joe Albert | Colfax |
| Eells, Walter Crosby | Mason County |
| Jayne, Clarence D. | Edwall |
| Wanamaker, Pearl Anderson | Mabana |

## WEST VIRGINIA

| | |
|---|---|
| Allen, James Edward, Jr. | Elkins |
| Ray, Joseph | Wheeling |

## WISCONSIN

| | |
|---|---|
| Adams, Romanzo | Bloomingdale |
| Benjamin, Harold Raymond Wayne | Gilmanton |
| Bleyer, Willard Grosvenor | Milwaukee |
| Brameld, Theodore Burghard Hurt | Neillsville |
| Bryant, Joseph Decatur | East Troy |
| Comstock, George Cary | Madison |
| Comstock, John Henry | Janesville |
| De Garmo, Charles | Muckwonago |
| Gesell, Arnold | Alma |
| Hanna, Delphine | Markeson |
| Havighurst, Robert James | De Pere |
| Hetzel, Ralph Dorn | Merrill |
| Keyes, Charles Henry | Banfield |
| Kraus, Mother M. Seraphine (Mary Katharine) | Marytown |
| Larson, Lars Moore | Vernon County |
| Lutkin, Peter Christian | Thompsonville |
| Madeleva, Sister Mary (Mary Evaline Wolff) | Cumberland |
| Miller, Paul Gerard | Pickett |
| Moehlman, Arthur Bernard | Racine |
| Murphy, John Benjamin | Appleton |
| Nash, George Williston | Janesville |
| Parkhurst, Helen | Durand |
| Russell, Harry Luman | Poynetti |
| Sabin, Ellen Clara | Sun Prairie |

Salisbury, Albert                          Lima
Sewall, May Eliza Wright Thompson          Milwaukee
Shuster, George Nauman                     Lancaster
Van Hise, Charles Richard                  Fulton

WYOMING

Wriston, Henry Merritt                     Laramie

FOREIGN COUNTRIES

*Austria*

Bettelheim, Bruno                          Vienna
Grossmann, Louis                           Vienna
Gruenberg, Sidonie Matsner                 Vienna
Harap, Henry                               n.a.

*Belgium*

Coppens, Charles                           Turnhout

*Bermuda*

Cooke, John Esten
Tucker, George

*Bohemia*

Neumann, John Nepomucene                   Prachatitz
Wise, Isaac Mayer                          Steingrub

*British Guiana*

Holmes, George Frederick                   Straebrock

*Canada*

Atkinson, Alfred                           Seaforth, Ontario
Bethune, Joanna Graham                     Fort Niagara, Ontario
Bowman, Isaiah                             Waterloo, Ontario
Burk, Frederic Lister                      Blenheim, Ontario
Carpenter, George Rice                     Eskimo River Mission
                                             Station, Labrador
Charters, Werrett Wallace                  Hartford, Ontario
Dett, Robert Nathaniel                     Drummondville, Quebec
Eby, Frederick                             Berlin (later, Kitchener),
                                             Ontario
Fairclough, Henry Rushton                  near Barrie, Ontario
Freeman, Frank Nugent                      Rockwood, Ontario
Hayakawa, Samuel Ichiye                    Vancouver, British Columbia
Johnstone, Edward Ransom                   Galt, Ontario
Kimball, Dexter Simpson                    New River, New Brunswick
Leffingwell, William Henry                 Woodstock, Ontario
Lillie, Frank Rattray                      Toronto, Ontario

| | |
|---|---|
| McKenzie, Robert Tait | Almonte, Ontario |
| McVicar, Peter | George, New Brunswick |
| Munro, William Bennett | Almonte, Ontario |
| Nutting, Mary Adelaide | Frost Village, Quebec |
| Pearce, Richard Mills, Jr. | Montreal, Quebec |
| Robb, Isabel Adams Hampton | Welland, Ontario |
| Sterling, John Ewart Wallace | Linwood, Ontario |
| Stewart, Isabel Maitland | Chatham, Ontario |
| Taylor, Harold Alexander | Toronto, Ontario |
| Woodbridge, Frederick James Eugene | Windsor, Ontario |

*China*

| | |
|---|---|
| Coulter, John Merle | Ning-Po |
| Gayley, Charles Mills | Shanghai |
| Glass, Hiram Bentley | Laichowfu (later, Yehsien) |
| Tewksbury, Donald George | Tunghsien |

*England*

| | |
|---|---|
| Bryant, John Collins | Ebley, Gloucestershire |
| Buckham, Matthew Henry | Hinckley, Leicestershire |
| Burnz, Eliza Boardman | Rayne |
| Carr, William George | Northampton |
| Cheever, Ezekiel | London |
| Cooper, Myles | Wha House Estate, Cumberland County |
| Cooper, Thomas | Westminster |
| Corlet, Elijah | London |
| Cowling, Donald John | Trevalga, Cornwall |
| Dove, David James | Portsmouth |
| Draper, John William | St. Helen's |
| Dunglison, Robley | Keswick |
| Dunster, Henry | Lancashire |
| Eliot, John | Widford, Hertfordshire |
| Jacobi, Mary Corinna Putnam | London |
| Jones, Thomas Jesse | Llanfacthraeth, Wales |
| Kiddle, Henry | Bath |
| Leipziger, Henry Marcus | Manchester |
| Lovell, John Epy | Colne, Lancashire |
| McDougall, William | Chadderton, Lancashire |
| Meiklejohn, Alexander | Rochdale |
| Mortimer, Mary | Trowbridge, Wiltshire |
| Mursell, James Lockhart | Derby |
| Pitman, Benn | Trowbridge, Wiltshire |
| Proud, Robert | Yorkshire |
| Roberts, Robert Jeffries | n.a. |
| Rogers, Elizabeth Ann | St. Erth, Heyle, Cornwall |
| Sisson, Edward Octavius | Gateshead |

| | |
|---|---|
| Smith, John Rubens | London |
| Soares, Theodore Gerald | Abridge |
| Talmage, James Edward | Hungerford, Berkshire |
| Titchener, Edward Bradford | Chichester |
| Tomlins, William Lawrence | London |
| Warshaw, Jacob | London |
| Whitworth, George Frederic | Boston |

*Estonia*

| | |
|---|---|
| Taba, Hilda | n.a. |

*France*

| | |
|---|---|
| Benezet, Anthony | St. Quentin |
| Clerc, Laurent | LaBalme |
| Crozet, Claude | Villenbrauche |
| Duchesne, Rose Philippine | Grenoble |
| Guerin, Anne Therese | Etables, Cotes-du-Nord |
| Neef, Francis Joseph Nicholas | Soultz, Alsace |
| Sorin, Edward Frederick | Ahuille |

*Germany*

| | |
|---|---|
| Adler, Felix | Alzey |
| Beck, Charles (Karl) | Heidelberg |
| Boas, Franz | Minden, Westphalia |
| Collitz, Hermann | Bleckede, Hanover |
| Collitz, Klara Hechtenberg | Rheydt, Rhineland |
| Damrosch, Frank Heino | Breslau |
| Dock, Christopher | n.a. |
| Follen, Karl (Charles) Theodore Christian | Ranrod, Hesse-Darmstadt |
| Gropius, Walter Adolf | Berlin |
| Guthe, Karl Eugen | Hanover |
| Hendrix, Herman Elert | Hauen |
| Kraus, John | Nassau |
| Kraus-Boelté, Maria | Mecklenburg-Schwerin |
| Krey, August Charles | n.a. |
| Leeser, Isaac | Neuenkirchen, Westphalia |
| Lieber, Francis | Berlin |
| Mannes, Clara Damrosch | Breslau, Silesia |
| Marwedel, Emma Jacobina Christiana | Münden |
| Mies van der Rohe, Ludwig | Aachen |
| Panofsky, Erwin | Hanover |
| Pastorius, Francis Daniel | Sommerhausen, Franconia |
| Pollock, Louise Plessner | Erfurt |
| Ritter, Frederic Louis | Strasbourg |
| Schurz, Margarethe Meyer | Hamburg |

| | |
|---|---|
| Soldan, Frank Louis | Frankfort-am-Main |
| Struck, Ferdinand Theodore | Hamburg |
| Ulich, Robert | Lam bei Riedermühl, Bavaria |
| Wittkower, Rudolf | Berlin |

*Greece*

| | |
|---|---|
| Anagnos, Michael | Papingo, Epirus |
| Sophocles, Evangelinus Apostolides | Tsangarada, Thessaly |

*India*

| | |
|---|---|
| Judd, Charles Hubbard | Bareilly |
| Travers, Robert Morris William | Bangalore |

*Ireland*

| | |
|---|---|
| Alison, Francis | County Donegal |
| Butler, Marie Joseph | Ballynunnery, County Kilkenny |
| Conaty, Thomas James | Kilmallough |
| Gregg, John Robert | Rockcorry, County Monaghan |
| Hughes, John Joseph | County Tyrone |
| Hunter, Thomas | Ardglass |
| Ireland, John | Burnchurch, County Kilkenny |
| Keane, John Joseph | Ballyshannon, County Donegal |
| Knox, Samuel | County Armagh |
| McGroarty, Susan (Sister Julia) | Inver, County Donegal |
| Maxwell, William Henry | Stewartstown, County Tyrone |
| Mullany, Patrick Francis (Brother Azarias) | near Killenaule, County Tipperary |
| Newell, McFadden Alexander | Belfast |
| Tennent, William | n.a. |
| Thompson, Robert Ellis | Lurgan |

*Italy*

| | |
|---|---|
| Covello, Leonard | Avigliano (Potenza) |
| Patri, Angelo | n.a. |

*Lithuania*

| | |
|---|---|
| Revel, Bernard | Kaunas |

*Mexico*

| | |
|---|---|
| Campa, Arthur Leon | Guaymas |
| Castañeda, Carlos Eduardo | Camargo |

*Moravia*

Zeisberger, David                          Zauchental

*Netherlands (Holland)*

Gantvoort, Arnold Johann                   Amsterdam
Gideonse, Harry David                      Rotterdam

*Norway*

Christiansen, Fredrik Melius               Eidsvold
Larsen, Peter Laurentius                   Oslo
Owre, Alfred                               Hammerfest

*Poland*

Broudy, Harry Samuel                       Filipowa
Wiener, Leo                                Bialystok

*Prussia*

Goldbeck, Robert                           Potsdam
Hanus, Paul Henry                          Hermsdorf, Upper Silesia
Rauch, Frederick Augustus                  Kirchbracht

*Rumania*

Kandel, Isaac Leon                         Botoshani
Klapper, Paul                              Jassy

*Russia*

Demiashkevich, Michael John                Mohilev
Gamoran, Emmanuel                          Beltz
Gruenberg, Benjamin Charles                Bessarabia
Scott, Miriam Finn                         Vilna

*Saxony*

Watteville, Henrietta Benigna              Berthelsdorf
    Justina von Zinzendorf

*Scotland*

Bell, Alexander Graham                     Edinburgh
Bishop, Robert Hamilton                    Whitburn County
Blair, James                               n.a.
Davidson, Thomas                           Deer, Aberdeenshire
Fraser, John                               Cromarty
Kinley, David                              Dundee
Lawson, Andrew Cowper                      Anstruther
MacAlister, James                          Glasgow
McCosh, James                              Carskoech, Ayrshire

| | |
|---|---|
| MacKenzie, James Cameron | Aberdeen |
| Maclean, John (1771–1814) | Glasgow |
| MacVicar, Malcolm | Dunglass, Argyleshire |
| Martin, Alexander | Nairn |
| Neilson, William Allan | Doune, Perthshire |
| Paterson, William Burns | Tullibody |
| Paterson, James Kennedy | Glasgow |
| Russell, William | Glasgow |
| Smith, William | Aberdeen |
| Swinton, William | Salton |
| Wilson, Peter | Ordiquhill |
| Witherspoon, John | Gifford |

*Sweden*

| | |
|---|---|
| Johnson, Henry | Norra Nörum |
| Oldberg, Oscar | Aefta |
| Posse, Nils | Stockholm |
| Seashore, Carl Emil | Mörlunda |

*Switzerland*

| | |
|---|---|
| Agassiz, Jean Louis Rodolphe | Motier |
| Bapst, John | Le Roche, Fribourg |
| Cajori, Florian | St. Aignan |
| Guyot, Arnold Henry | Boudevilliers |
| Hailmann, William Nicholas | Glarus |
| Krüsi, Johann Heinrich Hermann | Yverdon |
| Meyer, Adolf | Niederwenigen |
| Talbot, Marion | Thun |

*Turkey*

| | |
|---|---|
| Farnsworth, Charles Hubert | Cesareá |
| Goodell, Henry Hill | Constantinople |
| Zachos, John Celivergos | Constantinople |

*Wurtemberg, Duchy of*

| | |
|---|---|
| Memminger, Christopher Gustavus | Nayhingen |

# APPENDIX B:
## STATE OF MAJOR SERVICE

### ALABAMA

Abercrombie, John William
Battle, Archibald John
Carmichael, Oliver Cromwell
Councill, William Hooper
Curry, Jabez Lamar Monroe
Garland, Landon Cabell
Haynes, Benjamin Rudolph
Jewett, Milo Parker
Johnson, Marietta Louise Pierce
Moton, Robert Russa
Paterson, William Burns
Perry, William Flake
Petrie, George
Pinney, Norman
Powers, James Knox
Snavely, Guy Everett
Thach, Charles Coleman
Tutwiler, Henry
Tutwiler, Julia Strudwick
Washington, Booker Taliaferro

### ALASKA

Bunnell, Charles Ernest
Henderson, Lester Dale
Jackson, Sheldon
Wagner, Jonathan Howard

### ARIZONA

Atkinson, Alfred
Case, Charles Orlando
Fitz-Gerald, John Driscoll, II
Gammage, Grady
Hendrix, Herman Elert
Safford, Anson Peacely-Killen

### ARKANSAS

Corbin, Joseph Carter
Doyne, John James

Gates, Noah Putnam
Hill, Daniel Harvey
Shinn, Josiah Hazen
Smith, Thomas

### CALIFORNIA

Almack, John Conrad
Barnes, Earl
Brownell, William Arthur
Burk, Frederic Lister
Cajori, Florian
Campbell, Douglas Houghton
Cassidy, Rosalind
Cooper, Sarah Brown Ingersoll
Cubberly, Elwood Patterson
Dorsey, Susan Almira Miller
Durant, Henry
Eells, Walter Crosby
Espinosa, Aurelio Macedonio
Fairclough, Henry Rushton
Frye, Alexis Everett
Gayley, Charles Mills
Hanna, Paul Robert
Hayakawa, Samuel Ichiye
Hedrick, Earle Raymond
Hetherington, Clark Wilson
Hilgard, Ernest Ropriequet
Hills, Elijah Clarence
Howison, George Holmes
Hunt, Thomas Forsyth
Immel, Ray Keeslar
Jordan, David Starr
Kefauver, Grayson Neikirk
Kelley, Truman Lee
Keppel, Mark
Kerr, Clark
Keyes, Charles Henry
Lange, Alexis Frederick

[1500]

Lawson, Andrew Cowper
McConnell, Thomas Raymond
Marvin, John Gage
Marwedel, Emma Jacobina Christiana
Meriam, Junius Lathrop
Merrill, George Arthur
Millikan, Robert Andrews
Mills, Susan Lincoln Tolman
Moore, Ernest Carroll
Morphet, Edgar Leroy
Munro, William Bennett
Oppenheimer, J. Robert
Powell, Lawrence Clark
Proctor, William Martin
Quillen, Isaac James
Reinhardt, Aurelia Isabel Henry
Sanford, Robert Nevitt
Schevill, Rudolph
Sill, Edward Rowland
Simpson, Roy E.
Sproul, Robert Gordon
Sterling, John Ewart Wallace
Strong, Edward Kellogg, Jr.
Stowell, Thomas Blanchard
Swett, John
Taba, Hilda
Terman, Lewis Madison
Thomas, Frank Waters
Toland, Hugh Huger
Wahlquist, John Thomas
Wheeler, Benjamin Ide
Wiggin, Kate Douglas
Wilbur, Ray Lyman
Wood, William Christopher

COLORADO

Baker, James Hutchins
Bradford, Mary Carroll Craig
Cajori, Florian
Campa, Arthur Leon
Crabbe, John Grant
Douglass, Harl Roy
Ellis, Alston
Feder, Daniel Dunn
Gove, Aaron Estellus
Griffith, Emily
Hale, Horace Morrison

Hunter, Frederick Maurice
Shattuck, Joseph Cummings

CONNECTICUT

Anderson, William Gilbert
Andrews, Charles McLean
Andrews, Ethan Allen
Angell, James Rowland
Atwater, Wilbur Olin
Baker, George Pierce
Barnard, Henry
Beecher, Catharine Esther
Brownell, Thomas Church
Brubacher, John Seiler
Bryant, Ralph Clement
Cady, Sarah Louise Ensign
Camp, David Nelson
Chittenden, Russell Henry
Clap, Thomas
Clerc, Laurent
Comstock, John Lee
Cook, Albert Stanburrough
Crandall, Prudence
Cross, Wilbur Lucius
Cummings, Joseph
Daboll, Nathan
Dana, James Dwight
Day, Henry Noble
Day, Jeremiah
De Vane, William Clyde
Dodge, Richard Elwood
Dutton, Samuel Train
Dwight, Timothy (1752–1817)
Dwight, Timothy (1828–1916)
Emerson, Joseph
Fisher, Irving
Fisk, Wilbur
Gallaudet, Thomas Hopkins
Gesell, Arnold
Goodrich, Annie Warburton
Goodrich, Chauncey Allen
Gordy, Wilbur Fisk
Gould, James
Grace, Alonzo Gaskell
Griswold, Alfred Whitney
Gruhn, William Theodore
Gunn, Frederick William

Hadley, Arthur Twining
Hadley, James
Harris, Samuel
Hartranft, Chester David
Hill, Clyde Milton
Hine, Charles Daniel
Hooker, Worthington
Hull, Clark Leonard
Huntington, Ellsworth
Kingsley, James Luce
Ladd, George Trumbull
Lovell, John Epy
Morse, Jedidiah
Northend, Charles
Northrop, Birdsey Grant
Norton, John Pitkin
Olin, Stephen
Olmsted, Denison
Olney, Jesse
Parker, Horatio William
Phelps, William Lyon
Pierce, Sarah
Pierson, Abraham
Pirsson, Louis Valentine
Porter, Noah
Porter, Sarah
Reeve, Tapping
Rice, William North
Rogers, Henry Wade
Silliman, Benjamin
Silliman, Benjamin, Jr.
Smith, Nathan
Spaulding, Frank Ellsworth
Stiles, Ezra
Sumner, William Graham
Taft, Horace Dutton
Webster, Noah
Weigle, Luther Allan
Wheatley, William Alonzo
Winslow, Charles-Edward Amory
Woodbridge, William Channing
Woolsey, Theodore Dwight

DELAWARE

Alison, Francis
Gilbert, Eliphalet Wheeler
Groves, James Henry

Hall, Willard
Wallin, John Edward Wallace

DISTRICT OF COLUMBIA

Allen, Charles Ricketson
Allen, James Edward, Jr.
Armstrong, Wesley Earl
Barrows, Alice Prentice
Bell, Alexander Graham
Brawley, Benjamin Griffith
Brown, Elmer Ellsworth
Caliver, Ambrose
Carr, William George
Chambers, Merritt Madison
Claxton, Philander Priestley
Conaty, Thomas James
Crabtree, James William
Cushman, Frank
Eaton, John
Eells, Walter Crosby
Fay, Edward Allen
Frazier, Edward Franklin
Gallaudet, Edward Miner
Givens, Willard Earl
Gowan, Mary Olivia
Harris, William Torrey
Johnson, Mordecai Wyatt
Keane, John Joseph
Langston, John Mercer
Locke, Alain LeRoy
MacDonald, Arthur
McGrath, Earl James
Merriam, John Campbell
Miller, Kelly
Miner, Myrtilla
Moten, Lucy Ella
Pace, Edward Aloysius
Pollock, Louise Plessner
Powell, William Bramwell
Richards, Zalmon
Shahan, Thomas Joseph
Shields, Thomas Edward
Studebaker, John Ward
Tigert, John James
True, Alfred Charles
Ward, Lester Frank
Welling, James Clarke

Woodson, Carter Godwin
Wright, Arthur Davis
Wright, John Calvin
Zook, George Frederick

## FLORIDA

Bailey, Thomas David
Bethune, Mary McLeod
Cottingham, Harold Fred
English, John Colin
Forbes, John Franklin
Gibbs, Jonathan C.
Murphree, Albert Alexander
Russell, Albert Jonathan
Scates, Douglas Edgar
Sheats, William Nicholas
Shores, Louis
Tigert, John James
Walker, David Shelby
Wiles, Kimball

## GEORGIA

Aderhold, Omer Clyde
Andrews, Eliza Frances
Battle, Archibald John
Berry, Martha McChesney
Bond, Horace Mann
Bonnell, John Mitchell
Brittain, Marion Luther
Chapman, Paul Wilber
Clement, Rufus Early
Collins, Mauney Douglass
Du Bois, William Edward Burghardt
Evans, Lawton Bryan
Glenn, Gustavus Richard
Haygood, Atticus Green
Hope, John
Hunt, Henry Alexander
Laney, Lucy Craft
Mays, Benjamin Elijah
Orr, Gustavus John
Packard, Sophia B.
Parrish, Celestia Susannah
Pittman, Marvin Summers
Stewart, Joseph Spencer
Ware, Edmund Asa
Wright, Richard Robert

## HAWAII

Adams, Romanzo
Andrews, Lorrin
Armstrong, Richard
Long, Oren Ethelbirt
MacCaughey, Vaughan
Richards, William
Rogers, Elizabeth Ann
Wist, Benjamin Othello

## IDAHO

Axline, George Andrew
Bryan, Enoch Albert
Gault, Franklin Benjamin
Sisson, Edward Octavius

## ILLINOIS

Ahern, Mary Eileen
Allyn, Robert
Anderson, Archibald Watson
Baker, Edna Dean
Baldwin, Theron
Bateman, Newton
Beberman, Max
Belfield, Henry Holmes
Bennett, Charles Alpheus
Bettelheim, Bruno
Bevier, Isabel
Bigelow, Harry Augustus
Bloomfield, Leonard
Blunt, Katharine
Bobbitt, John Franklin
Bode, Boyd Henry
Boynton, Percy Holmes
Breasted, James Henry
Breckinridge, Sophonisba Preston
Broudy, Harry Samuel
Burgess, Theodore Chalon
Compton, Arthur Holly
Cook, John Williston
Cooley, Edwin Gilbert
Coulter, John Merle
Curme, George Oliver
Davenport, Eugene
Davis, Nathan Smith
De Boer, John James
Dewey, John

Dexter, Edwin Grant
Deyoe, George Percy
Downing, Elliot Rowland
Draper, Andrew Sloan
Edwards, Newton
Freeman, Frank Nugent
Gale, George Washington
Gardner, Helen
Goode, John Paul
Gray, William Scott
Gregg, John Robert
Gregory, John Milton
Gulliver, Julia Henrietta
Hale, William Gardner
Haley, Margaret Angela
Hamrin, Shirley
Hand, Harold Curtis
Harper, William Rainey
Harrington, Harry Franklin
Harrison, Elizabeth
Havighurst, Robert James
Heald, Henry Townley
Henry, David Dodds
Hill, Howard Copeland
Holzinger, Karl John
Hosic, James Fleming
Hovey, Charles Edward
Hutchins, Robert Maynard
Jackman, Wilbur Samuel
James, Edmund Janes
Johnson, Earl Shepard
Johnson, Franklin
Judd, Charles Hubbard
Judson, Harry Pratt
Kinley, David
Kirk, Samuel Alexander
Koos, Leonard Vincent
Lancour, Adlore Harold
Leffingwell, William Henry
Lillie, Frank Rattray
Long, Livingston Chester
Lutkin, Peter Christian
McConathy, Osbourne
Manly, John Matthews
Marshall, Leon Carroll
Mechem, Floyd Russell
Melby, Ernest Oscar

Merriam, Charles Edward
Mies van der Rohe, Ludwig
Monroe, Walter Scott
Morrison, Henry Clinton
Murphy, John Benjamin
Myers, George William
Norton, Mary Alice Peloubet
Noyes, William Albert
Oldberg, Oscar
Owen, William Bishop
Parker, Francis Wayland
Peabody, Selim Hobart
Powell, William Bramwell
Putnam, Alice Harvey Whiting
Reavis, William Claude
Ricker, Nathan Clifford
Rogers, Carl Ransom
Rogers, Henry Wade
Root, George Frederick
Sargent, Walter
Schlesinger, Hermann Irving
Scott, Walter Dill
Seybolt, Robert Francis
Sharp, Katharine Lucinda
Sill, Anna Peck
Small, Albion Woodbury
Smith, Bunnie Othanel
Smith, Eleanor
Snyder, Franklyn Bliss
Soares, Theodore Gerald
Spalding, John Lancaster
Steinhaus, Arthur H.
Stoddard, George Dinsmore
Sturtevant, Julian Monson
Sunderland, Eliza Jane Read
Taba, Hilda
Temple, Alice
Thurstone, Louis Leon
Tomlins, William Lawrence
Tompkins, Arnold
Turner, Jonathan Baldwin
Tyler, Ralph Winfred
Wells, William Harvey
Vaile, Edwin Orlando
Washburne, Carleton Wolsey
White, Leonard Dupee
White, Samuel Holmes

Willard, Frances Elizabeth Caroline
Witty, Paul Andrew
Young, Ella Flagg
Young, Jacob William Albert

## INDIANA

Baldwin, James
Birge, Edward Bailey
Blaker, Eliza Ann Cooper
Bogue, Benjamin Nathaniel
Brigance, William Norwood
Bryan, William Lowe
Burns, James Aloysius
Cotton, Fassett Allen
DuShane, Donald
Elliott, Edward Charles
Gillespie, Eliza Maria (Mother Angela)
Guerin, Anne Therese
Larrabee, William Clark
Madeleva, Sister Mary (Mary Evaline
    Wolff)
Mills, Caleb
Morrison, John Irwin
Rice, Thurman Brooks
Ridpath, John Clark
Sewall, May Eliza Wright Thompson
Smart, James Henry
Smith, Henry Lester
Sorin, Edward Frederick
Wells, Herman B.
White, Emerson Elbridge
Wirt, William Albert
Wylie, Andrew

## IOWA

Benton, Thomas Hart
Betts, George Herbert
Hammond, William Gardiner
Jessup, Walter Albert
King, William Fletcher
Knapp, Seaman Asahel
Larsen, Peter Laurentius
Lindquist, Everet Franklin
McCloy, Charles Harold
Pickard, Josiah Little
Seashore, Carl Emil
Seerley, Homer Horatio

Studebaker, John Ward
Welch, Adonijah Strong

## KANSAS

Bawden, William Thomas
Brandenburg, William Aaron
Butcher, Thomas Walter
Cloud, Henry Roe
Eisenhower, Milton Stover
Fairchild, Edward Thomson
Fairchild, George Thompson
Fraser, John Lawrence
Goodnow, Isaac Tichenor
Lindley, Ernest Hiram
McVicar, Peter
Markham, Walter Tipton
Strong, Frank
Waters, Henry Jackson
Wheeler, Raymond Holder

## KENTUCKY

Bowman, John Bryan
Breckinridge, Robert Jefferson
Bryan, Anna E.
Butler, Edward Mann
Butler, Noble
Carmichael, Omer
Cherry, Henry Hardin
Cooke, John Esten
Crabbe, John Grant
Frost, William Goodell
Green, Lewis Warner
Hailmann, William Nicholas
Halleck, Reuben Post
Henderson, Howard Andrew Millet
Hill, Patty Smith
Holley, Horace
Kent, Raymond Asa
McClellan, Henry Brainerd
McVey, Frank LeRond
Moore, James
Neef, Francis Joseph Nicholas
Patterson, James Kennedy
Peers, Benjamin Orr
Pettit, Katherine
Roark, Ruric Nevel
Smith, Zachariah Frederick

Spalding, Catherine
Stewart, Cora Wilson
Taylor, William Septimus
Wilson, Atwood Sylvester
Young, John Clarke

## LOUISIANA

Aswell, James Benjamin
Boyd, David French
Boyd, Thomas Duckett
Chambers, Henry Edward
Dillard, James Hardy
Dimitry, Alexander
Dinwiddie, Albert Bledsoe
Soulé, George

## MAINE

Chamberlain, Joshua Lawrence
Cleaveland, Parker
Fernald, Charles Henry
Hale, Florence
Harris, Samuel
Hyde, William DeWitt
Newman, Samuel Phillips
Smith, Payson
Smyth, William
Stetson, William Wallace
Thomas, Augustus Orloff
Woods, Leonard

## MARYLAND

Adams, Herbert Baxter
Baldwin, James Mark
Balliet, Thomas Minard
Barr, Frank Stringfellow
Benjamin, Harold Raymond Wayne
Bowman, Isaiah
Browne, William Hand
Cobb, Stanwood
Collitz, Hermann
Collitz, Klara Hechtenberg
Cook, Albert Samuel
Eisenhower, Milton Stover
Elliott, Aaron Marshall
Ely, Charles Wright
Gildersleeve, Basil Lanneau
Gilman, Daniel Coit

Glass, Hiram Bentley
Goucher, John Franklin
Halsted, William Stewart
Harris, Chapin Aaron
Hayden, Horace H.
Johnson, William Woolsey
Knox, Samuel
Meyer, Adolf
Mullanany, Patrick Francis (Brother
  Azarius)
Newell, McFadden Alexander
Nutting, Mary Adelaide
Phelps, Almira Hart Lincoln
Remsen, Ira
Robb, Isabel Adams Hampton
Sabin, Florence Rena
Seton, Elizabeth Ann Bayley
Tall, Lida Lee
Van Bokkelen, Libertus
Welch, William Henry
Woods, Albert Fred

## MASSACHUSETTS

Abbott, Jacob
Adams, Henry Brooks
Agassiz, Elizabeth Cabot Cary
Agassiz, Jean Louis Rodolphe
Ainsworth, Dorothy Sears
Alcott, Amos Bronson
Alcott, William Andrus
Alden, Joseph
Allen, Edward Ellis
Allen, Nathaniel Topliffe
Allport, Gordon Willard
Allyn, Harriet May
Ames, James Barr
Anagnos, Michael
Andrews, Jane
Archer, Gleason Leonard
Atwood, Wallace Walter
Babbitt, Irving
Bailey, Ebenezer
Baker, Benjamin Franklin
Baker, George Pierce
Baldwin, Maria Louise
Balliet, Thomas Minard
Bancroft, Cecil Franklin Patch

Banister, Zilpah Polly Grant
Bapst, John
Barnes, Harry Elmer
Bartholomew, William Nelson
Bascom, John
Bates, Katharine Lee
Beck, Charles Karl
Bell, Alexander Graham
Benne, Kenneth Dean
Bingham, Caleb
Birkhoff, George David
Boring, Edwin Garrigues
Bowditch, Henry Pickering
Boyden, Albert Gardner
Boyden, Frank Learoyd
Brackett, Jeffrey Richardson
Bradford, Edward Hickling
Brameld, Theodore Burghard Hurt
Brattle, William
Brooks, Charles
Brown, Alice Van Vechten
Burnham, William Henry
Burton, Warren
Burton, William Henry
Butterfield, Kenyon Leech
Byerly, William Elwood
Calkins, Mary Whiton
Capen, Elmer Hewitt
Carmichael, Leonard
Carter, James Gordon
Chadbourne, Paul Ansel
Chadwick, George Whitfield
Channing, Edward Tyrrell
Cheever, Ezekiel
Clapp, Cornelia Maria
Clapp, Margaret
Colburn, Dana Pond
Colburn, Warren
Collar, William Coe
Commager, Henry Steele
Compton, Karl Taylor
Comstock, Ada Louise
Conant, James Bryant
Cooke, Josiah Parsons
Coolidge, Julian Lowell
Corlet, Elijah
Crocker, Lucretia

Crosby, Alpheus
Cross, Anson Kent
Cutler, Elliott Carr
Cutter, Calvin
Davis, William Morris
Dewey, Chester
Dickinson, John Woodbridge
Dix, Dorothea Lynde
Dunster, Henry
Eliot, Charles William
Eliot, John
Elson, Louis Charles
Emerson, George Barrell
Farmer, Fannie Merritt
Farnum, Royal Bailey
Farrar, John
Fernald, Charles Henry
Fitton, James
Follen, Karl (Charles) Theodore
    Christian
Ford, Jeremiah Dennis Matthais
Fowle, William Bentley
Fuller, Sarah
Gilman, Arthur
Goodale, George Lincoln
Goodell, Henry Hill
Goodrich, Samuel Griswold
Goodwin, William Watson
Gould, Benjamin Apthorp
Grandgent, Charles Hall
Gray, Asa
Greene, Samuel Stillman
Greenleaf, Benjamin
Greenleaf, Simon
Greenwood, Isaac
Gregory, Samuel
Gropius, Walter Adolf
Gulick, Luther Halsey
Guthe, Karl Eugen
Hagar, Daniel Barnard
Hall, Granville Stanley
Hanus, Paul Henry
Hart, Albert Bushnell
Hart, William Richard
Hartwell, Edward Mussey
Hazard, Caroline
Henderson, Lawrence Joseph

Hill, Frank Alpine
Hill, Thomas
Hillard, George Stillman
Hitchcock, Edward (1793–1864)
Hitchcock, Edward (1828–1911)
Hocking, William Ernest
Homans, Amy Morris
Hopkins, Mark
Howard, Ada Lydia
Howe, Samuel Gridley
Hunt, Mary Hannah Hanchett
Hunt, William Morris
Hyatt, Alpheus
Inglis, Alexander James
James, William
Kelley, Truman Lee
King, Charles Francis
Kingsley, Clarence Darwin
Kirkland, John Thornton
Kirkpatrick, Edwin Asbury
Langdell, Christopher Columbus
Lanman, Charles Rockwell
Leach, Daniel Dyer
Lewis, Dioclesian
Lillie, Frank Rattray
Lowell, Abbott Lawrence
Lyon, Mary Mason
McCurdy, James Huff
Mahoney, John Joseph
Mann, Horace
Marble, Albert Prescott
Maslow, Abraham Harold
Mason, Lowell
Mason, Luther Whiting
Mather, Increase
Mayo, Amory Dwight
Meiklejohn, Alexander
Merrill, Helen Abbot
Minot, Charles Sedgwick
Morse, Jedidiah
Mowry, William Augustus
Munro, William Bennett
Murchison, Carl Allanmore
Neilson, William Allan
Nichols, Frederick George
Norton, Charles Eliot
Packard, Alpheus Spring

Paine, John Knowles
Palmer, Alice Elvira Freeman
Palmer, George Herbert
Parker, Richard Green
Parsons, Frank
Peabody, Elizabeth Palmer
Peabody, Endicott
Pearson, Eliphalet
Peirce, Benjamin
Peirce, Charles (Santiago) Sanders
Peirce, Cyrus
Peirce, James Mills
Pendleton, Ellen Fitz
Philbrick, John Dudley
Pickering, Edward Charles
Pierpont, John
Pike, Nicholas
Porter, Arthur Kingsley
Posse, Nils
Pound, Roscoe
Prang, Mary Amelia Dana Hicks
Quincy, Josiah
Reed, David Allen
Richards, Ellen Henrietta Swallow
Richards, Linda (Melinda Ann) Judson
Riesman, David
Roberts, Robert Jeffries
Rogers, Harriet Burbank
Rogers, William Barton
Runkle, John Daniel
Russell, William
Sachar, Abram Leon
Sargent, Dudley Allen
Sargent, Epes
Seelye, Julius Hawley
Seelye, Laurenus Clark
Shafer, Helen Almira
Shaler, Nathaniel Southgate
Sheldon, William Evarts
Sherwin, Thomas
Skinner, Burrhus Frederic
Smith, Harold Babbitt
Smith, John Rubens
Smith, Payson
Snedden, David
Sophocles, Evangelinus Apostolides
Sparks, Jared

Stanley, Albert Augustus
Stimson, Rufus Whittaker
Story, Joseph
Talbot, Marion
Tappan, Eva March
Taussig, Frank William
Taylor, Samuel Harvey
Thayer, Gideon French
Thompson, Charles Oliver
Ticknor, George
Tourjée, Eben
Trowbridge, John
Tyler, William Seymour
Ulich, Robert
Viguers, Ruth Hill
Walker, Francis Amasa
Ware, William Robert
Warren, John
Warren, John Collins
Warren, William Fairfield
Watson, Fletcher Guard
Wells, Webster
Wendell, Barrett
Wheelock, Lucy
Whipple, Guy Montrose
Whittlesey, Derwent Stainthorpe
Wiener, Leo
Wigglesworth, Edward
Williston, Arthur Lyman
Wilson, Guy Mitchell
Wilson, Howard Eugene
Winship, Albert Edward
Winthrop, John
Woolley, Mary Emma
Worcester, Joseph Emerson
Yale, Caroline Ardelia

MICHIGAN

Angell, James Burrill
Bowen, Wilbur Pardon
Brownson, Josephine Van Dyke
Cady, Calvin Brainerd
Courtis, Stuart Appleton
Crary, Isaac Edwin
Davis, Calvin Olin
Davis, Jesse Buttrick
Frieze, Henry Simmons

Henderson, Algo Donmyer
Henry, David Dodds
Hinsdale, Burke Aaron
Jefferson, Mark Sylvester William
Maddy, Joseph Edgar
Mechem, Floyd Russell
Miles, Manly
Miller, Edwin Lillie
Mitchell, Elmer Dayton
Moehlman, Arthur Bernard
Payne, William Harold
Perrin, Ethel
Pierce, John Davis
Pillsbury, Walter Bowers
Schorling, Raleigh
Silvius, George Harold
Stone, Lucinda Hinsdale
Tappan, Henry Philip
Thomas, Calvin
Trueblood, Thomas Clarkson
Welch, Adonijah Strong
Winchell, Alexander
Woody, Clifford

MINNESOTA

Arny, Clara Maude Brown
Bishop, Harriet E.
Brueckner, Leo John
Christiansen, Fredrik Melius
Coffman, Lotus Delta
Comstock, Ada Louise
Cowling, Donald John
Engelhardt, Fred
Folwell, William Watts
Green, Samuel Bowdlear
Ireland, John
Johnson, Palmer Oliver
Kiehle, David Litchard
Koos, Leonard Vincent
Krey, August Charles
Lord, Livingston Chester
McConnell, Thomas Raymond
McHugh, Anna (Antonia)
Molloy, Mary Aloysius
Neill, Edward Duffield
Northrop, Cyrus
Owre, Alfred

Paterson, Donald Gildersleeve
Phelps, William Franklin
Prosser, Charles Allen
Sanford, Maria Louise
Schweickhard, Dean Merrill
Smith, Dora Valentine
Strong, James Woodward
Weeks, Thomas Edwin
Wesley, Edgar Bruce
West, Willis Mason
Williamson, Edmund Griffith
Wrenn, Charles Gilbert
Wulling, Frederick John

## MISSISSIPPI

Dickey, Sarah Ann
Humphrey, George Duke
Jones, Lawrence Clifton
Lee, Stephen Dill
Revels, Hiram Rhoades
Waddel, John Newton
Whitfield, Henry Lewis

## MISSOURI

Baker, Samuel Aaron
Baldwin, Joseph
Bernard, Luther Lee
Blow, Susan Elizabeth
Brackett, Anna Callender
Brooks, Stratton Duluth
Carpenter, William Weston
Carrington, William Thomas
Chauvenet, William
Coppens, Charles
Dearmont, Washington Strother
Dobbs, Ella Victoria
Duchesne, Rose Philippine
Goldbeck, Robert
Goldstein, Max Aaron
Greenwood, James Mickleborough
Hammond, William Gardner
Harris, William Torrey
Hedrick, Earle Raymond
Hetherington, Clark Wilson
Jesse, Richard Henry
Kirk, John Robert
Lathrop, John Hiram

Laws, Samuel Spahr
Leigh, Edwin
London, Hoyt Hobson
Mumford, Frederick Blackman
Read, Daniel
Selvidge, Robert Washington
Soldan, Frank Louis
Warshaw, Jacob
Williams, Walter
Woodward, Calvin Milton

## MONTANA

Atkinson, Alfred
Craig, Oscar John
Hedges, Cornelius

## NEBRASKA

Alexander, Hartley Burr
Andrews, Elisha Benjamin
Bessey, Charles Edwin
Brownell, Herbert
Crabtree, James William
Henzlik, Frank Ernest
Lee, Mabel
Luckey, George Washington Andrew
Morgan, Thomas Jefferson
Pound, Louise
Saylor, John Galen
Thomas, Augustus Orloff
Thompson, Samuel Rankin
Wolfe, Harry Kirke

## NEVADA

Adams, Romanzo
Sibley, Frederick Hubbard
Stubbs, Joseph Edward
Whitaker, Ozi William
Wier, Jeanne Elizabeth

## NEW HAMPSHIRE

Abbot, Benjamin
Adams, Daniel
Adams, Ebenezer
Engelhardt, Fred
Fairchild, Edward Thomson
Haddock, Charles Brickett
Hetzel, Ralph Dorn

Hopkins, Ernest Martin
Leonard, Levi Washburn
Lord, Nathan
Orcutt, Hiram
Patterson, James Willis
Phillips, John
Richardson, Charles Francis
Richardson, Leon Burr
Smith, John
Smith, Nathan
Squires, James Duane
Tucker, William Jewett
Wentworth, George Albert
Wheelock, Eleazar
Wheelock, John
Wright, Arthur Davis
Young, John Wesley

NEW JERSEY

Apgar, Ellis A.
Atwater, Lyman Hotchkiss
Baldwin, James Mark
Butler, Howard Crosby
Dodds, Harold Willis
Douglass, Mabel Smith
Eisenhart, Luther Pfahler
Frelinghuysen, Theodore
Goddard, Henry Herbert
Gummere, John
Guyot, Arnold Henry
Hart, John Seely
Hibben, John Grier
Johnstone, Edward Ransom
Kendall, Calvin Noyes
McCosh, James
Mackenzie, James Cameron
Maclean, John (1771–1814)
Maclean, John (1800–1886)
McQuaid, Bernard John
Mather, Frank Jewett, Jr.
Monroe, Will Seymour
Panofsky, Erwin
Oppenheimer, J. Robert
Raymond, George Lansing
Sammartino, Peter
Seeley, Levi
Sloane, William Milligan

Smith, Samuel Stanhope
Stimson, John Ward
Stone, John Charles
Van Dyke, John Charles
Veblen, Oswald
Wilson, Thomas Woodrow
Witherspoon, John
Wood, De Volson
Young, Charles Augustus

NEW MEXICO

Hadley, Hiram
Hill, David Spence
Hodgin, Charles Elkanah
Larson, Lars Moore
Wagner, Jonathan Howard

NEW YORK

Abbott, Gorham Dummer
Adams, Charles Kendall
Adler, Felix
Alden, Joseph
Allen, James Edward, Jr.
Anderson, John Jacob
Anderson, Martin Brewer
Anthon, Charles
Axtelle, George Edward
Ayres, Leonard Porter
Bagley, William Chandler
Bailey, Liberty Hyde
Baldwin, James
Balliet, Thomas Minard
Bancroft, Jessie Hubbell
Bard, Samuel
Bardeen, Charles William
Barnard, Frederick Augustus Porter
Barnes, Harry Elmer
Barnes, Mary Downing Sheldon
Barrows, Anna
Beard, Charles Austin
Becker, Carl Lotus
Benedict, Erastus Cornelius
Benedict, Ruth Fulton
Bennett, Charles Edwin
Bestor, Arthur Eugene
Bethune, Joanna Graham
Blow, Susan Elizabeth

Boas, Franz
Bonser, Frederick Gordon
Brackett, Anna Callender
Bradbury, William Batchelder
Brickman, William Wolfgang
Briggs, Thomas Henry
Brigham, Albert Perry
Brown, Elmer Ellsworth
Brown, Goold
Brubacher, Abram Rorer
Bryant, John Collins
Bryant, Joseph Decatur
Bryson, Lyman Lloyd
Bulkley, John Williams
Burchenal, Elizabeth
Burgess, John William
Burnz, Eliza Boardman
Butler, Marie Joseph
Butler, Nicholas Murray
Butts, Robert Freeman
Calderone, Mary Steichen
Caldwell, Otis William
Calkins, Norman Allison
Carpenter, George Rice
Cartwright, Morse Adams
Case, Adelaide Teague
Caswell, Hollis Leland
Cattell, James McKeen
Chapman, John Gadsby
Chase, William Merritt
Clinton, De Witt
Cobb, Lyman
Cochran, David Henry
Coe, George Albert
Coleman, Satis Narrona Barton
Comfort, George Fisk
Comstock, Anna Botsford
Comstock, John Henry
Cooley, LeRoy Clark
Cooper, Hermann
Cooper, Myles
Corson, Juliet
Counts, George Sylvester
Covello, Leonard
Crane, Julia Ettie
Crane, Thomas Frederick
Currier, Enoch Henry

Dalton, John Call
Damrosch, Frank Heino
Dann, Hollis Ellsworth
Davenport, Charles Benedict
Davidson, Charles
Davidson, Thomas
Davies, Charles
Davis, Henry
Day, James Roscoe
De Garmo, Charles
Dewey, Chester
Dewey, John
Dewey, Melvil
Dickinson, George Sherman
Dodge, Ebenezer
Dodge, Grace Hoadley
Dow, Arthur Wesley
Draper, Andrew Sloan
Draper, John William
Drisler, Henry
Duer, William Alexander
Duggan, Stephen Pierce
Dutton, Samuel Train
Dwight, Francis
Dwight, Theodore William
Dykema, Peter William
Eaton, Amos
Ely, Richard Theodore
Engelhardt, Nicholaus John
Erskine, John
Eurich, Alvin Christian
Fairchild, Mary Salome Cutler
Farnsworth, Charles Hubert
Finegan, Thomas Edward
Finley, John Huston
Fischer, John Henry
Fisher, Ebenezer
Flexner, Abraham
Flint, Austin
Foshay, Arthur Wellesley
Fretwell, Elbert Kirtley
Fuertes, Estevan Antonio
Gamoran, Emmanuel
Gates, Arthur Irving
Giddings, Franklin Henry
Gideonse, Harry David
Gildersleeve, Virginia Crocheron

Goetschius, Percy
Graves, Frank Pierrepont
Griscom, John
Gruenberg, Benjamin Charles
Gruenberg, Sidonie Matsner
Hale, Benjamin
Hanchett, Henry Granger
Hanson, Howard Harold
Hardy, Mary Aloysia
Hart, Joseph Kinmont
Hawley, Gideon
Hayes, Carlton Joseph Huntley
Henri, Robert
Hewett, Waterman Thomas
Hill, Patty Smith
Hollingworth, Leta Anna Stetter
Hook, Sidney
Horne, Herman Harrell
Howland, Emily
Hughes, John Joseph
Hughes, William Leonard
Hunter, Thomas
Jacobi, Mary Corinna Putnam
Jacoby, Henry Sylvester
Jersild, Arthur Jones
Jessup, Walter Albert
Jewett, Milo Parker
Johnson, Alvin Saunders
Johnson, Henry
Johnson, Joseph French
Johnson, Samuel
Johnston, Richard Malcolm
Kandel, Isaac Leon
Kauffman, Treva Erdine
Kellas, Eliza
Kendrick, Asahel Clark
Keppel, Frederick Paul
Kiddle, Henry
Kilpatrick, William Heard
Kimball, Dexter Simpson
Kitson, Harry Dexter
Klapper, Paul
Kraus, John
Kraus-Boelté, Maria
Krüsi, Johann Heinrich Hermann
Lee, James Melvin
Leipziger, Henry Marcus

Leonard, Robert Josselyn
Levy, Florence Nightingale
Linville, Henry Richardson
Lloyd-Jones, Esther McDonald
Lodge, Gonzalez
Lomax, Paul Sanford
Lozier, Clemence Sophia Harned
MacCracken, Henry Mitchell
Mace, William Harrison
McGrath, Earl James
MacKenzie, James Cameron
McMurry, Frank Morton
MacVicar, Malcolm
Mahan, Dennis Hart
Mannes, Clara Damrosch
Mannes, David
Marble, Albert Prescott
Mason, John Mitchell
Mason, William
Matthews, James Brander
Maxwell, William Henry
Mearns, William Hughes
Melby, Ernest Oscar
Meyer, Adolphe Erich
Mezes, Sidney Edward
Mitchell, Maria
Monroe, Paul
Morgan, Lewis Henry
Mort, Paul R.
Mursell, James Lockhart
Muzzey, David Saville
Nash, Jay Bryan
Nevins, Allan
Newlon, Jesse Homer
Norsworthy, Naomi
North, Edward
Nott, Eliphalet
Orton, James
Osborn, Henry Fairfield
Osborne, Estelle Massey Riddle
Owre, Alfred
Packard, Silas Sadler
Page, David Perkins
Palmer, Horatio Raymond
Parkhurst, Helen
Patri, Angelo
Patterson, Edwin Wilhite

Peck, William Guy
Peet, Harvey Prindle
Peet, Isaac Lewis
Penny, George Barlow
Perrin, Porter Gale
Picket, Albert
Potter, Alonzo
Pratt, Caroline
Pritchett, Henry Smith
Quackenbos, George Payn
Quackenbos, John Duncan
Randall, Samuel Sidwell
Raymond, John Howard
Redway, Jacques Wardlaw
Reeve, William David
Renner, George Thomas, Jr.
Revel, Bernard
Rice, James Edward
Rice, Victor Moreau
Richards, Charles Russell
Richman, Julia
Ritter, Frederic Louis
Rivlin, Harry N.
Robinson, Frederick Bertrand
Robinson, James Harvey
Rose, Mary Davies Schwartz
Rosskopf, Myron Frederick
Rugg, Harold Ordway
Rusby, Henry Hurd
Russell, James Earl
Russell, William Fletcher
Sabin, Florence Rena
Sachs, Julius
Samaroff, Olga
Sanders, Charles Walton
Scott, Miriam Finn
Shedd, William Greenough Thayer
Sheldon, Edward Austin
Shuster, George Nauman
Sinnott, Edmund Ware
Skinner, Charles Rufus
Sloane, William Milligan
Smith, David Eugene
Smith, Nila Banton
Snedden, David Samuel
Steele, Joel Dorman
Stevens, Georgia Lydia

Stewart, Isabel Maitland
Stimson, John Ward
Stoddard, Francis Hovey
Stowell, Thomas Blanchard
Strang, Ruth May
Strayer, George Drayton
Stryker, Melancthon Woolsey
Sturtevant, Sarah Martha
Suhrie, Ambrose Leo
Swinton, William
Symonds, Percival Mallon
Tapper, Thomas
Tarr, Ralph Stockman
Taylor, Harold Alexander
Taylor, John Orville
Taylor, Joseph Schimmel
Tewksbury, Donald George
Thayer, Sylvanus
Thomas, Calvin
Thomson, James Bates
Thorndike, Edward Lee
Thurston, Robert Henry
Titchener, Edward Bradford
Tonne, Herbert Arthur
Town, Salem
Traxler, Arthur Edwin
Trent, William Peterfield
Tyler, Moses Coit
Valentine, Thomas Weston
Van Doren, Mark
Van Dusen, Henry Pitney
Van Rensselaer, Martha
Van Til, William
Vincent, John Heyl
Wadsworth, James
Wait, William Bell
Wald, Lillian D.
Warren, Samuel Edward
Washburn, Margaret Floy
Watson, James Madison
Watson, John Broadus
Webster, Horace
Weed, Ella
Weir, Irene
West, Charles Edwin
White, Andrew Dickson
White, John Stuart

Wilbur, Hervey Backus
Willard, Emma Hart
Williams, Jesse Feiring
Williamson, Charles Clarence
Wilson, Peter
Wilson, William Dexter
Wittkower, Rudolf
Wood, Thomas Denison
Woodbridge, Frederick James Eugene
Woodworth, Robert Sessions
Woolman, Mary Raphael Schenck
Youmans, Edward Livingston
Young, Andrew White
Zachos, John Celivergos

## NORTH CAROLINA

Alderman, Edwin Anderson
Allen, Arch Turner
Ashley, Samuel Stanford
Aycock, Charles Brantley
Bradley, Amy Morris
Brooks, Eugene Clyde
Brown, Charlotte Hawkins
Brownell, William Arthur
Cain, William
Caldwell, David
Caldwell, Joseph
Chavis, John
Colton, Elizabeth Avery
Craven, Braxton
Dougherty, Blanford Barnard
Dudley, James Benson
Few, William Preston
Forest, Julius Isaac
Graham, Edward Kidder
Graham, Frank Porter
Greenlaw, Edwin Almiron
Haydon, Glen
Joyner, James Yadkin
Knight, Edgar Wallace
McCorkle, Samuel Eusebius
McCrorey, Henry Lawrence
McDougall, William
McIver, Charles Duncan
Meserve, Charles Francis
Odum, Howard Washington
Poteat, William Louis

Rice, John Andrew
Ryan, Will Carson, Jr.
Sanders, Daniel Jackson
Shepard, James Edward
Smith, Henry Louis
Swain, David Lowry
Wait, Samuel
Wiley, Calvin Henderson
Wilson, Louis Round

## NORTH DAKOTA

Gillette, John Morris
Merrifield, Webster
Sprague, Homer Baxter
Ward, Joseph

## OHIO

Alberty, Harold Bernard
Andrews, Lorin
Arbuthnot, May Hill
Avery, Elroy McKendree
Bailey, Henry Turner
Bishop, John Remsen
Bishop, Robert Hamilton
Bode, Boyd Henry
Brown, Hallie Quinn
Brown, LeRoy Decatur
Charters, Werrett Wallace
Cutler, Elliott Carr
Dabney, Charles William
Dale, Edgar
Drake, Daniel
Duveneck, Frank
Dyer, Franklin Benjamin
Ellis, Alston
Elson, William Harris
Fairchild, James Harris
Fess, Simeon Davidson
Finney, Charles Grandison
Fiske, George Walter
Galloway, Samuel
Gantvoort, Arnold Johann
Garrett, William Robertson
Gehrkens, Karl Wilson
Gibson, William
Goff, Milton Browning
Good, Carter Victor

Good, Harry Gehman
Gordy, John Pancoast
Grossmann, Louis
Guilford, Nathan
Hancock, John
Hanna, Delphine
Harvey, Thomas Wadleigh
Henderson, Algo Donmyer
Holbrook, Alfred
Hullfish, Henry Gordon
Irwin, Robert Benjamin
Jones, Gilbert Haven
Lewis, Samuel
Lord, Asa Dearborn
McConnell, Wallace Robert
McGuffey, William Holmes
Mahan, Asa
Mann, Horace
Morgan, Arthur Ernest
Myers, Garry Cleveland
Myers, Phillip Van Ness
Oberteuffer, Delbert
Orton, Edward, Jr.
Orton, Edward Francis Baxter
Payne, Daniel Alexander
Picket, Albert
Pitman, Benn
Pressey, Sidney Leavitt
Ray, Joseph
Read, Gerald Howard
Rice, Fenelon Bird
Rickoff, Andrew Jackson
Robinson, Stillman Williams
Scarborough, William Sanders
Schneider, Herman
Shera, Jesse Hauk
Spencer, Platt Rogers
Stowe, Calvin Ellis
Tappan, Eli Todd
Thompson, William Oxley
Thwing, Charles Franklin
Venable, William Henry
Warner, William Everett
Wesley, Charles Harris
White, Emerson Elbridge
Wise, Isaac Mayer
Woolley, Helen Bradford Thompson

Zeisberger, David
Zirbes, Laura

OKLAHOMA

Boyd, David Ross
Boyd, Thomas Duckett
Brooks, Stratton Duluth
Hodge, Oliver
Loughridge, Robert McGill
Nash, Mell Achilles
Page, Inman Edward
Robertson, William Schenck

OREGON

Atkinson, George Henry
Campbell, Prince Lucien
Foster, William Trufant
Hunter, Frederick Maurice
Kerr, William Jasper
Magruder, Frank Abbott
Putnam, Rex

PENNSYLVANIA

Adler, Cyrus
Agnew, David Hayes
Alison, Francis
Allen, Edward Ellis
Apple, Thomas Gilmore
Atherton, George Washington
Aydelotte, Frank
Bache, Alexander Dallas
Barton, Benjamin Smith
Benezet, Anthony
Betts, Emmett Albert
Bodley, Rachel Littler
Bogle, Sarah Comly Norris
Bond, Horace Mann
Brickman, William Wolfgang
Brooks, Edward
Brumbaugh, Martin Grove
Burrowes, Thomas Henry
Charters, Werrett Wallace
Cheyney, Edward Potts
Coppée, Henry
Coppin, Fanny Marion Jackson
Crawford, James Pyle Wickersham
Dock, Christopher

Dod, Thaddeus
Dove, David James
Downey, John
Dunglison, Robley
Eakins, Thomas
Earhart, Will
Finegan, Thomas Edward
Foster, Thomas Jefferson
Franklin, Benjamin
Frost, John
Garrett, Emma
Gibson, William
Goff, Milton Browning
Gratz, Rebecca
Graves, Frank Pierrepont
Green, Jacob
Gross, Samuel David
Haldeman, Samuel Stehman
Hallowell, Anna
Hamerschlag, Arthur Acton
Heathcote, Charles William
Hetzel, Ralph Dorn
Himes, Charles Francis
Houston, Edwin James
Hughes, Ray Osgood
Hughes, William Leonard
Jones, Arthur Julius
Junkin, George
Keen, William Williams
Kent, Roland Grubb
Laird, Warren Powers
Leidy, Joseph
Lessenberry, David Daniel
Lewis, Enoch
Lyte, Eliphalet Oram
MacAlister, James
McCormick, Samuel Black
McKenzie, Robert Tait
McKown, Harry Charles
McMaster, John Bach
Magill, Edward Hicks
March, Francis Andrew
Marshall, Charles
Miller, Leslie William
Mitchell, Samuel Augustus
Morgan, John
Neef, Francis Joseph Nicholas

Neumann, John Nepomucene
Parrish, Edward
Pastorius, Francis Daniel
Pattee, Fred Lewis
Pearce, Richard Mills, Jr.
Penniman, James Hosmer
Pepper, William
Physick, Philip Syng
Poor, John
Pratt, Richard Henry
Proud, Robert
Pugh, Evan
Rambaut, Mary Lucinda Bonney
Raub, Albert Newton
Rauch, Frederick Augustus
Reid, Ira de Augustine
Rice, Joseph Mayer
Rorer, Sarah Tyson Heston
Rush, Benjamin
Ryan, Will Carson, Jr.
Sartain, Emily
Schaeffer, Nathan Christ
Schelling, Felix Emmanuel
Shippen, William, Jr.
Smith, Daniel B.
Smith, William
Stillé, Charles Janeway
Stoddard, John Fair
Struck, Ferdinand Theodore
Swain, Joseph
Tennent, William
Thomas, Martha Carey
Thompson, Robert Ellis
Trabue, Marion Rex
Valentine, Milton
Watteville, Henrietta Benigna Justina
  von Zinzendorf
Wheeler, Anna Johnson Pell
Wickersham, James Pyle
Wilson, Lucy Langdon Williams
Wood, George Bacon
Woodhouse, James

PUERTO RICO

Brumbaugh, Martin Grove
Cordero y Molina, Rafael
Hostos, Eugenio María de

Miller, Paul Gerard
Osuna, Juan Jóse

## RHODE ISLAND

Allyn, Robert
Andrews, Elisha Benjamin
Bicknell, Thomas Williams
Bushee, James
Colvin, Stephen Sheldon
Craig, Clara Elizabeth
Farnum, Royal Bailey
Greene, Samuel Stillman
Harkness, Albert
Howland, John
Kingsbury, John
Leach, Daniel Dyer
Manning, James
Maxcy, Jonathan
Messer, Asa
Mowry, William Augustus
Murlin, Lemuel Herbert
Poland, William Carey
Potter, Elisha Reynolds, Jr.
Robinson, Ezekiel Gilman
Sears, Barnas
Wayland, Francis
Wriston, Henry Merritt

## SOUTH CAROLINA

Cooper, Thomas
Grimké, Charlotte L. Forten
Johnson, David Bancroft
Lieber, Francis
Maxcy, Jonathan
Memminger, Christopher Gustavus
Thompson, Hugh Smith
Waddel, Moses
Wilkinson, Robert Shaw

## SOUTH DAKOTA

Beadle, William Henry Harrison
Blackburn, William Maxwell
Nash, George Williston
O'Gorman, Thomas
O'Harra, Cleophus Cisney
Slagle, Robert Lincoln
Ward, Joseph

Weeks, Ila Delbert
Young, Clark Montgomery

## TENNESSEE

Carmichael, Oliver Cromwell
Carrick, Samuel
Claxton, Philander Priestley
Cocking, Walter Dewey
Dabney, Charles William
Demiashkevitch, Michael John
Doak, Samuel
Fanning, Tolbert
Fleming, Walter Lynwood
Gage, Lucy
Garland, Landon Cabell
Garrett, William Robertson
Harap, Henry
Haynes, Benjamin Rudolph
Johnson, Charles Spurgeon
Kirby-Smith, Edmund
Kirkland, James Hampton
Lindsley, John Berrien
Lindsley, Philip
McMurry, Charles Alexander
Morgan, William Henry
Parkins, Almon Ernest
Payne, Bruce Ryburn
Payne, William Harold
Priestley, James
Roemer, Joseph
Stearns, Eben Sperry
Webb, William Robert
Witherspoon, John Alexander

## TEXAS

Bailey, Rufus William
Baldwin, Joseph
Blanton, Annie Webb
Bralley, Francis Marion
Bruce, William Herschel
Castañeda, Carlos Eduardo
Cooper, Oscar Henry
Eby, Frederick
Halsted, George Bruce
Hollingsworth, Orlando Newton
Hyer, Robert Stewart
Mezes, Sidney Edward

Roberts, Oran Milo
Sanchez, George Isidore
Sutton, William Seneca

## UTAH

Bennion, Milton
Cowles, LeRoy Eugene
Harris, Franklin Stewart
Kerr, William Jasper
McMurrin, Sterling Moss
Park, John Rocky
Pratt, Orson
Stewart, William Mitton
Talmage, James Edward
Travers, Robert Morris William
Wahlquist, John Thomas

## VERMONT

Buckham, Matthew Henry
Davis, Henry
Hall, Samuel Read
Jenne, James Nathaniel
Leigh, Robert Devore
Orcutt, Hiram
Partridge, Alden
Woodruff, Caroline Salome

## VIRGINIA

Alderman, Edwin Anderson
Armstrong, Samuel Chapman
Barrett, Janie Porter
Blair, James
Crozet, Claude
Davis, Noah Knowles
Dett, Robert Nathaniel
Eggleston, Joseph Dupuy, Jr.
Ewell, Benjamin Stoddert
Frissell, Hollis Burke
Garland, Landon Cabell
Gildersleeve, Basil Lanneau
Green, Lewis Warner
Hatcher, Orie Latham
Holmes, George Frederick
Jefferson, Thomas
Joynes, Edward Southey
Leeser, Isaac
McGuffey, William Holmes

Maupin, Socrates
Minor, John Barbee
Mitchell, Samuel Chiles
Munford, Mary Cooke Branch
Newcomb, John Lloyd
Painter, Franklin Verzelius Newton
Rogers, William Barton
Ruffner, Henry
Ruffner, William Henry
Sears, Barnas
Smith, Charles Alfonso
Smith, Francis Henney
Smith, Henry Louis
Tucker, George
Vawter, Charles Erastus
Wayland, John Walter
Wythe, George

## WASHINGTON

Bryan, Enoch Albert
Chandler, Joe Albert
Dewey, Henry Bingham
Eells, Cushing
Holland, Ernest Otto
Preston, Josephine Corliss
Showalter, Noah David
Suzzallo, Henry
Wanamaker, Pearl Anderson
Whitworth, George Frederic

## WEST VIRGINIA

Davis, John Warren
Martin, Alexander
Pendleton, William Kimbrough
Scott, John Work

## WISCONSIN

Adams, Charles Kendall
Barr, Arvil Sylvester
Bascom, John
Birge, Edward Asahiel
Bleyer, Willard Grosvenor
Chapin, Aaron Lucius
Comstock, George Cary
Cotton, Fassett Allen
Curti, Merle Eugene
Ely, Richard Theodore

Fillmore, John Comfort
Fitzpatrick, Edward Augustus
Frank, Michael
Harvey, Lorenzo Dow
Hyde, Grant Milnor
Kraus, Mother M. Seraphine (Mary
    Katharine)
Ladd, Azel Parkhurst
Lathrop, John Hiram
Leonard, Sterling Andrus
McMynn, John Gibson
Marlatt, Abby Lillian
Mortimer, Mary
O'Shea, Michael Vincent

Pickard, Josiah Little
Russell, Harry Luman
Sabin, Ellen Clara
Salisbury, Albert
Schurz, Margarethe Meyer
Van Hise, Charles Richard
Whitford, William Clarke

WYOMING

Hebard, Grace Raymond
Hoyt, John Wesley
Humphrey, George Duke
Jayne, Clarence D.

# APPENDIX C:
## FIELD OF WORK

CONTENTS

## ADMINISTRATION OF EDUCATION, FEDERAL GOVERNMENT

Allen, James Edward, Jr.
Barnard, Henry
Bawden, William Thomas
Brown, Elmer Ellsworth
Caliver, Ambrose
Claxton, Philander Priestley
Eaton, John
Harris, William Torrey
Kraus, John
McGrath, Earl James
McMurrin, Sterling Moss
Studebaker, John Ward
Tigert, John James
True, Alfred Charles
Wright, John Calvin

## ADMINISTRATION OF EDUCATION, STATES

Abercrombie, John William
Allen, Arch Turner
Allen, James Edward, Jr.
Andrews, Lorrin
Apgar, Ellis A.
Armstrong, Richard
Ashley, Samuel Stanford
Aswell, James Benjamin
Atkinson, George Henry
Aycock, Charles Brantley
Bailey, Thomas David
Baker, Samuel Aaron
Barnard, Henry
Bateman, Newton
Beadle, William Henry Harrison
Benton, Thomas Hart
Bicknell, Thomas Williams
Blanton, Annie Webb
Bradford, Mary Carroll Craig
Breckinridge, Robert Jefferson
Brittain, Marion Luther
Brooks, Eugene Clyde
Brown, LeRoy Decatur
Brumbaugh, Martin Grove
Bryan, Enoch Albert
Burrowes, Thomas Henry

Camp, David Nelson
Carrington, William Thomas
Case, Charles Orlando
Collins, Mauney Douglass
Cook, Albert Samuel
Cooper, Hermann
Cooper, Oscar Henry
Corbin, Joseph Carter
Cotton, Fassett Allen
Crabbe, John Grant
Dewey, Henry Bingham
Dickinson, John Woodbridge
Dimitry, Alexander
Downey, John
Doyne, John James
Draper, Andrew Sloan
Eggleston, Joseph Dupuy, Jr.
English, John Colin
Fairchild, Edward Thomson
Finegan, Thomas Edward
Finley, John Huston
Galloway, Samuel
Garrett, William Robertson
Gibbs, Jonathan C.
Glenn, Gustavus Richard
Goodnow, Isaac Tichenor
Grace, Alonzo Gaskell
Graves, Frank Pierrepont
Groves, James Henry
Haddock, Charles Brickett
Hale, Florence Maria
Hale, Horace Morrison
Hancock, John
Harvey, Thomas Wadleigh
Hawley, Gideon
Hedges, Cornelius
Henderson, Howard Andrew Millet
Henderson, Lester Dale
Hendrix, Herman Elert
Hill, Frank Alpine
Hine, Charles Daniel
Hodge, Oliver
Hollingsworth, Orlando Newton
Howland, John
Jackson, Sheldon
Joyner, James Yadkin
Kauffman, Treva Erdine

Kendall, Calvin Noyes
Kiehle, David Litchard
Kingsley, Clarence Darwin
Ladd, Azel Parkhurst
Larrabee, William Clark
Leach, Daniel Dyer
Lewis, Samuel
Long, Oren Ethelbirt
MacCaughey, Vaughan
McMynn, John Gibson
McVicar, Peter
Mann, Horace
Markham, Walter Tipton
Marvin, John Gage
Memminger, Christopher Gustavus
Miller, Paul Gerard
Mills, Caleb
Mowry, William Augustus
Nash, George Williston
Nash, Mell Achilles
Neill, Edward Duffield
Newell, McFadden Alexander
Northrop, Birdsey Grant
Orr, Gustavus John
Park, John Rocky
Patterson, James Willis
Peers, Benjamin Orr
Perry, William Flake
Pierce, John Davis
Potter, Elisha Reynolds, Jr.
Preston, Josephine Corliss
Putnam, Rex
Randall, Samuel Sidwell
Rice, Victor Moreau
Richards, William
Ruffner, William Henry
Russell, Albert Jonathan
Safford, Anson Peacely-Killen
Schaeffer, Nathan Christ
Schweickhard, Dean Merrill
Sears, Barnas
Shattuck, Joseph Cummings
Sheats, William Nicholas
Shinn, Josiah Hazen
Showalter, Noah David
Simpson, Roy E.
Sisson, Edward Octavius

Skinner, Charles Rufus
Smart, James Henry
Smith, Payson
Smith, Thomas
Smith, Zachariah Frederick
Snedden, David Samuel
Stetson, William Wallace
Stewart, Joseph Spencer
Stimson, Rufus Whittaker
Swett, John
Thomas, Augustus Orloff
Thompson, Hugh Smith
Van Bokkelen, Libertus
Wagner, Jonathan Howard
Walker, David Shelby
Wanamaker, Pearl Anderson
Weeks, Ila Delbert
White, Emerson Elbridge
Whitfield, Henry Lewis
Whitford, William Clarke
Wickersham, James Pyle
Wiley, Calvin Henderson
Wood, William Christopher

## ADMINISTRATION OF HIGHER EDUCATION

Abercrombie, John William
Aderhold, Omer Clyde
Adler, Cyrus
Agassiz, Elizabeth Cabot Cary
Alden, Joseph
Alderman, Edwin Anderson
Allyn, Robert
Anderson, Martin Brewer
Andrews, Elisha Benjamin
Andrews, Lorin
Angell, James Burrill
Angell, James Rowland
Apple, Thomas Gilmore
Archer, Gleason Leonard
Armstrong, Samuel Chapman
Aswell, James Benjamin
Atherton, George Washington
Atkinson, Alfred
Atwood, Wallace Walter
Axline, George Andrew

Aydelotte, Frank
Baker, Edna Dean
Baker, James Hutchins
Bapst, John
Barnard, Frederick Augustus Porter
Barr, Frank Stringfellow
Bascom, John
Bateman, Newton
Battle, Archibald John
Beadle, William Henry Harrison
Beecher, Catharine Esther
Berry, Martha McChesney
Bessey, Charles Edwin
Bethune, Mary McLeod
Birge, Edward Asahiel
Bishop, Robert Hamilton
Blackburn, William Maxwell
Blair, James
Blunt, Katharine
Bond, Horace Mann
Bonnell, John Mitchell
Bowman, Isaiah
Bowman, John Bryan
Boyd, David French
Boyd, David Ross
Boyd, Thomas Duckett
Boyden, Albert Gardner
Bralley, Francis Marion
Brandenburg, William Aaron
Brattle, William
Brittain, Marion Luther
Brooks, Eugene Clyde
Brooks, Stratton Duluth
Brown, Elmer Ellsworth
Brownell, Thomas Church
Brubacher, Abram Royer
Bruce, William Herschel
Bryan, Enoch Albert
Bryan, William Lowe
Buckham, Matthew Henry
Bunnell, Charles Ernest
Burgess, Theodore Chalon
Burk, Frederic Lister
Burns, James Aloysius
Burrowes, Thomas Henry
Butcher, Thomas Walter
Butler, Nicholas Murray

Butterfield, Kenyon Leech
Caldwell, Joseph
Campbell, Prince Lucien
Capen, Elmer Hewitt
Carmichael, Leonard
Carmichael, Oliver Cromwell
Carrick, Samuel
Chadbourne, Paul Ansel
Chamberlain, Joshua Lawrence
Chapin, Aaron Lucius
Cherry, Henry Hardin
Clap, Thomas
Clapp, Margaret
Claxton, Philander Priestley
Clement, Rufus Early
Cochran, David Henry
Coffman, Lotus Delta
Compton, Arthur Holly
Compton, Karl Taylor
Comstock, Ada Louise
Conant, James Bryant
Conaty, Thomas James
Cook, John Williston
Cooper, Myles
Cooper, Thomas
Coppée, Henry
Corbin, Joseph Carter
Cotton, Fassett Allen
Councill, William Hooper
Cowling, Donald John
Crabbe, John Grant
Crabtree, James William
Craig, Oscar John
Craven, Braxton
Cummings, Joseph
Dabney, Charles William
Davidson, Thomas
Davis, Henry
Davis, John Warren
Davis, Noah Knowles
Day, James Roscoe
Day, Jeremiah
Dinwiddie, Albert Bledsoe
Doak, Samuel
Dodds, Harold Willis
Dodge, Ebenezer
Dougherty, Blanford Barnard

Douglass, Mabel Smith
Doyne, John James
Drake, Daniel
Draper, Andrew Sloan
Dudley, James Benson
Duer, William Alexander
Dunster, Henry
Durant, Henry
Dwight, Timothy (1752–1817)
Dwight, Timothy (1828–1916)
Eells, Cushing
Eells, Walter Crosby
Eisenhower, Milton Stover
Eliot, Charles William
Ellis, Alston
Erskine, John
Eurich, Alvin Christian
Ewell, Benjamin Stoddert
Fairchild, Edward Thomson
Fairchild, George Thompson
Fairchild, James Harris
Farnum, Royal Bailey
Fess, Simeon Davidson
Few, William Preston
Finley, John Huston
Finney, Charles Grandison
Fischer, John Henry
Fisher, Ebenezer
Fisk, Wilbur
Fitzpatrick, Edward Augustus
Folwell, William Watts
Forbes, John Franklin
Foster, Thomas Jefferson
Foster, William Trufant
Foust, Julius Isaac
Fraser, John
Frelinghuysen, Theodore
Frost, William Goodell
Gale, George Washington
Gammage, Grady
Garland, Landon Cabell
Gault, Franklin Benjamin
Gideonse, Harry David
Gilbert, Eliphalet Wheeler
Gildersleeve, Virginia Crocheron
Gilman, Daniel Coit
Glenn, Gustavus Richard

Goff, Milton Browning
Goodell, Henry Hill
Goucher, John Franklin
Graham, Edward Kidder
Graham, Frank Porter
Green, Lewis Warner
Gregory, John Milton
Griswold, Alfred Whitney
Gulliver, Julia Henrietta
Hadley, Arthur Twining
Hadley, Hiram
Hagar, Daniel Barnard
Hale, Benjamin
Hale, Horace Morrison
Hamerschlag, Arthur Acton
Hamlin, Cyrus
Hanus, Paul Henry
Harper, William Rainey
Harris, Franklin Stewart
Harris, Samuel
Harrison, Elizabeth
Harvey, Lorenzo Dow
Haygood, Atticus Green
Hazard, Caroline
Heald, Henry Townley
Henderson, Algo Donmyer
Henry, David Dodds
Hetzel, Ralph Dorn
Hibben, John Grier
Hill, Daniel Harvey
Hill, David Spence
Hill, Thomas
Hitchcock, Edward (1793–1864)
Holbrook, Alfred
Holland, Ernest Otto
Holley, Horace
Hope, John
Hopkins, Ernest Martin
Hopkins, Mark
Hovey, Charles Edward
Howard, Ada Lydia
Hoyt, John Wesley
Humphrey, George Duke
Hunt, Henry Alexander
Hunter, Frederick Maurice
Hunter, Thomas
Hutchins, Robert Maynard

Hyde, William DeWitt
Hyer, Robert Stewart
James, Edmund Janes
Jefferson, Thomas
Jesse, Richard Henry
Jessup, Walter Albert
Jewett, Milo Parker
Johnson, Alvin Saunders
Johnson, David Bancroft
Johnson, Joseph French
Johnson, Mordecai Wyatt
Johnson, Samuel
Jones, Gilbert Haven
Jordon, David Starr
Judson, Harry Pratt
Junkin, George
Keane, John Joseph
Kellas, Eliza
Kent, Raymond Asa
Kerr, Clark
Kerr, William Jasper
Keyes, Charles Henry
King, William Fletcher
Kinley, David
Kirk, John Robert
Kirkland, James Hampton
Kirkland, John Thornton
Klapper, Paul
Knox, Samuel
Larsen, Peter Laurentius
Lathrop, John Hiram
Laws, Samuel Spahr
Lee, Stephen Dill
Leigh, Robert Devore
Lindley, Ernest Hiram
Lindsley, John Berrien
Lindsley, Philip
Lord, Livingston Chester
Lord, Nathan
Lowell, Abbot Lawrence
MacAlister, James
McCormick, Samuel Black
McCosh, James
McCracken, Henry Mitchell
McCrory, Henry Lawrence
McHugh, Anna (Antonia)
McIver, Charles Duncan

Maclean, John (1800–1886)
McVey, Frank LeRond
McVicar, Peter
Madeleva, Sister Mary (Mary Evaline Wolff)
Magill, Edward Hicks
Mahan, Asa
Mann, Horace
Manning, James
Martin, Alexander
Maslow, Abraham Harold
Mason, John Mitchell
Mather, Increase
Maupin, Socrates
Maxcy, Jonathan
Mays, Benjamin Elijah
Meiklejohn, Alexander
Melby, Ernest Oscar
Merrifield, Webster
Meserve, Charles Francis
Messer, Asa
Mezes, Sidney Edward
Mies van der Rohe, Ludwig
Millikan, Robert Andrews
Mills, Susan Lincoln Tolman
Mitchell, Samuel Chiles
Molloy, Mary Aloysius
Moore, Ernest Carroll
Moore, James
Morgan, Arthur Ernest
Morgan, Thomas Jefferson
Mortimer, Mary
Moton, Robert Russa
Mullany, Patrick Francis (Brother Azarias)
Mumford, Frederick Blackman
Murlin, Lemuel Herbert
Murphree, Albert Alexander
Myers, Phillip Van Ness
Nash, George Williston
Nash, Mell Achilles
Neill, Edward Duffield
Neilson, William Allan
Newcomb, John Lloyd
Northrop, Cyrus
Nott, Eliphalet
O'Harra, Cleophas Cisney
Olin, Stephen
Oppenheimer, J. Robert

Orton, Edward Francis Baxter
Owen, William Bishop
Page, Inman Edward
Palmer, Alice Elvira Freeman
Park, John Rocky
Partridge, Alden
Paterson, William Burns
Patterson, James Kennedy
Payne, Bruce Ryburn
Payne, Daniel Alexander
Payne, William Harold
Peabody, Selim Hobart
Pendleton, Ellen Fitz
Pendleton, William Kimbrough
Phelps, William Franklin
Pickard, Josiah Little
Pierson, Abraham
Pittman, Marvin Summers
Porter, Noah
Poteat, William Louis
Powers, James Knox
Priestley, James
Pritchett, Henry Smith
Pugh, Evan
Quincy, Josiah
Rauch, Frederick Augustus
Raymond, John Howard
Read, Daniel
Reed, David Allen
Reinhardt, Aurelia Isabel Henry
Remsen, Ira
Revel, Bernard
Revels, Hiram Rhoades
Rice, John Andrew
Roark, Ruric Nevel
Robinson, Ezekiel Gilman
Robinson, Frederick Bertrand
Rogers, Henry Wade
Rogers, William Barton
Ruffner, Henry
Runkle, John Daniel
Russell, James Earl
Russell, William Fletcher
Sabin, Ellen Clara
Sachar, Abram Leon
Sammartino, Peter
Sanders, Daniel Jackson

Scarborough, William Sanders
Schneider, Herman
Scott, John Work
Scott, Walter Dill
Seelye, Julius Hawley
Seelye, Laurenus Clark
Seerley, Homer Horatio
Shafer, Helen Almira
Shahan, Thomas Joseph
Shepard, James Edward
Showalter, Noah David
Shuster, George Nauman
Sibley, Frederick Hubbard
Sill, Anna Peck
Slagle, Robert Lincoln
Smart, James Henry
Smith, Francis Henney
Smith, Henry Louis
Smith, Samuel Stanhope
Smith, William
Snavely, Guy Everett
Snyder, Franklyn Bliss
Sorin, Edward Frederick
Sprague, Homer Baxter
Sproul, Robert Gordon
Stearns, Eben Sperry
Sterling, John Ewart Wallace
Stiles, Ezra
Stille, Charles Janeway
Stoddard, George Dinsmore
Stowell, Thomas Blanchard
Strong, Frank
Strong, James Woodward
Stryker, Melancthon Woolsey
Stubbs, Joseph Edward
Sturtevant, Julian Monson
Suzzallo, Henry
Swain, David Lowry
Swain, Joseph
Tall, Lida Lee
Talmage, James Edward
Tappan, Eli Todd
Tappan, Henry Philip
Taylor, Harold Alexander
Tennent, William
Thach, Charles Coleman
Thayer, Sylvanus

Thomas, Augustus Orloff
Thomas, Frank Waters
Thomas, Martha Carey
Thompson, Charles Oliver
Thompson, William Oxley
Thwing, Charles Franklin
Tigert, John James
Tompkins, Arnold
Tucker, William Jewett
Tutwiler, Julia Strudwick
Valentine, Milton
Van Hise, Charles Richard
Waddel, John Newton
Waddel, Moses
Wahlquist, John Thomas
Wait, Samuel
Walker, Francis Amasa
Ward, Joseph
Ware, Edmund Asa
Warren, William Fairfield
Washington, Booker Taliaferro
Waters, Henry Jackson
Wayland, Francis
Webster, Horace
Weeks, Ila Delbert
Welch, Adonijah Strong
Welling, James Clarke
Wells, Herman B.
Wesley, Charles Harris
Wheeler, Benjamin Ide
Wheelock, Eleazar
Wheelock, John
Wheelock, Lucy
White, Andrew Dickson
White, Emerson Elbridge
White, Samuel Holmes
Whitfield, Henry Lewis
Whitford, William Clarke
Whitworth, George Frederick
Wilbur, Ray Lyman
Wilkinson, Robert Shaw
Willard, Frances Elizabeth Caroline
Wilson, Thomas Woodrow
Wise, Isaac Mayer
Witherspoon, John
Woodruff, Caroline Salome
Woods, Albert Fred

Woods, Leonard
Woolley, Mary Emma
Woolsey, Theodore Dwight
Wright, Richard Robert
Wriston, Henry Merritt
Wylie, Andrew
Young, John Clarke

## ADMINISTRATION OF PUBLIC AND PRIVATE SCHOOLS

Abbot, Benjamin
Abbott, Gorham Dummer
Abbott, Jacob
Adams, Charles Kendall
Allen, Nathaniel Topliffe
Allyn, Robert
Anderson, John Jacob
Balliet, Thomas Minard
Bancroft, Cecil Franklin Patch
Belfield, Henry Holmes
Benedict, Erastus Cornelius
Benezet, Anthony
Berry, Martha McChesney
Bingham, Caleb
Bishop, Harriet E.
Bishop, John Remsen
Boyden, Frank Learoyd
Brackett, Anna Callender
Brown, Charlotte Hawkins
Brumbaugh, Martin Grove
Bulkley, John Williams
Bushee, James
Butler, Edward Mann
Cady, Sarah Louise Ensign
Caldwell, David
Calkins, Norman Allison
Carmichael, Omer
Chambers, Henry Edward
Clinton, De Witt
Cloud, Henry Roe
Cobb, Stanwood
Collar, William Coe
Cooley, Edwin Gilbert
Corlet, Elijah
Crandall, Prudence

Dickey, Sarah Ann
Dock, Christopher
Dod, Thaddeus
Dorsey, Susan Almira Miller
Dove, David James
DuShane, Donald
Dyer, Franklin Benjamin
Emerson, George Barrell
Emerson, Joseph
Evans, Lawton Bryan
Fowle, William Bentley
Franklin, Benjamin
Gould, Benjamin Apthorp
Gove, Aaron Estellus
Greene, Samuel Stillman
Greenwood, James Mickleborough
Griscom, John
Gummere, John
Gunn, Frederick William
Halleck, Reuben Post
Hancock, John
Harris, William Torrey
Harvey, Thomas Wadleigh
Johnson, Marietta Louise Pierce
Johnston, Richard Malcolm
Jones, Lawrence Clifton
Kellas, Eliza
Keppel, Mark
Kiddle, Henry
King, Charles Francis
Kingsbury, John
Lewis, Enoch
Lord, Asa Dearborn
Lovell, John Epy
McClellan, Henry Brainerd
McCorkle, Samuel Eusebius
MacKenzie, James Cameron
Marble, Albert Prescott
Maxwell, William Henry
Merrill, George Arthur
Neef, Francis Joseph Nicholas
Newlon, Jesse Homer
Northend, Charles
Packard, Sophia B.
Parkhurst, Helen
Pastorius, Francis Daniel
Patri, Angelo

Peabody, Endicott
Pearson, Eliphalet
Phelps, Almira Hart Lincoln
Philbrick, John Dudley
Pierce, Sarah
Pinney, Norman
Poor, John
Porter, Sarah
Powell, William Bramwell
Pratt, Caroline
Proud, Robert
Quackenbos, George Payn
Rambaut, Mary Lucinda Bonney
Randall, Samuel Sidwell
Richman, Julia
Rickoff, Andrew Jackson
Rogers, Elizabeth Ann
Sachs, Julius
Sewall, May Eliza Wright Thompson
Sheldon, William Evarts
Sherwin, Thomas
Soldan, Frank Louis
Stoddard, John Fair
Sunderland, Eliza Jane Read
Tatt, Horace Dutton
Taylor, Samuel Harvey
Thompson, Robert Ellis
Town, Salem
Tutwiler, Henry
Valentine, Thomas Weston
Venable, William Henry
Waddel, Moses
Washburne, Carleton Wolsey
Watteville, Henrietta Benigna
    Justina von Zinzendorf
Webb, William Robert
Wells, William Harvey
West, Charles Edwin
White, John Stuart
Willard, Emma Hart
Wilson, Lucy Langdon Williams
Wirt, William Albert
Young, Ella Flagg

ADULT EDUCATION

Bestor, Arthur Eugene
Bryson, Lyman Lloyd

Cartwright, Morse Adams
Griffith, Emily
Holbrook, Josiah
Jayne, Clarence D.
Keppel, Frederick Paul
Leipziger, Henry Marcus
Pettit, Katherine Rhoda
Robinson, Frederick Bertrand
Stewart, Cora Wilson
Vincent, John Heyl
Winship, Albert Edward

## ARCHITECTURE

Gropius, Walter Adolf
Laird, Warren Powers
Mies van der Rohe, Ludwig
Ricker, Nathan Clifford
Ware, William Robert

## ART

Bailey, Henry Turner
Bartholomew, William Nelson
Brown, Alice Van Vechten
Butler, Howard Crosby
Chapman, John Gadsby
Chase, William Merritt
Cross, Anson Kent
Dobbs, Ella Victoria
Dow, Arthur Wesley
Duveneck, Frank
Eakins, Thomas
Farnum, Royal Bailey
Gardner, Helen
Henri, Robert
Hunt, William Morris
Levy, Florence Nightingale
Mather, Frank Jewett, Jr.
Miller, Leslie William
Norton, Charles Eliot
Panofsky, Erwin
Poland, William Carey
Porter, Arthur Kingsley
Prang, Mary Amelia Dana Hicks
Raymond, George Lansing
Sargent, Walter
Sartain, Emily
Smith, John Rubens

Stimson, John Ward
Van Dyke, John Charles
Weir, Irene
Wittkower, Rudolf

## AUTHORS OF TEXTS AND CHILDREN'S LITERATURE

Anderson, John Jacob
Andrews, Ethan Allen
Andrews, Jane
Arbuthnot, May Hill
Archer, Gleason Leonard
Atwood, Wallace Walter
Avery, Elroy McKendree
Bailey, Liberty Hyde
Bailey, Rufus William
Baldwin, James
Bardeen, Charles William
Beard, Charles Austin
Beberman, Max
Becker, Carl Lotus
Bennett, Charles Edwin
Bingham, Caleb
Brueckner, Leo John
Cheever, Ezekiel
Cobb, Lyman
Colburn, Dana Pond
Colburn, Warren
Commager, Henry Steele
Comstock, John Lee
Coppens, Charles
Davies, Charles
Day, Henry Noble
Day, Jeremiah
Dodge, Richard Elwood
Elson, William Harris
Fowle, William Bentley
Frye, Alexis Everett
Goodrich, Samuel Griswold
Gordy, Wilbur Fisk
Gray, Asa
Greene, Samuel Stillman
Greenleaf, Benjamin
Halleck, Reuben Post
Harkness, Albert
Hart, John Seely
Hill, Howard Copeland

Hillard, George Stillman
Holmes, George Frederick
Houston, Edwin James
Hughes, Ray Osgood
Hunt, Mary Hannah Hanchett
Huntington, Ellsworth
Johnson, William Woolsey
Kraus, Mother M. Seraphine
  (Mary Katharine)
Lodge, Gonzalez
Lovell, John Epy
Lyte, Eliphalet Oram
McConnell, Wallace Robert
McGuffey, William Holmes
McMurry, Frank Morton
Magruder, Frank Abbott
Mitchell, Samuel Augustus
Morse, Jedidiah
Murray, Lindley
Muzzey, David Saville
Myers, George William
Myers, Phillip Van Ness
Olney, Jesse
Parker, Richard Green
Peck, William Guy
Peirce, James Mills
Phelps, Almira Hart Lincoln
Picket, Albert
Pierpont, John
Pike, Nicholas
Pinney, Norman
Quackenbos, George Payn
Quackenbos, John Duncan
Raub, Albert Newton
Ray, Joseph
Renner, George Thomas, Jr.
Robinson, James Harvey
Russell, William
Sanders, Charles Walton
Sargent, Epes
Smith, Charles Alfonso
Smyth, William
Soulé, George
Spaulding, Frank Ellsworth
Steele, Joel Dorman
Stoddard, John Fair
Stone, John Charles

Swinton, William
Tappan, Eva March
Tapper, Thomas
Tarr, Ralph Stockman
Tippett, James Sterling
Town, Salem
Viguers, Ruth Hill
Warren, Samuel Edward
Watson, James Madison
Webster, Noah
Wells, Webster
Wentworth, George Albert
West, Willis Mason
White, Emerson Elbridge
Wiggin, Kate Douglas
Willard, Emma Hart
Williams, Jesse Feiring
Woodbridge, William Channing
Worcester, Joseph Emerson
Young, Andrew White

CLASSICS
Alison, Francis
Andrews, Ethan Allen
Anthon, Charles
Beck, Charles (Karl)
Bennett, Charles Edwin
Burgess, Theodore Chalon
Cheever, Ezekiel
Crosby, Alpheus
Drisler, Henry
Fairclough, Henry Rushton
Frieze, Henry Simmons
Gildersleeve, Basil Lanneau
Goodwin, William Watson
Gould, Benjamin Apthorp
Hadley, James
Hale, William Gardner
Harkness, Albert
Inglis, Alexander James
Kendrick, Asahel Clark
Kent, Roland Grubb
Kingsley, James Luce
Lodge, Gonzalez
North, Edward
Palmer, George Herbert
Smith, John

Sophocles, Evangelinus Apostolides
Tyler, William Seymour
Wilson, Peter

## COMPARATIVE AND INTERNATIONAL EDUCATION

Brickman, William Wolfgang
Butts, Robert Freeman
Counts, George Sylvester
Duggan, Stephen Pierce
Dutton, Samuel Train
Eells, Walter Crosby
Goucher, John Franklin
Griffis, William Elliot
Hamlin, Cyrus
Kandel, Isaac Leon
Knight, Edgar Wallace
Monroe, Paul
Read, Gerald Howard
Russell, William Fletcher
Tewksbury, Donald George
Ulich, Robert

## CURRICULUM

Alberty, Harold Bernard
Barrows, Alice Prentice
Bobbitt, John Franklin
Burk, Frederic Lister
Caswell, Hollis Leland
Charters, Werrett Wallace
Dale, Edgar
Davis, Calvin Olin
Foshay, Arthur Wellesley
Fretwell, Elbert Kirtley
Harap, Henry
Hullfish, Henry Gordon
McKown, Harry Charles
McMurry, Charles Alexander
McMurry, Frank Morton
Meriam, Junius Lathrop
Parkhurst, Helen
Pratt, Caroline
Roemer, Joseph
Saylor, John Galen
Smith, Bunnie Othanel
Taba, Hilda
Tyler, Ralph Winfred

Wiles, Kimball

## EDUCATION OF MINORITIES

Armstrong, Samuel Chapman
Ashley, Samuel Stanford
Baldwin, Maria Louise
Barrett, Janie Porter
Benezet, Anthony
Bethune, Mary McLeod
Bond, Horace Mann
Brawley, Benjamin Griffith
Brown, Charlotte Hawkins
Brown, Hallie Quinn
Caliver, Ambrose
Chavis, John
Clement, Rufus Early
Cloud, Henry Roe
Coppin, Fanny Marion Jackson
Corbin, Joseph Carter
Cordero y Molina, Rafael
Councill, William Hooper
Covello, Leonard
Crandall, Prudence
Davis, John Warren
Dett, Robert Nathaniel
Dickey, Sarah Ann
Dillard, James Hardy
Drake, Daniel
Du Bois, William Edward Burghardt
Dudley, James Benson
Eliot, John
Frazier, Edward Franklin
Frissell, Hollis Burke
Frost, William Goodell
Gibbs, Jonathan C.
Grimké, Charlotte L. Forten
Haygood, Atticus Green
Henderson, Howard Andrew Millet
Hope, John
Hostos, Eugenio María de
Howland, Emily
Hunt, Henry Alexander
Johnson, Charles Spurgeon
Johnson, Mordecai Wyatt
Jones, Gilbert Haven
Jones, Lawrence Clifton
Jones, Thomas Jesse

Laney, Lucy Craft
Langston, John Mercer
Locke, Alain LeRoy
Loughridge, Robert McGill
McCrorey, Henry Lawrence
Mays, Benjamin Elijah
Meserve, Charles Francis
Miller, Kelly
Miner, Myrtilla
Morgan, Thomas Jefferson
Moten, Lucy Ella
Moton, Robert Russa
Munford, Mary Cooke Branch
Osuna, Juan Jóse
Packard, Sophia B.
Page, Inman Edward
Paterson, William Burns
Payne, Daniel Alexander
Pratt, Richard Henry
Reid, Ira de Augustine
Revels, Hiram Rhoades
Robertson, William Schenck
Sanchez, George Isidore
Sanders, Daniel Jackson
Scarborough, William Sanders
Shepard, James Edward
Ware, Edmund Asa
Washington, Booker Taliaferro
Wesley, Charles Harris
Wilkinson, Robert Shaw
Wilson, Atwood Sylvester
Woodson, Carter Godwin
Wright, Richard Robert
Zeisberger, David

## EDUCATION OF WOMEN

Abbott, Gorham Dummer
Abbott, Jacob
Bailey, Ebenezer
Baldwin, Theron
Banister, Zilpah Polly Grant
Barnard, Frederick Augustus Porter
Barrett, Janie Porter
Beecher, Catharine Esther
Bethune, Mary McLeod
Blunt, Katharine
Bodley, Rachel Littler

Bonnell, John Mitchell
Brackett, Anna Callender
Butler, Marie Joseph
Butler, Noble
Cady, Sarah Louise Ensign
Colton, Elizabeth Avery
Comstock, Ada Louise
Crandall, Prudence
Dickey, Sarah Ann
Douglass, Mabel Smith
Emerson, Joseph
Gildersleeve, Virginia Crocheron
Gillespie, Eliza Maria (Mother Angela)
Gilman, Arthur
Gregory, Samuel
Howard, Ada Lydia
Howland, Emily
Hunter, Thomas
Jewett, Milo Parker
Kellas, Eliza
Kingsbury, John
Leigh, Robert Devore
Lyon, Mary Mason
McClellan, Henry Brainerd
McHugh, Anna (Antonia)
McIver, Charles Duncan
Mahan, Asa
Mills, Susan Lincoln Tolman
Mitchell, Maria
Mortimer, Mary
Munford, Mary Cooke Branch
Orcutt, Hiram
Packard, Sophia B.
Palmer, Alice Elvira Freeman
Parrish, Celestia Susannah
Pendleton, Ellen Fitz
Phelps, Almira Hart Lincoln
Pierce, Sarah
Poor, John
Porter, Sarah
Rambaut, Mary Lucinda Bonney
Rogers, Elizabeth Ann
Sabin, Ellen Clara
Seelye, Laurenus Clark
Sewall, May Eliza Wright Thompson
Shields, Thomas Edward
Sill, Anna Peck

Stearns, Eben Sperry
Stone, Lucinda Hinsdale
Thomas, Martha Carey
Tutwiler, Julia Strudwick
Warren, William Fairfield
Watteville, Henrietta Benigna
    Justina von Zinzendorf
Weed, Ella
West, Charles Edwin
Whitaker, Ozi William
Willard, Emma Hart
Willard, Frances Elizabeth Caroline
Wilson, Lucy Langdon Williams
Woolley, Mary Emma

## EDUCATIONAL ADMINISTRATION

Anderson, Archibald Watson
Carpenter, William Weston
Chambers, Merritt Madison
Cocking, Walter Dewey
Dutton, Samuel Train
Edwards, Newton
Engelhardt, Fred
Engelhardt, Nickolaus Louis
Henderson, Algo Donmyer
Leonard, Robert Josselyn
McConnell, Thomas Raymond
McGrath, Earl James
Moehlman, Arthur Bernard
Morphet, Edgar Leroy
Morrison, Henry Clinton
Newlon, Jesse Homer
Reavis, William Claude
Strayer, George Drayton

## ENGINEERING

Cain, William
Elliott, Edward Charles
Fuertes, Estevan Antonio
Hamerschlag, Arthur Acton
Heald, Henry Townley
Jacoby, Henry Sylvester
Kimball, Dexter Simpson
Mahan, Dennis Hart
Millikan, Robert Andrews
Orton, Edward, Jr.
Peabody, Selim Hobart

Robinson, Stillman Williams
Sibley, Frederick Hubbard
Smith, Harold Babbitt
Thayer, Sylvanus
Thompson, Charles Oliver
Thurston, Robert Henry
Williston, Arthur Lyman
Wood, De Volson

## EVALUATION AND RESEARCH

Ayres, Leonard Porter
Barr, Arvil Sylvester
Courtis, Stuart Appleton
Flexner, Abraham
Good, Carter Victor
Holzinger, Karl John
Hull, Clark Leonard
Johnson, Palmer Oliver
Judd, Charles Hubbard
Kelley, Truman Lee
Lindquist, Everet Franklin
McCloy, Charles Harold
MacDonald, Arthur
Monroe, Walter Scott
Paterson, Donald Gildersleeve
Pressey, Sidney Leavitt
Rice, Joseph Mayer
Scates, Douglas Edgar
Seashore, Carl Emil
Stoddard, George Dinsmore
Strong, Edward Kellogg, Jr.
Symonds, Percival Mallon
Terman, Lewis Madison
Thorndike, Edward Lee
Thurstone, Louis Leon
Travers, Robert Morris William
Traxler, Arthur Edwin
Tyler, Ralph Winfred
Wallin, John Edward Wallace
Whipple, Guy Montrose
Woody, Clifford

## GUIDANCE AND COUNSELING

Cottingham, Harold Fred
Davis, Jesse Buttrick
Feder, Daniel Dunn
Hamrin, Shirley Austin

Hatcher, Orie Latham
Jones, Arthur Julius
Kefauver, Grayson Neikirk
Kitson, Harry Dexter
Lloyd-Jones, Esther McDonald
Parsons, Frank
Paterson, Donald Gildersleeve
Procter, William Martin
Rogers, Carl Ransom
Ryan, Will Carson, Jr.
Strang, Ruth May
Sturtevant, Sarah Martha
Trabue, Marion Rex
Traxler, Arthur Edwin
Wheatley, William Alonzo
Williamson, Edmund Griffith
Wrenn, Charles Gilbert

## HEALTH AND PHYSICAL EDUCATION

Ainsworth, Dorothy Sears
Alcott, William Andrus
Anderson, William Gilbert
Bancroft, Jessie Hubbell
Beck, Charles (Karl)
Bowen, Wilbur Pardon
Burchenal, Elizabeth
Burnham, William Henry
Calderone, Mary Steichen
Cassidy, Rosalind
Follen, Karl (Charles) Theodore Christian
Gruenberg, Benjamin Charles
Gulick, Luther Halsey
Hanna, Delphine
Hartwell, Edward Mussey
Hetherington, Clark Wilson
Hitchcock, Edward (1828–1911)
Homans, Amy Morris
Hughes, William Leonard
Hunt, Mary Hannah Hanchett
Lee, Mabel
Lewis, Dioclesian
McCloy, Charles Harold
McCurdy, James Huff
McKenzie, Robert Tait
Mitchell, Elmer Dayton
Nash, Jay Bryan

Oberteuffer, Delbert
Perrin, Ethel
Posse, Nils
Rice, Thurman Brooks
Roberts, Robert Jeffries
Sargent, Dudley Allen
Steinhaus, Arthur H.
Williams, Jesse Feiring
Winslow, Charles-Edward Amory
Wood, Thomas Denison

## HOME ECONOMICS

Arny, Clara Maude Brown
Barrows, Anna
Beecher, Catharine Esther
Bevier, Isabel
Blunt, Katharine
Corson, Juliet
Dodge, Grace Hoadley
Farmer, Fannie Merritt
Kauffman, Treva Erdine
Marlatt, Abby Lillian
Norton, Mary Alice Peloubet
Richards, Ellen Henrietta Swallow
Rorer, Sarah Tyson Heston
Rose, Mary Davies Swartz
Talbot, Marion
Van Rensselaer, Martha
Woolman, Mary Raphael Schenck

## JOURNALISM

Bleyer, Willard Grosvenor
Harrington, Harry Franklin
Hyde, Grant Milnor
Lee, James Melvin
Williams, Walter

## KINDERGARTEN AND CHILDHOOD EDUCATION

Arbuthnot, May Hill
Baker, Edna Dean
Bethune, Joanna Graham
Blaker, Eliza Ann Cooper
Blow, Susan Elizabeth
Bryan, Anna E.
Cooper, Sarah Brown Ingersoll
Gage, Lucy

Hailmann, William Nicholas
Hallowell, Anna
Harrison, Elizabeth
Hill, Patty Smith
Kraus, John
Kraus-Boelté, Maria
Marwedel, Emma Jacobina Christiana
Peabody, Elizabeth Palmer
Pollock, Louise Plessner
Putnam, Alice Harvey Whiting
Schurz, Margarethe Meyer
Scott, Miriam Finn
Temple, Alice
Wheelock, Lucy
Wiggin, Kate Douglas


## LANGUAGE ARTS

Baker, George Pierce
Bates, Katharine Lee
Betts, Emmett Albert
Boynton, Percy Holmes
Brigance, William Norwood
Brown, Goold
Browne, William Hand
Brubacher, Abram Royer
Carpenter, George Rice
Channing, Edward Tyrrell
Colton, Elizabeth Avery
Cook, Albert Stanburrough
Cross, Wilbur Lucius
Davidson, Charles
Davidson, Hannah Amelia Noyes
De Boer, John James
De Vane, William Clyde
Erskine, John
Gates, Arthur Irving
Gayley, Charles Mills
Gray, William Scott
Greenlaw, Edwin Almiron
Hart, John Seely
Hayakawa, Samuel Ichiye
Hosic, James Fleming
Immel, Ray Keeslar
Laubach, Frank Charles
Leigh, Edwin
Leonard, Sterling Andrus

Manly, John Matthews
Matthews, James Brander
Miller, Edwin Lillie
Murray, Lindley
Newman, Samuel Phillips
Pattee, Fred Lewis
Perrin, Porter Gale
Phelps, William Lyon
Pound, Louise
Richardson, Charles Francis
Russell, William
Sanford, Maria Louise
Schelling, Felix Emanuel
Sill, Edward Rowland
Smith, Charles Alfonso
Smith, Dora Valentine
Smith, Nila Banton
Spencer, Platt Rogers
Stewart, Cora Wilson
Stoddard, Francis Hovey
Strang, Ruth May
Traxler, Arthur Edwin
Trent, William Peterfield
Trueblood, Thomas Clarkson
Vaile, Edwin Orlando
Van Doren, Mark
Wendell, Barrett
Witty, Paul Andrew


## LEGAL EDUCATION

Ames, James Barr
Archer, Gleason Leonard
Bigelow, Harry Augustus
Dwight, Theodore William
Gould, James
Greenleaf, Simon
Hammond, William Gardiner
Langdell, Christopher Columbus
Mechem, Floyd Russell
Minor, John Barbee
Patterson, Edwin Wilhite
Pound, Roscoe
Reeve, Tapping
Rogers, Henry Wade
Story, Joseph
Wythe, George

## LIBRARY SCIENCE

Ahern, Mary Eileen
Bogle, Sarah Comly Norris
Dewey, Melvil
Fairchild, Mary Salome Cutler
Lancour, Adlore Harold
Powell, Lawrence Clark
Sharp, Katharine Lucinda
Shera, Jesse Hauk
Shores, Louis
Viguers, Ruth Hill
Williamson, Charles Clarence
Wilson, Louis Round

## MATHEMATICS

Adams, Daniel
Adams, Ebenezer
Beberman, Max
Birkhoff, George David
Brownell, William Arthur
Bruce, William Herschel
Brueckner, Leo John
Byerly, William Elwood
Cajori, Florian
Chauvenet, William
Colburn, Warren
Coolidge, Julian Lowell
Crozet, Claude
Daboll, Nathan
Davies, Charles
Day, Jeremiah
Eisenhart, Luther Pfahler
Farrar, John
Greenwood, Isaac
Halsted, George Bruce
Hedrick, Earle Raymond
Johnson, William Woolsey
Merrill, Helen Abbot
Myers, George William
Peck, William Guy
Peirce, Benjamin
Peirce, James Mills
Pike, Nicholas
Pratt, Orson
Ray, Joseph
Reeve, William David
Rosskopf, Myron Frederick

Schorling, Raleigh
Smith, David Eugene
Smyth, William
Stoddard, John Fair
Stone, John Charles
Veblen, Oswald
Warren, Samuel Edward
Wells, Webster
Wentworth, George Albert
Wheeler, Anna Johnson Pell
Wilson, Guy Mitchell
Winthrop, John
Young, Jacob William Albert
Young, John Wesley

## MEDICAL SCIENCES

Agnew, David Hayes
Bard, Samuel
Barton, Benjamin Smith
Bradford, Edward Hickling
Bryant, Joseph Decatur
Cooke, John Esten
Cutler, Elliott Carr
Dalton, John Call
Davis, Nathan Smith
Dunglison, Robley
Flint, Austin
Gibson, William
Goodrich, Annie Warburton
Gowan, Mary Olivia
Gregory, Samuel
Gross, Samuel David
Harris, Chapin Aaron
Halsted, William Stewart
Hayden, Horace H.
Hooker, Worthington
Jacobi, Mary Corinna Putnam
Jenne, James Nathaniel
Keen, William Williams
Leidy, Joseph
Lozier, Clemence Sophia Harned
Marshall, Charles
Maupin, Socrates
Meyer, Adolf
Minot, Charles Sedgwick
Morgan, John
Morgan, William Henry

Murphy, John Benjamin
Nutting, Mary Adelaide
Oldberg, Oscar
Osborne, Estelle Massey Riddle
Owre, Alfred
Parrish, Edward
Pearce, Richard Mills, Jr.
Pepper, William
Physick, Philip Syng
Richards, Linda (Melinda Ann) Judson
Robb, Isabel Adams Hampton
Rush, Benjamin
Rusby, Henry Hurd
Sabin, Florence Rena
Shippen, William, Jr.
Smith, Daniel B.
Smith, Nathan
Stewart, Isabel Maitland
Toland, Hugh Huger
Wald, Lillian D.
Warren, John
Warren, John Collins
Weeks, Thomas Edwin
Welch, William Henry
Witherspoon, John Alexander
Wood, George Bacon
Wulling, Frederick John

## MODERN LANGUAGES
Babbitt, Irving
Bloomfield, Leonard
Campa, Arthur Leon
Collitz, Hermann
Collitz, Klara Hechtenberg
Crane, Thomas Frederick
Crawford, James Pyle Wickersham
Curme, George Oliver
Elliott, Aaron Marshall
Espinosa, Aurelio Macedonio
Fitz-Gerald, John Driscoll, II
Ford, Jeremiah Denis Matthias
Grandgent, Charles Hall
Hewett, Waterman Thomas
Hills, Elijah Clarence
Joynes, Edward Southey
Magill, Edward Hicks
March, Francis Andrew

Scheville, Rudolph
Thomas, Calvin
Ticknor, George
Warshaw, Jacob
Wiener, Leo

## MUSIC
Baker, Benjamin Franklin
Birge, Edward Bailey
Bradbury, William Batchelder
Cady, Calvin Brainerd
Chadwick, George Whitfield
Christiansen, Fredrik Melius
Coleman, Satis Narrona Barton
Crane, Julia Ettie
Damrosch, Frank Heino
Dann, Hollis Ellsworth
Dett, Robert Nathaniel
Dickinson, George Sherman
Dykema, Peter William
Earhart, Will
Elson, Louis Charles
Erskine, John
Farnsworth, Charles Hubert
Fillmore, John Comfort
Gantvoort, Arnold Johann
Gehrkens, Karl Wilson
Goetschius, Percy
Goldbeck, Robert
Hanchett, Henry Granger
Hanson, Howard Harold
Haydon, Glen
Lutkin, Peter Christian
McConathy, Osbourne
Maddy, Joseph Edgar
Mannes, Clara Damrosch
Mannes, David
Mason, Lowell
Mason, Luther Whiting
Mason, William
Mursell, James Lockhart
Paine, John Knowles
Palmer, Horatio Richmond
Parker, Horatio William
Penny, George Barlow
Rice, Fenelon Bird
Ritter, Frederic Louis

Root, George Frederick
Samaroff, Olga
Smith, Eleanor
Stanley, Albert Augustus
Stevens, Georgia Lydia
Tapper, Thomas
Tomlins, William Lawrence
Tourjée, Eben

## PHILOSOPHY

Adler, Felix
Alcott, Amos Bronson
Alden, Joseph
Alexander, Hartley Burr
Atwater, Lyman Hotchkiss
Axtelle, George Edward
Bagley, William Chandler
Benne, Kenneth Dean
Bode, Boyd Henry
Brameld, Theodore Burghard Hurt
Broudy, Harry Samuel
Brubacher, John Seiler
Butler, Nicholas Murray
Calkins, Mary Whiton
Counts, George Sylvester
Davis, Noah Knowles
Demiashkevich, Michael John
Dewey, John
Hocking, William Ernest
Hook, Sidney
Horne, Herman Harrell
Howison, George Holmes
James, William
Kilpatrick, William Heard
Ladd, George Trumbull
Parker, Francis Wayland
Peirce, Charles (Santiago) Sanders
Ulich, Robert
Wilson, William Dexter
Woodbridge, Frederick James Eugene

## PSYCHOLOGY

Allport, Gordon Willard
Angell, James Rowland
Baldwin, James Mark
Bettelheim, Bruno
Boring, Edwin Garrigues

Bryan, William Lowe
Calkins, Mary Whiton
Carmichael, Leonard
Cattell, James McKeen
Colvin, Stephen Sheldon
Freeman, Frank Nugent
Gesell, Arnold
Goddard, Henry Herbert
Gruenberg, Sidonie Matsner
Hall, Granville Stanley
Havighurst, Robert James
Hilgard, Ernest Ropriequet
Hollingworth, Leta Anna Stetter
Hull, Clark Leonard
James, William
Jersild, Arthur Thomas
Judd, Charles Hubbard
Kelley, Truman Lee
Kirkpatrick, Edwin Asbury
Ladd, George Trumbull
McConnell, Thomas Raymond
McDougall, William
Maslow, Abraham Harold
Murchison, Carl Allanmore
Myers, Garry Cleveland
Norsworthy, Naomi
Pillsbury, Walter Bowers
Pressey, Sidney Leavitt
Rogers, Carl Ransom
Sanford, Robert Nevitt
Scott, Walter Dill
Seashore, Carl Emil
Skinner, Burrhus Frederic
Strong, Edward Kellogg, Jr.
Symonds, Percival Mallon
Terman, Lewis Madison
Thorndike, Edward Lee
Thurstone, Louis Leon
Titchener, Edward Bradford
Traxler, Arthur Edwin
Washburn, Margaret Floy
Watson, John Broadus
Wheeler, Raymond Holder
Whipple, Guy Montrose
Witty, Paul Andrew
Wolfe, Harry Kirke
Woodworth, Robert Sessions

Woolley, Helen Bradford Thompson

RELIGIOUS EDUCATION

Adler, Cyrus
Bapst, John
Bethune, Joanna Graham
Betts, George Herbert
Brownson, Josephine Van Dyke
Burns, James Aloysius
Butler, Marie Joseph
Case, Adelaide Teague
Coe, George Albert
Conaty, Thomas James
Duchesne, Rose Philippine
Finney, Charles Grandison
Fisher, Ebenezer
Fiske, George Walter
Fitton, James
Fitzpatrick, Edward Augustus
Gamoran, Emmanuel
Gillespie, Eliza Maria (Mother Angela)
Goodrich, Chauncey Allen
Gratz, Rebecca
Grossmann, Louis
Guerin, Anne Therese
Hardey, Mary Aloysia
Hartranft, Chester David
Hughes, John Joseph
Ireland, John
Johnson, Franklin
Keane, John Joseph
Kraus, Mother M. Seraphine (Mary
  Katharine)
Leeser, Isaac
McGroarty, Susan (Sister Julia)
McHugh, Anna (Antonia)
McQuaid, Bernard John
Madeleva, Sister Mary (Mary Evaline Wolff)
Mason, John Mitchell
Molloy, Mary Aloysius
Mullany, Patrick Francis (Brother
  Azarias)
Neumann, John Nepomucene
O'Gorman, Thomas
Pace, Edward Aloysius
Revel, Bernard
Sears, Barnas

Seton, Elizabeth Ann Bayley
Shahan, Thomas Joseph
Shedd, William Greenough Thayer
Shields, Thomas Edward
Soares, Theodore Gerald
Sorin, Edward Frederick
Spalding, Catherine
Spalding, John Lancaster
Stevens, Georgia Lydia
Stowe, Calvin Ellis
Tucker, William Jewett
Valentine, Milton
Van Dusen, Henry Pitney
Warren, William Fairfield
Weigle, Luther Allan
Wigglesworth, Edward
Wise, Isaac Mayer

SCIENCE

Agassiz, Elizabeth Cabot Cary
Agassiz, Jean Louis Rodolphe
Andrews, Eliza Frances
Bache, Alexander Dallas
Bailey, Liberty Hyde
Barton, Benjamin Smith
Bessey, Charles Edwin
Birge, Edward Asahiel
Bodley, Rachel Littler
Bowditch, Henry Pickering
Brigham, Albert Perry
Brownell, Herbert
Caldwell, Otis William
Campbell, Douglas Houghton
Chittenden, Russell Henry
Clapp, Cornelia Maria
Cleaveland, Parker
Compton, Arthur Holly
Compton, Karl Taylor
Comstock, Anna Botsford
Comstock, George Cary
Comstock, John Henry
Cooke, Josiah Parsons
Cooley, LeRoy Clark
Coppens, Charles
Coulter, John Merle
Cutter, Calvin
Dabney, Charles William

Dana, James Dwight
Davenport, Charles Benedict
Dewey, Chester
Dodge, Richard Elwood
Downing, Elliot Rowland
Draper, John William
Dunglison, Robley
Eaton, Amos
Fernald, Charles Henry
Glass, Hiram Bentley
Goodale, George Lincoln
Gray, Asa
Green, Jacob
Gruenberg, Benjamin Charles
Henderson, Lawrence Joseph
Himes, Charles Francis
Houston, Edwin James
Hyatt, Alpheus
Hyer, Robert Stewart
Jackman, Wilbur Samuel
Jordan, David Starr
Lawson, Andrew Cowper
Lillie, Frank Rattray
Maclean, John (1771-1814)
Merriam, John Campbell
Mitchell, Maria
Norton, John Pitkin
Noyes, William Albert
Olmsted, Denison
Oppenheimer, J. Robert
Orton, James
Osborn, Henry Fairfield
Packard, Alpheus Spring, Jr.
Peirce, Benjamin
Peirce, Charles (Santiago) Sanders
Phelps, Almira Hart Lincoln
Pickering, Edward Charles
Pirsson, Louis Valentine
Remsen, Ira
Rice, William North
Richardson, Leon Burr
Rogers, William Barton
Schlesinger, Hermann Irving
Shaler, Nathaniel Southgate
Silliman, Benjamin
Silliman, Benjamin, Jr.
Sinnott, Edmund Ware

Trowbridge, John
Watson, Fletcher Guard
Winchell, Alexander
Winthrop, John
Woodhouse, James
Youmans, Edward Livingston
Young, Charles Augustus

SOCIAL SCIENCES

Adams, Charles Kendall
Adams, Henry Brooks
Adams, Herbert Baxter
Adams, Romanzo
Allyn, Harriet May
Anderson, John Jacob
Andrews, Charles McLean
Atwood, Wallace Walter
Barnes, Harry Elmer
Barnes, Mary Downing Sheldon
Beard, Charles Austin
Becker, Carl Lotus
Benedict, Ruth Fulton
Bernard, Luther Lee
Boas, Franz
Bowman, Isaiah
Brackett, Jeffrey Richardson
Breasted, James Henry
Breckinridge, Sophonisba Preston
Brigham, Albert Perry
Burgess, John William
Castañeda, Carlos Eduardo
Cheyney, Edward Potts
Commager, Henry Steele
Cubberly, Elwood Patterson
Curti, Merle Eugene
Davis, William Morris
Dodge, Richard Elwood
Du Bois, William Edward Burghardt
Ely, Richard Theodore
Fisher, Irving
Fleming, Walter Lynwood
Frost, John
Frye, Alexis Everett
Giddings, Franklin Henry
Gillette, John Morris
Good, Harry Gehman
Goode, John Paul

Gordy, Wilbur Fisk
Graves, Frank Pierrepont
Guyot, Arnold Henry
Hailmann, William Nicholas
Hanna, Paul Robert
Hart, Albert Bushnell
Havighurst, Robert James
Hayes, Carlton Joseph Huntley
Heathcote, Charles William
Hill, Howard Copeland
Hughes, Ray Osgood
Huntington, Ellsworth
Jefferson, Mark Sylvester William
Johnson, Charles Spurgeon
Johnson, Earl Shepard
Johnson, Henry
Jones, Thomas Jesse
King, Charles Francis
Kinley, David
Knight, Edgar Wallace
Krey, August Charles
Lieber, Francis
McConnell, Wallace Robert
McMaster, John Bach
Mace, William Harrison
Mahoney, John Joseph
Marshall, Leon Carroll
Merriam, Charles Edward
Meyer, Adolphe Erich
Mitchell, Samuel Augustus
Monroe, Paul
Morgan, Lewis Henry
Morse, Jedidiah
Munro, William Bennett
Muzzey, David Saville
Nevins, Allan
Odum, Howard Washington
Olney, Jesse
Parkins, Almon Ernest
Petrie, George
Quillen, Isaac James
Redway, Jacques Wardlaw
Reid, Ira de Augustine
Renner, George Thomas, Jr.
Ridpath, John Clark
Riesman, David
Robinson, James Harvey

Rugg, Harold Ordway
Seybolt, Robert Francis
Sloane, William Milligan
Small, Albion Woodbury
Snedden, David Samuel
Sparks, Jared
Sumner, William Graham
Tarr, Ralph Stockman
Taussig, Frank William
Thompson, Robert Ellis
Tucker, George
Tyler, Moses Coit
Ward, Lester Frank
Wayland, John Walter
Wesley, Edgar Bruce
West, Willis Mason
White, Leonard Dupee
Whittlesey, Derwent Stainthorpe
Wier, Jeanne Elizabeth
Wilson, Howard Eugene
Woodbridge, William Channing
Woodson, Carter Godwin

SPECIAL EDUCATION

Allen, Edward Ellis
Anagnos, Michael
Bell, Alexander Graham
Bettelheim, Bruno
Bogue, Benjamin Nathaniel
Bradford, Edward Hickling
Clerc, Laurent
Currier, Enoch Henry
Ely, Charles Wright
Fay, Edward Allen
Fuller, Sarah
Gallaudet, Edward Miner
Gallaudet, Thomas Hopkins
Garrett, Emma
Goddard, Henry Herbert
Goldstein, Max Aaron
Howe, Samuel Gridley
Irwin, Robert Benjamin
Johnstone, Edward Ransom
Kirk, Samuel Alexander
Larson, Lars Moore
Lord, Asa Dearborn
MacDonald, Arthur

Peet, Harvey Prindle
Peet, Isaac Lewis
Rogers, Harriet Burbank
Wait, William Bell
Wallin, John Edward Wallace
Wilbur, Hervey Backus
Yale, Caroline Ardelia

## TEACHER EDUCATION

Almack, John Conrad
Anderson, Archibald Watson
Armstrong, Wesley Earle
Bagley, William Chandler
Baldwin, Joseph
Balliet, Thomas Minard
Barnard, Henry
Barnes, Earl
Benjamin, Harold Raymond Wayne
Bennion, Milton
Blanton, Annie Webb
Boyden, Albert Gardner
Brackett, Anna Callender
Bradley, Amy Morris
Briggs, Thomas Henry
Brooks, Charles
Brooks, Edward
Brown, Elmer Ellsworth
Brownell, Herbert
Brownell, William Arthur
Brubacher, Abram Royer
Brubacher, John Seiler
Brueckner, Leo John
Burk, Frederic Lister
Burton, William Henry
Butcher, Thomas Walter
Caldwell, Otis William
Calkins, Norman Allison
Camp, David Nelson
Charters, Werrett Wallace
Cherry, Henry Hardin
Colburn, Dana Pond
Colvin, Stephen Sheldon
Cook, John Williston
Cooper, Hermann
Cowles, LeRoy Eugene
Craig, Clara Elizabeth
Cubberly, Elwood Patterson

Dearmont, Washington Strother
De Garmo, Charles
Dexter, Edwin Grant
Dickinson, John Woodbridge
Dougherty, Blanford Barnard
Douglass, Harl Roy
Doyne, John James
Eby, Frederick
Fretwell, Elbert Kirtley
Gates, Noah Putnam
Gordy, John Pancoast
Gruhn, William Theodore
Hagar, Daniel Barnard
Hall, Samuel Read
Hand, Harold Curtis
Hanna, Paul Robert
Hanus, Paul Henry
Hart, Joseph Kinmont
Henzlik, Frank Ernest
Hill, Clyde Milton
Hill, David Spence
Hinsdale, Burke Aaron
Hodgin, Charles Elkanah
Holbrook, Alfred
Hovey, Charles Edward
Johnson, David Bancroft
Kefauver, Grayson Neikirk
Kiehle, David Litchard
Koos, Leonard Vincent
Krüsi, Johann Heinrich Hermann
Lange, Alexis Frederick
Lord, Livingston Chester
Luckey, George Washington Andrew
Lyte, Eliphalet Oram
McCorkle, Samuel Eusebius
McMurry, Charles Alexander
McMurry, Frank Morton
MacVicar, Malcolm
Mahoney, John Joseph
Mann, Horace
Mearns, William Hughes
Monroe, Walter Scott
Monroe, Will Seymour
Morrison, Henry Clinton
Mort, Paul R.
Moten, Lucy Ella
Newell, McFadden Alexander

O'Shea, Michael Vincent
Osuna, Juan Jóse
Owen, William Bishop
Page, David Perkins
Painter, Franklin Verzelius Newton
Parker, Francis Wayland
Parrish, Celestia Susannah
Payne, Bruce Ryburn
Payne, William Harold
Peirce, Cyrus
Phelps, William Franklin
Pittman, Marvin Summers
Rivlin, Harry N.
Roark, Ruric Nevel
Roemer, Joseph
Russell, James Earl
Salisbury, Albert
Saylor, John Galen
Schaeffer, Nathan Christ
Schorling, Raleigh
Seeley, Levi
Sheldon, Edward Austin
Showalter, Noah David
Smith, Bunnie Othanel
Smith, Henry Lester
Spaulding, Frank Ellsworth
Stewart, Joseph Spencer
Stewart, William Mitton
Stoddard, George Dinsmore
Stowell, Thomas Blanchard
Suhrie, Ambrose Leo
Sutton, William Seneca
Tall, Lida Lee
Taylor, Joseph Schimmel
Taylor, William Septimus
Thomson, James Bates
Van Til, William
Wheelock, Lucy
White, Samuel Holmes
Wickersham, James Pyle
Wist, Benjamin Othello
Woodruff, Caroline Salome
Zirbes, Laura

VOCATIONAL, BUSINESS, AND
INDUSTRIAL ARTS EDUCATION
Aderhold, Omer Clyde

Allen, Charles Ricketson
Alvord, Henry Elijah
Atkinson, Alfred
Atwater, Wilbur Olin
Barrett, Janie Porter
Bawden, William Thomas
Belfield, Henry Holmes
Bennett, Charles Alpheus
Berry, Martha McChesney
Bonser, Frederick Gordon
Bryan, Enoch Albert
Bryant, John Collins
Bryant, Ralph Clement
Burnz, Eliza Boardman
Butterfield, Kenyon Leech
Chapman, Paul Wilber
Dabney, Charles William
Davenport, Eugene
Deyoe, George Percy
Fanning, Tolbert
Green, Samuel Bowdlear
Gregg, John Robert
Hart, William Richard
Harvey, Lorenzo Dow
Haynes, Benjamin Rudolph
Hunt, Thomas Forsyth
Johnson, Joseph French
Knapp, Seaman Asahel
Lee, Stephen Dill
Leffingwell, William Henry
Lessenberry, David Daniel
Lomax, Paul Sanford
London, Hoyt Hobson
Markham, Walter Tipton
Miles, Manly
Mumford, Frederick Blackman
Nichols, Frederick George
Norton, John Pitkin
Packard, Silas Sadler
Pitman, Benn
Prosser, Charles Allen
Pugh, Evan
Rice, James Edward
Richards, Charles Russell
Russell, Harry Luman
Schneider, Herman
Selvidge, Robert Washington

Silvius, George Harold
Smith, Payson
Snedden, David Samuel
Soulé, George
Stewart, Joseph Spencer
Stimson, Rufus Whittaker
Struck, Ferdinand Theodore
Taylor, William Septimus
Thompson, Samuel Rankin

Tonne, Herbert Arthur
True, Alfred Charles
Vawter, Charles Erastus
Walker, Francis Amasa
Warner, William Everett
Waters, Henry Jackson
Williston, Arthur Lyman
Woodward, Calvin Milton
Wright, John Calvin

# APPENDIX D:
## CHRONOLOGY OF BIRTH YEARS

**1604**
Eliot, John

**1609**
Dunster, Henry

**1611**
Corlet, Elijah

**1614**
Cheever, Ezekiel

**1639**
Mather, Increase

**1645**
Pierson, Abraham

**1651**
Pastorius, Francis Daniel

**1656**
Blair, James

**1662**
Brattle, William

**1673**
Tennent, William

**1693**
Wigglesworth, Edward

**1696**
Dove, David James
Johnson, Samuel
[1546]

**1698**
Dock, Christopher

**1702**
Greenwood, Isaac

**1703**
Clap, Thomas

**1705**
Alison, Francis

**1706**
Franklin, Benjamin

**1711**
Wheelock, Eleazar

**1713**
Benezet, Anthony

**1714**
Winthrop, John

**1719**
Phillips, John

**1721**
Zeisberger, David

**1722**
Witherspoon, John

**1725**
Caldwell, David
Watteville, Henrietta Benigna Justina
    von Zinzendorf

**1726**

Wythe, George

**1727**

Smith, William
Stiles, Ezra

**1728**

Proud, Robert

**1735**

Cooper, Myles (or 1737)
Morgan, John

**1736**

Shippen, William, Jr.

**1738**

Manning, James

**1740**

Dod, Thaddeus

**1742**

Bard, Samuel

**1743**

Jefferson, Thomas
Pike, Nicholas

**1744**

Marshall, Charles
Reeve, Tapping

**1745**

Murray, Lindley
Rush, Benjamin

**1746**

McCorkle, Samuel Eusebius
Wilson, Peter

**1749**

Doak, Samuel

**1750**

Daboll, Nathan

Smith, Samuel Stanhope

**1752**

Dwight, Timothy
Pearson, Eliphalet
Poor, John
Smith, John

**1753**

Warren, John

**1754**

Wheelock, John

**1756**

Knox, Samuel

**1757**

Bingham, Caleb
Howland, John

**1758**

Webster, Noah

**1759**

Cooper, Thomas

**1760**

Carrick, Samuel

**1761**

Morse, Jedidiah

**1762**

Abbot, Benjamin
Chavis, John (or 1763)
Smith, Nathan

**1764**

Moore, James

**1765**

Adams, Ebenezer
Downey, John

**1766**

Barton, Benjamin Smith

**1767**

Pierce, Sarah

**1768**

Maxcy, Jonathan
Physick, Philip Syng
Wadsworth, James

**1769**

Clinton, De Witt
Duchesne, Rose Philippine
Hayden, Horace H.
Messer, Asa

**1770**

Bethune, Joanna Graham
Gould, James
Kirkland, John Thornton
Mason, John Mitchell
Neef, Francis Joseph Nicholas
Waddel, Moses
Woodhouse, James

**1771**

Davis, Henry
Maclean, John
Picket, Albert

**1772**

Quincy, Josiah

**1773**

Adams, Daniel
Caldwell, Joseph
Day, Jeremiah
Nott, Eliphalet

**1774**

Griscom, John
Seton, Elizabeth Ann Bayley

**1775**

Smith, John Rubens
Tucker, George

**1776**

Eaton, Amos
Lewis, Enoch

**1777**

Bishop, Robert Hamilton
Emerson, Joseph

**1778**

Kingsley, James Luce
Warren, John Collins

**1779**

Brownell, Thomas Church
Farrar, John
Silliman, Benjamin
Story, Joseph
Town, Salem

**1780**

Cleaveland, Parker
Duer, William Alexander
Hall, Willard

**1781**

Gratz, Rebecca
Holley, Horace

**1783**

Cooke, John Esten
Greenleaf, Simon

**1784**

Butler, Edward Mann
Dewey, Chester
Gummere, John
Worcester, Joseph Emerson

**1785**

Clerc, Laurent
Drake, Daniel
Hawley, Gideon
Partridge, Alden
Pierpont, John

Thayer, Sylvanus

**1786**

Greenleaf, Benjamin
Guilford, Nathan
Lindsley, Philip

**1787**

Comstock, John Lee
Frelinghuysen, Theodore
Gallaudet, Thomas Hopkins
Gould, Benjamin Apthorp
Willard, Emma Hart

**1788**

Gibson, William
Holbrook, Josiah

**1789**

Gale, George Washington
Sparks, Jared
Wait, Samuel
Wylie, Andrew

**1790**

Channing, Edward Tyrrell
Cordero y Molina, Rafael
Crozet, Claude
Goodrich, Chauncey Allen
Green, Jacob
Junkin, George
Leonard, Levi Washburn
Peirce, Cyrus
Ruffner, Henry

**1791**

Brown, Goold
Olmsted, Denison
Ticknor, George

**1792**

Finney, Charles Grandison
Fisk, Wilbur
Lord, Nathan
Mason, Lowell

Mitchell, Samuel Augustus
Smith, Daniel B.

**1793**

Bailey, Rufus William
Colburn, Warren
Gilbert, Eliphalet Wheeler
Goodrich, Samuel Griswold
Hitchcock, Edward
Phelps, Almira Hart Lincoln
Richards, William
Spalding, Catherine
Thayer, Gideon French

**1794**

Banister, Zilpah Polly Grant
Peet, Harvey Prindle
Webster, Horace
Woodbridge, William Channing

**1795**

Andrews, Lorrin
Bailey, Ebenezer
Brooks, Charles
Carter, James Gordon
Fowle, William Bentley
Hall, Samuel Read
Lovell, John Epy

**1796**

Follen, Karl (Charles) Theodore
    Christian
Haddock, Charles Brickett
Mann, Horace
Wayland, Francis

**1797**

Andrews, Ethan Allen
Anthon, Charles
Emerson, George Barrell
Hale, Benjamin
Hughes, John Joseph
Lyon, Mary Mason
Newman, Samuel Phillips
Olin, Stephen

Pierce, John Davis
Smyth, William
Wood, George Bacon

**1798**

Alcott, William Andrus
Beck, Charles (Karl)
Davies, Charles
Dunglison, Robley
Guerin, Anne Therese
Olney, Jesse
Parker, Richard Green
Russell, William

**1799**

Alcott, Amos Bronson
Lathrop, John Hiram
Lewis, Samuel
Mahan, Asa
Sherwin, Thomas

**1800**

Beecher, Catharine Esther
Benedict, Erastus Cornelius
Breckinridge, Robert Jefferson
Burton, Warren
Cobb, Lyman
Frost, John
Lieber, Francis
McGuffey, William Holmes
Maclean, John
Peers, Benjamin Orr
Potter, Alonzo
Spencer, Platt Rogers

**1801**

Baldwin, Theron
Howe, Samuel Gridley
Kingsbury, John
Swain, David Lowry
Woolsey, Theodore Dwight

**1802**

Bulkley, John Williams
Dix, Dorothea Lynde
Durant, Henry

Hopkins, Mark
Larrabee, William Clark
Mahan, Dennis Hart
Sears, Barnas
Stowe, Calvin Ellis
Young, Andrew White

**1803**

Abbott, Jacob
Crandall, Prudence
Memminger, Christopher Gustavus
Thomson, James Bates
Young, John Clarke

**1804**

Crary, Isaac Edwin
Frank, Michael
Peabody, Elizabeth Palmer
Pinney, Norman
Rogers, William Barton

**1805**

Armstrong, Richard
Burrowes, Thomas Henry
Bushee, James
Dimitry, Alexander
Fitton, James
Gross, Samuel David
Read, Daniel
Sanders, Charles Walton
Sophocles, Evangelinus Apostolides
Sturtevant, Julian Monson
Tappan, Henry Philip
Turner, Jonathan Baldwin

**1806**

Bache, Alexander Dallas
Green, Lewis Warner
Harris, Chapin Aaron
Hooker, Worthington
Leach, Daniel Dyer
Leeser, Isaac
Mills, Caleb
Morrison, John Irwin
Rauch, Frederick Augustus
Toland, Hugh Huger

## 1807

Abbott, Gorham Dummer
Agassiz, Jean Louis Rodolphe
Alden, Joseph
Cutter, Calvin
Guyot, Arnold Henry
Ray, Joseph
Scott, John Work
Taylor, John Orville
Taylor, Samuel Harvey
Tutwiler, Henry
Woods, Leonard

## 1808

Chapman, John Gadsby
Day, Henry Noble
Dwight, Francis
Hillard, George Stillman
Jewett, Milo Parker
Maupin, Socrates
Smith, Thomas

## 1809

Barnard, Frederick Augustus Porter
Hardey, Mary Aloysia
Kendrick, Asahel Clark
Loughridge, Robert McGill
Peirce, Benjamin
Randall, Samuel Sidwell
West, Charles Edwin

## 1810

Butler, Noble
Crosby, Alpheus
Eells, Cushing
Ewell, Benjamin Stoddert
Fanning, Tolbert
Garland, Landon Cabell
Gray, Asa
Greene, Samuel Stillman
Hart, John Seely
Page, David Perkins
Tyler, William Seymour

## 1811

Baker, Benjamin Franklin

Barnard, Henry
Draper, John William
Galloway, Samuel
Hamlin, Cyrus
Ladd, Azel Parkhurst
McCosh, James
Neumann, John Nepomucene
Payne, Daniel Alexander
Porter, Noah
Potter, Elisha Reynolds, Jr.
Pratt, Orson
Richards, Zalmon

## 1812

Flint, Austin
Haldeman, Samuel Stehman
Smith, Francis Henney
Waddel, John Newton
Wells, William Harvey

## 1813

Atwater, Lyman Hotchkiss
Dana, James Dwight
Gregory, Samuel
Lozier, Clemence Sophia Harned
Minor, John Barbee
Porter, Sarah
Sargent, Epes

## 1814

Goodnow, Isaac Tichenor
Harris, Samuel
Northend, Charles
Raymond, John Howard
Sorin, Edward Frederick
Stone, Lucinda Hinsdale

## 1815

Anderson, Martin Brewer
Bapst, John
Fisher, Ebenezer
Kraus, John
Leigh, Edwin
Marvin, John Gage
Miner, Myrtilla
Orcutt, Hiram
Roberts, Oran Milo

Robinson, Ezekiel Gilman
Van Bokkelen, Libertus
Walker, David Shelby

**1816**

Benton, Thomas Hart
Bradbury, William Batchelder
Gunn, Frederick William
Holbrook, Alfred
Lord, Asa Dearborn
Mortimer, Mary
Rambaut, Mary Lucinda Bonney
Sill, Anna Peck
Silliman, Benjamin, Jr.
Whitworth, George Frederic
Wilson, William Dexter

**1817**

Allyn, Robert
Chapin, Aaron Lucius
Cummings, Joseph
Davis, Nathan Smith
Fairchild, James Harris
Frieze, Henry Simmons
Krüsi, Johann Heinrich Hermann
Northrop, Birdsey Grant
Pendleton, William Kimbrough

**1818**

Agnew, David Hayes
Bishop, Harriet E.
Drisler, Henry
Hill, Thomas
Krüsi, Johann Heinrich Hermann
Mitchell, Maria
Morgan, Lewis Henry
Morgan, William Henry
Philbrick, John Dudley
Rice, Victor Moreau
Valentine, Thomas Weston

**1819**

Andrews, Lorin
Ashley, Samuel Stanford
Atkinson, George Henry
Dodge, Ebenezer
Orr, Gustavus John

Stearns, Eben Sperry
Stillé, Charles Janeway
Wiley, Calvin Henderson
Wise, Isaac Mayer

**1820**

Bonnell, John Mitchell
Camp, David Nelson
Chauvenet, William
Hagar, Daniel Barnard
Holmes, George Frederick
North, Edward
Peck, William Guy
Robertson, William Schenck
Root, George Frederick
Shedd, William Greenough Thayer
Wilbur, Hervey Backus
Zachos, John Celivergos

**1821**

Anderson, John Jacob
Bryant, John Collins
Coppée, Henry
Hadley, James
Harvey, Thomas Wadleigh
Hill, Daniel Harvey
Welch, Adonijah Strong
Youmans, Edward Livingston

**1822**

Agassiz, Elizabeth Cabot Cary
Bartholomew, William Nelson
Bateman, Newton
Calkins, Norman Allison
Craven, Braxton
Dwight, Theodore William
Gregory, John Milton
Harkness, Albert
Johnston, Richard Malcolm
Lindsley, John Berrien
Martin, Alexander
Norton, John Pitkin
Parrish, Edward
Phelps, William Franklin
Pitman, Benn
Revels, Hiram Rhoades
Runkle, John Daniel

## 1823

Allen, Nathaniel Topliffe
Bradley, Amy Morris
Burnz, Eliza Boardman
Chadbourne, Paul Ansel
Colburn, Dana Pond
Leidy, Joseph
Lewis, Dioclesian
McQuaid, Bernard John
Mayo, Amory Dwight
Neill, Edward Duffield
Patterson, James Willis
Perry, William Flake
Sheldon, Edward Austin

## 1824

Bowman, John Bryan
Gillespie, Eliza Maria (Mother Angela)
Hunt, William Morris
Kiddle, Henry
Kirby-Smith, Edmund
Laws, Samuel Spahr
McMynn, John Gibson
Newell, McFadden Alexander
Packard, Sophia B.
Peet, Isaac Lewis
Pickard, Josiah Little
Rickoff, Andrew Jackson
Ruffner, William Henry
Seelye, Julius Hawley
Tappan, Eli Todd
Winchell, Alexander

## 1825

Curry, Jabez Lamar Monroe
Dalton, John Call
Dickinson, John Woodbridge
Hancock, John
Magill, Edward Hicks
March, Francis Andrew
Mills, Susan Lincoln Tolman
Stoddard, John Fair
Valentine, Milton
Welling, James Clarke

Wickersham, James Pyle

## 1826

Battle, Archibald John
Langdell, Christopher Columbus
Miles, Manly
Packard, Silas Sadler
Quackenbos, George Payn

## 1827

Baldwin, Joseph
Bascom, John
Boyden, Albert Gardner
Cooke, Josiah Parsons
Fraser, John
Gibbs, Jonathan C.
Hovey, Charles Edward
Howland, Emily
McGroarty, Susan (Sister Julia)
Norton, Charles Eliot
Smith, Zachariah Frederick
Watson, James Madison

## 1828

Blackburn, William Maxwell
Browne, William Hand
Chamberlain, Joshua Lawrence
Cochran, David Henry
Dwight, Timothy
Hitchcock, Edward
Mason, Luther Whiting
Pugh, Evan
Whitford, William Clarke

## 1829

Angell, James Burrill
Apple, Thomas Gilmore
Cady, Sarah Louise Ensign
Crocker, Lucretia
Eaton, John
Hammond, William Gardiner
Howard, Ada Lydia
Langston, John Mercer
MacVicar, Malcolm
McVicar, Peter
Mason, William
Mowry, William Augustus

Orton, Edward Francis Baxter
Peabody, Selim Hobart
Rogers, Elizabeth Ann
Sprague, Homer Baxter
White, Emerson Elbridge

### 1830

Davis, Noah Knowles
Hunt, Mary Hannah Hanchett (or 1831)
King, William Fletcher
Orton, James
Safford, Anson Peacely-Killen
Swett, John
Whitaker, Ozi William
White, Samuel Holmes

### 1831

Bodley, Rachel Littler
Brooks, Edward
Gildersleeve, Basil Lanneau
Gilman, Daniel Coit
Goff, Milton Browning
Goodwin, William Watson
Hallowell, Anna
Hedges, Cornelius
Hoyt, John Wesley
Hunter, Thomas
Russell, Albert Jonathan
Warren, Samuel Edward

### 1832

Buckham, Matthew Henry
Gates, Noah Putnam
Pollock, Louise Plessner
Sheldon, William Evarts
Vincent, John Heyl
Ware, William Robert
White, Andrew Dickson
Wood, De Volson

### 1833

Andrews, Jane
Collar, William Coe
Comfort, George Fisk
Cooley, LeRoy Clark
Corbin, Joseph Carter
Folwell, William Watts

Hadley, Hiram
Hale, Horace Morrison
Knapp, Seaman Asahel
Larsen, Peter Laurentius
Lee, Stephen Dill
Park, John Rocky
Patterson, James Kennedy
Schurz, Margarethe Meyer
Strong, James Woodward
Swinton, William
Thompson, Samuel Rankin
Warren, William Fairfield

### 1834

Bicknell, Thomas Williams
Boyd, David French
Eliot, Charles William
Howison, George Holmes
Jackson, Sheldon
Joynes, Edward Southey
Northrop, Cyrus
Palmer, Horatio Richmond
Peirce, James Mills
Ritter, Frederic Louis
Rogers, Harriet Burbank
Soulé, George
Tourjée, Eben
Young, Charles Augustus

### 1835

Adams, Charles Kendall
Cooper, Sarah Brown Ingersoll
Coppens, Charles
Harris, William Torrey
Shattuck, Joseph Cummings
Tyler, Moses Coit
Wentworth, George Albert

### 1836

Apgar, Ellis A.
Brackett, Anna Callender
Fuller, Sarah
Greenwood, James Mickleborough
Hailmann, William Nicholas
Henderson, Howard Andrew Millet
Hollingsworth, Orlando Newton
Johnson, Franklin

Kraus-Boelté, Maria
Marble, Albert Prescott
Ogden, Robert Curtis
Payne, William Harold
Powell, William Bramwell
Prang, Mary Amelia Dana Hicks
Sanford, Maria Louise
Steele, Joel Dorman
Thompson, Charles Oliver
Thompson, Hugh Smith
Venable, William Henry

**1837**

Anagnos, Michael
Atherton, George Washington
Belfield, Henry Holmes
Coppin, Fanny Marion Jackson
Gallaudet, Edward Miner
Gilman, Arthur
Grimké, Charlotte L. Forten
Groves, James Henry
Hinsdale, Burke Aaron
Keen, William Williams
Kiehle, David Litchard
Parker, Francis Wayland
Seelye, Laurenus Clark
Ware, Edmund Asa
Woodward, Calvin Milton

**1838**

Adams, Henry Brooks
Beadle, William Henry Harrison
Capen, Elmer Hewitt
Dickey, Sarah Ann
Fairchild, George Thompson
Fernald, Charles Henry
Fuertes, Estevan Antonio
Himes, Charles Francis
Hyatt, Alpheus
Ireland, John
Robinson, Stillman Williams
Ward, Joseph

**1839**

Armstrong, Samuel Chapman
Bancroft, Cecil Franklin Patch
Ely, Charles Wright

Garrett, William Robertson
Goldbeck, Robert
Goodale, George Lincoln
Goodell, Henry Hill
Gove, Aaron Estellus
Hartranft, Chester David
Haygood, Atticus Green
Hostos, Eugenio María de
Keane, John Joseph
Morgan, Thomas Jefferson
Packard, Alpheus Spring, Jr.
Paine, John Knowles
Peirce, Charles (Santiago) Sanders
Raymond, George Lansing
Shafer, Helen Almira
Sunderland, Eliza Jane Read
Thurston, Robert Henry
Tucker, William Jewett
Wait, William Bell
Willard, Frances Elizabeth Caroline

**1840**

Andrews, Eliza Frances
Bowditch, Henry Pickering
Davidson, Thomas
MacAlister, James
McClellan, Henry Brainerd
MacCracken, Henry Mitchell
Pratt, Richard Henry
Raub, Albert Newton
Ridpath, John Clark
Spalding, John Lancaster
Sumner, William Graham
Walker, Francis Amasa

**1841**

Baldwin, James
Corson, Juliet
Hill, Frank Alpine
Johnson, William Woolsey
Putnam, Alice Harvey Whiting
Rice, Fenelon Bird
Richards, Linda (Melinda Ann) Judson
Sartain, Emily
Shaler, Nathaniel Southgate
Sill, Edward Rowland
Smart, James Henry

Tutwiler, Julia Strudwick
Vawter, Charles Erastus
Ward, Lester Frank

**1842**

Jacobi, Mary Corinna Putnam
James, William
Ladd, George Trumball
Lyte, Eliphalet Oram
Palmer, George Herbert
Richards, Ellen Henrietta Swallow
Soldan, Frank Louis
Webb, William Robert

**1843**

Blow, Susan Elizabeth
Fay, Edward Allen
Fillmore, John Comfort
Foster, Thomas Jefferson
Griffis, William Elliot
King, Charles Francis
O'Gorman, Thomas
Pepper, William
Ricker, Nathan Clifford
Salisbury, Albert
Trowbridge, John
Vaile, Edwin Orlando

**1844**

Alvord, Henry Elijah
Andrews, Elisha Benjamin
Atwater, Wilbur Olin
Avery, Elroy McKendree
Burgess, John William
Cook, John Williston
Crane, Thomas Frederick
Eakins, Thomas
Hall, Granville Stanley
Sewall, May Eliza Wright Thompson
Skinner, Charles Rufus
Thompson, Robert Ellis
Tomlins, William Lawrence

**1845**

Bessey, Charles Edwin
Bryant, Joseph Decatur
Day, James Roscoe

Goucher, John Franklin
Hine, Charles Daniel
Rice, William North
Winship, Albert Edward
Young, Ella Flagg

**1846**

Ames, James Barr
Craig, Oscar John
Elliott, Aaron Marshall
Garrett, Emma
Hewett, Waterman Thomas
Myers, Phillip Van Ness
Oldberg, Oscar
Pickering, Edward Charles
Poland, William Carey
Remsen, Ira
Stowell, Thomas Blanchard

**1847**

Bardeen, Charles William
Bell, Alexander Graham
Cain, William
Conaty, Thomas James
Ellis, Alston
Houston, Edwin James
Mullany, Patrick Francis (Brother
    Azarias)
Sanders, Daniel Jackson
Seeley, Levi
Stoddard, Francis Hovey
White, John Stuart

**1848**

Baker, James Hutchins
Bradford, Edward Hickling
Brown, LeRoy Decatur
Councill, William Hooper
Draper, Andrew Sloan
Duveneck, Frank
Elson, Louis Charles
Glenn, Gustavus Richard
Harvey, Lorenzo Dow
Homans, Amy Morris
Miller, Leslie William
Quackenbos, John Duncan
Seerley, Homer Horatio

Yale, Caroline Ardelia

**1849**

Byerly, William Elwood
Chase, William Merritt
Clapp, Cornelia Maria
Comstock, John Henry
Currier, Enoch Henry
De Garmo, Charles
Dutton, Samuel Train
Hale, William Gardner
Harrison, Elizabeth
Judson, Harry Pratt
Paterson, William Burns
Redway, Jacques Wardlaw
Roberts, Robert Jeffries
Rorer, Sarah Tyson Heston
Sachs, Julius
Sargent, Dudley Allen
Schaeffer, Nathan Christ
Shinn, Josiah Hazen
Stetson, William Wallace
Tompkins, Arnold

**1850**

Adams, Herbert Baxter
Barnes, Mary Downing Sheldon
Brown, Hallie Quinn
Davis, William Morris
Hartwell, Edward Mussey
Lanman, Charles Rockwell
Meserve, Charles Francis
Reed, David Allen
Sabin, Ellen Clara
Sloane, William Milligan
Stimson, John Ward
Stubbs, Joseph Edward
Welch, William Henry

**1851**

Adler, Felix
Birge, Edward Asahiel
Cady, Calvin Brainerd
Coulter, John Merle
Dewey, Melvil
Frissell, Hollis Burke
Gault, Franklin Benjamin

Gordy, John Pancoast
Jordan, David Starr
Kirk, John Robert
Lord, Livingston Chester
Moten, Lucy Ella
Powers, James Knox
Richardson, Charles Francis
Sheats, William Nicholas
Stanley, Albert Augustus
Stryker, Melancthon Woolsey
Wells, Webster

**1852**

Balliet, Thomas Minard
Cooper, Oscar Henry
Davidson, Charles
Davidson, Hannah Amelia Noyes
Halsted, William Stewart
Mace, William Harrison
Mackenzie, James Cameron
McMaster, John Bach
Matthews, James Brander
Maxwell, William Henry
Merrifield, Webster
Minot, Charles Sedgwick
Painter, Franklin Verzelius Newton
Scarborough, William Sanders

**1853**

Boyd, David Ross
Buttrick, Wallace
Cook, Albert Stanburrough
Forbes, John Franklin
Goetschius, Percy
Halsted, George Bruce
Hanchett, Henry Granger
Hart, William Richard
Jesse, Richard Henry
Johnson, Joseph French
Page, Inman Edward
Parrish, Celestia Susannah
Pattee, Fred Lewis
Rogers, Henry Wade
Thwing, Charles Franklin
True, Alfred Charles
Weed, Ella
Weeks, Thomas Edwin

Wright, Richard Robert

**1854**

Blaker, Eliza Ann Cooper
Boyd, Thomas Duckett
Carrington, William Thomas
Chadwick, George Whitfield
Comstock, Anna Botsford
Elson, William Harris
Ely, Richard Theodore
Fairchild, Edward Thomson
Frost, William Goodell
Gordy, Wilbur Fisk
Hanna, Delphine
Hart, Albert Bushnell
Kraus, Mother M. Seraphine (Mary
  Katharine)
Laney, Lucy Craft
Leipziger, Henry Marcus
Parsons, Frank
Small, Albion Woodbury
Tappan, Eva March
Thomas, Calvin
Wheeler, Benjamin Ide

**1855**

Brigham, Albert Perry
Bryan, Enoch Albert
Burnham, William Henry
Collitz, Hermann
Comstock, George Cary
Crane, Julia Ettie
Dabney, Charles William
Fairchild, Mary Salome Cutler
Giddings, Franklin Henry
Hanus, Paul Henry
Jackman, Wilbur Samuel
James, Edmund Janes
Luckey, George Washington Andrew
Palmer, Alice Elvira Freeman
Richman, Julia
Rusby, Henry Hurd
Thompson, William Oxley
Wendell, Barrett

**1856**

Baldwin, Maria Louise

Bruce, William Herschel
Chittenden, Russell Henry
Davenport, Eugene
Dillard, James Hardy
Dodge, Grace Hoadley
Gulliver, Julia Henrietta
Hadley, Arthur Twining
Harper, William Rainey
Hazard, Caroline
Johnson, David Bancroft
Larson, Lars Moore
Lowell, Abbott Lawrence
MacDonald, Arthur
Poteat, William Louis
Taylor, Joseph Schimmel
Trueblood, Thomas Clarkson
Van Dyke, John Charles
Washington, Booker Taliaferro
Wiggin, Kate Douglas
Wilson, Thomas Woodrow
Young, Clark Montgomery

**1857**

Cooley, Edwin Gilbert
Dorsey, Susan Almira Miller
Dow, Arthur Wesley
Farmer, Fannie Merritt
Gantvoort, Arnold Johann
Jacoby, Henry Sylvester
McMurry, Charles Alexander
Murphy, John Benjamin
Noyes, William Albert
Osborn, Henry Fairfield
Peabody, Endicott
Pritchett, Henry Smith
Rice, Joseph Mayer
Shahan, Thomas Joseph
Swain, Joseph
Thomas, Martha Carey
Van Hise, Charles Richard
West, Willis Mason
Wheelock, Lucy

**1858**

Bailey, Liberty Hyde
Bennett, Charles Edwin
Boas, Franz

Bryan, Anna E.
Doyne, John James
Dyer, Franklin Benjamin

Gayley, Charles Mills
Hodgin, Charles Elkanah
Hyde, William DeWitt
Kendall, Calvin Noyes
Keyes, Charles Henry
Lutkin, Peter Christian
McCormick, Samuel Black
Mechem, Floyd Russell
Nutting, Mary Adelaide
Schelling, Felix Emanuel
Smith, Eleanor
Talbot, Marion
Wolfe, Harry Kirke

### 1859

Aycock, Charles Brantley
Bates, Katharine Lee
Burgess, Theodore Chalon
Cajori, Florian
Campbell, Douglas Houghton
Damrosch, Frank Heino
Dearmont, Washington Strother
Dewey, John
Dudley, James Benson
Farnsworth, Charles Hubert
Frye, Alexis Everett
Green, Samuel Bowdlear
Halleck, Reuben Post
Jenne, James Nathaniel
Kirkland, James Hampton
Roark, Ruric Nevel
Smith, Henry Louis
Stewart, William Mitton
Strong, Frank
Taussig, Frank William

### 1860

Ahern, Mary Eileen
Anderson, William Gilbert
Bevier, Isabel
Bishop, John Remsen
Brackett, Jeffrey Richardson
Bryan, William Lowe
Butler, Marie Joseph

Case, Charles Orlando
Cattell, James McKeen
Chambers, Henry Edward
Curme, George Oliver
Hyer, Robert Stewart
McIver, Charles Duncan
Norton, Mary Alice Peloubet
Penniman, James Hosmer
Pirsson, Louis Valentine
Robb, Isabel Adams Hampton
Smith, David Eugene
Sutton, William Seneca
Thach, Charles Coleman
Woolman, Mary Raphael Schenck

### 1861

Alderman, Edwin Anderson
Allen, Edward Ellis
Baldwin, James Mark
Barnes, Earl
Brown, Elmer Ellsworth
Campbell, Prince Lucien
Cheyney, Edward Potts
Dann, Hollis Ellsworth
Fess, Simeon Davidson
Haley, Margaret Angela
Hebard, Grace Raymond
Hibben, John Grier
Kinley, David
Laird, Warren Powers
Lawson, Andrew Cowper
Murlin, Lemuel Herbert
Pace, Edward Aloysius
Penny, George Barlow
Taft, Horace Dutton

### 1862

Allen, Charles Ricketson
Bradford, Mary Carroll Craig
Brown, Alice Van Vechten
Brownell, Herbert
Brumbaugh, Martin Grove
Burk, Frederic Lister
Butler, Nicholas Murray
Claxton, Philander Priestley
Coe, George Albert
Cotton, Fassett Allen

Cross, Anson Kent
Cross, Wilbur Lucius
Evans, Lawton Bryan
Fairclough, Henry Rushton
Goode, John Paul
Grandgent, Charles Hall
Hunt, Thomas Forsyth
Joyner, James Yadkin
Kirkpatrick, Edwin Asbury
Lange, Alexis Frederick
McMurry, Frank Morton
Posse, Nils
Shields, Thomas Edward
Talmage, James Edward
Trent, William Peterfield
Weir, Irene
Wiener, Leo

**1863**

Adler, Cyrus
Andrews, Charles McLean
Calkins, Mary Whiton
Carpenter, George Rice
Collitz, Klara Hechtenberg
Finley, John Huston
Grossmann, Louis
Jefferson, Mark Sylvester William
Kerr, William Jasper
Lodge, Gonzalez
McCrorey, Henry Lawrence
Mezes, Sidney Edward
Miller, Kelly
Monroe, Will Seymour
Orton, Edward, Jr.
Parker, Horatio William
Robinson, James Harvey
Stewart, Joseph Spencer
Thomas, Augustus Orloff
Woolley, Mary Emma

**1864**

Bailey, Henry Turner
Barrows, Anna
Bennett, Charles Alpheus
Bowen, Wilbur Pardon
Cherry, Henry Hardin
Crabtree, James William

Dewey, Henry Bingham
Johnson, Marietta Louise Pierce
Kellas, Eliza
Merrill, Helen Abbot
Mitchell, Samuel Chiles
Myers, George William
Pendleton, Ellen Fitz
Russell, James Earl
Smith, Charles Alfonso
Tapper, Thomas
Tarr, Ralph Stockman
Van Rensselaer, Martha
Williams, Walter
Wilson, Lucy Langdon Williams
Witherspoon, John Alexander

**1865**

Babbitt, Irving
Barrett, Janie Porter
Breasted, James Henry
Brittain, Marion Luther
Crabbe, John Grant
Faust, Julius Isaac
Gulick, Luther Halsey
Henri, Robert
Kimball, Dexter Simpson
Manly, John Matthews
Munford, Mary Cooke Branch
Phelps, William Lyon
Rice, James Edward
Richards, Charles Russell
Sharp, Katharine Lucinda
Slagle, Robert Lincoln
Waters, Henry Jackson
Wilkinson, Robert Shaw
Wood, Thomas Denison
Young, Jacob William Albert

**1866**

Abercrombie, John William
Baker, George Pierce
Berry, Martha McChesney
Breckinridge, Sophonisba Preston
Davenport, Charles Benedict
Dobbs, Ella Victoria
Finegan, Thomas Edward
Flexner, Abraham

Gillette, John Morris
Goddard, Henry Herbert
Goodrich, Annie Warburton
Guthe, Karl Eugen
Hunt, Henry Alexander
Linville, Henry Richardson
McCurdy, James Huff
Mannes, David
Merrill, George Arthur
Meyer, Adolf
O'Harra, Cleophas Cisney
O'Shea, Michael Vincent
Owen, William Bishop
Petrie, George
Seashore, Carl Emil
Spaulding, Frank Ellsworth
Temple, Alice
Woodruff, Caroline Salome
Woods, Albert Fred
Wulling, Frederick John

**1867**

Bancroft, Jessie Hubbell
Bralley, Francis Marion
Burns, James Aloysius
Butcher, Thomas Walter
Eggleston, Joseph Dupuy, Jr.
Few, William Preston
Fisher, Irving
Gregg, John Robert
Hills, Elijah Clarence
Johnson, Henry
Keppel, Mark
McKenzie, Robert Tait
Moton, Robert Russa
Pratt, Caroline
Stone, John Charles
Titchener, Edward Bradford
Wald, Lillian D.
Woodbridge, Frederick James Eugene

**1868**

Adams, Romanzo
Betts, George Herbert
Birge, Edward Bailey
Butterfield, Kenyon Leech
Cubberly, Elwood Patterson

Dexter, Edwin Grant
Dodge, Richard Elwood
Downing, Elliot Rowland
DuBois, William Edward Burghardt
Hatcher, Orie Latham
Hill, Patty Smith
Hope, John
Mather, Frank Jewett, Jr.
Miller, Edwin Lillie
Millikan, Robert Andrews
Mumford, Frederick Blackman
Nash, George Williston
Pettit, Katherine Rhoda
Sargent, Walter
Snedden, David Samuel
Stimson, Rufus Whittaker
Whitfield, Henry Lewis
Williston, Arthur Lyman

**1869**

Angell, James Rowland
Aswell, James Benjamin
Brandenburg, William Aaron
Brooks, Stratton Duluth
Caldwell, Otis William
Colvin, Stephen Sheldon
Graves, Frank Pierrepont
Hamerschlag, Arthur Acton
Lindley, Ernest Hiram
McVey, Frank LeRond
Mannes, Clara Damrosch
Marlatt, Abby Lillian
Merriam, John Campbell
Monroe, Paul
Neilson, William Allan
Scott, Walter Dill
Showalter, Noah David
Sisson, Edward Octavius
Smith, Harold Babbitt
Soares, Theodore Gerald
Wheatley, William Alonzo
Woodworth, Robert Sessions

**1870**

Bennion, Milton
Blanton, Annie Webb
Bogle, Sarah Comly Norris

Brubacher, Abram Royer
Dougherty, Blanford Barnard
Duggan, Stephen Pierce
Goldstein, Max Aaron
Hetherington, Clark Wilson
Hosic, James Fleming
Johnstone, Edward Ransom
Levy, Florence Nightingale
Lillie, Frank Rattray
Murphree, Albert Alexander
Muzzey, David Saville
Owre, Alfred
Pound, Roscoe
Stevens, Georgia Lydia
Wier, Jeanne Elizabeth

**1871**

Axline, George Andrew
Brooks, Eugene Clyde
Christiansen, Fredrik Melius
Davis, Calvin Olin
Davis, Jesse Buttrick
Dinwiddie, Albert Bledsoe
Earhart, Will
Jones, Arthur Julius
Kilpatrick, William Heard
McDougall, William
Moore, Ernest Carroll
Morrison, Henry Clinton
Perrin, Ethel
Prosser, Charles Allen
Sabin, Florence Rena
Washburn, Margaret Floy

**1872**

Atwood, Wallace Walter
Butler, Howard Crosby
Colton, Elizabeth Avery
Fiske, George Walter
Meiklejohn, Alexander
Meriam, Junius Lathrop
Pillsbury, Walter Bowers
Pound, Louise
Schneider, Herman
Selvidge, Robert Washington
Sibley, Frederick Hubbard
Wayland, John Walter

**1873**

Alexander, Hartley Burr
Becker, Carl Lotus
Bleyer, Willard Grosvenor
Bode, Boyd Henry
Cook, Albert Samuel
Coolidge, Julian Lowell
Craig, Clara Elizabeth
Dykema, Peter William
Fitz-Gerald, John Driscoll, II
Ford, Jeremiah Denis Matthias
Hill, David Spence
Hocking, William Ernest
Jones, Thomas Jesse
Judd, Charles Hubbard
McHugh, Anna (Antonia)
Preston, Josephine Corliss
Smith, Payson
Tall, Lida Lee
Wagner, Jonathan Howard

**1874**

Bagley, William Chandler
Baker, Samuel Aaron
Beard, Charles Austin
Bigelow, Harry Augustus
Courtis, Stuart Appleton
Eby, Frederick
Elliott, Edward Charles
Fleming, Walter Lynwood
Greenlaw, Edwin Almiron
Holland, Ernest Otto
Horne, Herman Harrell
Johnson, Alvin Saunders
Kingsley, Clarence Darwin
Merriam, Charles Edward
Payne, Bruce Ryburn
Pearce, Richard Mills, Jr.
Rose, Mary Davies Schwartz
Schevill, Rudolph
Suhrie, Ambrose Leo
Thorndike, Edward Lee
Wirt, William Albert
Woolley, Helen Bradford Thompson

**1875**

Allen, Arch Turner

Bawden, William Thomas
Bethune, Mary McLeod
Bonser, Frederick Gordon
Boynton, Percy Holmes
Charters, Werrett Wallace
Coffman, Lotus Delta
Gruenberg, Benjamin Charles
Keppel, Frederick Paul
McConathy, Osbourne
Mearns, William Hughes
Miller, Paul Gerard
Munro, William Bennett
Proctor, William Martin
Shepard, James Edward
Stewart, Cora Wilson
Suzzallo, Henry
Wilbur, Ray Lyman
Woodson, Carter Godwin

**1876**

Blunt, Katharine
Bobbitt, John Franklin
Comstock, Ada Louise
Eisenhart, Luther Pfahler
Gage, Lucy
Graham, Edward Kidder
Hart, Joseph Kinmont
Hedrick, Earle Raymond
Huntington, Ellsworth
Leffingwell, William Henry
Smith, Henry Lester
Strayer, George Drayton
Wallin, John Edward Wallace
Whipple, Guy Montrose
Wilson, Guy Mitchell
Wilson, Louis Round
Wright, John Calvin

**1877**

Barrows, Alice Prentice
Briggs, Thomas Henry
Bryant, Ralph Clement
Burchenal, Elizabeth
Douglass, Mabel Smith
Gildersleeve, Virginia Crocheron
Hopkins, Ernest Martin

Jessup, Walter Albert
Kent, Roland Grubb
Norsworthy, Naomi
Patri, Angelo
Reinhardt, Aurelia Isabel Henry
Terman, Lewis Madison
Williamson, Charles Clarence
Winslow, Charles-Edward Amory

**1878**

Bowman, Isaiah
Bunnell, Charles Ernest
Coleman, Satis Narrona Barton
Fretwell, Elbert Kinley
Gardner, Helen
Henderson, Lawrence Joseph
Hill, Howard Copeland
Lee, James Melvin
Morgan, Arthur Ernest
Nichols, Frederick George
Richardson, Leon Burr
Stewart, Isabel Maitland
Thomas, Frank Waters
Warshaw, Jacob
Watson, John Broadus

**1879**

Atkinson, Alfred
Ayres, Leonard Porter
Bestor, Arthur Eugene
Boyden, Frank Learoyd
Cushman, Frank
Erskine, John
Foster, William Trufant
Hughes, Ray Osgood
Hunter, Frederick Maurice
Inglis, Alexander James
Marshall, Leon Carroll
Parkins, Almon Ernest
Young, John Wesley

**1880**

Archer, Gleason Leonard
Aydelotte, Frank
Brownson, Josephine Van Dyke
Cowles, LeRoy Eugene
Cowling, Donald John

Espinosa, Aurelio Macedonio
Freeman, Frank Nugent
Gesell, Arnold
Good, Harry Gehman
Griffith, Emily
Hale, Florence Maria
Hendrix, Herman Elert
Mahoney, John Joseph
Molloy, Mary Aloysius
Veblen, Oswald
Weigle, Luther Allan
Wood, William Christopher

**1881**

Bernard, Luther Lee
Cobb, Stanwood
Gruenberg, Sidonie Matsner
Kandel, Isaac Leon
Koos, Leonard Vincent
McConnell, Wallace Robert
Newcomb, John Lloyd
Reavis, William Claude
Snavely, Guy Everett
Sturtevant, Sarah Martha

**1882**

Bogue, Benjamin Nathaniel
Brawley, Benjamin Griffith
Crawford, James Pyle Wickersham
Dett, Robert Nathaniel
Engelhardt, Nickolaus Louis
Gehrkens, Karl Wilson
Harrington, Harry Franklin
Hayes, Carlton Joseph Huntley
Heathcote, Charles William
Hetzel, Ralph Dorn
Magruder, Frank Abbott
Monroe, Walter Scott
Newlon, Jesse Homer
Pittman, Marvin Summers
Samaroff, Olga
Schlesinger, Hermann Irving
Scott, Miriam Finn
Tigert, John James

**1883**

Allyn, Harriet May

Almack, John Conrad
Baker, Edna Dean
Brown, Charlotte Hawkins
Gropius, Walter Adolf
Irwin, Robert Benjamin
Jones, Gilbert Haven
Kent, Raymond Asa
Porter, Arthur Kingsley
Reeve, William David
Robinson, Frederick Bertrand
Wheeler, Anna Johnson Pell

**1884**

Arbuthnot, May Hill
Birkhoff, George David
Farnum, Royal Bailey
Fitzpatrick, Edward Augustus
Harris, Franklin Stewart
Hull, Clark Leonard
Jones, Lawrence Clifton
Kelley, Truman Lee
Laubach, Frank Charles
Myers, Garry Cleveland
Odum, Howard Washington
Osuna, Juan Jóse
Roemer, Joseph
Snyder, Franklyn Bliss
Strong, Edward Kellogg, Jr.
Woody, Clifford
Zirbes, Laura

**1885**

Collins, Mauney Douglass
DuShane, Donald
Englehardt, Fred
Gray, William Scott
Hill, Clyde Milton
Immel, Ray Keeslar
Klapper, Paul
Leonard, Robert Josselyn
Markham, Walter Tipton
Revel, Bernard
Ryan, Will Carson, Jr.
Taylor, William Septimus
Tippett, James Sterling
Wright, Arthur Davis
Zook, George Frederick

## 1886

Boring, Edwin Garrigues
Cloud, Henry Roe
Eells, Walter Crosby
Givens, Willard Earl
Graham, Frank Porter
Henderson, Lester Dale
Hollingworth, Leta Anna Stetter
Kitson, Harry Dexter
Knight, Edgar Wallace
Lee, Mabel
Locke, Alain LeRoy
McCloy, Charles Harold
Mies van der Rohe, Ludwig
Nash, Jay Bryan
Rugg, Harold Ordway
Russell, Harry Luman
Struck, Ferdinand Theodore
Williams, Jesse Feiring

## 1887

Benedict, Ruth Fulton
Bloomfield, Leonard
Case, Adelaide Teague
Compton, Karl Taylor
Covello, Leonard
Krey, August Charles
MacCaughey, Vaughan
Madeleva, Sister Mary (Mary Evaline
  Wolff)
Murchison, Carl Allanmore
Parkhurst, Helen
Schorling, Raleigh
Studebaker, John Ward
Thurstone, Louis Leon

## 1888

Arny, Clara Maude Brown
Bryson, Lyman Lloyd
Cutler, Elliott Carr
Davis, John Warren
Dickinson, George Sherman
Gowan, Mary Olivia
Leonard, Sterling Andrus
Pressey, Sidney Leavitt

Rice, John Andrew
Rice, Thurman Brooks
Seyboldt, Robert Francis
Sinnott, Edmund Ware

## 1889

Barnes, Harry Elmer
Carpenter, William Weston
Counts, George Sylvester
Dodds, Harold Willis
Edwards, Newton
Hyde, Grant Milnor
Kauffman, Treva Erdine
Long, Oren Ethelbirt
Mitchell, Elmer Dayton
Moehlman, Arthur Bernard
Patterson, Edwin Wilhite
Washburne, Carleton Wolsey
Wist, Benjamin Othello
Wriston, Henry Merritt

## 1890

Alberty, Harold Bernard
Brueckner, Leo John
Burton, William Henry
Cartwright, Morse Adams
Gates, Arthur Irving
Johnson, Mordecai Wyatt
Leigh, Robert Devore
Lomax, Paul Sanford
Nash, Mell Achilles
Nevins, Allan
Putnam, Rex
Russell, William Fletcher
Smith, Nila Banton
Trabue, Marion Rex
Ulich, Robert
Whittlesey, Derwent Stainthorpe

## 1891

Carmichael, Oliver Cromwell
Chapman, Paul Wilber
Cocking, Walter Dewey
Demiashkevich, Michael John
Maddy, Joseph Edgar
Melby, Ernest Oscar
Sproul, Robert Gordon

Wesley, Charles Harris
Wesley, Edgar Bruce
White, Leonard Dupee

## 1892

Barr, Arvil Sylvester
Compton, Arthur Holly
Douglass, Harl Roy
Gammage, Grady
Holzinger, Karl John
McKown, Harry Charles
Panofsky, Erwin
Paterson, Donald Gildersleeve
Schweickhard, Dean Merrill
Wheeler, Raymond Holder

## 1893

Axtelle, George Edward
Benjamin, Harold Raymond Wayne
Carmichael, Omer
Conant, James Bryant
Harap, Henry
Henzlik, Frank Ernest
Johnson, Charles Spurgeon
Mursell, James Lockhart
Simpson, Roy E.
Smith, Dora Valentine
Symonds, Percival Mallon

## 1894

Ainsworth, Dorothy Sears
Caliver, Ambrose
Frazier, Edward Franklin
Hullfish, Henry Gordon
Johnson, Earl Shepard
Mort, Paul R.
Shuster, George Nauman
Tewksbury, Donald George
Van Doren, Mark

## 1895

Brownell, William Arthur
Cassidy, Rosalind
Cooper, Hermann
English, John Colin
Gamoran, Emmanuel

Hughes, William Leonard
Mays, Benjamin Elijah
Morphet, Edgar Leroy
Strang, Ruth May
Wilson, Atwood Sylvester

## 1896

Brigance, William Norwood
Casteñada, Carlos Eduardo
Grace, Alonzo Gaskell
Hanson, Howard Harold
Haydon, Glen
Lessenberry, David Daniel
Perrin, Porter Gale

## 1897

Allport, Gordon Willard
Bailey, Thomas David
Barr, Frank Stringfellow
Curti, Merle Eugene
Good, Carter Victor
Haynes, Benjamin Rudolph
Henderson, Algo Donmyer
Humphrey, George Duke
Meyer, Adolphe Erich
Steinhaus, Arthur H.
Stoddard, George Dinsmore
Van Dusen, Henry Pitney
Warner, William Everett

## 1898

Brubacher, John Seiler
Carmichael, Leonard
De Vane, William Clyde
Scates, Douglas Edgar
Witty, Paul Andrew

## 1899

Aderhold, Omer Clyde
Armstrong, Wesley Earl
Chambers, Merritt Madison
Eisenhower, Milton Stover
Hutchins, Robert Maynard
Sachar, Abram Leon
Wahlquist, John Thomas
Wanamaker, Pearl Anderson

**1900**

Clement, Rufus Early
Dale, Edgar
Hamrin, Shirley Austin
Havighurst, Robert James
Kefauver, Grayson Neikirk
London, Hoyt Hobson
Renner, George Thomas, Jr.
Traxler, Arthur Edwin
Williamson, Edmund Griffith

**1901**

Carr, William George
Caswell, Hollis Leland
Deyoe, George Percy
Gideonse, Harry David
Hand, Harold Curtis
Hodge, Oliver
Johnson, Palmer Oliver
Lindquist, Everet Franklin
Lloyd-Jones, Esther McDonald
McConnell, Thomas Raymond
Oberteuffer, Delbert
Reid, Ira de Augustine
Weeks, Ila Delbert
Wilson, Howard Eugene
Wittkower, Rudolf

**1902**

Commager, Henry Steele
Eurich, Alvin Christian
Hanna, Paul Robert
Hook, Sidney
Jayne, Clarence D.
Jersild, Arthur Thomas
McGrath, Earl James
Rogers, Carl Ransom
Saylor, John Galen
Taba, Hilda
Tyler, Ralph Winfred
Wells, Herman B.
Wrenn, Charles Gilbert

**1903**

Bettelheim, Bruno
Betts, Emmett Albert
Chandler, Joe Albert
De Boer, John James

Osborne, Estelle Massey Riddle
Shera, Jesse Hauk
Smith, Bunnie Othanel
Viguers, Ruth Hill

**1904**

Bond, Horace Mann
Brameld, Theodore Burghard Hurt
Calderone, Mary Steichen
Gruhn, William Theodore
Heald, Henry Townley
Hilgard, Ernest Ropriquet
Kirk, Samuel Alexander
Oppenheimer, J. Robert
Rivlin, Harry N.
Sammartino, Peter
Shores, Louis
Skinner, Burrhus Frederic
Squires, James Duane
Tonne, Herbert Arthur

**1905**

Anderson, Archibald Watson
Broudy, Harry Samuel
Campa, Arthur Leon
Henry, David Dodds

**1906**

Glass, Hiram Bentley
Griswold, Alfred Whitney
Hayakawa, Samuel Ichiye
Powell, Lawrence Clark
Sanchez, George Isidore
Sterling, John Ewart Wallace

**1907**

Rosskopf, Myron Frederick

**1908**

Benne, Kenneth Dean
Lancour, Adlore Harold
Maslow, Abraham Harold
Silvius, George Harold

**1909**

Quillen, Isaac James
Riesman, David

Sanford, Robert Nevitt

**1910**

Butts, Robert Freeman
Clapp, Margaret
Feder, Daniel Dunn
Fischer, John Henry

**1911**

Allen, James Edward, Jr.
Kerr, Clark
Van Til, William

**1912**

Foshay, Arthur Wellesley
Watson, Fletcher Guard

**1913**

Brickman, William Wolfgang
Cottingham, Harold Fred
Read, Gerald Howard
Travers, Robert Morris William
Wiles, Kimball

**1914**

McMurrin, Sterling Moss
Taylor, Harold Alexander

**1925**

Beberman, Max

**N.A.**

Priestley, James

# APPENDIX E:
## IMPORTANT DATES IN
## AMERICAN EDUCATION

1635  Boston Latin Grammar School established.
1636  Harvard College founded.
1642  Massachusetts law requiring education of children.
1647  Massachusetts law providing for the establishment of schools.
c. 1650  Ezekiel Cheever's *Accidence*, Latin grammar, published.
1690  *New England Primer* had been published.
1693  College of William and Mary established.
1701  Yale College established.
1702  First schools established by the Society for the Propagation of the Gospel in Foreign Parts.
1729  Isaac Greenwood published the first American arithmetic book.
1746  College of New Jersey (later, Princeton University) founded.
1749  University of Pennsylvania established.
1751  Benjamin Franklin established the first American academy.
1754  King's College (later Columbia College) established.
1765  John Morgan established the first school of medicine.
1779  First professorship of law established at the College of William and Mary.
1781  Phillips Academy established in Andover, Massachusetts.
1783  Noah Webster's *Spelling Book* published.
1784  Jedidiah Morse wrote *Geography Made Easy*.
1784  Tapping Reeve established a law school in Litchfield, Connecticut.
1786  First Sunday school established in Hancock County, Virginia.
1802  First federal land grant made to Ohio.
1805  Free School Society of New York founded.
1806  Lancastrian montorial school established in New York City.
1809  Elizabeth Ann Bayley Seton founded the order of the Sisters of Charity of St. Joseph.
1811  Albert Picket published the first educational periodical.
1812  New York state established the office of superintendent of the common schools.
1816  Infant school established in Boston, Massachusetts.
1817  Thomas Hopkins Gallaudet founded the first American school for the deaf in Hartford, Connecticut.
1819  Dartmouth College case decision.
1819  University of Virginia founded.
1821  First high school established in Boston, Massachusetts.
1823  Samuel Read Hall established a normal school near Concord, Vermont.
1826  First lyceum formed in Massachusetts.
1827  Massachusetts law required establishment of high schools.
1829  Samuel Read Hall's *Lectures on Schoolkeeping* published.

1832  Samuel Gridley Howe established in Boston, Massachusetts, a school for the blind that later became the Perkins Institute.
1837  Horace Mann became secretary of the Massachusetts Board of Education.
1837  Mary Lyon founded Mount Holyoke College.
1837  Calvin E. Stowe's *Report on Elementary Instruction in Europe* published.
1838  Henry Barnard became secretary to the Connecticut Board of Education.
1839  First state normal school established in Lexington, Massachusetts.
1839  Henry Barnard organized the first teacher institute in Connecticut.
1845  State teachers' associations organized in Rhode Island, New York, and Massachusetts.
1847  David P. Page's *Theory and Practice of Teaching* published.
1848  Class for idiots established in Boston, Massachusetts.
1851  Massachusetts School for the Idiotic and Feeble-Minded established.
1852  First compulsory school laws passed in Massachusetts.
1856  Margaretha Schurz established a German kindergarten in Milwaukee, Wisconsin.
1857  National Teachers' Association (later, National Education Association) founded.
1857  Columbia Institute for the Deaf (later, Gallaudet College) founded.
1860  Elizabeth Peabody established the first English kindergarten in Boston, Massachusetts.
1861  Edward A. Sheldon opened the Oswego (New York) Normal School.
1862  Morrill Act passed establishing land grant colleges.
1867  Howard University established in Washington, D.C.
1867  National Department of Education (later, United States Office of Education) established.
1872  Kalamazoo (Michigan) case established taxation for other than elementary education.
1873  Susan Blow opened the first public-school kindergarten in St. Louis, Missouri.
1874  John H. Vincent established the Chautauqua (New York) Institution.
1879  Calvin M. Woodward established the Manual Training High School at Washington University in St. Louis, Missouri.
1881  Booker T. Washington appointed head of the Tuskegee (Alabama) Normal and Industrial Institute.
1888  G. Stanley Hall became the first president of Clark University.
1889  William T. Harris became the United States Commissioner of Education.
1890  J. McKeen Cattell wrote *Mental Tests and Measurement*.
1892  National Herbartian Society (later, National Society for the Study of Education) established.
1897  National Congress of Parents and Teachers founded.
1906  Carnegie Foundation for the Advancement of Teaching established.
1908  Frank Parsons founded the Boston Vocational Bureau.
1909  First junior high school established at Berkeley, California.
1909  First remedial speech class held in New York City.
1910  First junior college established at Fresno, California.
1911  School surveys initiated at Montclair, New Jersey.

1913 Bureau of educational research established in New York City.
1914 Smith-Lever Act supported agricultural education.
1916 John Dewey wrote *Democracy and Education.*
1916 American Federation of Teachers organized.
1917 Smith-Hughes Act supported vocational education.
1918 Commission on the Reorganization of Secondary Education published the *Cardinal Principles of Secondary Education.*
1926 American Association for Adult Education established.
1940 Eight-Year Study of high schools completed by the Progressive Education Association
1944 G.I. Bill enacted.
1953 Department of Health, Education and Welfare established.
1953 Station KUHT of Houston, Texas, inaugurated educational television.
1954 *Brown* v. *Board of Education of Topeka* decision rules against racially segregated schools,
1954 B. F. Skinner wrote "The Science of Learning and the Art of Teaching" in the *Harvard Educational Review.*
1958 National Defense Education Act passed.
1961 Collective bargaining election in New York City won by the United Federation of Teachers.
1962 United States Supreme Court ruled against prayer in public schools.
1965 Elementary and Secondary Education Act passed.
1970 National student strike followed deaths of students at Kent State and Jackson State universities.

# INDEX

Gayley, Charles Mills, 502

Gehrkens, Karl Wilson, 413, 503

General Beadle State College (Madison, S.Dak.), 103

General Education Board, 23, 219, 247, 378, 384, 426, 468, 486, 514, 597, 615, 728, 963, 1223, 1256

General Federation of Women's Clubs, 308, 1083, 1167, 1402

General Theological Seminary (New York, N.Y.), 1383

Genesee College (Lima, N.Y.), 337, 1245. *See also* Syracuse University

Geneseo, New York, 1334. *See also* State University of New York College at Geneseo

Geneva, New York, 408, 727, 923, 1362. *See also* Hobart College

Geneva, Ohio, 1224

Geneva College. *See* Hobart College

Genoa, Nebraska, 274

Genoa, New York, 98

*Gentes Herbaum*, 71

Geological Society of America, 175, 361, 781, 888, 971, 972, 1093, 1171, 1269, 1325, 1416

George Peabody College for Teachers (Nashville, Tenn.), 54, 113, 190, 237, 240, 248, 277, 366, 490, 499, 598, 642, 753, 754, 801, 845, 932, 994, 1005, 1007, 1114, 1133, 1166, 1181, 1228, 1248, 1299, 1327. *See also* Nashville, University of

Georgetown, D.C. *See* District of Columbia

Georgetown, Kentucky, 564

Georgetown, Maryland. *See* District of Columbia

Georgetown, South Carolina, 72

Georgetown, Texas. *See* Southwestern University

Georgetown College (Georgetown, Ky.), 907

Georgetown University (D.C.), 200, 379, 965

George Washington University (D.C.), 624, 1075, 1097, 1134, 1337, 1344, 1370

George Williams College (Downers Grove, Ill.), 1230

Georgia
  board of regents, 120
  chief state school officer, 176, 284, 517, 970
  department of education, 258, 995
  planning commission, 120

Georgia, University of (Athens, Ga.), 11, 258, 277, 284, 339, 441, 517, 719, 962, 966, 970, 1235, 1332, 1334

Georgia Association of Colleges, 11, 1042

Georgia College (Milledgeville, Ga.), 1256

Georgia Education Association, 11, 148, 176, 682, 971, 1235, 1446

Georgia High School Association, 1235

Georgia Institute of Technology (Atlanta, Ga.), 176, 736

Georgia Military College (Milledgeville, Ga.), 642

Georgia Normal and Industrial College. *See* Georgia College

Georgia School of Technology. *See* Georgia Institute of Technology

Georgia Southern College (Statesboro, Ga.), 808, 1042

Georgia State Agricultural and Industrial Association, 1446

Georgia State College of Agriculture. *See* North Georgia College

Georgia State Industrial College for Negroes. *See* Savannah State College

Georgia State Normal School (Athens, Ga.), 441, 995

Georgia Teachers Association. *See* Georgia Education Association

Georgia Teachers College. *See* Georgia Southern College

German Reformed church, 48, 1073

Germantown, Ohio, 155

Germantown, Pennsylvania, 20, 112, 146, 383, 391, 392, 728, 998, 1080, 1199, 1359

Germany, 13, 105, 140, 142, 194, 205, 284, 285, 296, 348, 361, 366, 383, 407, 469, 536, 557, 568, 610, 631, 701, 755, 763, 765, 766, 770, 785, 793, 797, 859, 868, 873, 885, 894, 931, 988, 998, 1042, 1043, 1073, 1104, 1117, 1156, 1184, 1195, 1199, 1217, 1251, 1318, 1350, 1379, 1385, 1423, 1429, 1456
  student in, 6, 9, 15, 18, 27, 30, 40, 45, 58, 78, 83, 98, 115, 131, 139, 142, 151, 161, 168, 183, 197, 204, 212, 215, 221, 233, 236, 240, 249, 252, 260, 264, 265, 266, 269, 278, 284, 285, 287, 288, 294, 299, 303, 306, 331, 338, 342, 344, 380, 393, 407, 411, 413, 418, 427, 428, 430, 432, 455, 461, 464, 467, 469, 470, 471, 484, 487, 503, 509, 516, 518, 521, 529, 530, 538, 544, 557, 566, 569, 571, 580, 581, 586, 587, 590, 600, 607, 627, 630, 637, 638, 648, 653, 667, 670, 673, 684, 699, 711, 712, 713, 721, 725, 726, 733, 739, 756, 773, 797, 800, 805, 806, 815, 816, 827, 830, 831, 832, 845, 846, 860, 874, 886, 887, 890, 903, 909, 911, 927, 929, 932, 935, 937, 939, 958, 968, 978, 979, 984, 985, 987, 988, 990, 991, 993, 1001, 1008, 1011, 1040, 1043, 1048, 1050, 1060, 1064, 1073, 1079, 1080, 1084, 1088, 1090, 1093, 1100, 1112, 1129, 1131, 1138, 1140, 1152, 1154, 1159, 1161, 1163, 1164, 1169, 1192, 1195, 1202, 1221, 1223, 1227, 1232, 1253, 1257, 1274, 1285, 1286, 1297, 1300, 1315, 1318, 1350, 1356, 1377, 1378, 1384, 1397, 1425, 1429, 1438, 1441, 1455

Gerontology Society, 615

Mooers, New York, 734
Mooers Forks, New York, 734
Moonlight schools, 324, 1233
Moore, Ernest Carroll, 912
Moore, James, 913
Moore County, North Carolina, 837
Moorhead, Minnesota, 292, 591
Moorhead State Normal School. *See* Moorhead State University
Moorhead State University (Moorhead, Minn.), 292, 524, 591, 712, 714, 810
Moor's Indian Charity School (Hanover, N.H.), 130, 332, 1206, 1380
Moral Education Society, 814
Moravia, 1457
Moravian church, 1359, 1457
Moravian College (Bethlehem, Pa.), 1359
More, Paul Elmer, 65
Morehead, Kentucky, 1233
Morehead State University (Morehead, Ky.), 1233
Morehouse College (Atlanta, Ga.), 167, 358, 481, 665, 715, 880, 1082
Morgan, Arthur Ernest, 914
Morgan, John, 915
Morgan, Lewis Henry, 916
Morgan, Thomas Jefferson, 917
Morgan, William Henry, 918
Morgan County, Illinois, 99
Morgan Park Theological Seminary. *See* Chicago, University of
Morganton, North Carolina, 25, 1005
Morgantown, West Virginia, 1158. *See also* West Virginia University
Morphet, Edgar Leroy, 918
Morrill Act (1862), 1064, 1314
Morrill Act (1890), 55
Morris, Illinois, 580
Morris, Minnesota, 535
Morrisania, New York, 1071
Morrison, Henry Clinton, 920
Morrison, John Irwin, 920
Morrison, Illinois, 899
Morristown, New Jersey, 401, 451, 556, 802, 847, 951, 1257
Morrisville, New York, 1245
Morrowville, Kansas, 113
Morse, Jedidiah, 921
Morse, Samuel F. B., 397, 921
Mort, Paul R., 922
Mortimer, Mary, 923
Moscheles, Ignaz, 161, 873, 1088
Moscow, Idaho. *See* Idaho, University of
Moscow, Michigan, 927
Moscow College (Pa.), 16
Mossy Creek, Tennessee, 388. *See also* Jefferson City, Tennessee
Moten, Lucy Ella, 923

Moton, Robert Russa, 924
Mott, Valentine, 343
Mound City, Missouri, 364
Moundsville, West Virginia, 867
Moundview, Missouri, 1165
Mountainville, New York, 895
Mount Berry, Georgia, 119
Mount Berry Schools, 119
Mount Calvary, Wisconsin, 764
Mount Desert, Maine, 452
Mount Dora, Florida, 267
Mount Gretna, Pennsylvania, 1152
Mount Hermon Female Seminary (Clinton, Miss.), 376
Mount Holly, New Jersey, 996
Mount Holyoke College (South Hadley, Mass.), 31, 84, 251, 267, 286, 354, 375, 445, 672, 817, 901, 1258, 1378, 1438, 1439, 1450
Mount Holyoke Seminary. *See* Mount Holyoke College
Mount Mary College (Milwaukee, Wis.), 465
Mount Morris, Illinois, 1331
Mount Morris, New York, 1322
Mount Pleasant, Iowa. *See* Iowa Wesleyan College
Mount Pleasant Normal School. *See* Central Michigan University
Mount St. James Seminary. *See* Holy Cross, College of the
Mount St. Mary's College and Seminary (Emmitsburg, Md.), 677, 1221
Mount St. Mary's of the West College (Cincinnati, Ohio), 1221
Mount Sterling, Illinois, 824
Mount Sterling, Ohio, 323
Mount Tirzah, North Carolina, 1361
Mount Vernon, Iowa, 749. *See also* Cornell College
Mount Vernon, New Hampshire, 7, 82, 990
Mount Vernon, New York, 1053, 1078, 1153
Mount Vernon, Ohio, 254, 1365
Mount Vernon School for Young Ladies (Boston, Mass.), 4, 41, 159
Mount Zion, Georgia, 719
Mowry, William Augustus, 925
Mrs. Cady's School for Girls (New Haven, Conn.), 222
Muckwonago, Wisconsin, 365
Mullany, Patrick Francis (Brother Azarius), 926
Multnomah County, Oregon, 57
Mumford, Frederick Blackman, 927
Mumford, New York, 715
Muncie, Indiana. *See* Ball State University
Muncie Normal School. *See* Ball State University
Munford, Mary Cooke Branch, 928
Munro, William Bennett, 929
Munsterberg, Hugo, 230

Oneida, Kansas, 864
Oneida, New York, 300, 372, 1092
Oneida Institute (Oneida, N.Y.), 491
Ong, Nebraska, 678
Onondaga, New York, 1126, 1457
Onondaga Hill, New York, 1357
Ontario, Oregon, 389
Opelika, Alabama, 193
Oppenheimer, J. Robert, 968
*Opportunity*, 709
*Oralism and Auralism*, 522
Orange, California, 61
Orange, Massachusetts, 897, 982
Orange, New Jersey, 81, 220, 611, 871, 890
Orangeburg, South Carolina, 661
Orange County, North Carolina, 261
Orange County, New York, 1241
Orchard Lake, Michigan, 155
Orcutt, Hiram, 969
Oregon
  state system of higher education, 685, 743
  superintendent of schools, 1066
Oregon, University of (Eugene, Ore.), 32, 112, 210, 234, 389, 961, 1042, 1066, 1251, 1379
Oregon City, Oregon, 56, 711
Oregon College of Education (Monmouth, Ore.), 112, 211, 1042, 1443
Oregon High School Principals Association, 1066
Oregon State Normal School. *See* Oregon College of Education
Oregon State University (Corvallis, Ore.), 254, 636, 743, 783, 854, 1249
Oregon Superintendents of the First Class Association, 1066
Orem, Utah, 322
Orient, Iowa, 125
Orient, New York, 1163
Orlando, Florida, 827
Orlando School of Musical Art (Orlando, Fla.), 592
Orphan Asylum Society (New York, N.Y.), 122
Orr, Gustavus John, 970
Orrville, South Carolina, 970
Orton, Edward, Jr., 971, 972
Orton, Edward Francis Baxter, 971
Orton, James, 972
Osage, Iowa, 102
Osborn, Henry Fairfield, 973
Osborn, Ohio, 731
Osborne, Estelle Massey Riddle, 975
O'Shea, Michael Vincent, 976
Oshkosh, Wisconsin. *See* Wisconsin-Oshkosh, University of
Oshkosh Normal School. *See* Wisconsin-Oshkosh, University of
Oskaloosa, Iowa, 144, 1165

Ossining, New York, 917
Osuna, Juan Jóse, 977
Oswego, New York, 92, 1316, 1357. *See also* State University of New York College at Oswego
Oswego County, New York, 1193
Oswego State Normal and Training School. *See* State University of New York College at Oswego
Otero, Miguel A., 573
Ottawa, Illinois, 923
Ottawa University (Ottawa, Kans.), 712
Otto, New York, 293
Ottumwa, Iowa, 840
Ouachita Parish, Louisiana, 54
Overisel, Michigan, 132
Ovid, New York, 470
Owego, New York, 718, 1174
Owen, William Bishop, 978
Owensboro, Kentucky, 1220. *See also* Kentucky Wesleyan College
Owre, Alfred, 979
Oxford, Georgia, 621, 691, 1235. *See also* Emory University
Oxford, Massachusetts, 1185
Oxford, Mississippi, 88. *See also* Mississippi, University of
Oxford, New York, 1071
Oxford, North Carolina, 1337, 1362, 1399
Oxford, Ohio, 496, 827, 1177. *See also* Miami University
Oxford, Pennsylvania, 1064
Oxford, South Carolina, 1399

Pace, Edward Aloysius, 979
Pacific, College of the (San Jose, Calif.). *See* Pacific, University of the (Stockton, Calif.)
Pacific, University of the (Stockton, Calif.), 596
Pacific Grove, California, 815, 1427
Pacific Kindergarten Normal School, 869
Pacific University (Forest Grove, Ore.), 57, 241, 420, 1062
Packard, Alpheus Spring, Jr., 980
Packard, Silas Sadler, 981
Packard, Sophia B., 982
Packard's Business College (New York, N.Y.), 981
*Packard's Monthly*, 981
Packer Collegiate Institute, 95
Page, David Perkins, 982, 1007
Page, Inman Edward, 983
Page County, Iowa, 1341
Pageville, South Carolina, 1301
Pahala, Hawaii, 1420
Paine, John Knowles, 984
Painesville, Ohio, 613, 768. *See also* Lake Erie College

Raleigh, North Carolina, 25, 62, 174, 178, 262, 286, 537, 721, 725, 890, 1176, 1399. *See also* North Carolina State University; St. Augustine's College; Shaw University

Rambaut, Mary Lucinda Bonney, 1071

Ramona, Kansas, 1149

Rancocas, New Jersey, 567

Randall, Samuel Sidwell, 1071

Randolph, Massachusetts, 1378

Randolph, New York, 293, 1325

Randolph, Ohio, 885

Randolph County, North Carolina, 330

Randolph-Macon College (Ashland, Va.), 330, 498, 642, 966

Randolph-Macon Woman's College (Lynchburg, Va.), 995

Rankin County, Mississippi, 1388

Ranvier, Louis Antoine, 151, 903

Rapid City, South Dakota, 964. *See also* South Dakota School of Mines and Technology

Raub, Albert Newton, 1072

Rauch, Frederick Augustus, 1073

Ray, Joseph, 592, 1074

Raymond, George Lansing, 1074

Raymond, John Howard, 1075

Raymond, Mississippi, 375

Raymond, Washington, 1443

Read, Daniel, 1076

Read, Gerald Howard, 172, 1077

Reading, Massachusetts, 1381, 1416

Reading, Pennsylvania, 82

Reading, Vermont, 1113

Readville, Maine, 460

Reagan, Ronald, 742

Reavis, William Claude, 1077

Red Fork, Oklahoma, 812

Redkey, Indiana, 1419

Redlands, California, 6, 824

Red Lion, Delaware, 560

Redman, John, 1128

Redmond, Oregon, 1066

*Red Ribbon Record*, 1358

Redway, Jacques Wardlaw, 1078

Red Wing, Minnesota, 500, 1451

Redwood City, California, 889

Redwood Falls, Minnesota, 721

Reed, David Allen, 1080

Reed College (Portland, Ore.), 61, 290, 291, 475, 609, 789, 1192

Reed's Ferry, New Hampshire, 1262

Reeve, Tapping, 533, 1080

Reeve, William David, 1081

Reformed Church, Theological Seminary of. *See* Franklin and Marshall College

Reformed Presbyterian Seminary (Philadelphia, Pa.), 1289

Rehoboth, Massachusetts, 1207

Reid, Ira de Augustine, 1082

Reinhardt, Aurelia Isabel Henry, 1083

Reistertown, Maryland, 298

Religious Education Association, 278, 323, 496, 931, 1217, 1366

Religious journals, 13, 22, 42, 48, 170, 257, 288, 291, 297, 311, 447, 464, 466, 496, 509, 512, 528, 582, 601, 602, 609, 621, 646, 677, 697, 777, 796, 871, 907, 918, 980, 1013, 1020, 1088, 1098, 1111, 1161, 1170, 1173, 1179, 1183, 1219, 1222, 1224, 1290, 1316, 1320, 1331, 1390, 1399, 1404, 1420, 1434

Remsen, Ira, 958, 1084

Renner, George Thomas, Jr., 1085

Reno, Nevada, 1185, 1252, 1383, 1393. *See also* Nevada, University of

Rensselaer, Indiana, 657

Rensselaer Polytechnic Institute (Troy, N.Y.), 29, 416, 488, 1349, 1425

Renton, Washington, 1059

Republic, Ohio, 613

*Research Bulletin of Commercial Education*, 1303

Revel, Bernard, 1086

Revels, Hiram Rhoades, 1087

*Review of Educational Research*, 1152

Revolutionary War, 86, 261, 306, 410, 675, 865, 915, 1012, 1081, 1128, 1181, 1207, 1347, 1363, 1380

Rhees, Rush, 596

Rhinebeck, New York, 401, 485, 1271

Rhinelander, Wisconsin, 593

Rhode Island
  board of education, 89, 782
  commissioner of education, 31, 128, 750, 1050
  department of education, 326
  legislature, 31, 128, 1050
  school committee, 675
  supreme court, 1050

Rhode Island, University of (Kingston, R.I.), 218

Rhode Island College (1765-1804). *See* Brown University

Rhode Island College (Providence, R.I.), 281, 325, 546, 721, 917

Rhode Island College of Agriculture and Mechanic Arts. *See* Rhode Island, University of

*Rhode Island Educational Magazine*, 1050

Rhode Island Historical Society, 600, 675

Rhode Island Institute of Instruction, 128, 546, 782, 926

Rhode Island Normal School. *See* Rhode Island College

*Rhode Island Schoolmaster*, 31. *See also Journal of Education*

Rhode Island School of Design (Providence, R.I.), 449, 1043

**Rhodes Scholar**, 63, 93, 237, 805, 1089, 1298

Ulich, Robert, 1318
Umatilla Indian Reservation (Pendleton, Ore.), 274
Underhill, Vermont, 1381
*Understanding the Child,* 804, 1134
Union, Connecticut, 967
Union City, Georgia, 284
Union City, Indiana, 627
Union College (Schenectady, N.Y.), 22, 169, 188, 303, 357, 491, 507, 509, 552, 574, 579, 616, 696, 759, 790, 877, 916, 957, 1049, 1075, 1109, 1164, 1271, 1275, 1360, 1375, 1389, 1433
Union County, Kentucky, 1220
Union Institute. *See* Duke University
Union of South Africa, 311
Union Square, New York, 1193
Union Station, Ohio, 978
Union Theological Seminary (New York, N.Y.), 82, 256, 278, 485, 512, 515, 553, 581, 722, 745, 779, 828, 850, 870, 934, 935, 1015, 1115, 1120, 1124, 1174, 1250, 1323, 1389, 1429
Uniontown, Maryland, 320
Uniontown, Pennsylvania. *See* Madison College
Unionville, Tennessee, 749
Unitarian church, 164, 332, 470, 597, 658, 791, 879, 1018, 1083, 1217, 1220, 1222, 1258, 1414, 1457
United Brethren in Christ church, 376
United Nations, 123, 153, 511, 538, 603, 1370
United Nations Educational, Cultural and Scientific Organization (UNESCO), 30, 113, 241, 245, 290, 347, 358, 424, 459, 515, 595, 709, 734, 770, 1069, 1240, 1409, 1459
United Negro College Fund, 881
United Presbyterian Seminary (Xenia, Ohio), 827
United States
  agriculture department, 33, 58, 97, 293, 295, 424, 760, 1127, 1151, 1310, 1432
  bureau of education. *See* office of education
  bureau of Indian affairs, 274, 396, 917, 1058, 1340
  bureau of reclamation, 623
  bureau of standards, 569, 958, 1061
  census bureau, 723, 1340
  civil service commission, 552, 1289, 1387
  coast and geodetic survey, 1061
  coast survey, 66, 88, 1016
  commissioner of education, 28, 29, 89, 183, 269, 417, 605, 833, 844, 1254, 1298, 1459
  diplomatic service, 44, 233, 269, 296, 339, 379, 424, 479, 514, 529, 571, 620, 703, 774, 943, 946, 1195, 1226, 1384, 1385, 1392
  employment service, 1306
  federal board for vocational education, 26,

792, 807, 950, 1063, 1204, 1277, 1445
  federal communications commission, 789
  food administration, 1397
  forest service, 199
  geodetic survey, 1017
  geological survey, 387, 1040, 1171, 1273, 1325, 1345
  house of representatives, 5, 54, 329, 339, 454, 494, 584, 774, 858, 1004, 1050, 1069, 1164, 1193, 1243, 1312
  information service, 1214
  interior department, 1134, 1397
  labor department, 6, 108, 538, 844
  marine hospital service, 965
  mint, 1128
  office of education, 9, 35, 52, 89, 96, 100, 102, 113, 177, 209, 229, 232, 288, 341, 417, 422, 561, 697, 719, 723, 755, 764, 815, 830, 919, 1098, 1134, 1335, 1386, 1445, 1459
  post office department, 379
  president, 703, 1413
  public health service, 561, 789
  senate, 273, 454, 483, 538, 617, 809, 1004, 1087, 1362, 1368
  state department, 379, 840
  supreme court, 1243
  tariff commission, 1274
  treasury department, 178, 478, 555, 1289, 1340, 1344
  veterans bureau, 374, 421
  vice-president, 703
  war department, 1151, 1166
United States Army Judge Advocate General School, 1002
United States Army School of Nursing (D.C.), 527
United States International University (San Diego, Calif.), 61, 804
United States Military Academy (West Point, N.Y.), 66, 309, 335, 355, 442, 641, 753, 779, 784, 855, 997, 1012, 1085, 1202, 1283, 1362, 1400
United States Naval Academy (Annapolis, Md.), 261, 276, 420, 718, 1198, 1294
United States Naval Observatory (D.C.), 1060
*United States Service Magazine,* 310
Universalist church, 460
*Universities Quarterly,* 730
University and Bellevue Hospital Medical College (New York, N.Y.), 828, 1436
University of the State of New York, 110, 273, 353, 372, 446, 457, 616, 832, 1179. *See also* New York, board of regents; commissioner of education; education department; superintendent of public instruction
University Park, Pennsylvania, 55
Upper Arlington, Ohio, 680

## ABOUT THE EDITOR

JOHN F. OHLES is professor of education at Kent State University, Kent, Ohio. He is the editor of *Principles and Practice of Teaching: Selected Readings* and the author of *Introduction to Teaching* as well as numerous articles.

---